TCP/IP & DISTRIBUTED SYSTEM

TCP/IP
&
DISTRIBUTED SYSTEM

by

VIVEK ACHARYA
Lecturer
Dept. of Computer Science
Mahakal Institute of Technology
Ujjain, Madhya Pradesh

FIREWALL MEDIA
(An Imprint of Laxmi Publications Pvt. Ltd.
An ISO 9001:2015 Company

BENGALURU • CHENNAI • GUWAHATI • HYDERABAD
KOCHI • KOLKATA • LUCKNOW • RANCHI
NEW DELHI

Printed and bound in India

First Edition : 2006 Reprint : 2007, 2008, Edition : 2026

ISBN *:* 978-81-7008-932-2

FTC-2855-829-TCP/IP & DISTRIBUTED SYSTEM

Price: ₹ 829.00

Branches

✆	Bengaluru	080-26 75 69 30
✆	Chennai	044-24 34 47 26
✆	Guwahati	0361-254 36 69
✆	Hyderabad	040-27 55 53 83
✆	Kochi	0484-405 13 03
✆	Kolkata	033-40 04 77 79
✆	Lucknow	0522-430 36 13
✆	Ranchi	0651-224 24 64

Published in India by

FIREWALL MEDIA

(An Imprint of Laxmi Publications Pvt. Ltd.)

An ISO 9001:2015 Company

113, GOLDEN HOUSE, GURUDWARA ROAD, DARYAGANJ,

NEW DELHI - 110002, INDIA

Corporate Office : B-33, Sector-5, Noida,

Gautambuddha Nagar (U.P.) - 201 301, INDIA

Telephone : +91-120-44 46 900

www.laxmipublications.com

info@laxmipublications.com

PREFACE

This book attempts to provide a unified overview of the broad field of Data-Communication, Computer Network and Distributed Systems.

The organization of the book reflects an attempt to break these subjects into comprehensible parts and to build piece by piece, a survey of the state of the art.

This book emphasizes basic principles and topics of fundamental importance concerning the technology and architecture of this field as well as providing a detailed discussion of lead-edge topics.

I have taken a bottom-up approach on TCP/IP layer addressing the issues related to the design of data communication, computer network and distributed systems.

This book is divided into five parts :

1. Computer Network: It is related to data communication on networks. Protocol, computer network model and data communication model on client-server architecture are covered.

2. Data Communication: This part is concerned with topics related to computer communication to exchange data. Fundamental topics like signal, there characteristics, transmission medium, encoding techniques and modulation are covered.

3. TCP/IP: TCP/IP protocol is the base line used to design this section. Physical layer, Network (IP) layer, Transport layer(TCP & UDP), Application layer are the contents of this part.

4. Distributed System: This part aims to convey insight into knowledge of principle and practice underlying the design of distributed systems.

5. Questionnaire: It covers both descriptive, solved and unsolved objective questions. 1000 question set provides a leading edge on the topics covered in this book. These are beneficial for the students preparing for various competitive exams and for those going for open and campus selection procedure.

This book is intended for the benefit of students of undergraduate, introductory post-graduate courses like B.E./B.Tech,. MCA, MCM, various diploma courses in computer sciences. It can be used for sole self-study purpose too.

Author

FOREWORD

The information technology industry is undergoing a climatic change at a rapid rate. In turn communication, computer network, TCP/IP and distributed system have undergone a transformation in all their products to step a rung higher in global enterprise information management.

This book has been structured to facilitate easier perception and acquiring an in depth knowledge of the subject. It has been designed to equally facilitate fresher B.E./B.Tech (CS, CE, IT, EC, ET), MCA, MCM, BBA, BCA and other computer related course students.

On completion of this book the reader should be able to appreciate the features and capabilities of Computer Networks, TCP/IP and Distributed System and the objective questions will edge students and will bring depth to the subjective knowledge of the reader.

This creation of Mr. Vivek Acharya is appreciable and it is going to benefit readers in all dimensions.

(Prof. D.S. Saxena)
Director
Mahakal Institute of Technology, Ujjain

CONTENTS

1
INTRODUCTION TO DATA COMMUNICATION

1.1 BASIC COMMUNICATION MODEL

Communication is the transfer of a *message* from one entity, called the *source* or *transmitter,* to another, called the *destination* or *receiver,* via a *channel* of some sort.

The transfer of a message could be followed by a *response* message from the original destination to complete one cycle in a *dialogue* between *corresponding entities.* The only way that a message source can be certain that the destination properly received the message is by some kind of *acknowledgement* response from the destination. This acknowledged form of dialogue is the basis of reliable communications—the source must get feedback that the destination correctly received the message.

Source: Device that generates the data to be passed on to the Destination device. It could be a user computer trying to make a query to a server computer.

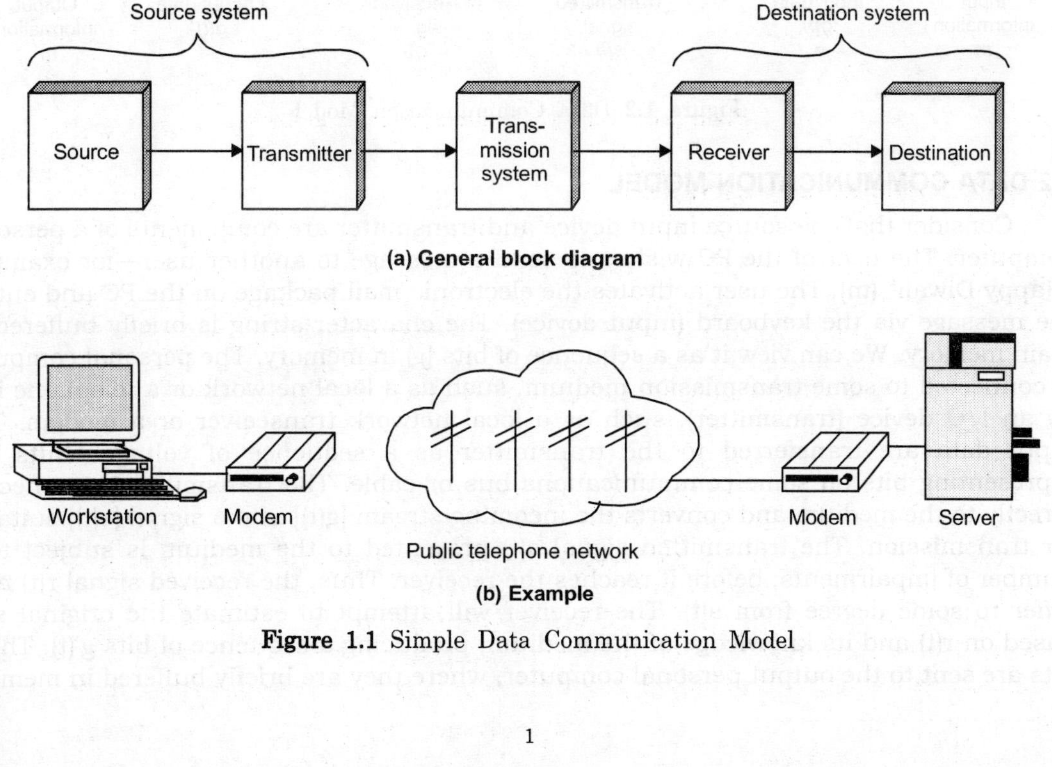

Figure 1.1 Simple Data Communication Model

Transmitter: If the data generated by the *Source device* has to be transmitted through *Transmission Channel* or Transmission System then it has to be presented in a form that is acceptable to the *Transmission system.* This job is done by the *Transmitter.* For example, a *modem* takes a digital bit stream from the attached computer and transforms that stream of bits into an analog signals which can be handled by the telephone network.

Transmission System: Thi s can be a single transmission line connecting the two systems communicating or a complex network to which numerous communicating systems are connected.

Receiver: This receives the signal from the transmission system and converts it into a form that is suitable to the destination device. For example, a *modem* accepts analog signal from a transmission channel and transforms it into digital bit stream.

Destination: Device to which the source device sends data.

Figure 1.2 provides a new view on the data communication model of Figure1.1. Let us trace through the details of this figure using electronic mail as an example.

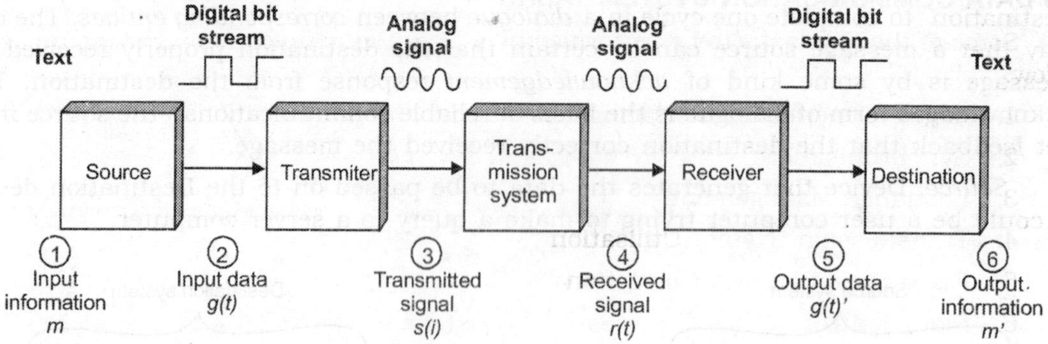

Figure 1.2 Data Communication Model

1.2 DATA COMMUNICATION MODEL

Consider that the source input device and transmitter are components of a personal computer. The user of the PC wishes to send a message to another user—for example, "Happy Diwali" (m). The user activates the electronic mail package on the PC and enters the message via the keyboard (input device). The character string is briefly buffered in main memory. We can view it as a sequence of bits (g) in memory. The personal computer is connected to some transmission medium, such as a local network or a telephone line by an I/O device (transmitter), such as a local network transceiver or a modem. The input data are transferred to the transmitter as a sequence of voltage shifts g(t) representing bits on some communications bus or cable. The transmitter is connected directly to the medium and converts the incoming stream [g(t)] into a signal [s(t)] suitable for transmission. The transmitted signal s(t) presented to the medium is subject to a number of impairments, before it reaches the receiver. Thus, the received signal r(t) may differ to some degree from s(t). The receiver will attempt to estimate the original s(t), based on r(t) and its knowledge of the medium, producing a sequence of bits g'(t). These bits are sent to the output personal computer, where they are briefly buffered in memory as a block of bits (g'). In many cases, the destination system will attempt to determine if an error has occurred and, if so, will cooperate with the source system to eventually obtain a complete, error-free block of data. These data are then presented to the user via an output device, such as a printer or a screen. The message (m'), as viewed by the user, will usually be an exact copy of the original message (m).

Now consider a telephone conversation. In this case, the input to the telephone is a message (m) in the form of sound waves. The sound waves are converted by the telephone into electrical signals of the same frequency. These signals are transmitted without modification over the telephone line. Hence, the input signal g(t) and the transmitted signal s(t) are identical. The signal s(t) will suffer some distortion over the medium, so that r(t) will not be identical to s(t). Nevertheless, the signal r(t) is converted back into a sound wave with no attempt at correction or improvement of signal quality. Thus m' is not an exact replica of m. However, the received sound message is generally comprehensible to the listener.

1.3 DATA COMMUNICATION SYSTEM TASKS

Some of the Key tasks to be performed by a Data Communications System are listed below.

1. Signal Generation Interfacing
2. Synchronisation
3. Exchange Management
4. Transmission System Utilisation
5. Error Detection and Correction
6. Flow Control
7. Addressing
8. Routing
9. Message Formatting

All the data that are transmitted over the transmitting system propagate as Electromagnetic signals. Hence the communicating device must be able to generate and receive these signals. Signal generation should be such that the resultant signal is capable of being propagated through the transmission medium and interpretable as data at the receiver.

A device must interface with the transmission system in order to communicate.

Unless the receiver and transmitter are in Synchronisation the receiver will not be able to make sense out of received signals. Receiver should know when the transmission of data starts, when it ends.

For meaningful data transaction there should be some kind management of data being exchanged. Both the transmitter and receiver should adhere to some common convention about the format of data, amount of data that can be sent at a time and so on. This requires, a prior definition of message formatting.

Transmission System Utilisation refers to the need to make efficient use of Transmission Channel, which are generally shared by many communicating devices. Various techniques (Multiplexing) are available to allocate the total capacity of a transmission channel among connected devices. Care should be taken to avoid probable Congestion in some kind of multiplexing.

In any communication system transmitted data is prone to error. Either it is because of transmitted signal getting distorted in the transmission medium leading to misinterpretation of signal or errors introduced by the intermediate devices. Error detection and Correction is required in cases where there is no scope for error in the data transaction. We can think of file transfer between two computers where there is a need for this. But in some cases it may not be very important as in the case of telephonic conversation.

There is a possibility of transmitter generating data faster than the receiver device capable of handling. To handle this there should be some kind of flow control mechanism agreed upon between the two communicating devices.

When more than two devices share a transmitting facility, a source system must somehow indicate the identity (or address) of the destination. The transmission system must ensure that the data being sent are routed only to the destination system.

The list of tasks explained above is not exhaustive one. But sure it indicates the complexities involved in a communication system. The data communication system must be designed to handle the above tasks as required so that meaningful communication can take place between two devices efficiently.

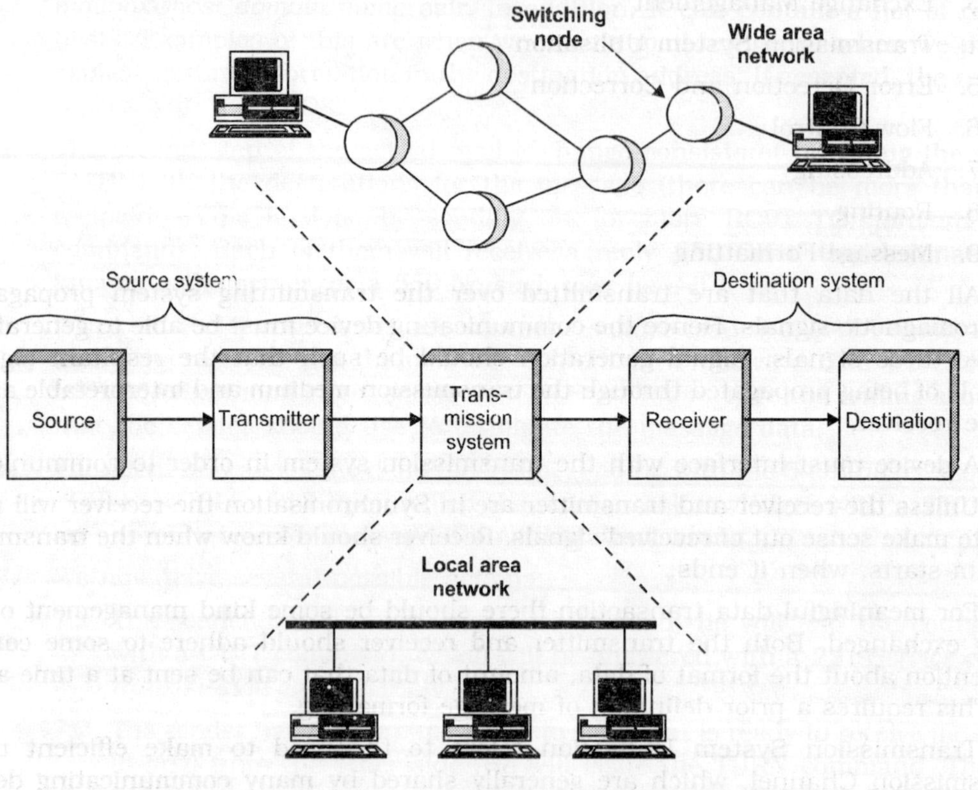

Figure 1.3 Data Communication Network Model

A communication network, in its simplest form, is a set of equipment and facilities that provides a communication service: the transfer of information between users located at various geographical points. Here we focus on networks that use electronic or optical technologies. Examples of such networks include telephone networks, computer networks, television broadcast networks, cellular telephone networks, and the Internet.

1.4 DATA COMMUNICATION NETWORKING

In its simplest form, data communication takes place between two devices that are directly connected by some form of point-to-point transmission medium. Often, however, it is impractical for two devices to be directly, point-to-point connected. This is so for one (or both) of the following reasons:

The devices are very far apart.

There is a set of devices, each of which may require a link to many of the others at various times. The solution to this problem is to attach each device to a communications network. Figure 1.3 relates this area to the communications model of Figure 1.1a and also suggests the two major categories into which communications networks are traditionally classified: *Wide-Area Networks* (WANs) and *Local-Area Networks* (LANs). The distinction between the two, both in terms of technology and application, has become somewhat blurred in recent years, but it remains a useful way of organizing the discussion.

2

DATA COMMUNICATION NETWORKS AND TECHNOLOGIES

2.1 WHAT IS AN INTERNETWORK ?

An *internet work* is a collection of individual networks, connected by intermediate networking devices, that functions as a single large network. Internetworking refers to the industry, products, and procedures that meet the challenge of creating and administering internet works.

Internetworking Challenges

Implementing a functional internet work is no simple task. Many challenges must be faced, especially in the areas of connectivity, reliability, network management, and flexibility. Each area is key in establishing an efficient and effective internet work.

The challenge when connecting various systems is to support communication among disparate technologies. Different sites, for example, may use different types of media operating at varying speeds, or may even include different types of systems that need to communicate. Because companies rely heavily on data communication, internetworks must provide a certain level of reliability. This is an unpredictable world, so many large internetworks include redundancy to allow for communication even when problems occur.

Furthermore, network management must provide centralized support and troubleshooting capabilities in an internetwork. Configuration, security, performance, and other issues must be adequately addressed for the internetwork to function smoothly. Security within an internetwork is essential. Many people think of network security from the perspective of protecting the private network from outside attacks. However, it is just as important to protect the network from internal attacks, especially because most security breaches come from inside. Networks must also be secured so that the internal network cannot be used as a tool to attack other external sites.

Early in the year 2000, many major web sites were the victims of Distributed Denial Of Service (DDOS) attacks. These attacks were possible because a great number of private networks currently connected with the Internet were not properly secured. These private networks were used as tools for the attackers .Because nothing in this world is stagnant, internetworks must be flexible enough to change with new demands.

Major Categories into which Communications Networks are Classified

1. Lan
2. Wan
3. Intranet
4. Extranet
5. Internet.

2.2 WHAT IS A LAN ?

A *LAN* is a high-speed data network that covers a relatively small geographic area. It typically connects workstations, personal computers, printers, servers, and other devices. LANs offer computer users many advantages, including shared access to devices and applications, file exchange between connected users, and communication between users via electronic mail and other applications.

A Local-Area Network or LAN is a communications network that interconnects a variety of devices and provides a means for information exchange among those devices.

Traditionally, LANs make use of a broadcast network approach rather than a switching approach. With a broadcast communication network, there are no intermediate switching nodes. At each station, there is a transmitter/receiver that communicates over a medium shared by other stations. A transmission from any one station is broadcast to and received by all other stations. Also in the case of LANs, data are usually transmitted in packets. Because the medium is shared, only one station at a time can transmit a packet.

2.3 LAN TRANSMISSION METHODS

LAN data transmissions fall into three classifications:

- unicast,
- multicast, and
- broadcast.

In each type of transmission, a single packet is sent to one or more nodes.

In a *unicast transmission*, a single packet is sent from the source to a destination on a network. First, the source node addresses the packet by using the address of the destination node. The package is then sent onto the network, and finally, the network passes the packet to its destination.

A *multicast transmission* consists of a single data packet that is copied and sent to a specific subset of nodes on the network. First, the source node addresses the packet by using a multicast address. The packet is then sent into the network, which makes copies of the packet and sends a copy to each node that is part of the multicast address.

A *broadcast transmission* consists of a single data packet that is copied and sent to all nodes on the network. In these types of transmissions, the source node addresses the packet by using the broadcast address. The packet is then sent on to the network, which makes copies of the packet and sends a copy to every node on the network.

2.4 LAN TOPOLOGIES

LAN topologies define the manner in which network devices are organized. Four common LAN topologies exist:

1. bus,
2. ring,
3. star, and
4. tree.

These topologies are logical architectures, but the actual devices need not be physically organized in these configurations. Logical bus and ring topologies, for example, are commonly organized physically as a star. A *bus topology* is a linear LAN architecture in which transmissions from network stations propagate the length of the medium and are received by all other stations.

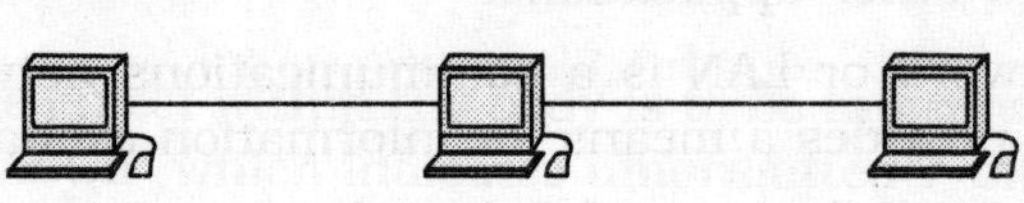

Figure 2.1 Some Networks Implement a Local Bus Topology

A *ring topology* is a LAN architecture that consists of a series of devices connected to one another by unidirectional transmission links to form a single closed loop. Both Token Ring/IEEE 802.5 and FDDI networks implement a ring topology. Figure 2.2 depicts a logical ring topology.

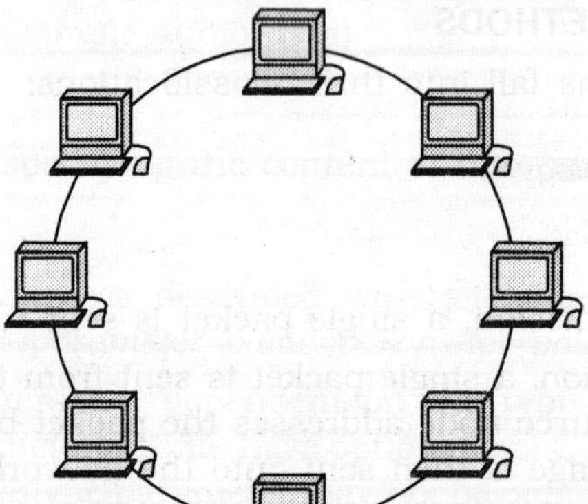

Figure 2.2 Some Networks Implement a Logical Ring Topology

A *star topology* is a LAN architecture in which the endpoints on a network are connected to a common central hub, or switch, by dedicated links. Logical bus and ring topologies are often implemented physically in a star topology.

A *tree topology* is a LAN architecture that is identical to the bus topology, except that branches with multiple nodes are possible in this case. Figure 2.3 illustrates a logical tree topology.

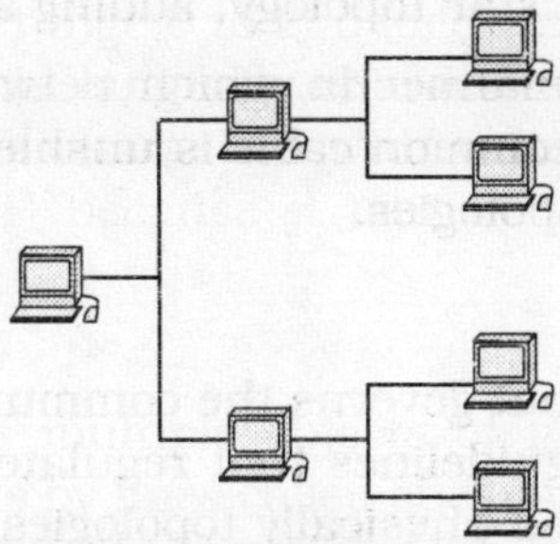

Figure 2.3 A Logical Tree Topology Can Contain Multiple Nodes

Advantages of a Linear Bus Topology

1. Easy to connect a computer or peripheral to a linear bus.
2. Requires less cable length than a star topology.

Disadvantages of a Linear Bus Topology

1. Entire network shuts down if there is a break in the main cable.
2. Terminators are required at both ends of the backboned cables.
3. It is difficult to identify the problem if the entire network shuts down.
4. Not good as a stand-alone solution in a large building.

Advantages of a Star Topology

1. Easy to install and wire.
2. No disruptions to the network when connecting or removing devices.
3. Easy to detect faults and to remove parts.

Disadvantages of a Star Topology

1. Requires more cable length than a linear topology.
2. If the hub fails, nodes attached are disabled.
3. More expensive than linear bus topologies because of the cost of the concentrators.

Advantages of a Tree Topology

1. Point-to-point wiring for individual segments.
2. Supported by several hardware and software vendors.

Disadvantages of a Tree Topology

Overall the type of cabling used limits length of each segment.

1. If the backbone line breaks, the entire segment goes down.
2. More difficult to configure and wire than other topologies.

Considerations when Choosing a Topology

- **Money.** A liner bus network may be the least expensive way to install a network;
- **Length of cable needed.** The linear bus network uses shorter lengths of cable.

- **Future growth.** With a star topology, adding another concentrator easily does expanding a network.
- **Cable type.** The most common cable is unshielded twisted pair, which is most often used with star topologies.

2.5 LAN PROTOCOLS

A protocol is a set of rules that governs the communications between computers on a network. These rules include guidelines that regulate the following characteristics of a network; access method, allowed physically topologies, types of cabling, and speeds of data transfer.

LAN protocols function at the lowest two layers of the OSI reference model the physical layer and the data link layer. Figure 2.4 illustrates how several popular LAN protocols map to the OSI reference model.

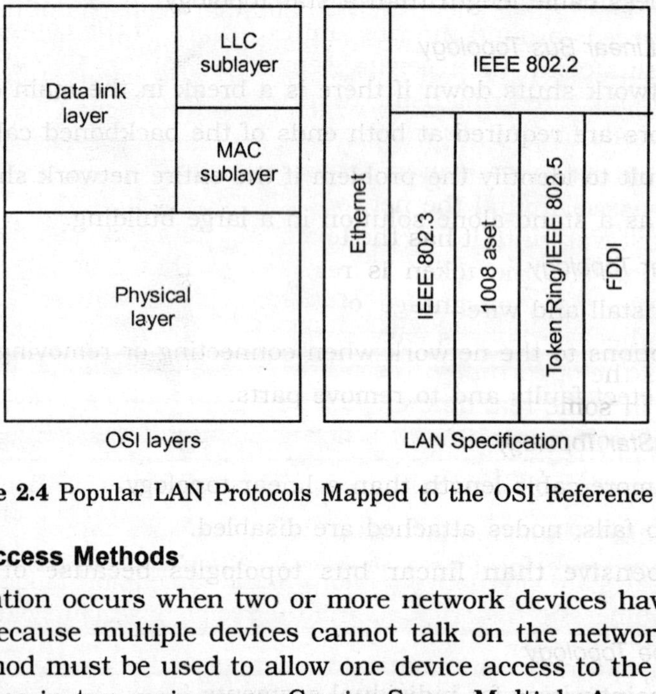

Figure 2.4 Popular LAN Protocols Mapped to the OSI Reference Model

2.5.1 Lan Media Access Methods

Media contention occurs when two or more network devices have data to send at the same time. Because multiple devices cannot talk on the network simultaneously, some type of method must be used to allow one device access to the network media at a time. This is done in two main ways: Carrier Sense Multiple Access Collision Detect (CSMA/CD) and token passing.

2.5.2 Ethernet

The Ethernet protocol is by far the most widely used. It uses an access method called CSMA/CD (Carrier Sense Multiple Access/Collision Detection). This protocol allows for linear bus, star, or tree topologies. Data can be transmitted over twisted pair, coaxial or fiber optic cable at a speed of 10 Mbps.

In networks using *CSMA/CD* technology such as Ethernet, network devices contend for the network media.

When a device has data to send, it first listens to see if any other device is currently using the network. If not, it starts sending its data. After finishing its transmission, it listens again to see if a collision occurred. A collision occurs when two devices send data simultaneously. When a collision happens, each device waits a random length of time before resending its data. In most cases, a collision will not occur again between the two devices. Because of this type of network contention, the busier a network becomes, the more collisions occur. This is why performance of Ethernet degrades rapidly as the number of devices on a single network increases.

2.5.3 Token Ring

IBM developed this protocol in the mid 1980s. The access method used involves token passing. In token ring the computers are connected so that the signal travels around the network from one computer to another in a logical ring. A single electronic token moves around the ring from one computer to next. If a computer does not have information to transmit, it simply passes the token on to the next workstation. If a computer wishes to transmit and receives an empty token, it attaches data to the token. The token then proceeds around the ring until it comes to the computer for which the data is meant. At this point, the receiving computer captures the data. The token ring protocol requires a star wired ring using twisted pair or fiber optic cable. It can operate at transmission speeds of 4 Mbps or 16 Mbps.

In *token-passing* networks such as Token Ring and FDDI, a special network packet called a token is passed around the network from device to device. When a device has data to send, it must wait until it has the token and then sends its data. When the data transmission is complete, the token is released so that other devices may use the network media. The main advantage of token-passing networks is that they are deterministic. In other words, it is easy to calculate the maximum time that will pass before a device has the opportunity to send data. This explains the popularity of token-passing networks in some real-time environments such as factories, where machinery must be capable of communicating at a determinable interval.

2.5.4 FDDI

Fiber Distributed Data Interface (FDDI) is a network protocol, used primarily to interconnect two or more local area networks, often over large distance. The access method used by FDDI involves token passing. FDDI uses a dual ring physical topology. Transmission normally occurs on one of the rings; however, if a break occurs, the system keeps information moving by automatically using portions of the second ring to create a new complete ring. A major advantage of FDDI is speed. It operates over fiber optic cable at 100 Mbps.

TABLE 1.1. Comparison Chart

Protocol	***Cable***	***Speed***	***Topology***
Ethernet	Twisted Pair, Coaxial, Fiber	10 Mbps	Linear Bus, Star, Tree
Fast Ethernet	Twisted Pair, Fiber	100 Mbps	Star
Local Talk	Twisted Pair	23 Mbps	Linear Bus or Star
Token Ring	Twisted Pair	4 Mbps-16 Mbps	Star-Wired Ring
FDDI	Fiber	100 Mbps	Dual Ring

2.6 LAN STANDARDS

802 IEEE committee responsible for setting standards concerning cabling, physical topologies, logical topologies and physical access methods for networking products. The Computer Society of IEEE's 802 project committee is divided into several sub-committees that deal with specific standards in these general areas. Specifically the Physical Layer and the Data Link Layer of the ISO's OSI model are addressed.

1. 802.1 This work defines an overall picture of LANs and connectivity.
2. 802.1B This set of standards specifically address the network management.
3. 802.1D Standards for bridges used to connect various types of LANs together were set up with 802.1D.
4. 802.2 Called the Logical Link Control (LLC) standards, this specification governs the communication of packets of information from one device to another on a network.
5. 802.3 Defines the way data has access to a network for multiple topology systems using CSMA/CD. A prime example is Ethernet and Star LAN Systems.
6. 802.4 Standards developed for a token passing scheme on a bus topology. The primary utilization of this specification was the Manufacturing Automation Protocol LANs developed by General Motors, operates at 10 Mbps.
7. 802.5 This standard defines token ring systems. It involves the token passing concept on a ring topology with twisted pair cabling. IBM's token ring system uses this specification; the speed is either 4 Mbps or 16 Mbps.
8. 802.6 Metropolitan Area Networks are defined by this group. MANs are networks that are larger than LANs typically falling within 50 Kilometres. They operate at speeds ranging from 1 Mbps up to about 200 Mbps.
9. 802.7 These are standards concerning broadband LANs.
10. 802.8 This group sets up standards for LANs using fiber optic cabling and access methods.
11. 802.9 This specification covers voice and digital data integration.
12. 802.10 These members set standards for interoperable security.
13. 802.11 Wireless LANs are the subject of this particular subcommittee's works. Both infrared and radio LANs are covered.

2.7 LAN DEVICES

Devices commonly used in LANs include repeaters, hubs, LAN extenders, bridges, LAN switches, and routers.

A *repeater* is a physical layer device used to interconnect the media segments of an extended network. A repeater essentially enables a series of cable segments to be treated as a single cable. Repeaters receive signals from one network segment and amplify, retime, and retransmit those signals to another network segment. These actions prevent signal deterioration caused by long cable lengths and large numbers of connected devices. Repeaters are incapable of performing complex filtering and other traffic processing. In addition, all electrical signals, including electrical disturbances and other errors, are repeated and amplified. The total number of repeaters and network segments that can be connected is limited due to timing and other issues. Figure 2.5 illustrates a repeater connecting two network segments.

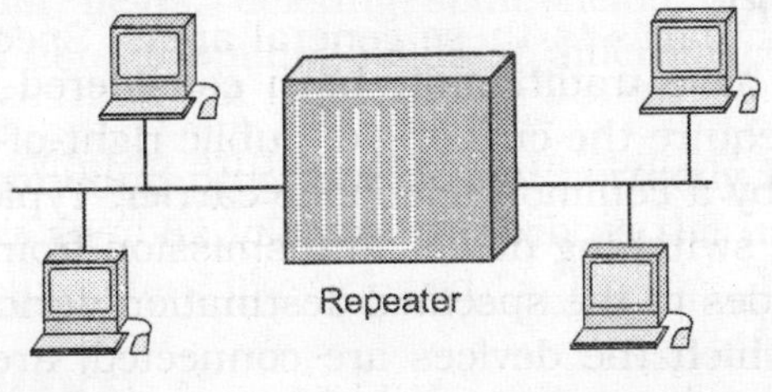

Figure 2.5 A Repeater Connects Two Network Segments

A *hub* is a physical layer device that connects multiple user stations, each via a dedicated cable. Electrical interconnections are established inside the hub. Hubs are used to create a physical star network while maintaining the logical bus or ring configuration of the LAN. In some respects, a hub functions as a multiport repeater.

A *LAN extender* is a remote-access multilayer switch that connects to a host router. LAN extenders forward traffic from all the standard network layer protocols (such as IP, IPX, and AppleTalk) and filter traffic based on the MAC address or network layer protocol type. LAN extenders scale well because the host router filters out unwanted broadcasts and multicasts. However, LAN extenders are not capable of segmenting traffic or creating security firewalls.

2.8 THE OSI MODEL AND INTERNET WORKING DEVICES

Repeaters

- Repeat signal by regenerating, retiming, and amplifying the signal
- Pass all signals between attached segments
- not read destination addresses of data packets
- allow for the connection of different types of media
- extend overall LAN distance effectively by repeating signals between LAN segments.

Bridges

Bridges are more discriminating as bridge reads the destination address of each data frame and decides whether the destination is local or remote and only allows packets with remote addresses to "cross the bridge" bridges also check the source address of each frame and adds it to a table of known local addresses forward-if-not-local.

Types of Bridges

- Transparent bridges (both LANs must be the same type)
- Translating bridges (multiprotocol bridges contain a format converter)
- Encapsulation bridges (bridges Ethernet & FDDI)

- Source routing bridges (source routing Token Ring to Ethernet)
- Bridge performance can be measured by the filtering rate (packets/sec) and the forwarding rate (packets/sec).

2.9 WIDE-AREA NETWORKS

Wide-area networks have traditionally been considered to be those that cover a large geographical area, require the crossing of public right-of-ways, and rely at least in part on circuits provided by a common telephone carrier. Typically, a WAN consists of a number of interconnected switching nodes. Transmission from any one device is routed through these internal nodes to the specified destination device. These nodes (including the boundary nodes to which the devices are connected) are not concerned with the

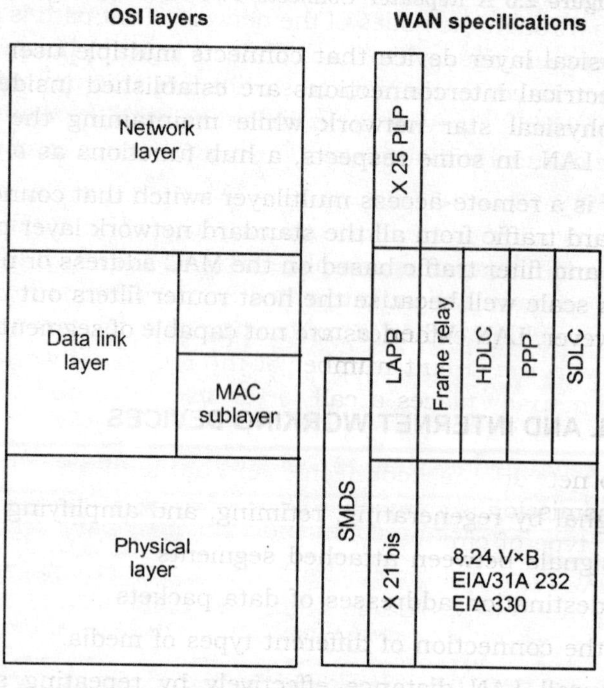

Figure 2.6 WAN Technologies Operate at the Lowest Levels of the OSI Model

content of the data; rather, their purpose is to provide a switching facility that will move the data from node to node until they reach their destination. Traditionally, WANs have been implemented using one of two technologies: circuit switching and packet switching. More recently, frame relay and ATM networks have assumed major roles. WAN technologies generally function at the lower three layers of the OSI reference model: the physical layer, the data link layer, and the network layer. Figure 2.6 illustrates the relationship between the common WAN technologies and the OSI model.

Point-to-point Link

A *point-to-point link* provides a single, pre-established WAN communications path from the customer premises through a carrier network, such as a telephone company, to a remote network. Point-to-point lines are usually leased from a carrier and thus are often called leased lines. Figure 2.7 illustrates a typical point-to-point link through a WAN.

Figure 2.7 A Typical Point-to-Point Link Operates Through a WAN to a Remote Network

2.9.1 WAN Networking Technologies

Circuit Switching

In a circuit-switched network, a dedicated communication path is established between two stations through the nodes of the network. That path is a connected sequence of physical links between nodes. On each link, a logical channel is *dedicated* to the connection. Data generated by the source station are transmitted along the dedicated path as rapidly as possible. At each node, incoming data are routed or switched to the appropriate outgoing channel without delay. The most common example of circuit switching is the telephone network.

Switched circuits allow data connections that can be initiated when needed and terminated when communication is complete. This works much like a normal telephone line works for voice communication. Integrated Services Digital Network (ISDN) is a good example of circuit switching. When a router has data for a remote site, the switched circuit is initiated with the circuit number of the remote network. In the case of ISDN circuits, the device actually places a call to the telephone number of the remote ISDN circuit.

When the two networks are connected and authenticated, they can transfer data. When the data transmission is complete, the call can be terminated. Figure 2.8 illustrates an example of this type of circuit.

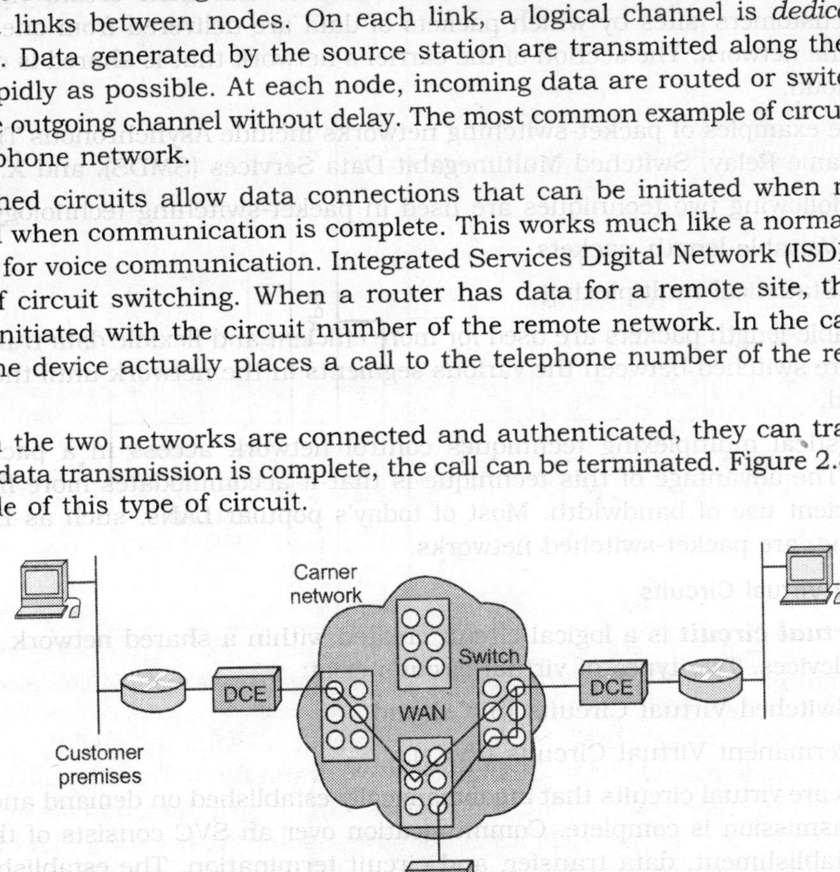

Figure 2.8 A Circuit-Switched WAN Undergoes a Process Similar to That Used for a Telephone Call

Packet Switching

A quite different approach is used in a packet-switched network. In this case, it is not necessary to dedicate transmission capacity along a path through the network. Rather, data are sent out in a sequence of small chunks, called packets. Each packet is passed through the network from node to node along some path leading from source to destination. At each node, the entire packet is received, stored briefly, and then transmitted to the next node. Packet-switched networks are commonly used for terminal-to-computer and computer-to-computer communications.

Packet switching is a WAN technology in which users share common carrier resources. Because this allows the carrier to make more efficient use of its infrastructure, the cost to the customer is generally much better than with point-to-point lines. In a packet switching setup, networks have connections into the carrier's network, and many customers share the carrier's network. The carrier can then create virtual circuits between customers' sites by which packets of data are delivered from one to the other through the network. The section of the carrier's network that is shared is often referred to as a cloud.

Some examples of packet-switching networks include Asynchronous Transfer Mode (ATM), Frame Relay, Switched Multimegabit Data Services (SMDS), and X.25.

The following two techniques are used in packet-switching technology:

- Variable-length packets
- Statistical multiplexing

Variable-length packets are used for more efficient and flexible data transfers. These packets are switched between the various segments in the network until the destination is reached.

Statistical multiplexing techniques control network access in a packet-switched network. The advantage of this technique is that it accommodates more flexibility and more efficient use of bandwidth. Most of today's popular LANs, such as Ethernet and Token Ring, are packet-switched networks.

2.9.2 WAN Virtual Circuits

A ***virtual circuit*** is a logical circuit created within a shared network between two network devices. Two types of virtual circuits exist:

1. Switched Virtual Circuits (SVCs) and
2. Permanent Virtual Circuits (PVCs).

SVCs are virtual circuits that are dynamically established on demand and terminated when transmission is complete. Communication over an SVC consists of three phases: circuit establishment, data transfer, and circuit termination. The establishment phase involves creating the virtual circuit between the source and destination devices. Data transfer involves transmitting data between the devices over the virtual circuit, and the circuit termination phase involves tearing down the virtual circuit between the source and destination devices. SVCs are used in situations in which data transmission between devices is sporadic, largely because SVCs increase bandwidth used due to the circuit establishment and termination phases, but they decrease the cost associated with constant virtual circuit availability.

PVC is a permanently established virtual circuit that consists of one mode: data transfer. PVCs are used in situations in which data transfer between devices is constant. PVCs decrease the bandwidth use associated with the establishment and termination of virtual circuits, but they increase costs due to constant virtual circuit availability. PVCs are generally configured by the service provider when an order is placed for service.

2.9.3 WAN Dialup Services

Dialup services offer cost-effective methods for connectivity across WANs. Two popular dialup implementations are dial-on-demand routing (DDR) and dial backup.

DDR is a technique whereby a router can dynamically initiate a call on a switched circuit when it needs to send data. In a DDR setup, the router is configured to initiate the call when certain criteria are met, such as a particular type of network traffic needing to be transmitted. When the connection is made, traffic passes over the line. The router configuration specifies an idle timer that tells the router to drop the connection when the circuit has remained idle for a certain period.

Dial backup is another way of configuring DDR. However, in dial backup, the switched circuit is used to provide backup service for another type of circuit, such as point-to-point or packet switching. The router is configured so that when a failure is detected on the primary circuit, the dial backup line is initiated. The dial backup line then supports the WAN connection until the primary circuit is restored. When this occurs, the dial backup connection is terminated.

2.9.4 WAN Devices

WANs use numerous types of devices that are specific to WAN environments. WAN switches, access servers, modems, CSU/DSUs, and ISDN terminal adapters are discussed in the following sections. Other devices found in WAN environments that are used in WAN implementations include routers, ATM switches, and multiplexers.

WAN Switch. A *WAN switch* is a multiport internetworking device used in carrier networks. These devices typically switch such traffic as Frame Relay, X.25, and SMDS, and operate at the data link layer of the OSI reference model.

Modem

A *modem* is a device that interprets digital and analog signals, enabling data to be transmitted over voice-grade telephone lines. At the source, digital signals are converted to a form suitable for transmission over analog communication facilities. At the destination, these analog signals are returned to their digital form. Figure 2.9 illustrates a simple modem-to-modem connection through a WAN.

Figure 2.9 A Modem Connection Through a WAN Handles Analog and Digital

CSU/DSU

A ***channel service unit/digital service unit (CSU/DSU)*** is a digital-interface device used to connect a router to a digital circuit like a T1. The CSU/DSU also provides signal timing for communication between these devices. ISDN

Terminal Adapter

An *ISDN terminal adapter* is a device used to connect ISDN Basic Rate Interface (BRI) connections to other interfaces, such as EIA/TIA-232 on a router. A terminal adapter is essentially an ISDN modem, although it is called a terminal adapter because it does not actually convert analog to digital signals.

2.10 OTHER INTERNETWORKS

Besides the above illustrated internetwork,a lot number of internetwork also exist, let's go through them.

2.10.1 Arpanet

Sometimes referred to as the "grand-daddy of packet networks", the ARPANET was built by DARPA in the late 60s to accommodate research equipment on packet-switching technology and to allow resource sharing for the Department of Defense's contractors. It soon became popular with researchers for collaboration through electronic mail and other services. It was developed into a research utility run by the Defense Communications Agency (DCA) by the end of 1975 and split in 1983 into MILNET for interconnection of military sites and ARPANET for interconnection of research sites.

In 1974, the ARPANET was based on 56 Kbps leased lines which interconnected *Packet-Switching Nodes* (PSN) scattered across the continental US and western Europe. These were minicomputers running a protocol known as *1822* and dedicated to the packet-switching task. Each PSN had at least two connections to other PSNs (to allow alternate routing in case of circuit failure) and up to 22 ports for user computer (*host*) connections. These 1822 systems offered reliable, flow-controlled delivery of a packet to a destination node. This is the reason why the original *NCP* protocol was a rather simple protocol. It was replaced by the TCP/IP protocols, which do not assume reliability of the underlying network hardware and can be used on other-than-1822 networks.

Data traffic rapidly exceeded the capacity of the 56 Kbps lines that made up the network, which were no longer able to support the necessary throughput. Today the ARPANET has been replaced by new technologies in its role of backbone on the research side of the connected Internet (see NSFNET later in this chapter), whereas MILNET continues to form the backbone of the military side.

2.10.2 NSFNET

NSFNET, the National Science Foundation Network, is a three-level internetwork in the United States consisting of:

- The *backbone*: a network that connects separately administered and operated mid-level networks and NSF-funded supercomputer centres. The backbone also has transcontinental links to other networks such as EBONE, the European IP backbone network.
- *Mid-level networks*: of three kinds (regional, discipline-based and supercomputer consortium networks).

First Backbone

Originally established by the National Science Foundation (NSF) as a communications network for researchers and scientists to access the NSF supercomputers, the first

NSFNET backbone used six DEC LSI/11 microcomputers as packet switches, interconnected by 56 Kbps leased lines.

Second Backbone

The need for a new backbone appeared in 1987, when the first one became overloaded within a few months (estimated growth at that time was 100% per year). Installed in 1988, the new network initially used 448 Kbps leased circuits to interconnect 13 *nodal switching systems* (NSS) supplied by IBM.

Third Backbone

In 1989, the NSFNET backbone circuits topology was reconfigured after traffic measurements and the speed of the leased lines increased to T1 (1.544 Mbps) using primarily fiber optics. Due to the constantly increasing need for improved packet switching and transmission capacities, three NSSs were added to the backbone and the link speed was upgraded. The migration of the NSFNET backbone from T1 to T3 (45Mbps) was completed in late 1992.

2.10.3 EBONE

EBONE, the Pan-European Multi-Protocol Backbone plays the same role in Europe for Internet traffic as the NSFNET backbone does in the United States. EBONE has kilobit and megabit links between five major centres.

2.10.4 CREN

Completed in October 1989, the merger of the two already well known networks CSNET (the Computer+Science Network) and BITNET (the *Because It's Time* Network) formed the Corporation for Research and Educational Networking. CREN draws on both of its historical CSNET and BITNET service families to provide a rich variety of network connection options:

1. *Phonenet*

Is the original CSNET network service and provides a store-and-forward electronic mail service using dial-up telephone lines (1200/2400 bps). It allows CSNET service members to exchange messages with other CREN members and with other major mail networks, including NSFNET, MILNET, etc.

2. *X.25NET*

Is a CSNET full-service Internet-connected network that uses TCP/IP protocols on top of X.25. It is the common method for international members to connect to CSNET, since they can use their local X.25 Public Data Network to reach Telenet in the US. It provides file transfer, remote login, and immediate electronic mail service between X.25Net hosts.

3. *Dial-Up IP*

Is an implementation of SLIP (Serial Line IP) that allows sites using the switched telephone network (9600 bps) to send IP packets, by means of a central server, to the Internet. Users of this method thus have the same services as X.25Net sites.

4. *Leased Line IP*

Used by many CREN members to connect to CREN. A variety of link speeds are supported up to T1 rates.

5. *RSCS/NJE Over Bisync*

Traditionally runs over leased lines at 9600 bps and provides interactive messages, unsolicited file transfer and electronic mail.

2.10.5 Cypress

Cypress is a leased-line network that provides a low-cost, protocol-independent, packet switching system used primarily for interconnecting small sites to the TCP/IP Internet. Originally established as part of a joint research project with CSNET, it is now independent of CSNET.

There are no restrictions on its use, outside those imposed by other networks. Thus commercial traffic can pass between two industrial sites across Cypress. Industrial sites cannot pass commercial traffic onto the Internet due to restrictions imposed by government agencies that control the backbone networks (for example NSFNET).

2.10.6 DRI

The Terrestrial Wideband Network is a wide area network whose purpose is to provide a platform for research on high-speed networking protocols and applications (this role was formerly played by the ARPANET). This system includes both connection-oriented as well as connectionless service, broadcast and multicast service and real-time conferencing.

2.10.7 European Academic Research Network (EARN)

EARN, started in 1983, was the first and largest network serving academic and research institutions in Europe, the Middle East and Africa. EARN was initially started with help from IBM. It evolved to become a non-profit non-commercial traffic-based network serving academic and research institutions.

2.11 THE INTERNET

First, the word *internet* (also *internetwork*) is simply a contraction of the phrase *interconnected network*. However when written with a capital "I" the Internet refers to a worldwide set of interconnected networks, so the Internet is an internet, but the reverse does not follow. The Internet consists of the following groups of networks (see the following sections for more information on some of these):

Backbones: large networks which exist primarily to interconnect other networks. Currently the backbones are NSFNET in the US, EBONE in Europe and large commercial backbones. Regional networks connecting, for example, universities and colleges. Commercial networks providing access to the backbones to subscribers, and networks owned by commercial organizations for internal use which also have connections to the Internet. Local networks, such as campus-wide university networks.

Internet is network of computers that offer access to people and information. Over 60 million people use Internet, and the number is expected to increase over 120 million within a few years. The kind of information freely available from internet includes Government documents, scientific data, hobbyist lists, business and personal information, advertising databases and much more.

Internet in India

In India Internet was started to serve the educational institutions to help in their research work. In 1986, IIT was linked up with Indian Institute of Science by ERNET, which later connected with foreign universities. On 15th August 1996 Government called VSNL and started its dial-up services as first Internet Service Provider. Now, there are more than 100 ISPs given license to provide Internet Service. Some of them are MTNL, Satyam Computers Ltd., Wintech, etc.

2.11.1 Internet Protocols

TCP/IP

Transfer Control Protocol and Internet Protocol are two sets of rules that allow computers and networks to communicate effectively. They regulate the flow of data and make sure that it reaches its destination safe and sound.

TCP and IP goes hand-in-hand to enable the safe delivery of data over a network, the data is split into a number of smaller packets. TCP/IP attaches a header to the data packet, which contains information like the address, its origin, length of the packet and so on. IP, on the other hand, works like a postal department and ensures that once the data packets reach the receiver's end, they are re-assembled in the same sequence they were broken up and are ready for the application they are meant for.

IP works as routing agent falls under the network layer which has function of making decision for transmitting data across device not connected to each other.

Layers

The two protocols TCP/IP are stacked over each other and occupy the network layer and the transport layer. These layers are a part of virtual model of networking called OPEN SYSTEM INTERCONNECTION (OSI) model. The OSI model consists of Physical, Data link, Network, Transport, Session, Presentation and Application layers.

The physical layer transmits data from one location to another and is made up of physical aspects of the network like cables and connectors. The data link layer ensures error-free transmission of data and consists of networking cards, modems, etc. The function of the network layer is to make routing decisions for transmitting data across devices that are not connected to each other.

As IP is a routing agent, it falls under this layer. The transport layer comes next and its primary function is to ensure error free transmission of data. Transfer Control Protocol or TCP falls under this layer. The remaining layers such as the Session, Presentation and Application layers from the application group, which synchronizes links across programs and converts network data to user readable formats.

TCP

As Transport layer protocol, TCP accepts message information from the applications, and divides it into multiple segments, and encapsulates each segment into a datagram. Each datagram is passed over to the network layer protocol (IP) for further transmission and routing. At the receiver's end, TCP reassembles the data and distributes it to the concerned application program.

TCP transmits data in the form of packets that comprise of a header and a data block. The header consists of information like the address of the packet, its origin, the length of the packet and more. The data block carries the payload, which is the text or pictures that we down load or browse off the Net.

Internet Protocol

Internet protocol or IP works like postal department. It routes data packets to the address mentioned in the header and fragments them. These are then marked so that the fragmentation sequence is maintained and are reassembled upon reaching their destination.

The routing of data grams over a network can occur over different paths and the possibility of some data grams arriving out of sequence is not ruled out. In addition, as data grams flow between various networks, they also face physical limitations in terms of the amount of data that can be transferred over a particular network.

IP is also attached to a small header on the data packet, which provides information about the handling of the datagram, identification of fragmented data grams and the like. The version field contains a 4, bit code that identifies the IP protocol used to create the datagram. The identification field proves the identity of a datagram. In case the datagram has been further fragmented, the fragment offset field specifies the other offset of the datagram.

The flag field contains information about the nature of fragmentation. It provides information about the current fragment and also gives the total number of the fragments. The header also has a field called 'Time to Live' or TTL that defines the number of routers a data packet can encounter en route to its destination computer, thereby avoiding chocked networks.

IP operates on gateway machines that move data from the department to the organization, then to the region and finally across the world.

2.11.2 IP Address & URL

To connect from one machine to another machine on the Internet, we need to know its IP address, which is an identifier for a particular machine on a particular network. These are referred as IP numbers or Internet addresses.

The IP address is represented by four decimal numbers separated by dots and is basically divided into the host computer section.

Classification to Internets

Class A: This comprises of very large networks with millions of nodes. They have their IP addresses ranging from 1.0.0.0 to 127.0.0.0. The first number before the dot defines the network with the remaining three sections assigned to hosts.

Class B: These are smaller networks and can have only about 65,000 nodes. Their IP addresses range from 128.0.0.0 to 191.0.0.0. The first two numbers are allocated to the network and the remaining two numbers for the hosts.

Class C: These are much smaller networks, which support a maximum of 254 nodes. The IP addresses range from 192.0.0.0 to 223.0.0.0. In this case, the first three numbers denote the network and the last one denotes the host.

To make the operation simpler, ordinary names are assigned to each address using the Domain Name System. Each Domain Name corresponds to a numeric IP address. The Internet uses the IP address to identify the network and the node and send data to the same. For example: As you type in the address www.yahoo.com form your browser, the Internet actually connects you to the IP number 204.71.200.74 (Which is the domain name for the web site).

Uniform Resource Locater (URL)

URL is the way to represent site name on the World Wide Web. URLs are similar to postal addresses or telephone numbers which are used to represent the destinations. Most URL consists of 3 parts:

- Service name
- Host name
- Request.

The most common service names you use in URLs are "http", "together", "ftp" and "news". These refer to Web servers, Gopher servers, FTP servers and Usenet news servers, respectively. A few URLs do not have a host name.

2.11.3 Domain Name Servers

Internet works on the numbering system. These numbers are called IP. When we connect to the net we have seen a set of 4 numbers being dialed *i.e.*, for each address on the Internet there is a unique set of these 32 bit numbers. Domain Name Servers are the servers, which maintain a distributed list of all domains against Internet Protocol address.

Earlier to Domain Name Servers there was a system of having a host table maintained by SRI-NIC. It was updated twice a week to include new sites. System would download the copy of this table through FTP.There are two types of servers as below:

- Resolver
- DNS.

There are a number of servers, which maintain the addresses of sites. When browser needs the address of any site, resolver queries the nearest name server, replies immediately if it knows the answer or it asks another server. Thus every server has two roles to play:

- As a server for name server
- Super server to extend functionality.

All web sites are arranged in 7 branches namely arpa, com, edu, net, gov, mil, org. Following this are 236 country name abbreviations like "in" for India. This helps to locate the site easily. The IP addresses of name servers at each of the domain name tags are maintained by 10 root servers.

- When a DNS fields a query that it cannot answer
- It sends a query to root server
- Root server says it does not know but a machine at say 195.95.251.10 might know
- DNS sends a query to the above machine
- Server at 195.95.251.10 knows the answer
- DNS returns answer to your PC.

Features of DNS

Cache: Name server caches all IP address for domain names that were requested recently. So that if requested again it responds immediately.

Load Balancing: Large sites like www.msn.com can have multiple addresses for same domain name. Name servers currently return all IP addresses leaving PC to choose at random. But some name servers will now evaluate all addresses to find out he one with least load.

2.11.4 Applications

FTP

File Transfer Protocol, which is the standard system for moving files on the Internet. With it, it is possible to send or receive files to and from a machine on the Internet. The machine to which we are connecting must have FTP server and its address generally starts with 'ftp' code.

FTP requires that we be directly linked to the machine in question. So we are unlikely to use FTP to transfer your files unless we or our client has dedicated FTP server permanently connected to the Net.

As FTP computer knows the name of the Internet services we are calling from, we only need to type 'username@' followed by return. Once logged on, we can get access to public accessible software. Here one can get all sorts of files inside them. Thus, numerous FTP servers all over the world allow the people anywhere on the Internet to log in and download whatever files have been placed on the FTP server.

Telnet

Telnet is a way of connecting to another machine on the Internet, and using it as if it were our own. In most cases we need to log-in and details of how to do this may be displayed after we have connected to it. A useful telnet site, especially if we are unable to access the full graphical splendor of the Web is: telnet.w3.org. This is a text based web browsing system.

The telnet command is a user interface to a protocol called, not surprisingly, TELNET. Both computers in order for the telnet program, to work must use the TELNET protocol. UNIX computer on the Internet uses the TELNET protocol, so this is rarely an issue. Telnet has many uses on the Internet:

- Hundreds of library catalogs are available only through direct connection to the library's computers. Using telnet server long distance charges of dial on directly to those computers; some don't even allow direct dialling.

- If you have accounts on more than one computer on the Internet, you can log into the one closest to you and use telnet to log into the others.

The World Wide Web

The World Wide Web is an architectural frame work for accessing linked documents spread out over thousands of machines all over the Internet. Its enormous popularity stems from the fact that it has a colorful graphical interface that is easy for beginners to use, and provides an enormous wealth of information on almost, every conceivable subject.

The Web began in 1989 at CERN, the European center for nuclear research. CERN has several accelerators at which large team of scientists from the participating European Countries carry out research in particle physics. The Web grew out of the need to have these large teams of internationally dispersed researchers collaborate using a constantly changing collection of reports, blueprints, drawings, photos, and other documents.

2.11.5 Hyper Text Transfer Protocol (HTTP)

The HTTP is a method used to make hyper text documents readable on the World Wide Web. Web servers and clients speak to each other using HTTP, so end users don't need to know anything about its intricacies.

HTTP is a stateless protocol, meaning that the client and the server programs speak to each other only once and that a connection is not retained. A web client program sends a single request to the web server for information, and the web sever responds with a single reply.

Web Server

Is a software program that sits on your server (The physical machine that is designed to store and serve web pages). Any server configured to communicate using TCP/IP uses ports. Not serial or parallel ports like the ones on the back of your computer, but the ones that look different and serve the same purpose. E.g. Port 80 is the default web server port and all hyper text transfer protocols.

As HTTP request comes to the server it checks the appropriate permissions and then either transmits the page or if the permissions are not adequate, it sends an error message.

The Web server has certain restrictions to what it can process. When the server receives a request for a page having embedded scripts, it cannot process these by itself. It therefore uses additional software that performs auxiliary processing called middleware.

Type of Web Servers

FTP Servers

FTP or File Server Transfer Protocol servers are Internet computers that use this protocol and provide data to Internet users for downloading. Firstly the user should log into FTP server, where the access rights are derived for different directories.

DNS Servers

Every computer in the Internet is provided with a specific IP address consisting of four numbers like 123.123.123.123. Since remembering the numbers is difficult, the

Internet users want to reach a specific computer on the WWW can also use description. A DNS server includes a database of IP Address. Mapping Web is referred by Internet software to retrieve the IP address.

Gopher Servers

In the past few years many new tools for searching for information on the Internet have developed. One of them is Gopher Server. It is a Client/Server system that teaches you to navigate through the Internet.

Usenet News Servers

It is a system where messages about any subject can be posted and other people on the Internet can reply to them. This topic includes politics, science, religion etc. There are more than 5000 active new groups,

2.11.6 Browsers

Browser is a kind of program, which can understand the hyper text protocol and present it into textual or graphical view. Some of the popular browsers are Internet Explorer, Netscape Navigator, Opera, Mosiac etc.

2.11.7 Search Engines

Searching on the net comprise the enormous and exhaustive task of connecting to each server and finding the requisite information on it. David Filo and Jerry Lang, studying electronics at Stanford University decided to do something about it. They decided to develop a universal database using which one could find information in a quick and simple way. Consequently the worlds first search engine Yahoo! was born in April 1994.

Today there exist a variety of search engines, all of them they would possibly cover almost a major part of the information on the web at any given time. Search engines are composed of databases that comprise indexing schemes, a query processor and 'spiders'. Spiders are programs that are designed to look up web pages which are listed in every database, follow up on each and every link and update their databases to reflect the updated information. The records in these databases consist of the Uniform Resource Locater or more simply, the dares where the website or page is located, the title of the page and the keywords for that page along with a short summary of the site in a few lines.

2.11.8 Hyper Text Markup Language (HTML)

It is language for describing how documents are to be formatted. The term "Markup" comes from the old days when copy editors actually marked up documents to tell the printer-in those days, Markup languages thus contain explicit commands for formatting. For example, in HTML, <B> means start boldface <\B> means leave bold face mode.

Documents written in a markup language can be contrasted to documents produced with WYSIWYG (What You See Is What You Get) word processor, such as MS-Word or MS-Perfect. These systems may store their files with hidden embedded markup so they can reproduce them later, but not all of them work this way. By embedding the markup commands within each HTML file and standardizing them, it becomes possible for any web browser to read and reformat any web page.

2.11.9 Shell Account PPP/SLIP Account

Shell account describes the authorization to access another computer at the operating system level. Shell accounts are useful to the user who needs data in textual format. In shell account, user has no direct IP-Link via SLIP/PPP.

PPP/SLIP

Computer using the TCP/IP Communication protocol to another TCP/IP computer over a modem or a serial line, both computers must be running on an additional protocol. This can either be PPP (point to point) or SLIP (special Line IP). Both protocols perform the same task but they are not interoperable (*i.e.*, both ends of the connection must be running on either PPP or SLIP). PPP was derived in 1991 by IETF (Internet Engineering Task Force).

2.11.10 Firewalls

For Networks integrated with the Internet, there is a need to ensure safety to our network. A study revealed that out of the 250,000 attacks on the Department's computer systems, about 65 percent succeed. To minimize such problems, the companies need to add a fire wall between the network and the Internet.

The firewall consists of hardware such as routers and host systems software. A firewall is basically a data packet between trusted and un-trusted networks. Any kind of network that uses TCP/IP for data transmission depends on source address, and the port number. A firewall uses these addresses and port numbers to control the flow of data packets between the trusted and un-trusted network.

Classification of Firewalls

- Packet filter,
- Application proxy or Application gateway,
- Packet Inspection Firewall.

1. Application filter firewall: It is the fastest and simplest of the three and is also one of the earliest. Usually the Router (hardware) based, in this system a packet filter compares the header information source and destination address, and port number-of each incoming or outgoing packet against a table of access control rules.

2. Application proxy firewall: Proxy firewalls are built on the principle that security can be reliable only if there is no direct connection between the trusted and un-trusted networks. An application firewall works by examining what application or service (such as e-mail or file transfer) a data packet is directed to. If the service is available to that packet, then it is allowed to pass through.

3. Packet inspection firewall: The content of the packets is also considered. This inspection of packet can be either based on its 'state' or 'session'. In Case of state filtering, the firewall only allows the incoming packet if it can be matched with an outbound request (or' invitation) for that packet.

In case of session filtering, the network station in tracked. Once the trusted user terminates the session, all incoming packets with identity pertaining to that session are rejected.

2.12 INTRANET

It is a network connecting as an affiliated set of clients using standard internet protocols, especially TCP/IP and HTTP. It is also defined as an IP-based network of nodes behind a firewall, or behind several firewalls connected by secure, possibly virtual, networks.

2.12.1 Introduction

A requirement for successful coordination is consistency of information. It is not very efficient if the existence or location of important information remains unknown to an individual who needs it. It also is not very efficient if a team tries to reach a consensus when each member is operating from a different information base that may be incompatible or inconsistent with the others on the team. Some information gets stale and requires attention to keep it current. Most of today's organizational structures and processes have been refined over centuries to solve these problems for paper-based information.

Information currency and integrity is a much simpler problem when the content does not change often, activities being coordinated are not large or complex, and the information is centrally collected and distributed. However, these are not common characteristics of most enterprises today. The distributed environments more commonly found today need to be able to coordinate information in a different way, and this requires a different set of management structures and processes than most organizations have inherited.

An Intranet offers new options for more effective coordination of organizational activities in a distributed decision-making environment. However, today's paper-based infrastructure inhibits exploitation of many Intranet enhancements and does not effectively control others. What is needed is an infrastructure that uses the Intranet to meet the requirements for organizational coordination by supporting the management of content in the distributed decision-making environment.

Constructing an effective Intranet infrastructure requires attention to three distinct areas:

- management,
- technical and
- content.

Management consists of the roles, policies, processes and organization needed to manage the life cycle of formal Intranet content.

The technical infrastructure consists of the networks, hardware and software required to support content development, publishing and access.

And, content requires processes to be developed to support special needs such as initial conversions, creation of database or application interfaces and development of "glossy" pages for high impact.

2.12.2 Intranets

An Intranet is a communication infrastructure. It is based on the communication standards of the Internet and the content standards of the World-Wide Web. Therefore, the tools used to create an Intranet are identical to those used for Internet and Web applications. The distinguishing feature of an Intranet is that access to information published on the Intranet is restricted to clients in the Intranet group.

2.12.3 Advantages of Intranet

Streamlining Business Process

Intranets are phenomenally powerful tools to streamline business process. From decision support, customer service and product engineering to distributed channel operations, from sales force automation and executive information systems, business applications based on intranets can substantially improve the efficiency of complex operations. This is possible because intranet applications are typically much less expensive to develop and deploy, and much easier to use than applications based on older proprietary platforms. Benefiting from a universal client interface the Web browser-intranet business applications can be deployed and managed from a central location. At the same time, standard based protocols and development technologies enable separate departments across a company to create intranet solutions that remain compatible and compliant with company wide systems and process.

Facilitating Information Dissemination

A key benefit of the intranet technology is its ability to provide up-to-date information quickly and cost-effectively to the entire user community. An intranet puts vital information at the fingertips of employees, regardless of their location or the location of the information. Information disseminated on an intranet enables a high degree of coherence for the entire company because communications are consistent. A 'news' section of an intranet, for example, can include recent company press releases regarding management strategies, partnerships, and new products. A finance section can keep employees informed of vital financial reports and forecasts. A customer section can allow customers to check the status of an order or repair. Vendors can submit invoices online and check procurement status.

By giving people the ability to access time-critical information, intranets improve the decision-making process by empowering individuals with the knowledge necessary for faster and better informed business decisions. Intranets allow the centralization of information, which makes it easier to maintain and keep data upto data. The benefit to the end-user is the simplicity and speed of information access. For example, the interactive capability enabled by hyper-text links makes it easy for users to gather all the information they need from Web pages quickly, just by clicking on a related icon or button. Providing instant and secure access to business-critical information saves time and increases productivity, and publishing information online eliminates the production, duplication and distribution costs associated with paper.

Enriching Communications and Collaboration

Intranet technologies enable teams to share knowledge and information regardless of their locations or time zones. Engineering groups can share research data, design concepts, schedules and other project materials for comments and reviews during a development process. Training groups can distribute training schedules and multimedia computer-associated training courses using Web-based technologies. Project terms can take advantage of intranet newsgroups and threaded discussion to communicate issues and solutions, and can use online chat technology when real-time interaction is required. With intranet teleconferencing, participants can share conference materials in a variety of formats, including text, graphics, audio and video.

2.13 NETWORKING TECHNOLOGIES

2.13.1 Frame Relay

Packet switching was developed at a time when digital long-distance transmission facilities exhibited a relatively high error rate compared to today's facilities. *Frame Relay* is a high-performance WAN protocol that operates at the physical and data link layers of the OSI reference model. Frame Relay is an example of a packet-switched technology. As a result, there is a considerable amount of overhead built into packet-switched schemes to compensate for errors. The overhead includes additional bits added to each packet to introduce redundancy and additional processing at the end stations and the intermediate switching nodes to detect and recover from errors. Frame Relay often is described as a streamlined version of X.25, offering fewer of the robust capabilities, such as windowing and retransmission of last data that are offered in X.25. This is because Frame Relay typically operates over WAN facilities that offer more reliable connection services and a higher degree of reliability than the facilities available during the late 1970s and early 1980s that served as the common platforms for X.25 WANs.

With modern high-speed telecommunication systems, this overhead is unnecessary and counterproductive. It is unnecessary because the rate of errors has been dramatically lowered and any remaining errors can easily be caught in the end systems by logic that operates above the level of the packet-switching logic; it is counterproductive because the overhead involved soaks up a significant fraction of the high capacity provided by the network.

Frame relay was developed to take advantage of these high data rates and low error rates. Whereas the original packet-switching networks were designed with a data rate to the end user of about 64 kbps(kilo bits per second, 1 kilo=10^3), frame relay networks are designed to operate efficiently at user data rates of up to 2 Mbps (Mega bits per second, 1 Mega=10^6). The key to achieving these high data rates is to strip out most of the overhead involved with error control.

2.13.2 Frame Relay Devices

Devices attached to a Frame Relay WAN fall into the following two general categories:

- Data terminal equipment (DTE)
- Data circuit-terminating equipment (DCE)

DTEs generally are considered to be terminating equipment for a specific network and typically are located on the premises of a customer. In fact, they may be owned by the customer. Examples of DTE devices are terminals, personal computers, routers, and bridges.

DCEs are carrier-owned internetworking devices. The purpose of DCE equipment is to provide clocking and switching services in a network, which are the devices that actually transmit data through the WAN. In most cases, these are packet switches. Figure 2.10 shows the relationship between the two categories of devices.

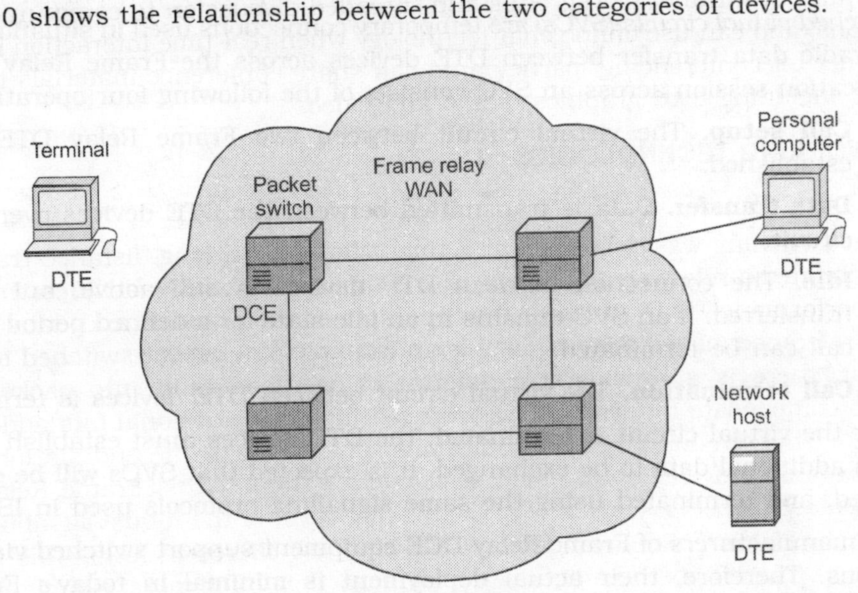

Figure 2.10 DCEs Generally Reside Within Carrier-Operated WANs

The connection between a DTE device and a DCE device consists of both a physical layer component and a link layer component. The physical component defines the mechanical, electrical, functional, and procedural specifications for the connection between the devices. One of the most commonly used physical layer interface specifications is the recommended standard (RS)-232 specification. The link layer component defines the protocol that establishes the connection between the DTE device, such as a router, and the DCE device, such as a switch. This chapter examines a commonly utilized protocol specification used in WAN networking: the Frame Relay protocol.

2.13.3 Frame Relay Virtual Circuits

Frame Relay provides connection-oriented data link layer communication. This means that a defined communication exists between each pair of devices and that these connections are associated with a connection identifier. This service is implemented by using a Frame Relay virtual circuit, which is a logical connection created between two data terminal equipment (DTE) devices across a Frame Relay packet-switched network (PSN).

Virtual circuits provide a bidirectional communication path from one DTE device to another and are uniquely identified by a data-link connection identifier (DLCI). A number of virtual circuits can be multiplexed into a single physical circuit for transmission across the network. This capability often can reduce the equipment and network complexity required to connect multiple DTE devices. A virtual circuit can pass through any number of intermediate DCE devices (switches) located within the Frame Relay PSN.

Frame Relay virtual circuits fall into two categories:

- Switched Virtual Circuits (SVCs) and
- Permanent Virtual Circuits (PVCs).

Switched Virtual Circuits

Switched virtual circuits (SVCs) are temporary connections used in situations requiring only sporadic data transfer between DTE devices across the Frame Relay network. A communication session across an SVC consists of the following four operational states:

- **Call setup.** The virtual circuit between two Frame Relay DTE devices is established.
- **Data transfer.** Data is transmitted between the DTE devices over the virtual circuit.
- **Idle.** The connection between DTE devices is still active, but no data is transferred. If an SVC remains in an idle state for a defined period of time, the call can be terminated.
- **Call termination.** The virtual circuit between DTE devices is terminated.

After the virtual circuit is terminated, the DTE devices must establish a new SVC if there is additional data to be exchanged. It is expected that SVCs will be established, maintained, and terminated using the same signalling protocols used in ISDN.

Few manufacturers of Frame Relay DCE equipment support switched virtual circuit connections. Therefore, their actual deployment is minimal in today's Frame Relay networks.

Previously not widely supported by Frame Relay equipment, SVCs are now the norm. Companies have found that SVCs save money in the end because the circuit is not open all the time.

Permanent Virtual Circuits

Permanent virtual circuits (PVCs) are permanently established connections that are used for frequent and consistent data transfers between DTE devices across the Frame Relay network. Communication across a PVC does not require the call setup and termination states that are used with SVCs. PVCs always operate in one of the following two operational states:

- **Data transfer state.** Data is transmitted between the DTE devices over the virtual circuit.
- **Idle state.** The connection between DTE devices is active, but no data is transferred. Unlike SVCs, PVCs will not be terminated under any circumstances when in an idle state.

DTE devices can begin transferring data whenever they are ready because the circuit is permanently established.

Data-Link Connection Identifier

Frame Relay virtual circuits are identified by *data-link connection identifiers (DLCIs).* DLCI values typically are assigned by the Frame Relay service provider (for example, the telephone company). Frame Relay DLCIs have local significance, which means that their values are unique in the LAN, but not necessarily in the Frame Relay WAN.

Congestion-Control Mechanisms

Frame Relay reduces network overhead by implementing simple congestion-notification mechanisms rather than explicit, per-virtual-circuit flow control. Frame Relay typically is implemented on reliable network media, so data integrity is not sacrificed because flow control can be left to higher-layer protocols. Frame Relay implements two congestion-notification mechanisms:

- Forward-Explicit Congestion Notification (FECN).
- Backward-Explicit Congestion Notification (BECN).

Frame Relay Discard Eligibility

The *Discard Eligibility (DE) bit* is used to indicate that a frame has lower importance than other frames. The DE bit is part of the Address field in the Frame Relay frame header.

Frame Relay Error Checking

Frame Relay uses a common error-checking mechanism known as the *Cyclic Redundancy Check (CRC).*

Frame Relay Local Management Interface

The *Local Management Interface (LMI)* is a set of enhancements to the basic Frame Relay specification. Frame Relay LMI extensions include global addressing, virtual circuit status messages, and multicasting. The LMI global addressing extension gives Frame Relay data-link connection identifier (DLCI) values global rather than local significance. DLCI values become DTE addresses that are unique in the Frame Relay WAN. The global addressing extension adds functionality and manageability to Frame Relay internetworks. Individual network interfaces and the end nodes attached to them, for example, can be identified by using standard address-resolution and discovery techniques. In addition, the entire Frame Relay network appears to be a typical LAN to routers on its periphery.

LMI virtual circuit status messages provide communication and synchronization between Frame Relay DTE and DCE devices. These messages are used to periodically report on the status of PVCs, which prevents data from being sent into black holes (that is, over PVCs that no longer exist).

The LMI multicasting extension allows multicast groups to be assigned. Multicasting saves bandwidth by allowing routing updates and address-resolution messages to be sent only to specific groups of routers. The extension also transmits reports on the status of multicast groups in update messages.

2.13.4 Frame Relay Network Implementation

A common private Frame Relay network implementation is to equip a T1 multiplexer with both Frame Relay and non-Frame Relay interfaces. Frame Relay traffic is forwarded out the Frame Relay interface and onto the data network. Non-Frame Relay traffic is forwarded to the appropriate application or service, such as a private branch exchange (PBX) for telephone service or to a video-teleconferencing application.

A typical Frame Relay network consists of a number of DTE devices, such as routers, connected to remote ports on multiplexer equipment via traditional point-to-point services such as T1, fractional T1, or 56-Kb circuits.

The majority of Frame Relay networks deployed today are provisioned by service providers that intend to offer transmission services to customers. This is often referred to as a public Frame Relay service. Frame Relay is implemented in both public carrier-provided networks and in private enterprise networks. The following section examines the two methodologies for deploying Frame Relay.

Public Carrier-Provided Networks

In public carrier-provided Frame Relay networks, the Frame Relay switching equipment is located in the central offices of a telecommunications carrier. Subscribers are charged based on their network use but are relieved from administering and maintaining the Frame Relay network equipment and service.

Generally, the DCE equipment also is owned by the telecommunications provider. DTE equipment either will be customer-owned or perhaps will be owned by the telecommunications provider as a service to the customer.

The majority of today's Frame Relay networks are public carrier-provided networks.

Private Enterprise Networks

More frequently, organizations worldwide are deploying private Frame Relay networks. In private Frame Relay networks, the administration and maintenance of the network are the responsibilities of the enterprise (a private company). All the equipment, including the switching equipment, is owned by the customer.

2.13.5 Uses of Frame Relay

For companies with numerous distributed offices, Frame Relay provides a cost effective way of providing a secure private IP based network. While some companies use VPNs over the Internet for inter-company communications, that option does expose the organization to some serious security issues, not the least of which is keeping viruses and hackers out of perhaps hundreds of individual internet connections at the offices. In contrast, Frame Relay privacy is guaranteed by the nature of the network, backed up by legislation.

Frame Relay is also used as a low cost carrier to replace the networks of leased lines previously used to connect ATM machines, POS terminals and other legacy devices to head office mainframes. These applications involve some kind of protocol conversion to spoof the equipment at both ends. Many Frame Relay connections are used for high-end Internet connections.

2.14 ATM

Asynchronous Transfer Mode (ATM), sometimes referred to as cell relay, is a culmination of all of the developments in circuit switching and packet switching over the past 25 years.

ATM can be viewed as an evolution from frame relay. The most obvious difference between frame relay and ATM is that frame relay uses variable-length packets, called frames, and ATM uses fixed-length packets, called cells. As with frame relay, ATM provides little overhead for error control, depending on the inherent reliability of the transmission system and on higher layers of logic in the end systems to catch and correct errors. By using a fixed-packet length, the processing overhead is reduced even further for ATM compared to frame relay. The result is that ATM is designed to work in the range of 10s and 100s of Mbps, compared to the 2-Mbps target of frame relay.

2.14.1 ATM Devices and the Network Environment

ATM is a cell-switching and multiplexing technology that combines the benefits of circuit switching (guaranteed capacity and constant transmission delay) with those of packet switching (flexibility and efficiency for intermittent traffic). It provides scalable bandwidth from a few megabits per second (Mbps) to many gigabits per second (Gbps). Because of its asynchronous nature, ATM is more efficient than synchronous technologies, such as *Time-Division Multiplexing (TDM)*.

With TDM, each user is assigned to a time slot, and no other station can send in that time slot. If a station has much data to send, it can send only when its time slot comes up, even if all other time slots are empty. However, if a station has nothing to transmit when its time slot comes up, the time slot is sent empty and is wasted. Because ATM is asynchronous, time slots are available on demand with information identifying the source of the transmission contained in the header of each ATM cell.

ATM Cell Basic Format

ATM transfers information in fixed-size units called *cells*. Each cell consists of 53 octets, or bytes. The first 5 bytes contain cell-header information, and the remaining 48 contain the payload (user information). Small, fixed-length cells are well suited to transferring voice and video traffic because such traffic is intolerant of delays that result from having to wait for a large data packet to download, among other things. Figure 2.11 illustrates the basic format of an ATM cell.

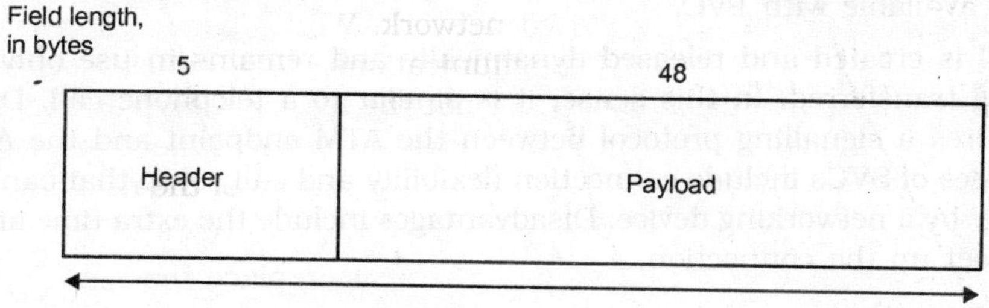

Figure 2.11 An ATM Cell Consists of a Header and Payload Data

ATM Devices

An *ATM network* is made up of an *ATM switch* and *ATM endpoints*. An ATM switch is responsible for cell transit through an ATM network. The job of an ATM switch is well defined: It accepts the incoming cell from an ATM endpoint or another ATM switch. It then reads and updates the cell header information and quickly switches the cell to an output interface toward its destination. An ATM endpoint (or end system) contains an ATM network interface adapter. Examples of ATM endpoints are workstations, routers, Digital Service Units (DSUs), LAN switches, and video coder-decoders (CODECs).

2.14.2 ATM Network Interfaces

An ATM network consists of a set of ATM switches interconnected by point-to-point ATM links or interfaces. ATM switches support two primary types of interfaces: UNI and NNI. The UNI connects ATM end systems (such as hosts and routers) to an ATM switch. The NNI connects two ATM switches.

Depending on whether the switch is owned and located at the customer's premises or is publicly owned and operated by the telephone company, UNI and NNI can be further subdivided into public and private UNIs and NNIs. A private UNI connects an ATM endpoint and a private ATM switch. Its public counterpart connects an ATM endpoint or private switch to a public switch. A private NNI connects two ATM switches within the same private organization. A public one connects two ATM switches within the same public organization.

An additional specification, the *broadband intercarrier interface (B-ICI)*, connects two public switches from different service providers.

2.14.3 ATM Services

Three types of ATM services exist:

- Permanent Virtual Circuits (PVC),
- Switched Virtual Circuits (SVC), and
- Connectionless service (which is similar to SMDS).

PVC allows direct connectivity between sites. In this way, a PVC is similar to a leased line. Among its advantages, PVC guarantees availability of a connection and does not require call setup procedures between switches. Disadvantages of PVCs include static connectivity and manual setup. Each piece of equipment between the source and the destination must be manually provisioned for the PVC. Furthermore, no network resiliency is available with PVC.

An SVC is created and released dynamically and remains in use only as long as data is being transferred. In this sense, it is similar to a telephone call. Dynamic call control requires a signalling protocol between the ATM endpoint and the ATM switch. The advantages of SVCs include connection flexibility and call setup that can be handled automatically by a networking device. Disadvantages include the extra time and overhead required to set up the connection.

ATM Virtual Connections

ATM networks are fundamentally connection-oriented, which means that a Virtual Channel (VC) must be set up across the ATM network prior to any data transfer. (A virtual channel is roughly equivalent to a virtual circuit.)

Two types of ATM connections exist:

- ***virtual paths,*** which are identified by virtual path identifiers, and
- ***virtual channels,*** which are identified by the combination of a VPI and a *Virtual Channel Identifier (VCI).*

A virtual path is a bundle of virtual channels, all of which are switched transparently across the ATM network based on the common VPI. All VPIs and VCIs, however, have only local significance across a particular link and are remapped, as appropriate, at each switch.

A transmission path is the physical media that transports virtual channels and virtual paths.

2.14.4 ATM Switching Operation

The basic operation of an ATM switch is straightforward: The cell is received across a link on a known VCI or VPI value. The switch looks up the connection value in a local translation table to determine the outgoing port (or ports) of the connection and the new VPI/VCI value of the connection on that link. The switch then retransmits the cell on that outgoing link with the appropriate connection identifiers. Because all VCIs and VPIs have only local significance across a particular link, these values are remapped, as necessary, at each switch.

2.14.5 ATM Reference Model

The ATM architecture uses a logical model to describe the functionality that it supports. ATM functionality corresponds to the physical layer and part of the data link layer of the OSI reference model.

The ATM reference model is composed of the following planes, which span all layers:

- **Control.** This plane is responsible for generating and managing signalling requests.
- **User.** This plane is responsible for managing the transfer of data.
- **Management.** This plane contains two components:

Layer management manages layer-specific functions, such as the detection of failures and protocol problems.

Plane management manages and coordinates functions related to the complete system.

The ATM reference model is composed of the following ATM layers:

Physical layer. Analogous to the physical layer of the OSI reference model, the ATM physical layer manages the medium-dependent transmission.

ATM layer. Combined with the ATM adaptation layer, the ATM layer is roughly analogous to the data link layer of the OSI reference model. The ATM layer is responsible for the simultaneous sharing of virtual circuits over a physical link (cell multiplexing) and passing cells through the ATM network (cell relay). To do this, it uses the VPI and VCI information in the header of each ATM cell.

ATM Adaptation Layer (AAL). Combined with the ATM layer, the AAL is roughly analogous to the data link layer of the OSI model. The AAL is responsible for isolating higher-layer protocols from the details of the ATM processes. The adaptation layer prepares user data for conversion into cells and segments the data into 48-byte cell payloads.

Finally, the higher layers residing above the AAL accept user data, arrange it into packets, and hand it to the AAL. Figure 2.12 illustrates the ATM reference model.

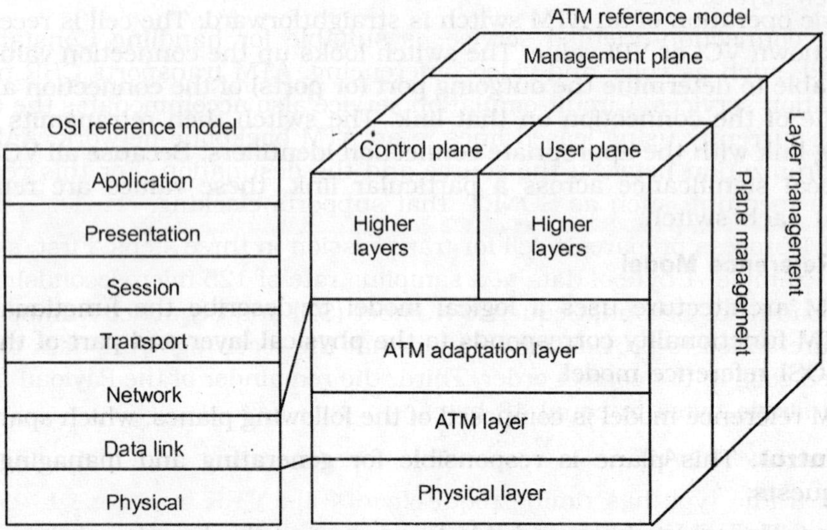

Figure 2.12 The ATM Reference Model Relates to the Lowest Two Layers of the OSI Reference Model

The ATM Physical Layer

The ATM physical layer has four functions: Cells are converted into a bitstream, the transmission and receipt of bits on the physical medium are controlled, ATM cell boundaries are tracked, and cells are packaged into the appropriate types of frames for the physical medium. For example, cells are packaged differently for SONET than for DS-3/E-3 media types.

The ATM physical layer is divided into two parts: the Physical Medium Dependent (PMD) sublayer and the Transmission Convergence (TC) sublayer.

The PMD sublayer provides two key functions. First, it synchronizes transmission and reception by sending and receiving a continuous flow of bits with associated timing information. Second, it specifies the physical media for the physical medium used, including connector types and cable. Examples of physical medium standards for ATM include Synchronous Digital Hierarchy/Synchronous Optical Network (SDH/SONET), DS-3/E3, 155 Mbps over Multi Mode Fiber (MMF) using the 8B/10B encoding scheme, and 155 Mbps 8B/10B over Shielded Twisted Pair (STP) cabling.

The TC sublayer has four functions: cell delineation, Header Error Control (HEC) sequence generation and verification, cell-rate decoupling, and transmission frame adaptation. The cell delineation function maintains ATM cell boundaries, allowing devices to locate cells within a stream of bits. HEC sequence generation and verification generates and checks the header error control code to ensure valid data. Cell-rate decoupling maintains synchronization and inserts or suppresses idle (unassigned) ATM cells to adapt the rate of valid ATM cells to the payload capacity of the transmission system. Transmission frame adaptation packages ATM cells into frames acceptable to the particular physical layer implementation.

ATM Adaptation Layers: AAL1

AAL1, a connection-oriented service, is suitable for handling Constant Bit Rate sources (CBR), such as voice and videoconferencing. ATM transports CBR traffic using circuit-emulation services. Circuit-emulation service also accommodates the attachment of equipment currently using leased lines to an ATM backbone network. AAL1 requires timing synchronization between the source and the destination. For this reason, AAL1 depends on a medium, such as SONET, that supports clocking.

The AAL1 process prepares a cell for transmission in three steps. First, synchronous samples (for example, 1 byte of data at a sampling rate of 125 microseconds) are inserted into the Payload field. Second, Sequence Number (SN) and Sequence Number Protection (SNP) fields are added to provide information that the receiving AAL1 uses to verify that it has received cells in the correct order. Third, the remainder of the Payload field is filled with enough single bytes to equal 48 bytes.

ATM Adaptation Layers : AAL2

Another traffic type has timing requirements like CBR but tends to be bursty in nature. This is called Variable Bit Rate (VBR) traffic. This typically includes services characterized as packetized voice or video that do not have a constant data transmission speed but that do have requirements similar to constant bit rate services. AAL2 is suitable for VBR traffic. The AAL2 process uses 44 bytes of the cell payload for user data and reserves 4 bytes of the payload to support the AAL2 processes.

ATM Adaptation Layers : AAL3/4

AAL3/4 supports both connection-oriented and connectionless data. It was designed for network service providers and is closely aligned with Switched Multimegabit Data Service (SMDS). AAL3/4 is used to transmit SMDS packets over an ATM network.

AAL3/4 prepares a cell for transmission in four steps. First, the Convergence Sublayer (CS) creates a Protocol Data Unit (PDU) by prepending a beginning/end tag header to the frame and appending a length field as a trailer. Second, the Segmentation And Reassembly (SAR) sublayer fragments the PDU and prepends a header to it. Then the SAR sublayer appends a CRC-10 trailer to each PDU fragment for error control. Finally, the completed SAR PDU becomes the Payload field of an ATM cell to which the ATM layer prepends the standard ATM header.

An AAL 3/4 SAR PDU header consists of Type, Sequence Number, and Multiplexing Identifier fields. Type fields identify whether a cell is the beginning, continuation, or end of a message. Sequence number fields identify the order in which cells should be reassembled. The Multiplexing Identifier field determines which cells from different traffic sources are interleaved on the same Virtual Circuit Connection (VCC) so that the correct cells are reassembled at the destination.

ATM Adaptation Layers : AAL5

AAL5 is the primary AAL for data and supports both connection-oriented and connectionless data. It is used to transfer most non-SMDS data, such as classical IP over ATM and LAN Emulation (LANE). AAL5 also is known as the Simple and Efficient Adaptation Layer (SEAL) because the SAR sublayer simply accepts the CS-PDU and segments it into 48-octet SAR-PDUs without reserving any bytes in each cell.

AAL5 prepares a cell for transmission in three steps. First, the CS sublayer appends a variable-length pad and an 8-byte trailer to a frame. The pad ensures that the resulting PDU falls on the 48-byte boundary of an ATM cell. The trailer includes the length of the frame and a 32-bit Cyclic Redundancy Check (CRC) computed across the entire PDU. This allows the AAL5 receiving process to detect bit errors, lost cells, or cells that are out of sequence. Second, the SAR sublayer segments the CS-PDU into 48-byte blocks. A header and trailer are not added (as is in AAL3/4), so messages cannot be interleaved. Finally, the ATM layer places each block into the Payload field of an ATM cell. For all cells except the last, a bit in the Payload Type (PT) field is set to 0 to indicate that the cell is not the last cell in a series that represents a single frame. For the last cell, the bit in the PT field is set to 1.

2.14.6 ATM Addressing

The ITU-T standard is based on the use of E.164 addresses (similar to telephone numbers) for public ATM (B-ISDN) networks. The ATM Forum extended ATM addressing to include private networks. It decided on the subnetwork or overlay model of addressing, in which the ATM layer is responsible for mapping network layer addresses to ATM addresses. This subnetwork model is an alternative to using network layer protocol addresses (such as IP and IPX) and existing routing protocols (such as IGRP and RIP). The ATM Forum defined an address format based on the structure of the OSI Network Service Access Point (NSAP) addresses.

2.14.7 ATM Connections

ATM supports two types of connections:

- point-to-point and
- point-to-multipoint.

Point-to-point connects two ATM end systems and can be unidirectional (one-way communication) or bidirectional (two-way communication). Point-to-multipoint connects a single-source end system (known as the root node) to multiple destination end systems (known as leaves). Such connections are unidirectional only. Root nodes can transmit to leaves, but leaves cannot transmit to the root or to each other on the same connection. Cell replication is done within the ATM network by the ATM switches where the connection splits into two or more branches.

It would be desirable in ATM networks to have bidirectional multipoint-to-multipoint connections. Such connections are analogous to the broadcasting or multicasting capabilities of shared-media LANs, such as Ethernet and Token Ring. A broadcasting capability is easy to implement in shared-media LANs, where all nodes on a single LAN segment must process all packets sent on that segment.

Unfortunately, a multipoint-to-multipoint capability cannot be implemented by using AAL5, which is the most common AAL to transmit data across an ATM network. Unlike AAL3/4, with its Message Identifier (MID) field, AAL5 does not provide a way within its cell format to interleave cells from different AAL5 packets on a single connection. This means that all AAL5 packets sent to a particular destination across a particular connection must be received in sequence; otherwise, the destination reassembly process will be incapable of reconstructing the packets.

This is why AAL5 point-to-multipoint connections can be only unidirectional. If a leaf node were to transmit an AAL5 packet onto the connection, for example, it would be received by both the root node and all other leaf nodes. At these nodes, the packet sent by the leaf could be interleaved with packets sent by the root and possibly other leaf nodes, precluding the reassembly of any of the interleaved packets.

ATM Signalling and Connection Establishment

When an ATM device wants to establish a connection with another ATM device, it sends a signalling-request packet to its directly connected ATM switch. This request contains the ATM address of the desired ATM endpoint, as well as any QoS parameters required for the connection.

ATM signalling protocols vary by the type of ATM link, which can be either UNI signals or NNI signals. UNI is used between an ATM end system and ATM switch across ATM UNI, and NNI is used across NNI links.

The ATM Forum UNI 3.1 specification is the current standard for ATM UNI signalling. The UNI 3.1 specification is based on the Q.2931 public network signalling protocol developed by the ITU-T. UNI signalling requests are carried in a well-known default connection: VPI = 0, VPI = 5.

The ATM Connection-Establishment Process

ATM signalling uses the one-pass method of connection setup that is used in all modern telecommunication networks, such as the telephone network. An ATM connection sctup proceeds in the following manner. First, the source end system sends a connection-signaling request. The connection request is propagated through the network. As a result, connections are set up through the network. The connection request reaches the final destination, which either accepts or rejects the connection request.

3

PROTOCOL AND PROTOCOL ARCHITECTURE

3.1 INTRODUCTION

When computers, terminals, and/or other data processing devices exchange data, for example, the transfer of a file between two computers. There must be a data path between the two computers, either directly or via a communication network. There must be a high degree of *cooperation between the two computer systems*. The exchange of information between computers for the purpose of cooperative action is generally referred to as ***computer communications.*** Similarly, when two or more computers are interconnected via a communication network, the set of computer stations is referred to as a ***computer network.***

What is an Internetwork?

An ***internetwork*** is a collection of individual networks, connected by intermediate networking devices, that functions as a single large network. Internetworking refers to the industry, products, and procedures that meet the challenge of creating and administering internetworks.

In discussing computer communications and computer networks, two concepts are Important:

1. Protocols
2. Protocol architecture or Computer Communications architecture

A *network protocol* is a set of rules for communicating between computers. Protocols govern format, timing, sequencing, and error control. Without these rules, the computer cannot make sense of the stream of incoming bits.

A protocol is used for communication *between entities* in different systems. For two entities to communicate successfully, they must *speak the same language.* What is communicated, how it is communicated, and when it is communicated must conform to some mutually acceptable convention or protocol between the entities involved.

The key elements of a protocol are:

- Syntax Includes such things as data format and signal levels.
- Semantics Includes control information for coordination and error handling.
- Timing Includes speed matching and sequencing.

Protocol is software that resides either in a computer's memory or in the memory of a transmission device, like a network interface card. When data is ready for transmission, this software is executed. The software prepares data for transmission and sets the transmission in motion. At the receiving end, the software takes the data off the wire and prepares it for the computer by taking off all the information added by the transmitting end.

It is clear that there must be a high degree of cooperation between the two computers. Instead of implementing the logic for this as a single module, the task is broken up into subtasks, each of which is implemented separately.

Instead of a single module for performing communications, there is a structured set of modules that implements the communications function. That structure is referred to as *protocol architecture*. Each module in a layer is defined by a protocol and a set of protocols which work together are termed as *protocol stack*. The terms protocol architecture and protocol stack are used interchangeably.

Two protocol architectures have served as the basis for the development of interoperable communications standards: the TCP/IP protocol suite and the OSI reference model. *TCP/IP is the most widely used interoperable architecture, and OSI has become the standard model for classifying communication functions.* Hence a brief introduction to both of them is given below.

3.2 THE OSI PROTOCOL ARCHITECTURE

The *Open System Interconnection (OSI)* model includes a set of protocols that attempt to define and standardize the data communications process. The OSI protocols were defined by the *International Organization for Standardization (ISO)*.

The OSI model is not a single definition of how data communications actually takes place in the real world. Numerous protocols may exist at each layer. The OSI model states how the process should be divided and what protocols should be used at each layer. If a network vendor implements one of the protocols at each layer, its network components should work with other vendors' offerings. The OSI model has seven layers.

3.2.1 Open System Interconnection Reference Model

The ***Open System Interconnection (OSI) reference model*** describes how information from a software application in one computer moves through a network medium to a software application in another computer. The OSI reference model is a conceptual model composed of seven layers, each specifying particular network functions. The model was developed by the International Organization for Standardization (ISO) in 1984, and it is now considered the primary architectural model for intercomputer communications. The OSI model divides the tasks involved with moving information between networked computers into seven smaller, more manageable task groups. A task or group of tasks is then assigned to each of the seven OSI layers. Each layer is reasonably self-contained so that the tasks assigned to each layer can be implemented independently. This enables the solutions offered by one layer to be updated without adversely affecting the other layers.

The following list details the seven layers of the Open System Interconnection (OSI) reference model:

Layer 7-Application
Layer 6-Presentation
Layer 5-Session
Layer 4-Transport
Layer 3-Network
Layer 2-Data link
Layer 1-Physical

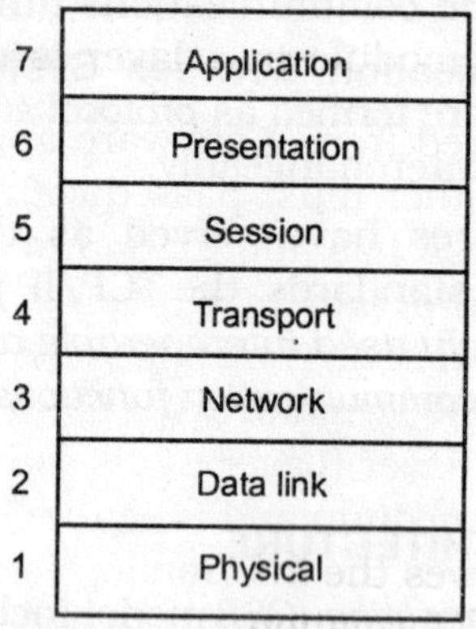

Figure 3.1 The Seven-layer OSI Reference Model

Characteristics of the OSI Layers

The seven layers of the OSI reference model can be divided into two categories: upper layers and lower layers.

The *upper layers* of the OSI model deal with application issues and generally are implemented only in software. The highest layer, the application layer, is closest to the end user. Both users and application layer processes interact with software applications that contain a communications component. The term upper layer is sometimes used to refer to any layer above another layer in the OSI model.

The *lower layers* of the OSI model handle data transport issues. The physical layer and the data link layer are implemented in hardware and software. The lowest layer, the physical layer, is closest to the physical network medium (the network cabling, for example) and is responsible for actually placing information on the medium.

3.2.2 Protocols

The OSI model provides a conceptual framework for communication between computers, but the model itself is not a method of communication. Actual communication is made possible by using communication protocols. In the context of data networking, a *protocol* is a formal set of rules and conventions that governs how computers exchange information over a network medium. A protocol implements the functions of one or more of the OSI layers.

A wide variety of communication protocols exist. Some of these protocols include LAN protocols, WAN protocols, network protocols, and routing protocols. *LAN protocols* operate at the physical and data link layers of the OSI model and define communication over the various LAN media. *WAN protocols* operate at the lowest three layers of the OSI model and define communication over the various wide-area media. *Routing protocols* are network layer protocols that are responsible for exchanging information between routers so that the routers can select the proper path for network traffic. Finally, *network protocols* are the various upper-layer protocols that exist in a given protocol suite. Many protocols rely on others for operation. For example, many routing protocols use network protocols to exchange information between routers. This concept of building upon the layers already in existence is the foundation of the OSI model.

3.2.3 OSI Model and Communication Between Systems

Information being transferred from a software application in one computer system to a software application in another must pass through the OSI layers. For example, if a software application in System A has information to transmit to a software application in System B, the application program in System A will pass its information to the application layer (Layer 7) of System A. The application layer then passes the information to the presentation layer (Layer 6), which relays the data to the session layer (Layer 5), and so on down to the physical layer (Layer 1). At the physical layer, the information is placed on the physical network medium and is sent across the medium to System B. The physical layer of System B removes the information from the physical medium, and then its physical layer passes the information up to the data link layer (Layer 2), which passes it to the network layer (Layer 3), and so on, until it reaches the application layer (Layer 7) of System B. Finally, the application layer of System B passes the information to the recipient application program to complete the communication process.

3.2.4 Interaction Between OSI Model Layers

A given layer in the OSI model generally communicates with three other OSI layers: the layer directly above it, the layer directly below it, and its peer layer in other networked computer systems. The data link layer in System A, for example, communicates with the network layer of System A, the physical layer of System A, and the data link layer in System B.

OSI Layer Services

One OSI layer communicates with another layer to make use of the services provided by the second layer. The services provided by adjacent layers help a given OSI layer communicate with its peer layer in other computer systems. Three basic elements are involved in layer services: the service user, the service provider, and the service access point (SAP). In this context, the *service user* is the OSI layer that requests services from an adjacent OSI layer. The *service provider* is the OSI layer that provides services to service users. OSI layers can provide services to multiple service users. The SAP is a conceptual location at which one OSI layer can request the services of another OSI layer.

OSI Model Layers and Information Exchange

The seven OSI layers use various forms of control information to communicate with their peer layers in other computer systems. This *control information* consists of specific requests and instructions that are exchanged between peer OSI layers.

Control information typically takes one of two forms: headers and trailers. *Headers* are prepended to data that has been passed down from upper layers. *Trailers* are appended to data that has been passed down from upper layers. An OSI layer is not required to attach a header or a trailer to data from upper layers.

Headers, trailers, and data are relative concepts, depending on the layer that analyzes the information unit. At the network layer, for example, an information unit consists of a Layer 3 header and data. At the data link layer, however, all the information passed down by the network layer (the Layer 3 header and the data) is treated as data. In other words, the data portion of an information unit at a given OSI layer potentially can contain headers, trailers, and data from all the higher layers. This is known as *encapsulation*. Figure 3.2 shows how the header and data from one layer are encapsulated into the header of the next lowest layer.

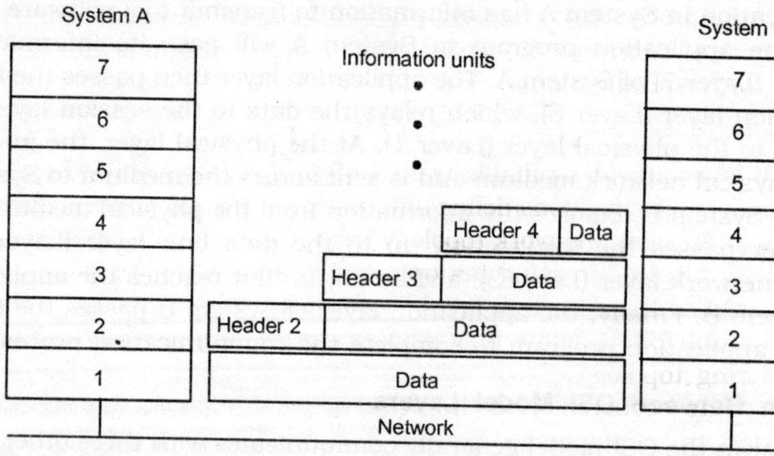

Figure 3.2 Headers and Data can be Encapsulated During Information Exchange

Information Exchange Process

The information exchange process occurs between peer OSI layers. Each layer in the source system adds control information to data, and each layer in the destination system analyzes and removes the control information from that data.

If System A has data from a software application to send to System B, the data is passed to the application layer. The application layer in System A then communicates any control information required by the application layer in System B by prepending a header to the data. The resulting information unit (a header and the data) is passed to the presentation layer, which prepends its own header containing control information intended for the presentation layer in System B. The information unit grows in size as each layer prepends its own header (and, in some cases, a trailer) that contains control information to be used by its peer layer in System B. At the physical layer, the entire information unit is placed onto the network medium.

The physical layer in System B receives the information unit and passes it to the data link layer. The data link layer in System B then reads the control information contained in the header prepended by the data link layer in System A. The header is then removed, and the remainder of the information unit is passed to the network layer. Each layer performs the same actions: The layer reads the header from its peer layer, strips it off, and passes the remaining information unit to the next highest layer. After the application layer performs these actions, the data is passed to the recipient software application in System B, in exactly the form in which it was transmitted by the application in System A.

3.2.5 Layers in Working

OSI Model Physical Layer

The physical layer defines the electrical, mechanical, procedural, and functional specifications for activating, maintaining, and deactivating the physical link between communicating network systems. Physical layer specifications define characteristics such as voltage levels, timing of voltage changes, physical data rates, maximum transmission distances, and physical connectors. Physical layer implementations can be categorized as either LAN or WAN specifications.

OSI Model Data Link Layer

The data link layer provides reliable transit of data across a physical network link. Different data link layer specifications define different network and protocol characteristics, including physical addressing, network topology, error notification, sequencing of frames, and flow control. Physical addressing (as opposed to network addressing) defines how devices are addressed at the data link layer. Network topology consists of the data link layer specifications that often define how devices are to be physically connected, such as in a bus or a ring topology. Error notification alerts upper-layer protocols that a transmission error has occurred, and the sequencing of data frames reorders frames that are transmitted out of sequence. Finally, flow control moderates the transmission of data so that the receiving device is not overwhelmed with more traffic than it can handle at one time.

The Institute of Electrical and Electronics Engineers (IEEE) has subdivided the data link layer into two sublayers:

- Logical Link Control (LLC) and
- Media Access Control (MAC).

The *Logical Link Control (LLC)* sublayer of the data link layer manages communications between devices over a single link of a network. LLC is defined in the IEEE 802.2 specification and supports both connectionless and connection-oriented services used by higher-layer protocols. IEEE 802.2 defines a number of fields in data link layer frames that enable multiple higher-layer protocols to share a single physical data link.

The *Media Access Control (MAC)* sublayer of the data link layer manages protocol access to the physical network medium. The IEEE MAC specification defines MAC addresses, which enable multiple devices to uniquely identify one another at the data link layer.

OSI Model Network Layer

The network layer defines the network address, which differs from the MAC address. Some network layer implementations, such as the Internet Protocol (IP), define network addresses in a way that route selection can be determined systematically by comparing the source network address with the destination network address and applying the subnet mask. Because this layer defines the logical network layout, routers can use this layer to determine how to forward packets. Because of this, much of the design and configuration work for internetworks happens at Layer 3, the network layer.

OSI Model Transport Layer

The transport layer accepts data from the session layer and segments the data for transport across the network. Generally, the transport layer is responsible for making sure that the data is delivered error-free and in the proper sequence. Flow control generally occurs at the transport layer.

Flow control manages data transmission between devices so that the transmitting device does not send more data than the receiving device can process. Multiplexing enables data from several applications to be transmitted onto a single physical link. Virtual circuits are established, maintained, and terminated by the transport layer. Error checking involves creating various mechanisms for detecting transmission errors, while error recovery involves acting, such as requesting that data be retransmitted, to resolve any errors that occur. The transport protocols used on the Internet are TCP and UDP.

OSI Model Session Layer

The session layer establishes, manages, and terminates communication sessions. Communication sessions consist of service requests and service responses that occur between applications located in different network devices. These requests and responses are coordinated by protocols implemented at the session layer. Some examples of session-layer implementations include Zone Information Protocol (ZIP), the AppleTalk protocol that coordinates the name binding process; and Session Control Protocol (SCP), the DECnet Phase IV session layer protocol.

OSI Model Presentation Layer

The presentation layer provides a variety of coding and conversion functions that are applied to application layer data. These functions ensure that information sent from the application layer of one system would be readable by the application layer of another system. Some examples of presentation layer coding and conversion schemes include common data representation formats, conversion of character representation formats, common data compression schemes, and common data encryption schemes.

Common data representation formats, or the use of standard image, sound, and video formats, enable the interchange of application data between different types of computer systems. Conversion schemes are used to exchange information with systems by using different text and data representations, such as EBCDIC and ASCII. Standard data compression schemes enable data that is compressed at the source device to be properly decompressed at the destination. Standard data encryption schemes enable data encrypted at the source device to be properly deciphered at the destination.

Presentation layer implementations are not typically associated with a particular protocol stack. Some well-known standards for video include QuickTime and Motion Picture Experts Group (MPEG). QuickTime is an Apple Computer specification for video and audio, and MPEG is a standard for video compression and coding.

Among the well-known graphic image formats are Graphics Interchange Format (GIF), Joint Photographic Experts Group (JPEG), and Tagged Image File Format (TIFF). GIF is a standard for compressing and coding graphic images. JPEG is another compression and coding standard for graphic images, and TIFF is a standard coding format for graphic images.

OSI Model Application Layer

The application layer is the OSI layer closest to the end user, which means that both the OSI application layer and the user interact directly with the software application.

This layer interacts with software applications that implement a communicating component. Such application programs fall outside the scope of the OSI model. Application layer functions typically include identifying communication partners, determining resource availability, and synchronizing communication.

When identifying communication partners, the application layer determines the identity and availability of communication partners for an application with data to transmit.When determining resource availability, the application layer must decide whether sufficient network resources for the requested communication exist. In synchronizing communication, all communication between applications requires cooperation that is managed by the application layer.

Some examples of application layer implementations include Telnet, File Transfer Protocol (FTP), and Simple Mail Transfer Protocol (SMTP).

Information Formats

The data and control information that is transmitted through internetworks takes a variety of forms. The terms used to refer to these information formats are not used consistently in the internetworking industry but sometimes are used interchangeably. Common information formats include frames, packets, datagrams, segments, messages, cells, and data units. A frame is an information unit whose source and destination are data link layer entities. A frame is composed of the data link layer header (and possibly a trailer) and upper-layer data. The header and trailer contain control information intended for the data link layer entity in the destination system. Data from upper-layer entities is encapsulated in the data link layer header and trailer. A *packet* is an information unit whose source and destination are network layer entities. A packet is composed of the network layer header (and possibly a trailer) and upper-layer data. The header and trailer contain control information intended for the network layer entity in the destination system. Data from upper-layer entities is encapsulated in the network layer header and trailer.

The term ***datagram*** usually refers to an information unit whose source and destination are network layer entities that use connectionless network service.

The term ***segment*** usually refers to an information unit whose source and destination are transport layer entities.

A ***message*** is an information unit whose source and destination entities exist above the network layer (often at the application layer).

A ***cell*** is an information unit of a fixed size whose source and destination are data link layer entities. Cells are used in switched environments, such as Asynchronous Transfer Mode (ATM) and Switched ultimegabit Data Service (SMDS) networks. A cell is composed of the header and payload. The header contains control information intended for the destination data link layer entity and is typically 5 bytes long. The payload contains upper-layer data that is encapsulated in the cell header and is typically 48 bytes long.

The length of the header and the payload fields always are the same for each cell.

Data unit is a generic term that refers to a variety of information units. Some common data units are service data units (SDUs), protocol data units, and bridge protocol data units (BPDUs). SDUs are information units from upper-layer protocols that define a service request to a lower-layer protocol. PDU is OSI terminology for a packet. BPDUs are used by the spanning-tree algorithm as hello messages.

Connection-oriented and Connectionless Network Services

In general, transport protocols can be characterized as being either connection-oriented or connectionless. Connection-oriented services must first establish a connection with the desired service before passing any data. A connectionless service can send the data without any need to establish a connection first. In general, connection-oriented services provide some level of delivery guarantee, whereas connectionless services do not.

Connection-oriented service involves three phases:

- connection establishment,
- data transfer, and
- connection termination.

During connection establishment, the end nodes may reserve resources for the connection. The end nodes also may negotiate and establish certain criteria for the transfer, such as a window size used in TCP connections. This resource reservation is one of the things exploited in some denial of service (DOS) attacks. An attacking system will send many requests for establishing a connection but then will never complete the connection. The attacked computer is then left with resources allocated for many never-completed connections. Then, when an end node tries to complete an actual connection, there are not enough resources for the valid connection.

The data transfer phase occurs when the actual data is transmitted over the connection. During data transfer, most connection-oriented services will monitor for lost packets and handle resending them. The protocol is generally also responsible for putting the packets in the right sequence before passing the data up the protocol stack.

When the transfer of data is complete, the end nodes terminate the connection and release resources reserved for the connection. Connection-oriented network services have more overhead than connectionless ones. Connection-oriented services must negotiate a connection, transfer data, and tear down the connection, whereas a connectionless transfer can simply send the data without the added overhead of creating and tearing down a connection. Each has its place in internetworks.

3.2.6 Internetwork Addressing

Internetwork addresses identify devices separately or as members of a group. Addressing schemes vary depending on the protocol family and the OSI layer. Three types of internetwork addresses are commonly used: data link layer addresses, Media Access Control (MAC) addresses, and network layer addresses.

Data Link Layer Addresses

A *data link layer address* uniquely identifies each physical network connection of a network device. Data-link addresses sometimes are referred to as *physical* or *hardware addresses*. Data-link addresses usually exist within a flat address space and have a pre-established and typically fixed relationship to a specific device.

End systems generally have only one physical network connection and thus have only one data-link address. Routers and other internetworking devices typically have multiple physical network connections and therefore have multiple data-link addresses.

Mac Addresses

Media Access Control (MAC) addresses consist of a subset of data link layer addresses. MAC addresses identify network entities in LANs that implement the IEEE MAC addresses of the data link layer. As with most data-link addresses, MAC addresses are unique for each LAN interface.

MAC addresses are 48 bits in length and are expressed as 12 hexadecimal digits. The first 6 hexadecimal digits, which are administered by the IEEE, identify the manufacturer or vendor and thus comprise the Organizationally Unique Identifier (OUI). The last 6 hexadecimal digits comprise the interface serial number, or another value administered by the specific vendor. MAC addresses sometimes are called *burned-in addresses (BIAs)* because they are burned into read-only memory (ROM) and are copied into random-access memory (RAM) when the interface card initializes.

Mapping Addresses

Because internetworks generally use network addresses to route traffic around the network, there is a need to map network addresses to MAC addresses. When the network layer has determined the destination station's network address, it must forward the information over a physical network using a MAC address. Different protocol suites use different methods to perform this mapping, but the most popular is Address Resolution Protocol (ARP).

Different protocol suites use different methods for determining the MAC address of a device. The following three methods are used most often. Address Resolution Protocol (ARP) maps network addresses to MAC addresses. The Hello protocol enables network devices to learn the MAC addresses of other network devices. MAC addresses either are embedded in the network layer address or are generated by an algorithm.

Network Layer Addresses

A *network layer address* identifies an entity at the network layer of the OSI layers.

Network addresses usually exist within a hierarchical address space and sometimes are called *virtual* or *logical addresses.*

The relationship between a network address and a device is logical and unfixed; it typically is based either on physical network characteristics (the device is on a particular network segment) or on groupings that have no physical basis (the device is part of an AppleTalk zone). End systems require one network layer address for each network layer protocol that they support. (This assumes that the device has only one physical network connection.) Routers and other internetworking devices require one network layer address per physical network connection for each network layer protocol supported. For example, a router with three interfaces each running AppleTalk, TCP/IP, and OSI must have three network layer addresses for each interface. The router therefore has nine network layer addresses.

Hierarchical Versus Flat Address Space

Internetwork address space typically takes one of two forms:

- hierarchical address space or
- flat address space.

A *hierarchical address space* is organized into numerous subgroups, each successively narrowing an address until it points to a single device. A *flat address space* is organized into a single group.

Hierarchical addressing offers certain advantages over flat-addressing schemes. Address sorting and recall is simplified using comparison operations.

Address Assignments

Addresses are assigned to devices as one of two types:

- static and
- dynamic.

Static addresses are assigned by a network administrator according to a preconceived internetwork addressing plan. A static address does not change until the network administrator manually changes it.

Dynamic addresses are obtained by devices when they attach to a network, by means of some protocol-specific process. A device using a dynamic address often has a different address each time that it connects to the network. Some networks use a server to assign addresses. Server-assigned addresses are recycled for reuse as devices disconnect. **"A device is therefore likely to have a different address each time that it connects to the network."**

Addresses versus Names

Internetwork devices usually have both a name and an address associated with them. Internetwork names typically are location-independent and remain associated with a device wherever that device moves (for example, from one building to another). Internetwork addresses usually are location-dependent and change when a device is moved (although MAC addresses are an exception to this rule). As with network addresses being mapped to MAC addresses, names are usually mapped to network addresses through some protocol. The Internet uses Domain Name System (DNS) to map the name of a device to its IP address. For example, it's easier for you to remember www.vivekricha.com instead of some IP address. Therefore, you type www.vivekricha.com into your browser when you want to access Vivek's web site. Your computer performs a DNS lookup of the IP address for Vivek's web server and then communicates with it using the network address.

3.2.7 Flow Control Basics

Flow control is a function that prevents network congestion by ensuring that transmitting devices do not overwhelm receiving devices with data. A high-speed computer, for example, may generate traffic faster than the network can transfer it, or faster than the destination device can receive and process it. The three commonly used methods for handling network congestion are buffering, transmitting source-quench messages, and windowing.

Buffering is used by network devices to temporarily store bursts of excess data in memory until they can be processed. Occasional data bursts are easily handled by buffering. Excess data bursts can exhaust memory, however, forcing the device to discard any additional datagrams that arrive.

Source-quench messages are used by receiving devices to help prevent their buffers from overflowing. The receiving device sends source-quench messages to request that the source reduce its current rate of data transmission. First, the receiving device begins discarding received data due to overflowing buffers. Second, the receiving device begins sending source-quench messages to the transmitting device at the rate of one message for each packet dropped. The source device receives the source-quench messages and lowers the data rate until it stops receiving the messages. Finally, the source device then gradually increases the data rate as long as no further source-quench requests are received.

Windowing is a flow-control scheme in which the source device requires an acknowledgement from the destination after a certain number of packets have been transmitted. With a window size of 3, the source requires an acknowledgement after sending three packets, as follows. First, the source device sends three packets to the destination device. Then, after receiving the three packets, the destination device sends an acknowledgement to the source. The source receives the acknowledgement and sends three more packets. If the destination does not receive one or more of the packets for some reason, such as overflowing buffers, it does not receive enough packets to send an acknowledgement. The source then retransmits the packets at a reduced transmission rate.

3.2.8 Error-Checking Basics

Error-checking schemes determine whether transmitted data has become corrupt or otherwise damaged while travelling from the source to the destination. Error checking is implemented at several of the OSI layers.

One common error-checking scheme is the cyclic redundancy check (CRC), which detects and discards corrupted data. Error-correction functions (such as data retransmission) are left to higher-layer protocols. A CRC value is generated by a calculation that is performed at the source device. The destination device compares this value to its own calculation to determine whether errors occurred during transmission. **First,** the source device performs a predetermined set of calculations over the contents of the packet to be sent. **Then,** the source places the calculated value in the packet and sends the packet to the destination. The destination performs the same predetermined set of calculations over the contents of the packet and then compares its computed value with that contained in the packet. If the values are equal, the packet is considered valid. If the values are unequal, the packet contains errors and is discarded.

3.3 THE TCP/IP PROTOCOL ARCHITECTURE

TCP/IP is a result of protocol research and development conducted on the experimental packet-switched network, ARPANET, funded by the Defense Advanced Research Projects Agency (DARPA) in the U.S, and is generally referred to as the TC/IP protocol suite. This protocol suite consists of a large collection of protocols that have been issued as Internet standards by the Internet Activities Board (IAB).

There is no official TCP/IP protocol model as there is in the case of OSI. However, based on the protocol standards that have been developed, we can organize the communication task for TCP/IP into five relatively independent layers;

- Application layer
- Transport layer (TCP)
- Internet layer (IP)
- Network access layer
- Physical layer.

The **physical layer** covers the physical interface between a data transmission device (e.g., workstation, computer) and a transmission medium or network. This layer is concerned with specifying the characteristics of the transmission medium, the nature of the signals, the data rate, and related matters.

The **network access layer** is concerned with the exchange of data between end system and the network to which it is attached. The sending computer must provide the network with the address of the destination computer, so that the network may route the data to the appropriate destination. The specific software used at this layer depends on the type of network to be used; different standards have been developed for circuit-switching, packet-switching (e.g., X.25), local area networks (e.g., Ethernet), and others. Thus, it makes sense to separate those functions having to do with network access into a separate layer. By doing this, the remainder of the communications software, above the network access layer, need not be concerned about the specifics of the network to be used. The same higher-layer software should function properly regardless of the particular network to which the computer is attached.

The network access layer is concerned with access to and routing data across a network for *two end systems attached to the same network.* In those cases where two devices are attached to different networks, procedures are needed to allow data to traverse multiple interconnected networks. This is the function of the **Internet layer.** The ***Internet Protocol (IP)*** is used at this layer to provide the routing function across multiple networks.

This protocol is implemented not only in the end systems but also in routers. A router is a processor that connects two or more *networks* and whose primary function is to relay data from one network to the other on its route from the source to the destination end system.

Regardless of the nature of the applications that are exchanging data, there is usually a requirement that data be exchanged reliably. That is, we would like to be assured that all of the data arrive at the destination application and that the data arrive in the same order in which they were sent. As we shall see, the mechanisms for providing reliability are essentially independent of the nature of the applications. Thus, it makes sense to collect those mechanisms in a common layer shared by all applications; this is referred to as the **transport layer.** The ***Transmission Control Protocol (TCP)*** is the most commonly used protocol to provide this functionality. This protocol model TCP/IP derived its name from the above two protocols.

Finally, the **application layer** contains the logic needed to support the various user applications. For each different type of application, such as file transfer, separate module is needed that is peculiar to that application.

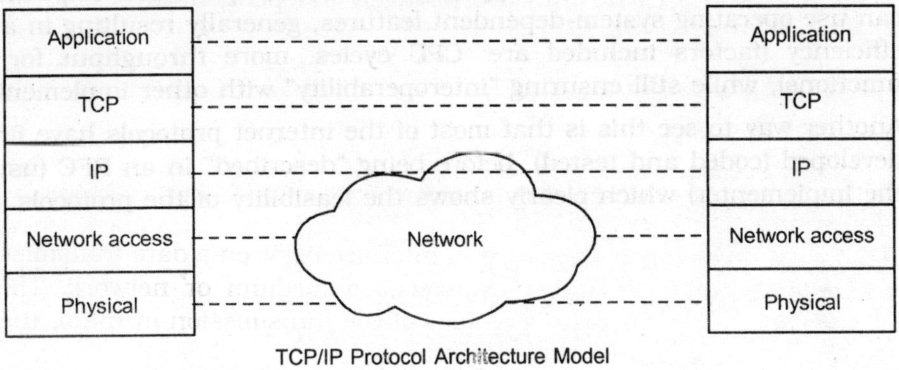

Figure 3.3 TCP/IP Protocol Architecture Model

Figure 3.3 shows how the TCP/IP protocols are implemented in end systems. Note that the physical and network access layers provide interaction between the end system and the network, whereas the transport and application layers are what is known as end-to-end protocols; they support interaction between two end systems. The *internet layer* has the flavor of both. At this layer, the end system communicates routing information to the network but also must provide some common functions between the two end systems.

3.3.1 Difference Between TCP/IP and OSI

One can only functionally position the internet model to the ISO OSI model because basic differences exist such as:

1. In the internet protocol suite, a layer represents a reasonable packaging of function.

   The ISO view, on the other hand, treats layers as rather narrow functional groups, attempting to force modularity by requiring additional layers for additional functions.

In the TCP/IP protocols, a given protocol can be used by other protocols within the same layer, whereas in the OSI model two separate layers would be defined in such circumstances. Examples of such "horizontal dependencies" are FTP, which uses the same common representation as TELNET on the "application layer," and ICMP, which uses IP for sending its datagrams on the "internetwork" layer.

In practice, what we are discussing here is the difference between a de jure standard, OSI, and a de facto standard, TCP/IP. The focus in the TCP/IP world is on agreeing on a protocol standard which can be made to work in diverse heterogeneous networks. The focus in the OSI world has always been more on the standard than the implementation of the standard.

2. Efficiency and feasibility. The OSI norms tend to be prescriptive (for instance the "layer N" must go through "all layers below it"), whereas the TCP/IP protocols are descriptive, and leave a maximum of freedom for the implementers. One of the advantages of the TCP/IP approach is that each particular implementation can use operating system-dependent features, generally resulting in a greater efficiency (factors included are: CPU cycles, more throughput for similar functions), while still ensuring "interoperability" with other implementations.

   Another way to see this is that most of the internet protocols have first been developed (coded and tested), before being "described" in an RFC (usually by the implementer) which clearly shows the feasibility of the protocols.

4

MODEL OF INTERNET

4.1 ARCHITECTURE OF INTERNET

First, the word *internet* (also *internetwork*) is simply a contraction of the phrase *interconnected network*. However when written with a capital "I" the Internet refers to a worldwide set of interconnected networks, so the Internet is an internet, but the reverse does not follow. The Internet consists of the following groups of networks (see the following sections for more information on some of these):

- Backbones: large networks which exist primarily to interconnect other networks. Currently the backbones are NSFNET in the US, EBONE in Europe and large commercial backbones.
- Regional networks connecting, for example, universities and colleges.
- Commercial networks providing access to the backbones to subscribers, and networks owned by commercial organizations for internal use which also have connections to the Internet.
- Local networks, such as campus-wide university networks.

Internet is network of computers that offer access to people and information. Over 60 million people use Internet, and the number is expected to increase over 120 million within a few years. The kind of information freely available from internet includes Government documents, scientific data, hobbyist lists, business and personal information, advertising databases and much more.

Its mainly based on the Client-Server Model. Client is a needy one agent and server is the provider with a ever working motto.

- ***Client:*** A client is a single-user workstation that provides presentation services and the appropriate computing, connectivity, and database services and interfaces relevant to the business need.
- ***Server:*** A server is one or more multiuser processors with shared memory providing computing, connectivity, and database services and interfaces relevant to the business need.

Client/server computing is an environment that satisfies the business need by appropriately allocating the application processing between the client and the server processors. The client requests services from the server; the server processes the request and returns the result to the client. The communications mechanism is a message passing *interprocess communication* (IPC) that enables (but does not require) distributed placement of the client and server processes. Client/server is a software model of computing, not a hardware definition.

Because the client/server environment is typically heterogeneous, the hardware platform and operating system of the client and server are not usually the same. In such cases, the communications mechanism may be further extended through a well-defined set of standard application program interfaces (APIs) and remote procedure calls (RPCs).

Client/server computing provides the capability to use the most cost-effective user interface, data storage, connectivity, and application services. Frequently, client/server products are deployed within the present organization but are not used effectively. The client/server model provides the technological means to use previous investments in concert with current technology options. There has been a dramatic decline in the cost of the technology components of client/server computing.

4.2 THE ADVANTAGE OF CLIENT/SERVER COMPUTING

The client/server computing model provides the means to integrate personal productivity applications for an individual employee or manager with specific business data processing needs to satisfy total information processing requirements for the entire enterprise. Major Advantages of Client/Server Computing are:

- Enhanced data sharing
- Integrated services
- Sharing resources among diverseplatforms
- Location independence of data and processing and
- Centralized management.

Data that is collected as part of the normal business process and maintained on a server is immediately available to all authorized users. Transparent network services ensure that the same data is available with the same currency to all designated users.

In the client/server model, all information that the client (user) is entitled to use is available at the desktop. There is no need to change into terminal mode or log into another processor to access information. All authorized information and processes are directly available from the desktop interface. The desktop tools-e-mail, spreadsheet, presentation graphics, and word processing-are available and can be used to deal with information provided by application and database servers resident on the network.

The client/server computing model provides opportunities to achieve true open system computing. Applications may be created and implemented without regard to the hardware platforms or the technical characteristics of the software. Thus, users may obtain client services and transparent access to the services provided by database, communications, and applications servers. Operating systems software and platform hardware are independent of the application and masked by the development tools used to build the application.

We are moving from the machine-centred computing era of the 1970s and 1980s to a new era in which PC-familiar users demand systems that are user-centered. Previously, a user logged into a mainframe, mini-, or microapplication. The syntax of access was unique in each platform.

As processing steers away from the central data center to the remote office and plant, workstation server, and local area network (LAN) reliability must approach that provided today by the centrally located mini- and mainframe computers. The most effective way to ensure this is through the provision of monitoring and support from these same central locations.

4.3 THE ROLE OF THE CLIENT

In the client/server model, the client is primarily a consumer of services provided by one or more server processors. The model provides a clear separation of functions based on the idea of servers acting as service providers responding to requests from clients. It is important to understand that a workstation can operate as a client in some instances while acting as a server in other instances.

The client almost always provides presentation services. User input and final output, if any, are presented at the client workstation. Current technology provides cost effective support for a graphical user interface (GUI).

Client Services

The ideal client/server platform operates in an open systems environment using a requester-server discipline that is based on well-defined standards. This enables multiple hardware and software platforms to interact.

Request for Service

Client workstations request services from the attached server. Whether this server is in fact the same processor or a network processor, the application format of the request is the same. NOS software translates or adds the specifics required by the targeted requester to the application request.

Interprocess communication (IPC) is the generic term used to describe communication between running processes. In the client/server model, these processes might be on the same computer, across the LAN, or across the WAN.

Remote Procedure Call (RPC)

Over the years, good programmers have developed modular code using structured techniques and subroutine logic. Today, developers want subroutines to be stored as a named objects "somewhere" and made available to everyone with the right to use them. Remote Procedure Calls (RPCs) provide this capability. RPCs standardize the way programmers must write calls, so that remote procedures can recognize and respond correctly.

4.4 THE SERVER

The server is a multiuser computer. There is no special hardware requirement that turns a computer into a server. The hardware platform should be selected based on application demands and economics. Servers for client/server applications work best when they are configured with an operating system that supports shared memory, application isolation, and preemptive multitasking. An operating system with preemptive multitasking enables a higher priority task to preempt or take control of the processor from a currently executing, lower priority task.

The server provides and controls shared access to server resources. Applications on a server must be isolated from each other so that an error in one cannot damage another. Preemptive multitasking ensures that no single task can take over all the resources of the server and prevent other tasks from providing service. There must be a means of defining the relative priority of the tasks on the server. These requirements are specific to the client/server implementation and not to the file server implementation. Because file servers execute only the single task of file service, they can operate in a more limited operating environment without the need for application isolation and preemptive multitasking.

4.4.1 The Role of the Server

Servers provide application, file, database, print, fax, image, communications, security, systems, and network management services. These are each described in some detail in the following sections.

It is important to understand that a server is an architectural concept, not a physical implementation description. Client and server functions can be provided by the same physical device. With the movement toward peer computing, every device will potentially operate as a client and server in response to requests for service.

Security at the server restricts access to software and data accessed from the server.

Communications access is controlled from the communications server. In most implementations, the use of a user login ID is the primary means of security. Using LAN Server, some organizations have implemented integrated Response Access/Control Facility (RACF) security by creating profiles in the MVS environment and downloading those to the LAN server for domain control. Systems and network management services for the local LAN are managed by a LAN administrator, but WAN services must be provided from some central location. Typically, remote LAN management is done from the central data center site by trained MIS personnel.

4.4.2 Server Functionality in Detail

The discussion in the following sections more specifically describes the functions provided by the server in a NOS environment.

- Request processing,
- File services,
- Fax/Print/Image services,
- Database services,
- Communications services and
- Security services.

Requests are issued by a client to the NOS services software resident on the client machine. These services format the request into an appropriate RPC and issue the request to the application layer of the client protocol stack. This request is received by the application layer of the protocol stack on the server.

File services handle access to the virtual directories and files located on the client workstation and to the server's permanent storage. These services are provided through the redirection software implemented as part of the client workstation operating environment.

High-quality printers, workstation-generated faxes, and plotters are natural candidates for support from a shared server. The server can accept input from many clients, queue it according to the priority of the request and handle it when the device is available.

Early database servers were actually file servers with a different interface. Products such as dBASE, Clipper, FoxPro, and Paradox execute the database engine primarily on the client machine and use the file services provided by the file server for record access and free space management. These are new and more powerful implementations of the original flat-file models with extracted indexes for direct record access. Currency control is managed by the application program, which issues lock requests and lock checks, and by the database server, which creates a lock table that is interrogated whenever a record access lock check is generated. Because access is at the record level, all records satisfying the primary key must be returned to the client workstation for filtering.

Client/server applications require LAN and WAN communication services. Basic LAN services are integral to the NOS. WAN services are provided by various communications server products.

Client/server applications require similar security services to those provided by host environments. Every user should be required to log in with a user ID and password. If passwords might become visible to unauthorized users, the security server should insist that passwords be changed regularly. The enterprise on the desk implies that a single logon ID and logon sequence is used to gain the authority once to access all information and process for the user has a need and right of access. Because data may be stored in a less physically secure area, the option should exist to store data in an encrypted form. A combination of the user ID and password should be required to decrypt the data.

4.5 THE NETWORK OPERATING SYSTEM

The Network Operating System (NOS) provides the services not available from the client OS.

4.5.1 The Server Operating System

Servers provide the platform for application, database, and communication services. There are six operating system platforms that have the greatest potentional and/or are prevalent today: NetWare, OS/2, Windows NT, MVS, VMS, and UNIX.

NetWare

NetWare is used by many organizations, large and small, for the provision of file, printer, and network services. NetWare is a self-contained operating system. It does not require a separate OS (as do Windows NT, OS/2, and UNIX) to run. Novell is taking steps to allow NetWare to run on servers with UNIX. The products will enable UNIX to simultaneously access information from both a NetWare and a UNIX server.

OS/2

OS/2 is the server platform for Intel products provided by IBM in the System Application Architecture (SAA) model. OS/2 provides the storage protection and preemptive multitasking services needed for the server platform. Several database and many application products have been ported to OS/2. The only network operating systems directly supported with OS/2 are LAN Manager and LAN Server. Novell supports the use of OS/2 servers running on separate processors from the NetWare server. The combination of Novell with an OS/2 database and application servers can provide the necessary environment for a production-quality client/server implementation. Appendix A describes such an implementation.

UNIX

UNIX is a primary player as a server system in the client/server model. Certainly, the history of UNIX in the distributed computing arena and its open interfaces provide an excellent opportunity for it to be a server of choice. To understand what makes it an open operating system, look at the system's components. UNIX was conceived in the early 1970s by AT&T employees as an operating environment to provide services to software developers who were discouraged by the incompatibility of new computers and the lack of development tools for application development. The original intention of the UNIX architecture was to define a standard set of services to be provided by the UNIX kernel. These services are used by a shell that provides the command-line interface. Functionality is enhanced through the provision of a library of programs. Applications are built up from the program library and custom code. The power and appeal of UNIX lie in the common definition of the kernel and shell and in the large amount of software that has been built and is available. Applications built around these standards can be ported to many different hardware platforms.

The objectives of the original UNIX were very comprehensive and might have been achieved except that the original operating system was developed under the auspices of AT&T. Legal ramifications of the consent decree governing the breakup of the Regional Bell Operating Companies (RBOCs) prevented AT&T from getting into the computer business. As a result, the company had little motivation early on to promote UNIX as a product.

5

DATA COMMUNICATION BASICS

5.1 DATA TRANSMISSION INTRODUCTION

Data transmission occurs between transmitter and receiver over some transmission medium. Transmission media may be classified as guided or unguided. In both cases, communication is in the form of electromagnetic waves *i.e.*signals are electromagnetic waves. With guided media, the waves are guided along a physical path examples of guided media are twisted pair, coaxial cable, and optical fiber. Unguided media provide a means for transmitting electromagnetic waves but do not guide them: examples are propagation through air, vacuum and seawater.

Direct link means the transmission path between two devices in which signals propagate directly from transmitter to receiver with no intermediate devices, other than amplifiers or repeaters used to increase signal strength. A guided transmission medium is point-to-point if, first, it provides a direct link between two devices and, second, those are the only two devices sharing the medium (Figure 5.1.a).

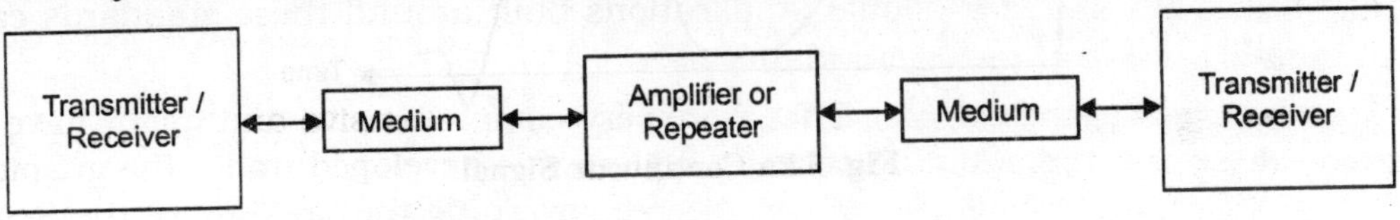

Figure 5.1a Point-to-Point Transmission Configuration

In a multipoint configuration, more than two devices share the same medium (Figure 5.1.b).

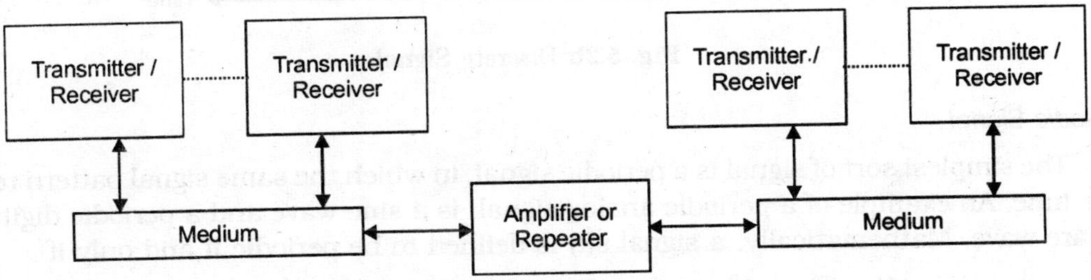

Figure 5.1b Multi-Point Transmission Configuration

A transmission may be *simplex, half-duplex,* or *full-duplex.* In **simplex** transmission, signals are transmitted in only one direction; one station is the transmitter and the other is the receiver. In **half-duplex** operation, both stations may transmit, but only one at a time. In **full-duplex** operation, both stations may transmit simultaneously. In the latter case, the medium is carrying signals in both directions at the same time.

The electromagnetic signal is generated by the transmitter and transmitted over a medium. The signal is a function of time, but it can also be expressed as a function of frequency; that is, the signal consists of components of different frequencies.

- **Data** : Entity that convey meaning.
- **Signal** : Electromagnetic encoding of data.
- **Signalling** : Act of propagating signal over a medium.
- **Transmission** : Communication of data by propagation and processing of signal.

5.2 TIME DOMAIN CONCEPT

Viewed as a function of time, an electromagnetic signal can be either continuous or discrete. A *continuous signal* is one in which the signal intensity or signal strength varies in a smooth fashion over time. In other words there are no breaks or discontinuities in the signal. A *discrete signal* is one in which the signal intensity maintains a constant level for some period of time and then changes to another constant level. Figure 5.2 shows of both kinds of signals. The continuous signal might represent speech, and the discrete signal might represent binary 1s and 0s.

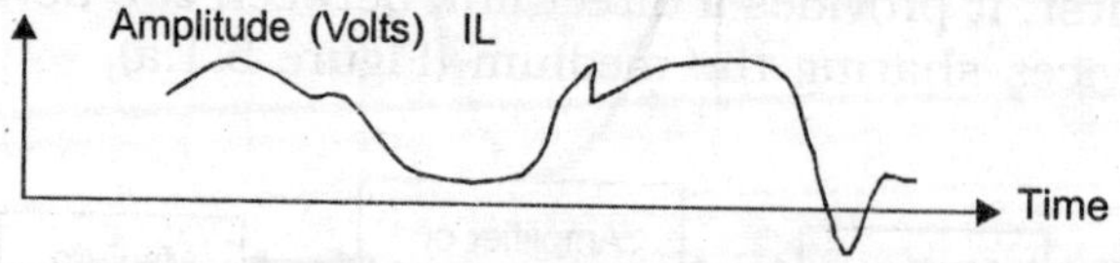

Fig. 5.2a Continuous Signal

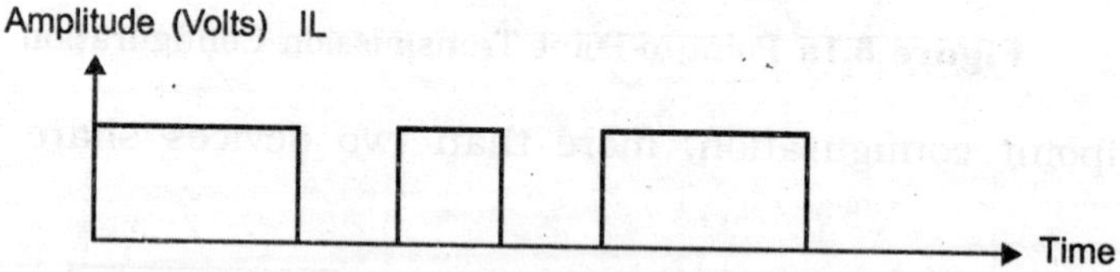

Fig. 5.2b Discrete Signal

Periodic Signal

The simplest sort of signal is a periodic signal, in which the same signal pattern repeats over time. An example of a periodic analog signal is a sine wave and a periodic digital is a square wave. Mathematically, a signal s(t) is defined to be periodic if and only if

$$s(t + T) = s(t) \qquad \text{for } -00 < t < +00$$

where the constant T is the period of the signal. (T is the smallest value that satisfies the equation.) Otherwise, the signal is *aperiodic.*

The *sine wave* is the fundamental continuous signal. A general sine wave can be represented by three parameters: amplitude (A), frequency (f), and phase (Φ). The amplitude is the peak value of strength of the signal over time; typically, this value is measured in volts or watts. The frequency is the rate (in cycles per second, or Hertz (Hz)) at which the signal repeats. An equivalent parameter is the period (T) of a signal, which is the amount of time it takes for one repetition; therefore, T = 1/f. Phase is a measure of the relative position in time within a single period of a signal, as illustrated below. The general sine wave can be written as

$$s(t) = A \sin (2\Pi ft + \Phi)$$

5.2.1 Frequency Domain Concepts

In practice, an electromagnetic signal will be made up of many frequencies. For example, the signal

$$s(t) = \sin (2\ \Pi\ f_1 t) + 1/3 \sin (2\ \Pi\ (3f_1)t)$$

is shown in Figure 5.3.

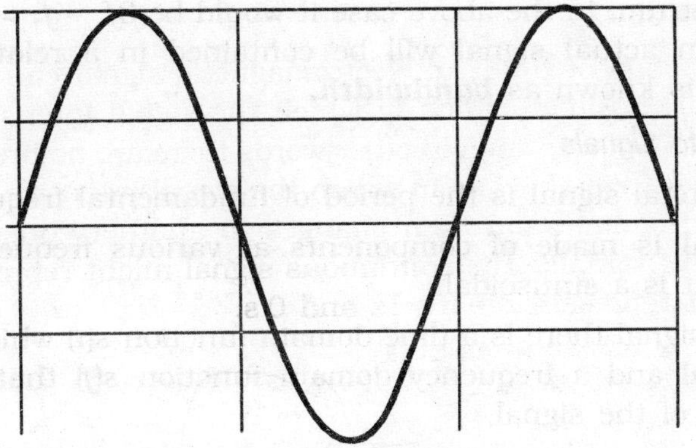

(a) sin $(2\pi f_1 t)$

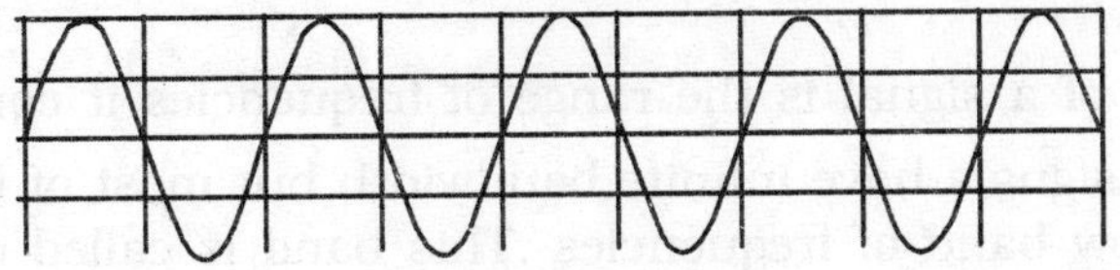

(b) 1/3 sin $(2\pi(3f_1)t)$

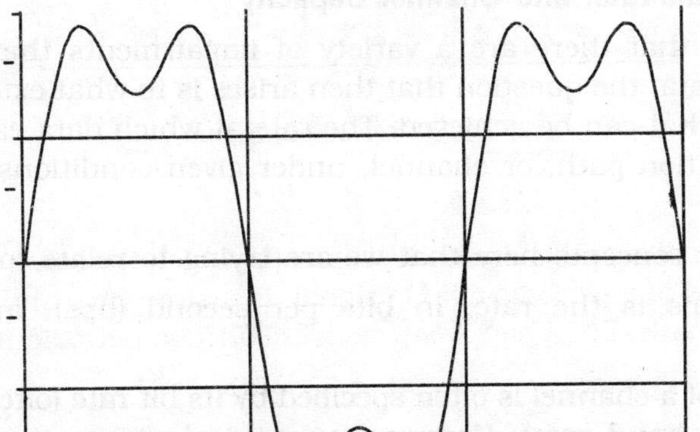

(c) S(t) = $(2\pi f_1 t)$ + 1/3 $(2\pi\ (3f_1)t)$

Figure 5.3 Addition of Frequency Components

The components of this signal are just sine waves of frequencies f_1 and $3f_1$; parts (*a*) and (*b*) of the figure show these individual components. There are several interesting points that can be made about this figure: the second frequency is an integer multiple of the first frequency. When all of the frequency components of a signal are integer multiples of one frequency, the latter frequency is referred to as the *fundamental frequency.*

The period of the total signal is equal to the period of the fundamental frequency. The period of the fundamental signal $sin(2 \Pi f_1 t)$ is $T = 1/f_1$, and the period of *s*(*t*) is also T, as can be seen from Figure 5.3c. It can be shown, using a discipline known as ***Fourier Analysis*** that any signal is made up of components at various frequencies, in which case each component is *sinusoid.* This result is of tremendous importance, because the effects of various transmission media on a signal can be expressed in terms of frequencies and the signal can be analysed to great extent.

The **Spectrum** of a signal is the range of frequencies that it contains. For the signal in Figure 5.3c, the spectrum extends from f_1 to $3f_1$. The *absolute bandwidth* of the signal is the width of spectrum; in the above case it would be $3f_1 - f_1 = 2f_1$ Hz. However most of the energy in an actual signal will be contained in a relatively narrow band of frequencies, which is known as ***bandwidth.***

Conclusions Related to Signals

1. Period of total signal is the period of fundamental frequency.
2. Any signal is made of components at various frequencies ,in which each component is a sinusoidal.
3. For each signal there is a time domain function *s*(*t*) which specifies amplitude of a signal and a frequency domain function *s*(*f*) that specifies constituent frequency of the signal.
4. Magnitude of frequency component of a signal becomes smaller for large frequency.
5. Spectrum of a signal is the range of frequencies it contains.
6. Most real signals have infinite bandwidth but most of the energy is contained in a narrow band of frequencies .This band is called effective Bandwidth.

5.2.2 Bandwidth Data-rate, and Channel Capacity

We have seen that there are a variety of impairments that distort or corrupt a signal. For digital data, the question that then arises is to what extent these impairments limit the data rate that can be achieved. The rate at which data can be transmitted over a given communication path, or channel, under given conditions, is referred to as the ***channel capacity.***

There are four concepts here that we are trying to relate to one another:

Data rate. This is the rate, in bits per second (bps), at which data can be communicated.

The data rate of a channel is often specified by its bit rate (often thought erroneously to be the same as baud rate). However, an equivalent measure channel capacity is bandwidth. In general, the maximum data rate a channel can support is directly proportional to the channel's bandwidth and inversely proportional to the channel's noise level.

Bandwidth. This is the maximum bandwidth of the transmitted signal as constrained by the nature of the transmission medium or transmission channel, expressed in cycles per second, or hertz (Hz). Bandwidth is the transmission capacity of a computer or communications channel. For pure digital transmission, it is measured in bits or bytes per second. When digital data is converted to frequencies for transmission over carrier-based networks, bandwidth is still stated in bits or bytes per second. However, when frequencies are used as the transmission signal rather than on-off pulses,bandwidth may also be measured in cycles per second, or Hertz. The bandwidth is the difference between the *lowest* and the *highest* frequencies transmitted. In this case, the frequency will be equal to or greater than the bits per second.

Baud Rate. The baud rate refers to the signalling rate at which data is sent through a channel and is measured in electrical transitions per second. In the EIA232 serial interface standard, one signal transition, at most, occurs per bit, and the baud rate and bit rate are identical. In this case, a rate of 9600 baud corresponds to a transfer of 9,600 data bits per second with a bit period of 104 microseconds (1/9600 sec.). If two electrical transitions were required for each bit, as is the case in non-return-to-zero coding, then at a rate of 9600 baud, only 4800 bits per second could be conveyed. The channel efficiency is the number of bits of useful information passed through the channel per second. It does not include framing, formatting, and error detecting bits that may be added to the information bits before a message is transmitted, and will always be less than one.

Baud rate is the transmission speed of a communications channel. Baud rate is commonly used to represent bits per second. For example, 4800 baud is 4,800 bits per second of data transfer. In a typical personal computer transmission, 10 bits are used for each character, thus 4800 baud is equivalent to 480 characters or bytes of data transmitted per second.

Bits Per Second and Baud

Data transmission rates expressed in bits/second are unambiguous and indicate the exact rate of data transfer. The *baud* rate, however, refers to the rate of transitions impressed onto a transmission line. As there are a number of ways to represent a bit (or a series of bits) as transitions on a transmission path, there is only a loose correlation between the bit rate as expressed in bits/second and the signalling rate as expressed in baud. Some encoding schemes, such as Manchester encoding, require two bauds per bit. Other schemes, such as a Nonreturn to Zero or NRZ encoding, use a single baud per bit. However, some schemes encode more than one bit with each baud and, thus, it may be seen that the baud rate of a data stream can be higher or lower than the bit rate. As a result, the bandwidth required to transmit at a given rate is a function of the encoding scheme used. However, the signalling rate rarely differs from the bit rate by more than a factor of 2 or 4 when wire-line transmission is used.

Error rate. The rate at which errors occur, where an error is the reception of a 1 when a 0 was transmitted, or the reception of a 0 when a 1 was transmitted.

The problem we are addressing is this: communications facilities are expensive, and, in general, the *greater the bandwidth of the transmission facility, the greater the cost.* Furthermore, all transmission channels of any practical interest are of limited bandwidth. The limitations arise from the physical properties of the transmission medium or from deliberate limitations at the transmitter on the bandwidth to prevent interference from other sources. Accordingly, we would like to make as efficient use as possible of a given bandwidth. For digital data, this means that we would like to *get as high a data rate as possible at a particular limit of error rate for a given bandwidth.* The main constraint on achieving this efficiency is noise.

Conclusions Related to Bandwidth and Data Rate

Let's we have the following signal:

$$s(t) = \sin(2\Pi f_1 t) + 1/3 \sin(2\Pi (3f_1)t + 1/5 \sin(2\Pi (5f_1)t)$$

Amplitude of the Kth frequency component kf_1 is $1/k$, so Bandwidth is :

$$5 f_1 - f_1 = 4 f_1, \text{ and } f_1 = 1 \text{ MHz and so B} = 4\text{MHz.}$$

So Time T = 1 msec., hence a bit occurs every 0.5 msec.

Respectively Data Rate is 2^*f_1, *i.e.* 2 Mbps.

1. Transmission medium will limit the Bandwidth that can be transmitted.
2. For any medium, greater bandwidth transmitted, greater will be cost.
3. Limiting the Bandwidth will increase distortion and errors at the reception side.
4. If we think bandwidth is centered about some frequency, referred as central frequency then higher the central frequency, higher is the potential bandwidth and higher is the data rate.

5.2.3 Analog and Digital Signals

Analog and digital signals are referred in **Three** Context:

1. Data
2. Signalling
3. Transmission.

Analog Data are function of time and occupy a limited frequency spectrum .Such data can be represented by an electromagnetic signal occupying same spectrum.

Digital Data is represented by digital signals with a different voltage level for each of the Two binary digits.

5.2.4 Nyquest Sampling Rate

To begin, let us consider the case of a channel that is noise-free. In this environment, the limitation on data rate is simply the bandwidth of the signal. A formulation of this limitation, due to **Nyquist,** states that if the signal with frequencies components not greater than ***W*** Hz (cycles per second) is given, then it is possible to represent completely that signal by sampling it at **2W** samples per second.

Extending this to the transmission media, given a transmission medium of bandwidth W Hz, the highest signal rate that can be carried by it is 2W samples per second.

Note that in the last paragraph, we referred to samples. If the signals to be transmitted are binary (two voltage levels), then each sample would represent a binary bit, and the data rate that can be supported by W Hz is 2W bps. As an example, consider a voice channel being used, via modem, to transmit digital data. Assume a bandwidth of 3100 Hz. Then the capacity, C, of the channel is 2W = 6200 bps. However, signals or samples with more than two levels can be used; that is, each signal element can represent more than one bit. For example, if four possible voltage levels are used as sampled signals, then each signal element can represent two bits. With multilevel signalling, the Nyquist formulation becomes

$$C = 2W \log_2 M$$

where M is the number of discrete signal or voltage levels. Thus, for M = 8, a value used with some modems, channel capacity C becomes 18,600 bps. So, for a given bandwidth, the data rate can be increased by increasing the number of different signals. However, this places an increased burden on the receiver: Instead of distinguishing one of two possible signals during each signal time, it must distinguish one of M possible signals. Noise and other impairments on the transmission line will limit the practical value of M.

Thus, all other things being equal, doubling the bandwidth doubles the data rate. Now consider the relationship between data rate, noise, and error rate. The presence of noise can corrupt one or more bits. If the data rate is increased, then the duration of bit becomes *shorter* so that more bits are affected by a given pattern of noise. Thus, at a given noise level, the higher the data rate, the higher the error rate.

5.2.5 Shannon Channel Capacity

All of these concepts can be tied together neatly in a formula developed by the mathematician **Claude Shannon.** As we have just illustrated, the higher the data rate, the more damage that unwanted noise can do. For a given level of noise, we would expect that greater signal strength would improve the ability to correctly receive data in the presence of noise. The key parameter involved in this reasoning is the signal-to-noise ratio (S/N), which is the ratio of the power in a signal to the power contained in the noise that is present at a particular point in the transmission. Typically, this ratio is measured at a receiver, as it is at this point that an attempt is made to process the signal and eliminate the unwanted noise. For convenience, this ratio is often reported in decibels:

$$(S/N)_{db} = 10 \log \text{(signal power/noise power)}$$

This expresses the amount, in decibels, that the intended signal exceeds the noise level. A high S/N will mean a high-quality signal and a low number of required intermediate repeaters.

The signal-to-noise ratio is important in the transmission of digital data because it sets the upper bound on the achievable data rate. **Shannon's** result is that the *theoretical maximum channel capacity*, in bits per second, obeys the equation

$$C = W \log_2 [1 + (S/N)]$$

where C is the capacity of the channel in bits per second and W is the bandwidth of the channel in hertz.

As an example, consider a voice channel being used, via modem, to transmit digital data. Assume a bandwidth of 3100 Hz. A typical value of S/N for a voice-grade line is 30 dB, or a ratio of 1000:1. Thus,

$$C = 3100 \log_2(1 + 1000)$$

$$C = 30{,}894 \text{ bps}$$

This represents the theoretical maximum channel capacity that can be achieved.

5.2.6 Data Rate Revisited

Let f_1 is 2 MHz of a signal $s(t)$.

$$S(t) = \sin(2 \Pi f_1 t) + 1/3 \sin(2 \Pi (3f_1)t)$$

Bandwidth is $3 * 2 f_1 - 2 f_1 = 4$ MHz. So data rate is 4 Mbps.

Time $T = 1/f_1$, Hence T = 0.5 msec.

Every bit will occur every 0.25 msec. Data Rate will be 4 Mbps.

So if W is the frequency, Rate will be 2W.

This says that our signal has more than two signal levels .Signals with more than two signal levels are used in communication.

With multilevel signal Nyquest Formula will be: $C = 2W \log_2 m$

Where m is number of discrete signal or voltage levels. For m = 8, C = 18600 bps.

Conclusions

1. For given bandwidth data rate can be increased by increasing the number of different signals. But it's a burden on receiver. It has to distinguish between m possible signals.
2. If data rate is increased, bits becomes "Shorter", so more bits are affected by a given pattern of noise. So at a given noise level, higher the data rate, higher the error rate.
3. $$(S/N)_{db} = 10 \log \frac{\text{Signal Power}}{\text{Noise Power}}$$

   Higher is the signal to noise ratio, higher will be quality of signal.

   S/N sets upper bond on the achievable data rate.

   $$C = W \log_2 (1 + S/N)$$

   W is bandwidth and C channel capacity.

5.3 COMMUNICATION MEDIA USED FOR DATA TRANSMISSION

The transmission medium is the physical path between transmitter and receiver in a data transmission system. Transmission media can be classified as guided or unguided. In both cases, communication is in the form of electromagnetic waves. With guided media, the waves are guided along a solid medium, such as copper twisted pair, copper coaxial cable, and optical fiber. The atmosphere and outer space are examples of unguided media that provide a means of transmitting electromagnetic signals but do not guide them; this form of transmission is usually referred to as *wireless transmission.*

The characteristics and quality of a data transmission are determined both by the characteristics of the medium and the characteristics of the signal. In the case of guided media, the medium itself is more important in determining the limitations of transmission.

For unguided media, the bandwidth of the signal produced by the transmitting.

Antenna is more important than the medium in determining transmission characteristics. One key property of signals transmitted by antenna is directionality. In general, signals at lower frequencies are omni directional; that is, the signal propagates in all directions from the antenna. At higher frequencies, it is possible to focus the signal into a directional beam.

In considering the design of data transmission systems, a key concern, generally, is data rate and distance: the greater the data rate and distance, the better. A number of design factors relating to the transmission medium and the signal determine the data rate and distance:

- **Bandwidth.** All other factors remaining constant, greater the bandwidth of the signal allowed over the transmission line, higher the data rate that can be achieved.
- **Transmission impairments.** Impairments, such as attenuation, limit the distance. For guided media, twisted pair generally suffers more impairment than coaxial cable, which in turn suffers more than optical fiber.
- **Interference.** Interference from competing signals in overlapping frequency bands can distort or wipe out a signal. Interference is of particular concern for unguided media, but it is also a problem with guided media. For guided media, interference can be caused by nearby cables. For example, twisted pair cables are often bundled together, and conduits often carry multiple cables. Interference can also be experienced from unguided transmissions. Proper shielding of a guided medium can minimize this problem.

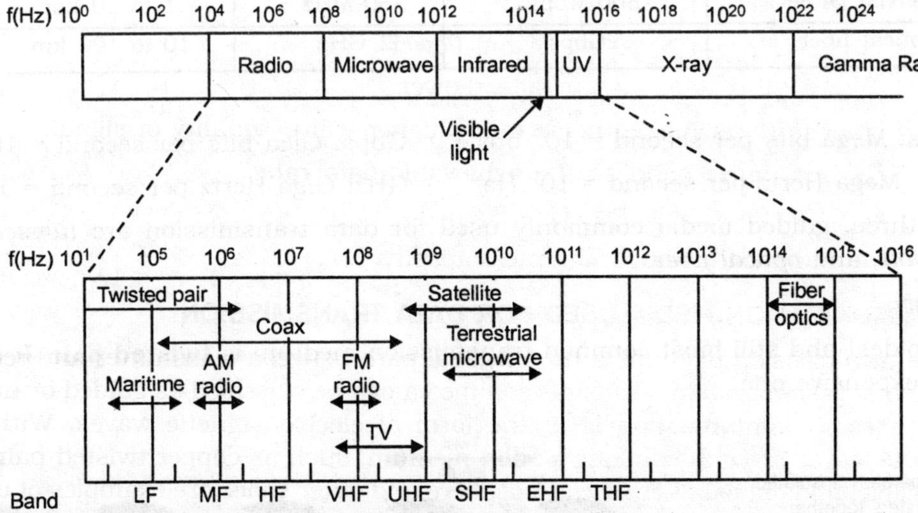

Figure 5.4 Electromagnetic Spectrum and Its Uses for Communication

- **Number of receivers.** A guided medium can be used to construct a point-to-point link or a shared link with multiple attachments. In the latter case, each attachment introduces some attenuation and distortion on the line, limiting distance and/or data rate.

Figure 5.4 depicts the electromagnetic spectrum and indicates the frequencies at which various guided media and unguided transmission techniques operate. In this section, we examine these guided and unguided alternatives.

There are several types of physical channels (communication media) through which data can be transmitted from one point to another. Some of the most common data transmission media are:

1. **Guided Transmission Medium**
   - 1.1 Twisted wire
   - 1.2 Coaxial cable
   - 1.3 Optical fiber
2. **Unguided Transmission Medium**

5.3.1 Guided Transmission Media

For guided transmission media, the transmission capacity, in terms of either data-rate or bandwidth, depends critically on the distance and on whether the medium is point-to-point or multipoint such as in a local area network (LAN). Table 5.1 indicates the type of performance typical for the common guided medium for long-distance point-to-point applications

TABLE 5.1. Point-to-point transmission characteristics of guided media

Transmission medium	*Total data rate*	*Bandwidth*	*Repeater spacing*
Twisted pair	4 Mbps	3 MHz	2 to 10 km
Coaxial cable	500 Mbps	350 MHz	1 to 10 km
Optical fiber	2Gbps	2 GHz	10 to 100 km

Mbps: Mega bits per second = 10^6 bps, Gbps: Giga bits per second = 10^9 bps

MHz: Mega Hertz per second = 10^6 Hz, GHz: Giga Hertz per second = 10^9 Hz

The three, guided media commonly used for data transmission are *twisted pair, coaxial cable,* and *optical fiber.*

Twisted Pair

The oldest and still most common transmission medium is **twisted pair**. It is also the least-expensive one.

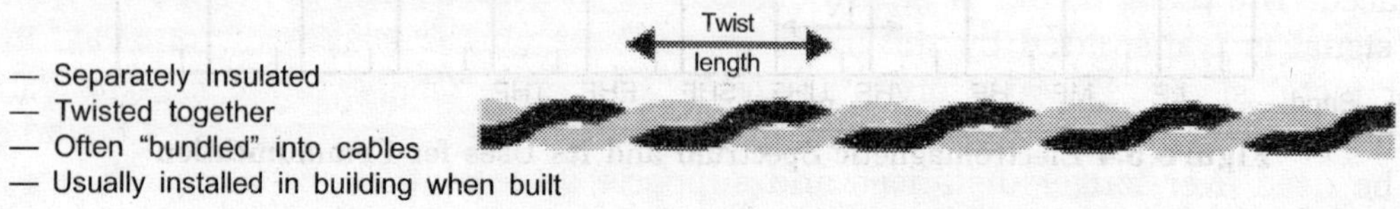

Figure 5.5 Twisted Pair Cable

A twisted pair consists of two insulated copper wires arranged in a regular spiral pattern. A wire pair acts as a single communication link. The twisting tends to decrease the cross-talk interference between adjacent pairs in a cable. Neighboring pairs in a bundle typically have somewhat different twist lengths to enhance the cross-talk interfere. Wire pairs are commonly used in local telephone communication, and for digital data transmission for short distances upto 1 Km. They are usually made of copper and a pair of wires is twisted together to reduce interference from adjacent wires. Wire pairs are normally used to connect terminals to the main computer upto short distances from the main computer. Data transmission speed of upto 9600 bits per second can be achieved if the distance is not more than 100 metres. However, for longer distances, local telephone lines are used. In this case, the typical speed of digital signal transmission is 1200 bits per second.

It is the most commonly used medium in the telephone network as well as being the workhorse for communications within buildings. In the telephone system, individual residential telephone sets are connected to the local telephone exchange, or *end office*, by twisted-pair wire. These are referred to as *subscriber loops*. Within an office building, each telephone is also connected to a twisted pair, which goes to the in-house private branch exchange (PBX) system. Twisted pair is much less expensive than the other commonly used guided transmission media (coaxial cable, optical fiber) and is easier to work with. It is more limited in terms of data rate and distance.

Advantages and Limitations of Wire Pairs

- Wire pairs are an inexpensive medium of data transmission.
- They are easy to install and use.

However, their use is limited because :

- They easily pick up noise signals which results in high error rates when the line length extends beyond 100 metres.

The twisted wire pairs that are used in networking are of the following types:

(a) Type 1 Two twisted pairs, each 22 gauge, shielded

(b) Type 2 Four pairs of telephone type twisted-pair wires with metallic shield plastic cover

(c) Type 3 Telephone type cable with 24 gauge wire

Coaxial Cable

Coaxial cable, like twisted pair, consists of two conductors, but is constructed differently to permit it to operate over a wider range of frequencies.A single coaxial cable has a diameter of from 0.4 to about 1 in. Coaxial cables are groups of specially wrapped and insulated wire lines that are able to transmit data at high rates. They consist of a central copper wire surrounded by a PVC insulation over which a sleeve of copper mesh is placed. The metal sleeve is again shielded by an outer shield of thick PVC material. The signal is transmitted by the inner copper wire and is electrically shielded by the outer metal sleeve. Because of its shielding, concentric construction, coaxial cable is much less susceptible to interference and cross-talk than is twisted pair. Coaxial cable can be used over longer distances and supports more stations on a shared line than twisted pair.

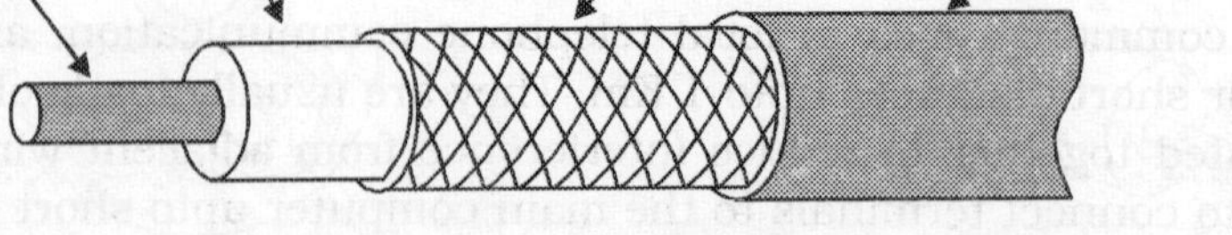

Figure 5.6 Coaxial Cable

Coaxial cable is perhaps the most versatile transmission medium and is enjoying widespread use in a wide variety of applications; the most important of these are :

1. Television distribution
2. Long-distance telephone transmission
3. Short-run computer system links
4. Local Area Networks

Coaxial cable is spreading rapidly as a means of distributing TV signals to individual homes—cable TV. A cable TV system can carry dozens or even hundreds of TV channels at ranges upto a few tens of miles.

Advantages and Limitations of Coaxial Cables

Coaxial cables are capable of transmitting digital signals at very high rates of 10 mega bits per second. They are extensively used in long distance telephone lines and as cables for closed circuit TV. In many cases, coaxial cables are packaged into a single large cable that can handle over 15,000 telephone calls simultaneously. Furthermore, coaxial cables have much higher noise immunity and can offer clean data transmission with less distortion or loss of signal. But coaxial cables are more expensive.

5.4 OPTICAL TRANSMISSION SYSTEM AND OPTICAL FIBER

An optical transmission system has three components; the light source, the transmission medium, and the detector. Conventionally, a pulse of light indicates a bit 1 and absence of light indicates bit 0. Transmission medium is an ultra thin fiber of glass. The transmitter generates the light pulses based on the input electrical signal. The detector regenerates the electrical signal based on the light signal it detects on the transmission medium. By attaching a light source to one end of an optical fiber and a detector to the other, we have a *unidirectional data transmission system* that accepts an electrical signal, converts and transmits it by light pulse, and then reconverts the output to an electrical signal at the receiving end.

An optical fiber is a thin (2 to 125 nm—nana meter—10^{-9} meter), flexible medium capable of conducting an optical ray. Various glasses and plastics can be used to make optical fibers. The lowest losses have been obtained using fibers of ultrapure fused silica. Ultrapure fiber is difficult to manufacture; higher-loss multicomponent glass fibers are more economical and still provide good performance. Plastic fiber is even less costly and can be used for short-haul links, for which moderately high losses are acceptable.

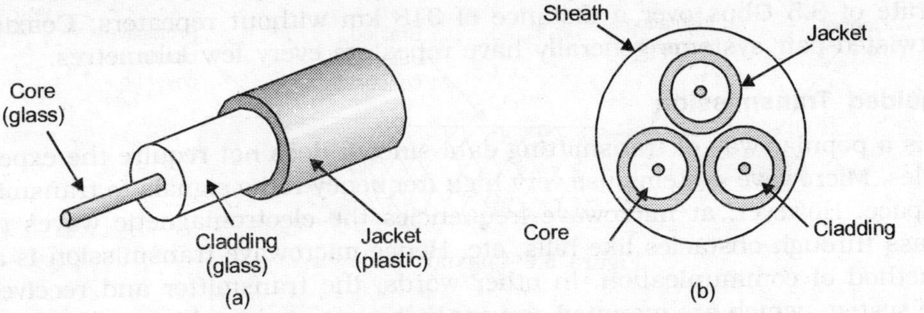

Figure 5.7 Optical Fiber

An optical fiber cable has a cylindrical shape and consists of three concentric sections: the core, the cladding, and the jacket. The *core is* the innermost section and consists of one or more very thin strands, or fibers, made of glass or plastic. Each fiber is surrounded by *its own cladding,* a glass or plastic coating that has optical properties different from those of the core. The outermost layer, surrounding one or a bundle of cladded fibers, is the *jacket.* The jacket is composed of plastic and other material layered to protect against moisture, abrasion, crushing and other environmental dangers. One of the most significant technological breakthroughs in data transmission has been the development of practical fiber optic communications systems. Optical fiber already enjoys considerable usc in *long distance telecommunications.* The continuing improvements in performance and decline in prices, together with the inherent advantages of optical fiber, have made it increasingly attractive for *local area networking* and *metropolitan networks.*

Advantages of Optical Fibers

1. The potential bandwidth, and hence data rate of optical fiber is immense; data rates of Gbps over tens of kilometres have been demonstrated. Compare this capability to the practical maximum of hundreds of Mbps over about 1 km for coaxial cable and just a few Mbps over 1 km or upto 100 Mbps over a few tens of metres for twisted pair.

2. Optical fibers are considerably thinner than coaxial cable or bundled twisted-pair cable - at least an order of magnitude thinner for comparable information-transmission capacity. For cramped conduits in buildings and underground along public rights-of-way, the advantage of small size is considerable. The corresponding reduction in weight reduces structural support requirements.

3. Attenuation is significantly lower for optical fiber than for coaxial cable or twisted pair and is constant over a wide range.

4. Optical fiber systems are not affected by external electromagnetic fields. Thus, the system is not vulnerable to interference, impulse noise, or cross-talk. By the same token, fibers do not radiate energy, thereby causing little interference with other equipment and thus providing a high degree of security from eavesdropping. In addition, fiber is inherently difficult to tap.

5. Fewer repeaters mean lower cost and fewer sources of error. The performance of optical fiber systems from this point of view has been steadily improving. For

example, AT&T has developed a fiber transmission system that achieves a data rate of 3.5 Gbps over a distance of 318 km without repeaters. Coaxial and twisted-pair systems generally have repeaters every few kilometres.

5.4.1 Unguided Transmission

This is a popular way of transmitting data since it does not require the expense of laying cables. Microwave systems use very high frequency radio signals to transmit data through space. However, at microwave frequencies the electromagnetic waves cannot bend or pass through obstacles like hills, etc. Hence microwave transmission is a line-of-sight method of communication. In other words, the transmitter and receiver of a microwave system, which are mounted on very high towers, should be in a line-of-sight. This may not be possible for very long distance transmission due to physical constraints. Moreover, the signals become weak after travelling a certain distance and require power amplification.

Wireless (Radio) Transmission

Radio encompasses the electromagnetic spectrum in the range of 3 KHz to 300 GHz. In radio communications the signal is transmitted into the air or space, using an antenna that radiates energy at some carrier frequency. For example, in QAM modulation the information sequence determines a point in the signal constellation that specifies the amplitude and phase of the cosine wave that is transmitted. Depending on the frequency and the antenna, this energy can propagate in either a unidirectional or omni-directional fashion. In the unidirectional case a properly aligned antenna receives the modulated signal, and an associated receiver in the direction of the transmission recovers the original information. In the omni directional case any receiver with an antenna in the area of coverage can pick up the signal.

Radio communication systems are subject to a variety of transmission impairments. The attenuation in radio links varies logarithmically with the distance. Attenuation for radio systems also increases with rainfall. Radio systems are subject to multipath fading and interference. Multipath fading refers to the interference that results at a receiver when two or more versions of the same signal arrive at slightly different times because of reflections from different objects. If the arriving signals differ in polarity, then they will cancel each other. Multipath fading can result in wide fluctuations in the amplitude and phase of the received signal. Interference refers to energy that appears at the receiver from sources other than the transmitter. Interference can be generated by other users of the same frequency band or by equipment that inadvertently transmits energy outside its band and into the bands of adjacent channels. Interference can seriously affect the performance of radio systems, and for this reason regulatory bodies apply strict requirements on the emission properties of electronic equipment.

Figure 5.4 gives the range of various frequency bands and their applications. The frequency bands are classified according to wavelengths. Thus the low frequency (LF) band spans the range 30 kHz to 300 kHz, which corresponds to a wavelength of 1 km to 10 km, whereas the extremely high frequency (EHF) band occupies the range from 30 to 300 GHz corresponding to wavelengths of 1 millimeter to 1 centimeter. Note that the progression of frequency bands in the logarithmic frequency scale have increasingly larger bandwidths, for example, the *band* from 10^{11} to 10^{12} Hz has a bandwidth of

0.9×10^{12} Hz, whereas the band from 10^5 to 10^6 Hz has a bandwidth of 0.9×10^6 Hz.

The propagation properties of radio waves vary with the frequency. Radio waves at the VLF, LF, and MF bands follow the surface of the earth in the form of ground waves. VLF waves can be detected at distances upto about 1000 km, and MF waves, for example, AM radio, at much shorter distances. Radio waves in the HF band are reflected by the ionosphere and can be used for long-distance communications. These waves are detectable only within certain specific distances from the transmitter. Finally, radio waves in the VHF band and higher are not reflected back by the ionosphere and are detectable only within line-of-sight.

5.4.2 Generalities of Transmission

Transmission over Short Distances (< 2 feet)

When the source and destination registers are part of an integrated circuit (within a microprocessor chip, for example), they are extremely close (thousandths of an inch). Consequently, the bus signals are at very low power levels, may traverse a distance in very little time, and are not very susceptible to external noise and distortion. This is the ideal environment for digital communications. However, it is not yet possible to integrate all the necessary circuitry for a computer (*i.e.*, CPU, memory, disk control, video and display drivers, etc.) on a single chip. When data is sent off-chip to another integrated circuit, the bus signals must be amplified and conductors extended out of the chip through external pins. Amplifiers may be added to the source register: Bus signals that exit microprocessor chips and other VLSI circuitry are electrically capable of traversing about one foot of conductor on a printed circuit board, or less if many devices are connected to it. Special buffer circuits may be added to boost the bus signals sufficiently for transmission over several additional feet of conductor length, or for distribution to many other chips (such as memory chips).

Transmission over Medium Distance (< 20 feet)

Computer peripherals such as a printer or scanner generally include mechanisms that cannot be situated within the computer itself. Our first thought might be just to extend the computer's internal buses with a cable of sufficient length to reach the peripheral. Doing so, however, would expose all bus transactions to external noise and distortion even though only a very small percentage of these transactions concern the distant peripheral to which the bus is connected.

If a peripheral can be located within 20 feet of the computer, however, relatively simple electronics may be added to make data transfer through a cable efficient and reliable. To accomplish this, a bus interface circuit is installed in the computer:

It consists of a holding register for peripheral data, timing and formatting circuitry for external data transmission, and signal amplifiers to boost the signal sufficiently for transmission through a cable. When communication with the peripheral is necessary, data is first deposited in the holding register by the microprocessor. This data will then be reformatted, sent with error-detecting codes, and transmitted at a relatively slow rate by digital hardware in the bus interface circuit. In addition, the signal power is greatly boosted before transmission through the cable. These steps ensure that the data will not be corrupted by noise or distortion during its passage through the cable. In addition, because only data destined for the peripheral is sent, the party-line transactions taking place on the computer's buses are not unnecessarily exposed to noise.

Data sent in this manner may be transmitted in byte-serial format if the cable has eight parallel channels (at least 10 conductors for half-duplex operation), or in bit-serial format if only a single channel is available.

Transmission over Long Distances (< 4000 feet)

When relatively long distances are involved in reaching a peripheral device, driver circuits must be inserted after the bus interface unit to compensate for the electrical effects of long cables:

This is the only change needed if a single peripheral is used. However, if many peripherals are connected, or if other computer stations are to be linked, a local area network (LAN) is required, and it becomes necessary to drastically change both the electrical drivers and the protocol to send messages through the cable. Because multiconductor cable is expensive, bit-serial transmission is almost always used when the distance exceeds 20 feet.

In either a simple extension cable or a LAN, a balanced electrical system is used for transmitting digital data through the channel. This type of system involves at least two wires per channel, neither of which is a ground. Note that a common ground return cannot be shared by multiple channels in the same cable as would be possible in an unbalanced system.

The basic idea behind a balanced circuit is that a digital signal is sent on two wires simultaneously, one wire expressing a positive voltage image of the signal and the other a negative voltage image. When both wires reach the destination, the signals are subtracted by a summing amplifier, producing a signal swing of twice the value found on either incoming line. If the cable is exposed to radiated electrical noise, a small voltage of the same polarity is added to both wires in the cable. When the signals are subtracted by the summing amplifier, the noise cancels and the signal emerges from the cable without noise:

A great deal of technology has been developed for LAN systems to minimize the amount of cable required and maximize the throughput. The costs of a LAN have been concentrated in the electrical interface card that would be installed in PCs or peripherals to drive the cable, and in the communications software, not in the cable itself (whose cost has been minimized). Thus, the cost and complexity of a LAN are not particularly affected by the distance between stations.

Transmission over Very Long Distances (> 4000 feet)

Data communications through the telephone network can reach any point in the world. The volume of overseas fax transmissions is increasing constantly, and computer networks that link thousands of businesses, governments, and universities are pervasive. Transmissions over such distances are not generally accomplished with a direct-wire digital link, but rather with digitally-modulated analog carrier signals. This technique makes it possible to use existing analog telephone voice channels for digital data, although at considerably reduced data rates compared to a direct digital link.

Transmission of data from your personal computer to a timesharing service over phone lines requires that data signals be converted to audible tones by a modem. An audio sine wave carrier is used, and, depending on the baud rate and protocol, will encode data by varying the frequency, phase, or amplitude of the carrier. The receiver's modem accepts the modulated sine wave and extracts the digital data from it. Several modulation techniques typically used in encoding digital data for analog transmission are shown below:

Similar techniques may be used in digital storage devices such as hard disk drives to encode data for storage using an analog medium.

5.5 LINE CODING

Line coding is the method used for converting a *binary information sequence* into a *digital signal* in a digital communications system. The selection of a line coding technique involves several considerations. Maximizing bit rate is the main concern in digital transmission when bandwidth is at a premium. However, in other situations, such as in LANs, other concerns are also of interest. For example, another important design consideration is the ease with which the bit timing information can be recovered from the digital signal. Also, some line coding methods have built-in error detecting capabilities, and other methods have better immunity to noise and interference. Finally, the complexity and the cost of the line code implementations are always factors in the selection for a given application.

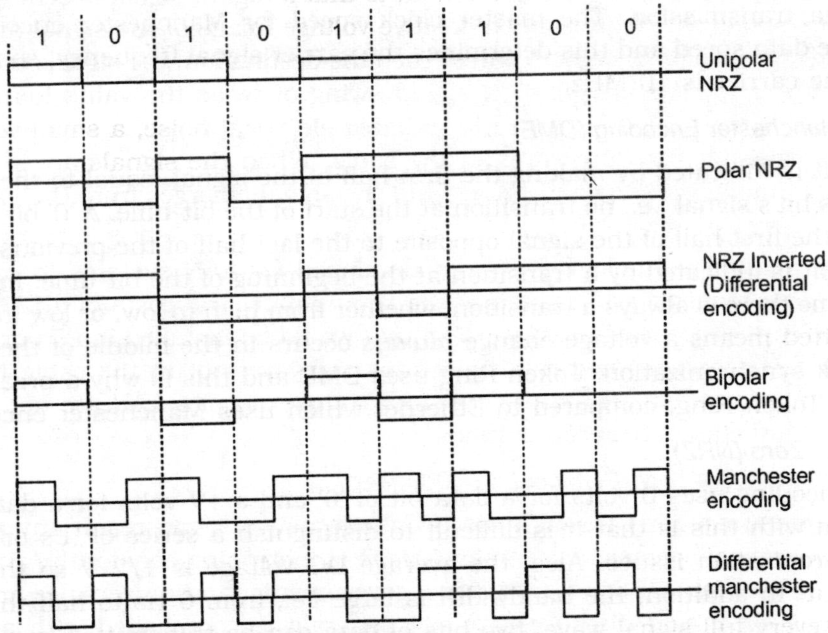

Figure 5.8 Line Coding Methods

Figure 5.8 shows various line codes that are used in practice. The figure shows the digital signals that are produced by the line codes for the binary sequence 101011100.

5.5.1 Data Encoding Techniques

In order to transport digital bits of data across carrier waves, encoding techniques have been developed each with their own pros and cons. This document briefly describes some of the more common techniques.

Manchester Phase Encoding (MPE)

802.3 Ethernet uses **Manchester Phase Encoding (MPE).** A data bit '1' from the level-encoded signal (*i.e.*, that from the digital circuitry in the host machine sending data) is represented by a full cycle of the *inverted* signal from the master clock which matches with the '0' to '1' rise of the phase-encoded signal (linked to the phase of the carrier signal which goes out on the wire). *i.e.*, -V in the first half of the signal and +V in the second half.

The data bit '0' from the level-encoded signal is represented by a full *normal* cycle of the master clock which gives the '1' to '0' fall of the phase-encoded signal. *i.e.*, +V in the first half of the signal and -V in the second half.

The above diagram shows graphically how MPE operates. The example at the bottom of the diagram indicates how the digital bit stream **10110** is encoded.

A transition in the middle of each bit makes it possible to synchronize the sender and receiver. At any instant either can be in one of three states: transmitting a 0 bit (-0.85 v), transmitting a 1 bit (0.85 v) or idle (0 volts). Having a normal clock signal as well as an inverted clock signal leads to regular transitions which means that synchronization of clocks is easily achieved even if there are a series of '0's or '1's. This results in highly reliable data transmission. The master clock speed for Manchester encoding always matches the data speed and this determines the carrier signal frequency, so for 10 Mbps Ethernet the carrier is 10 MHz.

Differential Manchester Encoding (DME)

A '1' bit is indicated by making the first half of the signal, equal to the last half of the previous bit's signal *i.e.*, no transition at the start of the bit-time. A '0' bit is indicated by making the first half of the signal opposite to the last half of the previous bit's signal *i.e.*, a zero bit is indicated by a transition at the beginning of the bit-time. In the middle of the bit-time there is always a transition, whether from high to low, or low to high. Each bit transmitted means a voltage change *always* occurs in the middle of the bit-time to ensure clock synchronization. Token Ring uses DME and this is why a preamble is not required in Token Ring, compared to Ethernet which uses Manchester encoding.

Non Return to Zero (NRZ)

NRZ encoding uses 0 volts for a data bit of '0' and a +V volts for a data bit of '1'. The problem with this is that it is difficult to distinguish a series of '1's or '0's due to clock synchronization issues. Also, the average DC voltage is 1/2 V so there is high power output. In addition, the bandwidth is large *i.e.*, from 0 Hz to half the data rate because for every full signal wave, two bits of data can be transmitted (remember that with MPE the data rate equals the bit rate which is even more inefficient!) *i.e.*, two bits of information are transmitted for every cycle (or hertz). After 50 m of cable attenuation the signal amplitude may have been reduced to 100 mV giving an induced noise tolerance of 100 mV.

Return to Zero (RZ)

With RZ a '0' bit is represented by 0 volts whereas a '1' data bit is represented by +V volts for half the cycle and 0 volts for the second half of the cycle. This means that the average DC voltage is reduced to 1/4 V plus there is the added benefit of there always being a voltage change even if there are a series of '1's. Unfortunately, the efficiency of bandwidth usage decreases if there are a series of '1's since now a '1' uses a whole cycle.

Non Return to Zero Invertive (NRZ-I)

With NRZ-I a '1' bit is represented by 0 volts or +V volts depending on the previous level. If the previous voltage was 0 volts then the '1' bit will be represented by +V volts, however if the previous voltage was +V volts then the '1' bit will be represented by 0 volts. A '0' bit is represented by whatever voltage level was used previously. This means that only a '1' bit can 'invert' the voltage, a '0' bit has no effect on the voltage, it remains the same as the previous bit whatever that voltage was.

This can be demonstrated in the following examples for the binary patterns **10110** and **11111:**

Note how that a '1' inverts the voltage whilst a '0' leaves it where it is. This means that the encoding is different for the same binary pattern depending on the voltage starting point.

The bandwidth usage is minimised with NRZ-I, plus there are frequent voltage changes required for clock synchronisation. With fibre there are no issues with power output so a higher clock frequency is fine whereas with copper NRZ-I would not be acceptable.

4B/5B

4B/5B encoding is sometimes called 'Block coding'. To get around this problem, an intermediate encoding takes place before the MLT-3 encoding. Each 4-bit 'nibble' of received data has an extra 5th bit added. If input data is dealt with in 4-bit nibbles there are $2^4 = 16$ different bit patterns. With 5-bit 'packets' there are $2^5 = 32$ different bit patterns. As a result, the 5-bit patterns can always have two '1's in them even if the data is all '0's a translation occurs to another of the bit patterns. This enables clock synchronisations required for reliable data transfer.

Notice that the clock frequency is 125 MHz. The reason for this is due to the 4B/5B encoding. A 100 MHz signal would not have been enough to give us 100 Mbps, we need a 125 MHz clock.

5B/6B

Same idea as 4B/5B but you can have DC balance (3 zero bits and 3 one bits in each group of 6) to prevent polarisation. 5B/6B Encoding is the process of encoding the scrambled 5-bit data patterns into predetermined 6-bit symbols. This creates a balanced data pattern, containing equal numbers of 0's and 1's, to provide guaranteed clock transitions synchronization for receiver circuitry, as well as an even power value on the line.

5B/6B encoding also provides an added error-checking capability. Invalid symbols and invalid data patterns, such as more than three 0's or three 1's in a row, are easily detected.

For 100 VG-AnyLAN for instance, the clock rate on each wire is 30 MHz, therefore 30 Mbits per second are transmitted on each pair giving a total data rate of 120 Mbits/sec. Since each 6-bits of data on the line represents 5 bits of real data due to the 5B/6B encoding, the rate of real data being transmitted is 25 Mbits/sec on each pair, giving a total rate of real data of 100 Mbits/sec. For 2-pair STP and fiber, the data rate is 120 Mbits/sec on the transmitting pair, for a real data transmission rate of 100 Mbits/sec.

8B/6T

8B/6T means send 8 data bits as six ternary (one of three voltage levels) signals. 3/4 (6/8) wave transitions transitions per bit *i.e.,* the carrier just needs to be running at 3/4 of the speed of the data rate.

The incoming data stream is split into 8-bit patterns. Each 8-bit data pattern with two voltage levels 0 volts and V volts is examined. This 8-bit pattern is then converted into a 6-bit pattern but using three voltage levels -V, 0 and V volts, so each 8-bit pattern has a unique 6T code. For example the bit pattern **0000 0000** (0x00) uses the code **+-00+-** and **0000 1110** (0x)E) uses the code **-+0-0+.** There are 3^6 = 729 possible patterns (symbols). The rules for the symbols are that there must be at least two voltage transitions (to maintain clock synchronisation) and the average DC voltage must be zero (this is called 'DC balance' that is the overall DC voltage is summed up to 0 V, the +V and -V transitions are evenly balanced either side of 0V) which stops any polarisation on the cable.

The maximum frequency that the 6T codes could generate on one carrier is 37.5 MHz. FCC rules do not allow anything above 30 MHz on cables and Category 3 cable does not allow anything above 16 MHz (which is what 100BaseT4 was designed for). The 100BaseT4 standard uses 8B/6T encoding on three pairs in a round robin fashion such that the maximum carrier frequency on any single pair is 37.5/3 = 12.5 MHz.

8B/10B

Each octet of data is examined and assigned a 10 bit code group. The data octet is split up into the 3 most significant bits and the 5 least significant bits. This is then represented as two decimal numbers with the least significant bits first *e.g.,* for the octet **101 00110** we get the decimal **6.5**. 10 bits are used to create this code group and the naming convention follows the format **/D6.5/.** There are also 12 special code groups which follow the naming convention **/Kx.y/.**

The 10 bit code groups must either contain five ones and five zeros, or four ones and six zeros, or six ones and four zeros. This ensures that not too many consecutive ones and zeros occurs between code groups thereby maintaining clock synchronisation. Two 'commas' are used to aid in bit synchronisation, these 'commas' are the 7 bit patterns **0011111** (+comma)and **1100000** (-comma). In order to maintain a DC balance, a calculation called the **Running Disparity** calculation is used to try to keep the number of '0's transmitted the same as the number of '1's transmitted. This uses 10 bits for each 8 bits of data and therefore drops the data rate speed relative to the line speed, for instance in order to gain a data rate of 1Gbps the line speed has to be 10/8 × 1 = 1.25 Gbps .

MLT–3

This scheme was specified by ANSI X3T9.5 committee. It is used by FDDI and TP-PMD to obtain 100 MB/s out of a 31.25 MHz signal. UTP is low pass in nature, meaning that it hinders high frequency signal (like a low-pass filter). So it is not feasible to merely increase the clock frequency by 10 to 100 MHz and use Manchester encoding to give us 100 Mbps. In addition, the FCC (Federal Communications Commission) have severely curtailed the power that is allowed to be emitted above 30 MHz. We have to use another encoding technique in order to transmit high data rates across UTP.

If you take an averaging spectrum analyser and look at the output signal of the 10 Mbps Ethernet phase-encoded signal, you will see a power peak at 10 MHz where there is a stream of '1's or '0's, you will see a smaller harmonic at 30 MHz and if there is a stream of '1's and '0's, you will see a peak at 5 MHz. Now 100 BaseT uses a master clock running at 125 MHz instead of 10 MHz. The equivalent peaks would then be at 125 MHz, 375 MHz and 62.5 MHz. Transmission electronics designed to work within the FCC rules will block the frequencies higher than 30 MHz.

To get around this issue we need to concentrate the signal power below 30MHz if possible. To do this the encoding method **Multi-Level Transition 3 (MLT-3)** is used. This involves using the pattern **1, 0, –1, 0**. If the next data signal is a '1' then the output 'transitions' to the next bit in the pattern *e.g.*, if the last output bit was a '–1', and the input bit is a '1', then the next output bit is a '0'. If the next data signal is a '0' then there is no transition which means that the next output bit is the same as last time, in our case a '0'.

The cycle length of the output signal is therefore going to be 1/4 that of the MPE method so that instead of the main signal peak being at 125 MHz as measured by the averaging spectrum analyser, it will be at 31.25 MHz which is near enough to be O K as far as FCC are concerned. 5 bits are transmitted for every 4 bits of data so that the data bit rate is actually 125 Mb/s for 100 Mb/s data throughput. There is an issue with this in that you can end up with a series of '0's or '1's which force the local circuitry to count the bits using its own free running clock rather than have the check of the clock synchronisation from the transmit source.

PAM-5

This employs multi-level amplitude signalling. To encode 8 bits, $2^8 = 256$ codes or symbols, are required since there are 256 possible pattern combinations. A five level signal (*e.g.* –2v, –1v, 0v, 1v and 2v) called **Pulse Amplitude Modulation 5** is used (This works in a similar manner to MLT-3). Bearing in mind that there are 4 separate pairs being used for transmission and reception of data, this gives us a possibility of $5^4 = 625$ codes to choose from when using all four pairs. Actually only four levels are used for data, the fifth level (0v) is used for the 4-dimensional 8-state Trellis Forward Error Correction used to recover the transmitted signal from the high noise.

If you plot time (nanoseconds) against voltage you will see an 'eye pattern' effect showing the different signal levels. Comparing a plot for MLT-3 against PAM-5 will demonstrate how that the separate levels for PAM-5 are less discreet. This **is** why extra convolution coding is used called **Trellis coding,** which uses **Viterbi decoding** for error detection and correction. 2 bits are represented per symbol and the symbol rate is

125 Mbps in each direction on a pair because the clock rate is set at 125 MHz. This gives 250 Mbps data per pair and therefore 1000 Mbps for the whole cable. This type of encoding is used by Gigabit Ethernet. The data signals have distinct and measurable amplitude and phases relative to a 'marker signal'. Using this two way matrix allows more data bits per cycle, in the case of Gigabit Ethernet 1000 Mbps is squeezed into 125 MHz signals. The electronics are more complex and the technology is more susceptible to noise.

5.6 COMMUNICATION TECHNOLOGIES

There are two types of communication technologies:-

1. **Synchronous line communications**
2. **Asynchronous line communications**

5.6.1 The Synchronization Problem

Serial Communication normally consists of transmitting binary data across an electrical or optical link such as RS 232 or V.35. The data, being binary, is usually represented by two physical states. For example, +5v may represent 1 and -5v represent 0. The accurate decoding of the data at the remote end is dependent on the sender and receiver maintaining synchronization during decoding. The receiver must sample the signal in phase with the sender.

If the sender and receiver were both supplied by exactly the same clock source, then transmission could take place forever with the assurance that signal sampling at the receiver was always in perfect synchronization with the transmitter. This is seldom the case, so in practice the receiver is periodically brought into synch. with the transmitter. It is left to the internal clocking accuracy of the transmitter and receiver to maintain sampling integrity between synchronization pulses.

Serialized data is not generally sent at a uniform rate through a channel. Instead, there is usually a burst of regularly spaced binary data bits followed by a pause, after which the data flow resumes. Packets of binary data are sent in this manner, possibly with variable-length pauses between packets, until the message has been fully transmitted. In order for the receiving end to know the proper moment to read individual binary bits from the channel, it must know exactly when a packet begins and how much time elapses between bits. When this timing information is known, the receiver is said to be synchronized with the transmitter, and accurate data transfer becomes possible. Failure to remain synchronized throughout a transmission will cause data to be corrupted or lost.

Two basic techniques are employed to ensure correct synchronization:

1. **Synchronous systems**
2. **Asynchronous systems**

5.6.2 Asynchronous Communications

In asynchronous systems, a separate timing channel is not used. The transmitter and receiver must be preset in advance to an agreed-upon baud rate. A very accurate local oscillator within the receiver will then generate an internal clock signal that is equal to the transmitter's within a fraction of a percent. For the most common serial protocol, data is sent in small packets of 10 or 11 bits, eight of which constitute message information. When the channel is idle, the signal voltage corresponds to a continuous logic '1'. A data packet always begins with a logic '0' (the start bit) to signal the receiver that a transmission is starting. The start bit triggers an internal timer in the receiver that generates the needed clock pulses. Following the start bit, eight bits of message data are sent bit by bit at the agreed upon baud rate. The packet is concluded with a parity bit and stop bit. One complete packet is illustrated below: This is the method most widely used for PC or simple terminal serial communications.

In asynch. serial communication, the electrical interface is held in the mark position between characters. The start of transmission of a character is signalled by a drop in signal level to the space level. At this point, the receiver starts its clock. After one bit time (the start bit) come 8 bits of true data followed by one or more stop bits at the mark level. The receiver tries to sample the signal in the middle of each bit time. The byte will be read correctly if the line is still in the intended state when the last stop bit is read.

Thus the transmitter and receiver only have to have **approximately the same clock rate.** A little arithmetic will show that for a 10 bit sequence, the last bit will be interpreted correctly even if the sender and receiver clocks differ by as much as 5%.

Asynch. is **relatively simple,** and therefore inexpensive. However, it has a **high overhead,** in that each byte carries at least two extra bits: a 25% loss of line bandwidth. A 56 kbps line can only carry 5600 bytes/second asynchronously, in ideal conditions.

5.6.3 Synchronous Communications

In synchronous systems, separate channels are used to transmit data and timing information. The timing channel transmits clock pulses to the receiver. Upon receipt of a clock pulse, the receiver reads the data channel and latches the bit value found on the channel at that moment. The data channel is not read again until the next clock pulse arrives. Because the transmitter originates both the data and the timing pulses, the receiver will read the data channel only when told to do so by the transmitter (via the clock pulse), and synchronization is guaranteed.

Techniques exist to merge the timing signal with the data so that only a single channel is required. This is especially useful when synchronous transmissions are to be sent through a modem. Two methods in which a data signal is self-timed are nonreturn-to-zero and biphase Manchester coding. These both refer to methods for encoding a data stream into an electrical waveform for transmission.

Synchronous communication is usually much **more efficient** in use of bandwidth than Asynch. The data field is usually large in comparison to the flag, control, address, and CRC fields, so there is very little overhead. A 56 kbps synchronous line can be expected to carry close to 7000 bytes per second (*i.e.*, 56000/8, whereas the asynch. data rate would be 56000/10). Another advantage of synchronous communications is that the frame structure allows for easy handling of control information. There is a natural position (usually at the start of the frame) for any special codes that are needed by the communication protocol.

5.7 WHAT IS MODULATION ?

Modulation is a prescribed method of encoding digital (or analog) signals onto a waveform (the carrier signal). Once encoded, the original signal may be recovered by an inverse process called demodulation. Modulation is performed to adapt the signal to a different frequency range than that of the original signal. Here's how it flows:

bits → modulator → audio → phone network → audio → demodulator → bits

Figure 5.9 Vivek's Sequence of Modulation to Demodulation

Over the past few years a major transition has occurred from simple analog Amplitude Modulation (AM) and Frequency/Phase Modulation (FM/PM) to new digital modulation techniques. Examples of digital modulation include

- QPSK (Quadrature Phase Shift Keying)
- FSK (Frequency Shift Keying)
- MSK (Minimum Shift Keying)
- QAM (Quadrature Amplitude Modulation).

Another layer of complexity in many new systems is multiplexing. Two principal types of multiplexing (or "multiple access") are TDMA (Time Division Multiple Access) and CDMA (Code Division Multiple Access). These are two different ways to add diversity to signals allowing different signals to be separated from one another.

5.7.1 Transmitting Information

To transmit a signal over the air, there are three main steps:

1. A pure carrier is generated at the transmitter.
2. The carrier is modulated with the information to be transmitted. Any reliably detectable change in signal characteristics can carry information.
3. At the receiver the signal modifications or changes are detected and demodulated.

5.7.2 Signal Characteristics that can be Modified

There are only **three** characteristics of a signal that can be changed over time:

1. amplitude,
2. phase or
3. frequency.

However, phase and frequency are just different ways to view or measure the same signal change.

In AM, the amplitude of a high-frequency carrier signal is varied in proportion to the instantaneous amplitude of the modulating message signal.

Frequency Modulation (FM) is the most popular analog modulation technique used in mobile communications systems. In FM, the amplitude of the modulating carrier is kept constant while its frequency is varied by the modulating message signal.

Amplitude and phase can be modulated simultaneously and separately, but this is difficult to generate, and especially difficult to detect. Instead, in practical systems the signal is separated into another set of independent components: *I* (In-phase) and *Q* (Quadrature). These components are orthogonal and do not interfere with each other.

5.7.3 Polar Display-Magnitude and Phase Represented Together

A simple way to view amplitude and phase is with the polar diagram. The carrier becomes a frequency and phase reference and the signal is interpreted relative to the carrier. The signal can be expressed in polar form as a magnitude and a phase. The phase is relative to a reference signal, the carrier in most communication systems. The magnitude is either an absolute or relative value. Both are used in digital communication systems. Polar diagrams are the basis of many displays used in digital communications, although it is common to describe the signal vector by its rectangular coordinates of *I* (In-phase) and *Q* (Quadrature).

5.7.4 Signal Changes or Modifications in Polar Form

Magnitude is represented as the distance from the centre and phase is represented as angle.

Amplitude Modulation (AM) changes only the magnitude of the signal. Phase Modulation (PM) changes only the phase of the signal. Amplitude and phase modulation can be used together. Frequency Modulation (FM) looks similar to phase modulation, though frequency is the controlled parameter, rather than relative phase.

Bit rate is the frequency of a system bit stream. Take, for example, a radio with an 8 bit sampler, sampling at 10 kHz for voice. The bit rate, the basic bit stream rate in the radio, would be eight bits multiplied by 10 K samples per second, or 80 Kbits per second. (For the moment we will ignore the extra bits required for synchronization, error correction, etc.).

The symbol rate is the bit rate divided by the number of bits that can be transmitted with each symbol. If one bit is transmitted per symbol, as with BPSK, then the symbol rate would be the same as the bit rate of 80 Kbits per second. If two bits are transmitted per symbol, as in QPSK, then the symbol rate would be half of the bit rate or 40 Kbits per second. Symbol rate is sometimes called baud rate. Note that baud rate is not the same as bit rate. These terms are often confused. If more bits can be sent with each symbol, then the same amount of data can be sent in a narrower spectrum.This is why modulation formats that are more complex and use a higher number of states can send the same information over a narrower piece of the RF spectrum.

5.7.5 Phase Shift Keying

One of the simplest forms of digital modulation is binary or Bi-Phase Shift Keying (BPSK). One application where this is used is for deep space telemetry. The phase of a constant amplitude carrier signal moves between zero and 180 degrees. On an *I* and *Q* diagram, the *I* state has two different values. There are two possible locations in the state diagram, so a binary one or zero can be sent. The symbol rate is one bit per symbol.

A more common type of phase modulation is **Quadrature Phase Shift Keying** (QPSK). It is used extensively in applications including CDMA (Code Division Multiple Access) cellular service, wireless local loop, Iridium (a voice/data satellite system) and DVB-S (Digital Video Broadcasting—Satellite). Quadrature means that the signal shifts between phase states which are separated by 90 degrees. The signal shifts in increments of 90 degrees from 45 to 135, –45, or –135 degrees. These points are chosen as they can be easily implemented using an *I/Q* modulator. Only two *I* values and two *Q* values are needed and this gives two bits per symbol. There are four states because $2^2 = 4$. It is therefore a more bandwidth-efficient type of modulation than BPSK, potentially twice as efficient.

5.7.6 Frequency Shift Keying

Frequency modulation and phase modulation are closely related. A static frequency shift of +1 Hz means that the phase is constantly advancing at the rate of 360 degrees per second (2 Πrad/sec), relative to the phase of the unshifted signal.

FSK (Frequency Shift Keying) is used in many applications including cordless and paging systems. Some of the cordless systems include DECT (Digital Enhanced Cordless Telephone) and CT2 (Cordless Telephone 2). In FSK, the frequency of the carrier is changed as a function of the modulating signal (data) being transmitted. Amplitude remains unchanged.In binary FSK (BFSK or 2FSK), a "1" is represented by one frequency and a "0" is represented by another frequency.

5.7.7 Minimum Shift Keying

Since a frequency shift produces an advancing or retarding phase, frequency shifts can be detected by sampling phase at each symbol period. Phase shifts of $(2N + 1)\ \pi/2$ radians are easily detected with an *I/Q* demodulator. At even numbered symbols, the polarity of the *I* channel conveys the transmitted data, while at odd numbered symbols the polarity of the *Q* channel conveys the data. This orthogonality between *I* and *Q* simplifies detection algorithms and hence reduces power consumption in a mobile receiver. The minimum frequency shift which yields orthogonality of *I* and *Q* is that which results in a phase shift of $\pm\ \pi/2$ radians per symbol (90 degrees per symbol). FSK with this deviation is called MSK (Minimum Shift Keying). The deviation must be accurate in order to generate repeatable 90 degree phase shifts. MSK is used in the GSM (Global System for Mobile Communications) cellular standard. A phase shift of +90 degrees represents a data bit equal to "1", while –90 degrees represents a "0". The peak-to-peak frequency shift of an MSK signal is equal to one-half of the bit rate.

FSK and MSK produce constant envelope carrier signals, which have no amplitude variations. This is a desirable characteristic for improving the power efficiency of transmitters. Amplitude variations can exercise nonlinearities in an amplifier's amplitude-transfer function, generating spectral regrowth, a component of adjacent channel power. Therefore, more efficient amplifiers (which tend to be less linear) can be used with constant-envelope signals, reducing power consumption.

5.7.8 Quadrature Amplitude Modulation

Another member of the digital modulation family is Quadrature Amplitude Modulation (QAM). QAM is used in applications including microwave digital radio, DVB-C (Digital Video Broadcasting—Cable) and modems. In 16-state Quadrature Amplitude Modulation (16QAM), there are four *I* values and four *Q* values. This results in a total of 16 possible states for the signal. It can transition from any state to any other state at every symbol time. Since $2^4 = 16$, four bits per symbol can be sent. This consists of two bits for *I* and two bits for *Q*. The symbol rate is one fourth of the bit rate. So this modulation format produces a more spectrally efficient transmission. It is more efficient than BPSK, QPSK or 8PSK. Note that QPSK is the same as 4QAM.

Another variation is 32QAM. In this case there are six *I* values and six *Q* values resulting in a total of 36 possible states (6x6=36). This is too many states for a power of two (the closest power of two is 32). So the four corner symbol states, which take the most power to transmit, are omitted. This reduces the amount of peak power the transmitter has to generate. Since $2^5 = 32$, there are five bits per symbol and the symbol rate is one fifth of the bit rate. The current practical limits are approximately 256QAM, though work is underway to extend the limits to 512 or 1024 QAM. A 256QAM system uses 16 *I*-values and 16 *Q*-values giving 256 possible states. Since $2^8 = 256$, each symbol can represent eight bits. A 256QAM signal that can send eight bits per symbol is very spectrally efficient. However, the symbols are very close together and are thus more subject to errors due to noise and distortion. Such a signal may have to be transmitted with extra power (to effectively spread the symbols out more) and this reduces power efficiency as compared to simpler schemes.

5.7.9 What is PCM?

Pulse code modulation (PCM) is used in the phone network to reduce the data rate required for voice grade audio to less than 64 Kb/s. It uses either u-law (North America) or A-law (Europe) as the compression method. Any given 8 kHz analog audio sample is converted to 4 bits of mantissa, 3 bits of exponent, and a sign bit. This code has a characteristic that quantization noise is proportional to signal amplitude and does not become objectionable to the average telephone user. For a conventional modem this noise floor limits the available dynamic range to about 36 dB which sets the maximum data rate. The least significant bit of the mantissa may be periodically stolen for signalling within the phone network (called robbed-bit signaling) further increasing the noise.

The 8-bit codes are processed through the telephone switching network in fixed time slots. There exists an ever increasing hierarchy of data rates to support this. A DSO is a 64 Kb/s time slot. 24 DSOs become a DS1. 4 DS1s become a DS2. 7 DS2s become a DS3, etc.

The physical layer of a DS1 (T1) may be remodulated as alternate mark inversion for passing over a wire pair as a method to concentrate local loops. Repeaters regenerate the signal every 6000-9000'. These signals may coexist with xDSL in the same wire bundle.

5.7.10 What is PAM?

Pulse Amplitude Modulation (PAM) is the physical layer of an ISDN or HDSL connection. The modulation consists of sending discrete amplitude levels (symmetric about 0 volts) at a regular rate. Both use the two binary one quaternary (2B1Q) line code. Four analog voltages (called quaternary symbols) are used to represent the four possible combinations of two bits. These symbols are assigned the names +3, +1, –1, and –3. So each amplitude level being held for one symbol time communicates two bits.

PAM differs from the other modulations in that it is base band modulation and does not use a carrier. Some versions of HDSL increase the number of levels to 16 which communicates four bits per symbol in the same bandwidth.

5.7.11 What is V.90?

V.90 is actually a variant of PAM. It has 256 PCM levels from which to choose a more limited set. The inner levels become more closely spaced so some of these must be excluded for reasons of limited signal-to-noise ratio. In addition, outer codes are excluded to keep transmit power on the local loop below 12 dBm, a formal limit established by the FCC. V.90 includes a spectral shaping algorithm to prevent sending signal at DC.

V.90 bypasses the problems associated with a conventional modem. It recognizes that with enough signal processing the original PCM samples sent by the phone company may be resolved as individual levels using a 16-bit A/D converter on the receiving end. Audio is sent through the digital network as 8-bit U-law or A-law samples. Of course, the telco D/A converter, reconstruction filter, and phone network blur the levels into one continuous signal, so it's up to the receiver to reconstruct what was sent. An additional problem is recovering symbol (*i.e.*, PCM sample) timing information which must be inferred from the residue of modulation at a frequency around 4 kHz. By just selecting a limited set of codes with say 64 levels, 6 bits per 8 kHz symbol may be sent for a data rate of 48 Kb/s. More levels, more data, but a maximum of about 53.3 Kb/s is a practical limit.

5.7.12 What is CAP?

Carrier less amplitude and phase (CAP) modulation is a proprietary standard. While the name specifies that the modulation is "carrier less" an actual carrier is imposed by the transmit band shaping filter through which the outbound symbols are filtered. Hence CAP is algorithmically identical to QAM. The upstream symbol rate is 136 K baud on a 113.2 KHz carrier, while the downstream symbol rate is 340 K baud on a 435.5 KHz carrier, 680 K baud on a 631 KHz carrier, or 952 K baud on a 787.5 KHz carrier. This allows the modem to be symbol rate adaptive to varying line conditions (see RADSL). The QAM modulation is also rate adaptive by varying the number of bits per symbol.

One advantage CAP claims to have is a lower peak-to-average signal power ratio relative to DMT. This means that the drivers and receivers may operate at lower power than DMT because they are not required to have the peak signal capacity that is required in the DMT circuitry. This is mitigated by the infrequency of the really high signal peaks in DMT which may be just considered to be another form of noise if they happen to clip.

CAP's principle advantage is its installed base of modems. It is actively being deployed in many trial markets and is available from several manufacturers.

5.7.13 What is DMT?

Discrete multitone (DMT) modulation is a method by which the usable frequency range is separated into 256 frequency bands (or channels) of 4.3125 KHz each. These are intimately connected to the FFT (fast Fourier transform) algorithm which DMT uses as its modulator and demodulator. The FFT is not perfect in separating the frequencies into individual bands, but it does well enough, and it generates spectra which are fully separable on the receiving end. By dividing the frequency spectrum into multiple channels

DMT is thought to perform better in the presence of interference sources such as AM radio transmitters. It is also better able to focus its transmit power on those portions of the spectrum in which it is profitable to send data.

The assignment of channels is less flexible, but typical settings might be channels 6-31 for upstream (24 KHz-136 KHz), 32-250 for downstream (136 KHz-1.1 MHz). The modulation used on any given frequency channel is QAM. Channels 16 and 64 are reserved for pilot tones which are used to recover timing. The number of bitsper symbol within each channel may bc independently selected allowing the modem to be rate adaptive.

The use of the FFT is considered to be somewhat substandard to other orthogonal transformations such as the discrete wavelet transform which do a better job of isolating the individual frequency spectra. The FFT is chosen for its computational efficiency.

While DMT is off to a slow start in the marketplace, it is expected to dominate for two reasons:

1. It is thought to perform better for technical reasons and
2. There is an ANSI standard behind it *i.e.*, Intel/Microsoft support.

6

DATA LINK LAYER

6.1 INTRODUCTION

The data link layer provides reliable transit of data across a physical network link. Different data link layer specifications define different network and protocol characteristics, including physical addressing, network topology, error notification, sequencing of frames, and flow control. Physical addressing (as opposed to network addressing) defines how devices are addressed at the data link layer. Network topology consists of the data link layer specifications that often define how devices are to be physically connected, such as in a bus or a ring topology. Error notification alerts upper-layer protocols that a transmission error has occurred, and the sequencing of data frames reorders frames that are transmitted out of sequence. Finally, flow control moderates the transmission of data so that the receiving device is not overwhelmed with more traffic than it can handle at one time.

The Institute of Electrical and Electronics Engineers (IEEE) has subdivided the data link layer into two sublayers:

1. Logical Link Control (LLC) and
2. Media Access Control (MAC).

Figure 6.1 illustrates the IEEE sublayers of the data link layer.

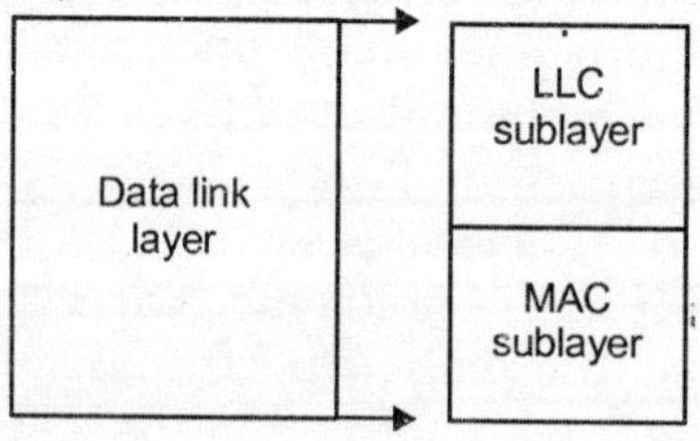

Figure 6.1 The Data Link Layer Contains Two Sublayers

The *Logical Link Control (LLC)* sublayer of the data link layer manages communications between devices over a single link of a network. LLC is defined in the IEEE 802.2 specification and supports both connectionless and connection-oriented services used by higher-layer protocols. IEEE 802.2 defines a number of fields in data link layer frames that enable multiple higher-layer protocols to share a single physical data link.

The *Media Access Control (MAC)* sublayer of the data link layer manages protocol access to the physical network medium. The IEEE MAC specification defines MAC addresses, which enable multiple devices to uniquely identify one another at the data link layer.

6.2 ETHERNET TERMINOLOGY

The term *Ethernet* refers to the family of local-area network (LAN) products covered by the IEEE 802.3 standard that defines what is commonly known as the CSMA/CD protocol. Ethernet has survived as the major LAN technology (it is currently used for approximately 85 percent of the world's LAN-connected PCs and workstations) because its protocol has the following characteristics:

- Is easy to understand, implement, manage, and maintain
- Allows low-cost network implementations
- Provides extensive topological flexibility for network installation
- Guarantees successful interconnection and operation of standards-compliant products, regardless of manufacturer.

The original Ethernet was developed as an experimental coaxial cable network in the 1970s by Xerox Corporation to operate with a data rate of 3 Mbps using a carrier sense multiple access collision detect (CSMA/CD) protocol for LANs with sporadic but occasionally heavy traffic requirements.

6.2.1 Ethernet Terminology

Ethernet follows a simple set of rules that govern its basic operation. To better understand these rules, it is important to understand the basics of Ethernet terminology. Ethernet devices attach to a common **medium** that provides a path along which the electronic signals will travel. Historically this medium has been coaxial copper cable, but today it is more commonly twisted pair or fiber optic cabling. In any case, we refer to a single shared medium as an Ethernet **segment**, and devices that attach to that segment are stations or **nodes.** The nodes communicate in short messages called **frames,** which are variable-sized chunks of information. Frames are analogous to sentences in human language. In English, we have rules for constructing our sentences. We know that each sentence must contain a subject and a predicate. The Ethernet protocol specifies a set of rules for constructing frames. There are explicit minimum and maximum lengths for frames, and a set of required pieces of information that must appear in the frame. Each frame must include, for example, both a **destination address** and a **source address,** which identify the recipient and the sender of the message. The address uniquely identifies the node, just as a name identifies a particular person. No two Ethernet devices should ever have the same address.

Since a signal on the Ethernet medium reaches every attached node, the destination address is critical to identify the intended recipient of the frame. For example, in the figure below, when computer B transmits to printer C, computers A and D will still receive and examine the frame. However, when a station first receives a frame, it checks the destination address to see if the frame is intended for itself. If it is not (*e.g.*, computers A and D), the station discards the frame without even examining its contents. One interesting thing about Ethernet addressing is the implementation of a **broadcast address.** A frame with a destination address equal to the broadcast address (simply called a broadcast, for short) is intended for every node on the network, and every node will both receive and process this type of frame.

6.2.2 Ethernet Network Nodes

Ethernet LANs consist of network nodes and interconnecting media. The network nodes fall into two major classes:

- **Data Terminal Equipment (DTE)**–Devices that are either the source or the destination of data frames. DTEs are typically devices such as PCs, workstations, file servers, or print servers that, as a group, are all often referred to as end stations.
- **Data Communication Equipment (DCE)**–Intermediate network devices that receive and forward frames across the network. DCEs may be either standalone devices such as repeaters, network switches, and routers, or communications interface units such as interface cards and modems.

LANs take on many topological configurations, but regardless of their size or complexity, all will be a combination of only three basic interconnection structures or network building blocks.

The simplest structure is the point-to-point interconnection. Only two network units are involved, and the connection may be DTE-to-DTE, DTE-to-DCE, or DCE-to-DCE. The cable in point-to-point interconnections is known as a network link. The maximum allowable length of the link depends on the type of cable and the transmission method that is used.

The original Ethernet networks were implemented with a coaxial bus structure. Segment lengths were limited to 500 metres, and upto 100 stations could be connected to a single segment. Individual segments could be interconnected with repeaters, as long as multiple paths did not exist between any two stations on the network and the number of DTEs did not exceed 1024. The total path distance between the most-distant pair of stations was also not allowed to exceed a maximum prescribed value.

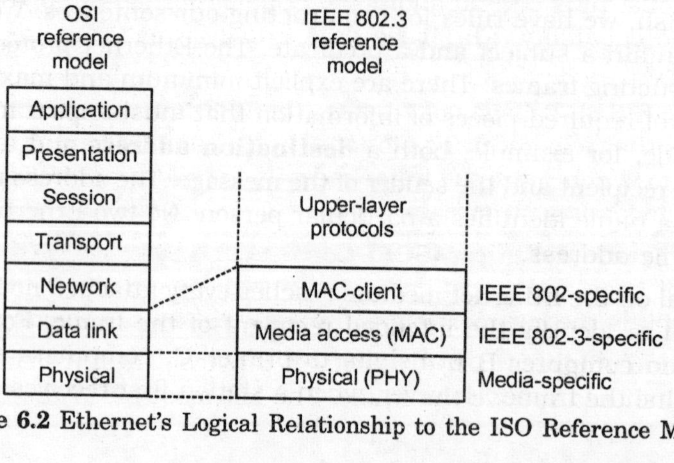

Figure 6.2 Ethernet's Logical Relationship to the ISO Reference Model

Figure 6.2 shows the IEEE 802.3 logical layers and their relationship to the OSI reference model. As with all IEEE 802 protocols, the ISO data link layer is divided into two IEEE 802 sublayers, the Media Access Control (MAC) sublayer and the MAC-client sublayer. The IEEE 802.3 physical layer corresponds to the ISO physical layer.

The MAC-client sublayer may be one of the following:

1. Logical Link Control (LLC), if the unit is a DTE. This sublayer provides the interface between the Ethernet MAC and the upper layers in the protocol stack of the end station. The LLC sublayer is defined by IEEE 802.2 standards.
2. Bridge entity, if the unit is a DCE. Bridge entities provide LAN-to-LAN interfaces between LANs that use the same protocol (for example, Ethernet to Ethernet) and also between different protocols (for example, Ethernet to Token Ring). Bridge entities are defined by IEEE 802.1 standards.

The MAC layer controls the node's access to the network media and is specific to the individual protocol. All IEEE 802.3 MACs must meet the same basic set of logical requirements, regardless of whether they include one or more of the defined optional protocol extensions. The only requirement for basic communication (communication that does not require optional protocol extensions) between two network nodes is that both MACs must support the same transmission rate.

The 802.3 physical layer is specific to the transmission data rate, the signal encoding, and the type of media interconnecting the two nodes. Gigabit Ethernet, for example, is defined to operate over either twisted-pair or optical fiber cable, but each specific type of cable or signal-encoding procedure requires a different physical layer implementation.

6.2.3 The Ethernet MAC Sublayer

The MAC sublayer has two primary responsibilities:

1. Data encapsulation, including frame assembly before transmission, and frame parsing/error detection during and after reception
2. Media access control, including initiation of frame transmission and recovery from transmission failure

6.2.4 The Basic Ethernet Frame Format

The IEEE 802.3 standard defines a basic data frame format that is required for all MAC implementations, plus several additional optional formats that are used to extend the protocol's basic capability. The basic data frame format contains the seven fields shown in Figure 6.3.

- **Preamble (PRE)**–Consists of 7 bytes. The PRE is an alternating pattern of ones and zeros that tells receiving stations that a frame is coming, and that provides a means to synchronize the frame-reception portions of receiving physical layers with the incoming bit stream.
- **Start Of Frame delimiter (SOF)**–Consists of 1 byte. The SOF is an alternating pattern of ones and zeros, ending with two consecutive 1-bits indicating that the next bit is the left-most bit in the left-most byte of the destination address.
- **Destination Address (DA)**–Consists of 6 bytes. The DA field identifies which station(s) should receive the frame. The left-most bit in the DA field indicates

whether the address is an individual address (indicated by a 0) or a group address (indicated by a 1). The second bit from the left indicates whether the DA is globally administered (indicated by a 0) or locally administered (indicated by a 1). The remaining 46 bits are a uniquely assigned value that identifies a single station, a defined group of stations, or all stations on the network.

- **Source Addresses (SA)**–Consists of 6 bytes. The SA field identifies the sending station. The SA is always an individual address and the left-most bit in the SA field is always 0.
- **Length/Type**–Consists of 4 bytes. This field indicates either the number of MAC-client data bytes that are contained in the data field of the frame, or the frame type ID if the frame is assembled using an optional format. If the Length/Type field value is less than or equal to 1500, the number of LLC bytes in the Data field is equal to the Length/Type field value. If the Length/Type field value is greater than 1536, the frame is an optional type frame, and the Length/Type field value identifies the particular type of frame being sent or received.
- **Data**–Is a sequence of *n* bytes of any value, where *n* is less than or equal to 1500. If the length of the Data field is less than 46, the Data field must be extended by adding a filler (a pad) sufficient to bring the Data field length to 46 bytes.
- **Frame Check Sequence (FCS)**–Consists of 4 bytes. This sequence contains a 32-bit cyclic redundancy check (CRC) value, which is created by the sending MAC and is recalculated by the receiving MAC to check for damaged frames. The FCS is generated over the DA, SA, Length/Type, and Data fields.

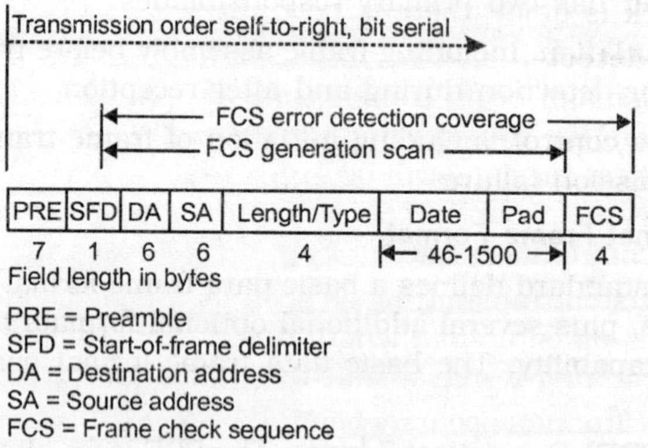

Figure 6.3 The Basic IEEE 802.3 MAC Data Frame Format

6.3 FRAME TRANSMISSION

Whenever an end station MAC receives a transmit-frame request with the accompanying address and data information from the LLC sublayer, the MAC begins the transmission sequence by transferring the LLC information into the MAC frame buffer.

- The preamble and start-of-frame delimiter are inserted in the PRE and SOF fields.

- The destination and source addresses are inserted into the address fields.
- The LLC data bytes are counted, and the number of bytes is inserted into the Length/Type field.
- The LLC data bytes are inserted into the Data field. If the number of LLC data bytes is less than 46, a pad is added to bring the Data field length upto 46.
- An FCS value is generated over the DA, SA, Length/Type, and Data fields and is appended to the end of the Data field.

After the frame is assembled, actual frame transmission will depend on whether the MAC is operating in half-duplex or full-duplex mode.

The IEEE 802.3 standard currently requires that all Ethernet MACs support half-duplex operation, in which the MAC can be either transmitting or receiving a frame, but it cannot be doing both simultaneously. Full-duplex operation is an optional MAC capability that allows the MAC to transmit and receive frames simultaneously.

6.3.1 Half Duplex Transmission -The CSMA/CD Access Method

The CSMA/CD protocol was originally developed as a means by which two or more stations could share a common media in a switch-less environment when the protocol does not require central arbitration, access tokens, or assigned time slots to indicate when a station will be allowed to transmit. Each Ethernet MAC determines for itself when it will be allowed to send a frame.

The CSMA/CD access rules are summarized by the protocol's acronym:

- **Carrier sense**–Each station continuously listens for traffic on the medium to determine when gaps between frame transmissions occur.
- **Multiple access**–Stations may begin transmitting any time they detect that the network is quiet (there is no traffic).
- **Collision detect**–If two or more stations in the same CSMA/CD network (collision domain) begin transmitting at approximately the same time, the bit streams from the transmitting stations will interfere (collide) with each other, and both transmissions will be unreadable. If that happens, each transmitting station must be capable of detecting that a collision has occurred before it has finished sending its frame.

  Each must stop transmitting as soon as it has detected the collision and then must wait a quasirandom length of time (determined by a back-off algorithm) before attempting to retransmit the frame.

The worst-case situation occurs when the two most-distant stations on the network both need to send a frame and when the second station does not begin transmitting until just before the frame from the first station arrives. The collision will be detected almost immediately by the second station, but it will not be detected by the first station until the corrupted signal has propagated all the way back to that station. The maximum time that is required to detect a collision (the collision window, or "slot time") is approximately equal to twice the signal propagation time between the two most-distant stations on the network.

This means that both the minimum frame length and the maximum collision diameter are directly related to the slot time. Longer minimum frame lengths translate to longer slot times and larger collision diameters; shorter minimum frame lengths correspond to shorter slot times and smaller collision diameters.

The trade-off was between the need to reduce the impact of collision recovery and the need for network diameters to be large enough to accommodate reasonable network sizes. The compromise was to choose a maximum network diameter (about 2500 metres) and then to set the minimum frame length long enough to ensure detection of all worst-case collisions.

The compromise worked well for 10 Mbps, but it was a problem for higher data-rate Ethernet developers. Fast Ethernet was required to provide backward compatibility with earlier Ethernet networks, including the existing IEEE 802.3 frame format and error-detection procedures, plus all applications and networking software running on the 10-Mbps networks.

Although signal propagation velocity is essentially constant for all transmission rates, the time required to transmit a frame is inversely related to the transmission rate. At 100 Mbps, a minimum-length frame can be transmitted in approximately one-tenth of the defined slot time, and any collision that occurred during the transmission would not likely be detected by the transmitting stations. This, in turn, meant that the maximum network diameters specified for 10-Mbps networks could not be used for 100-Mbps networks. The solution for Fast Ethernet was to reduce the maximum network diameter by approximately a factor of 10 (to a little more than 200 metres).

The same problem also arose during specification development for Gigabit Ethernet, but decreasing network diameters by another factor of 10 (to approximately 20 metres) for 1000-Mbps operation was simply not practical. This time, the developers elected to maintain approximately the same maximum collision domain diameters as 100-Mbps networks and to increase the apparent minimum frame size by adding a variable-length nondata extension field to frames that are shorter than the minimum length (the extension field is removed during frame reception).

6.3.2 Full Duplex Transmission-Optional Way to Higher Network Efficiency

Full-duplex operation is an optional MAC capability that allows simultaneous two-way transmission over point-to-point links. Full duplex transmission is functionally much simpler than half-duplex transmission because it involves no media contention, no collisions, no need to schedule retransmissions, and no need for extension bits on the end of short frames. The result is not only more time available for transmission, but also an effective doubling of the link bandwidth because each link can now support full-rate, simultaneous, two-way transmission.

Transmission can usually begin as soon as frames are ready to send. The only restriction is that there must be a minimum-length interframe gap between successive frames, as shown in Figure 6.4, and each frame must conform to Ethernet frame format standards.

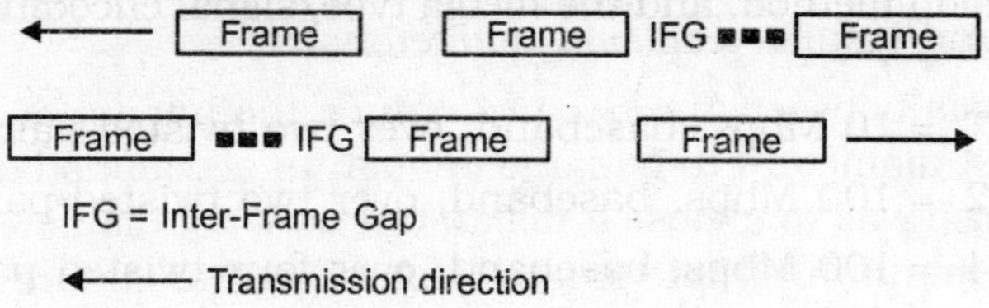

Figure 6.4 Full Duplex Operation Allows Simultaneous Two-Way Transmission on the Same Link

6.3.3 Flow Control

Full-duplex operation requires concurrent implementation of the optional flow-control capability that allows a receiving node (such as a network switch port) that is becoming congested to request the sending node (such as a file server) to stop sending frames for a selected short period of time. Control is MAC-to-MAC through the use of a pause frame that is automatically generated by the receiving MAC. If the congestion is relieved before the requested wait has expired, a second pause frame with a zero time-to-wait value can be sent to request resumption of transmission.

The full-duplex operation and its companion flow control capability are both options for all Ethernet MACs and all transmission rates. Both options are enabled on a link-by-link basis, assuming that the associated physical layers are also capable of supporting full-duplex operation.

Pause frames are identified as MAC control frames by an exclusive assigned (reserved) length/type value. They are also assigned a reserved destination address value to ensure that an incoming pause frame is never forwarded to upper protocol layers or to other ports in a switch.

6.3.4 Frame Reception

Frame reception is essentially the same for both half-duplex and full-duplex operations, except that full-duplex MACs must have separate frame buffers and data paths to allow for simultaneous frame transmission and reception.

Frame reception is the reverse of frame transmission. The destination address of the received frame is checked and matched against the station's address list (its MAC address, its group addresses, and the broadcast address) to determine whether the frame is destined for that station. If an address match is found, the frame length is checked and the received FCS is compared to the FCS that was generated during frame reception. If the frame length is okay and there is an FCS match, the frame type is determined by the contents of the Length/Type field. The frame is then parsed and forwarded to the appropriate upper layer.

6.3.5 The Ethernet Physical Layers

Because Ethernet devices implement only the bottom two layers of the OSI protocol stack, they are typically implemented as network interface cards (NICs) that plug into the host device's motherboard. The different NICs are identified by a three-part product name that is based on the physical layer attributes.

The naming convention is a concatenation of three terms indicating the transmission rate, the transmission method, and the media type/signal encoding. For example, consider this:

10Base–T = 10 Mbps, baseband, over two twisted-pair cables

100Base–T2 = 100 Mbps, baseband, over two twisted-pair cables

100Base–T4 = 100 Mbps, baseband, over four-twisted pair cables

1000Base–LX = 100 Mbps, baseband, long wavelength over optical fiber cable.

A question sometimes arises as to why the middle term always seems to be "Base." Early versions of the protocol also allowed for broadband transmission (for example, 10Broad), but broadband implementations were not successful in the marketplace. All current Ethernet implementations use baseband transmission.

Encoding for Signal Transmission

In baseband transmission, the frame information is directly impressed upon the link as a sequence of pulses or data symbols that are typically attenuated (reduced in size) and distorted (changed in shape) before they reach the other end of the link. The receiver's task is to detect each pulse as it arrives and then to extract its correct value before transferring the reconstructed information to the receiving MAC.

Filters and pulse-shaping circuits can help restore the size and shape of the received waveforms, but additional measures must be taken to ensure that the received signals are sampled at the correct time in the pulse period and at same rate as the transmit clock. The receive clock must be recovered from the incoming data stream to allow the receiving physical layer to synchronize with the incoming pulses. Compensating measures must be taken for a transmission effect known as baseline wander.

Clock recovery requires level transitions in the incoming signal to identify and synchronize on pulse boundaries. The alternating 1s and 0 s of the frame preamble were designed both to indicate that a frame was arriving and to aid in clock recovery. However, recovered clocks can drift and possibly lose synchronization if pulse levels remain constant and there are no transitions to detect (for example, during long strings of 0 s).

Baseline wander results because Ethernet links are AC-coupled to the transceivers and because AC coupling is incapable of maintaining voltage levels for more than a short time. As a result, transmitted pulses are distorted by a droop effect. In long strings of either 1s or 0 s, the droop can become so severe that the voltage level passes through the decision threshold, resulting in erroneous sampled values for the affected pulses.

Fortunately, encoding the outgoing signal before transmission can significantly reduce the effect of both these problems, as well as reduce the possibility of transmission errors. Early Ethernet implementations, up to and including 10Base-T, all used the Manchester encoding method. Each pulse is clearly identified by the direction of the midpulse transition rather than by its sampled level value.

6.3.6 The 802.3 Physical Layer Relationship to the ISO Reference Model

Although the specific logical model of the physical layer may vary from version to version, all Ethernet NICs generally conform to the generic model shown in Figure 6.5.

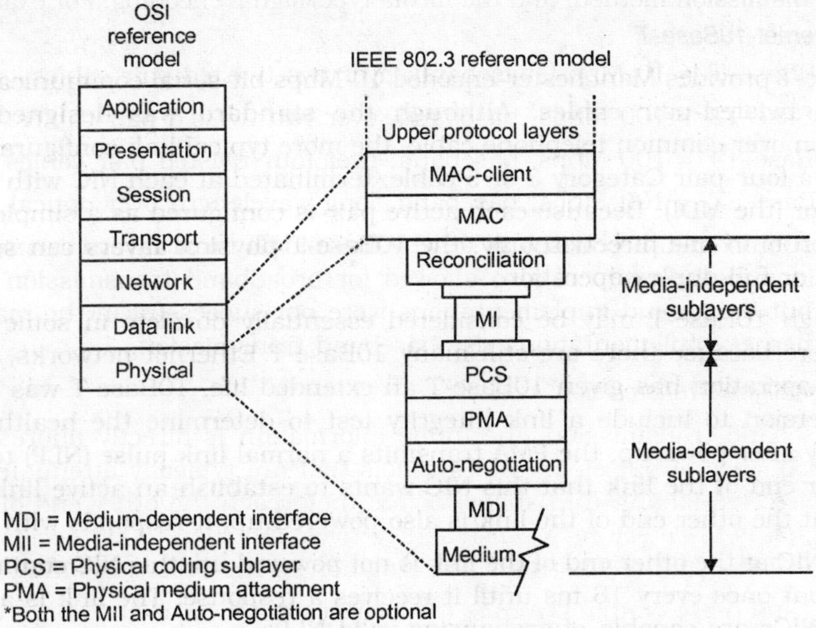

Figure 6.5 The Generic Ethernet Physical Layer Reference Model

The physical layer for each transmission rate is divided into sublayers that are independent of the particular media type and sublayers that are specific to the media type or signal encoding.

The reconciliation sublayer and the optional media-independent interface (MII in 10-Mbps and 100-Mbps Ethernet, GMII in Gigabit Ethernet) provide the logical connection between the MAC and the different sets of media-dependent layers. The MII and GMII are defined with separate transmit and receive data paths that are bit-serial for 10-Mbps implementations, nibble-serial (4 bits wide) for 100-Mbps implementations, and byte-serial (8 bits wide) for 1000-Mbps implementations. The media-independent interfaces and the reconciliation sublayer are common for their respective transmission rates and are configured for full-duplex operation in 10Base-T and all subsequent Ethernet versions.

The media-dependent physical coding sublayer (PCS) provides the logic for encoding, multiplexing, and synchronization of the outgoing symbol streams as well symbol code alignment, demultiplexing, and decoding of the incoming data.

The physical medium attachment (PMA) sublayer contains the signal transmitters and receivers (transceivers), as well as the clock recovery logic for the received data streams. The medium-dependent interface (MDI) is the cable connector between the signal transceivers and the link. The Auto-negotiation sublayer allows the NICs at each end of the link to exchange information about their individual capabilities, and then to negotiate and select the most favorable operational mode that they both are capable of supporting. Auto-negotiation is optional in early Ethernet implementations and is mandatory in later versions.

6.4 TYPES OF ETHERNET

10-Mbps Ethernet-10Base-T

10Base-T provides Manchester-encoded 10-Mbps bit-serial communication over two unshielded twisted-pair cables. Although the standard was designed to support transmission over common telephone cable, the more typical link configuration is to use two pair of a four-pair Category 3 or 5 cable, terminated at each NIC with an 8-pin RJ-45 connector (the MDI). Because each active pair is configured as a simplex link where transmission is in one direction only, the 10Base-T physical layers can support either half-duplex or full-duplex operation.

Although 10Base-T may be considered essentially obsolete in some circles, it is included here because there are still many 10Base-T Ethernet networks, and because full-duplex operation has given 10Base-T an extended life. 10Base-T was also the first Ethernet version to include a link integrity test to determine the health of the link. Immediately after powerup, the PMA transmits a normal link pulse (NLP) to tell the NIC at the other end of the link that this NIC wants to establish an active link connection: If the NIC at the other end of the link is also powered up, it responds with its own NLP.

If the NIC at the other end of the link is not powered up, this NIC continues sending an NLP about once every 16 ms until it receives a response. The link is activated only after both NICs are capable of exchanging valid NLPs.

100 Mbps-Fast Ethernet

Increasing the Ethernet transmission rate by a factor of ten over 10Base-T was not a simple task, and the effort resulted in the development of three separate physical layer standards for 100 Mbps over UTP cable: 100Base-TX and 100Base-T4 in 1995, and 100Base-T2 in 1997. Each was defined with different encoding requirements and a different set of media-dependent sublayers, even though there is some overlap in the link cabling.

Although not all three 100-Mbps versions were successful in the marketplace, all three have been discussed in the literature, and all three did impact future designs. As such, all three are important to consider here.

100Base-X

100Base-X was designed to support transmission over either two pairs of Category 5 UTP copper wire or two strands of optical fiber. Although the encoding, decoding, and clock recovery procedures are the same for both media, the signal transmission is different-electrical pulses in copper and light pulses in optical fiber.

The 100Base-X encoding procedure is based on the earlier FDDI optical fiber physical media-dependent and FDDI/CDDI copper twisted-pair physical media-dependent signalling standards developed by ISO and ANSI. The 100Base-TX physical media-dependent sublayer (TP-PMD) was implemented with CDDI semiconductor transceivers and RJ-45 connectors; the fiber PMD was implemented with FDDI optical transceivers and the Low Cost Fiber Interface Connector (commonly called the duplex SC connector).

100Base-T4

100Base-T4 was developed to allow 10Base-T networks to be upgraded to 100-Mbps operation without requiring existing four-pair Category 3 UTP cables to be replaced with the newer Category 5 cables. Two of the four pairs are configured for half-duplex operation and can support transmission in either direction, but only in one direction at a time. The other two pairs are configured as simplex pairs dedicated to transmission in one direction only. The simplex pair for the opposite direction provides carrier sense and collision detection. Full-duplex operation cannot be supported on 100Base-T4.

100Base-T2

The 100Base-T2 specification was developed as a better alternative for upgrading networks with installed Category 3 cabling than was being provided by 100Base-T4. Two important new goals were defined:

1. To provide communication over two pairs of Category 3 or better cable
2. To support both half-duplex and full-duplex operation

100Base-T2 uses a different signal transmission procedure than any previous twisted-pair Ethernet implementations. Instead of using two simplex links to form one full-duplex link, the 100Base-T2 dual-duplex baseband transmission method sends encoded symbols simultaneously in both directions on both wire pairs.

1000Base-T

- 1000Base-T Ethernet provides full-duplex transmission over four-pair Category 5 or better UTP cable. 1000Base-T is based largely on the findings and design approaches that led to the development of the Fast Ethernet physical layer implementations:
- 100Base-TX proved that binary symbol streams could be successfully transmitted over Category 5 UTP cable at 125 MBd.
- 100Base-T4 provided a basic understanding of the problems related to sending multilevel signals over four wire pairs.
- 100Base-T2 proved that PAM5 encoding, coupled with digital signal processing, could handle both simultaneous two-way data streams and potential crosstalk problems resulting from alien signals on adjacent wire pairs.
- 1000Base-T scrambles each byte in the MAC frame to randomize the bit sequence before it is encoded using a 4-D, 8-State Trellis Forward Error Correction (FEC) coding in which four PAM5 symbols are sent at the same time over four wire pairs. Four of the five levels in each PAM5 symbol represent 2 bits in the data byte. The fifth level is used for FEC coding, which enhances symbol recovery in the presence of noise and crosstalk. Separate scramblers for the master and slave PHYs create essentially uncorrelated data streams between the two opposite-travelling symbol streams on each wire pair.

1000Base-X

All three 1000Base-X versions support full-duplex binary transmission at 1250 Mbps over two strands of optical fiber or two STP copper wire-pairs. Transmission coding is based on the ANSI Fibre Channel 8B/10B encoding scheme. Each 8-bit data byte is mapped into a 10-bit code-group for bit-serial transmission. Like earlier Ethernet versions, each data frame is encapsulated at the physical layer before transmission, and link synchronization is maintained by sending a continuous stream of IDLE code-groups during interframe gaps. All 1000Base-X physical layers support both half-duplex and full-duplex operation.

6.5 ALTERNATIVE TECHNOLOGIES

The most common local area network alternative to Ethernet is a network technology developed by IBM, called **Token Ring.** Where Ethernet relies on the random gaps between transmissions to regulate access to the medium, Token ring implements a strict, orderly access method. A token ring network arranges nodes in a logical ring, as shown below. The nodes forward frames in one direction around the ring, removing a frame when it has circled the ring once. The ring initializes by creating a token, which is a special type of frame that gives a station permission to transmit. The token circles the ring like any frame until it encounters a station that wishes to transmit data. This station then "captures" the token by replacing the token frame with a data-carrying frame, which encircles the network. Once that data frame returns to the transmitting station, that station removes the data frame, creates a new token, and forwards that token on to the next node in the ring. Token ring nodes do not look for a carrier signal or listen for collisions; the presence of the token frame provides assurance that the station can transmit a data frame without fear of another station interrupting. Because a station transmits only a single data frame before passing the token along, each station on the ring will get a turn to communicate in a deterministic and fair manner. Token ring networks typically transmit data at either 4 or 16 Mbps.

6.5.1 Token Ring/IEEE 802.5

The Token Ring network was originally developed by IBM in the 1970s. It is still IBM's primary local-area network (LAN) technology. The related IEEE 802.5 specification is almost identical to and completely compatible with IBM's Token Ring network. In fact, the IEEE 802.5 specification was modelled after IBM Token Ring, and it continues to shadow IBM's Token Ring development. The term *Token Ring* generally is used to refer to both IBM's Token Ring network and IEEE 802.5 networks.

Token Ring and IEEE 802.5 networks are basically compatible, although the specifications differ in minor ways. IBM's Token Ring network specifies a star, with all end stations attached to a device called a multistation access unit (MSAU). In contrast, IEEE 802.5 does not specify a topology, although virtually all IEEE 802.5 implementations are based on a star. Other differences exist, including media type (IEEE 802.5 does not specify a media type, although IBM Token Ring networks use twisted-pair wire) and routing information field size.

Token Ring Operation

Token Ring and IEEE 802.5 are two principal examples of token-passing networks (FDDI is the other). *Token-passing networks* move a small frame, called a token, around the network. Possession of the token grants the right to transmit. If a node receiving the token has no information to send, it passes the token to the next end station. Each station can hold the token for a maximum period of time.

If a station possessing the token does have information to transmit, it seizes the token, alters 1 bit of the token (which turns the token into a start-of-frame sequence), appends the information that it wants to transmit, and sends this information to the next station on the ring. While the information frame is circling the ring, no token is on the network (unless the ring supports early token release), which means that other stations wanting to transmit must wait. Therefore, collisions cannot occur in Token Ring networks. If early token release is supported, a new token can be released when frame transmission is complete.

The information frame circulates the ring until it reaches the intended destination station, which copies the information for further processing. The information frame continues to circle the ring and is finally removed when it reaches the sending station. The sending station can check the returning frame to see whether the frame was seen and subsequently copied by the destination.

Unlike CSMA/CD networks (such as Ethernet), token-passing networks are *deterministic*, which means that it is possible to calculate the maximum time that will pass before any end station will be capable of transmitting. This feature and several reliability features, which are discussed in the section "Fault-Management Mechanisms," later in this chapter, make Token Ring networks ideal for applications in which delay must be predictable and robust network operation is important. Factory automation environments are examples of such applications.

Priority System

Token Ring networks use a sophisticated priority system that permits certain user-designated, high-priority stations to use the network more frequently. Token Ring frames have two fields that control priority: the priority field and the reservation field.

Only stations with a priority equal to or higher than the priority value contained in a token can seize that token. After the token is seized and changed to an information frame, only stations with a priority value higher than that of the transmitting station can reserve the token for the next pass around the network. When the next token is generated, it includes the higher priority of the reserving station. Stations that raise a token's priority level must reinstate the previous priority after their transmission is complete.

Fault-Management Mechanisms

Token Ring networks employ several mechanisms for detecting and compensating for network faults. For example, one station in the Token Ring network is selected to be the *active monitor*. This station, which potentially can be any station on the network, acts as a centralized source of timing information for other ring stations and performs a variety of ring-maintenance functions. One of these functions is the removal of continuously circulating frames from the ring. When a sending device fails, its frame may continue to circle the ring. This can prevent other stations from transmitting their own frames and essentially can lock up the network. The active monitor can detect such frames, remove them from the ring, and generate a new token.

The IBM Token Ring network's star topology also contributes to overall network reliability. Because all information in a Token Ring network is seen by active MSAUs, these devices can be programmed to check for problems and selectively remove stations from the ring, if necessary.

A Token Ring algorithm called *beaconing* detects and tries to repair certain network faults. Whenever a station detects a serious problem with the network (such as a cable break), it sends a beacon frame, which defines a failure domain. This domain includes the station reporting the failure, its nearest active upstream neighbor (NAUN), and everything in between. Beaconing initiates a process called *auto re-configuration*, in which nodes within the failure domain automatically perform diagnostics in an attempt to reconfigure the network around the failed areas. Physically, the MSAU can accomplish this through electrical reconfiguration.

Frame Format

Token Ring and IEEE 802.5 support two basic frame types: tokens and data/command frames. Tokens are 3 bytes in length and consist of a start delimiter, an access control byte, and an end delimiter. Data/command frames vary in size, depending on the size of the Information field. Data frames carry information for upper-layer protocols, while command frames contain control information and have no data for upper-layer protocols. Both formats are shown in Figure 6.6 (*a*).

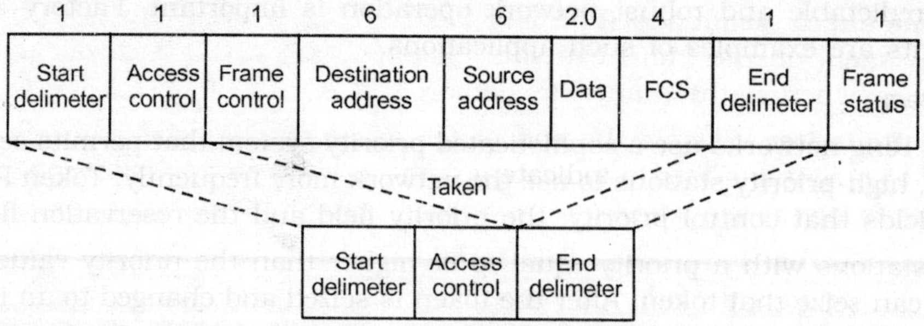

Figure 6.6a IEEE 802.5 and Token Ring Specify Tokens and Data/Command Frames

Token Frame Fields

The three token frame fields illustrated in Figure 6.6 are summarized in the descriptions that follow:

Start delimiter. Alerts each station of the arrival of a token (or data/command frame). This field includes signals that distinguish the byte from the rest of the frame by violating the encoding scheme used elsewhere in the frame.

Access-control byte. Contains the Priority field (the most significant 3 bits) and the Reservation field (the least significant 3 bits), as well as a token bit (used to differentiate a token from a data/command frame) and a monitor bit (used by the active monitor to determine whether a frame is circling the ring endlessly).

End delimiter. Signals the end of the token or data/command frame. This field also contains bits to indicate a damaged frame and identify the frame that is the last in a logical sequence.

Data/Command Frame Fields

Data/command frames have the same three fields as Token Frames, plus several others. The Data/command frame fields illustrated in Figure 6.6 are described in the following summaries:

Start delimiter. Alerts each station of the arrival of a token (or data/command frame). This field includes signals that distinguish the byte from the rest of the frame by violating the encoding scheme used elsewhere in the frame.

Access-control byte. Contains the Priority field (the most significant 3 bits) and the Reservation field (the least significant 3 bits), as well as a token bit (used to differentiate a token from a data/command frame) and a monitor bit (used by the active monitor to determine whether a frame is circling the ring endlessly).

Frame-control bytes. Indicates whether the frame contains data or control information. In control frames, this byte specifies the type of control information.

Destination and source addresses. Consists of two 6-byte address fields that identify the destination and source station addresses.

Data. Indicates that the length of field is limited by the ring token holding time, which defines the maximum time a station can hold the token.

Frame-check sequence (FCS). Is filed by the source station with a calculated value dependent on the frame contents. The destination station recalculates the value to determine whether the frame was damaged in transit. If so, the frame is discarded.

End Delimiter. Signals the end of the token or data/command frame. The end delimiter also contains bits to indicate a damaged frame and identify the frame that is the last in a logical sequence.

Frame Status. Is a 1-byte field terminating a command/data frame. The Frame Status field includes the address-recognized indicator and frame-copied indicator.

6.5.2 Fiber Distributed Data Interface

Fiber Distributed Data Interface (FDDI) is another token passing technology that operates over a pair of fiber optic rings, with each ring passing a token in opposite directions. FDDI networks offered transmission speeds of 100 Mbps, which initially made them quite popular for high-speed networking. With the advent of 100 Mbps Ethernet, which is cheaper and easier to administer, FDDI has waned in popularity.

A final network technology that bears mentioning is **Asynchronous Transfer Mode,** or ATM. ATM networks blur the line between local and wide area networking, being able to attach many different devices with high reliability and at high speeds, even across the country. ATM networks are suitable for carrying not only data, but voice and video traffic as well, making them versatile and expandable. While ATM has not gained acceptance as rapidly as originally predicted, it is nonetheless a solid network technology for the future.

The *Fiber Distributed Data Interface (FDDI)* specifies a 100-Mbps token-passing, dual-ring LAN using fiber-optic cable. FDDI is frequently used as high-speed backbone technology because of its support for high bandwidth and greater distances than copper. It should be noted that relatively recently, a related copper specification, called Copper Distributed Data Interface (CDDI), has emerged to provide 100-Mbps service over copper. CDDI is the implementation of FDDI protocols over twisted-pair copper wire. This chapter focuses mainly on FDDI specifications and operations, but it also provides a high-level overview of CDDI.

FDDI uses dual-ring architecture with traffic on each ring flowing in opposite directions (called counter-rotating). The dual rings consist of a primary and a secondary ring. During normal operation, the primary ring is used for data transmission, and the secondary ring remains idle. As will be discussed in detail later in this chapter, the primary purpose of the dual rings is to provide superior reliability and robustness.

FDDI Transmission Media

FDDI uses optical fiber as the primary transmission medium, but it also can run over copper cabling. As mentioned earlier, FDDI over copper is referred to as *Copper-Distributed Data Interface (CDDI).* Optical fiber has several advantages over copper media. In particular, security, reliability, and performance all are enhanced with optical fiber media because fiber does not emit electrical signals. A physical medium that does emit electrical signals (copper) can be tapped and therefore would permit unauthorized access to the data that is transiting the medium. In addition, fiber is immune to electrical interference from radio frequency interference (RFI) and electromagnetic interference (EMI). Fiber historically has supported much higher bandwidth (throughput potential) than copper, although recent technological advances have made copper capable of transmitting at 100 Mbps. Finally, FDDI allows 2 km between stations using multimode fiber, and even longer distances using a single mode.

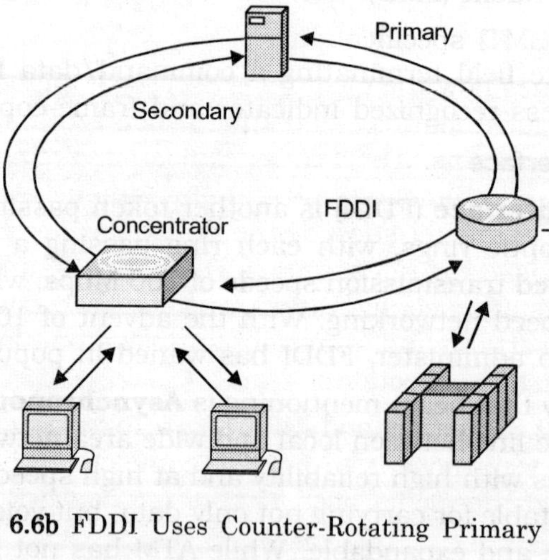

Figure 6.6b FDDI Uses Counter-Rotating Primary and Secondary Rings

FDDI defines two types of optical fiber:

1. single-mode and
2. multimode.

A *mode* is a ray of light that enters the fiber at a particular angle. *Multimode* fiber uses LED as the light-generating device, while *single-mode* fiber generally uses lasers.

Multimode fiber allows multiple modes of light to propagate through the fiber. Because these modes of light enter the fiber at different angles, they will arrive at the end of the fiber at different times. This characteristic is known as *modal dispersion*. Modal dispersion limits the bandwidth and distances that can be accomplished using multimode fibers. For this reason, multimode fiber is generally used for connectivity within a building or a relatively geographically contained environment.

Single-mode fiber allows only one mode of light to propagate through the fiber. Because only a single mode of light is used, modal dispersion is not present with single-mode fiber. Therefore, single-mode fiber is capable of delivering considerably higher performance connectivity over much larger distances, which is why it generally is used for connectivity between buildings and within environments that are more geographically dispersed.

FDDI Specifications

FDDI specifies the physical and media-access portions of the OSI reference model. FDDI is not actually a single specification, but it is a collection of four separate specifications, each with a specific function. Combined, these specifications have the capability to provide high-speed connectivity between upper-layer protocols such as TCP/IP and IPX, and media such as fiber-optic cabling.

FDDI's four specifications are:

1. the Media Access Control (MAC),
2. Physical Layer Protocol (PHY),
3. Physical-Medium Dependent (PMD), and
4. Station Management (SMT) specifications.

The *MAC* specification defines how the medium is accessed, including frame format, token handling, addressing, algorithms for calculating cyclic redundancy check (CRC) value, and error-recovery mechanisms. The *PHY* specification defines data encoding/decoding procedures, clocking requirements, and framing, among other functions. The *PMD* specification defines the characteristics of the transmission medium, including fiber-optic links, power levels, bit-error rates, optical components, and connectors. The *SMT* specification defines FDDI station configuration, ring configuration, and ring control features, including station insertion and removal, initialization, fault isolation and recovery, scheduling, and statistics collection.

FDDI is similar to IEEE 802.3 Ethernet and IEEE 802.5 Token Ring in its relationship with the OSI model. Its primary purpose is to provide connectivity between upper OSI layers of common protocols and the media used to connect network devices.

6.6 ETHERNET LIMITATIONS

A single shared cable can serve as the basis for a complete Ethernet network, which is what we discussed above. However, there are practical limits to the size of our Ethernet network in this case. A primary concern is the length of the shared cable. Electrical signals propagate along a cable very quickly, but they weaken as they travel, and electrical interference from neighboring devices (fluorescent lights, for example) can scramble the signal. A network cable must be short enough that devices at opposite ends can receive each other's signals clearly and with minimal delay. This places a distance limitation on the maximum separation between two devices (called the **network diameter**) on an Ethernet network. Additionally, since in CSMA/CD only a single device can transmit at a given time, there are practical limits to the number of devices that can coexist in a single network. Attach too many devices to one shared segment and contention for the medium will increase. Every device may have to wait an inordinately long time before getting a chance to transmit.

6.7 DEVICES

Engineers have developed a number of network devices that alleviate these difficulties. Many of these devices are not specific to Ethernet, but play roles in other network technologies as well.

6.7.1 Hubs

One of the most important technologies in delivering LAN technology to mainstream information system architecture is the intelligent hub. Recent enhancements in the capabilities of intelligent hubs have changed the way LANs are designed. Hubs owe their success to the efficiency and robustness of the 10Base-T protocol, which enables the implementation of Ethernet in a star fashion over Unshielded Twisted Pair. Now commonly used, hubs provide integrated support for the different standard topologies (such as Ethernet, Token-Ring, and FDDI) over different types of cabling. By repeating or amplifying signals where necessary, they enable the use of high-quality UTP cabling in virtually every situation. These intelligent hubs provide the necessary functionality to distribute a structured hardware and software system throughout networks, serve as network integration and control points, provide a single platform to support all LAN topologies, and deliver a foundation for managing all the components of the network.

There are three different types of hubs.

1. *Workgroup hubs* support one LAN segment and are packaged in a small footprint for small branch offices.
2. *Wiring closet hubs* support multiple LAN segments and topologies, include extensive management capabilities, and can house internetworking modules such as routers or bridges.
3. *Network center hubs*, at the high end, support numerous LAN connections, have a high-speed backplane with flexible connectivity options between LAN segments, and include fault tolerance features.

Hubs have evolved to provide tremendous flexibility for the design of the physical LAN topologies in large office buildings or plants. Various design strategies are now available. Hubs are also an effective vehicle to put management intelligence throughout the LANs in a corporation, allowing control and monitoring capabilities from a Network Management Center. This is particularly important as LANs in branch offices become supported by a central group.

6.7.2 Repeaters

The first popular Ethernet medium was a copper coaxial cable known as "thicknet." The maximum length of a thicknet cable was 500 metres. In large building or campus environments, a 500-metre cable could not always reach every network device. A **repeater** addresses this problem. Repeaters connect multiple Ethernet segments, listening to each segment and repeating the signal heard on one segment onto every other segment connected to the repeater. By running multiple cables and joining them with repeaters, you can significantly increase your network diameter.

6.7.3 Internetworking Devices-Bridges

Internetworking devices enable the interconnection of multiple LANs in an integrated network. This approach to networking is inevitably supplanting the terminal-to-host networks as the LAN becomes the preferred connectivity platform to all personal, workgroup, or corporate computing facilities.

Bridges provide the means to connect two LANs together-in effect, to extend the size of the LAN by dividing the traffic and enabling growth beyond the physical limitations of any one topology. Bridges operate at the data link layer of the OSI model, which makes them topology-specific. Thus, bridging can occur between identical topologies only (Ethernet-to-Ethernet, Token Ring-to-Token Ring). Source-Route Transparent bridging, a technology that enables bridging between Ethernet and Token-Ring LANs, is seldom used.

Although bridges may cost less, some limitations must be noted. Forwarding of broadcast packets can be detrimental to network performance. Bridges operate promiscuously, forwarding packets as required. In a large internetwork, broadcasts from devices can accumulate, effectively taking away available bandwidth and adding to network utilization. "Broadcast storms" are rarely predictable, and can bring a network completely to a halt. Complex network topologies are difficult to manage. Ethernet bridges implement a simple decision logic that requires that only a single path to a destination be active. Thus, in complex meshed topologies, redundant paths are made inoperative, a situation that rapidly becomes ineffective as the network grows.

Bridges and *switches* are data communications devices that operate principally at Layer 2 of the OSI reference model. As such, they are widely referred to as data link layer devices. Bridges became commercially available in the early 1980s. At the time of their introduction, bridges connected and enabled packet forwarding between homogeneous networks. More recently, bridging between different networks has also been defined and standardized.

Several kinds of bridging have proven important as internetworking devices.

1. *Transparent bridging* is found primarily in Ethernet environments.
2. *source-route bridging* occurs primarily in Token Ring environments.
3. *Translational bridging* provides translation between the formats and transit principles of different media types (usually Ethernet and Token Ring). Finally,
4. *Source-route transparent bridging* combines the algorithms of transparent bridging and source-route bridging to enable communication in mixed Ethernet/Token Ring environments.

Today, switching technology has emerged as the evolutionary heir to bridging-based internetworking solutions. Switching implementations now dominate applications in which bridging technologies were implemented in prior network designs. Superior throughput performance, higher port density, lower per-port cost, and greater flexibility have contributed to the emergence of switches as replacement technology for bridges and as complements to routing technology.

Bridging and switching occur at the link layer, which controls data flow, handles transmission errors, provides physical (as opposed to logical) addressing, and manages access to the physical medium. Bridges provide these functions by using various link layer protocols that dictate specific flow control, error handling, addressing, and media-access algorithms. Examples of popular link layer protocols include Ethernet, Token Ring, and FDDI.

Bridges and switches are not complicated devices. They analyze incoming frames, make forwarding decisions based on information contained in the frames, and forward the frames toward the destination. In some cases, such as source-route bridging, the entire path to the destination is contained in each frame. In other cases, such as transparent bridging, frames are forwarded one hop at a time toward the destination. Upper-layer protocol transparency is a primary advantage of both bridging and switching. Because both device types operate at the link layer, they are not required to examine upper-layer information. This means that they can rapidly forward traffic representing any network layer protocol. It is not uncommon for a bridge to move AppleTalk, DECnet, TCP/IP, XNS, and other traffic between two or more networks.

Bridges are capable of filtering frames based on any Layer 2 fields. For example, a bridge can be programmed to reject (not forward) all frames sourced from a particular network. Because link layer information often includes a reference to an upper-layer protocol, bridges usually can filter on this parameter. Furthermore, filters can be helpful in dealing with unnecessary broadcast and multicast packets.

By dividing large networks into self-contained units, bridges and switches provide several advantages. Because only a certain percentage of traffic is forwarded, a bridge or switch diminishes the traffic experienced by devices on all connected segments. The bridge or switch will act as a firewall for some potentially damaging network errors and will accommodate communication between a larger number of devices than would be supported on any single LAN connected to the bridge. Bridges and switches extend the effective length of a LAN, permitting the attachment of distant stations that was not previously permitted.

Although bridges and switches share most relevant attributes, several distinctions differentiate these technologies. Bridges are generally used to segment a LAN into a couple of smaller segments. Switches are generally used to segment a large LAN into many smaller segments. Bridges generally have only a few ports for LAN connectivity, whereas switches generally have many. Small switches such as the Cisco Catalyst 2924XL have 24 ports capable of creating 24 different network segments for a LAN. Larger switches such as the Cisco Catalyst 6500 can have hundreds of ports. Switches can also be used to connect LANs with different media-for example, a 10-Mbps Ethernet LAN and a 100-Mbps Ethernet LAN can be connected using a switch. Some switches support cut-through switching, which reduces latency and delays in the network, while bridges support only store-and-forward traffic switching. Finally, switches reduce collisions on network segments because they provide dedicated bandwidth to each network segment.

Transparent Bridging

Transparent bridges were first developed at Digital Equipment Corporation (Digital) in the early 1980s.

Operation

Transparent bridges are so named because their presence and operation are transparent to network hosts. When transparent bridges are powered on, they learn the workstation locations by analyzing the source address of incoming frames from all attached networks. For example, if a bridge sees a frame arrive on port 1 from Host A, the bridge concludes that Host A can be reached through the segment connected to port 1. Through this process, transparent bridges build a table (the learning process), such as the one in Figure 6.7

Host address	Network address
15	1
17	1
12	2
13	2
18	1
9	1
14	3

Figure 6.7 Transparent Bridges Build a Table that Determines a Host's Accessibility

The bridge uses its table as the basis for traffic forwarding. When a frame is received on one of the bridge's interfaces, the bridge looks up the frame's destination address in its internal table. If the table contains an association between the destination address and any of the bridge's ports aside from the one on which the frame was received, the frame is forwarded out the indicated port. If no association is found, the frame is flooded to all ports except the inbound port. Broadcasts and multicasts also are flooded in this way.

Transparent bridges successfully isolate intrasegment traffic, thereby reducing the traffic seen on each individual segment. This is called *filtering* and occurs when the source and destination MAC addresses reside on the same bridge interface. Filtering usually improves network response times, as seen by the user. The extent to which traffic is reduced and response times are improved depends on the volume of intersegment traffic relative to the total traffic, as well as the volume of broadcast and multicast traffic.

Bridging Loops

Without a bridge-to-bridge protocol, the transparent-bridge algorithm fails when multiple paths of bridges and local-area networks (LANs) exist between any two LANs in the internetwork. Figure 6.9 illustrates such a bridging loop. Suppose that Host A sends a frame to Host B. Both bridges receive the frame and correctly learn that Host A is on segment 2. Each bridge then forwards the frame onto segment 2. Unfortunately, not only will Host B receive two copies of the frame (once from bridge 1 and once from bridge 2), but each bridge now believes that Host A resides on the same segment as Host B. When

Host B replies to Host A's frame, both bridges will receive and subsequently filter the replies because the bridge table will indicate that the destination (Host A) is on the same network segment as the frame's source.

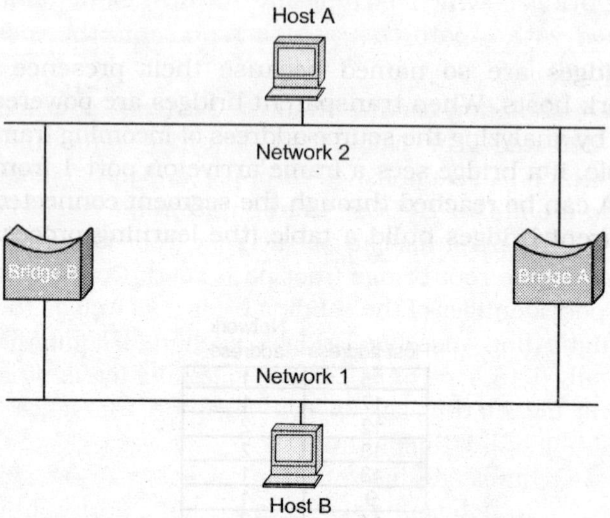

Figure 6.8 Bridging Loops Can Result in Inaccurate Forwarding and Learning in

In addition to basic connectivity problems, the proliferation of broadcast messages in networks with loops represents a potentially serious network problem. Referring again to Figure 6.8, assume that Host A's initial frame is a broadcast. Both bridges forward the frames endlessly, using all available network bandwidth and blocking the transmission of other packets on both segments.

A topology with loops, such as that shown in Figure 6.8, can be useful as well as potentially harmful. A loop implies the existence of multiple paths through the internetwork, and a network with multiple paths from source to destination can increase overall network fault tolerance through improved topological flexibility.

Spanning-Tree Algorithm

The *spanning-tree algorithm (STA)* was developed by Digital Equipment Corporation, a key Ethernet vendor, to preserve the benefits of loops while eliminating their problems. Digital's algorithm subsequently was revised by the IEEE 802 committee and was published in the IEEE 802.1d specification. The Digital algorithm and the IEEE 802.1d algorithm are not compatible. The STA designates a loop-free subset of the network's topology by placing those bridge ports that, if active, would create loops into a standby (blocking) condition. Blocking bridge ports can be activated in the event of a primary link failure, providing a new path through the internetwork.

The STA uses a conclusion from graph theory as a basis for constructing a loop-free subset of the network's topology. Graph theory states the following:

1. For any connected graph consisting of nodes and edges connecting pairs of nodes,
2. A spanning tree of edges maintains the connectivity of the graph but contains no loops.

The STA calls for each bridge to be assigned a unique identifier. Typically, this identifier is one of the bridge's *Media Access Control (MAC)* addresses, plus an administratively assigned priority. Each port in every bridge also is assigned a unique identifier (within that bridge), which is typically its own MAC address. Finally, each bridge port is associated with a path cost, which represents the cost of transmitting a frame onto a LAN through that port.

The spanning-tree calculation occurs when the bridge is powered up and whenever a topology change is detected. The calculation requires communication between the spanning-tree bridges, which is accomplished through *configuration messages* (sometimes called *bridge protocol data units*, or *BPDUs*). Configuration messages contain information identifying the bridge that is presumed to be the root (root identifier) and the distance from the sending bridge to the root bridge (root path cost). Configuration messages also contain the bridge and port identifier of the sending bridge, as well as the age of information contained in the configuration message.Bridges exchange configuration messages at regular intervals (typically 1 to 4 seconds). If a bridge fails (causing a topology change), neighboring bridges will detect the lack of configuration messages and will initiate a spanning-tree recalculation. All transparent-bridge topology decisions are made locally by each bridge. Bridges exchange configuration messages with neighboring bridges, and no central authority exists to determine network topology or administration.

Source Route Bridging

The source-route bridging (SRB) algorithm was developed by IBM and was proposed to the IEEE 802.5 committee as the means to bridge between all LANs.

SRB Algorithm

SRBs are so named because they assume that the complete source-to-destination route is placed in all inter-LAN frames sent by the source. SRBs store and forward the frames as indicated by the route appearing in the appropriate frame field. Figure 6.9 illustrates a sample SRB network. In Figure 6.10, assume that Host X wants to send a frame to Host Y. Initially, Host X does not know whether Host Y resides on the same LAN or a different LAN. To determine this, Host X sends out a test frame. If that frame returns to Host X without a positive indication that Host Y has seen it, Host X assumes that Host Y is on a remote segment.

To determine the exact remote location of Host Y, Host X sends an explorer frame. Each bridge receiving the explorer frame (Bridges 1 and 2, in this example) copies the frame onto all outbound ports. Route information is added to the explorer frames as they travel through the internetwork. When Host X's explorer frames reach Host Y, Host Y replies to each individually, using the accumulated route information. Upon receipt of all response frames, Host X chooses a path based on some predetermined criteria.

In the example in Figure 6.9, this process will yield two routes:

1. LAN 1 to Bridge 1 to LAN 3 to Bridge 3 to LAN 2.
2. LAN 1 to Bridge 2 to LAN 4 to Bridge 4 to LAN 2.

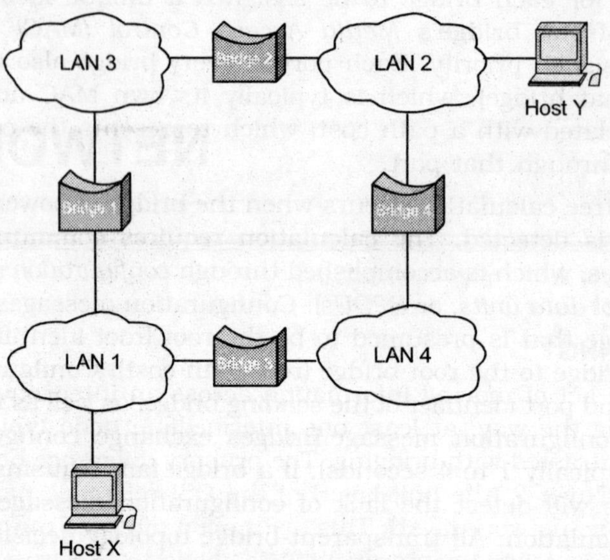

Figure 6.9 An SRB Network Contains LANs and Bridges

Host X must select one of these two routes. The IEEE 802.5 specification does not mandate the criteria that Host X should use in choosing a route, but it does make several suggestions, including the following:

1. First frame received.
2. Response with the minimum number of hops.
3. Response with the largest allowed frame size.
4. Various combinations of the preceding criteria.

In most cases, the path contained in the first frame received is used.After a route is selected, it is inserted into frames destined for Host Y in the form of a *routing information field (RIF)*. A RIF is included only in those frames destined for other LANs. The presence of routing information within the frame is indicated by setting the most significant bit within the Source Address field, called the *routing information indicator (RII)* bit.

7

NETWORK LAYER

7.1 WHAT IS ROUTING?

Routing is the act of moving information across an internetwork from a source to a destination. Along the way, at least one intermediate node typically is encountered. Routing is often contrasted with bridging. The primary difference between the two is that bridging occurs at Layer 2 (the link layer) of the OSI reference model, whereas routing occurs at Layer 3 (the network layer). This distinction provides routing and bridging with different information to use in the process of moving information from source to destination, so the two functions accomplish their tasks in different ways.

7.1.1 Routing Components

Routing involves two basic activities:

1. Determining optimal routing paths and
2. Transporting information groups (typically called packets) through an internetwork.

In the context of the routing process, the latter of these is referred to as packet switching.

Path Determination

Routing protocols use metrics to evaluate what path will be the best for a packet to travel. A metric is a standard of measurement, such as path bandwidth, that is used by routing algorithms to determine the optimal path to a destination. To aid the process of path determination, routing algorithms initialize and maintain routing tables, which contain route information. Route information varies depending on the routing algorithm used.

Routing algorithms fill routing tables with a variety of information. Destination/next hop associations tell a router that a particular destination can be reached optimally by sending the packet to a particular router representing the "next hop" on the way to the final destination. When a router receives an incoming packet, it checks the destination address and attempts to associate this address with a next hop.

Routing tables also can contain other information, such as data about the desirability of a path. Routers compare metrics to determine optimal routes, and these metrics differ depending on the design of the routing algorithm used. Routers communicate with one another and maintain their routing tables through the transmission of a variety of messages.

1. The routing update message is one such message that generally consists of all or a portion of a routing table. By analyzing routing updates from all other routers, a router can build a detailed picture of network topology.
2. A link-state advertisement, another example of a message sent between routers, informs other routers of the state of the sender's links. Link information also can be used to build a complete picture of network topology to enable routers to determine optimal routes to network destinations.

Switching

Switching algorithms is the same for most routing protocols. In most cases, a host determines that it must send a packet to another host. Having acquired a router's address by some means, the source host sends a packet addressed specifically to a router's physical (Media Access Control [MAC]-layer) address, this time with the protocol (network layer) address of the destination host.

As it examines the packet's destination protocol address, the router determines that it either knows or does not know how to forward the packet to the next hop. If the router does not know how to forward the packet, it typically drops the packet. If the router knows how to forward the packet, it changes the destination physical address to that of the next hop and transmits the packet.

The next hop may be the ultimate destination host. If not, the next hop is usually another router, which executes the same switching decision process. As the packet moves through the internetwork, its physical address changes, but its protocol address remains constant. The International Organization for Standardization (ISO) terminology that is useful in describing network devices.

Network devices without the capability to forward packets between subnetworks are called **end systems (ESs)**. Network devices with these capabilities are called **intermediate systems (ISs)**. ISs are further divided into those that can communicate within routing domains (intradomain ISs) and those that communicate both within and between routing domains (interdomain ISs).

7.1.2 Routing Algorithms Characteristics

Routing algorithms can be differentiated on the basis of several key characteristics.

First, the particular goals of the algorithm designer affect the operation of the resulting routing protocol.

Second, various types of routing algorithms exist, and each algorithm has a different impact on network and router resources.

Finally, routing algorithms use a variety of metrics that affect calculation of optimal routes. The following sections analyze these routing algorithm attributes.

Design Goals Routing algorithms often have one or more of the following design goals:

1. Optimality
2. Simplicity and low overhead

3. Robustness and stability
4. Rapid convergence
5. Flexibility.

Optimality refers to the capability of the routing algorithm to select the best route, which depends on the metrics and metric weightings used to make the calculation. For example, one routing algorithm may use a number of hops and delays, but it may weigh delay more heavily in the calculation. Routing protocols must define their metric calculation algorithms strictly.

Routing algorithms must be ***robust***, which means that they should perform correctly in the face of unusual or unforeseen circumstances, such as hardware failures, high load conditions, and incorrect implementations. Because routers are located at network junction points, they can cause considerable problems when they fail. The best routing algorithms are often those that have withstood the test of time and that have proven stable under a variety of network conditions.

In addition, routing algorithms must converge rapidly. ***Convergence*** is the process of agreement, by all routers, on optimal routes. When a network event causes routes to either go down or become available, routers distribute routing update messages that permeate networks, stimulating recalculation of optimal routes and eventually causing all routers to agree on these routes. Routing algorithms that converge slowly can cause routing loops or network outages.

Let a packet arrives at Router 1 at time t1. Router 1 already has been updated and thus knows that the optimal route to the destination calls for Router 2 to be the next stop. Router 1 therefore forwards the packet to Router 2, but because this router has not yet been updated, it believes that the optimal next hop is Router 1. Router 2 therefore forwards the packet back to Router 1, and the packet continues to bounce back and forth between the two routers until Router 2 receives its routing update or until the packet has been switched the maximum number of times allowed.

Routing algorithms should also be **flexible,** which means that they should quickly and accurately adapt to a variety of network circumstances. Assume, for example, that a network segment has gone down. As many routing algorithms become aware of the problem, they will quickly select the next-best path for all routes normally using that segment. Routing algorithms can be programmed to adapt to change in network bandwidth, router queue size, and network delay, among other variables.

Algorithm Types

Routing algorithms can be classified by type.

1. Static versus dynamic
2. Single-path versus multipart
3. Flat versus hierarchical
4. Host-intelligent versus router-intelligent
5. Intradomain versus interdomain
6. Link-state versus distance vector

Static Versus Dynamic

Static routing algorithms are hardly algorithms at all, but are table mappings established by the network administrator before the beginning of routing. These mappings do not change unless the network administrator alters them. Algorithms that use static routes are simple to design and work well in environments where network traffic is relatively predictable and where network design is relatively simple.

Because static routing systems cannot react to network changes, they generally are considered unsuitable for today's large, constantly changing networks. Most of the dominant routing algorithms today are *dynamic routing algorithms*, which adjust to changing network circumstances by analyzing incoming routing update messages. If the message indicates that a network change has occurred, the routing software recalculates routes and sends out new routing update messages.

Dynamic routing algorithms can be supplemented with static routes where appropriate. A router of last resort (a router to which all unroutable packets are sent), for example, can be designated to act as a repository for all unroutable packets, ensuring that all messages are at least handled in some way.

Single-Path Versus Multipath

Some sophisticated routing protocols support multiple paths to the same destination. Unlike single-path algorithms, these multipath algorithms permit traffic multiplexing over multiple lines. The advantages of multipath algorithms are obvious: They can provide substantially better throughput and reliability. This is generally called load sharing.

Flat Versus Hierarchical

Some routing algorithms operate in a flat space, while others use routing hierarchies. In a *flat routing system*, the routers are peers of all others. In a hierarchical routing system, some routers form what amounts to a routing backbone. Packets from nonbackbone routers travel to the backbone routers, where they are sent through the backbone until they reach the general area of the destination. At this point, they travel from the last backbone router through one or more nonbackbone routers to the final destination.

Routing systems often designate logical groups of nodes, called domains, autonomous systems, or areas. In *hierarchical systems*, some routers in a domain can communicate with routers in other domains, while others can communicate only with routers within their domain. In very large networks, additional hierarchical levels may exist, with routers at the highest hierarchical level forming the routing backbone.

Host-Intelligent Versus Router-Intelligent

Some routing algorithms assume that the source end node will determine the entire route. This is usually referred to as *source routing*. In source-routing systems, routers merely act as store-and-forward devices, mindlessly sending the packet to the next stop. Other algorithms assume that hosts know nothing about routes. In these algorithms, routers determine the path through the internet work based on their own calculations. In the first system, the hosts have the routing intelligence. In the latter system, routers have the routing intelligence.

Intradomain Versus Interdomain

Some routing algorithms work only within domains; others work within and between domains. The nature of these two algorithm types is different. It stands to reason, therefore, that an optimal intradomain-routing algorithm would not necessarily be an optimal interdomain-routing algorithm.

Link-State Versus Distance Vector

Link-state algorithms (also known as shortest path first algorithms) flood routing information to all nodes in the internetwork. Each router, however, sends only the portion of the routing table that describes the state of its own links. In link-state algorithms, each router builds a picture of the entire network in its routing tables. Distance vector algorithms (also known as Bellman-Ford algorithms) call for each router to send all or some portion of its routing table, but only to its neighbors. In essence, **link-state algorithms send small updates everywhere, while distance vector algorithms send larger updates only to neighboring routers.** *Distance vector* algorithms know only about their neighbors.

7.1.3 Routing Metrics

Routing tables contain information used by switching software to select the best route

But questions are:

1. But how are routing tables built?.
2. What is the specific nature of the information that they contain?
3. How do routing algorithms determine that one route is preferable to others?

Routing algorithms have used many different metrics to determine the best route. Sophisticated routing algorithms can base route selection on multiple metrics, combining them in a single (hybrid) metric.

All the following metrics have been used:

Path length is the most common routing metric. Some routing protocols allow network administrators to assign arbitrary costs to each network link. In this case, path length is the sum of the costs associated with each link traversed. Other routing protocols define hop count, a metric that specifies the number of passes through internetworking products, such as routers, that a packet must take en route from a source to a destination.

Reliability, in the context of routing algorithms, refers to the dependability (usually described in terms of the bit-error rate) of each network link. Some network links might go down more often than others. After a network fails, certain network links might be repaired more easily or more quickly than other links. Any reliability factors can be taken into account in the assignment of the reliability ratings, which are arbitrary numeric values usually assigned to network links by network administrators.

Routing delay refers to the length of time required to move a packet from source to destination through the internetwork. Delay depends on many factors, including the bandwidth of intermediate network links, the port queues at each router along the way, network congestion on all intermediate network links, and the physical distance to be travelled. Because delay is a conglomeration of several important variables, it is a common and useful metric.

Bandwidth refers to the available traffic capacity of a link. All other things being equal, a 10-Mbps Ethernet link would be preferable to a 64-kbps leased line. Although bandwidth is a rating of the maximum attainable throughput on a link, routes through links with greater bandwidth do not necessarily provide better routes than routes through slower links. For example, if a faster link is busier, the actual time required to send a packet to the destination could be greater.

Load refers to the degree to which a network resource, such as a router, is busy. Load can be calculated in a variety of ways, including CPU utilization and packets processed per second. Monitoring these parameters on a continual basis can be resource-intensive itself.

Communication cost is another important metric, especially because some companies may not care about performance as much as they care about operating expenditures. Although line delay may be longer, they will send packets over their own lines rather than through the public lines that cost money for usage time.

Rounted Protocols

Two terms are a bit confusing. Routed Protocols, and Routing Protocols.

Routed protocols are transported by **routing protocols** across an internetwork.

In general, routed protocols also are referred to as network protocols. These network protocols perform a variety of functions required for communication between user applications in source and destination devices, and these functions can differ widely among protocol suites. Network protocols occur at the upper five layers of the OSI reference model: the network layer, the transport layer, the session layer, the presentation layer, and the application layer.

Confusion about the terms *routed protocol* and *routing protocol* is common. **Routed protocols** are protocols that are routed over an internetwork. Examples of such protocols are the Internet Protocol (IP), DECnet, AppleTalk, Novell NetWare, OSI, Banyan VINES, and Xerox Network System (XNS). **Routing protocols,** on the other hand, are protocols that implement routing algorithms. Put simply, routing protocols are used by intermediate systems to build tables used in determining path selection of routed protocols. Examples of these protocols include Interior Gateway Routing Protocol (IGRP), Enhanced Interior Gateway Routing Protocol (Enhanced IGRP), Open Shortest Path First (OSPF), Exterior Gateway Protocol (EGP), Border Gateway Protocol (BGP), Intermediate System-to-Intermediate System (IS-IS), and Routing Information Protocol (RIP).

7.1.4 Routing Algorithms

In this section, we discuss the Vector-Distance and Link-State, Shortest Path First routing algorithms.

Vector-Distance

The term *Vector-Distance* refers to a class of algorithms that gateways use to update routing information. Each router begins with a set of routes for those networks or subnets to which it is directly attached, and possibly some additional routes to other networks or hosts if the network topology is such that the routing protocol will be unable to produce the desired routing correctly. This list is kept in a *routing table*, where each entry identifies a destination network or host and gives the "distance" to that network. The distance is called a *metric* and is typically measured in "hops".

Periodically, each router sends a copy of its routing table to any other router it can reach directly. When a report arrives at router B from router A, B examines the set of destinations it receives and the distance to each. B will update its routing table if:

1. A knows a shorter way to reach a destination.
2. A lists a destination that B does not have in its table.
3. A's distance to a destination, already routed through A from B, has changed.

This kind of algorithm is easy to implement, but it has a number of disadvantages:

1. When routes change rapidly, that is, a new connection appears or an old one fails, the routing topology may not stabilize to match the changed network topology because information propagates slowly from one router to another and while it is propagating, some routers will have incorrect routing information.
2. Another disadvantage is that each router has to send a copy of its entire routing table to every neighbor at regular intervals. Of course, one can use longer intervals to reduce the network load but that introduces problems related to how well the network responds to changes in topology.

Vector-distance algorithms using hop counts as a metric do not take account of the link speed or reliability. Such an algorithm will use a path with hop count 2 that crosses two slow-speed lines, instead of using a path with hop count 3 that crosses three token-rings and may be substantially faster.

The most difficult task in a vector-distance algorithm is to prevent instability. Different solutions are available:

Counting to Infinity

Let us choose a value of 16 to represent infinity. Suppose a network becomes inaccessible; all the immediately neighboring routers time out and set the metric to that network to 16. We can consider that all the neighboring routers have a piece of hardware that connects them to the vanished network, with a cost of 16. Since that is the only connection to the vanished network, all the other routers in the system will converge to new routes that go through one of those routers with a direct but unavailable connection. Once convergence has happened, all the routers will have metrics of 16 for the vanished network. Since 16 indicates infinity, all routers then regard the network as unreachable.

Link State; Shortest Path First

The growth in networking over the past few years has pushed the currently available *Interior Gateway Protocols*, which use vector-distance algorithms, past their limits. The primary alternative to vector-distance schemes is a class of protocols known as *Link State, Shortest Path First*.

The important features of these routing protocols are:

1. A set of physical networks is divided into a number of areas.
2. All routers within an area have an identical database.

Each router's database describes the complete topology (which routers are connected to which networks) of the routing domain. The topology of an area is represented with a database called a *Link State Database* describing all of the links that each of the routers in the area has.

Each router uses its database to derive the set of optimum paths to all destinations from which it builds its routing table. The algorithm used to determine the optimum paths is called a *Shortest Path First (SPF)* algorithm.

In general, a link state protocol works as follows. Each router periodically sends out a description of its connections (the state of its links) to its neighbors (routers are neighbors if they are connected to the same network). This description, called a *Link State Advertisement (LSA)*, includes the configured cost of the connection. The LSA is flooded throughout the router's domain. Each router in the domain maintains an identical synchronized copy of a database composed of this link state information. This database describes both the topology of the router's domain and routes to networks outside of the domain such as routes to networks in other autonomous systems. Each router runs an algorithm on its topological database resulting in a shortest-path tree. This shortest-path tree contains the shortest path to every router and network the gateway can reach. From the shortest-path tree, the cost to the destination and the next hop to forward a datagram to be used to build the router's routing table.

Link-state protocols, in comparison with vector-distance protocols, send out updates when there is news, and may send out regular updates as a way of ensuring neighbor routers that a connection is still active. More importantly, the information exchanged is the state of a router's links, not the contents of the routing table. This means that link-state algorithms use fewer network resources than their vector-distance counterparts, particularly when the routing is complex or the autonomous system is large. They are, however, compute-intensive. In return, users get faster response to network events, faster route convergence, and access to more advanced network services.

7.1.5 How Routers Work ?

One of the tools a router uses to decide where a packet should go is a **configuration table.** A configuration table is a collection of information, including:

- Information on which connections lead to particular groups of addresses.
- Priorities for connections to be used.
- Rules for handling both routine and special cases of traffic.

A configuration table can be a simple as a half-dozen lines in the smallest routers, but can grow to massive size and complexity in the very large routers that handle the bulk of Internet messages.

A router, then, has two separate but related jobs. **First,** the router ensures that information doesn't go where it's not needed. **Second,** the router makes sure that information does make it to the intended destination. In performing these two jobs, a router is extremely useful in dealing with two separate computer networks. It joins the two networks, passing information from one to the other and, in some cases, performing translations of various **protocols** between the two networks. It also protects the networks from one another, preventing the traffic on one from unnecessarily spilling over to the other. As the number of networks attached to one another grows, the configuration table for handling traffic among them grows, and the processing power of the router is increased.

Packet Transfer

Internet data, whether in the form of a Web page, a downloaded file or an e-mail message, travels over a system known as a packet-switching network. In this system, the data in a message or file is broken up into packages about 1,500 bytes long. Each of these packages gets a wrapper that includes information on the sender's address, the receiver's address, the package's place in the entire message, and how the receiving computer can be sure that the package arrived intact. Each data package, called a **packet,** is then sent off to its destination via the best available route — a route that might be taken by all the other packets in the message or by none of the other packets in the message. In a network designed for data there are two **huge advantages to the packet-switching plan. First,** the network can balance the load across various pieces of equipment on a millisecond-by-millisecond basis. **Second,** if there is a problem with one piece of equipment in the network while a message is being transferred, packets can be routed around the problem, ensuring the delivery of the entire message.

- The routers that make up the main part of the Internet can reconfigure the paths that packets take because they look at the information surrounding the data packet, and they tell each other about line conditions, such as delays in receiving and sending data and traffic on various pieces of the network.

In addition to routing packets from one point to another, the How Stuff Works router has rules limiting how computers from outside the network can connect to computers inside the network, how the How Stuff Works network appears to the outside world, and other security functions. While most companies also have a special piece of hardware or software called a **firewall** to enforce security, the rules in a router's configuration table are important to keeping a company's — or a family's — network secure.

One of the crucial tasks for any router is knowing when a packet of information stays on its local network. For this, it uses a mechanism called a **subnet mask.** The subnet mask looks like an IP address and usually reads "255.255.255.0". This tells the router that all messages with the sender and receiver having an address sharing the first three groups of numbers are on the same network, and shouldn't be sent out to another network. Here's an example: The computer at address 15.57.31.40 sends a request to the computer at 15.57.31.52. The router, which sees all the packets, matches the first three groups in the address of both sender and receiver (15.57.31) , and keeps the packet on the local network. (For more on how the addresses work, see the sidebar "Logical and Physical addresses" in the next section.)

How Routers Know where to Send Data? Routers are one of several types of devices that make up the "plumbing" of a computer network. Hubs, switches and routers all take signals from computers or networks and pass them along to other computers and networks, but a router is the only one of these devices that examines each bundle of data as it passes and makes a decision about exactly where it should go. To make these decisions, routers must first know about two kinds of information: addresses and network structure.

You can think of this address as a **logical address** because it describes a way someone can get a message to you. This logical address is connected to a **physical address** that you generally only see when you're buying or selling a piece of property.

Every piece of equipment that connects to a network, whether an office network or the Internet, has a physical address. This is an address that's unique to the piece of equipment that's actually attached to the network cable. For example, if your desktop computer has a network interface card (NIC) in it, the NIC has a physical address permanently stored in a special memory location. This physical address, which is also called the MAC address (for Media Access Control) has two parts, each 3 bytes long. The first 3 bytes identify the company that made the NIC. The second 3 bytes are the serial number of the NIC itself.

Logical addresses for computer networks work in exactly the same way. You may be using the addressing schemes, or protocols, from several different types of networks simultaneously. If you're connected to the Internet (and if you're reading this, you probably are), then you have an address that's part of the TCP/IP network protocol. If you also have a small network set up to exchange files between several family computers, then you may also be using the Microsoft NetBEUI protocol. If you connect to your company's network from home, then your computer may have an address that follows Novell's IPX/SPX protocol. All of these can coexist on your computer. Since the driver software that allows your computer to communicate with each network uses resources like memory and CPU time, you don't want to load protocols you won't need, but there's no problem with having all the protocols your work requires running at the same time.

Routers understand the Protocols. The first and most basic job of the router is to know where to send information addressed to your computer. Most of the routers that forward message to you don't know your computer's MAC address, but they know enough to keep the message flowing. Routers are programmed to understand the most common network protocols. That means they know the format of the addresses, how many bytes are in the basic package of data sent out over the network, and how to make sure all the packages reach their destination and get reassembled. For the routers that are part of the Internet's main "backbone," this means looking at, and moving on, millions of information packages every second. And simply moving the package along to its destination isn't all that a router will do. It's just as important, in today's computerized world, that they keep the message flowing by the best possible route.

Depending on the time of day and day of the week, some parts of the huge public packet-switched network may be busier than others. When this happens, the routers that make up this system will communicate with one another so that traffic not bound for the crowded area can be sent by less congested network routes. This lets the network function at full capacity without excessively burdening already-busy areas.

Tracing a Message. If you're using a Microsoft-Windows-based system, you can see just how many routers are involved in your Internet traffic by using a program you have on your computer. The program is called **Traceroute,** and that describes what it does—it traces the route that a packet of information takes to get from your computer to another computer connected to the Internet. To run this program, click on the "MS-DOS Prompt" icon on the "Start". Then, at the **"C:\WINDOWS>"** prompt, type **"tracert www.vivekricha.com"**.

The first number shows how many routers are between your computer and the router shown. In this instance, there were a total of 14 routers involved in the process The next three numbers show how long it takes a packet of information to move from your computer to the router shown and back again. Next, in this example, starting with step six, comes the "name" of the router or server. This is something that helps people looking at the list but is of no importance to the routers and computers as they move traffic along the Internet. Finally, you see the Internet Protocol (IP) address of each computer or router. The final picture of this trace route shows that there were 14 routers between me and the Web server and that it took, on average, a little more than 2.5 seconds for information to get from my computer to the server and back again.

7.2 OPEN SYSTEM INTERCONNECTION ROUTING PROTOCOL

The International Organization for Standardization (ISO) developed a complete suite of routing protocols for use in the Open System Interconnection (OSI) protocol suite. These include Intermediate System-to-Intermediate System (IS-IS), End System-to-Intermediate System (ES-IS), and Interdomain Routing Protocol (IDRP). This chapter addresses the basic operations of each of these protocols.

IS-IS originally was developed to route in ISO Connectionless Network Protocol (CLNP) networks. A version has since been created that supports both CLNP and Internet Protocol (IP) networks; this version usually is referred to as Integrated IS-IS (it also has been called Dual IS-IS).

The world of OSI networking uses some specific terminology, such as *end system (ES)*, which refers to any nonrouting network nodes, and *intermediate system (IS)*, which refers to a router. These terms form the basis for the ES-IS and IS-IS OSI protocols. The ES-IS protocol enables ESs and ISs to discover each other. The IS-IS protocol provides routing between ISs.

Other important OSI networking terms include area, domain, Level 1 routing, and Level 2 routing. An *area* is a group of contiguous networks and attached hosts that is specified to be an area by a network administrator or manager. A *domain* is a collection of connected areas. Routing domains provide full connectivity to all end systems within them. *Level 1 routing* is routing within a Level 1 area, while *Level 2 routing* is routing between Level 1 areas.

7.2.1 End System-to-Intermediate System

End System-to-Intermediate System (ES-IS) is an OSI protocol that defines how end systems (hosts) and intermediate systems (routers) learn about each other, a process known as configuration. **Configuration** must happen before routing between ESs can occur.

ES-IS is more of a discovery protocol than a routing protocol. It distinguishes among three different types of subnetworks:

- point-to-point subnetworks,

- broadcast subnetworks, and
- general topology subnetworks.

Point-to-point subnetworks, such as WAN serial links, provide a point-to-point link between two systems. Broadcast subnetworks, such as Ethernet and IEEE 802.3, direct a single physical message to all nodes on the subnetwork. General topology subnetworks, such as X.25, support an arbitrary number of systems. Unlike broadcast subnetworks, however, the cost of an *n*-way transmission scales directly with the subnetwork size on a general topology subnetwork.

ES-IS Configuration. *ES-IS configuration* is the process whereby ESs and ISs discover each other so that routing between ESs can occur. ES-IS configuration information is transmitted at regular intervals through two types of messages: ES hello messages (ESHs) and IS hello messages (ISHs). ESHs are generated by ESs and are sent to every IS on the subnetwork. ISHs are generated by ISs and are sent to all ESs on the subnetwork. These hello messages primarily are intended to convey the subnetwork and network layer addresses of the systems that generate them. Where possible, ES-IS attempts to send configuration information simultaneously to many systems. On broadcast subnetworks, ES-IS hello messages are sent to all ISs through a special multicast address that designates all end systems. When operating on a general topology subnetwork, ES-IS generally does not transmit configuration information because of the high cost of multicast transmissions.

ES-IS Addressing Information. The ES-IS configuration protocol conveys both OSI network layer addresses and OSI subnetwork addresses. OSI network layer addresses identify either the network service access point (NSAP), which is the interface between OSI Layer 3 and Layer 4, or the network entity title (NET), which is the network layer entity in an OSI IS. OSI subnetwork addresses, or subnetwork point-of-attachment addresses (SNPAs) are the points at which an ES or IS is physically attached to a subnetwork. The SNPA address uniquely identifies each system attached to the subnetwork. In an Ethernet network, for example, the SNPA is the 48-bit Media Access Control (MAC) address. Part of the configuration information transmitted by ES-IS is the NSAP-to-SNPA or NET-to-SNPA mapping.

7.2.2 Intermediate System-to-Intermediate System

Intermediate System to Intermediate System (IS-IS) is a similar protocol to OSPF: it also uses a Link State, Shortest Path First algorithm However, IS-IS is an OSI protocol used for routing *Connectionless Network Protocol (CLNP)* packets within a routing domain. CLNP is the OSI protocol most comparable to IP.

Intermediate System-to-Intermediate System (IS-IS) is an OSI link-state hierarchical routing protocol that floods the network with link-state information to build a complete, consistent picture of network topology. To simplify router design and operation, IS-IS distinguishes between Level 1 and Level 2 ISs. Level 1 ISs communicate with other Level 1 ISs in the same area. Level 2 ISs route between Level 1 areas and form an intradomain routing backbone. Hierarchical routing simplifies backbone design because Level 1 ISs need to know only how to get to the nearest Level 2 IS. The backbone routing protocol also can change without impacting the intra-area routing protocol.

OSI Routing Operation. Each ES lives in a particular area. OSI routing begins when the ESs discover the nearest IS by listening to ISH packets. When an ES wants to send a packet to another ES, it sends the packet to one of the ISs on its directly attached network. The router then looks up the destination address and forwards the packet along the best route. If the destination ES is on the same subnetwork, the local IS will know this from listening to ESHs and will forward the packet appropriately. The IS also might provide a redirect (RD) message back to the source to tell it that a more direct route is available. If the destination address is an ES on another subnetwork in the same area, the IS will know the correct route and will forward the packet appropriately. If the destination address is an ES in another area, the Level 1 IS sends the packet to the nearest Level 2 IS. Forwarding through Level 2 ISs continues until the packet reaches a Level 2 IS in the destination area. Within the destination area, ISs forward the packet along the best path until the destination ES is reached.

Link-state update messages help ISs learn about the network topology. First, each IS generates an update specifying the ESs and ISs to which it is connected, as well as the associated metrics. The update then is sent to all neighboring ISs, which forward (flood) it to their neighbors, and so on. (Sequence numbers terminate the flood and distinguish old updates from new ones.) Using these updates, each IS can build a complete topology of the network. When the topology changes, new updates are sent.

IS-IS Metrics. IS-IS uses a single required default metric with a maximum path value of 1024. The metric is arbitrary and typically is assigned by a network administrator. Any single link can have a maximum value of 64, and path links are calculated by summing link values. Maximum metric values were set at these levels to provide the granularity to support various link types while at the same time ensuring that the shortest-path algorithm used for route computation will be reasonably efficient. IS-IS also defines three optional metrics (costs): delay, expense, and error. The delay cost metric reflects the amount of delay on the link. The expense cost metric reflects the communications cost associated with using the link. The error cost metric reflects the error rate of the link. IS-IS maintains a mapping of these four metrics to the quality of service (QoS) option in the CLNP packet header. IS-IS uses these mappings to compute routes through the internetwork.

Integrated IS-IS. *Integrated IS-IS* is a version of the OSI IS-IS routing protocol that uses a single routing algorithm to support more network layer protocols than just CLNP. Integrated IS-IS sometimes is called Dual IS-IS, named after a version designed for IP and CLNP networks. Several fields are added to IS-IS packets to allow IS-IS to support additional network layers. These fields inform routers about the reachability of network addresses from other protocol suites and other information required by a specific protocol suite. Integrated IS-IS implementations send only one set of routing updates, which is more efficient than two separate implementations.

Integrated IS-IS represents one of two ways of supporting multiple network layer protocols in a router; the other is the ships-in-the-night approach. Ships-in-the-night routing advocates the use of a completely separate and distinct routing protocol for each network protocol so that the multiple routing protocols essentially exist independently. The different types of routing information basically pass like ships in the night. Integrated routing has the capability to route multiple network layer protocols through tables calculated by a single routing protocol, thus saving some router resources. Integrated IS-IS uses this approach.

Here is an overview of some of the more important aspects of IS-IS routing. Where possible, comparisons are made with equivalent concepts used in OSPF but it is dangerous to draw too close a parallel, since there are fundamental differences between the two protocols.

- Routers are divided into Level 1 routers, which know nothing of the topology outside their areas, and Level 2 routers, which do know about the higher-level topology, but know nothing about the topology inside the areas unless they are also Level 1 routers.
- A Level 1 router may belong to more than one area, but unlike OSPF this is not for routing purposes but for ease of management of the domain, and would normally be short term: A Level 1 router recognizes another as a neighbor if they are both in the same area.
- A Level 2 router recognizes all other Level 2 routers as neighbors. A Level 2 router may also be a Level 1 router in one area, but not more.
- A Level 1 router in IS-IS cannot have a link to an external router (in OSPF an internal router can be an AS border router).
- There is a Level 2 backbone containing all Level 2 routers, but unlike in OSPF, it must be physically connected.
- The OSI addressing scheme explicitly identifies the target area for a packet, allowing simple selection of routing choices as follows:
  - o Level 2 routers route towards the area without regard to its internal structure.
  - o Level 1 routers route towards the destination if it is within their area, or to the nearest Level 2 router if it is not.
- Multiaccess networks use a Designated Router concept. To avoid the "$n(n-1)/2$" problem described under OSPF, IS-IS implements a *pseudo-node* for the LAN. Each LAN-attached router is regarded as having a link to the pseudo-node but no link to any of the other routers on the LAN. The Designated Router then acts on behalf of the pseudo-node.

7.2.3 Interdomain Routing Protocol

The *Interdomain Routing Protocol (IDRP)* is an OSI protocol that specifies how routers communicate with routers in different domains. IDRP is designed to operate seamlessly with CLNP, ES-IS, and IS-IS. **IDRP is based on the Border Gateway Protocol (BGP)**, an interdomain routing protocol that originated in the IP community. IDRP features include the following:

1. Support for CLNP quality of service (QoS)
2. Loop suppression by keeping track of all RDs traversed by a route
3. Reduction of route information and processing by using confederations, the compression of RD path information, and other means

4. Reliability by using a built-in reliable transport
5. Security by using cryptographic signatures on a per-packet basis
6. Route servers

IDRP Terminology. IDRP introduces several environment-specific terms. These include border intermediate system (BIS), routing domain (RD), routing domain identifier (RDI), routing information base (RIB), and confederation.

A *BIS* is an IS that participates in interdomain routing and, as such, uses IDRP. An *RD* is a group of ESs and ISs that operate under the same set of administrative rules and that share a common routing plan. An *RDI* is a unique RD identifier. An *RIB* is a routing database used by IDRP that is built by each BIS from information received from within the RD and from other BISs. A RIB contains the set of routes chosen for use by a particular BIS. A *confederation* is a group of RDs that appears to RDs outside the confederation as a single RD. The confederation's topology is not visible to RDs outside the confederation. Confederations must be nested within one another and help reduce network traffic by acting as internetwork firewalls. Figure 7.1 illustrates the relationship between IDRP entities.

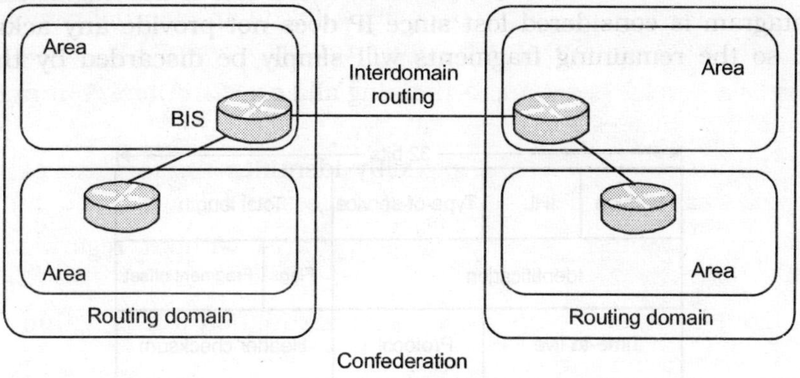

Figure 7.1 Domains Communicate via Border Intermediate Systems (BISs)

IDRP Routing. An IDRP route is a sequence of RDIs, some of which can be confederations. Each BIS is configured to know the RD and the confederations to which it belongs. It learns about other BISs, RDs, and confederations through information exchanges with each neighbor. As with distance-vector routing, routes to a particular destination accumulate outward from the destination. Only routes that satisfy a BIS's local policies and that have been selected for use will be passed on to other BISs. Route recalculation is partial and occurs when one of three events occurs: an incremental routing update with new routes is received, a BIS neighbor goes down, or a BIS neighbor comes up.

7.3 INTERNET PROTOCOL (IP)

The Internet Protocol (IP) is a network-layer (Layer 3) protocol that contains addressing information and some control information that enables packets to be routed. IP is documented in RFC 791 and is the primary network-layer protocol in the Internet protocol suite. Along with the Transmission Control Protocol (TCP), IP represents the heart of the Internet protocols. IP has two primary responsibilities: providing connectionless, best-effort delivery of datagrams through an internetwork; and providing fragmentation and reassembly of datagrams to support data links with different maximum-transmission unit (MTU) sizes.

7.3.1 IP Datagram

The Internet datagram (IP datagram) is the base transfer packet in the Internet protocol suite. It has a header containing information for IP, and data that is relevant only to the higher level protocols. The IP datagram is encapsulated in the underlying network's frame, which usually has a maximum length or frame limitation, depending on the hardware used. For Ethernet, this will typically be 1500 bytes. Instead of limiting the IP datagram length to some maximum size, IP can deal with *fragmentation* and *re-assembly* of its datagrams. In particular, the IP standard does not impose a maximum size, but states that all subnetworks should be able to handle datagrams of at least 576 bytes.Fragments of a datagram all have a header, basically copied from the original datagram, and data following it. They are treated as normal IP datagrams while being transported to their destination. Note, however, that if one of the fragments gets lost, the complete datagram is considered lost since IP does not provide any acknowledgement mechanism, so the remaining fragments will simply be discarded by the destination host.

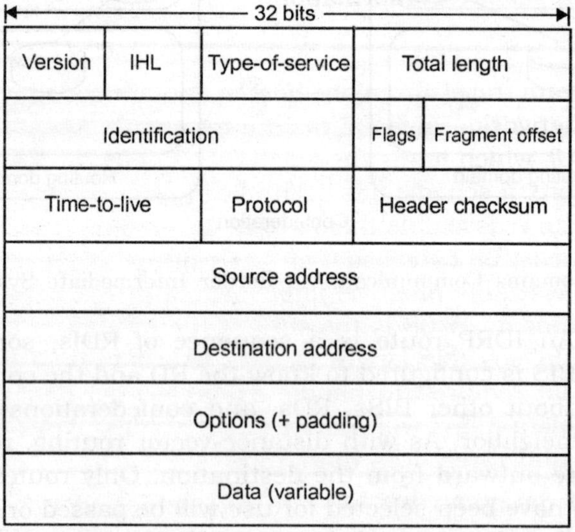

Figure 7.2 Fields Comprise an IP Packet

Version. Indicates the version of IP currently used.

IP Header Length (IHL). Indicates the datagram header length in 32-bit words.

Type-of-Service. Specifies how an upper-layer protocol would like a current datagram to be handled, and assigns datagrams various levels of importance.

Total Length. Specifies the length, in bytes, of the entire IP packet, including the data and header.

Identification. Contains an integer that identifies the current datagram. This field is used to help piece together datagram fragments.

Flags. Consists of a 3-bit field of which the two low-order (least-significant) bits control fragmentation. The low-order bit specifies whether the packet can be fragmented. The middle bit specifies whether the packet is the last fragment in a series of fragmented packets. The third or high-order bit is not used.

Fragment Offset. Indicates the position of the fragment's data relative to the beginning of the data in the original datagram, which allows the destination IP process to properly reconstruct the original datagram.

Time-to-Live. Maintains a counter that gradually decrements down to zero, at which point the datagram is discarded. This keeps packets from looping endlessly.

Protocol. Indicates which upper-layer protocol receives incoming packets after IP processing is complete.

Header Checksum. Helps ensure IP header integrity.

Source Address. Specifies the sending node.

Destination Address. Specifies the receiving node.

Options. Allows IP to support various options, such as security.

Data. Contains upper-layer information.

7.3.2 Fragmentation

When an IP datagram travels from one host to another, it can cross different physical networks. Physical networks have a maximum frame size, called the *Maximum Transmission Unit (MTU)*, which limits the length of a datagram that can be placed in one physical frame. Therefore, a scheme has been put in place to fragment long IP datagram into smaller ones, and to reassemble them at the destination host. IP requires that each link has an MTU of at least 68 bytes, so if any network provides a lower value than this, fragmentation and re-assembly must be implemented in the network interface layer in a way that is transparent to IP. 68 is the sum of the maximum IP header length of 60 bytes and the minimum possible length of data in a non-final fragment (8 bytes). IP implementations are not required to handle unfragmented datagram larger than 576 bytes, but most implementations will handle larger values, typically slightly more than 8192 bytes or higher, and rarely less than 1500.

An unfragmented datagram has all-zero fragmentation information. That is, the more fragments flag bit is zero and the fragment offset is zero. When fragmentation is to be done, the following steps are performed:

1. The DF flag bit is checked to see if fragmentation is allowed. If the bit is set, the datagram will be discarded and an error will be returned to the originator using ICMP.

2. Based on the MTU value, the data field is split into two or more parts. All newly created data portions must have a length which is a multiple of 8 bytes, with the exception of the last data portion.

3. All data portions are placed in IP datagram. The header of these datagram are copies of the original one, with some modifications:
   - 3.1 The more fragments flag bit is set in all fragments except the last.
   - 3.2 The fragment offset field in each is set to the location this data portion occupied in the original datagram, relative to the beginning of the original unfragmented datagram. The offset is measured in 8-byte units.
   - 3.3 If options were included in the original datagram, the high order bit of the option type byte determines whether or not they will be copied to all fragment datagram or just to the first one. For instance, source route options have to be copied in all fragments and therefore they have this bit set.
   - 3.4 The header length field is of the new datagram is set.
   - 3.5 The total length field of the new datagram is set.
   - 3.6 The header checksum field is re-calculated.
4. Each of these fragmented datagram is now forwarded as a normal IP datagram. IP handles each fragment independently, that is, the fragments may traverse different routers to the intended destination, and they may be subject to further fragmentation if they pass through networks that have smaller MTUs.

At the destination host, the data has to be reassembled into one datagram. The identification field of the datagram was set by the sending host to a unique number (for the source host, within the limits imposed by the use of a 16-bit number). As fragmentation doesn't alter this field, incoming fragments at the receiving side can be identified, if this ID field is used together with the Source and Destination IP addresses in the datagram. The Protocol field is also be checked for this identification.

In order to reassemble the fragments, the receiving host allocates a buffer in storage as soon as the first fragment arrives. A timer routine is then started. When the timer timeouts and not all of the fragments have been received, the datagram is discarded. The initial value of this timer is called the IP datagram time-to-live (TTL) value. It is implementation dependent, and some implementations allow it to be configured; for example AIX Version 3.2 provides an *ipfragttl* option with a default value of 60 seconds.

When subsequent fragments of the datagram arrive, before the timer expires, the data is simply copied into the buffer storage, at the location indicated by the fragment offset field. As soon as all fragments have arrived, the complete original unfragmented datagram is restored, and processing continues, just as for unfragmented datagrams.

Note: IP does not provide the reassembly timer. It will treat each and every datagram, fragmented or not, the same way, that is, as individual messages. It is up to the higher layer to implement a timeout and to look after any missing fragments. The higher layer could be TCP for a connection-oriented transport network or the application for connectionless transport networks based upon UDP and IP. The netstat command may be used on some TCP/IP hosts to list details of fragmentation that is occurring. An example of this is the netstat -i command in TCP/IP for OS/2.

7.3.3 Internet Timestamp

A timestamp is an option forcing some (or all) of the routers on the route to the destination to put a timestamp in the option data. The timestamps are measured in seconds and can be used for debugging purposes. They cannot be used for performance measurement for two reasons:

1. They are insufficiently precise because most IP datagrams will be forwarded in less than one second.
2. They are insufficiently accurate because IP routers are not required to have synchronized clocks.

A 32-bit timestamp recorded in milliseconds since midnight UT (GMT). The originating host must compose this option with a large enough data area to hold all the timestamps. If the timestamp area becomes full, no further timestamps are added.

7.3.4 Addressing

Internet addresses can be symbolic or numeric. The symbolic form is easier to read, for example: vivekricha@yahoo.com. The numeric form is a 32-bit unsigned binary value which is usually expressed in a dotted decimal format. For example, 9.167.5.8 is a valid Internet address. The numeric form is used by the IP software. The mapping between the two is done by the *Domain Name System.* We shall first look at the numeric form, which is called the IP address.

To be able to identify a host on the internet, each host is assigned an address, the *IP address*, or *Internet Address*. When the host is attached to more than one network, it is called *multi-homed* and it has one IP address for each network interface. The IP address consists of a pair of numbers:

IP address = <network number><host number>

The *network number* part of the IP address is centrally administered by the Internet Network Information Center (the InterNIC) and is unique throughout the Internet. IP addresses are 32-bit numbers usually represented in a *dotted decimal* form (as the decimal representation of four 8-bit values concatenated with dots). For example *128.2.7.9* is an IP address with 128.2 being the network number and 7.9 being the host number. The rules used to divide an IP address into its network and host parts are explained below.

The binary format of the IP address 128.2.7.9 is:

10000000 00000010 00000111 00001001

IP addresses are used by the IP protocol to uniquely identify a host on the internet. IP datagrams (the basic data packets exchanged between hosts) are transmitted by some physical network attached to the host and each IP datagram contains a *source IP address* and a *destination IP address.* To send a datagram to a certain IP destination, the target IP address must be translated or mapped to a physical address. This may require transmissions on the network to find out the destination's physical network address (for example, on LANs the Address Resolution Protocol, is used to translate IP addresses to physical MAC addresses).

The first bits of the IP address specify how the rest of the address should be separated into its network and host part. The terms *network address* and *netID* are sometimes used instead of network number. Similarly, the terms *host address* and *hostID* are sometimes used instead of host number. As with any other network-layer protocol, the IP addressing scheme is integral to the process of routing IP datagrams through an internetwork. Each IP address has specific components and follows a basic format. These IP addresses can be subdivided and used to create addresses for subnetworks, as discussed in more detail later in this chapter.

Each host on a TCP/IP network is assigned a unique 32-bit logical address that is divided into two main parts: the network number and the host number. The network number identifies a network and must be assigned by the Internet Network Information Center (InterNIC) if the network is to be part of the Internet. An Internet Service Provider (ISP) can obtain blocks of network addresses from the InterNIC and can itself assign address space as necessary. The host number identifies a host on a network and is assigned by the local network administrator.

IP Address Format. The 32-bit IP address is grouped eight bits at a time, separated by dots, and represented in decimal format (known as *dotted decimal notation*). Each bit in the octet has a binary weight (128, 64, 32, 16, 8, 4, 2, 1). The minimum value for an octet is 0, and the maximum value for an octet is 255. Figure 7.3 illustrates the basic format of an IP address.

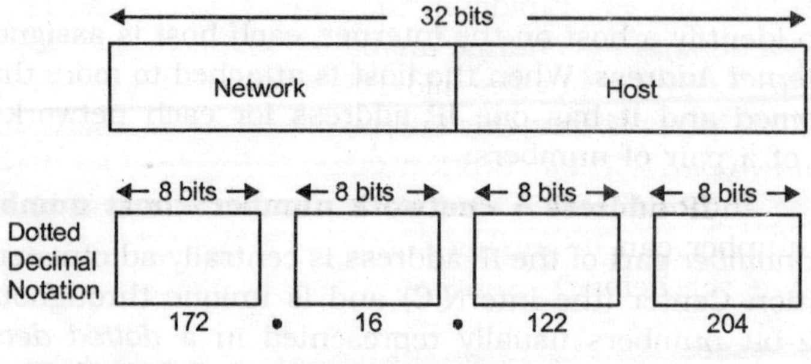

Figure 7.3 An IP Address Consists of 32 bits, Grouped into Four Octets

IP Address Classes. IP addressing supports five different address classes: A, B,C, D, and E. Only classes A, B, and C are available for commercial use. The left-most (high-order) bits indicate the network class. Table 7.1 Provides reference information about the five IP address classes.

TABLE 7.1. Reference information about the five IP address classes

IP address class	*Format*	*Purpose*	*High-order bit(s)*	*Address range*	*No. Bits network/ host*	*Max. Hosts*
A	N.H.H.H	Few large organizations	0	1.0.0.0 to 126.0.0.0	7/24	16,777, (2^{24} – 2)
B	N.N.H.H	Medium-size organizations	1, 0	128.1.0.0 to 191.254.0.0	14/16	65, 543 (2^{16} – 2)

C	N.N.N.H	Relatively small organizations	1, 1, 0	192.0.1.0 to 223.255.254.0	22/8	245 ($2^8 - 2$)
D	N/A	Multicast groups (RFC 1112)	1, 1, 1,0	224.0.0.0 to 239.255.255.255	N/A (not for commercial use)	N/A
E	N/A	Experimental	1, 1, 1, 1	240.0.0.0 to 254.255.255.255	N/A	N/A

[1]N = Network number, H = Host number. [2]One address is reserved for the broadcast address, and one address is reserved for the network.

The class of address can be determined easily by examining the first octet of the address and mapping that value to a class range in the following table. In an IP address of 172.31.1.2, for example, the first octet is 172. Because 172 falls between 128 and 191, 172.31.1.2 is a Class B address.

It is clear that a class A address will only be assigned to networks with a huge number of hosts, and that class C addresses are suitable for networks with a small number of hosts. However, this means that medium-sized networks (those with more than 254 hosts or where there is an expectation that there may be more than 254 hosts in the future) must use Class B addresses. The number of small- to medium-sized networks has been growing very rapidly in the last few years and it was feared that, if this growth had been allowed to continue unabated, all of the available Class B network addresses would have been used by the mid-1990s. One point to note about the split of an IP address into two parts is that this split also splits the responsibility for selecting the IP address into two parts. The network number is assigned by the InterNIC, and the host number by the authority which controls the network. As we shall see in the next section, the host number can be further subdivided: this division is controlled by the authority which owns the network, and *not* by the InterNIC.

7.3.5 Special IP Addresses

As noted above, any component of an IP address with a value

1. "all bits 0" or all "all bits 1" has a special meaning all bits 0 stands for "this": "this" host (IP address with <host number>=0) or "this" network (IP address with <network number>=0) and is only used when the real value is not known. This form is only used in source addresses when the host is trying to determine its IP addresses from a remote server.

2. all bits 1 stands for "all": "all" networks or "all" hosts. For example, 128.2.255.255 (a class B address with a host number of 255.255) means all hosts on network 128.2. These are used in broadcast messages, as described below.

There is another address of special importance: the "all bits 1" class A network number 127 is reserved for the *loopback address*. Anything sent to an address with 127 as the value of the high order byte, for example 127.0.0.1, must not be routed via a network but must be routed directly from the IP implementation's output driver to its input driver.

Unicast, Broadcast and Multicasting. The majority of IP addresses refer to a single recipient: these are called *unicast* addresses. However, as noted above, there are two special types of IP address which are used for addressing multiple recipients: broadcast addresses and multicast addresses. These addresses are used for sending messages to multiple recipients. Any protocol which is *connectionless* may send broadcast or multicast messages as well as unicast messages. A protocol which is *connection-oriented* can only use unicast addresses because the connection exists between a specific pair of hosts.

Broadcasting

There are a number of addresses which are used for IP broadcasting: all use the convention that "all-bits 1" indicates "all". Broadcast addresses are never valid as source addresses, only as destination addresses. **The different types of broadcast addresses are listed here:**

1. Limited broadcast address

The address 255.255.255.255 (all bits 1 in all parts of the IP address) is used on networks which support broadcasting, such as token rings, and it refers to all hosts on the subnet. It does not require the host to know any IP configuration information at all. All hosts on the local network will recognize the address, but routers will never forward it.

2. Network-directed broadcast address

If the network number is a valid network number, the network is not subnetted and the host number is all ones (for example, 128.2.255.255), then the address refers to all hosts on the specified network. Routers should forward these broadcast messages unless configured otherwise. This is used in ARP requests on unsubnetted networks.

3. Subnet-directed broadcast address

If the network number is a valid network number, the subnet number is a valid subnet number and the host number is all ones, then the address refers to all hosts on the specified subnet. Since the sender's subnet and the target subnet may have different subnet mask, the sender must somehow find out the subnet mask in use at the target. The actual broadcast is performed by the router which receives the datagram into the subnet.

4. All-subnets-directed broadcast address

If the network number is a valid network number, the network is subnetted and the local part is all ones (for example, 128.2.255.255), then the address refers to all hosts on all subnets in the specified network. In principle routers may propagate broadcasts for all subnets but are not required to do so. In practice, they do not; there are few circumstances where such a broadcast would be desirable, and it can lead to problems, particularly if a host has been incorrectly configured with no subnet mask. Consider the wasted resource involved if a host 9.180.214.114 in the subnetted Class A network 9 thought that it was not subnetted and used 9.255.255.255 as a "local" broadcast address instead of 9.180.214.255 and all of the routers in the network respected the request to forward the request to all clients.

If routers do respect all-subnets-directed broadcast address they use an algorithm called *Reverse Path Forwarding* to prevent the broadcast messages from multiplying out of control. See RFC 922 for more details on this algorithm.

Multicasting

Broadcasting has a major disadvantage: its lack of selectivity. If an IP datagram is broadcast to a subnet, every host on the subnet will receive it, and have to process it to determine whether the target protocol is active. If it is not, the IP datagram is discarded. Multicasting avoids this overhead by using groups of IP addresses.

Each group is represented by a 28-bit number, which is included in a Class D address. Recall that a class D address has the format: So *multicast group addresses* are IP addresses in the range 224.0.0.0 to 239.255.255.255. For each multicast address there is a set of zero or more hosts which are listening to it. This set is called the *host group*. There is no requirement for any host to be a member of a group to send to that group. There are two kinds of host group:

1. **Permanent.** The IP address is permanently assigned by IANA. The membership of a host group is not permanent: a host may leave or join the group at will.
2. **Transient.** Any group which is not permanent is transient and is available for dynamic assignment as needed. Transient groups cease to exist when their membership drops to zero.

Multicasting on a single physical network which supports the use of multicasting is simple. To join a group, a process running on a host must somehow inform its network device drivers that it is wishes to be a member of the specified group. The device driver software itself must map the multicast address to a physical multicast address and enable the reception of packets for that address. The device driver must also ensure that the receiving process does not receive any spurious datagrams by checking the destination address in the IP header before passing it to the IP layer.

For example, Ethernet supports multi-casting if the high-order byte of the 48-byte address is X'01' and IANA owns an Ethernet address block, which consists of the addresses between X'00005E000000' and X'00005EFFFFFF'. The lower half of this range has been assigned by IANA for multicast addresses, so on an Ethernet LAN there is a range of physical addresses between X'01005E000000' and X'01005E7FFFFF' which is used for IP multicasting. This range has 23 usable bits, so the 28-bit multicast addresses are mapped to the Ethernet addresses by considering the low-order 23 bits, that is 32 multicast addresses are mapped to each Ethernet address. Because of this non-unique mapping, filtering by the device driver is required. There are two other reasons why filtering might still be needed:

1. Some LAN adapters are limited to a finite number of concurrent multicast addresses and if this is exceeded they must receive all multicasts.
2. Other LAN adapters tend to filter according to a hash table value rather than the whole address, which means that there is a chance that two multicast addresses with the same hash value might be in use at the same time and the filter might "leak".

Despite this requirement for software filtering of multicast packets, multicasting still causes much less overhead for hosts that are not interested. In particular, those hosts that are not in any host group are not listening to any multicast addresses and all multicast messages are filtered by the network interface hardware.

Multicasting is not limited to a single physical network. There are two aspects to multicasting across physical networks:

1. A mechanism for deciding how widespread the multicast is (remember that unlike unicast addresses and broadcast addresses) multicast addresses cover the entire Internet.
2. A mechanism for deciding whether a multicast datagram needs to be forwarded to a particular network.

7.3.6 The IP Exhaustion Problem

The number of networks on the Internet has been approximately doubling annually for a number of years. However, the usage of the Class A, B and C networks differs greatly: nearly all of the new networks assigned in the late 1980s were Class B, and in 1990 it became apparent that if this trend continued, the last Class B network number would be assigned during 1994. On the other hand, Class C networks were hardly being used.

The reason for this trend was that most potential users found a Class B network to be large enough for their anticipated needs, since it accommodates up to 65534 hosts, whereas a class C network, with a maximum of 254 hosts, severely restricts the potential growth of even a small initial network. Furthermore, most of the class B networks being assigned were small ones. There are relatively few networks that would need as many as 65,534 host addresses, but very few for which 254 hosts would be an adequate limit. In summary, although the Class A, Class B and Class C divisions of the IP address are logical and easy to use (because they occur on byte boundaries), with hindsight they are not the most practical because Class C networks are too small to be useful for most organizations while Class B networks are too large to be densely populated by any but the largest organizations.

Private Internets. Approach to conservation of the IP address space is described as - *Address Allocation for Private Internets.* Briefly, it relaxes the rule that IP addresses are globally unique by reserving part of the address space for networks which are used exclusively within a single organization and which do not require IP connectivity to the Internet. There are three ranges of addresses which have been reserved by IANA for this purpose:

1. *10* A single Class A network
2. *172.16 through 172.31* 16 contiguous Class B networks
3. *192.168.0 through 192.168.255* 256 contiguous Class C networks

Any organization may use any addresses in these ranges without reference to any other organization. However, because these addresses are not globally unique, they cannot be referenced by hosts in another organization and they are not defined to any external routers. Routers in networks not using private addresses, particularly those operated by Internet service providers, are expected to quietly discard all routing information regarding these addresses. Routers in an organization using private addresses are expected to limit all references to private addresses to internal links; they should neither advertise routes to private addresses to external routers nor forward IP datagrams containing private addresses to via external routers. Hosts having only a private IP address do not have IP-layer connectivity to the Internet. This may be desirable and may even be a reason for using private addressing. All connectivity to external Internet hosts must be provided with application gateways.

Classless Inter-Domain Routing (CIDR). There is a major problem with the use of a range of Class C addresses instead of a single Class B addresses: each network must be routed separately. Standard IP routing understands only the class A, B and C network classes. Within each of these types of network, subnetting can be used to provided better granularity of the address space within each network, but there is no way to specify that multiple class C networks are actually related. The result of this is termed the *routing table explosion* problem: a Class B network of 3000 hosts requires one routing table entry at each backbone router, but if the same network is addressed as a range of Class C networks, it requires 16 entries.

The solution to this problem is a scheme called *Classless Inter-Domain Routing (CIDR)*. CIDR is a *proposed standard protocol* with a status of *elective*.

CIDR does not route according to the class of the network number (hence the term classless) but solely according to the high order bits of the IP address which are termed the *IP prefix*. Each CIDR routing entry contains a 32 bit IP address and a 32 bit network mask, which together give the length and value of the IP prefix. This can be represented as <IP_address network_mask>. For example <194.0.0.0 254.0.0.0> represents the 7 bit IP prefix B'1100001'. CIDR handles the routing for a group of networks with a common prefix with a single routing entry. This is the reason why multiple Class C network numbers assigned to a single organization have a common prefix. This process of combining multiple networks into a single entry is termed *address aggregation* or *address summarization*. It is also called *supernetting* because routing is based upon network masks which are shorter than the *natural* network mask of the IP address, in contrast to *subnetting* where the network masks are longer than the natural mask.

Unlike subnet masks, which are normally contiguous but may have a discontiguous local part, supernet masks are *always* contiguous. If IP addresses are represented with a tree showing the routing topology, with each leaf of the tree representing a group of networks which are considered as a single unit (called a *routing domain*) and the IP addressing scheme is chosen so that each fork in this tree corresponds to an increase in the length of the IP prefix, then CIDR allows address aggregation to be performed very efficiently. For example, if a router in North America routes all European traffic via a single link, then a single routing entry for <194.0.0.0 254.0.0.0> includes the group of Class C network addresses assigned to Europe as described above. This single entry takes the place of all the entries for all of the assigned network numbers in this range which is a possible maximum of 2(superscript 17) or 131,072 numbers. At the European end of this link, there are routing entries with longer prefixes which map to the European network topology but this routing information is not needed at the American end of the link. CIDR uses a *longest match is best* approach, so if the router in the US needs to make an exception for one range of addresses, such as the 64 network range <95.1.64.0 255.555.192.0> it needs just one additional entry, since this entry overrides the more general (shorter) one for those networks it contains. It is apparent from this example that as the usage of the IP address space increases, particularly the Class C address space, the benefits of CIDR increase as well, provided that the assignment of addresses follows the network topology. The existing state of the IP address space does not follow such a scheme since it pre-dates the development of CIDR. However, new Class C addresses are being assigned in such a way as to enable CIDR, and this should have the effect of alleviating the routing table explosion problem in the near term. In the longer term, a restructuring of the IP address space along topological lines may be necessary. This would involve the re-numbering of a large number of networks, implying an enormous amount of implementation effort, and so would be a gradual process.

It is an over-simplification to assume that routing topology can be represented as a simple tree; although most routing domains have a single attachment which provides access to the rest of the Internet, there are also many domains which have multiple attachments. Routing domains of these two types are called *single-homed* and *multi-homed.* Furthermore, the topology is not static. Not only are new organizations joining the Internet at an ever-increasing rate, but existing organizations may change places within the topology, for example if they change between service providers for commercial or other reasons. Although such cases complicate the practical implementation of CIDR-based routing and reduce the efficiency of address aggregation that can be achieved, they do not invalidate the approach.

The current Internet address allocation policies and the assumptions on which those policies were based is described in *RFC 1518 - An Architecture for IP Address Allocation with CIDR.* They can be summarized as follows:

1. IP address assignment reflects the physical topology of the network and not the organizational topology; wherever organizational and administrative boundaries do not match the network topology, they should *not* be used for the assignment of IP addresses.
2. In general, network topology will closely follow continental and national boundaries and therefore IP addresses should be assigned on this basis.
3. There will be a relatively small set of networks which carry a large amount of traffic between routing domains and which will be interconnected in a non-hierarchical way and which will cross national boundaries. These are referred to as *transit routing domains (TRDs).* Each TRD will have a unique IP prefix. TRDs will not be organized in a hierarchical way where there is no appropriate hierarchy. However, wherever a TRD is wholly within a continental boundary, its IP prefix should be an extension of the continental IP prefix.
4. There will be many organizations which have attachments to other organizations which are for the private use of those two organizations and which do not carry traffic intended for other domains (transit traffic). Such private connections do not have a significant effect on the routing topology and can be ignored.
5. The great majority of routing domains will be single-homed. That is, they will be attached to a single TRD. They should be assigned addresses which begin

with that TRD's IP prefix. All of the addresses for all single-homed domains attached to a TRD can therefore be aggregated into a single routing table entry for all domains outside that TRD.

There are a number of address assignment schemes which can be used for multi-homed domains. These include:

1. The use of a single IP prefix for the domain. External routers must have an entry for the organization which lies partly or wholly outside the normal hierarchy. Where a domain is multi-homed, but all of the attached TRDs themselves are topologically nearby, it would be appropriate for the domain's IP prefix to include those bits common to all of the attached TRDs. For example, if all of the TRD's were wholly within the United States, an IP prefix implying an exclusively North American domain would be appropriate.
2. The use of one IP prefix for each attached TRD, with hosts in the domain having IP addresses containing the IP prefix of the most appropriate TRD. The organization appears to be a set of routing domains.
3. Assigning an IP prefix from one of the attached TRDs. This TRD becomes a default TRD for the domain but other domains may explicitly route by one of the alternative TRDs.
4. The use of IP prefixes to refer to sets of multi-homed domains having the TRD attachments. For example there may be an IP prefix to refer to single-homed domains attached to network A, one to refer to single-homed domains attached to network B and one to refer to dual-homed domains attached to networks A and B.

Each of these has various advantages, disadvantages and side effects. For example, the first approach tends to result in inbound traffic entering the target domain closer to the sending host than the second approach, and therefore in a larger proportion of the network costs being incurred by the receiving organization.

Because multi-homed domains may vary greatly in character and none of the above schemes is suitable for all such domains, there is no single policy which is best and RFC 1518 does not specify any rules for choosing between them.

CIDR Implementation

The implementation of CIDR in the Internet is primarily based on *Border Gateway Protocol Version 4*. In future CIDR will also be implemented by a variant of the ISO standard *Inter-Domain Routing Protocol (IDRP, ISO 10747)*, called IDRP for IP, which is closely related to BGP-4.

Network service providers are divided into four types:

Type 1 Those which cannot employ any default inter-domain routing.

Type 2 Those which use default inter-domain routing but which require explicit routes for a substantial proportion of the assigned IP network numbers.

Type 3 Those which use default inter-domain routing and supplement it with a small number of explicit routes.

Type 4 Those which perform all inter-domain routing using only default routes.

The CIDR implementation involves an implementation beginning with the Type 1 network providers, then the Type 2 and finally the Type 3 ones. CIDR has already been widely deployed in the backbone and over 9,000 class-based routes have been replaced by approximately 2,000 CIDR-based routes.

IP Subnet Addressing. IP networks can be divided into smaller networks called subnetworks (or subnets). Subnetting provides the network administrator with several benefits, including extra flexibility, more efficient use of network addresses, and the capability to contain broadcast traffic (a broadcast will not cross a router).

Subnets are under local administration. As such, the outside world sees an organization as a single network and has no detailed knowledge of the organization's internal structure.A given network address can be broken up into many subnetworks. For example, 172.16.1.0, 172.16.2.0, 172.16.3.0, and 172.16.4.0 are all subnets within network 171.16.0.0. (All 0s in the host portion of an address specifies the entire network.)

IP Subnet Mask

A subnet address is created by "borrowing" bits from the host field and designating them as the subnet field. The number of borrowed bits varies and is specified by the subnet mask. Figure 7.4 shows how bits are borrowed from the host address field to create the subnet address field.

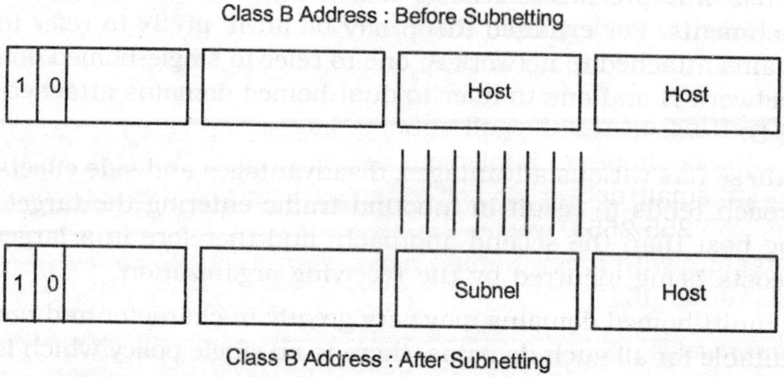

Figure 7.4 Bits are Borrowed from the Host Address Field to Create the Subnet Address Field

Subnet masks use the same format and representation technique as IP addresses. The subnet mask, however, has binary 1s in all bits specifying the network and subnetwork fields, and binary 0s in all bits specifying the host field. Subnet mask bits should come from the high-order (left-most) bits of the host field.

Various types of subnet masks exist for Class B and C subnets.

The default subnet mask for a Class B address that has no subnetting is 255.255.0.0, while the subnet mask for a Class B address 171.16.0.0 that specifies eight bits of subnetting is 255.255.255.0. The reason for this is that eight bits of subnetting or 2^8 – 2 (1 for the network address and 1 for the broadcast address) = 254 subnets possible, with $2^8 - 2 = 254$ hosts per subnet. The subnet mask for a Class C address 192.168.2.0 that specifies five bits of subnetting is 255.255.255.248.With five bits available for subnetting, $2^5 - 2 = 30$ subnets possible, with $2^3 - 2 = 6$ hosts per subnet.

Two simple guidelines exist for remembering logical AND operations: Logically "ANDing" a 1 with a 1 yields the original value, and logically "ANDing" a 0 with any number yields 0.

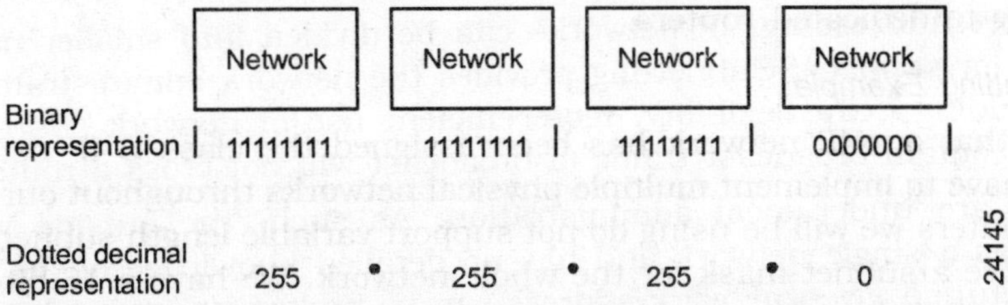

Figure 7.5 A Sample Subnet Mask Consists of all Binary 1s and 0s.

Types of Subnetting

There are three types of subnetting:

1. static,
2. variable length and

Variable length is the more flexible of the two. Which type of subnetting is available depends upon the routing protocol being used; native IP routing supports only static subnetting, as does the widely used RIP protocol.

Static Subnetting

Static subnetting means that all subnets in the subnetted network use the same subnet mask. This is simple to implement and easy to maintain, but it implies wasted address space for small networks. For example, a network of four hosts that uses a subnet mask of 255.255.255.0 wastes 250 IP addresses. It also makes the network more difficult to reorganize with a new subnet mask. Currently, almost every host and router supports static subnetting.

Variable Length Subnetting

When variable length subnetting is used, the subnets that make up the network may use different subnet masks. A small subnet with only a few hosts needs a subnet mask that accommodates only these few hosts. A subnet with many hosts attached may need a different subnet mask to accommodate the large number of hosts. The possibility to assign subnet masks according to the needs of the individual subnets will help conserve network addresses. Also, a subnet can be split into two parts by adding another bit to the subnet mask. Other subnets in the network are unaffected by the change. Not every host and router supports variable length subnetting. Only networks of the size needed will be allocated and routing problems will be solved by isolating networks with routers that support variable subnetting. A host that does not support this kind of subnetting would have to route to a router that supports variable subnetting.

Mixing Static and Variable Length Subnetting

At first sight, it appears that the presence of a host which only supports static subnetting would prevent variable length subnetting from being used anywhere in the network. Fortunately this is not the case. Provided that the routers between subnets with different subnet masks are using variable length subnetting, the routing protocols employed are able to hide the difference between subnet masks from the hosts in a subnet. Hosts can continue to use basic IP routing and offload all of the complexities of the subnetting to dedicated routers.

A Static Subnetting Example

Assume that our IP network has been assigned the class B IP network number 129.112. We have to implement multiple physical networks throughout our network. And some of the routers we will be using do not support variable length subnetting. We must therefore choose a subnet mask for the whole network. We have a 16-bit local address for our whole network and must divide it into two parts appropriately. At the moment, we do not anticipate having more than 254 physical networks, nor more than 254 hosts per network, so a logical subnet mask to use is 255.255.255.0 (which also has the advantage of being an "easily readable" one). This decision should be made with care, since it will be difficult to change it later. If the number of networks or hosts grows beyond the planned numbers, we may have to implement variable length subnetting to make the best use of the 65,534 local addresses we have.

Obtaining a Subnet Mask

Usually, hosts will store the subnet mask to be used in a configuration file. However, sometimes this cannot be done, as for example in the case of a diskless workstation. The ICMP protocol includes two messages, address mask request and address mask reply, which allow hosts to obtain the correct subnet mask from a server.

Addressing Routers and Multi-homed Hosts

Whenever a host has a physical connection to multiple networks or subnets, it is described as being *multi-homed.* All routers are multi-homed since their purpose is to join networks or subnets. A multi-homed host always has different IP addresses associated with each network adapter, since each adapter is in a different subnet or network.

There is one apparent exception to this rule: with some systems (for example VM and MVS) it is possible to specify the same IP address for multiple point-to-point links (such as channel-to-channel adapters) if the routing protocol used is limited to the basic IP routing algorithm. For example, a VM "hypervisor" system running TCP/IP connected to a token-ring LAN via a 3172 Interconnect Controller may run a number of "guest" VM and/or MVS systems. A very cost-effective solution for connecting these guests to the token-ring is to connect them to the hypervisor's TCP/IP with virtual channel-to-channel connections. The IP addresses can be chosen so that the channel-to-channel connected systems constitute their own subnet, in which case the hypervisor acts as a router. Because the routing protocols available on VM and MVS only support static subnetting, it may be difficult to find an additional subnet number if the address space is constrained. Therefore, the channel-to-channel connected systems may be given IP addresses in the same subnet as the token ring, in which case the hypervisor is taking the place of a bridge, and is *not* multi-homed. One disadvantage of this configuration is that other hosts on the LAN need static definitions to route datagrams for the hosts on the far side of the "bridge" via the hypervisor because the 3172 is not aware that it has this bridging responsibility.

7.4 COMMONLY USED PROTOCOLS

7.4.1 Address Resolution Protocol (ARP)

The address resolution protocol is responsible for converting the higher-level protocol addresses (IP addresses) to physical network addresses.

ARP Overview

On a single physical network, individual hosts are known on the network by their physical hardware address. Higher-level protocols address destination hosts in the form of a symbolic address (IP address in this case). When such a protocol wants to send a datagram to destination IP address w.x.y.z, the device driver does not understand this address.

Therefore, a module (ARP) is provided that will translate the IP address to the physical address of the destination host. It uses a lookup table (sometimes referred to as the *ARP cache*) to perform this translation.

When the address is not found in the ARP cache, a broadcast is sent out on the network, with a special format called the *ARP request.* If one of the machines on the network recognizes its own IP address in the request, it will send an *ARP reply* back to the requesting host. The reply will contain the physical hardware address of the host and source route information (if the packet has crossed bridges on its path). Both this address and the source route information are stored in the ARP cache of the requesting host. All subsequent datagrams to this destination IP address can now be translated to a physical address, which is used by the device driver to send out the datagram on the network. ARP was designed to be used on networks that support hardware broadcast. This means, for example, that ARP will not work on an X.25 network.

ARP Detailed Concept

ARP is used on IEEE 802 networks as well as on the older DIX Ethernet networks to map IP addresses to physical hardware addresses. To do this, it is closely related to the device driver for that network. The implementation depends to a large extent on the device driver for a network type and they are usually coded together in the *adapter microcode.*

ARP Packet Generation

If an application wishes to send data to a certain IP destination address, the IP routing mechanism first determines the IP address of the "next hop" of the packet (it can be the destination host itself, or a router) and the hardware device on which it should be sent. The ARP module tries to find the address in this ARP cache. If it finds the matching pair, it gives the corresponding 48-bit physical address back to the caller (the device driver) which then transmits the packet. If it doesn't find the pair in its table, it *discards the packet* (assumption is that a higher-level protocol will retransmit) and generates a network *broadcast* of an ARP request.

1. Hardware address space: Specifies the type of hardware; examples are Ethernet or Packet Radio Net.
2. Protocol address space: Specifies the type of protocol, same as EtherType field in the IEEE 802 header (IP or ARP).

1. Hardware address length: Specifies the length (in bytes) of the hardware addresses in this packet. For IEEF 802.3 and IEEE 802.5 this will be 6.
2. Protocol address length: Specifies the length (in bytes) of the protocol addresses in this packet. For IP this will be 4.
3. Operation code: Specifies whether this is an ARP request (1) or reply (2).
4. Source/target hardware address: Contains the physical network hardware addresses. For IEEE 802.3 these are 48-bit addresses.
5. Source/target protocol address: Contains the protocol addresses. For TCP/IP these are the 32-bit IP addresses.

For the ARP request packet, the target hardware address is the only undefined field in the packet.

ARP Packet Reception

When a host receives an ARP packet (either a broadcast request or a point-to-point reply), the receiving device driver passes the packet to the ARP module.The requesting host will receive ARP reply, and will follow the same algorithm to treat it. As a result of this, the triplet <protocol type, protocol address, hardware address> for the desired host will be added to its lookup table (ARP cache). The next time a higher-level protocol wants to send a packet to that host, the ARP module will find the target hardware address and the packet will be sent to that host.

Note that because the original ARP request was a broadcast on the network, all hosts on that network will have updated the sender's hardware address in their table (only if it was already in the table).

ARP and Subnets

The ARP protocol remains unchanged in the presence of subnets. Remember that each IP datagram first goes through the IP routing algorithm. This algorithm selects the hardware device driver which should send out the packet. Only then, the ARP module associated with that device driver is consulted.

Proxy-ARP Concept

Consider one IP network, which is divided into subnets, interconnected by routers. We use the "old" IP routing algorithm, which means that no host knows about the existence of multiple physical networks. Consider hosts A and B which are on different physical networks within the same IP network, and a router R between the two subnetworks: When host A wants to send an IP datagram to host B, it first has to determine the physical network address of host B through the use of the ARP protocol. As host A cannot differentiate between the physical networks, his IP routing algorithm thinks that host B is on the local physical network and sends out a broadcast ARP request. Host B doesn't receive this broadcast, but router R does. Router R understands subnets, that is, it runs the "subnet" version of the IP routing algorithm and it will be able to see that the destination of the ARP request (from the target protocol address field) is on another physical network. If router R's routing tables specify that the next hop to that other network is through a different physical device, it will reply to the ARP *as if it were host B*, saying that the network address of host B is that of the router R itself. Host A receives this ARP reply, puts it in his cache and will send future IP packets for host B to the router R. The router will forward such packets to the correct subnet.

The result is transparent subnetting:

- Normal hosts (such as A and B) don't know about subnetting, so they use the "old" IP routing algorithm.
- The routers between subnets have to:
  1. Use the "subnet" IP algorithm.
  2. Use a modified ARP module, which can reply on behalf of other hosts.

7.4.2 RARP Overview

Some network hosts, such as diskless workstations, do not know their own IP address when they are booted. To determine their own IP address, they use a mechanism similar to ARP (Address Resolution Protocol), but now the hardware address of the host is the known parameter, and the IP address the queried parameter. It differs more fundamentally from ARP in the fact that a "RARP server" must exist on the network which maintains a database of mappings from hardware address to protocol address.

RARP Concept

The reverse address resolution is performed the same way as the ARP address resolution. The same packet format is used as for ARP. And of course, the "physical" header of the frame will now indicate RARP as the higher-level protocol instead of ARP or IP in the *EtherType* field. Some differences arise from the concept of RARP itself:

- ARP only assumes that every host knows the mapping between its own hardware address and protocol address. RARP requires one or more server hosts on the network to maintain a database of mappings between hardware addresses and protocol addresses so that they will be able to reply to requests from client hosts.
- Due to the size this database can take, part of the server function is usually implemented outside the adapter's microcode, with optionally a small cache in the microcode. The microcode part is then only responsible for reception and transmission of the RARP frames, the RARP mapping itself being taken care of by server software running as a normal process in the host machine.
- The nature of this database also requires some software to create and update the database manually.

In case there are multiple RARP servers on the network, the RARP requester only uses the first RARP reply received on its broadcast RARP request, and discards the others.

7.4.3 Dynamic Host Configuration Protocol (DHCP)

The Dynamic Host Configuration Protocol (DHCP) provides a framework for passing configuration information to hosts on a TCP/IP network. DHCP is based on the BOOTP protocol, adding the capability of automatic allocation of reusable network addresses and additional configuration options. DHCP consists of two components:

1. A protocol that delivers host-specific configuration parameters from a DHCP server to a host.
2. A mechanism for the allocation of network addresses to hosts.

IP requires the setting of many parameters within the protocol implementation software. Because IP can be used on many dissimilar kinds of network hardware, values for those parameters cannot be guessed at or assumed to have correct defaults. The use of a distributed address allocation scheme based on a polling/defense mechanism, for discovery of network addresses already in use, cannot guarantee unique network addresses because hosts may not always be able to defend their network addresses.

DHCP supports three mechanisms for IP address allocation:

1. Automatic allocation: DHCP assigns a permanent IP address to the host.
2. Dynamic allocation: DHCP assigns an IP address for a limited period of time. Such a network address is called a *lease*. This is the only mechanism that allows automatic reuse of addresses that are no longer needed by the host to which it was assigned.
3. Manual allocation: The host's address is assigned by a network administrator.

Configuration Parameters Repository

DHCP provides persistent storage of network parameters for network clients. The model of DHCP persistent storage is that the DHCP service stores a key-value entry for each client, where the key is some unique identifier, for example an IP subnet number and a unique identifier within the subnet, and the value contains the configuration parameters for this particular client.

Allocating a New Network Address

This section describes the client/server interaction if the client does not know its network address. Assume that the DHCP server has a block of network addresses from which it can satisfy requests for new addresses. Each server also maintains a database of allocated addresses and leases in permanent local storage.

1. The client broadcasts a DHCPDISCOVER message on its local physical subnet. The DHCPDISCOVER message may include some options like network address suggestion or lease duration etc.
2. Each server may respond with a DHCPOFFER message that includes an available network address and other configuration options.
3. The client receives one or more DHCPOFFER messages from one or more servers. The client chooses one based on the configuration parameters offered and broadcasts a DHCPREQUEST message which includes the "server identifier" option to indicate which message it has selected.
4. The servers receive the DHCPREQUEST broadcast from the client. Those servers not selected by the DHCPREQUEST message use the message as notification that the client has declined that server's offer. The server selected in the DHCPREQUEST message commits the binding for the client to persistent storage and responds with a DHCPACK message containing the configuration

parameters for the requesting client. The combination of client hardware and assigned network address constitute a unique identifier for the client's lease and are used by both the client and server to identify a lease referred to in any DHCP messages. The "your IP address" field in the DHCPACK messages is filled in with the selected network address.

5. The client receives the DHCPACK message with configuration parameters. The client performs a final check on the parameters, for example with ARP for allocated network address, and notes the duration of the lease and the lease identification cookie specified in the DHCPACK message. At this point, the client is configured. If the client detects a problem with the parameters in the DHCPACK message, the client sends a DHCPDECLINE message to the server and restarts the configuration process. The client should wait a minimum of ten seconds before restarting the configuration process to avoid excessive network traffic in case of looping.

   If the client receives a DHCPNAK message, the client restarts the configuration process.

6. The client may choose to relinquish its lease on a network address by sending a DHCPRELEASE message to the server. The client identifies the lease to be released by including its network address and its hardware address.

7.4.4 ICMP

When a router or a destination host must inform the source host about errors in datagram processing, it uses the Internet Control Message Protocol (ICMP). ICMP can be characterized as follows:

- ICMP uses IP as if ICMP were a higher-level protocol (that is, ICMP messages are encapsulated in IP datagrams). However, ICMP is an integral part of IP and must be implemented by every IP module.
- ICMP is used to report some errors, *not* to make IP reliable. Datagrams may still be undelivered without any report on their loss. Reliability must be implemented by the higher-level protocols that use IP.
- ICMP can report errors on any IP datagram with the exception of ICMP messages, to avoid infinite repetitions.
- For fragmented IP datagrams, ICMP messages are only sent about errors on fragment zero. That is, ICMP messages never refer to an IP datagram with a non-zero fragment offset field.
- ICMP messages are never sent in response to datagrams with a destination IP address that is a broadcast or a multicast address.
- ICMP messages are never sent in response to a datagram which does not have a source IP address which represents a unique host. That is, the source address cannot be zero, a loopback address, a broadcast address or a multicast address.
- ICMP messages are never sent in response to ICMP error messages. They may be sent in response to ICMP query messages (ICMP types 0, 8, 9, 10 and 13 through 18).

- RFC 792 states that ICMP messages "may" be generated to report IP datagram processing errors, *not* "must". In practice, routers will almost always generate ICMP messages for errors, but for destination hosts, the number of ICMP messages generated is implementation dependent.

ICMP Messages

ICMP messages are sent in IP datagrams. The IP header will always have a Protocol number of 1, indicating ICMP and a type of service of zero (routine). The IP data field will contain the actual ICMP message.

Each of the messages is explained below.

1. *Destination unreachable*

If this message is received from an intermediate router, it means that the router regards the destination IP address as unreachable. If this message is received from the destination host, it means that the protocol specified in the protocol number field of the original datagram is not active, or that protocol is not active on this host or if the specified port is inactive.

2. *Source quench*

If this message is received from an intermediate router, it means that the router does not have the buffer space needed to queue the datagrams for output to the next network. If this message is received from the destination host, it means that the incoming datagrams are arriving too quickly to be processed.

3. *Redirect*

If this message is received from an intermediate router, it means that the host should send future datagrams for the network to the router whose IP address is given in the ICMP message. This preferred router will always be on the same subnet as the host which sent the datagram and the router which returned the IP datagram. The router will forward the datagram to its next hop destination. If the router IP address matches the source IP address in the original datagram header it indicates a routing loop. This ICMP will not be sent if the IP datagram contains a source route.

4. *Echo and echo reply*

Echo is used to detect if another host is active on the network. The sender initializes the identifier and sequence number (which is used if multiple echo requests are sent), adds some data to the data field and sends the ICMP echo to the destination host. The ICMP header code field is zero. The recipient changes the type to Echo Reply and returns the datagram to the sender. This mechanism is used by the Ping command to determine if a destination host is reachable .

5. *Router advertisement and router solicitation*

Each router on a subnet is responsible for advertising its own preference level. Larger values imply higher preference, smaller values imply lower. The default is zero, which is in the middle of the possible range. A value of X'80000000' –2(superscript 31) indicates that the router should never be used as a default router.

The default behavior is to send advertisements every 10 minutes with a TTL value of 1800 (30 minutes). Routers also reply to solicitation messages they receive. They may reply directly to the soliciting host, or they may wait a short random interval and reply with a multicast. Hosts may send solicitation messages when they start until they receive a response. Solicitation messages are sent to the all-routers multicast address (224.0.0.2) or the limited broadcast address (255.255.255.255). Typically, three solicitation messages are sent at 3-second intervals. Alternatively a host may wait for periodic advertisements. Each time a host receives an advertisement, it updates its default router if the new advertisement has one with a higher preference value and sets the TTL timer for the entry to match the value in the advertisement. When the host receives a new advertisement for its current default router, it resets the TTL value to that in the new advertisement. This also provides a mechanism for routers to declare themselves unavailable: they send an advertisement with a TTL value of zero.

6. *Time exceeded*

If this message is received from an intermediate router, it means that the time-to-live field of an IP datagram has expired. If this message is received from the destination host, it means that the IP fragment reassembly time-to-live timer has expired while the host is waiting for a fragment of the datagram.

7. *Parameter problem*

Indicates that a problem was encountered during processing of the IP header parameters. The pointer field points to the byte in the original IP datagram where the problem was encountered.

8. *Timestamp request and timestamp reply*

These two messages are for performance measurements and for debugging. They are not used for clock synchronization. The sender initializes the identifier and sequence number (which is used if multiple timestamp requests are sent), sets the originate timestamp and sends it to the recipient. The receiving host fills in the receive and transmit timestamps, changes the type to Timestamp reply and returns it to the recipient. The receiver has two timestamps in case there is a perceptible time difference between the receipt and transmit times, but in practice, most implementations will perform the two (receipt and reply) in one operation and will set the two timestamps to the same value. Timestamps are the number of milliseconds elapsed since midnight UT (GMT).

9. *Information request and information reply*

An Information Request is issued by a host to obtain an IP address for an attached network. The sender fills in the request with the destination IP address in the IP header set to zero (meaning this network) and waits for a reply from a server authorized to assign IP addresses to other hosts. The ICMP header code field is zero. The reply will contain IP network addresses in both the source and destination fields of the IP header.

10. *Address mask request and address mask reply*

An Address Mask Request is used by a host to determine the subnet mask in use on an attached network. Most hosts will be configured with their subnet mask(s), but some, such as diskless workstations, must obtain this information from a server. A host uses RARP to obtain its IP address. To obtain a subnet mask, the host broadcasts an Address Mask Request. Any host on the network which has been configured to send Address Mask Replies will fill in the subnet mask, convert the packet to an Address Mask Reply and return it to the sender.

ICMP applications

There are two simple and widely used applications which are based on ICMP: Ping and Traceroute. Ping uses the ICMP Echo and Echo Reply messages to determine whether a host is reachable. Traceroute sends IP datagrams with low TTL values so that they expire en route to a destination. It uses the resulting ICMP Time Exceeded messages to determine where in the internet the datagrams expired and pieces together a view of the route to a host.

7.5 BASIC IP ROUTING

The fundamental function for routers is present in *all* IP implementations:

An *incoming* IP datagram that specifies a "destination IP address" other than the local host's IP address(es), is treated as a normal *outgoing* IP datagram.

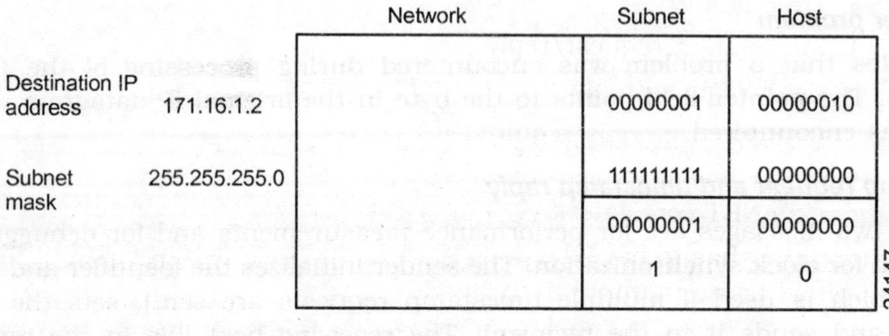

Figure 7.6 Applying a Logical AND the Destination IP Address and the Subnet Mask Produces the Subnetwork Number

This outgoing IP datagram is subject to the IP routing algorithm of the local host, which selects the *next hop* for the datagram (the next host to send it to). This new destination can be located on any of the physical networks to which the intermediate host is attached. If it is a physical network other than the one on which the host originally received the datagram, then the net result is that the intermediate host has *forwarded* the IP datagram from one physical network to another.

The normal IP routing table contains information about the locally attached networks and the IP addresses of other routers located on these networks, plus the networks they attach to. It can be extended with information on IP networks that are farther away, and can also contain a default route, but it still remains a table with limited information; that is, it represents only a part of the whole internet. That is why this kind of router is called a *router with partial routing information.*

Some considerations apply to these routers with partial information:

1. They do not know about all internetworks.
2. They allow local sites autonomy in establishing and modifying routes.
3. A routing entry error in one of the routers may introduce inconsistencies, thereby making part of the network unreachable.

Some error reporting should be implemented by routers with partial information via the Internet Control Message Protocol (ICMP) .They should be able to report the following errors back to the source host:

1. Unknown IP destination network by an ICMP *Destination Unreachable* message.
2. Redirection of traffic to more suitable routers by sending ICMP *Redirect* messages.
3. Congestion problems (too many incoming datagrams for the available buffer space) by an ICMP *Source Quench* message.
4. The "Time-to-Live" field of an IP datagram has reached zero. This is reported with an ICMP *Time Exceeded* message.
5. Also, the following base ICMP operations and messages should be supported:
   - 5.1 Parameter problem
   - 5.2 Address mask
   - 5.3 Time stamp
   - 5.4 Information request/reply
   - 5.5 Echo request/reply

A more intelligent router is required if:

1. The router has to know routes to *all* possible IP networks, as was the case for the ARPANET *core* gateways.
2. The router has to have dynamic routing tables, which are kept up-to-date with minimal or no manual intervention.
3. The router has to be able to advertise local changes to other routers.

These more advanced forms of routers use additional protocols to communicate with each other. The reasons for this multiplicity of different protocols are basically fourfold:

1. Using Internet terminology, there is a concept of a group of networks, called an *Autonomous System (AS)*, which is administered as a unit. The AS concept arose because the TCP/IP protocols were developed with the ARPANET already in place. Routing within an AS and routing outside an AS are treated as different issues and are addressed by different protocols.
2. Over two decades several routing protocols were tested in the Internet. Some of them performed well, others had to be abandoned.
3. The emergence of Autonomous Systems of different sizes called for different routing solutions. For small to medium sized ASs a group of routing protocols based upon Distance Vector (RIP, for example) became very popular. However, such protocols do not perform well for large interconnected networks. Link State protocols like OSPF are much better suited for such networks.

4. To exchange routing information between ASs border gateway protocols were developed.

Before discussing the various routing protocols, we will review the routing architectures used in the early Internet, since this will help in understanding the role played by the differing routing protocols. This overview will also show the difference between *Interior* and *Exterior* routing. We will then discuss the various protocols used for the two types of routing.

7.5.1 IP Routing

An important function of the IP layer is *IP routing*. It provides the basic mechanism for routers to interconnect different physical networks. This means that an internet host can function as a normal host and a router simultaneously. A basic router of this type is referred to as a *router with partial routing information*, because the router only has information about four kinds of destination:

1. Hosts which are directly attached to one of the physical networks to which the router is attached.
2. Hosts or networks for which the router has been given explicit definitions.
3. Hosts or networks for which the router has received an ICMP redirect message
4. A default destination for everything else.

The last two items allow a basic router to begin with a very limited amount of information and to increase its information because a more sophisticated router will issue an ICMP redirect message if it receives a datagram and it knows of a better router on the same network for the sender to use. This process is repeated each time a basic router of this type is restarted.

7.5.2 Direct and Indirect Destinations

If the destination host is attached to a network to which the source host is also attached, an IP datagram can be sent directly, simply by encapsulating the IP datagram in the physical network frame. This is called *direct routing.*

Indirect routing occurs when the destination host is not on a network directly attached to the source host. The only way to reach the destination is via one or more routers. The address of the first of these routers (the *first hop*) is called an *indirect route.* The first hop address is the only information needed by the source host: the router which receives a datagram has responsibility for the second hop and so on. A host can tell whether a route is direct or indirect by examining the network number and subnet number parts of the IP address.

1. If they match one of the IP addresses of the source host, the route is a direct one. The host needs to be able to address the target correctly using a lower-level protocol than ARP. This can either be done automatically using a network-specific protocol, such as ARP.

For "indirect" routes, the only knowledge required is the IP address of a router leading to the destination network.

7.5.3 IP Routing Table

Each host keeps the set of mappings between destination IP addresses and the IP addresses of the next hop routers for those destinations in a table called the *IP routing table.*

Three types of mappings can be found in this table:

1. Direct routes, for locally attached networks
2. Indirect routes, for networks reachable via one or more routers
3. A default route, which contains the IP address of a router to be used for all IP addresses which are not covered by the direct and indirect routes.

7.6 AUTONOMOUS SYSTEM DEFINITION

For the purpose of routing,a group of networks and routers controlled by a single administrative authority is called autonomous system. Routers within an autonomous system are free to choose their own mechanisms for discovering, propagating, validating and checking the consistency of routes. To make networks that are hidden inside autonomous systems reachable throughout the Internet, each autonomous system must agree to advertise network reachability information to other autonomous systems. Usually one router in the autonomous system takes the responsibility for advertising routes and interact directly with one of the backbone router. To make it possible for automated routing algorithms to distinguish among autonomous systems, each is assigned an autonomous system number by the central authority that is charged with assigning all internet addresses.

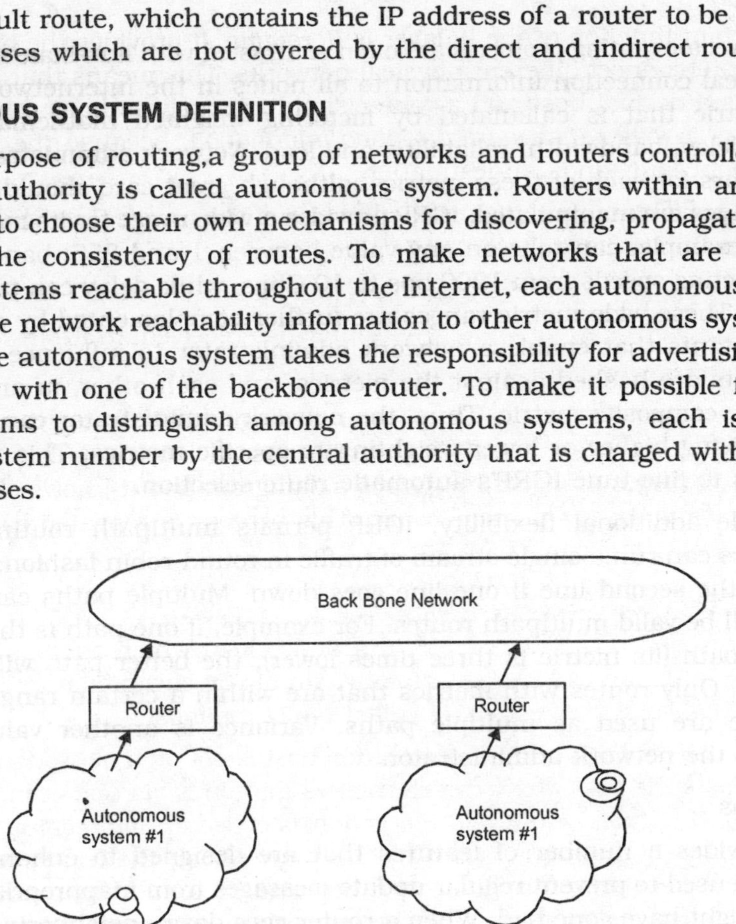

Figure 7.7

7.7 INTERIOR ROUTING PROTOCOLS

Interior routing protocols or *interior gateway protocols (IGPs)* are used to exchange routing information between routers within a single autonomous system. They are also used by routers which run *exterior routing protocols* to collect network-reachability information for the autonomous system. The *Interior Gateway Routing Protocol (IGRP)* is a routing protocol that was developed in the mid-1980s by Cisco Systems,

7.7.1 IGRP Protocol Characteristics

IGRP is a *distance vector* Interior Gateway Protocol (IGP). Distance vector routing protocols mathematically compare routes using some measurement of distance. This measurement is known as the distance vector. Routers using a distance vector protocol must send all or a portion of their routing table in a routing-update message at regular intervals to each of their neighboring routers. As routing information proliferates through the network, routers can identify new destinations as they are added to the network, learn of failures in the network, and, most importantly, calculate distances to all known destinations.

Distance vector routing protocols are often contrasted with link-state routing protocols, which send local connection information to all nodes in the internetwork. IGRP uses a composite metric that is calculated by factoring weighted mathematical values for internetwork delay, bandwidth, reliability, and load. Network administrators can set the weighting factors for each of these metrics, although great care should be taken before any default values are manipulated. IGRP provides a wide range for its metrics. Reliability and load, for example, can take on any value between 1 and 255; bandwidth can take on values reflecting speeds from 1200 bps to 10 Gbps, while delay can take on any value from 1 to 2^{24}. These wide metric ranges are further complemented by a series of user-definable constants that enable a network administrator to influence route selection. These constants are hashed against the metrics, and each other, in an algorithm that yields a single, composite metric. Thus, the network administrator can influence route selection by giving higher or lower weighting to specific metrics. This flexibility allows administrators to fine-tune IGRP's automatic route selection.

To provide additional flexibility, IGRP permits multipath routing. Dual equal-bandwidth lines can run a single stream of traffic in round-robin fashion, with automatic switchover to the second line if one line goes down. Multiple paths can have unequal metrics yet still be valid multipath routes. For example, if one path is three times better than another path (its metric is three times lower), the better path will be used three times as often. Only routes with metrics that are within a certain range or variance of the best route are used as multiple paths. Variance is another value that can be established by the network administrator.

Stability Features

IGRP provides a number of features that are designed to enhance its stability. *Holddowns* are used to prevent regular update messages from inappropriately reinstating a route that might have gone bad. When a router goes down, neighboring routers detect this via the lack of regularly scheduled update messages. These routers then calculate new routes and send routing update messages to inform their neighbors of the route change. This activity begins a wave of triggered updates that filter through the network. These triggered updates do not instantly arrive at every network device. Thus, it is possible for a device that has yet to be informed of a network failure to send a regular update message, which advertises a failed route as being valid to a device that has just been notified of the network failure. In this case, the latter device would contain (and potentially advertise) incorrect routing information. Holddowns tell routers to hold down any changes that might affect routes for some period of time. The holddown period usually is calculated to be just greater than the period of time necessary to update the entire network with a routing change.

Split horizons derive from the premise that it is never useful to send information about a route back in the direction from which it came. Figure 7.8 illustrates the split-horizon rule. Router 1 (R1) advertises that it has a route to Network A. There is no reason for Router 2 (R2) to include this route in its update back to R1 because R1 is closer to Network A. The split-horizon rule says that R2 should strike this route from any updates that it sends to R1. The split-horizon rule helps prevent routing loops. Consider, for example, the case in which R1's interface to Network A goes down. Without split horizons, R2 continues to inform R1 that it can get to Network A (through R1). If R1 does not have sufficient intelligence, it actually might pick up R2's route as an alternative to its failed direct connection, causing a routing loop. Although holddowns should prevent this, split horizons are implemented in IGRP because they provide extra algorithm stability.

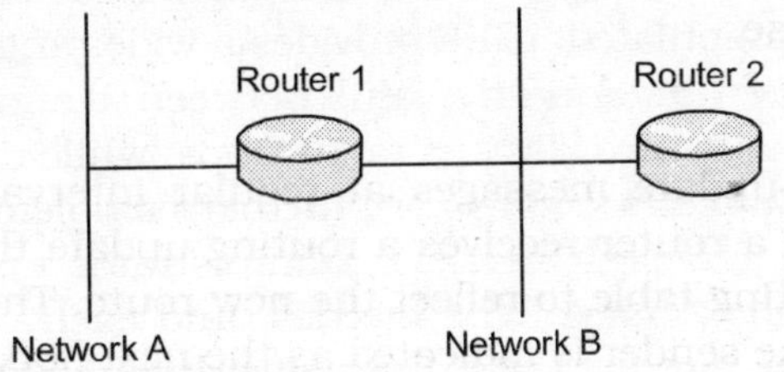

Figure 7.8 The Split-Horizon Rule Helps Protect Against Routing Loops

Split horizons should prevent routing loops between adjacent routers, but *poison-reverse updates* are necessary to defeat larger routing loops. Increases in routing metrics generally indicate routing loops. Poison-reverse updates then are sent to remove the route and place it in holddown. In Cisco's implementation of IGRP, poison-reverse updates are sent if a route metric has increased by a factor of 1.1 or greater.

Timers

IGRP maintains a number of timers and variables containing time intervals. These include an update timer, an invalid timer, a hold-time period, and a flush timer. The *update timer* specifies how frequently routing update messages should be sent. The IGRP default for this variable is 90 seconds. The *invalid timer* specifies how long a router should wait in the absence of routing-update messages about a specific route before declaring that route invalid. The IGRP default for this variable is three times the update period. The *hold-time variable* specifies the holddown period. The IGRP default for this variable is three times the update timer period plus 10 seconds. Finally, the *flush timer* indicates how much time should pass before a route should be flushed from the routing table. The IGRP default is seven times the routing update period.

The most widely used IGPs are:

1. Routing Information Protocol.
2. The Open Shortest Path First protocol.
3. The Hello protocol.

7.7.2 Routing Information Protocol

The Routing Information Protocol, or RIP, as it is more commonly called, is one of the most enduring of all routing protocols. RIP is also one of the more easily confused protocols because a variety of RIP-like routing protocols proliferated, some of which even used the same name! RIP and the myriad RIP-like protocols were based on the same set of algorithms that use distance vectors to mathematically compare routes to identify the best path to any given destination address.

Today's open standard version of RIP, sometimes referred to as IP RIP. As IP-based networks became both more numerous and greater in size, it became apparent to update RIP.There are two versions of RIP. Version 1 (RIP-1) is a widely deployed protocol with a number of known limitations. Version 2 (RIP-2) is an enhanced version designed to alleviate the limitations of RIP while being highly compatible with it. The term RIP is used to refer to Version 1, while RIP-2 refers to Version 2. Whenever the reader encounters the term RIP in TCP/IP literature, it is safe to assume that it is referring to Version 1 unless explicitly stated otherwise.

Routing Updates

RIP sends routing-update messages at regular intervals and when the network topology changes. When a router receives a routing update that includes changes to an entry, it updates its routing table to reflect the new route. The metric value for the path is increased by 1, and the sender is indicated as the next hop. RIP routers maintain only the best route (the route with the lowest metric value) to a destination. After updating its routing table, the router immediately begins transmitting routing updates to inform other network routers of the change. These updates are sent independently of the regularly scheduled updates that RIP routers send.

RIP Routing Metric

RIP uses a single routing metric (hop count) to measure the distance between the source and a destination network. Each hop in a path from source to destination is assigned a hop count value, which is typically 1. When a router receives a routing update that contains a new or changed destination network entry, the router adds 1 to the metric value indicated in the update and enters the network in the routing table. The IP address of the sender is used as the next hop.

RIP Stability Features

RIP prevents routing loops from continuing indefinitely by implementing a limit on the number of hops allowed in a path from the source to a destination. The maximum number of hops in a path is 15. If a router receives a routing update that contains a new or changed entry, and if increasing the metric value by 1 causes the metric to be infinity (that is, 16), the network destination is considered unreachable. The downside of this stability feature is that it limits the maximum diameter of a RIP network to less than 16 hops.

RIP includes a number of other stability features that are common to many routing protocols. These features are designed to provide stability despite potentially rapid changes in a network's topology. For example, RIP implements the split horizon and holddown mechanisms to prevent incorrect routing information from being propagated.

RIP Timers

RIP uses numerous timers to regulate its performance. These include a routing-update timer, a route-timeout timer, and a route-flush timer. The routing-update timer clocks the interval between periodic routing updates. Generally, it is set to 30 seconds, with a small random amount of time added whenever the timer is reset. This is done to help prevent congestion, which could result from all routers simultaneously attempting to update their neighbors. Each routing table entry has a route-timeout timer associated with it. When the route-timeout timer expires, the route is marked invalid but is retained in the table until the route-flush timer expires.

RIP Packet Format

1-octet command field	1-octet version number field	2-octet zero field	2-octet AFI field	2-octet zero field	4-octet IP address field	4-octet zero field	4-octet zero field	4-octet metric field

Figure 7.9 An IP RIP Packet Consists of Nine Fields

The following descriptions summarize the IP RIP packet format fields illustrated in Figure.

Command—Indicates whether the packet is a request or a response. The request asks that a router send all or part of its routing table. The response can be an unsolicited regular routing update or a reply to a request. Responses contain routing table entries. Multiple RIP packets are used to convey information from large routing tables.

Version number—Specifies the RIP version used. This field can signal different potentially incompatible versions.

Zero—This field is not actually used by RFC 1058 RIP; it was added solely to provide backward compatibility with prestandard varieties of RIP. Its name comes from its defaulted value: zero.

Address Family Identifier (AFI)—Specifies the address family used. RIP is designed to carry routing information for several different protocols. Each entry has an address-family identifier to indicate the type of address being specified. The AFI for IP is 2.

Address—Specifies the IP address for the entry.

Metric—Indicates how many internetwork hops (routers) have been traversed in the trip to the destination. This value is between 1 and 15 for a valid route, or 16 for an unreachable route.

RIP is generally implemented with a daemon named *routed*. RIP is also supported by *gated* daemons. RIP is a straightforward implementation of vector-distance routing for local networks. RIP communication uses UDP as a transport protocol, with port number 520 as the destination port for a description of UDP and ports). RIP operates in one of two modes: *active* (normally used by routers) and *passive* (normally used by hosts).

Basic Operation

1. When RIP is started it sends a message to each of its neighbors (on well-known UDP port 520) asking for a copy of the neighbor's routing table. This message

is a query (command set to 1) with an address family of 0 and a metric of 16. The neighboring routers return a copy of their routing tables.

2. When RIP is in active mode it sends all or part of its routing table to all of its neighbor routers (by broadcasting and/or by sending it on any point-to-point links to its neighbors). This is done every 30 seconds. The routing table is sent as a reply (command is 2, even though it is unsolicited).
3. When RIP discovers a metric has changed, it broadcasts the change to other routers.
4. When RIP receives a reply, the message is validated and the local routing table is updated if necessary.

To improve performance and reliability, RIP specifies that once a router (or host) learns a route from another router, it must keep that route until it learns of a better one (with a strictly lower cost). This prevents routes from oscillating between two or more equal cost paths.

1. When RIP receives a request, other than one for the entire table, it is returned as the response with the metric for each entry set to the value from the local routing table. If no route exists in the local table, the metric is set to 16.
2. RIP routes learned from other routers time out unless they are re-advertised within 180 seconds (6 broadcast cycles). When a route times out, its metric is set to infinity, the invalidation of the route is broadcast to the router's neighbors, and 60 seconds later, the route is deleted from the local routing table.

RIP has the following specific limitations:

1. The maximum cost allowed in RIP is 16 which means that the network is unreachable. Thus RIP is inadequate for large networks (that is, those in which legitimate hop counts approach 16).
2. RIP does not support variable length subnet masks *(variable subnetting)*. There is no facility in a RIP message to specify a subnet mask associated with the IP address.
3. RIP has no facilities to ensure that routing table updates come from authorized routers. It is an unsecure protocol.
4. RIP only uses fixed metrics to compare alternative routes. It is not appropriate for situations where routes need to be chosen based on real-time parameters such as measured delay, reliability, or load.

The protocol depends upon *counting to infinity* to resolve certain unusual situations. As described earlier (Vector Distance), the resolution of a loop would require either much time (if the frequency of updates was limited) or much bandwidth (if updates were sent whenever changes were detected). As the size of the routing domain grows, the instability of the vector-distance algorithm in the face of changing topology becomes apparent. RIP specifies mechanisms to minimize the problems with counting to infinity (these are described below) which allows RIP to be used for larger routing domains, but eventually RIP will be unable to cope. There is no fixed upper limit, but the practical maximum depends upon the frequency of changes to the topology, the details of the network topology itself, and what is deemed as an acceptable maximum time for the routing topology to stabilize.

7.7.3 The Hello Protocol

OSPF includes a quite separate protocol for negotiation between routers which is also called the Hello protocol. The communication in the Hello protocol is via Hello messages which are carried via IP datagrams. Hello uses protocol number 63 (reserved for "any local network").

The Hello protocol is significant partly because of its wide deployment during the early expansion of the Internet and partly because it provides an example of a vector-distance algorithm that does not use hop counts like RIP but, instead, network delays as a metric for the distance.

A *Distributed Computer Network (DCN)* physical host is a processor which supports a number of cooperating sequential Processes, each of which is given a unique 8-bit identifier called its port ID. Every DCN host contains one or more internet processes, each of which supports a virtual host given a unique 8-bit identifier called its host ID. There is a one-to-one correspondence between internet addresses and host IDs. Each DCN physical host is identified by a host ID for the purpose of detecting loops in routing updates, which establish the minimum-delay paths between the virtual hosts.

Each physical host contains two tables:

1. *Host table*

This contains estimates of round-trip delay and logical-clock offset (that is, the difference between the logical clock of this host and the logical clock of the sender's host). It is indexed by the host number. The host table is maintained dynamically using updates generated by periodic (from 1 to 30 seconds) Hello messages.

2. *Net table*

This contains an entry for every neighbor network that may be connected to the local network and certain other networks that are not neighbors. Each entry contains the network number, as well as the host number of the router (located on the local network) to that network. The Net table is fixed at configuration time for all hosts except those that support the GGP or EGP routing protocols. In these cases the Net table is updated as part of the routing operation. The delay and offset estimates are updated by Hello messages exchanged on the links connecting physical neighbors.

Let us consider the two main steps of the Hello protocol.

1. Round-Trip Delay Calculation and
2. Host Updates

Round-Trip Delay Calculation

Periodically each host sends a Hello message to its neighbor on each of the communication links common to both of them. For each of these links the sender keeps a set of state variables, including a copy of the source-address field of the last Hello message received. When constructing a Hello message the sender sets the destination-address field to this state variable and the source-address field to its own address. It then fills in the date and time fields from its clock and the time stamp from another state variable. It finally copies the delay and offset values from its host table into the message.

Round-trip delay calculations are performed on the host receiving the Hello message. Each link has an internal state variable assigned, which is updated as each Hello message is received; this variable takes the value of the time field, minus the current time-of-day. When the next Hello message is transmitted, the value assigned to the time stamp field is computed as the low-order 16-bits of this variable minus the current time-of-day. The round trip delay is computed as the low-order 16-bits of the current time-of-day minus the value of the timestamp field.

Host Updates

When a Hello message arrives which results in a valid round trip-delay calculation, a host update process is performed. This consists of adding the round trip delay to each of the "Delay n" entries in the Hello message in turn and comparing each of these calculated delays to the delay field of the corresponding host table. Each entry is then updated according to the following rules:

1. If the link connects to another host on the same network and the port ID of the link output process matches the port ID field of the entry, then update the entry.
2. If the link connects to another host on the same network and the port ID of the link output process does not match the port ID field of the entry *and* the calculated delay is less than the host delay field of the host table by at least a specified switching threshold (currently 100 milliseconds), then update the entry. For example, if host A sends host B a Hello message, and if B's current delay to reach a given destination, D, is greater than the delay from A to D plus the delay from B to A, B changes its route and sends traffic to D via A.

The purpose of the switching threshold is to avoid (together with minimum delay specification) unnecessary switching between links and transient loops which can occur due to normal variations in propagation delays.

7.7.4 Open Shortest Path First (OSPF)

Open Shortest Path First (OSPF) is a routing protocol developed for Internet Protocol (IP) networks by the Interior Gateway Protocol (IGP) working group of the Internet Engineering Task Force (IETF). The working group was formed in 1988 to design an IGP based on the Shortest Path First (SPF) algorithm for use in the Internet. Similar to the Interior Gateway Routing Protocol (IGRP), OSPF was created because in the mid-1980s, the Routing Information Protocol (RIP) was increasingly incapable of serving large, heterogeneous internet works.

OSPF has two primary characteristics.

1. The first is that the protocol is open, which means that its specification is in the public domain. The OSPF specification is published as Request For Comments (RFC) 1247.
2. The second principal characteristic is that OSPF is based on the SPF algorithm, which sometimes is referred to as the Dijkstra algorithm, named for the person credited with its creation.

OSPF is a link-state routing protocol that calls for the sending of link-state advertisements (LSAs) to all other routers within the same hierarchical area. Information on attached interfaces, metrics used, and other variables is included in OSPF LSAs. As OSPF routers accumulate link-state information, they use the SPF algorithm to calculate the shortest path to each node.

As a link-state routing protocol, OSPF contrasts with RIP and IGRP, which are distance-vector routing protocols. Routers running the distance-vector algorithm send all or a portion of their routing tables in routing-update messages to their neighbors.

Routing Hierarchy

Unlike RIP, OSPF can operate within a hierarchy. The largest entity within the hierarchy is the autonomous system (AS), which is a collection of networks under a common administration that share a common routing strategy. OSPF is an intra-AS (interior gateway) routing protocol, although it is capable of receiving routes from and sending routes to other ASs.

An AS can be divided into a number of areas, which are groups of contiguous networks and attached hosts. Routers with multiple interfaces can participate in multiple areas. These routers, which are called Area Border Routers, maintain separate topological databases for each area.A topological database is essentially an overall picture of networks in relationship to routers. The topological database contains the collection of LSAs received from all routers in the same area. Because routers within the same area share the same information, they have identical topological databases.

The term *domain* sometimes is used to describe a portion of the network in which all routers have identical topological databases. Domain is frequently used interchangeably with AS. An area's topology is invisible to entities outside the area. By keeping area topologies separate, OSPF passes less routing traffic than it would if the AS were not partitioned. Area partitioning creates two different types of OSPF routing, depending on whether the source and the destination are in the same or different areas. Intra-area routing occurs when the source and destination are in the same area; interarea routing occurs when they are in different areas.

An OSPF backbone is responsible for distributing routing information between areas. It consists of all Area Border Routers, networks not wholly contained in any area, and their attached routers. The backbone itself is an OSPF area, so all backbone routers use the same procedures and algorithms to maintain routing information within the backbone that any area router would. The backbone topology is invisible to all intra-area routers, as are individual area topologies to the backbone.

Areas can be defined in such a way that the backbone is not contiguous. In this case, backbone connectivity must be restored through virtual links. Virtual links are configured between any backbone routers that share a link to a nonbackbone area and function as if they were direct links.AS border routers running OSPF learn about exterior routes through exterior gateway protocols (EGPs), such as Exterior Gateway Protocol (EGP) or Border Gateway Protocol (BGP), or through configuration information.

Open Shortest Path First Protocol (OSPF) Version 2

OSPF says that any router implementing a protocol other than simple IP-based routing must implement OSPF (this does not preclude a router implementing other protocols as well, of course). OSPF is an interior routing protocol, but it is designed to operate with a suitable exterior protocol, such as BGP. Much of the complexity of OSPF is directed towards a single purpose: ensuring that the topological databases are the same for all of the routers within an area. Because the database is the basis for all routing choices, if routers were to have independent databases, they could make mutually conflicting decisions.

OSPF communicates using IP. It is a *Link-State, Shortest Path First* protocol . OSPF supports different kinds of networks such as point-to-point networks, broadcast networks, such as Ethernet and token-ring, and non-broadcast networks, such as X.25.

The OSPF specification makes use of *state machines* to define the behavior of routers complying with the protocol. Aspects of a router's operation which are important to OSPF, such as its network interfaces and its neighboring routers, are described as being in one of a finite number of *states* (for example, a neighbor may be in the down state). There is a separate state machine for each separate component (for example, two network interfaces have separate state machines) and the state of one is independent of the state of another. The possible states are sufficient to describe all possible conditions relevant to the protocol, so a state machine is always in one, and only one, of its possible states. State changes occur only as a result of *events*. There is a finite set of events for each type of state machine which is sufficient to describe all possible occurrences relevant to the protocol. The behavior of the state machine in response to an event is defined for all possible combinations of state and event. For example, if the state machine for a network interface experiences an InterfaceDown event, the state machine changes to the down state unconditionally. The InterfaceDown event is generated by the OSPF implementation whenever it receives an indication from a lower-level protocol that the interface is not functioning.

Here are some definitions which are necessary to understand the sequence of operations described later in this section:

1. *Area*

A set of networks within a single autonomous system that have been grouped together. The topology of an area is hidden from the rest of the autonomous system, and each area has a separate topological database . Routing within the autonomous system takes place on two levels, depending on whether the source and destination of a packet reside in the same area (*intra-area routing*) or different areas (*inter-area routing*).

- Intra-area routing is determined only by the area's own topology. That is, the packet is routed solely on information obtained within the area; no routing information obtained outside the area can be used.
- Inter-area routing is always done via the *backbone*.

The division of an autonomous system into areas enables a significant reduction in the volume of routing traffic required to manage the routing database for a large autonomous system.

2. *Backbone*

The backbone consists of those networks not contained in any area, their attached routers, and those routers that belong to multiple areas. The backbone *must* be logically contiguous. If it is not physically contiguous, the separate components must be connected using *virtual links* (see below). The backbone is responsible for the distribution of routing information between areas. The backbone itself has all the properties of an area; its topology is separate from that of the areas.

3. *Area border router*

A router connected to multiple areas. An area border router has a copy of the topological database for each area that it is connected to. An area border router is always part of the backbone. Area border routers are responsible for the propagation of inter-area routing information into the areas to which they are connected.

4. *Internal router*

A router which is not an area border router.

5. *AS Border Router (ASBR)*

A router which exchanges routing information with routers belonging to other autonomous systems. All routers in the AS know the path to all AS boundary routers. An ASBR may be an area border router *or* an internal router. It need not be part of the backbone.

6. *Virtual link*

A virtual link is part of the backbone. Its endpoints are two area border routers which share a common non-backbone area. The link is treated like a point-to-point link with metrics cost equal to the intra-area metrics between the endpoints of the links. The routing through the virtual link is done using normal intra-area routing.

7. *Transit area*

An area through which a virtual route is physically connected.

8. *Stub area*

An area configured to use default routing for inter-AS routing. A stub area can be configured where there is only a single exit from the area, or where any exit may be used without preference for routing to destinations outside the autonomous system. By default inter-AS routes are copied to all areas, so the use of stub areas can reduce the storage requirements of routers within those areas for autonomous systems where a lot of inter-AS routes are defined.

9. *Multiaccess network*

A physical network that supports the attachment of multiple routers. Each pair of routers on such a network is assumed to be able to communicate directly.

10. *Hello protocol*

The part of the OSPF protocol used to establish and maintain neighbor relationships.

11. *Neighboring routers*

Two routers that have interfaces to a common network. On multiaccess networks, neighbors are dynamically discovered by the Hello protocol. Each neighbor is described by a state machine which describes the conversation between this router and its neighbor.

A brief outline of the meaning of the states follows.

Down

Initial state of a neighbor conversation. It indicates that there has been no recent information received from the neighbor.

Attempt

A neighbor on a non-broadcast network appears down and an attempt should be made to contact it by sending regular Hello packets.

Init

A Hello packet has recently been received from the neighbor. However, bidirectional communication has not yet been established with the neighbor (that is, the router itself did not appear in the neighbor's Hello packet).

2-way

In this state, communication between the two routers is bidirectional. Adjacencies can be established, and neighbors in this state or higher are eligible to be elected as (backup) designated routers.

ExStart

The two neighbors are about to create an adjacency.

Exchange

The two neighbors are telling each other what they have in their topological databases.

Loading

The two neighbors are synchronizing their topological databases.

Full

The two neighbors are now fully adjacent; their databases are synchronized.

12. *Adjacency*

A relationship formed between selected neighboring routers for the purpose of exchanging routing information. *Not* every pair of neighboring routers become adjacent. In particular, not every pair of routers will stay synchronized. If all neighbors were to be synchronized, the number of synchronized pairs on a multiaccess network such as a LAN would be $n(n-1)/2$ where n is the number of routers on the LAN. In large networks, the synchronization traffic would swamp the network, rendering it unusable. The concept of adjacencies is used to limit the number of synchronized pairs to $2n-1$, ensuring that the amount of synchronization traffic is manageable.

13. *Link state advertisement*

Refers to the local state of a router or network. This includes the state of the router's interfaces and adjacencies. Each link state advertisement is flooded throughout the routing domain. The collected link state advertisements of all routers and networks form the area's topological database.

14. *Flooding*

The process of ensuring that each link state advertisement is passed between adjacent routers to reach every router in the area. The flooding procedure is reliable.

15. *Designated router*

Each multi-access network that has at least two attached routers, has a Designated Router. The Designated Router generates a link state advertisement for the multi-access network. It is elected by the Hello protocol. It becomes adjacent to all other routers on the network. Since the topological databases of all routers are synchronized through adjacencies, the Designated Router plays a central part in the synchronization process.

16. *Backup designated router*

In order to make the transition to a new Designated Router smoother, there is a Backup Designated Router for each multi-access network. The Backup Designated Router is also adjacent to all routers on the network, and becomes Designated Router when the previous Designated Router fails. Because adjacencies already exist between the Backup Designated Router and all other routers attached to the network, new adjacencies do not have to be formed when the Backup Designated Router takes over from the Designated Router, shortening the time required for the takeover considerably. The Backup designated router is elected using the Hello protocol.

17. *Interface*

The connection between a router and one of its attached networks. Each interface has state information associated with it which is obtained from the underlying lower-level protocols and the OSPF protocol itself. A brief description of each state is given here.

Down

The interface is unavailable. This is the initial state of an interface.

Loopback

The interface is looped back to the router. It cannot be used for regular data traffic.

Waiting

The router is trying to determine the identity of the Designated Router or its backup.

Point-to-Point

The interface is to a point-to-point network or is a virtual link. The router forms an adjacency with the router at the other end.

DR Other

The interface is on a multiaccess network but this router is neither the Designated Router nor its backup. The router forms adjacencies with the Designated Router and its backup.

Backup

The router is the Backup Designated Router. It will be promoted to Designated Router if the present Designated Router fails. The router forms adjacencies with every other router on the network.

DR

The router itself is the Designated Router. The router forms adjacencies with every other router on the network. The router must also originate a network links advertisement for the network node.

18. *Type Of Service (TOS) metrics*

In each type of link state advertisement, different metrics can be advertised for each IP Type of Service. A metric for TOS 0 (used for OSPF routing protocol packets) must always be specified. Metrics for other TOS values can be specified; if they are not, these metrics are assumed equal to the metric specified for TOS 0.

19. *Link state database*

Also called the *directed graph* or the *topological database*. It is created from the link state advertisements generated by the routers in the area.

20. *Shortest-path tree*

Each router runs the Shortest Path First (SPF) algorithm on the Link State Database to obtain its shortest-path tree. The tree gives the route to any destination network or host as far as the area boundary. It is used to build the routing table.

21. *Routing table*

The routing table contains entries for each destination: network, subnet or host. For each destination, there is information for one or more types of service (TOS). For each combination of destination and type of service, there are entries for one or more optimum paths to be used.

22. *Area ID*

A 32-bit number identifying a particular area. The backbone has an Area ID of zero.

23. *Router ID*

A 32-bit number identifying a particular router. Each router within the AS has a single router ID. One possible implementation is to use the lowest numbered IP address belonging to a router as its router ID.

24. *Router priority*

An 8-bit unsigned integer, configurable on a per-interface basis indicating this router's priority in the selection of the (backup) Designated Router. A Router Priority of zero indicates that this router is ineligible to be the Designated Router.

Overview of OSPF Operation

The basic sequence of operations performed by OSPF routers is:

1. Discovering OSPF neighbors.
2. Electing the Designated Router.
3. Forming adjacencies.
4. Synchronizing databases.
5. Calculating the routing table.
6. Advertising Link States.

Routers will go through these steps when they first come up, and will repeat these steps in response to events which occur in the network. Each router must perform each of these steps for each network it is connected to, except for the calculation of the routing table. Each router generates and maintains a single routing table for all networks.

Each of these steps is described in the following sections.

Discovering OSPF Neighbors

When OSPF routers start, they initiate and sustain relationships with their neighbors using the Hello protocol. The Hello protocol also ensures that communication between neighbors is bidirectional. Hello packets are sent periodically out to all router interfaces. Bidirectional communication is indicated when the router sees itself in the neighbor's Hello packet. On a broadcast network, Hello packets are sent using multicast; neighbors are then discovered dynamically. On non-broadcast networks each router that may potentially become a Designated Router has a list of all routers attached to the network and will send Hello packets to all other potential Designated Routers when its interface to the non-broadcast network first becomes operational.

Determining the Designated Router

This is done using the Hello protocol. A brief description of the process is given here. See RFC 1583 for a full description. The router examines the list of its neighbors, discards any with which it does not have bidirectional communication or which have a Router Priority of zero, and records the Designated Router, Backup Designated Router and Router Priority declared by each one. The router adds itself to the list, using the Router Priority configured for the interface and zero (unknown) for the Designated Router and Backup Designated Router values, if the calculating router has just come up.

The following rules are used to determine the Backup Designated Router:

1. If one or more routers declare themselves to be the Backup Designated Router and not to be the Designated Router, then the one with the higher Router Priority wins.
2. In the event of a tie, the router with the highest Router ID wins.
3. If no router has declared itself to be the Backup Designated Router, then the Router with the highest Router Priority is elected unless it has declared itself to be the Designated Router.
4. Again, in the event of a tie, the router with the highest Router ID wins.

Because the calculating router is in the list, it may determine that it is to become the Backup Designated Router. A similar process is followed for the Designated Router:

1. If one or more routers declare themselves to be the Designated Router, then the one with the higher Router Priority wins.
2. In the event of a tie, the router with the highest Router ID wins.
3. If no router has declared itself to be the Backup then the Backup Designated Router becomes the Designated Router.

The actual process is considerably more complex than this, because the Hello messages transmitted include changes to the fields recorded on other routers, and these changes cause events in those routers which in turn will trigger state changes or other actions. The intent behind the mechanism is twofold:

1. That when a router comes up, it should not usurp the position of (Backup) Designated Router from the current holder even if it has a higher Router priority.
2. That the promotion of a Backup Designated Router to Designated Router should be orderly and require the Backup to accept its responsibilities.

The algorithm does not always result in the router with the highest priority being the Designated Router, nor in the one with the second highest priority being the Backup.

The Designated Router has the following responsibilities:

1. The Designated Router generates the network links advertisement on behalf of the network. This advertisement is *flooded* throughout the area and describes this network to all routers in all networks in this area.
2. The Designated Router becomes adjacent to other routers on the network. These adjacencies are central to the flooding procedure used to ensure that link state advertisements reach all routers in the area and therefore that the topological database used by all routers remains the same.

The Backup Designated Router has the following responsibility

1. The Designated Router becomes adjacent to all other routers on the network. This ensures that it can take over from the Designated Router rapidly.

Forming Adjacencies

After a neighbor has been discovered, bidirectional communication ensured, and (on a multiaccess network) a Designated Router elected, a decision is made regarding whether or not an adjacency should be formed with the neighbor:

1. On multiaccess networks, all routers become adjacent to both the Designated Router and the Backup Designated Router.
2. On point-to-point links (or virtual links), the router always forms an adjacency with the router at the other end.

If the decision is made to not form an adjacency, the state of the neighbor communication remains in the 2-way state. Adjacencies are established using *Database Description* packets. These contain a summary of the sender's link state database. Multiple packets may be used to describe the database: for this purpose a poll-response procedure is used. The router with the higher router ID will become the master, the other will become the slave. Database Description packets sent by the master (*polls*) are acknowledged by Database Description packets sent by the slave (*responses*). The packets contain sequence numbers to ensure a match between polls and responses. This is called the *Database Exchange Process.*

Synchronization of Databases

After the Database Exchange Process is over, each router has a list of those link advertisements for which the neighbor has more up-to-date instances. These are then requested in *Link State Request* packets. The response to a Link State Request packet is a Link State Update packet which contains some or all of the link state advertisements requested. At most one Link State Request can be outstanding: if no response is received. the requester must retry the request.

Calculating the Routing Table

Using its attached areas' link state databases as input, a router runs the SPF algorithm to build its routing table. The routing table is always built from scratch: updates are never made to an existing routing table. An old routing table is not discarded until changes between the two tables have been identified. Briefly, the calculation consists of the steps listed below.The intra-area routes are calculated building the shortest path tree for each attached area using the router itself as the root of the tree. The router also calculates whether the area can act as a transit area for virtual links.

1. The inter-area routes are calculated through examination of summary link advertisements. For area border routers (which are part of the backbone) only link advertisements corresponding to the backbone are used (that is, an area border router will always route inter-area traffic through the backbone).
2. If the router is connected to one or more transit areas, the router replaces any routes it has calculated by routes through transit areas if these are superior.
3. AS external routes are calculated through examination of AS external link advertisements. The locations of the AS boundary routers are already known because these are determined like any other intra-area or inter-area routes.

When the algorithm produces multiple equal cost routes, OSPF can distribute the load across them evenly. The maximum supported number of equal cost routes is implementation dependent.

Advertising Link States

A router periodically advertises its link state, so the absence of a recent advertisement indicates to a router's neighbors that the router is down. All routers which have established bidirectional communication with a neighbor run an inactivity timer to detect such an occurrence. If the timer is not reset, it will eventually pop, and the associated event places the state machine corresponding to that neighbor in the down state. This means that communication must be re-established from the beginning, including re-synchronization of databases. A router also re-issues its advertisements when its state changes.

A router can issue several link state advertisements into each area. These are propagated throughout the area by the flooding procedure. Each router issues a Router Links Advertisement. If the router is also the Designated Router for one or more of the networks in the area, then it will originate Network Links Advertisements for those networks. Area border routers issue one Summary Link Advertisement for each known inter-area destination. AS boundary routers originate one AS External Link Advertisement for each known external destination. Destinations are advertised one at a time so that the change in any single route can be flooded without reflooding the entire collection of routes. During the flooding procedure, many link state advertisements can be carried by a single Link State Update packet.

Summary of Features for OSPF

OSPF is a complex routing protocol, as will be clear from the preceding sections. The benefits of this complexity (over RIP) are as follows:

1. Because of the synchronized Link State databases, OSPF routers will converge much faster than RIP routers after topology changes. This effect becomes more pronounced as autonomous systems get larger.
2. It includes *Type of Service (TOS)* routing that is designed to compute separate routes for each type of service. For any destination, multiple routes can exist, each route supporting one or more different Types of Service.
3. It uses weighted metrics for different speed links. For example, a T1 1.544 Mbps link might be assigned a metric of 1 and a 9600 bps SLIP link might be assigned a metric of 10.
4. It provides load balancing since an OSPF gateway can use more than one equal minimum cost path to a destination.
5. A subnet mask is associated with each route, allowing variable-length subnetting and supernetting
6. All exchanges between routers may be authenticated by the use of passwords.
7. OSPF supports host-specific routes, network-specific routes as well as subnet routes.
8. OSPF allows contiguous networks and hosts to be grouped together into *areas* within an AS, simplifying the topology and reducing the amount of routing information which must be exchanged. Knowledge of an area's topology remains hidden from other areas.
9. It minimizes broadcasts by allowing a more complex graph topology in which multiaccess networks have a *Designated Router* which is responsible for describing that network to the other networks in the area.
10. It allows external routing information exchange, that is, routing information learned from another autonomous system.
11. It allows routing within the AS to be configured according to a virtual topology rather than just the physical interconnections. Areas can be joined using virtual links which cross other areas without requiring complicated routing.

7.7.5 Enhanced IGRP

The Enhanced Interior Gateway Routing Protocol (EIGRP) represents an evolution from its predecessor IGRP. This evolution resulted from changes in networking and the demands of diverse, large-scale internetworks. Enhanced IGRP integrates the capabilities of link-state protocols into distance vector protocols. Additionally, EIGRP contains several important protocols that greatly increase its operational efficiency relative to other routing protocols. DUAL enables EIGRP routers to determine whether a path advertised by a neighbor is looped or loop-free, and allows a router running EIGRP to find alternate paths without waiting on updates from other routers.

Enhanced IGRP provides compatibility and seamless interoperation with IGRP routers. An automatic-redistribution mechanism allows IGRP routes to be imported into Enhanced IGRP, and vice versa, so it is possible to add Enhanced IGRP gradually into an existing IGRP network. Because the metrics for both protocols are directly translatable, they are as easily comparable as if they were routes that originated in their own autonomous systems (ASs). In addition, Enhanced IGRP treats IGRP routes as external routes and provides a way for the network administrator to customize them.

Enhanced IGRP Capabilities and Attributes

Key capabilities that distinguish Enhanced IGRP from other routing protocols include fast convergence, support for variable-length subnet mask, support for partial updates, and support for multiple network layer protocols. A router running Enhanced IGRP stores all its neighbors' routing tables so that it can quickly adapt to alternate routes. If no appropriate route exists, Enhanced IGRP queries its neighbors to discover an alternate route. These queries propagate until an alternate route is found.Its support for variable-length subnet masks permits routes to be automatically summarized on a network number boundary. In addition, Enhanced IGRP can be configured to summarize on any bit boundary at any interface.

Enhanced IGRP does not make periodic updates. Instead, it sends partial updates only when the metric for a route changes. Propagation of partial updates is automatically bounded so that only those routers that need the information are updated. As a result of these two capabilities, Enhanced IGRP consumes significantly less bandwidth than IGRP.

Enhanced IGRP includes support for AppleTalk, IP, and Novell NetWare. The AppleTalk implementation redistributes routes learned from the Routing Table Maintenance Protocol (RTMP). The IP implementation redistributes routes learned from OSPF, Routing Information Protocol (RIP), Intermediate System-to-Intermediate System (IS-IS), Exterior Gateway Protocol (EGP), or Border Gateway Protocol (BGP). The Novell implementation redistributes routes learned from Novell RIP or Service Advertisement Protocol (SAP).

Underlying Process and Technologies

To provide superior routing performance, Enhanced IGRP employs four key technologies that combine to differentiate it from other routing technologies: neighbor discovery/recovery, reliable transport protocol (RTP), DUAL finite-state machine, and protocol-dependent modules.

The *neighbor discovery/recovery* mechanism enables routers to dynamically learn about other routers on their directly attached networks. Routers also must discover when their neighbors become unreachable or inoperative. This process is achieved with low overhead by periodically sending small hello packets. As long as a router receives hello packets from a neighboring router, it assumes that the neighbor is functioning, and the two can exchange routing information.

Reliable Transport Protocol (RTP) is responsible for guaranteed, ordered delivery of Enhanced IGRP packets to all neighbors. It supports intermixed transmission of multicast or unicast packets. For efficiency, only certain Enhanced IGRP packets are transmitted reliably. On a multiaccess network that has multicast capabilities, such as Ethernet, it is not necessary to send hello packets reliably to all neighbors individually. For that reason, Enhanced IGRP sends a single multicast hello packet containing an indicator that informs the receivers that the packet need not be acknowledged. Other types of packets, such as updates, indicate in the packet that acknowledgement is required. RTP contains a provision for sending multicast packets quickly when unacknowledged packets are pending, which helps ensure that convergence time remains low in the presence of varying speed links.

The *DUAL finite-state machine* embodies the decision process for all route computations by tracking all routes advertised by all neighbors. DUAL uses distance information to select efficient, loop-free paths and selects routes for insertion in a routing table based on feasible successors. A *feasible successor* is a neighboring router used for packet forwarding that is a least-cost path to a destination that is guaranteed not to be part of a routing loop. When a neighbor changes a metric, or when a topology change occurs, DUAL tests for feasible successors. If one is found, DUAL uses it to avoid recomputing the route unnecessarily. When no feasible successors exist but neighbors still advertise the destination, a recomputation (also known as a diffusing computation) must occur to determine a new successor. Although recomputation is not processor-intensive, it does affect convergence time, so it is advantageous to avoid unnecessary recompilations.

Protocol-dependent modules are responsible for network layer protocol-specific requirements. The IP-Enhanced IGRP module, for example, is responsible for sending and receiving Enhanced IGRP packets that are encapsulated in IP. Likewise, IP-Enhanced IGRP is also responsible for parsing Enhanced IGRP packets and informing DUAL of the new information that has been received. IP-Enhanced IGRP asks DUAL to make routing decisions, the results of which are stored in the IP routing table. IP-Enhanced IGRP is responsible for redistributing routes learned by other IP routing protocols.

Routing Concepts

Enhanced IGRP relies on four fundamental concepts: neighbor tables, topology tables, route states, and route tagging. Each of these is summarized in the discussions that follow.i

Neighbor Tables

When a router discovers a new neighbor, it records the neighbor's address and interface as an entry in the *neighbor table.* One neighbor table exists for each protocol-dependent module. When a neighbor sends a hello packet, it advertises a hold time, which is the amount of time that a router treats a neighbor as reachable and operational. If a hello packet is not received within the hold time, the hold time expires and DUAL is informed of the topology change. The neighbor-table entry also includes information required by RTP. Sequence numbers are employed to match acknowledgements with data packets, and the last sequence number received from the neighbor is recorded so that out-of-order packets can be detected. A transmission list is used to queue packets for possible retransmission on a per-neighbor basis. Round-trip timers are kept in the neighbor-table entry to estimate an optimal retransmission interval.

Topology Tables

The *topology table* contains all destinations advertised by neighboring routers. The protocol-dependent modules populate the table, and the table is acted on by the DUAL finite-state machine. Each entry in the topology table includes the destination address and a list of neighbors that have advertised the destination. For each neighbor, the entry records the advertised metric, which the neighbor stores in its routing table. An important rule that distance vector protocols must follow is that if the neighbor advertises this destination, it must use the route to forward packets.

The metric that the router uses to reach the destination is also associated with the destination. The metric that the router uses in the routing table, and to advertise to other routers, is the sum of the best-advertised metric from all neighbors and the link cost to the best neighbor.

Route States

A topology-table entry for a destination can exist in one of two states: active or passive. A destination is in the *passive state* when the router is not performing a recomputation; it is in the *active state* when the router is performing a recomputation. If feasible successors are always available, a destination never has to go into the active state, thereby avoiding a recomputation.A recomputation occurs when a destination has no feasible successors. The router initiates the recomputation by sending a query packet to each of its neighboring routers. The neighboring router can send a reply packet, indicating that it has a feasible successor for the destination, or it can send a query packet, indicating that it is participating in the recomputation. While a destination is in the active state, a router cannot change the destination's routing-table information. After the router has received a reply from each neighboring router, the topology-table entry for the destination returns to the passive state, and the router can select a successor.

Route Tagging

Enhanced IGRP supports internal and external routes. Internal routes originate within an Enhanced IGRP AS. Therefore, a directly attached network that is configured to run Enhanced IGRP is considered an internal route and is propagated with this information throughout the Enhanced IGRP AS. External routes are learned by another routing protocol or reside in the routing table as static routes. These routes are tagged individually with the identity of their origin.

External routes are tagged with the following information:

1. Router ID of the Enhanced IGRP router that redistributed the route
2. AS number of the destination
3. Configurable administrator tag
4. ID of the external protocol
5. Metric from the external protocol
6. Bit flags for default routing

Route tagging allows the network administrator to customize routing and maintain flexible policy controls. Route tagging is particularly useful in transit ASs, where Enhanced IGRP typically interacts with an interdomain routing protocol that implements more global policies, resulting in a very scalable, policy-based routing.

Enhanced IGRP Packet Types

Enhanced IGRP uses the following packet types: hello and acknowledgement, update, query and reply.

Hello packets are multicast for neighbor discovery/recovery and do not require acknowledgement. An *acknowledgement* packet is a hello packet that has no data. Acknowledgment packets contain a nonzero acknowledgement number and always are sent by using a unicast address.

Update packets are used to convey reach ability of destinations. When a new neighbor is discovered, unicast update packets are sent so that the neighbor can build up its topology table. In other cases, such as a link-cost change, updates are multicast. Updates always are transmitted reliably.

Query and reply packets are sent when a destination has no feasible successors. *Query* packets are always multicast. Reply packets are sent in response to query packets to instruct the originator not to recompute the route because feasible successors exist. *Reply* packets are unicast to the originator of the query. Both query and reply packets are transmitted reliably.

7.8 EXTERIOR ROUTING PROTOCOLS

Exterior Routing Protocols or *Exterior Gateway Protocols (EGPs)* are used to exchange routing information between routers in different autonomous systems.

Two ERPs are in common use

1. Exterior Gateway Protocol.
2. Border Gateway Protocol.

EGP is being replaced progressively by BGP.

7.8.1 Exterior Gateway Protocol (EGP)

EGP is a *standard protocol*. The Exterior Gateway Protocol is the protocol used for exchange of routing information between *exterior* gateways (not belonging to the same autonomous system).

EGP gateways may only forward reachability information for networks within their autonomous system. This routing information must be collected by this EGP gateway, usually via an *Interior Gateway Protocol* (IGP), used to exchange information between gateways within an autonomous system.

EGP is based on periodic polling using *Hello/I Hear You* message exchanges, to monitor neighbor reach ability and poll requests to solicit update responses. EGP restricts exterior gateways by allowing them to advertise only those destination networks reachable entirely within that gateway's autonomous system. Thus, an exterior gateway using EGP passes along information to its EGP neighbors but does not advertise reachability information about its EGP neighbors (gateways are neighbors if they exchange routing information) outside the autonomous system. It has three main features:

1. It supports a *neighbor acquisition protocol.* Two gateways may be regarded as neighbors if they are connected by an *internet* which is transparent to them. EGP does not specify the way in which one gateway initially decides that it wants to become a neighbor of another. To become a neighbor it must send an *Acquisition confirm* message as a response to an *Acquisition Request* message. This step is necessary to obtain routing information from another gateway.
2. It supports a *neighbor reachability protocol.* It is used by a gateway to keep real-time information as to the reachability of its neighbors. The EGP protocol provides two message types for that purpose: a *Hello* message and an *I Hear You* message (response to Hello).
3. It supports update messages (also called *network reachability (NR) messages*) that carry routing information. No gateway is required to send NR messages to any other gateway, except as a response to a *poll request.*

To perform these three basic functions, EGP defines 10 message types:

1. *Acquisition request*

Request a gateway to become a neighbor (or peer)

2. *Acquisition confirm*

Positive response to acquisition request

3. *Acquisition refuse*

Negative response to acquisition request

4. *Cease request*

Request termination of neighbor relationship

5. *Cease confirm*

Confirmation response to cease request

6. *Hello*

Request neighbor to respond if alive

7. *I hear uou*

Response to Hello message

8. *Poll request*

Request network routing table

9. *Routing update*

Network reachability information

10. *Error*

Response to Incorrect Message

The EGP routing information messages associate a *distance* qualifier to each route. But, EGP *does not interpret these distance values*. They merely serve as an indication of the reachability or unreachability of a network (a value of 255 means that the network is unreachable). The value cannot be used to compute the shorter of two routes unless those routes are both contained within a single autonomous system. For this reason, EGP cannot be used as a routing algorithm. As a result there will be only one path from the exterior gateway to any network. EGP is gradually being replaced by the more functional Border Gateway Protocol (BGP). For a more detailed description of BGP refer to the next section.

7.8.2 Border Gateway Protocol (BGP)

The *Border Gateway Protocol (BGP)* is an interautonomous system routing protocol. An autonomous system is a network or group of networks under a common administration and with common routing policies. BGP is used to exchange routing information for the Internet and is the protocol used between Internet service providers (ISP). Customer networks, such as universities and corporations, usually employ an Interior Gateway Protocol (IGP) such as RIP or OSPF for the exchange of routing information within their networks. Customers connect to ISPs, and ISPs use BGP to exchange customer and ISP routes. When BGP is used between autonomous systems (AS), the protocol is referred to as External BGP (EBGP). If a service provider is using BGP to exchange routes within an AS, then the protocol is referred to as Interior BGP (IBGP).

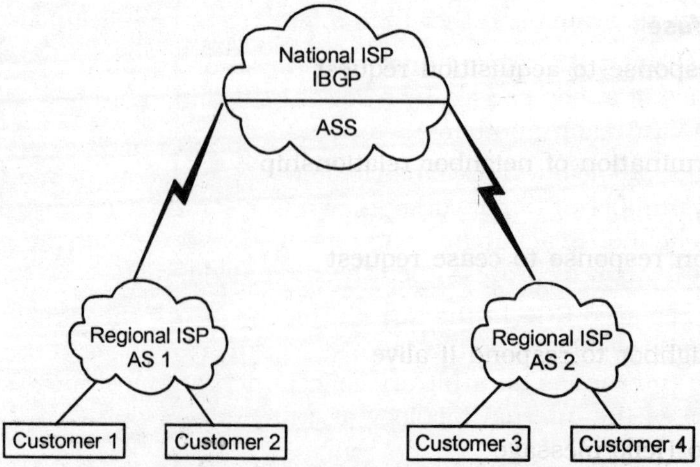

Figure 7.10 External and Interior BGP

BGP is a very robust and scalable routing protocol, as evidenced by the fact that BGP is the routing protocol employed on the Internet. At the time of this writing, the Internet BGP routing tables number more than 90,000 routes. To achieve scalability at this level, BGP uses many route parameters, called attributes, to define routing policies and maintain a stable routing environment.

In addition to BGP attributes, classless interdomain routing (CIDR) is used by BGP to reduce the size of the Internet routing tables. For example, assume that an ISP owns the IP address block 195.10.x.x from the traditional Class C address space. This block consists of 256 Class C address blocks, 195.10.0.x through 195.10.255.x. Assume that the ISP assigns a Class C block to each of its customers. Without CIDR, the ISP would advertise 256 Class C address blocks to its BGP peers. With CIDR, BGP can supernet the address space and advertise one block, 195.10.x.x. This block is the same size as a traditional Class B address block. The class distinctions are rendered obsolete by CIDR, allowing a significant reduction in the BGP routing tables.

BGP neighbors exchange full routing information when the TCP connection between neighbors is first established. When changes to the routing table are detected, the BGP routers send to their neighbors only those routes that have changed. BGP routers do not send periodic routing updates, and BGP routing updates advertise only the optimal path to a destination network.

There are four different versions of BGP defined. Where BGP is specified without a version number, it normally refers to BGP Version 3 unless the document pre-dates the publication of the BGP-3 definition.

Border Gateway Protocol Version 3 (BGP-3)

BGP-3 is an *inter-Autonomous System* (inter-AS) routing protocol based on experience gained from EGP. Unlike other routing protocols which communicate via packets or datagrams, BGP-3 is ***connection oriented;*** it uses TCP as a transport protocol. The well-known port number is 179.

Recall that the EGP was designed as a protocol to exchange *reachability* information between autonomous systems, rather than a true *routing* protocol.Flowbacks of EGP are:

1. Because inter-AS routing information is not available, EGP cannot detect the presence of a loop caused by a set of EGP routers all believing that one of the others can reach another AS to which none of them is connected.
2. A further problem with EGP has to do with the amount of information exchanged; as the number of IP networks known to the NSFNET increased, the size of the EGP Neighbor Reachability (NR) messages became quite large and the amount of time it took to process them became significant.

BGP-3 has replaced EGP in the NSFNET backbone for these reasons. Compare this to the Core System role played by the ARPANET in the early days of the Internet. Instead, BGP-3 views the Internet as an arbitrary collection of autonomous systems, and it does not take account of the internal topology of an AS nor of the IGP (or possibly multiple IGPs) used within an AS.

Path Selection

Each BGP speaker must evaluate different paths to a destination from the border router(s) for an AS connection, select the best one that complies with the routing policies in force and then advertise that route to all of its BGP neighbors at that AS connection. BGP-3 is a vector-distance protocol but, unlike traditional vector-distance protocols such as RIP where there is a single metric, BGP-3 determines a preference order by applying a function mapping each path to a preference value and selects the path with the highest value. The function applied is generated by the BGP-3 implementation according to configuration information.

Routing Policies

A BGP-3 implementation should be able to control which routes it announces. The granularity of this control should be at least at the network level for the announced routes and at the AS level for the recipients. For example, BGP-3 should allow a policy of announcing a route to a specific network to a specific adjacent AS.

BGP-3 should allow a weighting policy for paths. Each AS can be assigned a weight and the preferred path to a destination is then the one with the lowest aggregate weight. BGP-3 should allow a policy of excluding an AS from all possible paths. This can be done with a variant of the previous policy; each AS to be excluded is given an "infinite" weight and the route selection process refuses to consider paths of infinite weight.

Routing Information Exchange

BGP-3 only advertises routes that it uses itself to its neighbors. That is, BGP-3 conforms to the normal Internet hop-by-hop paradigm, even though it has additional information in the form of AS paths and theoretically could be capable of informing a neighbor of a route it would not use itself. When two BGP speakers form a BGP session, they begin by exchanging their entire routing tables. Routing information is exchanged via UPDATE messages (see below for the format of these messages). Since the routing information contains the complete AS path to each listed destination in the form of a list of AS numbers in addition to the usual reachability and next hop information used in traditional vector distance protocols, it can be used to suppress routing loops and to eliminate the *counting-to-infinity* problem found in RIP. After BGP neighbors have performed their initial exchange of their complete routing databases, they only exchange updates to that information.

BGP-3 Message Formats

All BGP-3 messages have a common basic format. They vary between 19 and 4096 bytes in length, are transmitted over TCP and are processed in their entirety (that is, a BGP speaker does not begin to process the message until it has received the whole message).

BGP OSPF Interaction

There is a *proposed standard protocol* with a status of *elective* defining how BGP-3 (an exterior routing protocol) should interact with OSPF (an interior routing protocol). Any host or router which dynamically exchanges information between BGP-3 and OSPF should adhere to this standard.

BGP Path Selection

BGP could possibly receive multiple advertisements for the same route from multiple sources. BGP selects only one path as the best path. When the path is selected, BGP puts the selected path in the IP routing table and propagates the path to its neighbors. BGP uses the following criteria, in the order presented, to select a path for a destination:

If the path specifies a next hop that is inaccessible, drop the update.

1. Prefer the path with the largest weight.
2. If the weights are the same, prefer the path with the largest local preference.
3. If the local preferences are the same, prefer the path that was originated by BGP running on this
4. Router.
5. If no route was originated, prefer the route that has the shortest AS_ path.
6. If all paths have the same AS_ path length, prefer the path with the lowest origin type (where IGP
7. Is lower than EGP, and EGP is lower than incomplete).
8. If the origin codes are the same, prefer the path with the lowest MED attribute.
9. If the paths have the same MED, prefer the external path over the internal path.
10. If the paths are still the same, prefer the path through the closest IGP neighbor.
11. Prefer the path with the lowest IP address, as specified by the BGP router ID.

8

TRANSPORT LAYER

8.1 INTRODUCTION TO TRANSPORT LAYER

The transport layer accepts data from the session layer and segments the data for transport across the network. Generally, the transport layer is responsible for making sure that the data is delivered error-free and in the proper sequence. Flow control generally occurs at the transport layer.

Flow control manages data transmission between devices so that the transmitting device does not send more data than the receiving device can process. Multiplexing enables data from several applications to be transmitted onto a single physical link. Virtual circuits are established, maintained, and terminated by the transport layer. Error checking involves creating various mechanisms for detecting transmission errors, while error recovery involves acting, such as requesting that data be retransmitted, to resolve any errors that occur. The transport protocols used on the Internet are TCP and UDP.

Regardless of the nature of the applications that are exchanging data, there is usually a requirement that data be exchanged reliably. That is, we would like to be assured that all of the data arrive at the destination application and that the data arrive in the same order in which they were sent. As we shall see, the mechanisms for providing reliability are essentially independent of the nature of the applications. Thus, it makes sense to collect those mechanisms in a common layer shared by all applications; this is referred to as the **transport layer.**

8.2 TRANSMISSION CONTROL PROTOCOL

TCP provides a different service than UDP. TCP offers a connection-oriented byte stream, instead of a connectionless datagram delivery service. TCP guarantees delivery, whereas UDP does not.TCP is used by network applications that require guaranteed delivery and cannot be bothered with doing time-outs and retransmissions.

The two most typical network applications that use TCP are File Transfer Protocol (FTP) and the TELNET. Other popular TCP network applications include X-Window System, rcp (remote copy), and the r-series commands. TCP's greater capability is not without cost: it requires more CPU and network bandwidth. The internals of the TCP module are much more complicated than those in a UDP module.

Similar to UDP, network applications connect to TCP ports. Well-defined port numbers are dedicated to specific applications. For instance, the TELNET server uses port number 23. The TELNET client can find the server simply by connecting to port 23 of TCP on the specified computer. When the application first starts using TCP, the TCP module on the client's computer and the TCP module on the server's computer start communicating with each other. These two end-point TCP modules contain state information that defines a virtual circuit. This virtual circuit consumes resources in both TCP end-points. The virtual circuit is full duplex; data can go in both directions simultaneously. The application writes data to the TCP port, the data traverses the network and is read by the application at the far end.

TCP packetizes the byte stream at will. It does not retain the boundaries between writes. For example, if an application does 5 writes to the TCP port, the application at the far end might do 10 reads to get all the data. Or it might get all the data with a single read. There is no correlation between the number and size of writes at one end to the number and size of reads at the other end.

TCP is a sliding window protocol with time-out and retransmits. Outgoing data must be acknowledged by the far-end. TCP acknowledgements can be piggybacked on data. Both receiving ends can flow control the far end, thus preventing a buffer overrun. As with all sliding window protocols, the protocol has a window size. The window size determines the amount of data that can be transmitted before an acknowledgement is required. For TCP, this amount is not a number of TCP segments but a number of bytes.

The **TCP provides reliable transmission of data in an IP environment.** TCP corresponds to the transport layer of the OSI reference model. Among the services TCP provides are stream data transfer, reliability, efficient flow control, full-duplex operation, and multiplexing.

With stream data transfer, **TCP delivers an unstructured stream of bytes** identified by sequence numbers. This service benefits applications because they do not have to chop data into blocks before handing it off to TCP. Instead, TCP groups bytes into segments and passes them to IP for delivery.

TCP offers reliability by providing connection-oriented, end-to-end reliable packet delivery through an internetwork. It does this by sequencing bytes with a forwarding acknowledgement number that indicates to the destination the next byte the source expects to receive. Bytes not acknowledged within a specified time period are retransmitted. The reliability mechanism of TCP allows devices to deal with lost, delayed, duplicate, or misread packets. A time-out mechanism allows devices to detect lost packets and request retransmission.

TCP offers efficient flow control, which means that, when sending acknowledgements back to the source, the receiving TCP process indicates the highest sequence number it can receive without overflowing its internal buffers.

Full-duplex operation means that TCP processes can both send and receive at the same time.

Finally, **TCP's multiplexing** means that numerous simultaneous upper-layer conversations can be multiplexed over a single connection.

8.2.1 TCP Connection Establishment

To use reliable transport services, TCP hosts must establish a connection-oriented session with one another. Connection establishment is performed by using a "three-way handshake" mechanism.

A three-way handshake synchronizes both ends of a connection by allowing both sides to agree upon initial sequence numbers. This mechanism also guarantees that both sides are ready to transmit data and know that the other side is ready to transmit as well. This is necessary so that packets are not transmitted or retransmitted during session establishment or after session termination. Each host randomly chooses a sequence number used to track bytes within the stream it is sending and receiving. Then, the three-way handshake proceeds in the following manner:

The first host (Host A) initiates a connection by sending a packet with the initial sequence number (X) and SYN bit set to indicate a connection request. The second host (Host B) receives the SYN, records the sequence number X, and replies by acknowledging the SYN (with an ACK = X + 1). Host B includes its own initial sequence number (SEQ = Y). An ACK = 20 means the host has received bytes 0 through 19 and expects byte 20 next. This technique is called *forward acknowledgement*. Host A then acknowledges all bytes Host B sent with a forward acknowledgement indicating the next byte Host A expects to receive (ACK = Y + 1). Data transfer then can begin.

8.2.2 Positive Acknowledgement and Retransmission (PAR)

A simple transport protocol might implement a reliability-and-flow-control technique where the source sends one packet, starts a timer, and waits for an acknowledgement before sending a new packet. If the acknowledgement is not received before the timer expires, the source retransmits the packet. Such a technique is called *positive acknowledgement and retransmission* (PAR).

By **assigning each packet a sequence number,** PAR enables hosts to track lost or duplicate packets caused by network delays that result in premature retransmission. The sequence numbers are sent back in the acknowledgements so that the acknowledgements can be tracked.

PAR is an inefficient use of bandwidth, however, because a host must wait for an acknowledgement before sending a new packet, and only one packet can be sent at a time.

8.2.3 TCP Sliding Window

A ***TCP sliding window*** **provides more efficient use of network bandwidth** than PAR because it enables hosts to send multiple bytes or packets before waiting for an acknowledgement. In TCP, the receiver specifies the current window size in every packet. Because TCP provides a byte-stream connection, window sizes are expressed in bytes. This means that a window is the number of data bytes that the sender is allowed to send before waiting for an acknowledgement. Initial window sizes are indicated at connection setup, but might vary throughout the data transfer to provide flow control. A window size of zero, for instance, means "Send no data."

In a TCP sliding-window operation, for example, the sender might have a sequence of bytes to send (numbered 1 to 10) to a receiver who has a window size of five. The sender then would place a window around the first five bytes and transmit them together. It would then wait for an acknowledgement.The receiver would respond with an ACK = 6, indicating that it has received bytes 1 to 5 and is expecting byte 6 next. In the same packet, the receiver would indicate that its window size is 5. The sender then would move the sliding window five bytes to the right and transmit bytes 6 to 10. The receiver would respond with an ACK = 11, indicating that it is expecting sequenced byte 11 next. In this packet, the receiver might indicate that its window size is 0 (because, for example, its internal buffers are full). At this point, the sender cannot send any more bytes until the receiver sends another packet with a window size greater than 0.

8.2.4 TCP Packet Format

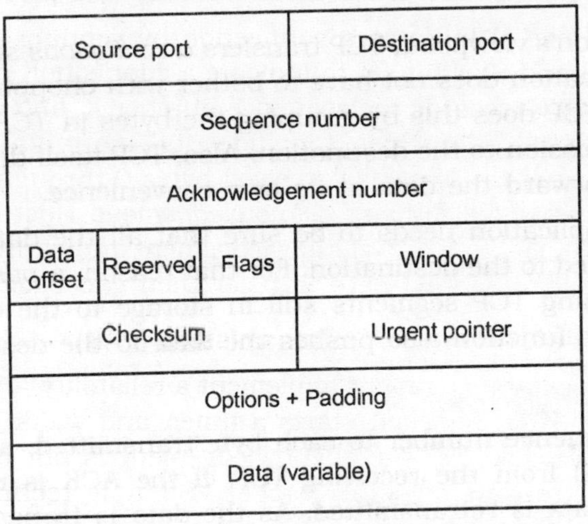

Figure 8.1 Twelve Fields Comprise a TCP Packet

TCP Packet Field Descriptions

The following descriptions summarize the TCP packet fields illustrated in Figure 8.1.

Source Port* and *Destination Port–Identifies points at which upper-layer source and destination processes receive TCP services.

Sequence Number–Usually specifies the number assigned to the first byte of data in the current message. In the connection-establishment phase, this field also can be used to identify an initial sequence number to be used in an upcoming transmission.

Acknowledgement Number–Contains the sequence number of the next byte of data the sender of the packet expects to receive.

Data Offset–Indicates the number of 32-bit words in the TCP header.

Reserved–Remains reserved for future use.

Flags–Carries a variety of control information, including the SYN and ACK bits used for connection establishment, and the FIN bit used for connection termination.

Window–Specifies the size of the sender's receive window (that is, the buffer space available for incoming data).

Checksum–Indicates whether the header was damaged in transit.

Urgent Pointer–Points to the first urgent data byte in the packet.

Options-Specifies various TCP options.

Data–Contains upper-layer information.

As noted above, the primary purpose of TCP is *to provide reliable logical circuit or connection service between pairs of processes.* It does *not* assume reliability from the lower-level protocols (such as IP) so TCP must guarantee this itself.

8.2.5 TCP can be Characterized by the Following Facilities it Provides for the Applications Using it

Stream Data Transfer

From the application's viewpoint, TCP transfers *a contiguous stream of bytes* through the internet. The application does not have to bother with chopping the data into basic blocks or datagrams. TCP does this by grouping the bytes in *TCP segments*, which are passed to IP for transmission to the destination. Also, TCP itself decides how to segment the data and it may forward the data at its own convenience.

Sometimes, an application needs to be sure that all the data passed to TCP has actually been transmitted to the destination. For that reason, a *push* function is defined. It will push all remaining TCP segments still in storage to the destination host. The normal *close connection* function also pushes the data to the destination.

Reliability

TCP assigns a sequence number to each byte transmitted, and expects a positive acknowledgement (ACK) from the receiving TCP. If the ACK is not received within a timeout interval, the data is retransmitted. As the data is transmitted in blocks (TCP segments) only the sequence number of the first data byte in the segment is sent to the destination host. The receiving TCP uses the sequence numbers to rearrange the segments when they arrive out of order, and to eliminate duplicate segments.

Flow Control

The receiving TCP, when sending an ACK back to the sender, also indicates to the sender the number of bytes it can receive beyond the last received TCP segment, without causing overrun and overflow in its internal buffers. This is sent in the ACK in the form of the highest sequence number it can receive without problems. This mechanism is also referred to as a *window*-mechanism and we will discuss it in more detail later in this chapter.

Multiplexing

Is achieved through the use of ports, just as with UDP.

Logical Connections

The reliability and flow control mechanisms described above require that TCP initializes and maintains certain status information for each "data stream". The combination of this status, including sockets, sequence numbers and window sizes, is called a logical connection. Each connection is uniquely identified by the pair of sockets used by the sending and receiving processes.

Full Duplex

TCP provides for concurrent data streams in both directions.

8.2.6 Acknowledgement and Retransmissions

TCP sends data in variable length segments. Sequence numbers are based on a byte count. Acknowledgements specify the sequence number of the next byte that the receiver expects to receive.

Now suppose that a segment gets lost or corrupted. In this case, the receiver will acknowledge all further well-received segments with an acknowledgement referring to the first byte of the missing packet. The sender will stop transmitting when it has sent all the bytes in the window. Eventually, a timeout will occur and the missing segment will be retransmitted. Suppose a window size of 1500 bytes, and segments of 500 bytes.

A problem now arises, since the sender does know that segment 2 is lost or corrupted, but doesn't know anything about segments 3 and 4. The sender should at least retransmit segment 2, but it could also retransmit segments 3 and 4 (since they are within the current window). It is possible that:

Segment 3 has been received, and for segment 4 we don't know: it could be received, but ACK didn't reach us yet, or it could be lost also. Segment 3 was lost, and we received the ACK 1500 upon the reception of segment 4. Each TCP implementation is free to react to a timeout as the implementers wish. It could retransmit only segment 2, but in case 2 above, we will be waiting again until segment 3 times out. In this case, we lose all of the throughput advantages of the window mechanism. Or TCP might immediately resend all of the segments in the current window. Whatever the choice, maximal throughput is lost. This is because the ACK does not contain a second acknowledgment sequence number indicating the actual frame received.

8.2.7 Variable Timeout Intervals

Each TCP should implement an algorithm to adapt the timeout values to be used for the round trip time of the segments. To do this, TCP records the time at which a segment was sent, and the time at which the ACK is received. A weighted average is calculated over several of these round trip times, to be used as a timeout value for the next segment(s) to be sent.

This is an important feature, since delays may be variable on an internet, depending on multiple factors, such as the load of an intermediate low-speed network or the saturation of an intermediate IP gateway.

8.2.8 Establishing a TCP Connection

Before any data can be transferred, a connection has to be established between the two processes. One of the processes (usually the server) issues a passive OPEN call, the other an active OPEN call. The passive OPEN call remains dormant until another process tries to connect to it by an active OPEN. On the network, three TCP segments are exchanged: This whole process is known as three-way handshake. Note that the exchanged TCP segments include the initial sequence numbers from both sides, to be used on subsequent data transfers.

Closing the connection is done implicitly by sending a TCP segment with the FIN bit (no more data) set. As the connection is full-duplex (that is, we have two independent data streams, one in each direction), the FIN segment only closes the data transfer in one direction. The other process will now send the remaining data it still has to transmit and also ends with a TCP segment where the FIN bit is set. The connection is deleted (status information on both sides) once the data stream is closed in both directions. TCP Segments Carried by IP Datagrams TCP segments are transported in IP datagrams with the following parameter settings:

Type of Service = 00000000
Precedence = routine
Delay = normal
Throughput = normal
Time to Live = 00111100 (1 minute)

8.2.9 TCP Application Programming Interface

The TCP application programming interface is not fully defined. The following function calls are described:

Open

To establish a connection, takes several parameters:

1. Active/passive.
2. Foreign socket.
3. Local port number.
4. Timeout value (optional).
5. Returns a local connection name, which is used to reference this particular connection in all other functions.

Send

Causes data in a referenced user buffer to be sent over the connection. Can optionally set the URGENT flag or the PUSH flag.

Receive

Copies incoming TCP data to a user buffer.

Close

Closes the connection; causes a push of all remaining data and a TCP segment with FIN flag set.

Status

Is an implementation-dependent call that could return information such as:

1. Local and foreign socket

2. Send and receive window sizes
3. Connection state
4. Local connection name

Abort

Causes all pending Send and Receive operations to be aborted, and a RESET to be sent to the foreign TCP.

8.3 USER DATAGRAM PROTOCOL (UDP)

The User Datagram Protocol (UDP) is a connectionless transport-layer protocol that belongs to the Internet protocol family. UDP is basically an interface between IP and upper-layer processes. UDP protocol ports distinguish multiple applications running on a single device from one another.

Unlike the TCP, **UDP adds no reliability, flow-control, or error-recovery functions to IP.** Because of UDP's simplicity, UDP headers contain fewer bytes and consume less network overhead than TCP.

UDP is useful in situations where the reliability mechanisms of TCP are not necessary, such as in cases where a higher-layer protocol might provide error and flow control.

UDP is the transport protocol for several well-known application-layer protocols, including Network File System (NFS), Simple Network Management Protocol (SNMP), Domain Name System (DNS), and Trivial File Transfer Protocol (TFTP).The UDP packet format contains four fields, as shown in Figure 8.2 These include source and destination ports, length, and checksum fields.

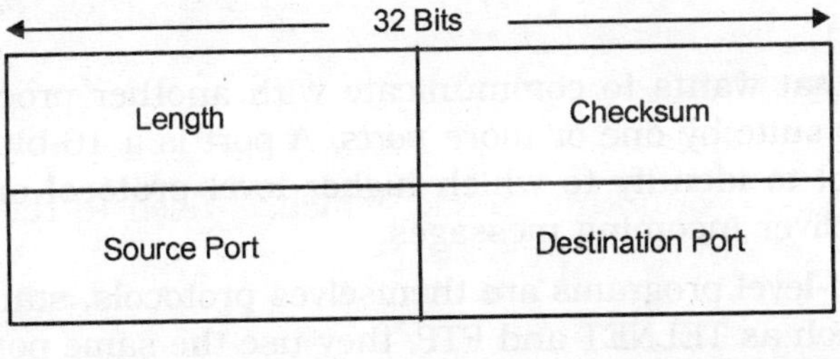

Figure 8.2 A UDP Packet Consists of Four Fields

Source and destination ports contain the 16-bit UDP protocol port numbers used to demultiplex datagrams for receiving application-layer processes. A length field specifies the length of the UDP header and data. Checksum provides an (optional) integrity check on the UDP header and data.

8.4 WHY DO BOTH TCP AND UDP EXIST, INSTEAD OF JUST ONE OR THE OTHER?

They supply different services. Most applications are implemented to use only one or the other. You, the programmer, choose the protocol that best meets your needs. If you need a reliable stream delivery service, TCP might be best. If you need a datagram service, UDP might be best. If you need efficiency over long-haul circuits, TCP might be best. If you need efficiency over fast networks with short latency, UDP might be best. If your needs do not fall nicely into these categories, then the "best" choice is unclear. However, applications can make up for deficiencies in the choice. For instance if you choose UDP and you need reliability, then the application must provide reliability. If you choose TCP and you need a record oriented service, then the application must insert markers in the byte stream to delimit records.

8.5 HOW DOES A CLIENT ON ONE COMPUTER REACH THE SERVER ON ANOTHER?

The path of communication between an application and UDP is through UDP ports. These ports are numbered, beginning with zero. An application that is offering service (the server) waits for messages to come in on a specific port dedicated to that service. The server waits patiently for any client to request service. For instance, the SNMP server, called an SNMP agent, always waits on port 161. There can be only one SNMP agent per computer because there's only one UDP port number 161. This port number is well known; it is a fixed number, an internet assigned number. If an SNMP client wants service, it sends its request to port number 161 of UDP on the destination computer.

When an application sends data out through UDP it arrives at the far end as a single unit. For example, if an application does 5 writes to the UDP port, the application at the far end will do 5 reads from the UDP port. Also, the sizes of each write matches the size of each read.UDP preserves the message boundary defined by the application. It never joins two application messages together, or divides a single application message into parts.

8.6 PORTS AND SOCKETS

In this section we will introduce the concepts of *port* and *socket.*

8.6.1 Ports

Each *process* that wants to communicate with another process identifies itself to the TCP/IP protocol suite by one or more *ports.* A port is a 16-bit number, used by the host-to-host protocol to identify to which higher-level protocol or application program (process) it must deliver incoming messages.

As some higher-level programs are themselves protocols, standardized in the TCP/IP protocol suite, such as TELNET and FTP, they use the same port number in all TCP/IP implementations. Those "assigned" port numbers are called *well-known ports* and the standard applications *well-known services.*

The "well-known" ports are controlled and assigned by the Internet Assigned Numbers Authority (IANA) and on most systems can only be used by system processes or by programs executed by privileged users. The assigned "well-known" ports occupy port numbers in the range 0 to 1023. The ports with numbers in the range 1024-65535 are not controlled by the IANA and on most systems can be used by ordinary user-developed programs.

Confusion due to two different applications trying to use the same port numbers on one host is avoided by writing those applications to request an available port from TCP/IP. Because this port number is dynamically assigned, it may differ from one invocation of an application to the next.

8.6.2 Sockets

Let us first consider the following terminologies:

1. A *socket* is a special type of *file handle* which is used by a process to request network services from the operating system.
2. A socket address is the triple:

   {protocol, local-address, local-process}

   In the TCP/IP suite, for example:

   {*tcp, 172.16.2.1, 12345*}
3. A *conversation* is the communication link between two processes.
4. An *association* is the 5-tuple that completely specifies the two processes that comprise a connection:

   {*protocol, local-address, local-process, foreign-address, foreign-process*}

   In the TCP/IP suite, for example:

   {*tcp, 172.16.2.2, 1500, 193.44.234.5, 21*}

   could be a valid association.

   A *half-association* is either:

   {*protocol, local-address, local-process*}

   or

   {*protocol, foreign-address, foreign-process*}

   which specify each half of a connection.
5. The half-association is also called a *socket* or a *transport address*. That is, a socket is an end point for communication that can be named and addressed in a network.

   The socket interface is one of several *application programming interfaces (APIs)* to the communication protocols.

Basic Socket Calls

The following lists some basic socket interface calls. In the next section we shall see an example scenario of using these socket interface calls.

Initialize a socket

int *sockfd* = socket(int *family*, int *type*, int *protocol*)

where:

Family stands for *addressing family*. It can take on values such as AF_UNIX, AF_INET, AF_NS and AF_IUCV. Its purpose is to specify the method of addressing used by the socket.

type stands for the type of socket interface to be used. It can take on values such as SOCK_STREAM, SOCK_DGRAM, SOCK_RAW, and SOCK_SEQPACKET.

Protocol can be UDP, TCP, IP or ICMP.

sockfd is an integer (similar to a file descriptor) returned by the socket call.

Bind (Register) a socket to a port address

int bind(int *sockfd*, struct sockaddr **localaddr*, int *addrlen*)

where:

sockfd is the same integer returned by the socket call.

localaddr is the local address returned by the bind call.

Note that after the bind call, we now have values for the first three parameters inside our 5-tuple association:

{*protocol, local-address, local-process, foreign-address, foreign-process*}

Indicate readiness to receive connections

FORMAT: int listen (int *sockfd*, int *queue-size*)

where:

sockfd is the same integer returned by the socket call.

queue-size indicates the number of connection requests which can be queued by the system while the local process has not yet issued the accept call.

Accept a connection

int accept(int *sockfd*, struct sockaddr **foreign-address*, int *addrlen*)

where:

sockfd is the same integer returned by the socket call.

foreign-address is the address of the foreign (client) process returned by the accept call.

This accept call is issued by a server process rather than a client process. If there is a connection request waiting on the queue for this socket connection, accept takes the first request on the queue and creates another socket with the same properties as *sockfd*; otherwise, accept will block the caller process until a connection request arrives.

Request connection to the server

int connect (int *sockfd*, struct sockaddr **foreign-address*, int *addrlen*)

where:

sockfd is the same integer returned by the socket call.

foreign-address is the address of the foreign (server) process returned by the connect call. Note that this call is issued by a client process rather than a server process.

Send and/or receive data

The read(), readv(*sockfd*, char **buffer*, int *addrlen*), recv(), readfrom(), send(*sockfd*, *msg*, *len*, *flags*), write() calls can be used to receive and send data in an established socket association (or connection).

Note that these calls are similar to the standard read and write file I/O system calls.

Close a socket

int close(int *sockfd*)

where:

sockfd is the same integer returned by the socket call.

The socket interface is differentiated by the different services that are provided. Stream, datagram, and raw sockets each define a different service available to applications.

Stream socket interface (SOCK_STREAM): It defines a reliable connection-oriented service (over TCP for example). Data is sent without errors or duplication and is received in the same order as it is sent. Flow control is built-in to avoid data overruns. No boundaries are imposed on the exchanged data, which is considered to be a stream of bytes. An example of an application that uses stream sockets is the File Transfer Program (FTP).

Datagram socket interface (SOCK_DGRAM): It defines a connectionless service (over UDP for example). Datagrams are sent as independent packets. The service provides no guarantees; data can be lost or duplicated, and datagrams can arrive out of order. No disassembly and reassembly of packets is performed. An example of an application that uses datagram sockets is the Network File System (NFS).

Raw socket interface (SOCK_RAW): It allows direct access to lower-layer protocols such as IP and ICMP. This interface is often used for testing new protocol implementations. An example of an application that uses raw sockets is the Ping command.

9

APPLICATION LAYER

9.1 DOMAIN NAME SYSTEM, AND THE IMPLEMENTATION OF NAME SERVERS

Internet works on the numbering system. These numbers are called IP. When we connect to the net we have seen a set of 4 numbers being dialled *i.e.* for each address on the Internet there is a unique set of these 32 bit numbers. Domain Name Servers are the servers, which maintain a distributed list of all domains against Internet Protocol address.

Earlier to Domain Name Servers there was a system of having a host table maintained by SRI-NIC. It was updated twice a week to include new sites. System would download the copy of this table through FTP. There are two types of servers as below:

1. Resolver
2. DNS.

There are a number of servers, which maintain the addresses of sites. When browser needs the address of any site, resolver queries the nearest name server, replies immediately if it knows the answer or it asks another server. Thus every server has two roles to play:

1. As a server for name server
2. Super server to extend functionality.

All web sites are arranged in 7 branches namely arpa, com, edu, net, gov, mil, org. Following this are 236 country name abbreviations like ".in" for India. This helps to locate the site easily. The IP addresses of name servers at each of the domain name tags are maintained by 10 root servers.

When a DNS fields a query that it cannot answer :

1. It sends a query to root server.
2. Root server says it does not know but a machine at say 195.95.251.10 might know.
3. DNS sends a query to the above machine.
4. Server at 195.95.251.10 knows the answer.
5. DNS returns answer to your PC.

9.1.1 The Distributed Name Space

The Domain Name System uses the concept of a *distributed name space*. Symbolic names are grouped into *zones of authority*, or more commonly *zones*. In each of these zones, one or more hosts has the task of maintaining a database of symbolic names and IP addresses and providing a server function for clients who wish to translate between symbolic names and IP addresses. These local *name servers* are then (through the internet on which they are connected) logically interconnected into a hierarchical tree of *domains*. Each zone contains a part or a *subtree* of the hierarchical tree and the names within the zone are administered independently of names in other zones. Authority over zones in vested in the name servers. Normally, the name servers which have authority for a zone will have domain names belonging to that zone, but this is not required. Where a domain contains a subtree which falls in a different zone, the name server(s) with authority over the superior domain are said to *delegate authority* to the name server(s) with authority over the subdomain. Name servers may also delegate authority to themselves; in this case, the domain name space is still divided into zones moving down the domain name tree, but authority for two zones is held by the same server.

The division of the domain name space into zones is accomplished using resource records stored in the Domain Name System:

Start of Authority (SOA) Records. Defines the start of a zone.

Name Server (NS) Records. Marks the end of a zone started by an SOA record and points to a name server having authority for the next zone.

In this context, the start of a domain is closer to the root of the tree than the end. At the root, there can be no higher name servers to delegate authority: authority for the zone encompassing the root of the name space is vested in a set of *root name servers*. The results of this scheme are:

1. Rather than having a central server for the database, the work that is involved in maintaining this database is off-loaded to hosts throughout the name space.
2. Authority for creating and changing symbolic host names and responsibility for maintaining a database for them is delegated to the organization owning the zone (within the name space) containing those host names.
3. From the user's standpoint, there is a single database that deals with these address resolutions. The user may be aware that the database is distributed, but generally need not be concerned about this.

Although domains within the namespace will frequently map in a logical fashion to networks and subnets within the IP addressing scheme, this is not a requirement of the Domain Name System. Consider a router between two subnets: it has two IP addresses, one for each network adapter, but it would not normally have two symbolic names.

9.1.2 Domain Resolution

Domain resolution is a client/server process. The client function (called the *resolver* or *name resolver*) is transparent to the user and is called by an application to resolve symbolic high-level names into real IP-addresses or vice versa. The name server (also called a *domain name server*) is a server application providing the translation between high-level machine names and the IP addresses. The former shows a program called a *full resolver*, which is a program distinct from the user program, which forwards all queries to a name server for processing. Responses are cached by the name server for future use, and often by the name server. The latter shows a *stub resolver*, which is a routine linked with the user program, which forwards the queries to a name server for processing. Responses are cached by the name server but not usually by the resolver although this is implementation dependent. On UNIX, the stub resolver is implemented by two library routines: gethostbyname (and gethostbyaddr) for converting host names to IP addresses and vice versa. Other platforms have the same or equivalent routines. Stub resolvers are much more common than full resolvers.

Domain Name Resolver Operation

Domain name queries can be one of two types:

1. *recursive* or
2. *iterative* (also termed *non-recursive*).

A flag bit in the domain name query specifies whether the client desires a recursive query and a flag bit in the response specifies whether the server supports recursive queries. The difference between a recursive and an iterative query arises when the server receives a request for which it cannot supply a complete answer by itself. A recursive query requests that the server should issue a query itself to determine the requested information and return the complete answer to the client. An iterative query means that the name server should return what information it has available and also a list of additional servers for the client to contact to complete the query.

Domain name responses can be one of two types:

1. *authoritative* and
2. *non-authoritative*.

A flag bit in the response indicates which type a response is. When a name server receives a query for a domain in a zone over which it has authority, it returns all of the requested information in a response with the authoritative answer flag set. When it receives a query for a domain over which it does not have authority, its actions depend upon the setting of the recursion desired flag in the query.

1. If the recursion desired flag is set and the server supports recursive queries, it will direct its query to another name server. This will either be a name server with authority for the domain given in the query, or it will be one of the root name servers. If the second server does not return an authoritative answer (for example if it has delegated authority to another server) the process is repeated. When a server (or a full resolver program) receives a response, it will cache it to improve the performance of repeat queries. The cache entry is stored for a maximum length of time specified by the originator in a 32-bit *time-to-live (TTL)* field contained in the response. 172,800 seconds (two days) is a typical TTL value.

2. If the recursion desired flag is not set or the server does not support recursive queries, it will return whatever information it has in its cache and also a list of additional name servers to be contacted for authoritative information.

9.1.3 Domain Name Server Operation

Each name server has *authority* for zero or more zones. There are three types of name server:

1. **Primary.** A primary name server loads a zone's information from disk, and has authority over the zone.
2. **Secondary.** A secondary name server has authority for a zone, but obtains its zone information from a primary server using a process called *zone transfer.* To remain synchronized, the secondary name servers query the primary on a regular basis (typically every three hours) and re-execute the zone transfer if the primary has been updated. A name server can operate as a primary or a secondary name server for multiple domains, or a primary for some domains and as a secondary for others. A primary or secondary name server performs all of the functions of a caching only name server.
3. **Caching-only.** A name server that does not have authority for any zone is called a caching-only name server. A caching-only name server obtains all of its data from primary or secondary name servers as required. It requires at least one NS record to point to a name server from which it can initially obtain information.

When a domain is registered with the root and a separate zone of authority established, the following rules apply:

- The domain must be registered with the root administrator.
- There must be an identified administrator for the domain.
- There must be at least two name servers with authority for the zone which are accessible from outside and inside the domain to ensure no single point of failure).

It is also recommended that name servers which delegate authority also apply these rules, since the delegating name servers are responsible for the behavior of name servers under their authority.

9.1.4 Domain System Resource Records

The Domain Name System's distributed database is composed of *resource records (RRs).* They provide a mapping between domain names and *network objects.* The most common network objects are the addresses of Internet hosts, but the Domain Name System is designed to accommodate a wide range of different objects. The general format of a resource record is:

name ttl class type rdata

where:

name

Is the domain name to be defined. The domain name system is very general in its rules for the composition of domain names. However, it recommends a syntax for domain names which will minimize the likelihood of applications which use a DNS resolver (that is, nearly all TCP/IP applications) from misinterpreting a domain name. A domain name adhering to this recommended syntax will consist of a series of labels consisting of alphanumeric characters or hyphens, each label having a length of between 1 and 63 characters, starting with an alphabetic character. Each pair of labels is separated by a dot (period) in human readable form, but not in the form used within DNS messages. Domain names are not case-sensitive.

ttl

Is the *time-to-live (TTL)* time in seconds that this resource record will be valid in a name server cache. This is stored in the DNS as an unsigned 32-bit value. 86400 (one day) is a typical value for records pointing to IP addresses.

class

1. Identifies the protocol family. Commonly used values are:
2. IN
3. The Internet system
4. CH
5. The Chaos system

type

Identifies the type of the resource in this resource record.

Rdata

The value depends on the type, for example:

1. A ,A 32-bit IP address (if the class is IN)'
2. CNAME ,A domain name
3. MX ,A 16-bit preference value (low values being preferred) followed by a domain name.
4. NS ,A host name
5. PTR ,A domain name

9.1.5 Domain Name System Messages

All messages in the Domain Name System protocol use a single format. This frame is sent by the resolver to the name server. Only the header and the question section are used to form the query. Replies and/or forwarding of the query use the same frame, but with more sections filled in (the answer/authority/additional sections).

Header Format

The header section is always present and has a fixed length of 12 bytes. The other sections are of variable length.

1. **ID.** A 16-bit identifier assigned by the program. This identifier is copied in the corresponding reply from the name server and can be used for differentiation of responses when multiple queries are outstanding at the same time.

2. **Parameters.** A 16-bit value in the following format.
3. **QR.** Flag identifying a query (0) or a response(1).
4. **Op code.** 4-bit field specifying the kind of query:

   0 standard query (QUERY)

   1 inverse query (IQUERY)

   2 server status request (STATUS) Other values are reserved for future use

AA

Authoritative answer flag. If set in a response, this flag specifies that the responding name server is an authority for the domain name sent in the query.

TC

Truncation flag. Set if message was longer than permitted on the physical channel.

RD

Recursion desired flag. This bit signals to the name server that recursive resolution is asked for. The bit is copied to the response.

RA

Recursion available flag. Indicates whether the name server supports recursive resolution.

Zero

3 bits reserved for future use. Must be zero.

Rcode

4-bit response code. Possible values are:

0 No error.

1 Format error. The server was unable to interpret the message.

2 Server failure. The message was not processed because of a problem with the server.

3 Name error. The domain name in the query does not exist. This is only valid if the AA bit is set in the response.

4 Not implemented. The requested type of query is not implemented by name server

5 Refused. The server refuses to respond for policy reasons. Other values are reserved for future use.

QDcount

An unsigned 16-bit integer specifying the number of entries in the question section.

ANcount

An unsigned 16-bit integer specifying the number of RRs in the answer section.

NScount

An unsigned 16-bit integer specifying the number of name server RRs in the authority section.

ARcount

An unsigned 16-bit integer specifying the number of RRs in the additional records section.

Message Compression

In order to reduce the message size, a compression scheme is used to eliminate the repetition of domain names in the various RRs. Any duplicate domain name or list of labels is replaced with a pointer to the previous occurrence. The pointer has the form of a 2-byte field:

1. The first 2 bits distinguish the pointer from a normal label, which is restricted to a 63-byte length plus the length byte ahead of it (which has a value of <64).
2. The offset field specifies an offset from the start of the message. A zero offset specifies the first byte of the ID field in the header.
    1. If compression is used in an Rdata field of an answer, authority or additional section of the message, the preceding RDlength field contains the real length after compression is done.

9.1.6 Transport

Domain Name System Messages are transmitted either as datagrams (UDP) or via stream connection (TCP).

UDP Usage

Server port 53 (decimal).

Messages carried by UDP are restricted to 512 bytes. Longer messages are truncated and the TC bit is set in the header. Since UDP frames can be lost, a retransmission strategy is required.

TCP Usage

Server port 53 (decimal).

In this case, the message is preceded by a 2-byte field indicating the total message frame length.

9.2 TELNET

The TELNET protocol provides a standardized interface, through which a program on one host (the TELNET client) may access the resources of another host (the TELNET server) as though the client were a local terminal connected to the server. For example, a user on a workstation on a LAN may connect to a host attached to the LAN as though the workstation were a terminal attached directly to the host. Of course, TELNET may be used across WANs as well as LANs.

TELNET Operation

TELNET protocol is based on three ideas:

1. The ***Network Virtual Terminal (NVT)* concept.** An NVT is an imaginary device having a basic structure common to a wide range of real terminals. Each host maps its own terminal characteristics to those of an NVT, and assumes that every other host will do the same.
2. A **symmetric view of terminals** and processes.
3. **Negotiation of terminal options.** The principle of negotiated options is used by the TELNET protocol, because many hosts wish to provide additional services, beyond those available with the NVT. Various options may be negotiated. Server and client use a set of conventions to establish the operational characteristics of their TELNET connection via the "DO, DON'T, WILL, WON'T" mechanism discussed later in this chapter.

The two hosts begin by verifying their mutual understanding. Once this initial negotiation is complete, they are capable of working on the minimum level implemented by the NVT. After this minimum understanding is achieved, they can negotiate additional options to extend the capabilities of the NVT to reflect more accurately the capabilities of the real hardware in use. Because of the symmetric model used by TELNET, both the host and the client may propose additional options to be used.

Network Virtual Terminal

The NVT has a printer (or display) and a keyboard. The keyboard produces outgoing data, which is sent over the TELNET connection. The printer receives the incoming data. The basic characteristics of an NVT, unless they are modified by mutually agreed options are:

1. The data representation is 7-bit ASCII transmitted in 8-bit bytes.
2. The NVT is a half-duplex device operating in a line-buffered mode.
3. The NVT provides a local echo function.

All of these may be negotiated by the two hosts. For example, a local echo is preferred because of the lower network load and superior performance but there is an option for using a remote echo, although no host is required to use it.

TELNET Options

There is an extensive set of TELNET options, and the reader should consult *STD 1-Official Internet Protocol Standards* for the standardization state and status for each of them.

TELNET Command Structure

The communication between client and server is handled with internal commands, which are not accessible by users. All internal TELNET commands consist of 2 or 3-byte sequences, depending on the command type. The Interpret As Command (IAC) character is followed by a command code. If this command deals with option negotiation, the command will have a third byte to show the code for the referenced option.

Option Negotiation

Using internal commands, TELNET in each host is able to negotiate options. The starting base of negotiation is the NVT capability: each host to be connected must agree to this minimum. Every option can be negotiated by the use of the four command codes WILL, WON'T, DO, DON'T described above. In addition, some options have sub-options: if both parties agree to the option, they use the SB and SE commands to manage the sub-negotiation.

Telnet Basic Commands

The primary goal of the TELNET protocol is the provision of a standard interface for hosts over a network. To allow the connection to start, the TELNET protocol defines a standard representation for some functions:

IP	Interrupt Process
AO	Abort Output
AYT	Are You There
EC	Erase Character
EL	Erase Line
SYNCH	Synchronize

9.3 FILE TRANSFER PROTOCOL (FTP)

Copying files from one machine to another is one of the most frequently used operations. The data transfer between client and server can be in either direction. The client may send a file to the server machine. It may also request a file from this server. To access remote files, the user must identify himself to the server. At this point the server is responsible for authenticating the client before it allows the file transfer. From an FTP user's point of view, the link is connection-oriented. In other words, it is necessary to have both hosts up and running TCP/IP to establish a file transfer.

Overview of FTP

FTP uses TCP as a transport protocol to provide reliable end-to-end connections. Two connections are used: the first is for **login** and follows the TELNET protocol and the second is for **managing the data transfer.** As it is necessary to log into the remote host, the user must have a user name and a password to access files and directories. The user who initiates the connection assumes the client function, while the server function is provided by the remote host. On both sides of the link the FTP application is built with a protocol interpreter (PI), a data transfer process (DTP), and a user interface.

The user interface communicates with the protocol interpreter, which is in charge of the control connection. This protocol interpreter has to communicate the necessary information to its own file system. On the opposite side of the link, the protocol interpreter, besides its function of responding to the TELNET protocol, has to initiate the data connection. During the file transfer, the data management is performed by DTPs. After a user's request is completed, the server's PI has to close the control connection.

FTP Operations

When using FTP, the user will perform some or all of the following operations:

1. Connect to a remote host.
2. Select a directory.
3. List files available for transfer.
4. Define the transfer mode.
5. Copy files to or from the remote host.
6. Disconnect from the remote host.
7. Connect to the Remote Host.

To execute a file transfer, the user begins by logging into the remote host. This is the primary method of handling the security. The user must have a user ID and password for the remote host, unless using Anonymous FTP which is described in Anonymous FTP.

There are **three commands** which are used:

1. Open Selects the remote host and initiates the login session.
2. User Identifies the remote user ID.
3. Pass Authenticates the user.

Select a Directory

When the control link is established, the user may use the cd (change directory) subcommand to select a remote directory to work with. Obviously, user can only access directories for which the remote user ID has the appropriate authorization. The user may select a local directory with the lcd (local change directory) command. The syntax of theses commands depends upon the operating system in use.

List Files Available for Transfer

This is done using the dir or ls subcommands.

Specifying the Transfer Mode

Transferring data between dissimilar systems often requires transformations of the data as part of the transfer process. The user has to decide on two aspects of the data handling:

1. The way the bits will be moved from one place to another.
2. The different representations of data upon the system's architecture.

This is controlled using **two** subcommands:

Mode. Specifies whether the file is to be treated as having a record structure in a byte stream format.

Block. Logical record boundaries of the file are preserved.

Stream. The file is treated as a byte stream. This is the default, and provides more efficient transfer but may not produce the desired results when working with a record-based file system.

Copy Files

1. **Get.** Copies a file from the remote host to the local host.
2. **Put.** Copies a file from the local host to the remote host.

End the Transfer Session

1. **Quit.** Disconnects from the remote host and terminates FTP. Some implementations use the BYE subcommand.
2. **Close.** Disconnects from the remote host but leaves the FTP client running. An open command may be issued to work with a new host.

Reply Codes

In order to manage these operations, the client and server conduct a dialogue using the TELNET convention. The client issues commands, and the server responds with *reply codes*. The responses also include comments for the benefit of the user, but the client program uses only the codes. Reply codes are three digits long, with the first digit being the most significant.

Example

For each user command, shown like **this**, the FTP server responds with a message beginning with a 3-digit reply code, shown like this:

1.	**FTP foreignhost**	220 service ready
2.	**USERNAME cms01**	331 user name okay
3.	**PASSWORD xyxyx**	230 user logged in
4.	**TYPE Image**	200 command okay

9.4 TRIVIAL FILE TRANSFER PROTOCOL (TFTP)

TFTP is an extremely simple protocol to transfer files. It is implemented on the internet UDP layer (User Datagram Protocol) and lacks most of the features of FTP. The only thing it can do is read/write a file from/to a server. **It has no provisions for user authentication: it is an unsecure protocol.**

USAGE

The Command

TFTP<hostname>takes you to the interactive prompt where you can enter subcommands:

Connect <host> specify destination host ID

Mode <ascii/binary> specify the type of transfer mode

Get <remote filename> [<local filename>] retrieve a file

Put <remote filename> [<local filename>] store a file

Verbose toggle verbose mode, which displays additional information during file transfer, on or off

Quit exit TFTP

Protocol Description

Any transfer begins with a request to read or write a file. If the server grants the request, the connection is opened and the file is sent in blocks of 512 bytes (fixed length). Blocks of the file are numbered consecutively, starting at 1. Each data packet must be acknowledged by an acknowledgement packet before the next one can be sent. Termination of the transfer is assumed on a data packet of less than 512 bytes. Almost all errors will cause termination of the connection (lack of reliability). If a packet gets lost in the network, a timeout will occur, after which a retransmission of the last packet (data or acknowledgement) will take place.

TFTP Packets

Only five types of packets exist:

Opcode	Operation
1	Read Request (RRQ)
2	Write Request (WRQ)
3	Data (DATA)
4	Acknowledgement (ACK)
5	Error (ERROR).

The TFTP header contains the *opcode* associated with the packet.

Data Modes

There are three modes of transfer :

1. **NetASCII.** US-ASCII as defined in *USA Standard Code for Information Interchange* with modifications specified in *RFC 854 - Telnet Protocol Specification* and extended to use the high order bit. That is, it is an 8-bit character set, unlike US-ASCII which is 7-bit.
2. **Octet.** Raw 8-bit bytes, also called binary.
3. **Mail.** This mode was originally defined in RFC 783 and was declared obsolete by RFC 1350. It allowed for sending mail to a user rather than transferring to a file.

The mode used is indicated in the Request for Read/Write packet (RRQ/WRQ).

9.5 NETWORK FILE SYSTEM (NFS)

The SUN Microsystems Network File System (NFS) protocol enables machines to share file systems across a network. The NFS protocol is designed to be machine-, operating system-, and transport protocol-independent. This is achieved through implementation on top of Remote Procedure Call. RPC establishes machine independence by using the External Data Representation convention.

Concept

NFS allows authorized users to access files located on remote systems as if they were local. Two protocols serve this purpose:

The ***Mount* protocol** to specify the remote host and file system to be accessed and where to locate them in the local file hierarchy.

The **NFS protocol** to do the actual file I/O to the remote file system.

Both Mount and NFS protocol are RPC applications (caller/server concept) and are ***transported by UDP.***

Mount Protocol

The Mount protocol is an RPC-application shipped with NFS. It is program number 100005. The Mount protocol is transported by UDP. Mount is an RPC-server program and **provides a total of six procedures**:

NULL	Does nothing, useful for server response testing.
MOUNT	Mount function, returns a file handle pointing to the directory.
DUMP	Returns the list of all mounted file systems.
UMOUNT	Removes a mount list entry.
UNMTALL	Removes all mount list entries for this client.
EXPORT	Returns information about the available file systems.

The *MOUNT*-call returns a file handle to the directory. The file handle is a 32-byte field, which will be used subsequently by the client to access files. File handles are a fundamental part of NFS because each directory and file will be referenced through a handle. Some implementations will encrypt the handles for security reasons. The user interface to this RPC application is provided through the MOUNT command. The user issues a MOUNT command to locate the remote file system in his own file hierarchy.

The *UMOUNT* command removes the remote file system from the local file hierarchy. Following the example above:

UMOUNT /u/vm/first will remove the /u/vm/first directory.

NFS Protocol

NFS is the RPC application program providing file I/O functions to a remote host, once it has been requested through a MOUNT command. It has program number **100003** and sometimes uses IP **port 2049**. As this is not an officially assigned port and several versions of NFS (and mount) already exist, port numbers may change. It is advised to go to Portmap (port number 111) to obtain the port numbers for both Mount and NFS. The NFS protocol is transported by UDP. The NFS program supports **18 procedures,** providing for all basic I/O operations such as:

LOOKUP. Searches for a file in the current directory and if found, returns a file handle pointing to it plus information on the file's attributes.

READ and WRITE. Basic read/write primitives to access the file.

RENAME. Renames a file.

REMOVE. Deletes a file.

MKDIR and RMDIR. Creation/deletion of subdirectories.

GET and SET-ATTR. Gets or sets file attributes.

Other functions are also provided. These correspond to most of the file I/O primitives used in the local operating system to access local files. In fact, once the remote directory is mounted, the local operating system just has to "re-route" the file I/O primitives to the remote host. This makes all file I/Os look alike, regardless of whether the file is located locally or remotely. The user can operate his normal commands and programs on both kinds of files; in other words, this *NFS protocol is completely transparent to the user.*

NFS File System

NFS assumes a hierarchical file system (directories). Files are unstructured streams of uninterpreted bytes; that is, files are seen as a contiguous byte stream, without any record-level structure. With NFS, all file operations are ***synchronous.*** This means that the file-operation call only returns when the server has completed all work for this operation. In case of a write request, the server will physically write the data to disk and if necessary, update any directory structure, before returning a response to the client. This ensures file integrity.

NFS also specifies that servers should be ***stateless.*** That is, a server does not need to maintain any extra information about any of its clients in order to function correctly. In case of a server failure, clients only have to retry a request until the server responds, without having to reiterate a mount operation.

9.6 SIMPLE MAIL TRANSFER PROTOCOL (SMTP)

Electronic mail (E-mail) is probably the most widely used TCP/IP application. The basic Internet mail protocols provide mail (note) and message exchange between TCP/IP hosts; facilities have been added for the transmission of data which cannot be represented as 7-bit ASCII text.

There are three *standard protocols* which apply to mail of this kind. Each is *recommended.* The term SMTP is frequently used to refer to the combined set of protocols, since they are so closely inter-related, but strictly speaking SMTP is just one of the three. Normally, it is evident from the context which of the three protocols is being referred to. The **three standards** are:

1. A standard for exchange of mail between two computers, which specifies the protocol used to send mail between TCP/IP hosts. This standard is SMTP itself.
2. A standard on the format of the mail messages.First standard describes the syntax of mail header fields and defines a set of header fields and their interpretation. Second standard describes how a set of document types other than plain text ASCII can be used in the mail body . The official protocol name for this standard is MAIL.
3. A standard for the routing of mail using the Domain Name System. The official protocol name for this standard is DNS-MX.

The RFC 821 standard dictates that data sent via SMTP is 7-bit ASCII data, with the high-order bit cleared to zero. This is adequate in most instances for the transmission of English text messages, but is inadequate for non-English text or non-textual data. There are two approaches to overcoming these limitations:

1. Multipurpose Internet Mail Extensions (MIME), defined in RFC 1521 and RFC 1522, which specifies a mechanism for encoding text and binary data as 7-bit

ASCII within the mail envelope defined by RFC 822.

2. SMTP Service Extensions, which define a mechanism to extend the capabilities of SMTP beyond the limitations imposed by RFC 821.

How SMTP Works

SMTP is based on *end-to-end delivery*; an SMTP client will contact the destination host's SMTP server directly to deliver the mail. It will keep the mail item being transmitted until it has been successfully copied to the recipient's SMTP. This is different from the store-and-forward principle that is common in many mailing systems, where the mail item may pass through a number of intermediate hosts in the same network on its way to the destination and where successful transmission from the sender only indicates that the mail item has reached the first intermediate hop.

In various implementations, there is a possibility to exchange mail between the TCP/IP SMTP mailing system and the locally used mailing systems. These applications are called *mail gateways* or *mail bridges*. Sending mail through a mail gateway may alter the end-to-end delivery specification, since SMTP will only guarantee delivery to the mail-gateway host, not to the real destination host, which is located beyond the TCP/IP network. When a mail gateway is used, the SMTP end-to-end transmission is host-to-gateway, gateway-to-host or gateway-to-gateway; the behavior beyond the gateway is not defined by SMTP. CSNET provides an interesting example of mail gateway service. Started as a low-cost facility to interconnect scientific and corporate research centers, CSNET operates a mail gateway service that allows subscribers to send and receive mail across the Internet using only a dial-up modem. The mail gateway polls the subscribers at regular times, delivers mail that was addressed to them and picks up the outgoing mail. Although this is not a direct end-to-end delivery, it has been proved to be a very useful system.

Each message has:

1. **A header, or envelope,** the structure of which is strictly defined by RFC 822. The mail header is terminated by a null line (that is, a line with nothing preceding the <CRLF> sequence). However, some implementations (for example VM, which does not support zero-length records in files) may interpret this differently and accept a blank line as a terminator.
2. Contents Everything after the null (or blank) line is the message body which is a sequence of lines containing ASCII characters (that is, characters with a value less than 128 decimal).

As usual, the client SMTP is the one which initiates the session (that is, the sending SMTP) and the server is the one which responds (the receiving SMTP) to the session request. However, since the client SMTP frequently acts as a server for a user mailing program, it is often simpler to refer to the client as the sender-SMTP and to the server as the receiver-SMTP.

Mail Header Format

The user normally doesn't have to worry about the message header, since it is taken care of by SMTP itself. A short reference is included below for completeness.

The syntax is written in a form known as the augmented Backus-Naur Form (BNF). RFC 822 describes how to parse a mail header to a *canonical representation*, unfolding continuation lines, deleting insignificant spaces, removing comments and so on. The syntax is powerful, but relatively difficult to parse. A basic description is given here, which should be adequate for the reader to interpret the meaning of simple mail headers that he or she encounters.

Briefly, the header is a list of lines, of the form:

Field-name : Field-value

Fields begin in column 1: lines beginning with white space characters (SPACE or TAB) are continuation lines which are unfolded to create a single line for each field in the canonical representation. Strings enclosed in ASCII quotation marks indicate single tokens within which special characters such as the colon are not significant. Many important field values (such as those for the "To" and "From" fields) are "mailboxes". The most common forms for these are:

1. vivekricha@yahoo.co.in
2. The vivekricha <vivekricha@yahoo.co.in>
3. "The vivekricha" <vivekricha@yahoo.co.in>

The string "the vivekricha" is intended for human recipients and is the name of the mailbox owner. The string "vivekricha@yahoo.co.in" is the machine-readable address of the mailbox (the angle brackets are used to delimit the address but are not part of it). One can see that this form of addressing is closely related to the Domain Name System concept. In fact, the client SMTP uses the Domain Name System to determine the IP address of the destination mailbox.

Some frequently used fields are:

Keyword	**value**
1. to	Primary recipients of the message.
2. cc	Secondary ("carbon-copy") recipients of the message.
3. from	Identity of sender.
4. reply-to	the mailbox to which responses are to be sent. This field is added by the Return-path Address and route back to the originator.
5. Originator.	This field is added by the final transport system that delivers the mail.
6. Subject	Summary of the message. This is usually provided by the user.

Mail Exchange

The SMTP design is based on the model of communication. As a result of a user mail request, the sender-SMTP establishes a two-way connection with a receiver-SMTP. The receiver-SMTP can be either the ultimate destination or an intermediate (mail gateway). The sender-SMTP will generate commands which are replied to by the receiver-SMTP.

SMTP Mail Transaction Flow

Although mail commands and replies are rigidly defined, the exchange can easily be followed in. All exchanged commands/replies/data are text lines, delimited by a <CRLF>. All replies have a numeric code at the beginning of the line.

1. The sender SMTP establishes a TCP connection with the destination SMTP and then waits for the server to send a *220 Service ready* message or a *421 Service not available* message when the destination is temporarily unable to proceed.
2. HELO (HELO is an abbreviation for hello) is sent, to which the receiver will identify himself by sending back its domain name. The sender-SMTP can use this to verify if it contacted the right destination SMTP. If the sender-SMTP supports SMTP Service Extensions, it may substitute an EHLO command in place of the HELO command. A receiver-SMTP which does not support service extensions will respond with a *500 Syntax error, command unrecognized* message. The sender-SMTP should then retry with HELO, or if it cannot transmit the message without one or more service extensions, it should send a QUIT message. If a receiver-SMTP supports service extensions, it responds with a multi-line *250 OK* message which includes a list of service extensions which it supports.
3. The sender now initiates the start of a mail transaction by sending a MAIL command to the receiver. This command contains the reverse-path which can be used to report errors. Note that a path can be more than just the *user mailbox@host domain name* pair. In addition, it can contain a list of routing hosts. Examples of this are when we pass a mail bridge, or when we provide explicit routing information in the destination address. If accepted, the receiver replies with a *250 OK*.
4. The second step of the actual mail exchange consists of providing the server SMTP with the destinations for the message (there can be more than one recipient). This is done by sending one or more RCPT TO:*<forward-path>* commands. Each of them will receive a reply *250 OK* if the destination is known to the server, or a *550 No such user here* if it isn't.
5. When all RCPT commands are sent, the sender issues a *DATA* command to notify the receiver that the message contents are following. The server replies with *354 Start mail input, end with <CRLF>.<CRLF>*. Note the ending sequence that the sender should use to terminate the message data.
6. The client now sends the data line by line, ending with the 5-character sequence <CRLF>.<CRLF> line upon which the receiver acknowledges with a *250 OK* or an appropriate error message if anything went wrong.
7. We now have several possible actions:

   7.1 The sender has no more messages to send; he will end the connection with a QUIT command, which will be answered with a *221 Service closing transmission channel* reply.

   7.2 The sender has no more messages to send, but is ready to receive messages (if any) from the other side. He will issue the TURN command. The two SMTPs now switch their role of sender/receiver and the sender (previously the receiver) can now send messages by starting with step 3 above.

The sender has another message to send, and simply goes back to step 3 to send a new MAIL command.

The SMTP destination address (a mailbox address),

In its general form *local-part@domain-name*, can take several forms:

1. user@host For a direct destination on the same TCP/IP network.
2. user%remote-host@gateway-host, for a user on a non-SMTP destination remote-host, via the mail gateway gateway-host.
3. @host-a, @host-b: user@host-c, for a *relayed* message. This contains explicit routing Information. The message will first be delivered to host-a, who will resend (relay) the Message to host-b. Host-b will then forward the message to the real destination host-c.

SMTP and the Domain Name System

If the network is using the domain concept, an SMTP cannot simply deliver mail sent to VIVEKRICHA.COM by opening a TCP connection to VIVEKRICHA.COM It must first query the name server to find out to which host (again a domain name) it should deliver the message.

For message delivery, the name server stores resource records (RRs) known as MX RRs. They map a domain name to two values:

1. A preference value. As multiple MX resource records may exist for the same domain name, a preference (priority) is assigned to them. The lowest preference value corresponds to the most preferred record. This is useful whenever the most preferred host is unreachable; the sending SMTP then tries to contact the next (less preferred) host.
2. A host name.

It is also possible that the name server responds with an empty list of MX RRs. This means that the domain name is in the name server's authority, but has no MX assigned to it. In this case, the sending SMTP may try to establish the connection with the host name itself.

9.6.1 Post Office Protocol Mail Servers

Since an SMTP mail receiver is a server program, and SMTP is an end-to-end application rather than a store-and-forward one, it is necessary for the server to be available when a client (sender) wishes to transmit mail. If the SMTP server resides on an end-user workstation or PC, that workstation must be running the server when the client wishes to send. Some clients, such as the SMTP service virtual machine on VM (which are themselves servers for a user mail program) can periodically retry the server for a finite period of time, others such as the MAIL program on DOS cannot. In either case, if the server is unavailable it will sooner or later be regarded as unreachable by the SMTP client and the sending process will fail. This is not generally a problem for multi-user systems because the systems are normally unavailable only for relatively short periods of time. For single-user systems, however, this is not the case, and a method for ensuring that the user has an accessible mailbox on a different server is required. There are a number of other reasons why it may be desirable to off-load mail server functions from a user workstation, including a lack of resources on small workstations, the lack of, or expense of, continuous TCP/IP connectivity and so on.

The simplest approach, of course, is for the user to use a multi-user host system for mail functions, but this is frequently not desirable — perhaps the user does not use a host system for any other purpose, or the user wants access to workstation files when composing mail messages without uploading them. Alternatively, the end-user may run a client program which communicates with a server program on a host. This server program acts as both a sender and a receiver SMTP. The end users mailbox resides on the server, and mail to other users is sent by the server system.

An intermediate approach is to off-load the SMTP server function from the end-user workstation, but not the SMTP client function. That is, the user sends mail directly from the workstation, but has a mailbox which resides on a server system. The user must then connect to the mail server system to collect mail from the mailbox. The Post Office Protocol (POP) describes how a program running on an end-user workstation may receive mail stored on a mail server system. POP uses the term "maildrop" to refer to a mailbox managed by a POP server. Post Office Protocol Version 3 is a *draft standard protocol* and its status is *elective*. The older Post Office Protocol Version 2 is an *historic protocol* with a status of *not recommended*.

9.7 MULTIPURPOSE INTERNET MAIL EXTENSIONS (MIME)

Electronic mail as presented by SMTP is probably the most widely used TCP/IP application. However, SMTP is limited to 7-bit ASCII text with a maximum line length of 1000 characters which results in a number of limitations.

1. **SMTP cannot transmit executable files or other binary objects.** There are a number of ad hoc methods of encapsulating binary items in SMTP mail items, for example:
    1. Encoding the file as pure hexadecimal
    2. The UNIX UUencode and UUdecode utilities which are used to encode binary data in the UUCP mailing system to overcome the same limitations of 7-bit transport
    3. The Andrew Toolkit representation
2. **SMTP cannot transmit text data which includes national language characters** since these are represented by codepoints with a value of 128 (decimal) or higher in all character sets based on ASCII.
3. **SMTP servers may reject mail messages over a certain size.** Any given server may have permanent and/or transient limits on the maximum amount of mail data it can accept from a client at any given time.
4. **SMTP gateways which translate from ASCII to EBCDIC and vice versa** do not use a consistent set of code page mappings, resulting in translation problems.
5. **Some SMTP implementations** or other mail transport agents (MTAs) in the Internet **do not adhere completely to the SMTP standards** defined in RFC 821. Common problems include:

1. Removal of trailing white space characters (TABs and SPACEs)
2. Padding of all lines in a message to the same length
3. Wrapping of lines longer than 76 characters
4. Changing of new line sequences between different conventions (for instance <CR> characters may be converted to <CRLF> sequences)
5. Conversion of TAB characters to multiple SPACEs.

9.7.1 MIME Introduction

MIME is a standard which includes mechanisms to solve these problems in a manner which is highly compatible with existing RFC 822 standards. Because mail messages are frequently forwarded through mail gateways, it is not possible for an SMTP client to distinguish between a server which manages the destination mailbox and one which acts as a gateway to another network. Since mail which passes through a gateway may be tunnelled through further gateways, some or all of which may be use a different set of messaging protocols, it is not possible in the general case for a sending SMTP to determine the lowest common denominator capability common to all stages of the route to the destination mailbox. For this reason, MIME assumes the worst: 7-bit ASCII transport. Thus, a MIME message is one which can be routed through any number of networks.

MIME is a *standard protocol* is described in two parts:

1. Protocols for including objects other than US ASCII text mail messages within the bodies of messages.
2. A protocol for encoding non-US ASCII text in the header fields of mail messages.

The MIME standard was designed with the following general order of priorities:

1. Compatibility with existing standards.
2. Robustness across existing practice.
3. Ease of extension.

MIME does *not* require mail items to be encoded—the decision is left to the user and/or the mail program. For binary data, transmitted across (7-bit) SMTP, encoding is invariably required, but for data consisting mostly of text, this may not be the case. The preferred encoding mechanism for "mostly text" data is such that, at a minimum, it is "mail-safe" with any compliant SMTP agent on an ASCII system and at maximum is mail-safe with all known gateways and MTAs. The reason why MIME does not require maximum encoding is that the encoding hampers readability when the mail is transmitted to non-MIME compliant systems. One standard categorizes elements of mail bodies into seven *content-types* which have *subtypes*. The content-type/subtype pairs in turn have parameters which further describe the object concerned. The RFC defines a mechanism for registering new values for these and other MIME fields with the Internet Assigned Numbers Authority (IANA). One consequence of this approach is that, "some of the mechanisms [used in MIME] may seem somewhat strange or even baroque at first. In particular, compatibility was always favored over elegance."

How MIME Works ?

A MIME-compliant message must contain a header field with the following verbatim text:

MIME-Version: 1.0

In the case of MIME header field names is never significant but the case of field values may be, depending on the field name and the context. For the MIME fields described below, the values are case-insensitive unless stated otherwise.

The general syntax for MIME header fields is :

MIME-Version: 1.0 (this is a comment)

Is valid since parenthetical phrases are treated as comments and ignored.

Five Header Fields are Defined for Mine

1. *MIME-version*

As noted above, this must have the value "1.0"

2. *Content-type*

This describes how the object within the body is to be interpreted. The default value is "text/plain; charset=us-ASCII" which indicates unformatted 7-bit ASCII text data (that is a message body by the RFC 822 definition).

3. *Content-transfer-encoding*

This describes how the object within the body was encoded so that it could be included in the message in a mail-safe form.

4. *Content-description*

A plain text description of the object within the body which is useful when the object is not readable (for example audio data).

5. *Content-ID*

A world-unique value specifying the content of this part of this message.

The Content-Type Field

The body of the message is described with a *Content-Type* field of the form: Content-Type: *type/subtype ;parameter=value ;parameter=value*

The allowable parameters are dependent on the type and subtype. Some type/subtype pairs have no parameters, some have optional ones, some have mandatory ones and some have both. The subtype parameter may *not* be omitted, but the whole field may be, in which case the default value is *text/plain.*

There are seven standard content-types:

1. *text*

A single subtype is defined:

plain

Unformatted text. The character set of the text may be specified with the *charset* parameter. The following values are permitted.

us-ascii

The text consists of ASCII characters in the range 0 to 127 (decimal). The text consists of ISO characters in the range 0 to 255 (decimal). All of the ISO-8859 character sets are ASCII-based with national language characters and so on in the range 128 to 255. Note, if the text contains no characters with values above 127, the character set should be specified as "us-ascii" because it can be adequately represented in that character set.

2. *multipart*

The message body contains multiple objects of independent data types. In each case, the body is divided into parts by lines called encapsulation boundaries. The contents of the boundary are defined with a parameter in the content-type field, for example:

Content-Type: multipart/mixed; boundary = "1995021309105517"

The boundary should not appear in any of the parts of the message. It is case-sensitive and consists of 1–70 characters from a set of 75 which are known to be very robust through mail gateways, and it may not end in a space. (The example uses a 16-digit decimal timestamp.) Each encapsulation boundary consists of the boundary value prefixed by a <CRLF> sequence and two hyphens (for compatibility with RFC 934). The final boundary which marks the end of the last part also has a suffix of two hyphens. Within each part there is a MIME header, which like ordinary mail headers is terminated by the sequence *<CRLF><CRLF>* but which may be blank. The header fields define the content of the encapsulated message.

Four Subtypes are Defined

mixed

The different parts are independent but are to be transmitted together. They should be presented to the recipient in the order that they appear in the mail message.

parallel

This differs from the mixed subtype only in that no order is ascribed to the parts and the receiving mail program may, for example, display all of them in parallel.

alternative

The different parts are alternative versions of the same information. They are ordered in increasing faithfulness to the original, and the recipient's mail system should display the "best" version to the user.

digest

This is a variant on multipart/mixed where the default type/subtype is message instead of text/plain.

The Content-Transfer-Encoding Field

As already noted, SMTP agents and mail gateways can severely constrain the contents of mail messages which can be transmitted safely. The MIME types described above list a rich set of different types of object which can be included in mail messages and the majority of these do not fall within these constraints. Therefore, it is necessary to encode data of these types in a fashion which can be transmitted, and to decode them on receipt. Standard defines two forms of encoding which are mail safe. The reason for two forms rather than one is that it is not possible, given the small set of characters known to be mail safe, to devise a form which can both encode text data with minimal impact to the readability of the text and yet can encode binary data which consists of characters distributed randomly across all 256 byte values compactly enough to be practical.

These two encodings are used only for bodies and not for headers. ***The Content-Transfer-Encoding:*** field defines the encoding used. Although cumbersome, this field name emphasizes that the encoding is a feature of the transport process and not an intrinsic property of the object being mailed. Although there are only two encodings defined, this field can take on *five* values (as usual, the values are case insensitive). Three of the values actually specify that no encoding has been done; where they differ is that they imply different reasons why this is the case. This is a subtle but important point. MIME is not restricted to SMTP as a transport agent, despite the prevalence of (broadly) SMTP-compliant mail systems on the Internet. It therefore allows a mail agent to transmit data which is not mail-safe by the standards of SMTP . If such a mail item reaches a gateway to a more restrictive system, the "encoding" mechanism specified allows the gateway to decide on an item-by-item basis whether the body must be encoded to be transmitted safely.

The five "encodings" are:

1. 7bit (the default if the "Content-Transfer-Encoding:" header is omitted).
2. 8bit
3. Binary
4. Quoted-Printable
5. Base64.

These are described in the sections that follow.

7bit Encoding

7bit "encoding" means that no encoding has been done and the body consists of lines of ASCII text with a length of not greater than 1000 characters. It is therefore known to be mail-safe with any mail system that *strictly* conforms with standards . This is the default. 7bit encoding does *not* guarantee that the contents are truly mail safe for two reasons. First, gateways to EBCDIC networks have a smaller set of mail-safe characters, and secondly because of the many non-conforming SMTP implementations. The Quoted-Printable encoding is designed to overcome these difficulties for text data.

8bit Encoding

8bit "encoding" implies that lines are short enough for SMTP transport, but that there may be non-ASCII characters (that is, octets with the high-order bit set). Where SMTP agents support the *SMTP Service Extension for 8bit-MIME transport.* 8bit encoding is possible. Otherwise, SMTP implementations should set the high-order bit to zero, so 8bit encoding is not valid.

Binary Encoding

Binary "encoding" indicates that non-ASCII characters may be present and that the lines may be too long for SMTP transport (that is, there may be sequences of 999 or more characters without a CRLF sequence). There are currently no standards for the transport of unencoded binary data by mail based on the TCP/IP protocol stack, so the only case where it is valid to use binary encoding in a MIME message sent on the Internet or other TCP/IP based network is in the header of an external-body part (see the message/external-body type above). Binary encoding would be valid if MIME were used in conjunction with other mail transport mechanisms, or with a hypothetical SMTP Service Extension which did support long lines.

Quoted-Printable Encoding

This is the first of the two "real" encodings and it is intended to leave text files largely readable in their encoded form.

1. It represents non-mail safe characters by the hexadecimal representation of their ASCII characters.
2. It introduces reversible (soft) line breaks to keep all lines in the message to a length of 76 characters or less.

Quoted-Printable encoding uses the equals sign as a "quote character" to indicate both of these cases. It has five rules which are summarized as follows:

1. Any character except one which is part of a new line sequence (that is, a X'0D0A' sequence on a text file) can be represented by "=XX" where XX are two uppercase hexadecimal digits. If none of the other rules apply, the character must be represented like this.
2. Any character in the range X '21' to X '7E' exceptX '3D' ("=") may be represented as the ASCII character.
3. ASCII TAB (X '09') and SPACE (X '20') may be represented as the ASCII character except when it is the last character on the line.
4. A line break must be represented by a <CRLF> sequence (X '0D0A'). When encoding binary data, X'0D0A' is not a line break and should be coded, according to rule 1, as "=0D=0A".
5. Encoded lines may not be longer than 76 characters (excluding the <CRLF>). If a line is longer than this, a soft line break must be inserted at or before column 75. A soft line break is the sequence "=<CRLF>" (X '3D0D0A').

Base64 Encoding

This encoding is intended for data which does not consist mainly of text characters. Quoted-printable replaces each non-text character with a 3-byte sequence which is grossly inefficient for binary data. Base64 encoding works by treating the input stream as a bit stream, regrouping the bits into shorter bytes, padding these short bytes to 8 bits and then translating these bytes to characters which are known to be mail-safe. As noted in the previous section, there are only 73 safe characters, so the maximum byte length usable is 6 bits which can be represented by 64 unique characters (hence the name Base64). Since the input and output are both byte streams, the encoding has to be done in groups of 24 bits (that is 3 input bytes and 4 output bytes).

Conversion between Encodings

The Base64 encoding can be freely translated to and from the binary encoding without ambiguity since both treat the data as an octet-stream. This is also true for the conversion from Quoted-Printable to either of the other two (in the case of the Quoted-Printable to Binary conversion the process can be viewed as involving an intermediate binary encoding) by converting the quoted character sequences to their 8-bit form, deleting the soft line breaks and replacing hard linebreaks with <CRLF> sequences. This is not strictly true of the reverse process since Quoted-Printable is actually a record-based system: there is a semantic difference between a hard line break and an imbedded "=0D=0A" sequence (for example when decoding Quoted-Printable on a EBCDIC record-based system such as VM, hard line breaks map to record boundaries but =0D=0A sequences map to X'0D25' sequences).

Multiple Encodings

MIME does *not* allow nested encodings. Any Content-Type that recursively includes other Content-Type fields (notable the multipart and message types) may not use a Content-Transfer-Encoding other than 7bit, 8bit or binary. All encodings must be done at the innermost level. The purpose of this restriction is to simplify the operation of user mail agents. If nested encodings are not permitted, the structure of the entire message is always visible to the mail agent without the need to decode the outer layer(s) of the message.

This simplification for user mail agents has a price: complexity for gateways. Because a user agent may specify an encoding of 8bit or binary, a gateway to a network where these encodings are not safe must encode the message before passing it to the second network. The obvious solution, to simply encode the message body and to change the "Content-Transfer-Encoding:" field, is not allowed for the multipart or message types since it would violate the restriction described above. The gateway must therefore correctly parse the message into its components and re-encode the innermost parts as necessary.

There is one further restriction: messages of type message/partial must *always* have 7bit encoding (8bit and binary are also disallowed). The reason for this is that if a gateway needs to re-encode a message, it requires the entire message to do so, but the parts of the message may not all be available together (parts may be transmitted serially because the gateway is incapable of storing the entire message at once or they may even be routed independently via different gateways). Therefore message/partial body parts must be mail safe across lowest common denominator networks; that is, they must be 7bit encoded.

Using Non-ASCII Characters in Message Headers

All of the mechanisms above refer exclusively to bodies and not to headers. The contents of message headers must be still be coded in US-ASCII. For header fields which include human-readable text, this is not adequate for languages other than English. A mechanism to include national language characters is defined by the second part of MIME. This mechanism differs from the Quoted-Printable encoding, which would be used in a message body for the following reasons:

1. The format of message headers is strictly codified by RFC 822 standard , so the

encoding used by MIME for header fields must work within a narrower set of constraints than that used for bodies.

2. Message relaying programs frequently change message headers, for example re-ordering header fields, deleting some fields but not others, re-ordering mailboxes within lists or spilling fields at different positions than the original message.

3. Some message handling programs do not correctly handle some of the more arcane features of RFC 822 standard (such as the use of the "\" character to "quote" special characters like "<"and ">.").

9.8 NETWORK MANAGEMENT

With the growth in size and complexity of the TCP/IP-based internets the need for network management became very important. The current network management framework for TCP/IP-based internets consists of:

1. SMI—(Structure and Identification of Management Information). describes how managed objects contained in the MIB are defined.
2. MIB-II—(Management Information Base) describes the managed objects contained in the MIB.
3. SNMP—(Simple Network Management Protocol) defines the protocol used to manage these objects.

The Internet Architecture Board issued an RFC detailing its recommendation, which adopted two different approaches:

1. In the short term SNMP should be used.

   The IAB recommends that all IP and TCP implementations be network manageable. At the current time, this implies implementation of the Internet MIB-II , and at least the recommended management protocol SNMP

2. In the long term, use of the emerging OSI network management protocol (CMIP) would be investigated. This is known as *CMIP over TCP/IP* (CMOT-Common Management Information Protocol over TCP/IP).

Both the SNMP and CMOT use the same basic concepts in describing and defining management information called *Structure and Identification of Management Information* (SMI) and *Management Information Base* (MIB) .

9.8.1 Simple Network Management Protocol

The *Simple Network Management Protocol (SNMP)* is an application layer protocol that facilitates the exchange of management information between network devices. It is part of the Transmission Control Protocol/Internet Protocol (TCP/IP) protocol suite. SNMP enables network administrators to manage network performance, find and solve network problems, and plan for network growth.

Two versions of SNMP exist:

1. **SNMP version 1 (SNMPv1) and**
2. **SNMP version 2 (SNMPv2).**

Both versions have a number of features in common, but SNMPv2 offers enhancements, such as additional protocol operations. Standardization of yet another version of SNMP-SNMP Version 3 (SNMPv3)-is pending.

SNMP Basic Components

An SNMP-managed network consists of three key components:

1. managed devices,
2. agents, and
3. network-management systems (NMSs).

A *managed device* is a network node that contains an SNMP agent and that resides on a managed network. Managed devices collect and store management information and make this information available to NMSs using SNMP. Managed devices, sometimes called network elements, can be routers and access servers, switches and bridges, hubs, computer hosts, or printers.

An *agent* is a network-management software module that resides in a managed device. An agent has local knowledge of management information and translates that information into a form compatible with SNMP.

An *NMS* executes applications that monitor and control managed devices. NMSs provide the bulk of the processing and memory resources required for network management. One or more NMSs must exist on any managed network.

SNMP Basic Commands

Managed devices are monitored and controlled using four basic SNMP commands:

1. **read,**
2. **write,**
3. **trap,** and
4. **traversal** operations.

The **read** command is used by an NMS to monitor managed devices. The NMS examines different variables that are maintained by managed devices.

The **write** command is used by an NMS to control managed devices. The NMS changes the values of variables stored within managed devices.

The **trap** command is used by managed devices to asynchronously report events to the NMS. When certain types of events occur, a managed device sends a trap to the NMS.

Traversal operations are used by the NMS to determine which variables a managed device supports and to sequentially gather information in variable tables, such as a routing table.

9.8.2 SNMP Management Information Base

A ***Management Information Base (MIB)*** is a collection of information that is organized hierarchically. MIBs are accessed using a network-management protocol such as SNMP. They are comprised of managed objects and are identified by object identifiers.

A managed object (sometimes called a MIB object, an object, or a MIB) is one of any number of specific characteristics of a managed device. Managed objects are comprised of one or more object instances, which are essentially variables. Two types of managed objects exist:

1. scalar and
2. tabular.

Scalar objects define a single object instance. ***Tabular objects*** define multiple related object instances that are grouped in MIB tables. **An example** of a managed object is atInput, which is a scalar object that contains a single object instance, the integer value that indicates the total number of input AppleTalk packets on a router interface. An object identifier (or object ID) uniquely identifies a managed object in the MIB hierarchy. The MIB hierarchy can be depicted as a tree with a nameless root, the levels of which are assigned by different organizations. Figure 9.1 illustrates the MIB tree.

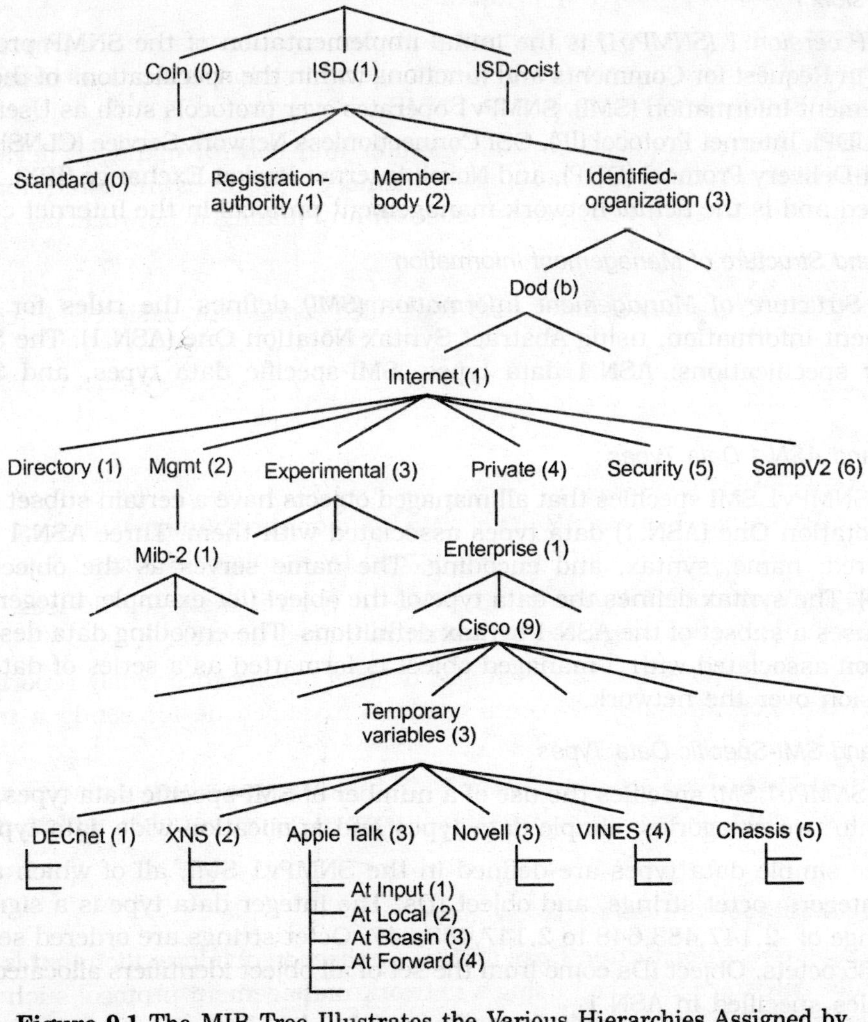

Figure 9.1 The MIB Tree Illustrates the Various Hierarchies Assigned by

The top-level MIB object IDs belong to different standards organizations, while lower-level object IDs are allocated by associated organizations. Vendors can define private branches that include managed objects for their own products. MIBs that have not been standardized typically are positioned in the experimental branch. The managed object atInput can be uniquely identified either by the object name-iso.identified-organization.dod.internet.private.enterprise.cisco.temporary variables. AppleTalk.atInput-or by the equivalent object descriptor, 1.3.6.1.4.1.9.3.3.1.

SNMP and Data Representation

SNMP must account for and adjust to incompatibilities between managed devices. Different computers use different data representation techniques, which can compromise the capability of SNMP to exchange information between managed devices. SNMP uses a subset of Abstract Syntax Notation One (ASN.1) to accommodate communication between diverse systems.

SNMP Version 1

SNMP version 1 (SNMPv1) is the initial implementation of the SNMP protocol. It is described in Request for Comments and functions within the specifications of the Structure of Management Information (SMI). SNMPv1 operates over protocols such as User Datagram Protocol (UDP), Internet Protocol (IP), OSI Connectionless Network Service (CLNS), AppleTalk Datagram-Delivery Protocol (DDP), and Novell Internet Packet Exchange (IPX). SNMPv1 is widely used and is the *actual* network-management protocol in the Internet community.

SNMPv1 and Structure of Management Information

The *Structure of Management Information (SMI)* defines the rules for describing management information, using Abstract Syntax Notation One (ASN.1). The SMI makes three key specifications: ASN.1 data types, SMI-specific data types, and SNMP MIB tables.

SNMPv1 and ASN.1 Data Types

The SNMPv1 SMI specifies that all managed objects have a certain subset of Abstract Syntax Notation One (ASN.1) data types associated with them. Three ASN.1 data types are required: name, syntax, and encoding. The name serves as the object identifier (object ID). The syntax defines the data type of the object (for example, integer or string). The SMI uses a subset of the ASN.1 syntax definitions. The encoding data describes how information associated with a managed object is formatted as a series of data items for transmission over the network.

SNMPv1 and SMI-Specific Data Types

The *SNMPv1 SMI* specifies the use of a number of SMI-specific data types, which are divided into two categories: simple data types and application-wide data types.

Three simple data types are defined in the SNMPv1 SMI, all of which are unique values: integers, octet strings, and object IDs. The integer data type is a signed integer in the range of -2,147,483,648 to 2,147,483,647. Octet strings are ordered sequences of 0 to 65,535 octets. Object IDs come from the set of all object identifiers allocated according to the rules specified in ASN.1.

SNMP MIB Tables

The SNMPv1 SMI defines highly structured tables that are used to group the instances of a tabular object (that is, an object that contains multiple variables). Tables are composed of zero or more rows, which are indexed in a way that allows SNMP to retrieve or alter an entire row with a single **Get, GetNext,** or **Set** command.

SNMPV1 Protocol Operations

SNMP is a simple request/response protocol. The network-management system issues a request, and managed devices return responses. This behavior is implemented by using one of four protocol operations: Get, GetNext, Set, and Trap. The Get operation is used by the NMS to retrieve the value of one or more object instances from an agent. If the agent responding to the Get operation cannot provide values for all the object instances in a list, it does not provide any values. The GetNext operation is used by the NMS to retrieve the value of the next object instance in a table or a list within an agent. The Set operation is used by the NMS to set the values of object instances within an agent. The Trap operation is used by agents to asynchronously inform the NMS of a significant event.

SNMP Version 2

SNMP version 2 (SNMPv2) is an evolution of the initial version, SNMPv1. Originally, SNMPv2 was published as a set of proposed Internet standards in 1993; currently, it is a draft standard. As with SNMPv1, SNMPv2 functions within the specifications of the Structure of Management Information (SMI). In theory, SNMPv2 offers a number of improvements to SNMPv1, including additional protocol operations.

SNMPV2 and Structure of Management Information

The Structure of Management Information (SMI) defines the rules for describing management information, using ASN.1.It makes certain additions and enhancements to the SNMPv1 SMI-specific data types, such as including bit strings, network addresses, and counters. Bit strings are defined only in SNMPv2 and comprise zero or more named bits that specify a value. Network addresses represent an address from a particular protocol family. SNMPv1 supports only 32-bit IP addresses, but SNMPv2 can support other types of addresses as well. Counters are non-negative integers that increase until they reach a maximum value and then return to zero. In SNMPv1, a 32-bit counter size is specified. In SNMPv2, 32-bit and 64-bit counters are defined.

SMI Information Modules

The SNMPv2 SMI also specifies information modules, which specify a group of related definitions. Three types of SMI information modules exist: MIB modules, compliance statements, and capability statements. MIB modules contain definitions of interrelated managed objects. Compliance statements provide a systematic way to describe a group of managed objects that must be implemented for conformance to a standard. Capability statements are used to indicate the precise level of support that an agent claims with respect to a MIB group. An NMS can adjust its behavior toward agents according to the capabilities statements associated with each agent.

SNMPV2 Protocol Operations

The Get, GetNext, and Set operations used in SNMPv1 are exactly the same as those used in SNMPv2. However, SNMPv2 adds and enhances some protocol operations. The SNMPv2 Trap operation, for example, serves the same function as that used in SNMPv1, but it uses a different message format and is designed to replace the SNMPv1 Trap.

SNMPv2 also defines two new protocol operations: GetBulk and Inform. The GetBulk operation is used by the NMS to efficiently retrieve large blocks of data, such as multiple rows in a table. GetBulk fills a response message with as much of the requested data as will fit. The Inform operation allows one NMS to send trap information to another NMS and to then receive a response. In SNMPv2, if the agent responding to GetBulk operations cannot provide values for all the variables in a list, it provides partial results.

SNMP Management

SNMP is a distributed-management protocol. A system can operate exclusively as either an NMS or an agent, or it can perform the functions of both. When a system operates as both an NMS and an agent, another NMS might require that the system query manage devices and provide a summary of the information learned, or that it report locally stored management information.

SNMP Security

SNMP lacks any authentication capabilities, which results in vulnerability to a variety of security threats. These include masquerading occurrences, modification of information, message sequence and timing modifications, and disclosure. Masquerading consists of an unauthorized entity attempting to perform management operations by assuming the identity of an authorized management entity. Modification of information involves an unauthorized entity attempting to alter a message generated by an authorized entity so that the message results in unauthorized accounting management or configuration management operations. Message sequence and timing modifications occur when an unauthorized entity reorders, delays, or copies and later replays a message generated by an authorized entity. Disclosure results when an unauthorized entity extracts values stored in managed objects, or learns of notifiable events by monitoring exchanges between managers and agents. Because SNMP does not implement authentication, many vendors do not implement Set operations, thereby reducing SNMP to a monitoring facility.

SNMP Interoperability

As presently specified, SNMPv2 is incompatible with SNMPv1 in two key areas: message formats and protocol operations. SNMPv2 messages use different header and protocol data unit (PDU) formats than SNMPv1 messages. SNMPv2 also uses two protocol operations that are not specified in SNMPv1. Furthermore, RFC 1908 defines two possible SNMPv1/v2 coexistence strategies: proxy agents and bilingual network-management systems.

Common Management Information Protocol Over TCP/IP (CMOT)

CMOT is the network management architecture that has been developed to move towards a closer relationship with the Open System Interconnection (OSI) network management standards named Common Management Information Protocol (CMIP). With these premises CMOT, as in the OSI model, can be divided into an organizational model, functional model and informational model.

In the organizational and informational models the same OSI concept is used in CMOT and in SNMP. The object identification is formed using the subtree related to the DoD with subdivisions in management, directory, experimental and private. All the management objects are defined in the Management Information Base (MIB) being represented by the Structure and Identification of Management Information (SMI), a subset of the ASN.1 (OSI Abstract Syntax Notation 1).

In the functional model CMOT adopted the OSI model that divides the management components into managers and agents. The agent collects information, performs commands and executes tests and the manager receives data, generates commands and sends instructions to the agents. This manager and agent are formed by a set of specific management information per communication layer named the Layer Management Entities (LME).

All the LME are coordinated by a System Management Application Process (SMAP) that can communicate between different systems over the Common Management Information Protocol (CMIP). In the OSI approach the management can occur only over fully established connections between the managers and the agents. CMOT allows management information exchange over connectionless services (datagram). But to maintain the same service interface required by CMIP, called Common Management Information Services (CMIS), the CMOT architecture defined a new communication layer, the Lightweight Presentation Protocol (LPP). This layer has been defined to provide the presentation services required for the CMIP so that the entirely defined network management standards defined by OSI will fit in the TCP/IP CMOT architecture.

9.8.3 Remote Monitoring

Remote Monitoring (RMON) is a standard monitoring specification that enables various network monitors and console systems to exchange network-monitoring data. RMON provides network administrators with more freedom in selecting network-monitoring probes and consoles with features that meet their particular networking needs.

The RMON specification defines a set of statistics and functions that can be exchanged between RMON-compliant console managers and network probes. As such, RMON provides network administrators with comprehensive network-fault diagnosis, planning, and performance-tuning information.

9.9 WORLD WIDE WEB

The World Wide Web is a global hypertext system which was initially developed in 1989 by Tim Berners Lee at the European Laboratory for Particle Physics, CERN in Switzerland. In 1993 the Web started to grow rapidly which was mainly due to the NCSA (National Center for Supercomputing Applications) developing a Web browser program called Mosaic, an X Windows-based application. This application provided the first graphical user interface to the Web and made browsing more convenient. Today there are Web browsers and servers available for nearly all platforms. You can get them either from an FTP site for free or buy a licensed copy. The rapid growth in popularity of the Web is due to the flexible way people can navigate through world-wide resources in the Internet and retrieve them. To get an idea of the growth of the Web, here are some statistics:

1. June 1993—only 130 Web sites available
2. December 1994—over 11500 Web sites available

The number of Web servers is growing very rapidly (between 50 and 100 daily) and the traffic over port 80, which is the *well known* Web port, on the NSF backbone has a phenomenal rate of growth too. There are already some companies doing business on the Web. You can look at prospectuses and product offerings and of course order products over the Web. Most of the multinational companies have a Web server in place to distribute product specific information, their portfolio or simply to get in contact with customers. A *page* is just the Web term for a document and the *home page* is a starting point to a collection of documents. It is, if you will, the table of contents of a Web site. From there you can easily explore and search the whole Web. Please see http://www.vivekricha.com which is the Vivek's home page.

Presenting a document in hypertext has certain advantages for the user. For example, if you want more information about a particular subject mentioned, you can usually "just click on it" to read further details. Subjects with a link to another document can be easily identified through highlighting. In fact, documents can be and often are linked to other documents by completely different authors, much like footnoting, but you can get the referenced document or graphic instantly displayed. A document on the Web could include links to other documents residing on different Web sites. If you activate the link, mostly done by a mouse click, the other document is automatically retrieved from the corresponding server and displayed. This document could include links to other resources as well and so on.

The standard communication protocol between Web servers and clients is the Hypertext Transfer Protocol (HTTP) which is a draft Internet standard. The HTTP is a generic stateless object-oriented protocol. The IETF has set up a working group to improve the performance of HTTP. Web browsers can also use many other Internet protocols like FTP, Gopher, WAIS and NNTP (Network News Transfer Protocol) for example. So you don't need a particular client product to get access to all these other resources also available on the Net. How the Web browser can differentiate between all these different protocols and which protocols are supported is explained later in this section.

An HTTP transaction consists basically of :

1. *Connection*

The establishment of a connection by the client to the server. TCP/IP port 80 is the well-known port, but other non-reserved ports may be specified in the URL.

2. *Request*

The sending, by the client, of a request message to the server.

3. *Response*

The sending, by the server, of a response to the client.

4. *Close*

The closing of the connection by either or both parties.

The standard markup language for Web documents is HTML (Hypertext Markup Language) which is a draft Internet standard and is presently under construction by several IETF working groups. HTML is an SGML (Standard Generalized Markup Language) application. If you want to create a Web document you have to use the HTML tags to build the logical structure of the document, for example headers, lists and paragraphs.

All documents, images, audio or video clips on the Web are called resources. To address and identify the access method for these resources the Web uses URLs (Uniform Resource Locators). URL is an Internet standards track protocol . The global framework for building new addressing schemes to encode names and addresses of objects. The standard introduces the term URI (Universal Resource Identifiers) as a more theoretical model for building these schemes. URIs which refer to an object address (IP address and path information) mapped to an access method using an existing network protocol like HTTP or FTP for example are known as URLs. Therefore an URL is a specific form of a URI. In general, URLs are written as follows:

<scheme>:<scheme-specific-part>

An URL contains the name of the scheme being used (<scheme>) followed by a colon and then a string (the <scheme-specific-part>) whose interpretation depends on the scheme. The following schemes are covered by the RFC standard , and other schemes may follow in the future:

1. ftp—File Transfer protocol
2. http—HyperText Transfer Protocol
3. gopher—The Gopher protocol
4. mailto—Electronic mail address
5. news—USENET news
6. nntp—USENET news using NNTP access
7. telnet—Interactive sessions
8. wais—Wide Area Information Servers
9. file—Host-specific file names
10. prospero—Prospero Directory Service
11. According to the definition the HTTP URL looks like this: http://<host>:<port>/<path>?<searchpart>

Where:

host

The fully qualified domain name of a network host or a dotted decimal IP address (for example, www.ibm.com).

port

The port number to connect to. If this parameter is omitted in an HTTP URL, it defaults to 80.

path

The path specifies the HTTP selector, a route to an HTML document for example.

? searchpart

The searchpart is a query string which is indicated with a preceding question mark.

Way to Access the Web

Use a Web browser on your own machine. This is the best option but your corporate LAN must have access to the Internet. In most cases these networks have no direct Internet access, but are connected via a firewall to the Internet. In this case you have to specify either a SOCKS server or a proxy gateway where you are registered to get Internet access. Another way to get connected is the use of the SLIP protocol. With this you set up your own modem connection to an Internet access provider.

10

DISTRIBUTED SYSTEM

10.1 INTRODUCTION

Distributed system is one in which components located at networked computers communicate and coordinate their actions only by passing messages. This definition leads to the following characteristics of distributed systems: concurrency of components, lack of global clock and independent failure of components. Sharing of resources is the main motivation for constructing distributed systems. Resources may be managed by servers and accessed by clients or they may be encapsulated as objects and accessed by other client objects.

Example of distributed system is:

Internet, WWW, intranet

Following are the **challenges** arising from the construction of distributed system:-

1. Heterogeneity of components,
2. Openness,
3. Security,
4. Scalability,
5. Failure Handling,
6. Concurrency of components and
7. Transparency

We use the term **SERVICES** for a distinct part of a computer system that manages a collection of related resources and present their functionality to users and applications as we access shared files through a file service. The only access to a service is via the set of operations that it exports,ex. A file service provides read, write, and delete operations on files.

Resources in a distributed system are encapsulated in computers and can only be accessed from other computers by communication. For effective sharing, each resource must be managed by a program that offers a communication interface enabling the resources to be accessed and updated reliably and consistently. By default the term client and server refers to processes rather than the computer that they execute upon.

In a distributed system written in an object-oriented language, resources may be encapsulated as objects and accessed by client objects, in which case we speak of a client object invoking a method upon a server object. The Object Oriented (OO) paradigm is well suited both for description and implementation of distributed systems. The advantages of such an approach are in increased decomposition of systems into modules (refinement), and in data abstraction. Since standards are emerging based round these techniques.

10.2 CHALLENGES OF DISTRIBUTED SYSTEM

Heterogeneity

Many distributed systems arose out of the need to integrate legacy stand-alone software systems into a larger more comprehensive system. Since the individual systems were often developed independently of each other, they may have been based on different architectural principles and even different programming and operating system technologies. This creates another common problem of distribution: integration of heterogeneous technologies. For example, one system might use a 16-bit integer format with the most significant bit in the leftmost position, while its peer may use a 32-bit format with the most significant bit in the rightmost position.

Internet enables users to access services and run application over a heterogeneous collection of computers and networks. Heterogeneity applies to following:

1. networks
2. computer hardware
3. operating systems
4. programming languages
5. implementation by different programmers.

Network heterogeneity is masked by the IP protocol. Programming languages are different, example integer representation in one language is different in one language than other and also usage differs from programmers to programmers.

Middleware is the solution to each problem related to heterogeneity. Its a software layer that provides a programming abstraction as well masking the heterogeneity of the underlying networks, Hardware, Operation system and programming languages. CORBA, Java RMI are example of the middleware. Middleware is implemented over IP layer which they mask the difference of underlying networks. But all middleware deals with the difference in operating systems and hardware.

Openness

It's a characteristic that determines whether the system can be extended and re-implemented in various ways. Openness can be determined primarily by the degree to which new resource sharing services can be added and made available for use by a variety of client programs. It needs specification and documents of key software interfaces of the components of a system i.e., the interfaces are published. Open system can be extended at the hardware level by the addition of computers to the network and at the software level by the introduction of new services and the reimplementation of old ones enabling application programs to share resources. and also open systems are Independent of individual of vendors.

Security

Challenge is to send sensitive information in am message over a network in a secure manner. It also includes -knowing the identity of the users or other agents on whose behalf the message was send. Secondly we have to identify a remote user or other agent correctly.

Scalability

A system is scalable if it remains effective when there is a significant increase in the number of users, resources.

Failure Handling

A failure is an event that occurs when a component fails to behave according to its specification. This is usually because the system experiencing the failure has reached some invalid state. We refer to such an undesirable state as an error. The underlying cause of an error is called a fault. For example, a bit in memory that is stuck at "high" is a fault. This will result in an error when a "low" value is written to that bit. When the value of that bit is read and used in a calculation, the outcome will be a failure.

Of course, this classification is a relative one. A fault is typically a failure at some lower level of abstraction (that is, the stuck-high bit may be the result of a lower-level fault due to an impurity in the manufacturing process).

When a failure occurs, it is first necessary to detect it and then to perform some basic failure handling. The latter involves diagnosis (determining the underlying cause of the fault), fault removal, and failure recovery. Each of these activities can be quite complex.

Consider, for example, failure diagnosis. A single fault can often lead to many errors and many different cascading failures, each of which may be reported independently. A key difficulty lies in sorting through the possible flurry of consequent error reports, correlating them, and determining the basic underlying cause (the fault).

The property of distributed system is that some components fail while others continue to function. Following techniques for dealing with failure are:

1. Detecting failure, example checksum can be used to detect corrupt data in a message or a file.
2. Masking failure example, messages can be retransmitted when they fail to arrive.

Concurrency

There is a possibility that several clients will attempt to access a shared resource at the same time. The process that manages a shared resource could take one client request at a time. This approach may limit the thoughput, Therefore services and applications generally allows multiple client requests to be processed concurrently. Let's suppose that each resource is encapsulated as an object and that invocations are executed in concurrent threads. In this case it is possible that several threads may be executing concurrently within an object, in which case their operations on the object may conflict with one another and produce inconsistent results.

So any object that represents a shared resource in a distributed system must be responsible for ensuring that it operates correctly in a concurrent environment .This applies not only to servers but also to objects in applications. Therefore an object to be safe in a concurrent environment ,its operation must be synchronized in such a way that its data remains consistent. This can be achieved by a technique which is used in most of the operating systems like semaphores.

Transparency

Its a secrecy from the user and application programmer of the separation of components in a distributed system, so that system is perceived as a whole rather than as a collection of independent components. Transparency is of following types:

1. Access transparency enables local and remote resources to be accessed using identical operations.
2. Location transparency enables resources to be accessed without the knowledge of their location.
3. Concurrency transparency enables multiple instances of resources to be used to increase reliability and performance without knowledge of the replicas by users or application programmers.
4. Failure transparency enables the secrecy of faults, allowing users and application programs to complete their tasks despite the failure of hardware or software components.
5. Scaling transparency allows the system and applications to expand in scale without change to the system structure or the application algorithms.

Hardware for distributed systems is important, but it is software that largely determines what a distributed system actually looks like. Distributed systems are very much like traditional operating systems. First, they act as **resource managers** for the underlying hardware, allowing multiple users and applications to share resources such as CPUs, memories, peripheral devices, the network, and data of all kinds. Second, and perhaps more important, is that distributed systems attempt to hide the intricacies and heterogeneous nature of the underlying hardware by providing a virtual machine on which applications can be easily executed. To understand the nature of distributed systems, we will therefore first take a look at operating systems in relation to distributed computers. Operating systems for distributed computers can be roughly divided into two categories: tightly coupled systems and loosely-coupled systems. In tightly-coupled systems, the operating system essentially tries to maintain a single, global view of the resources it manages. Loosely-coupled systems can be thought of as a collection of computers each running their own operating system. However, these operating systems work together to make their own services and resources available to the others. This distinction between tightly-coupled and loosely-coupled systems is related to the hardware classification given in the previous section. A tightly coupled operating system is generally referred to as a **distributed operating system (DOS)**, and is used for managing multiprocessors and homogeneous multicomputers. Like traditional uniprocessor operating systems, the main goal of a distributed operating system is to hide the intricacies of managing the underlying hardware such that it can be shared by multiple processes. The loosely-coupled **network operating system (NOS)** is used for heterogeneous multicomputer systems. Although managing the underlying hardware is an important issue for NOS, the distinction from traditional operating systems comes from the fact local services are made available to remote clients. In the following sections we will first take a look at tightly-coupled and loosely-coupled operating systems. To actually come to a distributed system, enhancements to the services of network operating systems are needed such that a better support for distribution transparency is provided. These enhancements lead to what is known as **middleware**, and lie at the heart of modern distributed systems. Middleware is also discussed in this section Figure 101. summarizes the main issues with respect to DOS, NOS, and middleware.

10.3 MODELS OF DISTRIBUTED SYSTEM

Following are the **models of distributed system:-**

1. Architectural model, its concerned with the placement of its parts and relationships between them. Example includes the client-server model and the peer-process model.
2. Fundamental models are concerned with the formal description of properties common in all the architectural models.

As we lack a global clock in distributed system. So all communication between processes is achieved by means of messages. Message communication over computer network is affected by delays, failure and security attacks. Three models which deals these issues are:

(*a*) Interaction model, it deals with the performance and with the difficulty of setting time limits in a distributed system example message delivery.

(*b*) Failure model, it attempts to give specification of the faults that can be exhibited by processes and communication channels.

(*c*) Security model, It deals with the possible threats to processes and communication channels. It introduces the concept of secure channel, which is secure against those threats.

Architectural models are build around the concept of process and object. It first simplifies and abstracts the functions of the individual components of the distributed system. Processes are classified as server processes, client processes and peer processes.

Software architecture refers to the structuring of software as layers or modules in a single computer and more recently in terms of services offered and requested between processes located in the same or different computers. Process and service oriented view can be expressed in terms of service layers. Server process accepts request from other processes. A distributed service can be provided by one or more server processes interacting with each other and with client processes in order to maintain a consistent system wide view of the service's resources.

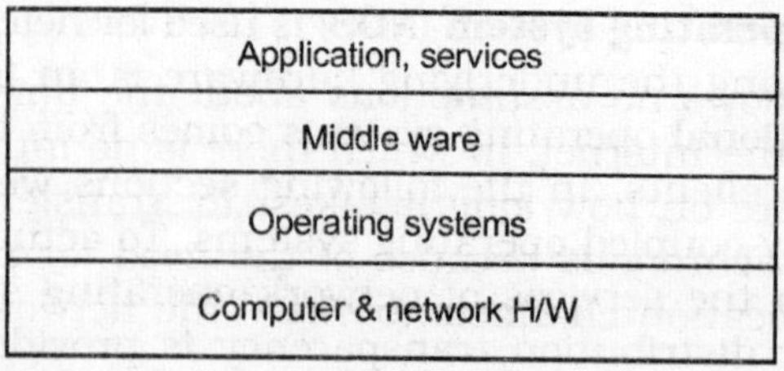

Figure 10.1 Software and Hardware Service Layers in Distributed Systems

Platform

Lowest layer H/W and S/W layers are often referred as Platform for distributed systems and applications. They provides services to the layers above them, which are implemented independently in each computer.

Middleware

It's a layer of software whose task is to mask heterogeneity and to provide a convenient programming model to application programmers'. It's a set of computers that interact with each other to implement communication and resource sharing support for distributed applications. It provides building blocks for the construction of software components that can work with one another in a distributed system.

Interfaces and Objects

Set of functions available in a process is specified by one or more interface definitions. Each server process is seen as a single entity with a fixed interface defining the functions that can invoke in it. Many objects can be encapsulated in server or peer processes and references to them are passed to other processes so that their methods can be accessed by remote invocation. This is the approach adopted by CORBA and Java with its remote method invocation (RMI) mechanism.

Fundamental Model

Models of distributed system share common properties. All of them are composed of processes that communicate with one another by sending messages over a computer network. A. Interaction model, Interacting processes perform all of the activities in a distributed system. Each process has its own state, consisting of the set of data that it can access and update, including the variables in its program. The state belonging to each process is completely private—*i.e.*, cannot be accessed or updated by other process. Messages are transmitted between processes to transfer information between them and to coordinate their activities.

Synchronous Distributed Systems

Its hard to set time limits on the time taken for process execution, message delivery or clock drift. For a Synchronous distributed system its required for the processes to perform tasks with well known resource requirements for which they can be guaranteed sufficient processor cycles and network capacity and for processes to be supplied with clock with bounded drift rates.

Asynchronous Distributed Systems

Asynchronous model allows no assumptions about the time intervals involved in any execution. This models the Internet, in which there is no intrinsic bound on server or network load and therefore on how long it takes, to ,transfer file using ftp. Actual distributed systems are Asynchronous because of the need for processes to share the processors and for communication channels to share the network.

Application Program Interface to UDP

It provides a message passing abstraction—the simplest form of interprocess communication. This enables a sending process to transmit a single message to a receiving process. The independent packets containing these messages are called datagrams. In java and Unix API the sender specifies the destination using a socket-an indirect reference to a particular port used by the destination process at a destination computer.

Application Program Interface to TCP

It provides the abstraction of a two way stream between pairs of processes. The information communicated consists of a stream of data items with no message boundaries. Stream provides a building block for producer-consumer communication.

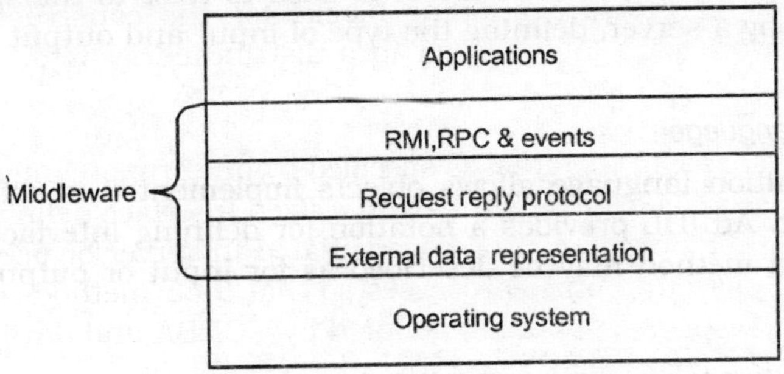

Figure 10.2 Middleware Layer

Programming models followed in distributed systems are concerned with those applications that are composed of cooperating programs running in several different computers. Such programs need to be able to invoke operations in other processes often running in different computers. Following models are applied to distributed systems:

1. Remote Procedure Call (RPC), it allows client programs to call procedures in server programs running in separate processes and generally in different computers from client.
2. Remote Method Invocation (RMI), objects in different processes communicate with one another by means of RMI. It's an extension of local method invocation that allows an object living in one process to invoke the methods of an object living in another process.

Middleware layer uses protocols used on messages between processes to provide its higher-level abstractions such as remote invocations and events. Middleware provides Location Transparency and independence from the details of communication protocols, O/Ss, and computer hardware.

Interfaces

Languages provide a means to organize a program as a set of modules that can communicate with one another. Communication between modules can be by means of procedure calls between modules or by direct access to the variables in another modules. To control the interaction between modules an Interface is defined for each module. Interface of a module specifies the procedures and the variables that can be accessed from other modules. Modules are implemented to hide all the information about them except them which is available through its interface. As long as the interface remains the same, implementation may be changed without affecting the users of the module.

In a distributed program, the modules can run in separate processes. It's not possible for a module running in one process to access the variables in a module in another process. The parameter-passing mechanisms used in local procedure calls are not suited when the callers and procedures are in different processes. So the specification of a procedure or a method in the interface of the module in a distributed program describes the parameters as input or output or sometimes both.

Service Interface: In a client -server model, each server provides a set of procedures that are available for use by clients.example,a file server provides procedures for reading and writing files. The term service interface is used to refer to the specifications of the procedures offered by a server, defining the type of input and output arguments of each of the procedures.

Interface Definition Language

Interface definition language allows objects implemented in different language to invoke one another. An IDL provides a notation for defining interfaces I which each of the parameters of a method may be described as for input or output .

Communication

How we are going to communicate distributed objects?

Following are the models used to facilitate communication between distributed objects.

1. **Object Model :** An object oriented program consists of collection of interacting objects, each of which consists of set of data and a set of methods. An object communicates with other objects by invoking their methods ,generally passing arguments and receiving results. Objects can encapsulated their data and the code of their methods. In distributed systems, an object's data should be accessible only via its methods. Objects can be accessed via object references. To invoke a method in an object, the object reference and method name are given together with any necessary arguments. Interface provides a definition of the signature of a set of methods without specifying their implementation. An object will provide a particular interface if its class contains code that implements the methods of that interface. Actions in object-oriented program is initiated by an object invoking a method in another object. An invocation can include additional information. The receiver executes the appropriate method and then returns control to the invoking object, sometimes supplying a result.

2. **Distributed Objects :** Distributed object system adopt the client-server architecture.Objects are managed by servers and their clients invoke their methods using remote method invocation. In RMI, the client's request to invoke a method of an object is send in a message to the server managing the object. The invocation is carried out by executing a method of the object at the server and the result is returned to the client in another message. Having client and server objects in different processes enforce encapsulation. *i.e.,* the state of an object can be accesses only by the methods of the object, which indicates that its not possible for unauthorized methods to act on the state.
3. **Distributed Objects Model :** Each process contains a collection of objects, some of which can receive both local and remote invocations. Method invocation in the same computer or in distributed computers is known as remote method invocation.

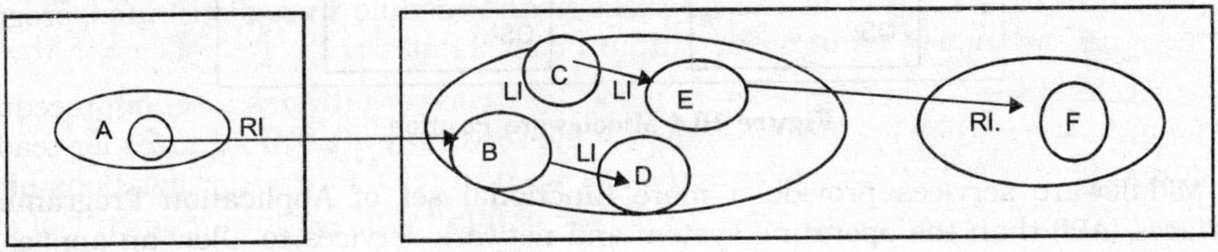

Remote Invocation RI , Local Invocation LI.

Figure 10.3 Remote and Local Method Invocation

Objects that can receive remote invocations are referred to as remote objects.In the above Figure 10.3 objects B and F are remote objects .All objects can receive local invocations, although they can receive them only from other objects that hold references to them. Example object C must have a reference to object E so that it can invoke one of it's methods. Any object that can receive an RMI to have a remote object reference. A remote object reference is an identifier that can be used thought a distributed system to refer to a particular unique remote object.

10.4 MIDDLEWARE

It's a layer of software whose task is to mask heterogeneity and to provide a convenient programming model to application programmers'. It's a set of computers that interact with each other to implement communication and resource sharing support for distributed applications. It provides building blocks for the construction of software components that can work with one another in a distributed system.

Middleware is connectivity software that consists of a set of enabling services that allow multiple processes running on one or more machines to interact across a network. Middleware is essential to migrating mainframe applications to client/server applications and to providing for communication across heterogeneous platforms. The most widely-publicized middleware initiatives are the Open Software Foundation's Distributed Computing Environment (DCE), Object Management Group's Common Object Request Broker Architecture (CORBA), and Microsoft's COM/DCOM. As outlined in Figure 10.4, middleware services are sets of distributed software that exist between the application and the operating system and network services on a system node in the network.

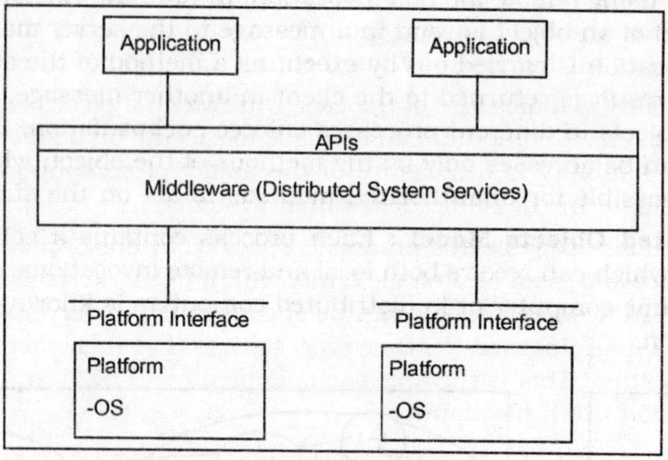

Figure 10.4 Middleware Position

Middleware services provide a more functional set of Application Programming Interfaces (API) than the operating system and network services to allow an application to :

- locate transparently across the network, providing interaction with another application or service
- be independent from network services
- be reliable and available
- scale up in capacity without losing function

Advantages of Middleware Layer/Distributed Computing Environment

1. DCE provides services that can be found in other computer networking environments, but packages them so as to make them much easier to use. For example, the DCE Remote Procedure Call (RPC) facility provides a way of communicating between software modules running on different systems that is much simpler to code than older methods, such as using socket calls.
2. DCE provides new capabilities that go beyond what was available previously. The DCE Security Service provides a reliable way of determining if a user of a distributed system should be allowed to perform a certain action, for example. This is very useful for most distributed applications, yet the design and implementation effort entailed in providing such a capability would be prohibitive for an individual developer.
3. DCE integrates components in a manner that makes them more valuable together than separately. For example, the DCE RPC uses threads in such a way that a developer can implement a multi-threaded server without ever explicitly creating or destroying a thread.

4. DCE supports both portability and interoperability by providing the developer with capabilities that hide differences among the various hardware, software and networking elements an application will deal with in a large network. For example, the RPC automatically converts data from the format used by one computer to that used by another.
5. Portability is a measure of the ease with which a piece of software that executes on one type of computer can be made to execute on a different type of computer. Interoperability is a measure of the ability of computers of different types to participate in the same distributed system.

Set of functions available in a process is specified by one or more interface definitions. Each server process is seen as a single entity with a fixed interface defining the functions that can invoke in it. Many objects can be encapsulated in server or peer processes and references to them are passed to other processes so that their methods can be accessed by remote invocation. This is the approach adopted by CORBA and Java with its remote method invocation (RMI) mechanism.

The role of middleware is to ease the task of designing, programming and managing distributed applications by providing a simple, consistent and integrated distributed programming environment. Essentially, middleware is a distributed software layer, or 'platform' which abstracts over the complexity and heterogeneity of the underlying distributed environment with its multitude of network technologies, machine architectures, operating systems and programming languages.

Different Middleware Platforms Support Different Programming Models

Perhaps the most popular model is *object based middleware* in which applications are structured into (potentially distributed) objects that interact via location transparent method invocation. Prime examples of this type of middleware are the OMG's CORBA and Microsoft's Distributed COM. Both of these platforms offer an *interface definition language* (IDL) which is used to abstract over the fact that objects can be implemented in any suitable programming language, an *object request broker* which is responsible for transparently directing method invocations to the appropriate target object, and a set of *services* (*e.g.* naming, time, transactions, replication etc.) which further enhance the distributed programming environment.

Not all middleware is object based, however. Two other popular paradigms are *event based middleware* and *message oriented middleware* both of which mainly employ 'single shot' communications rather than the request-reply style communication found in object based middleware. **Event based middleware** is particularly suited to the construction of non-centralized distributed applications that must monitor and react to changes in their environment. Examples are process control, Internet news channels and stock tracking. It is claimed that event based middleware has potentially better scaling properties for such applications than object based middleware. **Message oriented middleware,** on the other hand, is biased toward applications in which messages need to be persistently stored and queued. Workflow and messaging applications are good examples.

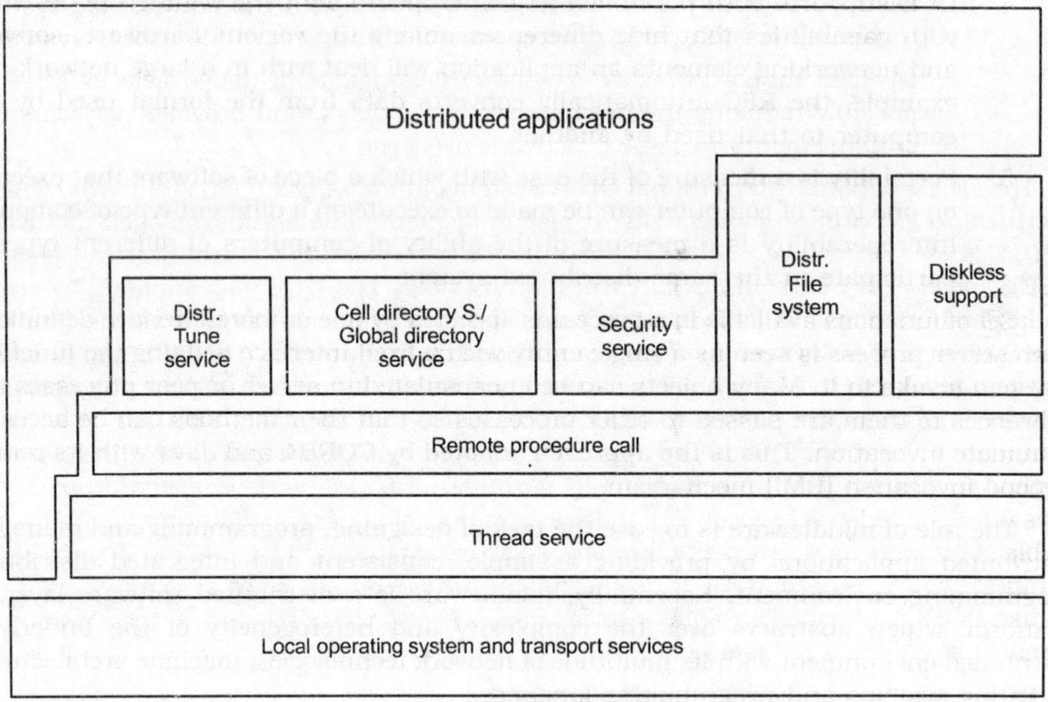

Figure 10.5 Distributed Computing Environment Architecture

DCE services are organized into two categories:

1. *Fundamental distributed services* provide tools for software developers to create the end-user services needed for distributed computing. They include
   a. Remote Procedure Call, which provides portability, network *independence*, and secure distributed applications.
   b. Directory services, which provide full X.500 support and a single naming model to allow programmers and maintainers to identify and access distributed resources more easily.
   c. Time service, which provides a mechanism to monitor and track clocks in a distributed environment and accurate time stamps to reduce the load on system administrator.
   d. Security service, which provides the network with authentication, authorization, and user account management services to maintain the *integrity*, privacy, and authenticity of the distributed system.
   e. Thread service, which provides a simple, portable, programming model for building concurrent applications.
2. *Data-sharing services* provide end users with capabilities built upon the fundamental distributed services. These services require no programming on the part of the end user and facilitate better use of information. They include

a. Distributed file system, which interoperates with the network file system to provide a high-performance, scalable, and secure file access system.

b. Diskless support, which allows low-cost workstations to use disks on servers, possibly reducing the need/cost for local disks, and provides performance enhancements to reduce network overhead.

The DCE supports International Open Systems Interconnect (OSI) standards, which are critical to global interconnectivity. It also implements ISO standards such as CCITT X.500, Remote Operations Service Element (ROSE), Association Control Service Element (ACSE), and the ISO session and presentation services. The DCE also supports Internet standards such as the TCP/IP transport and network protocols, as well as the Domain Name System and Network Time Protocol provided by the Internet. The DCE can be used by system vendors, software developers, and end users. It can be used on any network hardware and transport software, including TCP/IP, OSI, and X.25. The DCE is written in standard C and uses standard operating system service interfaces like POSIX and X/Open guidelines. This makes the DCE portable to a wide variety of platforms. DCE allows for the extension of a network to large numbers of nodes, providing an environment capable of supporting networks of numerous low-end computers (*i.e.*, PCs and Macintosh machines), which is important if downsizing and distributing of processing is desired. Because DCE is provided in source form, it can be tailored for specific applications if desired.

DCE works internally **with** the **client/server model** and is well-suited for development of applications that are structured according to this model. Most DCE services are especially optimized for a structuring of distributed computing systems into a "cell" (a set of nodes/platforms) that is managed together by one authority.

For DCE, intra-cell communication is optimized and relatively secure and transparent. Inter-cell communication, however, requires more specialized processing and more complexity than its intra-cell counterpart, and requires a greater degree of programming expertise.

When using the thread services provided by DCE, the application programmer must be aware of thread synchronization and shared data across threads. While different threads are mutually asynchronous up to a static number defined at initialization, an individual thread is synchronous. The complexity of thread programming should be considered if these services are to be used.

Message Oriented Middleware

Message-oriented middleware (MOM) is a client/server infrastructure that increases the interoperability, portability, and flexibility of an application by allowing the application to be distributed over multiple heterogeneous platforms. It reduces the complexity of developing applications that span multiple operating systems and network protocols by insulating the application developer from the details of the various operating system and network interfaces—Application Programming Interfaces (APIs) that extend across diverse platforms and networks are typically provided by the MOM.

Message-oriented middleware, as shown in Figure 10.6, is software that resides in both portions of a client/server architecture and typically supports asynchronous calls between the client and server applications. Message queues provide temporary storage when the destination program is busy or not connected. MOM reduces the involvement of application developers with the complexity of the master-slave nature of the client/server mechanism.

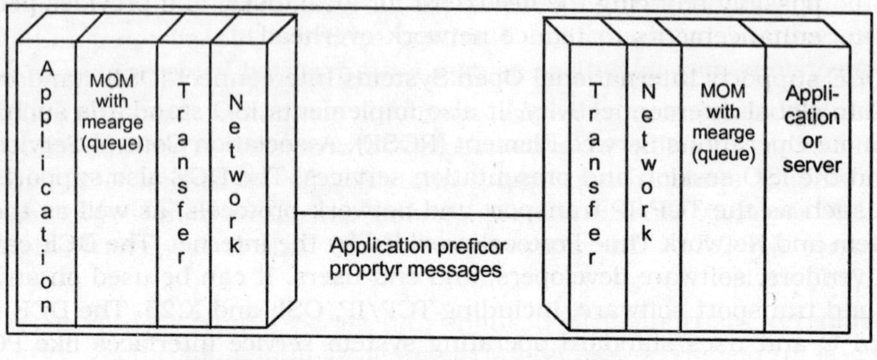

Figure 10.6 Message-Oriented Middleware

MOM increases the flexibility of architecture by enabling applications to exchange messages with other programs without having to know what platform or processor the other application resides on within the network. The aforementioned messages can contain formatted data, requests for action, or both. Nominally, MOM systems provide a message queue between interoperating processes, so if the destination process is busy, the message is held in a temporary storage location until it can be processed. MOM is typically asynchronous and peer-to-peer, but most implementations support synchronous message passing as well.

Application hands off to the messaging middleware application the responsibility of notifying a server that some action needs to be taken. MOM is also well-suited for object-oriented systems because it furnishes a conceptual mechanism for peer-to-peer communications between objects. MOM insulates developers from connectivity concerns-the application developers write to APIs that handle the complexity of the specific interfaces.

Asynchronous and synchronous mechanisms each have strengths and weaknesses that should be considered when designing any specific application. The asynchronous mechanism of MOM, unlike Remote Procedure Call (RPC), which uses a synchronous, blocking mechanism, does not guard against overloading a network. As such, a negative aspect of MOM is that a client process can continue to transfer data to a server that is not keeping pace. Message-oriented middleware's use of message queues, however, tends to be more flexible than RPC-based systems, because most implementations of MOM can default to synchronous and fall back to asynchronous communication if a server becomes unavailable.

10.5 THE VARIOUS ELEMENTS OF DCE ARE AS FOLLOWS

- **Remote Procedure Call (RPC) and Presentation Services:** Interface Definition Languages (IDLs) and RPCs enable programmers to transfer control and data across a network in a transparent manner that helps to mask the network's complexity. DCE uses the RPC originally developed by the HP Apollo Network

Computing System (NCS), with some enhancements by DEC and IBM. NCS also provides the Network Data Representation (NDR), a virtual data representation. NDR enables data to be exchanged between various vendor products transparently. Conversions (as necessary) will take place with no intervention by the caller. Naming, security, file system, and data type conversions may take place as data is transported between various platforms.

- **Naming:** User-oriented names, specifying computers, files, and people should be easily accessible in a distributed environment. These directory services must offer standard appearance and rules for all clients. DCE supports the X.500 directory services standard, adding extensions from DEC's Domain Name Service (DECdns). The standardized X.500 code is Siemens Nixdorf's DIR-X X.500 service.
- **Security:** Distributed applications and services must identify users, control access to resources, and guard the integrity of all applications. DCE uses the Kerberos authentication service, developed by MIT as part of its Athena networking project and enhanced by Hewlett-Packard. This service is one of the major challenges to making products available quickly, because very few products today are developed with an awareness of this specification.
- **Threads:** This terminology represents a method of supporting parallel execution by managing multiple threads of control within a process operating in a distributed environment. Threads enable systems to start up multiple processes and forget about them until they are completed. This is especially important for network servers that may have to handle many requests from many clients at the same time. They must be able to do this without waiting for the previous request to complete. DCE is using DEC's Concert Multithread Architecture (CMA) implementation.
- **Time Service:** A time service synchronizes all system clocks of a distributed environment so that executing applications can depend on equivalent clocking among processes. Consider that many machines operating in many time zones may provide processes as part of a single application solution. It is essential that they agree on the time in order to manage scheduled events and time-sequenced events. DCE is using a modification of DEC's Distributed Time Synchronization Service (DECdts).
- **Distributed File Services:** By extending the local file system throughout the network, users gain full access to files on remote configurations. DCE uses Sun's Network File System (NFS) Version 2 and provides next-generation capabilities with the Andrew File System (AFS), developed at Carnegie-Mellon University and commercialized by Transarc Corp. Diskless operations under AFS are supported by development work done by Hewlett-Packard.
- **PC Integration:** Integration enables PCs using MS-DOS, Windows NT, and OS/2 to access file and print services outside the MS-DOS environment. DCE uses Microsoft's LAN Manager/X.
- **Management:** Although partly addressed by the previous components, management is so complex in a distributed, heterogeneous configuration that

OSF has defined a new architecture: distributed management environment (DME). DME provides a common framework for the management of stand-alone and distributed systems. This framework provides consistent tools and techniques for managing different types of systems and enables vendors to build system management applications that work on a variety of platforms. OSF will base DME on technology from Hewlett-Packard's OpenView product.

- **Communications:** DCE is committed to support the OSI protocol stack.

10.6 WELL KNOWN MIDDLEWARE

Some named middleware/DCE are :

1. CORBA,
2. Java-RMI,
3. LEGION and
4. DCOM.

The Common Object Request Broker Architecture (CORBA) is a *specification* of a standard architecture for object request brokers (ORBs). A standard architecture allows vendors to develop ORB products that support application portability and interoperability across different programming languages, hardware platforms, operating systems, and ORB implementations: "Using a CORBA-compliant ORB, a client can transparently invoke a method on a server object, which can be on the same machine or across a network. The ORB intercepts the call, and is responsible for finding an object that can implement the request, passing it the parameters, invoking its method, and returning the results of the invocation. The client does not have to be aware of where the object is located, its programming language, its operating system or any other aspects that are not part of an object's interface". The "vision" behind CORBA is that distributed systems are conceived and implemented as distributed objects. The interfaces to these objects are described in a high- vel, architecture-neutral specification language that also supports object-oriented design abstraction. When combined with the Object Management Architecture, CORBA can result in distributed systems that can be rapidly developed, and can reap the benefits that result from using high-level building blocks provided by CORBA, such as maintainability and adaptability.

The CORBA specification was developed by the Object Management Group (OMG), an industry group with over six hundred member companies representing computer manufacturers, independent software vendors, and a variety of government and academic organizations. Thus, CORBA specifies an industry/consortium standard, not a "formal" standard in the IEEE/ANSI/ISO sense of the term. The OMG was established in 1988, and the initial CORBA specification emerged in 1992. Since then, the CORBA specification has undergone significant revision, with the latest major revision CORBA ORBs are middleware mechanisms, as are all ORBs. CORBA can be thought of as a generalization of remote procedure call (RPC) that includes a number of refinements of RPC, including:

1. a more abstract and powerful interface definition language
2. direct support for a variety of object-oriented concepts
3. a variety of other improvements and generalizations of the more primitive RPC

CORBA products provide a framework for the development and execution of *distributed applications*. But why would one want to develop a distributed application in the first place? As you will see later, distribution introduces a whole new set of difficult issues. However, sometimes there is no choice; some applications by their very nature are distributed across multiple computers because of one or more of the following reasons:

1. The *data* used by the application are distributed
2. The *computation* is distributed
3. The *users* of the application are distributed.

Data are Distributed

Some applications must execute on multiple computers because the data that the application must access exist on multiple computers for administrative and ownership reasons. The owner may permit the data to be accessed remotely but not stored locally. Or perhaps the data cannot be co-located and must exist on multiple heterogeneous systems for historical reasons.

Computation is Distributed

Some applications execute on multiple computers in order to take advantage of multiple processors computing in parallel to solve some problem. Other applications may execute on multiple computers in order to take advantage of some unique feature of a particular system. Distributed applications can take advantage of the scalability and heterogeneity of the distributed system.

Users are Distributed

Some applications execute on multiple computers because users of the application communicate and interact with each other via the application. Each user executes a piece of the distributed application on his or her computer, and shared objects, typically execute on one or more servers. A typical architecture for this kind of application is illustrated below.

10.7 CORBA AND THE OBJECT MANAGEMENT ARCHITECTURE

It is impossible to understand CORBA without appreciating its role in the Object Management Architecture (OMA), shown in Figure 10.7. The OMA is itself a specification (actually, a collection of related specifications) that defines a broad range of services for building distributed applications. The OMA goes far beyond RPC in scope and complexity. The distinction between CORBA and the OMA is an important one because many services one might expect to find in a middleware product such as CORBA (*e.g.*, naming, transaction, and asynchronous event management services) are actually specified as services in the OMA.

OMA services are partitioned into three categories: CORBA Services, CORBA Facilities, and Application Objects. The ORB (whose details are specified by CORBA) is a communication infrastructure through which applications access these services, and through which objects interact with each other. CORBA Services, CORBA Facilities, and Application Objects define different categories of objects in the OMA; these objects (more accurately object *types*) define a range of functionality needed to support the development of distributed software systems.

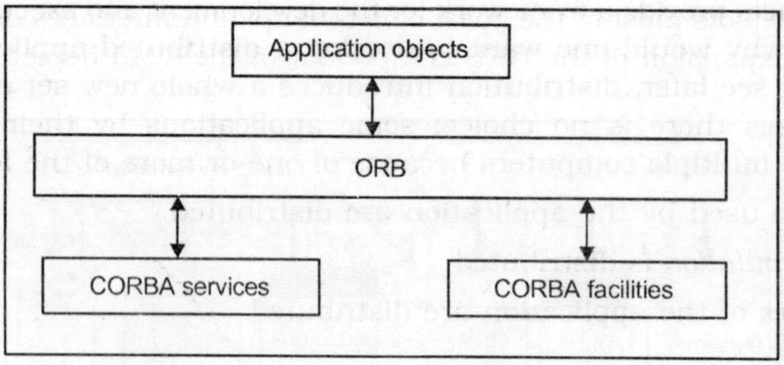

Figure 10.7 Object Management Architecture

1. CORBA Services are considered fundamental to building non-trivial distributed applications. These services currently include asynchronous event management, transactions, persistence, externalization, concurrency, naming, relationships, and lifecycle. Table 10.1 summarizes the purpose of each of these services.
2. CORBA Facilities may be useful for distributed applications in some settings, but are not considered as universally applicable as CORBA Services. These "facilities" include: user interface, information management, system management, task management, and a variety of "vertical market" facilities in domains such as manufacturing, distributed simulation, and accounting.

Application Objects provide services that are particular to an application or class of applications. These are not (currently) a topic for standardization within the OMA, but are usually included in the OMA reference model for completeness, *i.e.*, objects are either application-specific, support common facilities, or are basic services.

TABLE 10.1. Overview of CORBA services

Naming service	Provides the ability to bind a name to an object. Similar to other forms of directory service.
Event service	Supports asynchronous message-based communication among objects. Supports chaining of event channels, and a variety of producer/consumer roles.
Lifecycle service	Defines conventions for creating, deleting, copying and moving objects.
Persistence service	Provides a means for retaining and managing the persistent state of objects.
Transaction service	Supports multiple transaction models, including mandatory "flat" and optional "nested" transactions.
Concurrency service	Supports concurrent, coordinated access to objects from multiple clients.
Relationship service	Supports the specification, creation and maintenance of relationships among objects.
Externalization service	Defines protocols and conventions for externalizing and internalizing objects across processes and across ORBs.

Figure 10.8 depicts most of the basic components and interfaces defined by CORBA. This figure is an expansion of the ORB component of the OMA depicted in Figure 10.6.

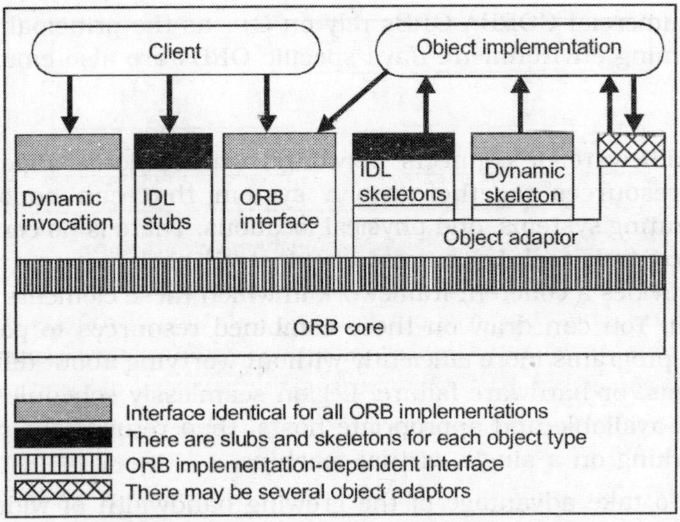

Figure 10.8 Structure of CORBA Interfaces

One element that is crucial to the understanding of CORBA is the interface definition language (IDL) processor. All objects are defined in CORBA (actually, in the OMA) using IDL. IDL is an object-oriented interface definition formalism that has some syntactic similarities with C++. Unlike C++, IDL can only define interfaces; it is not possible to specify behavior in IDL. Language mappings are defined from IDL to C, C++, Ada95, and Smalltalk80.

An important point to note is that CORBA specifies that clients and object implementations can be written in different programming languages and execute on different computer hardware architectures and different operating systems, and that clients and object implementations cannot detect any of these details about each other. Put another way, the IDL interface completely defines the interface between clients and objects; all other details about objects (such as their implementation language and location) can be made "transparent."

A large and growing number of implementations of CORBA are available in the marketplace, including implementations from most major computer manufacturers and independent software vendors. CORBA ORBs are also being developed by university research and development projects, for example Stanford's Fresco, Xerox Arc's ILU, Cornell's Electra, and others.

At the same time, it must be noted that not all CORBA ORBs are equally mature, nor has the OMA sufficiently matured to support the vision that lies behind CORBA. While CORBA and OMA products are maturing and are being used in increasingly complex and demanding situations, the specifications and product implementations are not entirely stable. This is in no small way a result of the dynamism of distributed object technology and middleware in general and is no particular fault of the OMG. Fortunately techniques exist for evaluating technology in the face of such dynamism.

Dependencies include the following:

1. TCP/IP is needed to support the CORBA-defined inter-ORB interoperability protocol (IIOP).
2. Most commercial CORBA ORBs rely on C++ as the principal client and server programming environment. Java-specific ORBs are also emerging.

10.8 LEGION

Legion is middleware; it connects networks, workstations, supercomputers, and other computer resources together into a system that can encompass different architectures, operating systems, and physical locations. There is no central "big brother" that oversees and controls each Legion resource: instead, each resource is an independent element. Legion provides a coherent framework in which these elements can be combined into a *metasystem*. You can draw on these combined resources to parallelize complex problems and run programs more efficiently without worrying about different languages, conflicting platforms, or hardware failure. Legion seamlessly schedules and distributes your processes on available and appropriate hosts, then returns the results. You have the illusion of working on a single, virtual machine.

Legion aims to take advantage of the growing bandwidth of wide- and local-area networks without compromising network security and functionality and without asking you to handle the complex arrangements between incompatible platforms and architectures.

A primary Legion feature is its scalability: it is designed to handle trillions of objects over enormous distances and in a widely variegated computing environment via a scalable software architecture. Legion uses a totally distributed system that easily encompasses disparate elements rather than a rigid centralized structure. This means that you have access to a potentially huge wealth of shared resources.

There are some core components and libraries that are necessary, but system administrators, users, and developers are free to customize Legion and choose which implementations best suit individual needs. Legion has extensible, replaceable components that will permit it to evolve over time to accommodate new and perhaps unexpected requirements of future users: we have designed Legion to be flexible enough to work with unpredicted resources and unpredicted users.

Legion does not replace your operating system, but acts as a middle layer between it and other Legion resources. Legion consists of libraries, source code, and executable binary files that run in user space in existing operating systems. Legion is designed to work on a variety of architectures and to run applications on multiple platforms.

The current release of Legion runs on:

1. Sun Workstation/Solaris 5.x (solaris)
2. SGI/IRIX 5.x or 6.5 n32 build (sgi_n32)
3. SGI/IRIX 5.x or 6.5 n64 build (sgi_n64)
4. x86/Red Hat Linux 5.x (linux)
5. DEC Alpha/Red Hat Linux 5.x (alpha_linux)
6. DEC Alpha/OSFI v4 (alpha_DEC)

7. IBM RS6000/AIX 4.2.1 or 4.3 (rs6000)
8. HPUX 11.x (hppa_hpux)
9. CRAY UNICOS (as a virtual host only).

10.9 DISTRIBUTED COM

It is an extension to COM that allows network-based component interaction. While COM processes can run on the same machine but in different address spaces, the DCOM extension allows processes to be spread across a network. With DCOM, components operating on a variety of platforms can interact, as long as DCOM is available within the environment.

10.10 INTERFACE DEFINITION LANGUAGE

Overview of IDL

1. IDL is a 'contractual' language that lets you specify a component's (object's) boundaries and its interfaces with potential clients
2. CORBA IDL is language nuetral and totally declarative (*i.e* does not define implementations details)
3. Provides operating system and programming language independent interfaces to all services and objects that resides on the CORBA bus.

Structure of Corba IDL

1. **Modules** provide a namespace to group a set of class descriptions (or interfaces interfaces in OMG terminology). A module is identified by the keyword **module**
2. **Interfaces** define a set of methods (operations in OMG terminology) that a client can invoke on an object. Think of this as a class definition without the implementation section. An inteface can declare one or more exceptions that indicate that an operation did not perform successfully. An inteface may have attributes.
3. **Operation** is a CORBA equivalent of a method. It denotes a service that clients can invoke.

   The IDL defines the operation's signature, which means method's parameters and the results it returns.
4. **Data types** are used to describe accepted values of CORBA parameters, attributes, exceptions, and return values.
   a. Open a UNIX shell and type at the Unix command prompt:

      module add java
   b. To compile the interfaces and produce client stubs and server skeletons, type in the Unix shell

      idlj-fall-oldImplBase Filename.idl
   c. The idl-compiler creates a subdirectories for the interfaces. Have a look at the code the compiler produced and try to understand how the compiler maps CORBA IDL to Java code. You will see that quite a few files are

generated for these simple example. Most of them contain all sorts of infrastructure allowing remote method invocations. The options **-fall** and allows idlj compiler to generate additional files. The **-oldImpBase** option allow the idlj compiler to generate pre jdk1.4 files.

The most interesting files to look at are the files *InterfaceName*.java for a Corba IDL containing an interface *InterfaceName*.

This was true when we were writing distributed systems using RPC; it is true when writing with COM; and it is also true for CORBA. In all these cases, the Interface Definition Language provides the mechanics for separating object interfaces from their implementations. IDL provides abstraction, creating something that is considered apart from its concrete existence.

It also gives us a common set of data types that we will use to define more complex data types. We will use all of these types to define the capabilities of our distributed service. Another wonderful aspect of IDL is that it abstracts away programming language dependence and hardware dependence. This article examines the OMG IDL built-in types and keywords. IDL is a specification language. It allows us to separate the specification of the object (how you interact with it) from the implementation. This is a contract that says "Ms. Client, if you call this method, passing these parameters, then I, Mr. Server, will return to you this array of strings." Client programmers using this interface have no idea what implementation details lie behind the interface.

IDL BASIC TYPES. The OMG Interface Definition Language has several fundamental types that should look familiar. Here is a table of these built-in types:

TABLE 10.2. IDL basic types

Type	*Range*	*Minimum size in bits*
short	-2^{15} to $2^{15}-1$	16
unsigned short	0 to 2^{16}-1	16
long	-2^{31} to $2^{31}-1$	32
unsigned long	0 to $2^{32}-1$	32
long long	-2^{63} to $2^{63}-1$	64
unsigned long long	0 to $2^{64}-1$	64
float	IEEE single-precision	32
double	IEEE double-precision	64
long double	IEEE double extended floating point	exponent of 15 bits and signed fraction of 64 bits
char	ISO Latin–1	8
wchar	Encodes wide characters from any wide character set, such as Unicode	Implementation dependent
string	ISO Latin–1, except ASCII NUL	Variable
Boolean	TRUE or FALSE	Unspecified
octet	0 to 255	8
any	Self-describing data type that can represent any IDL type	Variable

An IDL file contains one or more interface definitions. Each interface definition is composed of an interface header and an interface body. The interface header is demarcated by square brackets. The interface body is contained in curly brackets. This is illustrated in the following example interface:

```
[
/*Interface attributes go here. */
]
interface INTERFACENAME
{
/*The interface body goes here. */
}
```

10.11 APPLICATION PROGRAMMING INTERFACE (API)

It is an older technology that facilitates exchanging messages or data between two or more different software applications. API is the virtual interface between two internetworking software functions, such as a word processor and a spreadsheet. This technology has been expanded from simple subroutine calls to include features that provide for interoperability and system modifiability in support of the requirement for data sharing between multiple applications. An API is the software that is used to support system-level integration of multiple commercial-off-the-shelf (COTS) software products or newly-developed software into existing or new applications. APIs are also a type of Middleware that provide for data sharing across different platforms; this is an important feature when developing new or upgrading existing distributed systems.

An API is a set of rules for writing function or subroutine calls that access functions in a library. Programs that use these rules or functions in their API calls can communicate with any others that use the API, regardless of the others' specifics. APIs work with a wide spectrum of application dialogues (*i.e.*, interprogram communication schemes) to facilitate information exchange. These include database access, client/server, peer-to-peer, real-time, event-driven, store and forward, and transaction processing. APIs combine error recovery, data translation, security, queuing, and naming with an easy-to-learn interface that comprises simple but powerful actions/commands (verbs). To invoke an API, a program calls a SEND-type function, specifying parameters for destination name, pointers to the data, and return confirmation options. The API takes the data and does all the communications-specific work transparent to the application.

There are four types of APIs that are enablers of data sharing between different software applications on single or distributed platforms:

1. Remote Procedure Calls (RPCs)
2. Standard Query Language (SQL)
3. file transfer
4. message delivery.

Using RPCs, programs communicate via procedures (or tasks) that act on shared data buffers. SQL is a non-procedural data access language that allows data sharing between applications by access into a common database. File transfer allows for data sharing by sending formatted files between applications. Message delivery provides data sharing by direct interprogram communications via small formatted messages between loosely- or tightly-coupled applications. Current standards that apply to APIs include the ANSI standard SQL API. There are ongoing efforts to define standards for the other types.

APIs can be developed for all computing platforms and operating systems or purchased for most platforms and operating systems. All four API types can be used both on homogeneous and multi-platform applications. However, because of the added complexity required to share data across multiple platforms, RPC, SQL or file transfer APIs are better used to facilitate communication between different applications on homogeneous platform systems. These APIs communicate data in different formats (*e.g.,* shared data buffers, database structures, and file constructs). Each data format requires different network commands and parameters to communicate the data properly and can cause many different types of errors. Therefore, in addition to the knowledge required to perform the data sharing tasks, these types of APIs must account for hundreds of network parameters and hundreds of possible error conditions that each application must understand if it is to deliver robust interprogram communications. A message delivery API, in contrast, will offer a smaller subset of commands, network parameters, and error conditions because this API deals with only one format (messages). Because of this reduced complexity, message delivery APIs are a better choice when applications require data sharing across multiple platforms.

10.11.1 COM

It defines **an application programming interface (API)** to allow for the creation of components for use in integrating custom applications or to allow diverse components to interact. However, in order to interact, components must adhere to a binary structure specified by Microsoft. As long as components adhere to this binary structure, components written in different languages can interoperate.

Distributed COM is an extension to COM that allows network-based component interaction. While COM processes can run on the same machine but in different address spaces, the DCOM extension allows processes to be spread across a network. With DCOM, components operating on a variety of platforms can interact, as long as DCOM is available within the environment.

It is best to consider COM and DCOM as a single technology that provides a range of services for component interaction, from services promoting component integration on a single platform, to component interaction across heterogeneous networks. In fact, COM and its DCOM extensions are merged into a single runtime. This single runtime provides both local and remote access.COM is a binary compatibility specification and associated implementation that allows clients to invoke services provided by COM-compliant components (COM objects). As shown in Figure 10.9, services implemented by COM objects are exposed through a set of interfaces that represent the only point of contact between clients and the object.

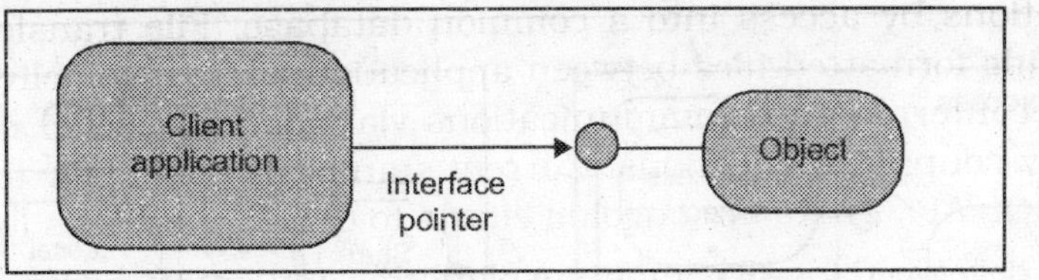

Figure 10.9 Client Using COM Object Through an Interface Pointer

COM defines a binary structure for the interface between the client and the object. This binary structure provides the basis for interoperability between software components written in arbitrary languages. As long as a compiler can reduce language structures down to this binary representation, the implementation language for clients and COM objects does not matter—the point of contact is the run-time binary representation. Thus, COM objects and clients can be coded in any language that supports Microsoft's COM binary structure. A COM object can support any number of interfaces. An interface provides a grouped collection of related methods. For example, Figure 10.10 depicts a COM object that emulates a clock. IClock, IAlarm and ITimer are the interfaces of the clock object. The IClock interface can provide the appropriate methods (not shown) to allow setting and reading the current time. The IAlarm and ITimer interfaces can supply alarm and stopwatch methods.

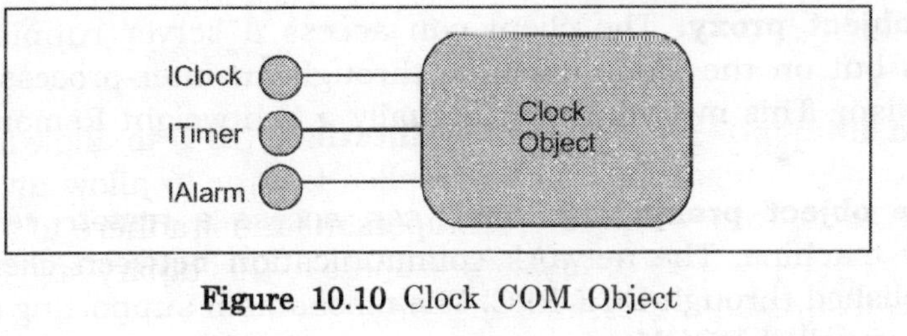

Figure 10.10 Clock COM Object

COM objects and interfaces are specified using Microsoft Interface Definition Language (IDL), an extension of the DCE Interface Definition Language standard. To avoid name collisions, each object and interface must have a unique identifier. Interfaces are considered logically immutable. Once an interface is defined, it should not be changed-new methods should not be added and existing methods should not be modified. This restriction on the interfaces is not enforced, but it is a rule that component developers should follow. Adhering to this restriction removes the potential for version incompatibility-if an interface never changes, then clients depending on the interface can rely on a consistent set of services. If new functionality has to be added to a component, it can be exposed through a different interface. For our clock example, we can design an enhanced clock COM object supporting the IClock2 interface that inherits from IClock. IClock2 may expose new functionality. Every COM object runs inside of a server. A single server can support multiple COM objects. As shown in Figure 10.11, there are three ways in which a client can access COM objects provided by a server:

1. **In-process server:** The client can link directly to a library containing the server. The client and server execute in the same process. Communication is accomplished through function calls.

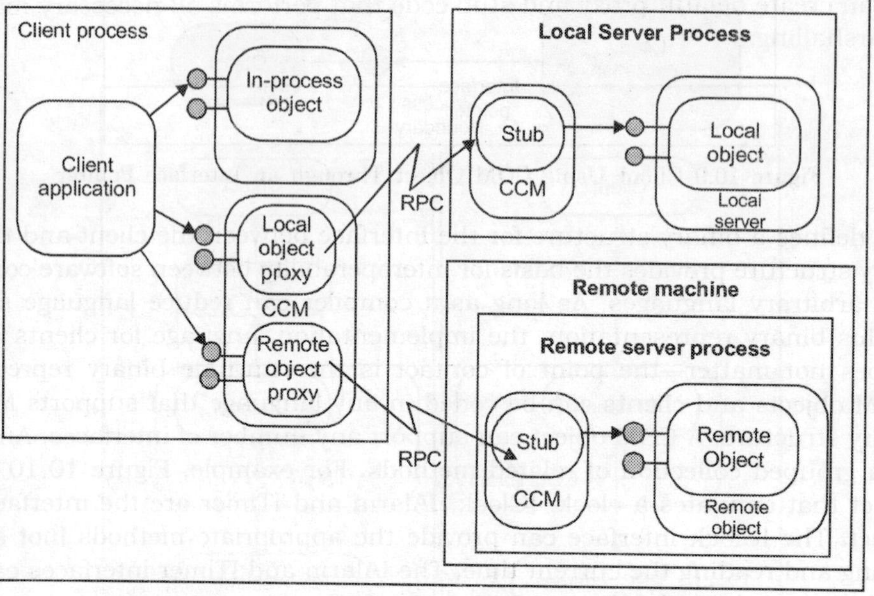

Figure 10.11 Three Methods for Accessing COM Objects

2. **Local object proxy:** The client can access a server running in a different process but on the same machine through an inter-process communication mechanism. This mechanism is actually a lightweight Remote Procedure Call (RPC).
3. **Remote object proxy:** The client can access a remote server running on another machine. The network communication between client and server is accomplished through DCE RPC. The mechanism supporting access to remote servers is called DCOM.

If the client and server are in the same process, the sharing of data between the two is simple. However, when the server process is separate from the client process, as in a local server or remote server, COM must format and bundle the data in order to share it. This process of preparing the data is called marshalling. Marshalling is accomplished through a "proxy" object and a "stub" object that handle the cross-process communication details for any particular interface (depicted in Figure 10.12). COM creates the "stub" in the object's server process and has the stub manage the real interface pointer. COM then creates the "proxy" in the client's process, and connects it to the stub. The proxy then supplies the interface pointer to the client.

The client calls the interfaces of the server through the proxy, which marshals the parameters and passes them to the server stub. The stub unmarshals the parameters and makes the actual call inside the server object. When the call completes, the stub marshals return values and passes them to the proxy, which in turn returns them to the client. The same proxy/stub mechanism is used when the client and server are on different machines. However, the internal implementation of marshalling and unmarshalling differs depending on whether the client and server operate on the same machine (COM) or on different machines (DCOM). Given an IDL file, the Microsoft IDL compiler can create default proxy and stub code that performs all necessary marshalling and unmarshalling.

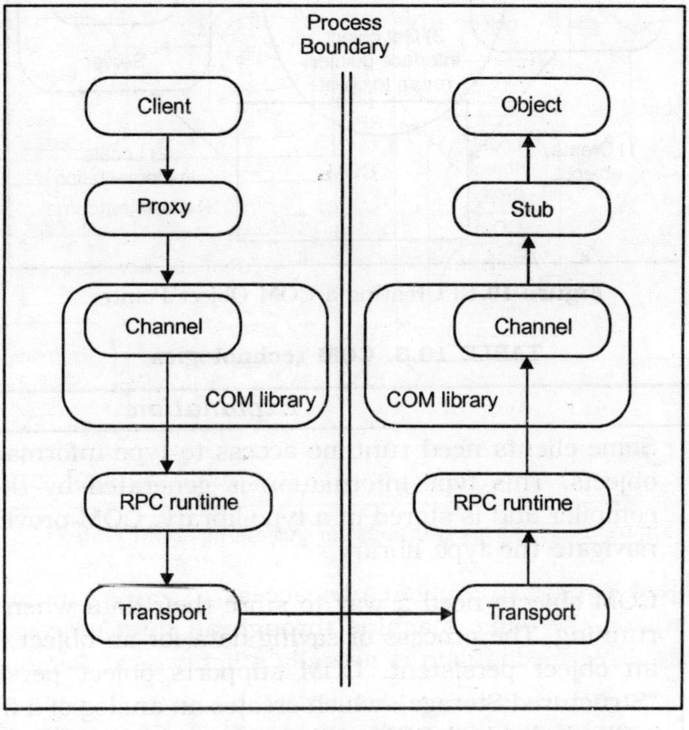

Figure 10.12 Cross-process Communication in COM

All COM objects are registered with a component database. As shown in Figure 10.13, when a client wishes to create and use a COM object:

1. It invokes the COM API to instantiate a new COM object.
2. COM locates the object implementation and initiates a server process for the object.
3. The server process creates the object, and returns an interface pointer at the object.
4. The client can then interact with the newly instantiated COM object through the interface pointer.

An important aspect in COM is that objects have no identity, *i.e.* a client can ask for a COM object of some type, but not for a particular object. Every time that COM is asked for a COM object, a new instance is returned. The main advantage of this policy is that COM implementations can pool COM objects and return these pooled objects to requesting clients. Whenever a client has finished using an object the instance is returned to the pool. However, there are mechanisms to simulate identity in COM such as monikers (reviewed later).

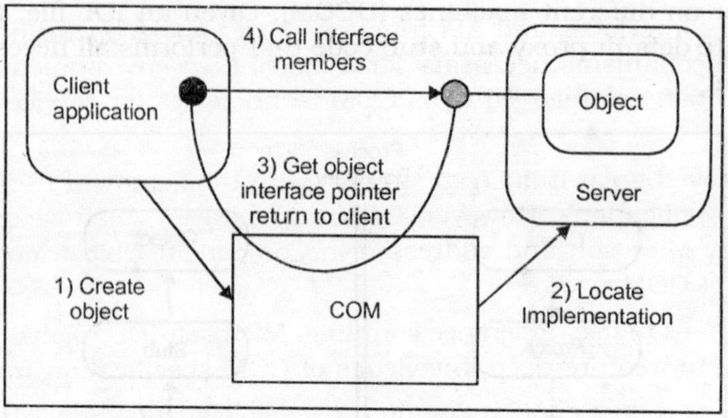

Figure 10.13 Creating a COM Object Pointer

TABLE 10.3. COM technologies

Service	*Explanation*
Type Information	Some clients need runtime access to type information about COM objects. This type information is generated by the Microsoft IDL compiler and is stored in a type library. COM provides interfaces to navigate the type library.
Structured Storage and Persistence	COM objects need a way to store their data when they are not running. The process of saving data for an object is called making an object persistent. COM supports object persistence through "Structured Storage", which creates an analog of a file system within a file. Individual COM objects can store data within the file, thus providing persistence.
Monikers	Clients often require a way to allow them to connect to the exact same object instance with the exact same state at a later point in time. This support is provided via "monikers". A moniker is a COM object that knows how to create and initialize the content of a single COM object instance. A moniker can be asked to bind to the COM object it represents, such as a COM object residing on specific machine on the network, or a group of cells inside a spreadsheet.
Uniform Data Transfer	COM objects often need to pass data amongst themselves. Uniform Data Transfer provides for data transfers and notifications of data changes between a source called the data object, and something that uses the data, called the consumer object.
Connectable Objects	Some objects require a way to notify clients that an event that has occurred. COM allows such objects to define outgoing interfaces to clients as well as incoming interfaces. The object defines an interface it would like to use (*e.g.*, a notification interface) and the client implements the interface. This enables two-way communication between the client and the component.

COM includes interfaces and API functions that expose operating system services, as well as other mechanisms necessary for a distributed environment (naming, events, etc.). These are sometimes referred to as COM technologies (or services), and are shown in Table 10.2.

COM has enjoyed great industrial support with thousands of ISVs developing COM components and applications. However, COM suffers from some weaknesses that have been recognized by Microsoft and addressed in Component Object Model+, which is the ongoing upgrade of COM.

1. COM is hard to use. Reference counting, Microsoft IDL, Global Unique Identifiers (GUID), etc. require deep knowledge of COM specification from developers.
2. COM is not robust enough for enterprise deployments. Services such as security, transactions, reliable communications, and load balancing are not integrated in COM.

Both issues were partially mitigated by add-ons of COM, complexity by integrated development environments and robustness by MTS. However, to further address those problems, the company is working to turn COM+ and the MTS (Microsoft Transaction Server) into one programming model that will simplifying the lives of developers building distributed, enterprise-wide COM applications. COM+ integrates seamlessly with all COM-aware languages (basically Microsoft languages). Users write components in their favorite language. Thc tool chosen and the COM+ runtime take care of turning these classes into COM components.

A number of issues must be evaluated when considering COM, DCOM, and COM+. They include :

1. ***Platform support.*** COM and DCOM are best supported on Windows 95 and NT platforms. However, Microsoft has released a version of COM/DCOM for MacOS that supports OLE-style compound documents and the creation of ActiveX controls. Software AG, a Microsoft partner, has released DCOM for some UNIX operating systems, concretely OS/390, HP-UX 11.0, SUN Solaris, AIX 4.2, 4.3, Tru64 Unix 4.0 and Linux. However, DCOM over non-Windows platforms has few supporters. Until DCOM for alternate platforms has solidified, the technology is best applied in environments that are primarily Windows-based.
2. ***Platform specificity of COM/DCOM components.*** Because COM and DCOM are based on a native binary format, components written to these specifications are not platform independent. Thus, either they must be recompiled for a specific platform, or an interpreter for the binary format must become available. Depending on your perspective, the use of a binary format may be either an advantage (faster execution, better use of native platform capabilities) or a disadvantage (ActiveX controls, unlike Java applets, are NOT machine independent).
3. ***Security.*** Because COM/DCOM components have access to a version of the Microsoft Windows API, "bad actors" can potentially damage the user's computing environment. In order to address this problem, Microsoft employs "Authenticode" which uses public key encryption to digitally sign components. Independent

certification authorities such as VeriSign issue digital certificates to verify the identity of the source of the component. However, even certified code can contain instructions that accidentally, or even maliciously, compromise the user's environment.

4. ***Support for distributed objects.*** COM/DCOM provides basic support for distributed objects. There is currently no support for situations requiring real time processing, high reliability, or other such specialized component interaction.
5. ***Stability of APIs.*** In October of 1996 Microsoft turned over COM/DCOM, parts of OLE, and ActiveX to the Open Group (a merger of Open Software Foundation and X/Open). The Open Group has formed the Active Group to oversee the transformation of the technology into an open standard. The aim of the Active Group is to promote the technology's compatibility across systems (Windows, UNIX, and MacOS) and to oversee future extension by creating working groups dedicated to specific functions. However, it is unclear how much control Microsoft will relinquish over the direction of the technology. Certainly, as the inventor and primary advocate of COM and DCOM, Microsoft is expected to have strong influence on the overall direction of the technology and underlying APIs.
6. ***Long-term system maintainability.*** Microsoft is actively supporting COM and DCOM technology and pushing it in distributed and Web-based directions. Microsoft is also trying to preserve existing investments in COM technology while introducing incremental changes. Microsoft, for example, has ensured backward compatibility of COM+. Although this affirmation is in general true, COM objects that access local information in the registry or in system folders may require modification. In general, the PC community has not been faced with the concern of very long-lived systems, and vendors often provide support only for recent releases.

10.12 REMOTE PROCEDURE CALL (RPC)

It is a client/server infrastructure that increases the interoperability, portability and flexibility of an application by allowing the application to be distributed over multiple heterogeneous platforms. It reduces the complexity of developing applications that span multiple operating systems and network protocols by insulating the application developer from the details of the various operating system and network interfaces—function calls are the programmer's interface when using RPC.

The concept of RPC has been discussed in literature as far back as 1976, with full-scale implementations appearing in the late 1970s and early 1980s. In order to access the remote server portion of an application, special function calls, RPCs, are embedded within the client portion of the client/server application program. Because they are embedded, RPCs do not stand alone as a discreet middleware layer. When the client program is compiled, the compiler creates a local stub for the client portion and another stub for the server portion of the application. These stubs are invoked when the application requires a remote function and typically support synchronous calls between clients and servers. These relationships are shown in Figure 10.14. By using RPC, the complexity involved in the development of distributed processing is reduced by keeping the semantics of a remote call the same whether or not the client and server are collocated on the same system. However, RPC increases the involvement of an application developer with the complexity of the master-slave nature of the client/server mechanism. RPC increases the flexibility of an architecture by allowing a client component of an application to employ a function call to access a server on a remote Asynchronous ("call/nowait") implementations are available but are currently the exception.

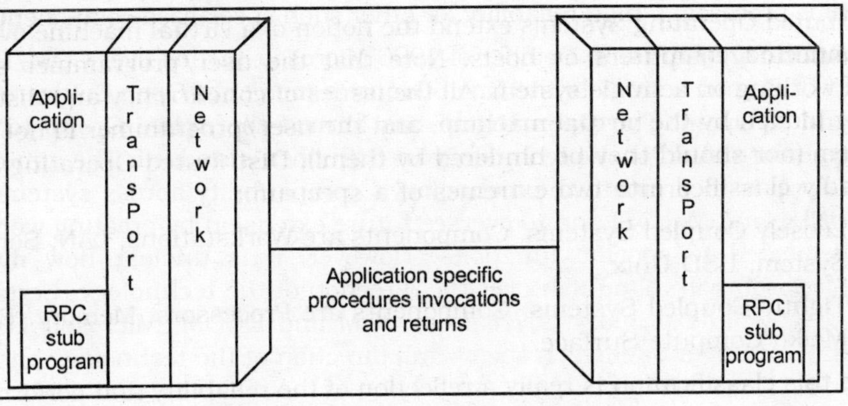

Figure 10.14 Remote Procedure Calls

RPC is typically implemented in one of two ways:

1. within a broader, more encompassing propriety product
2. by a programmer using a proprietary tool to create client/server RPC stubs.

RPC is appropriate for client/server applications in which the client can issue a request and wait for the server's response before continuing its own processing. Because most RPC implementations do not support peer-to-peer, or asynchronous, client/server interaction, RPC is not well-suited for applications involving distributed objects or object-oriented programming.

Asynchronous and synchronous mechanisms each have strengths and weaknesses that should be considered when designing any specific application. In contrast to asynchronous mechanisms employed by Message Oriented Middleware, the use of a synchronous request-reply mechanism in RPC requires that the client and server are always available and functioning (*i.e.*, the client or server is not blocked). In order to allow a client/server application to recover from a blocked condition, an implementation of a RPC is required to provide mechanisms such as error messages, request timers, retransmissions, or redirection to an alternate server. The complexity of the application using an RPC is dependent on the sophistication of the specific RPC implementation (*i.e.*, the more sophisticated the recovery mechanisms supported by RPC, the less complex the application utilizing the RPC is required to be). RPCs that implement asynchronous mechanisms are very few and are difficult (complex) to implement.

When utilizing RPC over a distributed network, the performance (or load) of the network should be considered. One of the strengths of RPC is that the synchronous, blocking mechanism of RPC guards against overloading a network, unlike the asynchronous mechanism of Message Oriented Middleware (MOM). However, when recovery mechanisms, such as retransmissions, are employed by an RPC application, the resulting load on a network may increase, making the application inappropriate for a congested network. Also, because RPC uses static routing tables established at compile-time, the ability to perform load balancing across a network is difficult and should be considered when designing an RPC-based application.

10.13 DISTRIBUTED OPERATING SYSTEMS

Distributed Operating Systems extend the notion of a virtual machine over a number of interconnected computers or hosts. Note that the user/programmer still has the illusion of working on a single system. All the issues of concurrency and distribution are completely hidden by the virtual machine, and the user/programmer is not at liberty to exploit them (nor should they be hindered by them!). Distributed Operating Systems are often broadly classified into two extremes of a spectrum:

1. Loosely Coupled Systems. Components are Workstations, LAN, Servers. *e.g.* V-System, BSD Unix.
2. Tightly Coupled Systems. Components are Processors, Memory, Bus, I/O *e.g.* Meiko Compute Surface.

Often this classification is really a reflection of the reliability and performance of the communications sub-system. Frequently, shared memory systems are regarded as more tightly coupled than message passing systems. Another way of looking at these classifications is to think of tightly coupled systems as being **dependent,** and loosely coupled systems as **independent,** where the dependency is in terms of system availability in the face of failure of some single host. In tightly coupled systems, it is reasonable to consider shared memory (or at least hierarchical cache mechanisms) as a communications mechanism. In loosely coupled systems, only message passing can be considered. Distributed systems have been around since the early 1970s. These can be categorised by whether they are:

1. Network Operating Systems *e.g.* 4.xBSD Unix These are conventional centralized operating systems with networking facilities added as operating system services, but distinct from other (i/o) services.
2. Distributed Operating Systems *e.g.* MACH These systems allow a distributed set of processors to appear as a single system.
3. Distributed Human Access *e.g.* OS + X Windows A set of systems running centralized operating system services are made to appear as a single system to the human user.
4. Distributed File Systems *e.g.* Unix + NFS Rather than providing a global human view of the systems, we provide the systems with a global view of storage, and therefore any programs too with the same view.
5. Distributed Processing Environments *e.g.* V-System/Amoeba The axis of distribution is the processor rather than terminal/window I/O or the storage system.

In practice, the most widespread systems are those combining distributed file access and distributed Human access: The workstation/fileserver/compute server model has evolved in the last ten years predominately due to costs of LAN access with enough performance to provide realistic remote disk/file access and memory/bitmap display costs dropping low enough to make window based software realistic on the desktop. Slowly, some more useful distributed tools are emerging: Since distributed systems have existed mainly in a Research and Development environment, there has been some work on tools to help with Software development in a distributed environment. These include:

1. Automated Software distribution (BSD rdist).
2. Shared views of data (single editor, multiple reviewers!), conferencing.
3. Generation of multiple executables for different architectures from a single Program Source development tree (including multiple source code revisions control trees).
4. Distributed Make facilities (ability to compile independent source files separately and automatically on multiple workstations).

Enslow's classic classification [REF] uses three axes of distribution:

1. Processors Any interesting distributed system has processing capability in more than one place.
2. Control The programs that make up the system have components in more than one processor. Another way of saying this is that the thread of control crosses more than one address space.
3. Data The data required for a given task is located at more than one place - perhaps replicated for reliability reasons, or partitioned for performance reasons.

If we apply these models to the systems above, we can see the choices made in the distribution of services. Distribution of services is rather different from distribution of the Operating System itself. In some systems [e.g. Sun NFS/Newcastle Connection] an operating system service [File access] has been distributed from within the operating system. In others [*e.g.* printing], the service has been distributed above (outside) the operating system.

The ODP standards, and this text, assume a model where distributed applications are running in multiple processes in multiple computers linked by communications. The application programmer will be supported by a programming environment and run-time system that will make many aspects of distribution in the system transparent. For instance the programmer may not have to worry about where the parts of the application are running, this can all be taken care of, if required; this is called *location transparency*. There is another approach to supporting applications in a distributed system, that is by using a distributed operating system. On every computer system with an operating system the O/S provides an interface which the programs use to obtain services, such as input and output.

In a distributed operating system this interface is enhanced so that a program may be run on any computer in the distributed system and access data on any other computer. The operating system provides data, execution and location transparency, often through an extended naming scheme. The advantage of a distributed operating system is that is uses an interface below that of the application program. This means the existing programming environments may be used, the programmer may use the system with little or no extra training, and in some cases existing software may be used. The disadvantage is that a number of problems are left for the programmer and user to handle, for instance concurrency; and because of the advantage above, programmers are given little support for this. Essentially, the Distributed Operating System dictates the policies of distribution for all aspects of programming. This means that the programmer is not able to use the distributed functionality in an application specific way to optimize a solution.

Another major disadvantage is that the distributed system is tied to a style of operating system interface. There are lots of different operating systems today, to meet different requirements (real or imaginary); there is no reason why future distributed systems will not need different operating system interfaces. Consequently it is not possible to build a truly heterogeneous open distributed system by building it on top of an homogeneous distributed operating system.

The ODP model provides an application interface to the distributed system. This interface is extremely simple and is concerned with aspects of distribution only. The application may still be run on any local operating system that is appropriate. The ODP model does include the use of distributed operating systems, but would require any particular type of distributed operating system to interwork with other types through ODP and with also with non-distributed operating systems. The applications would see no difference. One popular implementors specification for some parts of ODP is the Common Object Request Broker Architecture.

Network Operating Systems

In contrast to distributed operating systems, network operating systems do not assume that the underlying hardware is homogeneous and that it should be managed as if it were a single system. Instead, they are generally constructed from a collection of uniprocessor systems, each with its own operating system. The machines and their operating systems may be different, but they are all connected to each other in a computer network. Also, network operating systems provide facilities to allow users to make use of the services available on a specific machine. It is perhaps easiest to describe network operating systems by taking a closer look at some services they typically offer. Neither a distributed operating system or a network operating system really qualifies as a distributed system according to our definition. A distributed operating system is not intended to handle a collection of *independent* computers, while a network operating system does not provide a view of a *single coherent system.* The question comes to mind whether it is possible to develop a distributed system that has the best of both worlds: the scalability and openness of network operating systems and the transparency and related ease of use of distributed operating systems. The solution is to be found in an additional layer of software that is used in network operating systems to more or less hide the heterogeneity of the collection of underlying platforms but also to improve distribution transparency. Many modern distributed systems are constructed by means of such an additional layer of what is called **middleware.** In this section we take a closer look at what middleware actually constitutes by explaining some of its features.

Positioning Middleware

Many distributed applications make direct use of the programming interface offered by network operating systems. For example, communication is often expressed through operations on sockets, which allow processes on different machines to pass each other messages (Stevens, 1998). In addition, applications often make use of interfaces to the local file system. As we explained, a problem with this approach is that distribution is hardly transparent. A solution is to place an additional layer of software between applications and the network operating system, offering a higher level of abstraction. Such a layer is accordingly called **middleware.** It sits in the middle between applications and the network operating system. Each local system forming part of the underlying network operating system is assumed to provide local resource management in addition to simple communication means to connect to other computers. In other words, middleware itself will not manage an individual node; this is left entirely to the local operating system.

10.14 SHARING OF INFORMATION

Distributed system allows the sharing of information in the form of files throughout an Intranet. A well designed file service provides access to files stored at a server with performance and reliability similar to files stored on local disk. A distributed file system enables programs to store and access remote files exactly as they do local ones, allowing users to access files from any computer in an Intranet. Two distributed systems that have been in widespread use for a decade or more:

1. NFS
2. AFS

10.15 THE NETWORK FILE SYSTEM

Authentication and Naming facilities: NFS is simplistic in its notion of 'naming' and permissions. By default (and in many implementations) it requires a flat set of machines sharing the file systems (except for root whose ownerships vanish across an NFS mount). This means simply that two different users could have read/write permissions over each others files on different servers if they mounted each others file stores.. This causes problems when adding existing systems to the file store (without some gateway/uid-mapping service).

10.15.1 AFS

The Andrew File System was developed at Carnegie Mellon University (and named Andrew are the founder's first name), as part of a large project in next generation distributed systems in the mid 1980s. It has two main components; Vice and Venus:

1. Vice provides the shared file system
2. Venus provides the redirector function for clients

AFS has two main advantages over some other systems in terms of scaling:

1. Prefix naming—path name prefixes are used to provide location
2. Whole File Caching—the First access to a file causes it to appear in its entirety on the client machines local disk.

The development of the 3 versions of AFS through time is an instructive lesson in good distributed systems design, since the later phases solved problems that were perceived in the earlier versions by a series of refinements which were not precluded in any way by earlier designs. We look at this development next.

AFS is a distributed file system that enables co-operating hosts (clients and servers) to efficiently share file system resources across both local area and wide area networks. AFS is marketed, maintained, and extended by Transarc Corporation. AFS is based on a distributed file system originally developed at the Information Technology Center at Carnegie-Mellon University that was called the "Andrew File System".

"Andrew" was the name of the research project at CMU - honoring the founders of the University. Once Transarc was formed and AFS became a product, the "Andrew" was dropped to indicate that AFS had gone beyond the Andrew research project and had become a supported, product quality file system. However, there were a number of existing cells that rooted their file system as /afs. At the time, changing the root of the file system was a non-trivial undertaking. So, to save the early AFS sites from having to rename their file system, AFS remained as the name and file system root.

10.16 MUTUAL EXCLUSION

Systems involving multiple processes are often most easily programmed using critical regions. When a process has to read or update certain shared data structures, it first enters a critical region to achieve mutual exclusion and ensure that no other process will use the shared data structures at the same time. In singleprocessor systems, critical regions are protected using semaphores, monitors, and similar constructs. We will now look at a few examples of how critical regions and mutual exclusion can be implemented in distributed systems.

A Centralized Algorithm

The most straightforward way to achieve mutual exclusion in a distributed system is to simulate how it is done in a one-processor system. One process is elected as the coordinator (*e.g.,* the one running on the machine with the highest network address). Whenever a process wants to enter a critical region, it sends a request message to the coordinator stating which critical region it wants to enter and asking for permission. If no other process is currently in that critical region, the coordinator sends back a reply granting permission. When the reply arrives, the requesting process enters the critical region. Now suppose that another process, 2, asks for permission to enter the same critical region. The coordinator knows that a different process is already in the critical region, so it cannot grant permission. The exact method used to deny permission is system dependent. The coordinator just refrains from replying, thus blocking process 2, which is waiting for a reply. Alternatively, it could send a reply saying "permission denied." Either way, it queues the request from 2 for the time being and waits for more messages.

When process 1 exits the critical region, it sends a message to the coordinator releasing its exclusive access. The coordinator takes the first item off the queue of deferred requests and sends that process a grant message. If the process was still blocked (*i.e.,* this is the first message to it), it unblocks and enters the critical region. If an explicit message has already been sent denying permission, the process will have to poll for incoming traffic or block later. Either way, when it sees the grant, it can enter the critical region. It is easy to see that the algorithm guarantees mutual exclusion: the coordinator only lets one process at a time into each critical region. It is also fair, since requests are granted in the order in which they are received. No process ever waits forever (no starvation). The scheme is easy to implement, too, and requires only three messages per use of a critical region (request, grant, release). It can also be used for more general resource allocation rather than just managing critical regions.

The centralized approach also has shortcomings. The coordinator is a single point of failure, so if it crashes, the entire system may go down. If processes normally block after making a request, they cannot distinguish a dead coordinator from "permission denied" since in both cases no message comes back. In addition, in a large system, a single coordinator can become a performance bottleneck.

A Distributed Algorithm

Having a single point of failure is frequently unacceptable, so researchers have looked for distributed mutual exclusion algorithms. Our algorithm requires that there be a total ordering of all events in the system. That is, for any pair of events, such as messages, it must be unambiguous which one actually happened first. Lamport's algorithm is one way to achieve this ordering and can be used to provide timestamps for distributed mutual exclusion.

The Algorithm Works as Follows

When a process wants to enter a critical region, it builds a message containing the name of the critical region it wants to enter, its process number, and the current time. It then sends the message to all other processes, conceptually including itself. The sending of messages is assumed to be reliable; that is, every message is acknowledged. Reliable group communication if available, can be used instead of individual messages. When a process receives a request message from another process, the action it takes depends on its state with respect to the critical region named in the message.

Three cases have to be distinguished:

1. If the receiver is not in the critical region and does not want to enter it, it sends back an *OK* message to the sender.
2. If the receiver is already in the critical region, it does not reply. Instead, it queues the request.
3. If the receiver wants to enter the critical region but has not yet done so, it compares the timestamp in the incoming message with the one contained in the message that it has sent everyone. The lowest one wins. If the incoming message is lower, the receiver sends back an *OK* message. If its own message has a lower timestamp, the receiver queues the incoming request and sends nothing. After sending out requests asking permission to enter a critical region, a process sits back and waits until everyone else has given permission. As soon as all the permissions are in, it may enter the critical region. When it exits the critical region, it sends *OK* messages to all processes on its queue and deletes them all from the queue. Let us try to understand why the algorithm works. If there is no conflict, it clearly works. However, suppose that two processes try to enter the same critical region simultaneously, Process 0 sends everyone

a request with timestamp 8, while at the same time, process 2 sends everyone a request with timestamp 12. Process 1 is not interested in entering the critical region, so it sends *OK* to both senders. Processes 0 and 2 both see the conflict and compare timestamps. Process 2 sees that it has lost, so it grants permission to 0 by sending *OK*. Process 0 now queues the request from 2 for later processing and enters the critical region. When it is finished, it removes the request from 2 from its queue and sends an *OK* message to process 2, allowing the latter to enter its critical region.

The algorithm works because in the case of a conflict, the lowest timestamp wins and everyone agrees on the ordering of the timestamps. Note that the situation would have been essentially different if process 2 had sent its message earlier in time so that process 0 had gotten it and granted permission before making its own request. In this case, 2 would have noticed that it itself was in a critical region at the time of the request, and queued it instead of sending a reply.

As with the centralized algorithm discussed above, mutual exclusion is guaranteed without deadlock or starvation. The number of messages required per entry is now $2(2^{n-1}\ \pi +1)$, where the total number of processes in the system is n. Best of all, no single point of failure exists.

Unfortunately, the single point of failure has been replaced by n points of failure. If any process crashes, it will fail to respond to requests. This silence will be interpreted (incorrectly) as denial of permission, thus blocking all subsequent attempts by all processes to enter all critical regions. Since the probability of one of the n processes failing is at least n times as large as a single coordinator failing, we have managed to replace a poor algorithm with one that is more than n times worse and requires much more network traffic to boot.

The algorithm can be patched up by the same trick that we proposed earlier. When a request comes in, the receiver always sends a reply, either granting or denying permission. Whenever either a request or a reply is lost, the sender times out and keeps trying until either a reply comes back or the sender concludes that the destination is dead. After a request is denied, the sender should block waiting for a subsequent *OK* message.

Another problem with this algorithm is that either a group communication primitive must be used, or each process must maintain the group membership list itself, including processes entering the group, leaving the group, and crashing. The method works best with small groups of processes that never change their group memberships.

Finally, recall that one of the problems with the centralized algorithm is that making it handle all requests can lead to a bottleneck. In the distributed algorithm, *all* processes are involved in *all* decisions concerning entry into critical regions. If one process is unable to handle the load, it is unlikely that forcing everyone to do exactly the same thing in parallel is going to help much. Various minor improvements are possible to this algorithm. For example, getting permission from everyone to enter a critical region is really overkill. All that is needed is a method to prevent two processes from entering the critical region at the same time. The algorithm can be modified to allow a process to enter a critical region when it has collected permission from a simple majority of the other processes, rather than from all of them. Of course, in this variation, after a process has granted permission to one process to enter a critical region, it cannot grant the same permission to another process until the first one has released that permission. Other improvements are also possible, such as proposed by Maekawa , but these easily become more intricate. Nevertheless, this algorithm is slower, more complicated, more expensive, and less robust that the original centralized one.

10.17 CLOCKS AND TIME IN DISTRIBUTED SYSTEMS

Underlying communications services often deliver a bit-level clock to time data on and off the wire. In some systems (*e.g.* E1/Megastream, or the UK electricity clock cycle) this is globally guaranteed to some level of accuracy. However, higher level protocols usually rely on networks built out of LANs connected via routers and long haul links. In such systems, applications may be attached to different networks. Hence although each network may have its own bit level clock, there is no common bit level clock available to both applications. Hence a clock is needed at a higher level available to both end points. A high level clock synchronization mechanism is then often useful to provide coordinated time. Examples of such systems are the Network Time Protocol and the Digital Time Service, which use periodic exchanges of timestamped messages to estimate network transit delays, and therefore derive clock differences. A hierarchy of time servers is formed based on the measured accuracy and reliability of reports. Now a days, enterprises will even site atomic or satellite fed Global Positioning System receiver based clocks at a number of key places on the network to support such a service. Few distributed systems make use of this, but it could be very powerful in optimizing performance. However, havign global application level agreement on time can save application level handshake phases in many situations.

10.18 TRANSACTIONS

We have seen that concurrent access to a shared object by separate clients can lead to consistency problems. The mechanism that is employed to avoid these problems is *atomic* transactions. With knowledge that the service is shared, the client program may be written, specifying that some sequence of operations on the shared object are not to be interleaved with operations by other clients. Essentially, a group of operations are structured into a single *atomic* operation which is called a transaction. The **four properties** of an Atomic Operation are referred to conventionally the useful form :

1. Atomicity,
2. Consistency,
3. Independence and
4. Durability.

A major consequence of transactions is the requirement for mechanisms for failure recovery. If the client or the server fail *during* a transaction, the transaction must appear to have either:

1. Completed Successfully
2. Failed Completely

This means that the state of the system at each end must be *recoverable.* The Transaction is a mechanism that was devised for database systems. Its purpose it to maximize *consistency* of stored data. This consistency must be maintained in the face of failures, and without placing unnecessary restrictions on any concurrency between different applications accessing the data. Its properties include:

1. A Transaction consists of an arbitrary sequence of operations, bracketed by a StartTransaction, and an EndTransaction.
2. The transaction is said to be *atomic* if:
   2.1 either all the operations succeed, and the overall transaction succeeds.
   2.2 none appear to succeed, and the transaction fails—*failure atomicity.*
3. If more than one transaction is executed concurrently, then the effect must be the same as if the separate transactions had been executed one at a time (but in no specific order). This property of concurrent transactions is known as *serial equivalence*(the transactions are *serializable.* This is achieved through use of some concurrency control mechanism such as locking, timestamp or optimistic concurrency control (see below).
4. If one of some concurrent transactions fails (does not complete), its results (intermediate or terminal) are not hidden from the other transactions.

Transaction services are sometimes offered on file systems as well as database systems. In an Open Distributed System, transactions are a way of offering this failure atomicity on any object in the system (ref Persistent Objects). To provide a transaction service, certain functions are required:

1. The transaction must be *recoverable.* Either the transaction can be reversed (the is an inverse operation, and the current operation is reliably logged), or else some previous version of the data/object is available.
2. When each operation is invoked after the transaction is started, it is logged or else the operation is made on a *tentative* version of the data.
3. When the client ends the transaction, if all the operations have succeeded, the server will return to the client that the transaction is *committed.*
4. If the client finds some fault or error, it may ABORT the transaction. This causes the server to wind back the state of the data as if no operation had been invoked.
5. If the server fails for some reason (lack of resources/error), it must wind back to the same previous state (this may be after a restart) and report to the client that the transaction has failed.

All of these functions require stable storage (*i.e.* disk/battery backed RAM etc). Transactions are another tool to make programming distributed applications easier. The Atomicity property means that the programmer does not have to concern himself with consistency. They can group operations in a transaction arbitrarily, without concern for what failures may occur in the client, server or network. They are guaranteed that the stable storage holding the data will either contain successful results, or no change. The serializability of concurrent transactions means that each application programmer is sealed off from others. They need not concern themselves with the ORDER in which operations are invoked in different applications. Applications are shielded from handling errors caused by other applications by the way transactions hide tentative intermediate updates.

A Commit Log

A commit log is used to track the necessary state to make decisions during an n-phase commit process, or else to unroll back to any pre-committed state.

1. It either contains inverse operations or records the state of the object prior to the start of the transaction. These can be used to revert in the case of abort or failure during the transaction.
2. It also contains an effective duplicate of the operations and parameters of the transaction, since it must be feasible to replay the transaction if there is a system failure immediately after commitment.

This log must be in stable storage to maximize reliability. In case two above, failure of a distributed transaction service includes network failure. Network failure can be seen as temporary or long term inability for the application and transaction service to contact each other (loss of messages or network partitioning).

2 Phase Commits

Although a distributed system could suffer a number of failures of a different kind simultaneously, the normal approach to increased reliability is to consider this unlikely, and deal with network failures and service failures separately. This has lead to the *two phase commit* protocol. Transaction Agent (TA) acts on behalf of all the servers (S) involved in sub transactions in this transaction.

10.19 REPLICATION/REDUNDANCY

Many distributed systems are (ironically) less reliable than centralized ones. A distributed file system without replication has more failure modes than a centralized one, since the network between client machines and the file server can fail as well as the file server itself. Replication mechanisms for objects in a distributed system can be subdivided into two main classes.

1. Hot or Cold Standby.
2. Active replicas with Voting.

When the objects are changing rapidly, for instance in a rapidly updated filesystem, the second approach is essential. Replicated services lead to the requirement for *distributed two phase locking*. If several copies of an object are held replicated, the two phase locking mechanism described above must be extended to deal with this. If locks are granted independently on copies of the object, then it might be possible for two separate transactions to acquire locks on separate copies and create inconsistencies in the replicated file. There are a range of solutions. One is to designate a primary object, and locks always apply there—this can reduce availability of the object if the primary fails. Another extreme is propagate a lock for access to all copies of an object. This is costly. Cost is reduced by only insisting that a write lock must be applied at all sites, and a read at any one.

Replicated servers are wrapped up in "meta-servers", so that the replication is transparent. However, this leads to the requirement to map any transaction to the meta-server, into a transaction or set of them to the servers within. This is called "nested" transactions. The idea is generalized in most real distributed system platforms, to provide a way of creating hierarchically structured servers built out of other servers. The idea is to get the same gain for a distributed system that hierarchical modularization gains for single programs. There is a consequence of this that the fault/failure models must reflect the nesting of services, and some care is needed in making sure that a system built out of nested servers does not have less fault tolerance than a monolithic one.

10.20 REPLICATION

Many systems in safety critical areas use replication of vital components to improve reliability. It is important to note that such systems also provide high availability. These two characteristics are not the same thing: A low level technique for increasing integrity of information on a disk is to mirror the disk and use a simple comparator. If the data ever differs, we then force a failure. This means that the *integrity* of the data is twice as good, but even if the comparator has 0 failures, a failure of either disk means the whole system fails. Thus the system has 1/2 the availability, at best. In a distributed system, this is even more critical to appreciate, since the network that connects components may be far less reliable even than the components themselves. Network partitioning will reduce the availability of distributed replicated objects. A third characteristic of replicated services is that they may provide better performance for read access, but are generally slower for update access. To see why, we must consider how the replication is made transparent whilst providing exactly the same view of the data to all clients' consistency must be maintained, and the mechanisms for maintaining consistency have a cost. This cost is simply because a replication system is usually implemented by making all the operations that applied to a unique object into *atomic* operations which have a set of sub-operations on each of the replicated object. Thus locks or optimistic concurrency control, with rollback and recovery are required with all the overheads described in the previous section. In some systems (such as name and directory servers) updates are far less frequent than reads. In these services, the master/slave model of replication is simpler. A master service holds the state which is downloaded to slaves. Multiple slaves provide higher performance and availability for reading. Updates only happen on the master, which then restarts the slaves one by one with the new version. There are other systems in which it doesn't matter if the information is only slightly out of date: *e.g.* the latest weather. Then we can afford to propagate updates lazily (*i.e.* as a read request to a replicant server arrives). The design tradeoff here are similar to those for cache designs. Some systems allow write access to proceed even when network partitioning means that consistency cannot be maintained. This is so that availability is maintained. This is a reasonable engineering tradeoff. In this case, we need a scheme to deal with the rejoining of the distributed system after repair. This will be based on voting about versions of objects. Various schemes exist for distributed voting between replicated but possibly inconsistent servers and clients:

1. Majority Consensus The normal majority consensus algorithm is used for clients updating replicated servers:

   a. A client has previously read some version of some item (time stamped).

b. When the client updates, it submits the new version to some server together with the old ones.

c. This server then either broadcasts to all the others or simply chains through them.

To ensure that the servers converge on an update being accepted or rejected, there is now a voting phase, while the update is :

a. The servers recursively ask the next server if this is ok.

b. If the update's timestamp is more recent than each servers stored value, they ok it.

c. When the number of ok's in the consensus message is a majority of the servers, the update starts to be applied.

Suitable use of timeouts ensures that we can operate this scheme even with a minority of servers unavailable.

2. Weighted Voting Weighted voting schemes allow for weights to be associated with the different replicated objects, both for read and update access. Then read operations need some quorum of votes before they proceed, while updates need some different quorum. In this way, we can get higher read availability but for older copies, whilst maintaining high integrity for writing. This is an important properties in distributed systems, since there are often system objects which are rarely updated, but frequently read (e.g. executables on workstation disks).

11

APPENDICES

11.1 INTEGRATED SERVICES DIGITAL NETWORK

Integrated Services Digital Network (ISDN) is comprised of digital telephony and data-transport services offered by regional telephone carriers. ISDN involves the digitization of the telephone network, which permits voice, data, text, graphics, music, video, and other source material to be transmitted over existing telephone wires. The emergence of ISDN represents an effort to standardize subscriber services, user/network interfaces, and network and internetwork capabilities. ISDN applications include high-speed image applications (such as Group IV facsimile), additional telephone lines in homes to serve the telecommuting industry, high-speed file transfer, and videoconferencing. Voice service is also an application for ISDN. This chapter summarizes the underlying technologies and services associated with ISDN.

The History of ISDN

ISDN has been in the making for over a decade and is just beginning to become widely available in the United States. Europe and Japan have enjoyed large-scale deployment of ISDN services for years. North America has just over 70 percent deployment, with availability in most major metropolitan areas.

The International Telecommunications Union Telecommunications Standardization Sector (ITU-TSS), formerly known as the International Telephone and Telegraph Consultative Committee (CCITT), is a United Nations organization that coordinates international telecommunications. It was the intention of the ITU-TSS to standardize global telecommunications by implementing ISDN. The idea of standardization is widely accepted but the implementation of ISDN has been slow in coming. AT&T and Northern Telecom are the two major manufacturers of ISDN switches used by telephone companies. Each manufacturer took different steps to provide the ITU-TSS standards for their equipment, and the end result has been incompatibilities with hardware and software. The incongruities stifled the expansive deployment of ISDN since telephone companies have resisted purchasing products that are incompatible with their existing equipment.

National ISDN 1 (NISDN-1) is a United States-specific implementation of ISDN that was adopted by the telecommunications industry in 1991. NISDN-1 was intended to provide conformity to service users regardless of the equipment or software utilized. However, it wasn't until November 1992 that the Transcontinental ISDN Project 1992 (TRIP '92) was held in Reston, Virginia. TRIP '92 was a trade show with exhibits from vendors, proving that ISDN standardized products and services were available along with applications to support them. Also, the exposition featured the "Golden Splice" event which marked the advent of transcontinental ISDN service.

Basics of ISDN

Integrated Services Digital Network (ISDN) is a fully digital communications technology implemented throughout the infrastructure of the existing worldwide telephone network. ISDN uses a standard phone line (a copper wire pair) in a home or office and converts it from a single analog circuit into multiple high speed digital circuits capable of transmitting audio, still images, motion video, and text data simultaneously. ISDN services make possible videoconferencing and other real time data-intensive applications, and it does so at a price comparable to standard analog service.

Standard telephone service requires a separate phone line for each device to be used simultaneously. Not only can multiple lines be expensive, but the amount of information that can be transmitted is limited with analog service; current technology allows 56 kilobits per second (Kbps). ISDN, however, provides multiple channels to operate concurrently on the same pair of wires, and each channel is capable of transmitting at 64 Kbps. Additionally, digital transmissions allow for reduced noise and interference on the carrier channels.

ISDN provides services and capabilities not available through standard telephone service. ISDN furnishes these services through a digital package when a call is initiated. The digital packet includes information regarding: 1) who is calling, 2) the type of call (data/voice/etc...), and 3) the number dialled, if more than one number is used for a single ISDN line. [1] With the information provided, ISDN equipment can determine how to handle a call, based on user-defined preferences. Calls can be accepted, rejected or even rerouted. Data calls can even be routed to an Internet Protocol (IP) address.

ISDN Devices

ISDN devices include terminals, terminal adapters (TAs), network-termination devices, line-termination equipment, and exchange-termination equipment. ISDN terminals come in two types. Specialized ISDN terminals are referred to as terminal equipment type 1 (TE1). Non-ISDN terminals, such as DTE, that predate the ISDN standards are referred to as terminal equipment type 2 (TE2). TE1s connect to the ISDN network through a four-wire, twisted-pair digital link. TE2s connect to the ISDN network through a TA. The ISDN TA can be either a standalone device or a board inside the TE2. If the TE2 is implemented as a standalone device, it connects to the TA via a standard physical-layer interface. Examples include EIA/TIA-232-C (formerly RS-232-C), V.24, and V.35.

Beyond the TE1 and TE2 devices, the next connection point in the ISDN network is the network termination type 1 (NT1) or network termination type 2 (NT2) device. These are network-termination devices that connect the four-wire subscriber wiring to the conventional two-wire local loop. In North America, the NT1 is a customer premises equipment (CPE) device. In most other parts of the world, the NT1 is part of the network provided by the carrier. The NT2 is a more complicated device that typically is found in digital private branch exchanges (PBXs) and that performs Layer 2 and 3 protocol functions and concentration services. An NT1/2 device also exists as a single device that combines the functions of an NT1 and an NT2. ISDN specifies a number of reference points that define logical interfaces between functional groups, such as TAs and NT1s. ISDN reference points include the following:

R—The reference point between non-ISDN equipment and a TA.

S—The reference point between user terminals and the NT2.

T—The reference point between NT1 and NT2 devices.

U—The reference point between NT1 devices and line-termination equipment in the carrier network.

The U reference point is relevant only in North America, where the NT1 function is not provided by the carrier network.

Figure 11.1 illustrates a sample ISDN configuration and shows three devices attached to an ISDN switch at the central office. Two of these devices are ISDN-compatible, so they can be attached through an S reference point to NT2 devices. The third device (a standard, non-ISDN telephone) attaches through the reference point to a TA. Any of these devices also could attach to an NT1/2 device, which would replace both the NT1 and the NT2. In addition, although they are not shown, similar user stations are attached to the far-right ISDN switch.

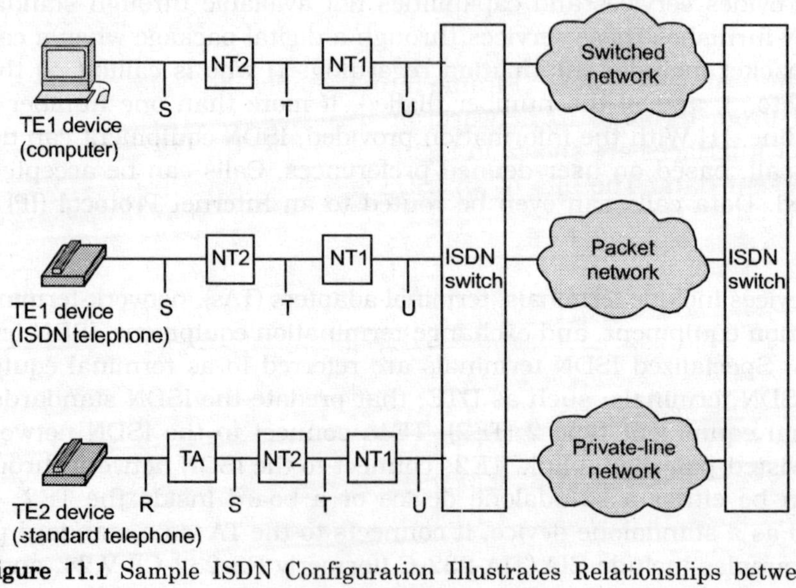

Figure 11.1 Sample ISDN Configuration Illustrates Relationships between Devices and Reference Points

Services

There are two types of services associated with ISDN:

1. BRI
2. PRI

ISDN BRI Service

The ISDN Basic Rate Interface (BRI) service offers two B channels and one D channel (2B+D). BRI B-channel service operates at 64 kbps and is meant to carry user data; BRI D-channel service operates at 16 kbps and is meant to carry control and signalling information, although it can support user data transmission under certain circumstances. The D channel signalling protocol comprises Layers 1 through 3 of the OSI reference model. BRI also provides for framing control and other overhead, bringing its total bit rate to 192 kbps.

The BRI physical layer specification is International Telecommunication Union-Telecommunications Standards Section (ITU-T) (formerly the Consultative Committee for International Telegraph and Telephone [CCITT]).

ISDN PRI Service

ISDN Primary Rate Interface (PRI) service offers 23 B channels and 1 D channel in North America and Japan, yielding a total bit rate of 1.544 Mbps (the PRI D channel runs at 64 kbps). ISDN PRI in Europe, Australia, and other parts of the world provides 30 B channels plus one 64-kbps D channel and a total interface rate of 2.048 Mbps. The PRI physical layer specification is ITU-T I.

ISDN Specifications

This section describes the various ISDN specifications for Layer 1, Layer 2, and Layer 3.

Layer 1

ISDN physical layer (Layer 1) frame formats differ depending on whether the frame is outbound (from terminal to network) or inbound (from network to terminal). Both physical layer interfaces are shown in Figure 11.2. The frames are 48 bits long, of which 36 bits represent data. The bits of an ISDN physical layer frame are used as follows:

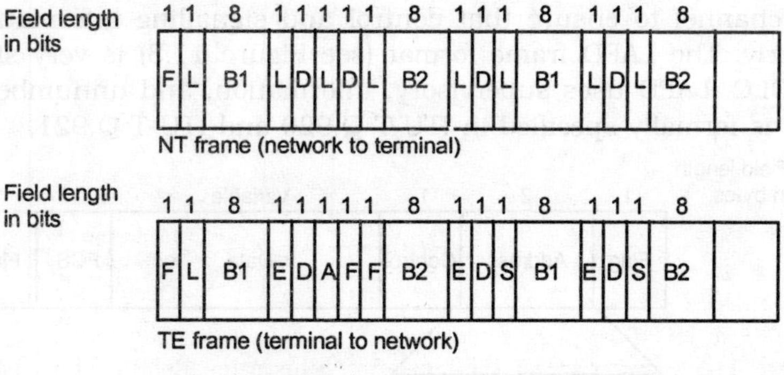

A = Activation bit
B1 = B1 channel bits
D = D channel (4 bits × 4000 frames sec. = 16 kbps)
E = Ethe of previous D bit
F = Framing bit
L = Load balancing
S = Spare bit

Figure 11.2 ISDN Physical Layer Frame Formats Differ Depending on their

1. **F**-Provides synchronization
2. **L**-Adjusts the average bit value

3. **E**-Ensures contention resolution when several terminals on a passive bus contend for a channel
4. **A**-Activates devices
5. **S**-Is unassigned
6. **B1, B2,** and **D**-Handle user data

Multiple ISDN user devices can be physically attached to one circuit. In this configuration, collisions can result if two terminals transmit simultaneously. Therefore, ISDN provides features to determine link contention. When an NT receives a D bit from the TE, it echoes back the bit in the next E-bit position. The TE expects the next E bit to be the same as its last transmitted D bit.

Terminals cannot transmit into the D channel unless they first detect a specific number of ones (indicating "no signal") corresponding to a pre-established priority. If the TE detects a bit in the echo (E) channel that is different from its D bits, it must stop transmitting immediately. This simple technique ensures that only one terminal can transmit its D message at one time. After successful D-message transmission, the terminal has its priority reduced by requiring it to detect more continuous ones before transmitting. Terminals cannot raise their priority until all other devices on the same line have had an opportunity to send a D message. Telephone connections have higher priority than all other services, and signalling information has a higher priority than nonsignalling information.

Layer 2

Layer 2 of the ISDN signalling protocol is Link Access Procedure, D channel (LAPD). LAPD is similar to High-Level Data Link Control (HDLC) and Link Access Procedure Balanced (LAPB). As the expansion of the LAPD acronym indicates, this layer is used across the D channel to ensure that control and signalling information flows and is received properly. The LAPD frame format (see Figure 11.3) is very similar to that of HDLC; like HDLC, LAPD uses supervisory, information, and unnumbered frames. The LAPD protocol is formally specified in ITU-T Q.920 and ITU-T Q.921.

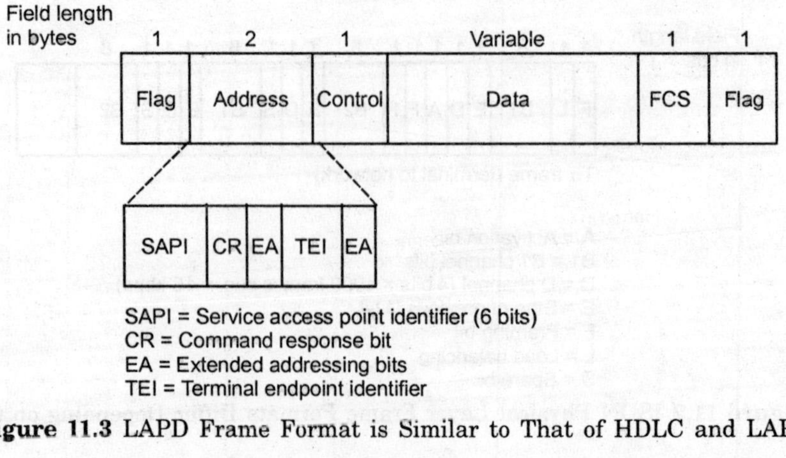

Figure 11.3 LAPD Frame Format is Similar to That of HDLC and LAPB

The LAPD Flag and Control fields are identical to those of HDLC. The LAPD Address field can be either 1 or 2 bytes long. If the extended address bit of the first byte is set, the address is 1 byte; if it is not set, the address is 2 bytes. The first Address-field byte contains the service access point identifier (SAPI), which identifies the portal at which LAPD services are provided to Layer 3. The C/R bit indicates whether the frame contains a command or a response. The Terminal Endpoint Identifier (TEI) field identifies either a single terminal or multiple terminals. A TEI of all ones indicates a broadcast.

Layer 3

Two Layer 3 specifications are used for ISDN signalling: ITU-T (formerly CCITT) I.450 (also known as ITU-T Q.930) and ITU-T I.451 (also known as ITU-T Q.931). Together, these protocols support user-to-user, circuit-switched, and packet-switched connections. A variety of call-establishment, call-termination, information, and miscellaneous messages are specified, including SETUP, CONNECT, RELEASE, USER INFORMATION, CANCEL, STATUS, and DISCONNECT. These messages are functionally similar to those provided by the X.25 protocol. Figure 11.4, from ITU-T I.451, shows the typical stages of an ISDN circuit-switched call.

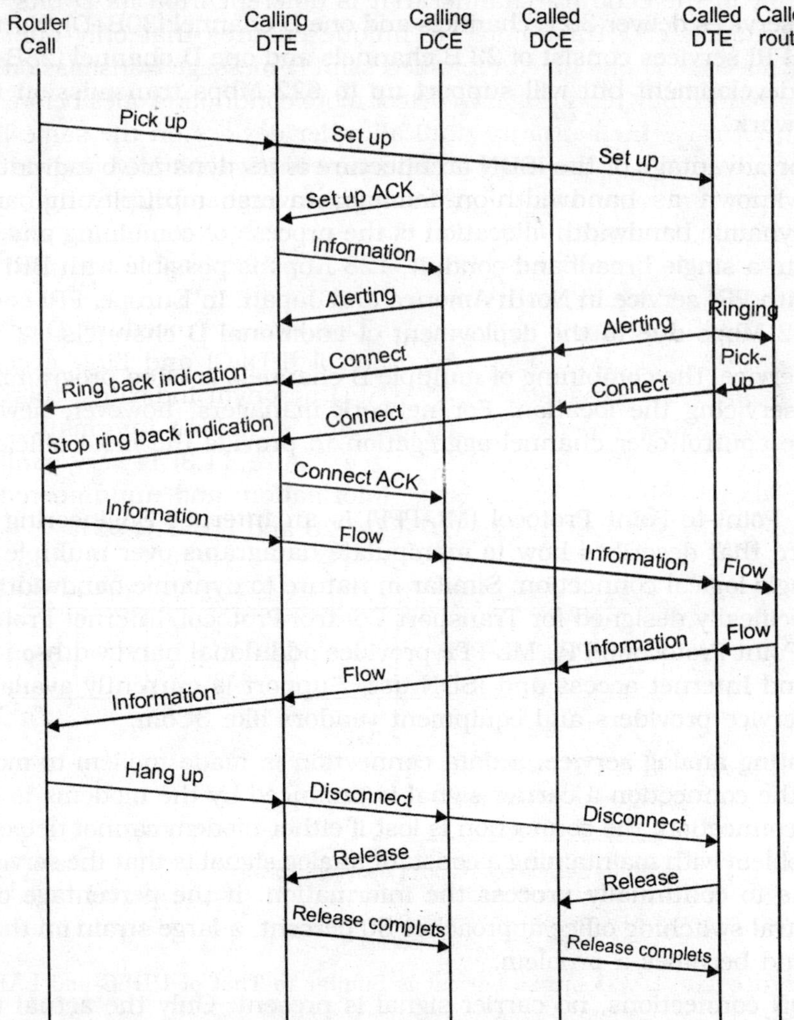

Figure 11.4 An ISDN Circuit-Switched Call Moves through Various Stages to its Destination

How ISDN Works

ISDN carries voice and data on bearer (B) channels which transmit at 64 Kbps each. (H channels, which are the functional equivalent to B channels, are available and provide faster bit rates.) A data (D) channel, sometimes referred to as a delta channel, operates at 16 or 64 Kbps and provides signalling to construct and tear down a connection, request network services, and route data over the B channels. The D channel can also be used to transmit user packet or frame data at times when bandwidth on the D channel is not required for signalling and control. Utilizing the D channel in this way provides the most efficient use of ISDN.

ISDN has three different services: 1) Basic Rate Interface (BRI), 2) Primary Rate Interface (PRI), and 3) Broadband (B-ISDN) . BRI is the most common service and was intended to be the most widely available for residential customers. BRI services provide two B channels and one D channel (2B+D). PRI services are implemented differently in North America and Japan than in Europe where they are the most common services. European PRI services deliver 30 B channels and one D channel (30B+D). North American and Japanese PRI services consist of 23 B channels and one D channel (23B+D). B-ISDN is still under development but will support up to 622 Mbps transmission rates over a fiber optic network.

One major advantage of the ISDN architecture is its dynamic bandwidth allocation feature. Also known as bandwidth-on-demand, inverse multiplexing, and channel aggregation, dynamic bandwidth allocation is the process of combining any or all of the B channels into a single broadband conduit. 128 Kbps is possible with BRI service and 1.536 Mbps with PRI service in North America and Japan. In Europe, PRI configurations can reach 1.92 Mbps due to the deployment of additional B channels.

For PRI service, the combining of multiple B channels is often programmed into the ISDN switch servicing the location. For network managers, however, new controllers allow real time control over channel aggregation to provide the most efficient use of a network.

Multilink Point-to-Point Protocol (ML-PPP) is an Internet Engineering Task Force (IETF) standard that describes how to manipulate datagrams over multiple B channels to create a single logical connection. Similar in nature to dynamic bandwidth allocation, ML-PPP is specifically designed for Transport Control Protocol/Internet Protocol's (TCP/IP's) Point-to-Point Protocol (PPP). ML-PPP provides additional bandwidth-on-demand for remote LAN and Internet access and ISDN use. Support is currently available through major ISDN service providers and equipment vendors like 3Com.

With existing analog service, a data connection is made modem-to-modem. At all times during the connection a carrier signal is produced by the modems to indicate the presence of a connection; the connection is lost if either modem cannot detect the carrier signal. The problem with maintaining a constant analog signal is that the service provider's equipment has to continually process the information. If the percentage of data calls through a central switching office approaches 50 percent, a large strain on the equipment is produced and becomes a problem.

With ISDN connections, no carrier signal is present. Only the actual user data is transmitted and it transfers at a fraction of the time compared to analog service. Therefore, implementing ISDN switches can actually reduce traffic overhead for service providers which reduces their service costs. In addition, ISDN technology swaps one analog line with two digital connections without physically replacing any wires.

Benefits of ISDN

1. ISDN affords many benefits to service providers and customers. The increasing popularity of ISDN allows pricing that continues to fall and compete with standard analog service. Some of the many benefits are:
2. Simultaneous audio, video, and data services over a single pair of copper wires reduces infrastructure and maintenance costs for service and subscribers.
3. ISDN BRI service can use data compression which boosts the 128 Kbps transmission rate to between 256 Kbps and 632 Kbps, depending upon the compression ratio used.
4. Digital transmissions produce clearer and quieter voice telephone service and more reliable and accurate connectivity than analog technology.
5. Remote computer users benefit from high performance ISDN connections at home or on the road.
6. ISDN's dynamic bandwidth allocation feature accommodates the bandwidth-intensive applications.
7. Up to eight different devices can be operated simultaneously over a single ISDN line.
8. LAN protocols such as IP and IPX are better supported by ISDN connections across WANs due to faster connect times (between 1 and 4 seconds) than analog service (between 10 and 40 seconds).
9. ISDN is compatible with other WAN services like X.25, Frame Relay, Switched Multi-megabit Data Services (SMDS) and higher speed services like Asynchronous Transfer Mode (ATM). [4]

Digital Service Comparison

Switched 56 Service (SW56)

SW56 provides 56 Kbps transmission rates for data-only applications over existing public phone lines. It is a low-cost alternative to dedicated leased lines and is used primarily for intermittent data swapping between WANs. SW56 is also used to connect ISDN networks in areas where ISDN is not yet available.

X.25 Switched Service

X.25 is a widely used protocol standard using synchronous data transmission over the public switched network. It provides data rates up to 56 Kbps and most commonly supports applications for order entry, electronic messaging, point-of-sales transactions and credit card verification. ISDN supports X.25 services over the D channel. X.25 is efficient at handling bursty LAN environment traffic and also provides data security and error detection/correction facilities. Due to its low speed, however, it is not a viable alternative for high speed LAN and WAN applications.

Switched Multi-megabit Data Services (SMDS)

SMDS uses a connectionless networking scheme to connect multi-node LANs through the public telephone network. SMDS is standardized and supports all major networking protocols and therefore can be utilized as the backbone for Ethernet, Token Ring, and FDDI networks. SMDS uses a fixed 53-byte datagram complete with addressing information for data transmission. Data is routed over the least congested path in an SMDS network, providing faster transmission, added security, and increased flexibility to reconfigure network sites. Deployment of SMDS service is very low; between 200 and 500 customers in North America.

Frame Relay Service

Frame relay service is similar to ISDN in that it is a standards-based technology defined by both the American National Standards Institute (ANSI) and ITU-TSS. Frame relay operates from between 56/64 Kbps to 1.544 Mbps and can easily handle peak volume traffic flow in the LAN environment, due to its bandwidth-on-demand capability. It typically is applied in LAN-to-LAN internetworking and IBM host access and data file transfer environments. Frame relay is relatively more expensive (as much as 12 times more) than ISDN since it requires a dedicated access line, and it is not as widely deployed as ISDN services.

Cable Service

Cable services, although still under development, will eventually provide residential customers with WAN connections of speeds between 500 Kbps and 30 Mbps. In addition to fast on-line access with built-in TCP/IP-ready WAN links, customers will be able enjoy interactive television. When services are available they will be delivered over standard coaxial cable, just as current services are provided. Eventually, fiber optic or a hybrid fiber-coaxial cable will provide services. Cable service has two main disadvantages. The first is the reputation for unreliability over existing cable networks. The second is that bandwidth is shared over cable, causing poor overall response for multiple users on a single cable. Also, current cable networks are not optimized for two-way data communications, and internetworking standards are not in place.

Asynchronous Transfer Mode (ATM)

Broadband ISDN is based on ATM technology, which is emerging as a popular method of simultaneously transmitting audio, video, and data. ATM has transmission rates between 1.544 Mbps and 622 Mbps. ATM standards are defined by ITU-TSS, but many details of the implementation of the standards remain in question and ATM WAN services are not yet widely available.

Point-to-Point Dedicated Leased Services

Private leased lines currently make up the majority of all worldwide WAN connections. Point-to-point leased lines consist of a dedicated digital connection between two points, providing security and control. Transmission rates vary between 56 Kbps and 1.544 Mbps in the United States (T1 rates). in Europe, E1 rates deliver between 64 Kbps and 2.048 Mbps. Leased line services provide a fixed bandwidth at a fixed speed. In many cases, leased lines are used at under 20 percent of their total capacity. Also, leased lines are not efficient at handling bursty network traffic.

11.2 DIGITAL SUBSCRIBER LINE

Digital Subscriber Line (DSL) technology is a modern technology that uses existing twisted-pair telephone lines to transport high-bandwidth data, such as multimedia and video, to service subscribers. The term *xDSL* covers a number of similar yet competing forms of DSL technologies, including ADSL, SDSL, HDSL, HDSL-2, G.SHDL, IDSL, and VDSL. xDSL is drawing significant attention from implementers and service providers because it promises to deliver high-bandwidth data rates to dispersed locations with relatively small changes to the existing telco infrastructure.

xDSL services are dedicated, point-to-point, public network access over twisted-pair copper wire on the local loop (last mile) between a network service provider's (NSP) central office and the customer site, or on local loops created either intrabuilding or intracampus. Currently, most DSL deployments are ADSL, mainly delivered to residential customers. This chapter focus mainly on defining ADSL.

Asymmetric Digital Subscriber Line

Asymmetric Digital Subscriber Line (ADSL) technology is asymmetric. It allows more bandwidth downstream-from an NSP's central office to the customer site-than upstream from the subscriber to the central office. This asymmetry, combined with always-on access (which eliminates call setup), makes ADSL ideal for Internet/intranet surfing, video-on-demand, and remote LAN access. Users of these applications typically download much more information than they send.

ADSL transmits more than 6 Mbps to a subscriber and as much as 640 kbps more in both directions. Such rates expand existing access capacity by a factor of 50 or more without new cabling. ADSL can literally transform the existing public information network from one limited to voice, text, and low-resolution graphics to a powerful, ubiquitous system capable of bringing multimedia, including full-motion video, to every home this century.

ADSL will play a crucial role over the next decade or more as telephone companies enter new markets for delivering information in video and multimedia formats. New broadband cabling will take decades to reach all prospective subscribers. Success of these new services depends on reaching as many subscribers as possible during the first few years. By bringing movies, television, video catalogs, remote CD-ROMs, corporate LANs, and the Internet into homes and small businesses, ADSL will make these markets viable and profitable for telephone companies and application suppliers alike.

ADSL Capabilities

An ADSL circuit connects an ADSL modem on each end of a twisted-pair telephone line, creating three information channels: a high-speed downstream channel, a medium-speed duplex channel, and a basic telephone service channel. The basic telephone service channel is split off from the digital modem by filters, thus guaranteeing uninterrupted basic telephone service, even if ADSL fails. The high-speed channel ranges from 1.5 to 9 Mbps, and duplex rates range from 16 to 640 kbps. Each channel can be submultiplexed to form multiple lower-rate channels.

ADSL modems provide data rates consistent with North American T1 1.544 Mbps and European E1 2.048 Mbps digital hierarchies , and can be purchased with various speed ranges and capabilities. The minimum configuration provides 1.5 or 2.0 Mbps downstream and a 16 kbps duplex channel; others provide rates of 6.1 Mbps and 64 kbps for duplex. Products with downstream rates up to 8 Mbps and duplex rates up to 640 kbps are available today. ADSL modems accommodate Asynchronous Transfer Mode (ATM) transport with variable rates and compensation for ATM overhead, as well as IP protocols.

Downstream data rates depend on a number of factors, including the length of the copper line, its wire gauge, the presence of bridged taps, and cross-coupled interference. Line attenuation increases with line length and frequency, and decreases as wire diameter increases. Ignoring bridged taps, ADSL performs.

Many applications envisioned for ADSL involve digital compressed video. As a real-time signal, digital video cannot use link- or network-level error control procedures commonly found in data communications systems. Therefore, ADSL modems incorporate forward error correction that dramatically reduces errors caused by impulse noise. Error correction on a symbol-by-symbol basis also reduces errors caused by continuous noise coupled into a line.

ADSL Technology

ADSL depends on advanced digital signal processing and creative algorithms to squeeze so much information through twisted-pair telephone lines. In addition, many advances have been required in transformers, analog filters, and analog/digital (A/D) converters. Long telephone lines may attenuate signals at 1 MHz (the outer edge of the band used by ADSL) by as much as 90 dB, forcing analog sections of ADSL modems to work very hard to realize large dynamic ranges, separate channels, and maintain low noise figures. On the outside, ADSL looks simple-transparent synchronous data pipes at various data rates over ordinary telephone lines. The inside, where all the transistors work, is a miracle of modern technology.

To create multiple channels, ADSL modems divide the available bandwidth of a telephone line in one of two ways: frequency-division multiplexing (FDM) or echo cancellation. FDM assigns one band for upstream data and another band for downstream data. The downstream path is then divided by time-division multiplexing into one or more high-speed channels and one or more low-speed channels. The upstream path is also multiplexed into corresponding low-speed channels. Echo cancellation assigns the upstream band to overlap the downstream, and separates the two by means of local echo cancellation, a technique well known in V.32 and V.34 modems. With either technique, ADSL splits off a 4 kHz region for basic telephone service at the DC end of the band.

An ADSL modem organizes the aggregate data stream created by multiplexing downstream channels, duplex channels, and maintenance channels together into blocks, and it attaches an error correction code to each block. The receiver then corrects errors that occur during transmission, up to the limits implied by the code and the block length. At the user's option, the unit also can create superblocks by interleaving data within subblocks; this allows the receiver to correct any combination of errors within a specific span of bits. This, in turn, allows for effective transmission of both data and video signals.

Signalling and Modulation

This section includes the following:

1. CAP and DMT Modulated ADSL
2. ADSL Standards and Associations

CAP and DMT Modulated ADSL

DMT and *CAP* are line-coding methods for modulating the electrical signals sent over the copper wire in the local loop. Carrierless Amplitude and Phase (CAP) is a common line-coding method. CAP is a well-understood technology because of its similarity with QAM. Although CAP is well-understood and relatively inexpensive, some argue that it is difficult to scale because it is a single-carrier modulation technique and is susceptible to narrowband interference. DMT uses multiple carriers. At this point, DMT is capable of more speed than CAP. This is one reason that the ANSI committee T1E1.4 accorded it standards status in document T1.413.

This standard calls for 256 subbands of 4 KHz each, thereby occupying 1.024 GHz. Each subband can be modulated with QAM 64 for clean subbands, down to QPSK. If each of the subbands can support QAM-64 modulation, then the forward channel supports 6.1 Mbps. On the return path are 32 subbands, with a potential for 1.5 Mbps.

CAP and DMT Compared

CAP is a single-carrier technique that uses a wide passband. DMT is a multiple-carrier technique that uses many narrowband channels. The two have a number of engineering differences, even though, ultimately, they can offer similar service to the network layers discussed previously.

Adaptive Equalization

Adaptive equalizers are amplifiers that shape frequency response to compensate for attenuation and phase error. Adaptive equalization requires that the modems learn line characteristics and do so by sending probes and looking at the return signals. The equalizer then knows how it must amplify signals to get a nice, flat frequency response. The greater the dynamic range, the more complex the equalization. ADSL requires 50 dB of dynamic range, complicating adaptive equalization. Only with recent advances in digital signal processing (number crunching) has it become possible to have such equalization in relatively small packaging.

Adaptive equalization is required for CAP because noise characteristics vary significantly across the frequency passband. Adaptive equalization is not needed for DMT because noise characteristics do not vary across any given 4 KHz subband. A major issue in comparing DMT with CAP is determining the point at which the complexity of adaptive equalization surpasses the complexity of DMT's multiple Fourier transform calculations. This is determined by further implementation experience.

Power Consumption

Although DMT clearly scales and does not need adaptive equalization, other factors must be considered. First, with 256 channels, DMT has a disadvantage regarding power consumption (and, therefore, cost) when compared with CAP. DMT has a high peak-to-average power ratio because the multiple carriers can constructively interfere to yield a strong signal. DMT has higher computational requirements, resulting in more transistors than the transceiver chips. Numbers are mostly proprietary at this point, but it is estimated that a single transceiver will consume 5 W of power, even with further advances. Power consumption is important because hundreds or thousands (as carriers dearly hope) of transceivers might be at the central office, or CEV. This would require much more heat dissipation than CAP requires.

Latency

Another issue for DMT is that latencies are somewhat higher than with CAP (15). Because each subband uses only 4 KHz, no bit can travel faster than permitted by a QAM-64. The trade-off between throughput and latency is a historical one in data communications and has normally been settled in the marketplace.

Speed

DMT appears to have the speed advantage over CAP. Because narrow carriers have relatively few equalization problems, more aggressive modulation techniques can be used on each channel. For CAP to achieve comparable bit rates, it might be necessary to use more bandwidth, far beyond 1 MHz. This creates new problems associated with high frequencies on wires and would reduce CAP's current advantage in power consumption.

Additional DSL Technologies

This section discusses the following DSL technologies:

1. SDSL
2. HDSL
3. HDSL-2
4. G.SHDSL
5. ISDN Digital Subscriber Line (DSL)
6. VDSL.

SDSL

Symmetric Digital Subscriber Line (SDSL) is a rate-adaptive version of HDSL and, like HDSL, is symmetric. It allows equal bandwidth downstream from an NSP's central office to the customer site as upstream from the subscriber to the central office. SDSL supports data only on a single line and does not support analog calls. SDSL uses 2B1Q line coding and can transmit up to 1.54 Mbps to and from a subscriber, or can be configured to offer a variable range of bandwidth up to 1.45 Mbps.

The symmetry that SDSL offers, combined with always-on access (which eliminates call setup), makes it a favorable WAN technology for small to medium businesses and branch offices, and can be an affordable alternative to dedicated leased lines and Frame Relay services. Because traffic is symmetrical, file transfer, web hosting, and distance-learning applications can effectively be implemented with SDSL.

HDSL

Originally developed by Bellcore, high bit-rate DSL (HDSL)/T1/E1 technologies have been standardized by ANSI in the United States and by ETSI in Europe. The ANSI standard covers two-pair T1 transmission, with a data rate of 784 kbps on each twisted pair. ETSI standards exist both for a two-pair E1 system, with each pair carrying 1168 kbps, and a three-pair E1 system, with 784 kbps on each twisted pair.

HDSL became popular because it is a better way of provisioning T1 or E1 over twisted-pair copper lines than the long-used technique known as Alternative Mark Inversion (AMI). HDSL uses less bandwidth and requires no repeaters up to the CSA range. By using adaptive line equalization and 2B1Q modulation, HDSL transmits 1.544 Mbps or 2.048 Mbps in bandwidth ranging from 80ntrast to the 1.5 MHz required by AMI. (AMI is still the encoding protocol used for the majority of T1.)T1 service can be installed in a day for less than $1,000 by installing HDSL modems at each end of the line. Installation via AMI costs much more and takes more time because of the requirement to add repeaters between the subscriber and the CO. Depending on the length of the line, the cost to add repeaters for AMI could be up to $5,000 and could take more than a week.

HDSL is heavily used in cellular telephone buildouts. Traffic from the base station is backhauled to the CO using HDSL in more than 50 percent of installations. Currently, the vast majority of new T1 lines are provisioned with HDSL. However, because of the embedded base of AMI, less than 30 percent of existing T1 lines are provisioned with HDSL. HDSL does have drawbacks. First, no provision exists for analog voice because it uses the voice band. Second, ADSL achieves better speeds than HDSL because ADSL's asymmetry deliberately keeps the crosstalk at one end of the line. Symmetric systems such as HDSL have crosstalk at both ends.

HDSL-2

HDSL-2 is an emerging standard and a promising alternative to HDSL. The intention is to offer a symmetric service at T1 speeds using a single-wire pair rather than two pairs. This will enable it to operate for a larger potential audience. It will require more aggressive modulation, shorter distances (about 10,000 feet), and better phone lines.

Much of the SDSL equipment in the market today uses the 2B1Q line code developed for Integrated Services Digital Network. The Bell companies have insisted that using this SDSL at speeds higher than 768 kbps can cause interference with voice and other services that are offered on copper wire within the same wire bundle.

The biggest advantage of HDSL-2, which was developed to serve as a standard by which different vendors' equipment could interoperate, is that it is designed not to interfere with other services. However, HDSL-2 is full rate only, offering services only at 1.5 Mbps.

G.SHDSL

G.SHDSL is a standards-based, multirate version of HDSL-2 and offers symmetrical service. The advantage of HDSL-2, which was developed to serve as a standard by which different vendors' equipment could interoperate, is that it is designed not to interfere with other services. However, the HDSL-2 standard addresses only services at 1.5 Mbps.

Multirate HDSL-2 is part of Issue 2 of the standard known as G.SHDSL, and is ratified by the ITU. G.SHDSL builds upon the benefits of HDSL-2 by offering symmetrical rates of 2.3 Mbps.

ISDN Digital Subscriber Line

ISDN digital subscriber line (IDSL) is a cross between ISDN and xDSL. It is like ISDN in that it uses a single-wire pair to transmit full-duplex data at 128 kbps and at distances of up to RRD range. Like ISDN, IDSL uses a 2B1Q line code to enable transparent operation through the ISDN "U" interface. Finally, the user continues to use existing CPE (ISDN BRI terminal adapters, bridges, and routers) to make the CO connections.

The big difference is from the carrier's point-of-view. Unlike ISDN, ISDL does not connect through the voice switch. A new piece of data communications equipment terminates the ISDL connection and shuts it off to a router or data switch. This is a key feature because the overloading of central office voice switches by data users is a growing problem for telcos.

The limitation of ISDL is that the customer no longer has access to ISDN signalling or voice services. But for Internet service providers, who do not provide a public voice service, ISDL is an interesting way of using POTS dial service to offer higher-speed Internet access, targeting the embedded base of more than five million ISDN users as an initial market.

VDSL

Very-High-Data-Rate Digital Subscriber Line (VDSL) transmits high-speed data over short reaches of twisted-pair copper telephone lines, with a range of speeds depending on actual line length. The maximum downstream rate under consideration is between 51 and 55 Mbps over lines up to 1000 feet (300 m) in length. Downstream speeds as low as 13 Mbps over lengths beyond 4000 feet (1500 m) are also common. Upstream rates in early models will be asymmetric, just like ADSL, at speeds from 1.6 to 2.3 Mbps. Both data channels will be separated in frequency from bands used for basic telephone service and Integrated Services Digital Network (ISDN), enabling service providers to overlay VDSL on existing services. Currently, the two high-speed channels are also separated in frequency. As needs arise for higher-speed upstream channels or symmetric rates, VDSL systems may need to use echo cancellation.

Advantages of ADSL

When you connect to the Internet, you might connect through a regular modem, through a local-area network connection in your office, or through a cable modem. A growing number of people, though, are reaching the Internet through a **Digital Subscriber Line (DSL)** connection—a very high-speed connection using the same wires as a regular telephone line.

Here are some advantages of DSL:

1. You can leave your Internet connection open and still use the phone line for voice calls.
2. The speed is much higher than a regular modem (1.5 Mps vs. 56 kps)

3. DSL doesn't necessarily require new wiring; it can use the phone line you already have.

Many companies that offer DSL will provide the modem as part of the installation.

But there are disadvantages:

1. A DSL connection works better when you are closer to the provider's central office.
2. The connection is faster for receiving data than it is for sending data over the Internet.
3. The service is not available everywhere.

A standard telephone installation in the U.S. consists of a pair of copper wires that the phone company installs in your home. The pair of copper wires has lots of room for carrying more than your phone conversations. The wires are capable of handling a much greater **bandwidth**, the range of frequencies, than that demanded for voice. DSL exploits this "extra capacity" to carry information on the wire without disturbing the line's ability to carry conversations. The entire plan is based on matching particular frequencies to specific tasks.

To understand DSL, you first need to know a couple of things about a normal telephone line—the kind that telephone professionals call **POTS**, for Plain Old Telephone Service. One of the ways that POTS makes the most of the telephone company's wires and equipment is by limiting the frequencies that the switches, telephones and other equipment will carry. Human voices, speaking in normal conversational tones, can be carried in a frequency range of 0 to 3,400 hertz, or cycles per second. This range of frequencies is tiny. For example, compare this to the range of most stereo speakers, which cover from roughly 20 hertz to 20,000 hertz. And the wires themselves have the potential to handle frequencies up to several million hertz in most cases. The use of such a small portion of the wire's total bandwidth is historical—remember that the telephone system has been in place, using a pair of copper wires to each home, for about a century. By limiting the frequencies carried over the lines, the telephone system can pack lots of wires into a very small space without worrying about interference from one line causing problems on another. Modern equipment that sends digital, rather than analog, data can safely use much more of the telephone line's capacity. DSL does just that.

11.3 VIRTUAL PRIVATE NETWORKS

Virtual private networks (VPNs) are a fairly quixotic subject; there is no single defining product, nor even much of a consensus among VPN vendors as to what comprises a VPN. Consequently, everyone knows what a VPN is, but establishing a single definition can be remarkably difficult. Some definitions are sufficiently broad as to enable one to claim that Frame Relay qualifies as a VPN when, in fact, it is an overlay network. Although an overlay network secures transmissions through a public network, it does so passively via logical separation of the data streams.

VPNs provide a more active form of security by either encrypting or encapsulating data for transmission through an unsecured network. These two types of security-encryption and encapsulation-form the foundation of virtual private networking. However, both *encryption* and *encapsulation* are generic terms that describe a function that can be performed by a myriad of specific technologies. To add to the confusion, these two sets of technologies can be combined in different implementation topologies. Thus, VPNs can vary widely from vendor to vendor.

This Appendices provides an overview of building VPNs using the Layer 2 Tunneling Protocol (L2TP), and it explores the possible implementation topologies.

Layer 2 Tunneling Protocol

The Internet Engineering Task Force (IETF) was faced with competing proposals from Microsoft and Cisco Systems for a protocol specification that would secure the transmission of IP datagrams through uncontrolled and untrusted network domains. Microsoft's proposal was an attempt to standardize the Point-to-Point Tunneling Protocol (PPTP), which it had championed. The IETF combined the best elements of each proposal and specified the open standard L2TP.

The simplest description of L2TP's functionality is that it carries the *Point-to-Point Protocol (PPP)* through networks that aren't point-to-point. PPP has become the most popular communications protocol for remote access using circuit-switched transmission facilities such as POTS lines or ISDN to create a temporary point-to-point connection between the calling device and its destination.

L2TP simulates a point-to-point connection by encapsulating PPP datagrams for transportation through routed networks or internetworks. Upon arrival at their intended destination, the encapsulation is removed, and the PPP datagrams are restored to their original format. Thus, a point-to-point communications session can be supported through disparate networks. This technique is known as *tunneling*.

Operational Mechanics

In a traditional remote access scenario, a remote user (or client) accesses a network by directly connecting a *network access server (NAS)*. Generally, the NAS provides several distinct functions: It terminates the point-to-point communications session of the remote user, validates the identity of that user, and then serves that user with access to the network. Although most remote access technologies bundle these functions into a single device, L2TP separates them into two physically separate devices: the *L2TP Access Server (LAS)* and the *L2TP Network Server (LNS)*.

As its names imply, the L2TP Access Server supports authentication, and ingress. Upon successful authentication, the remote user's session is forwarded to the LNS, which lets that user into the network. Their separation enables greater flexibility for implementation than other remote access technologies.

Implementation Topologies

L2TP can be implemented in two distinct topologies:

1. Client-aware tunneling.
2. Client-transparent tunneling.

The distinction between these two topologies is whether the client machine that is using L2TP to access a remote network is aware that its connection is being tunneled.

Client-Aware Tunneling

The first implementation topology is known as client-aware tunneling. This name is derived from the remote client initiating (hence, being "aware" of) the tunnel. In this scenario, the client establishes a logical connection within a physical connection to the LAS. The client remains aware of the tunneled connection all the way through to the LNS, and it can even determine which of its traffic goes through the tunnel.

Client-Transparent Tunneling

Client-transparent tunneling features L2TP access concentrators distributed geographically close to the remote users. Such geographic dispersion is intended to reduce the long-distance telephone charges that would otherwise be incurred by remote users dialling into a centrally located LAC.

The remote users need not support L2TP directly; they merely establish a point-to-point communication session with the LAC using PPP. Ostensibly, the user will be encapsulating IP datagrams in PPP frames. The LAC exchanges PPP messages with the remote user and establishes an L2TP tunnel with the LNS through which the remote user's PPP messages are passed.

The LNS is the remote user's gateway to its home network. It is the terminus of the tunnel; it strips off all L2TP encapsulation and serves up network access for the remote user.

Adding More Security

As useful as L2TP is, it is important to recognize that it is not a panacea. It enables flexibility in delivering remote access, but it does not afford a high degree of security for data in transit. This is due in large part to the relatively nonsecure nature of PPP. In fairness, PPP was designed explicitly for point-to-point communications, so securing the connection should not have been a high priority.

An additional cause for concern stems from the fact that L2TP's tunnels are not cryptographic. Their data payloads are transmitted in the clear, wrapped only by L2TP and PPP framing. However, additional security may be afforded by implementing the IPSec protocols in conjunction with L2TP. The IPSec protocols support strong authentication technologies as well as encryption.

11.4 IPv6

One of the newest major standards on the horizon is IPv6. Although IPv6 has not officially become a standard, it is worth some overview. It is very possible that this information will change as we move closer to IPv6 as a standard, so you should use this as a guide into IPv6, not the definitive information. A number of books are now being published that cover in detail this emerging standard; if you are looking for more details you should refer to these books. All the RFCs available on the Internet have the raw details on how this standard is developing. However, these documents are difficult to interpret at first glance and require some commitment to going through any number of RFCs pertaining to many subjects all related to IPv6 development.

Internet Protocol Version 4 is the most popular protocol in use today (see Chapter 08, "Internet Protocols"), although there are some questions about its capability to serve the Internet community much longer. IPv4 was finished in the 1970s and has started to show its age. The main issue surrounding IPv6 is addressing-or, the lack of addressing-because many experts believe that we are nearly out of the four billion addresses available in IPv4. Although this seems like a very large number of addresses, multiple large blocks are given to government agencies and large organizations. IPv6 could be the solution to many problems, but it is still not fully developed and is not a standard-yet! Many of the finest developers and engineering minds have been working on IPv6 since the early 1990s. Hundreds of RFCs have been written and have detailed some major areas, including expanded addressing, simplified header format, flow labelling, authentication, and privacy.

Expanded addressing moves us from 32-bit address to a 128-bit addressing method. It also provides newer unicast and broadcasting methods, injects hexadecimal into the IP address, and moves from using "." to using ":" as delimiters. Figure 11.5 shows the IPv6 packet header format.

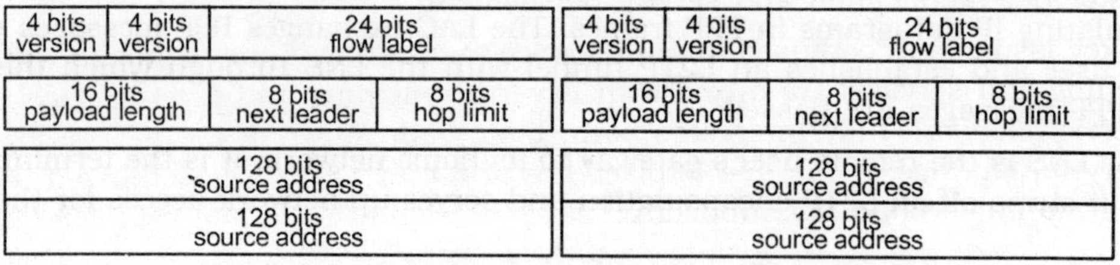

Figure 11.5 IPv6 Packet Header Format

Description of IPV6 Packet Header

The simplified header is 40 bits long and the format consists of Version, Class, Flow Label, Payload Length, Next Header, Hop Limit, Source Address, Destination Address, Data, and Payload fields.

Hexadecimal "Hex"

At its simplest, hex numbers are base 16. Decimal is base 10, counting from 0 to 9, as we do in decimal, and then adding a column to make 10. Counting in hex goes from 0 to F before adding a column. The characters A through F represent the decimal values of 10 through 15.

Counting in hex goes as follows: 0 1 2 3 4 5 6 7 8 9 A B C D E F 10 11 12 13 14 15 16 17 18 19 1A 1B 1C 1D 1E 1F 20 21 and up, as far as you want to go.

Addressing Description

Let's look at an example of IPv6 address. The address is an eight-part hex address separated by colons (" :"). Each part *n* can equal a 16-bit number and is eight parts long, providing a 128-bit address length (16 ¥ 8 = 128),

Addresses are n:n:n:n:n:n:n:n n = 4 digit hexadecimal integer, 16 ¥ 8 = 128 address.

1080:0:0:0:8:800:200C:417A Unicast address

FF01:0:0:0:0:0:0:101 Multicast address

Broadcasting Methods

Included in IPv6 are a number of new broadcasting methods:

1. Unicast
2. Multicast
3. Anycast

11.5 MULTISERVICE ACCESS TECHNOLOGIES

Multiservice networking is emerging as a strategically important issue for enterprise and public service provider infrastructures alike. The proposition of multiservice networking is the combination of all types of communications, all types of data, voice, and video over a single packet-cell-based infrastructure. The benefits of multiservice networking are reduced operational costs, higher performance, greater flexibility, integration and control, and faster new application and service deployment.

A key issue often confused in multiservice networking is the degree to which Layer 2 switching and services are mixed with Layer 3 switching and services. An intelligent multiservice network fully integrates both, taking advantage of the best of each; most multiservice offerings in the marketplace are primarily Layer 2 based, from traditional circuit switching technology suppliers.

The Importance of Voice Over IP

Of the key emerging technologies for data, voice, and video integration, voice over IP (Internet Protocol) is arguably very important. The most quality of service (QoS) sensitive of all traffic, voice is the true test of the engineering and quality of a network. Demand for Voice over IP is leading the movement for QoS in IP environments, and will ultimately lead to use of the Internet for fax, voice telephony, and video telephony services. Voice over IP will ultimately be a key component of the migration of telephony to the LAN infrastructure.

Significant advances in technology have been made over the past few years that enable the transmission of voice traffic over traditional public networks such as Frame Relay (Voice over Frame Relay) as well as Voice over the Internet through the efforts of the Voice over IP Forum and the Internet Engineering Task Force (IETF). Additionally, the support of Asynchronous Transfer Mode (ATM) for different traffic types and the ATM Forum's recent completion of the Voice and Telephony over ATM specification will quicken the availability of industry-standard solutions.

Packet Voice

All packet voice systems follow a common model. The packet voice transport network, which may be IP based, Frame Relay, or ATM, forms the traditional "cloud." At the edges of this network are devices or components that can be called *voice agents*. It is the mission of these devices to change the voice information from its traditional telephony form to a form suitable for packet transmission. The network then forwards the packet data to a voice agent serving the destination or called party.

This voice agent connection model shows that there are two issues in packet voice networking that must be explored to ensure that packet voice services meet user needs. The first issue is voice coding—how voice information is transformed into packets, and how the packets are used to re-create the voice. Another issue is the signalling associated with identifying who the calling party is trying to call and where the called party is in the network.

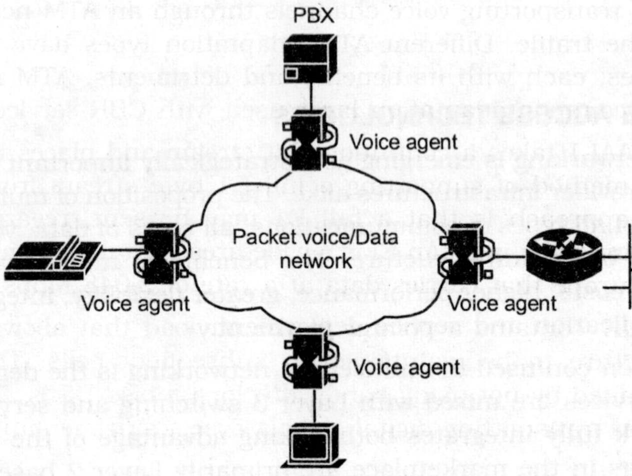

Figure 11.6 This Diagram Displays the Packet Voice Model

Packet Voice Transport

Integrating voice and data networks should include an evaluation of these three packet voice transport technologies:

1. Voice over ATM (VoATM)
2. Voice over Frame Relay (VoFR)
3. Voice over IP (VoIP)

There are two basic models for integrating voice over data-

1. transport and
2. translate.

Transport is the transparent support of voice over the existing data network. Simulation of tie lines over ATM using circuit emulation is a good example.

Translate is the translation of traditional voice functions by the data infrastructure. An example is the interpretation of voice signalling and the creation of Switched Virtual Circuits (SVCs) within ATM. Translate networking is more complex than transport networking, and its implementation is a current topic for many of the standards committees.

11.5.1 Voice Over ATM

The ATM Forum and the ITU have specified different classes of services to represent different possible traffic types for VoATM. Designed primarily for voice communications, Constant Bit Rate (CBR) and Variable Bit Rate (VBR) classes have provisions for passing real-time traffic and are suitable for guaranteeing a certain level of service. CBR, in particular, allows the amount of bandwidth, end-to-end delay, and delay variation to be specified during the call setup. Designed principally for bursty traffic, Unspecified Bit Rate (UBR) and available bit rate (ABR) are more suitable for data applications. UBR, in particular, makes no guarantees about the delivery of the data traffic.

The method of transporting voice channels through an ATM network is dependent on the nature of the traffic. Different ATM adaptation types have been developed for different traffic types, each with its benefits and detriments. ATM Adaptation Layer 1 (AAL1) is the most common adaptation layer used with CBR services.

Unstructured AAL1 takes a continuous bit stream and places it within ATM cells. This is a common method of supporting a full E1 byte stream from end to end. The problem with this approach is that a full E1 may be sent, regardless of the actual number of voice channels in use. (An EI is a wide-area digital transmission scheme used predominantly in Europe that carries data at a rate of 2.048 Mbps.)

Structured AAL1 contains a pointer in the payload that allows the digital signal level 0 (DS0) structure to be maintained in subsequent cells. This allows network efficiencies to be gained by not using bandwidth for unused DS0s. (A DS0 is a framing specification used in transmitting digital signals over a single channel at 64 kbps on a T1 facility.)

The remapping option allows the ATM network to terminate structured AAL1 cells and remap DS0s to the proper destinations. This eliminates the need for Permanent Virtual Circuits (PVCs) between every possible source/destination combination. The major difference from the above approach is that a PVC is not built across the network from edge to edge.

VOATM Signalling

In it voice signalling is carried through the network transparently. PVCs are created for both signalling and voice transport. First, a signalling message is carried transparently over the signaling PVC from end station to end station. Second, coordination between the end systems allow the selection of a PVC to carry the voice communication between end stations.

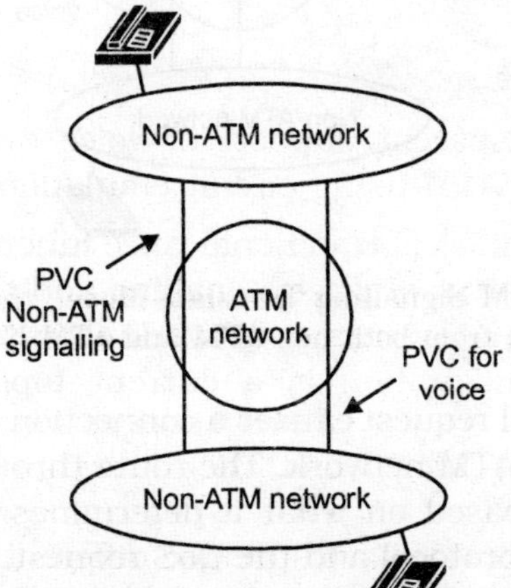

Figure 11.7 The VoATM Signalling Transport Model Describes the Transport Method, in which Voice Signalling is Carried through the Network Transparently

At no time is the ATM network participating in the interpretation of the signalling that takes place between end stations. However, as a value-added feature, some products are capable of understanding Channel Associated Signalling (CAS) and can prevent the sending of empty voice cells when the end stations are on-hook. In the translate model, the ATM network interprets the signalling from both non-ATM and ATM network devices. PVCs are created between the end stations and the ATM network. This contrasts with the previous model, in which the PVCs are carried transparently across the network.

A signalling request from an end station causes the ATM network to create an SVC with the appropriate QoS to the desired end station. The creation of an SVC versus the prior establishment of PVCs is clearly more advantageous for three reasons:

1. SVCs are more efficient users of bandwidth than PVCs.
2. QoS for connections do not need to be constant, as with PVCs.
3. The ability to switch calls within the network can lead to the elimination of the tandem Private Branch Exchange (PBX) and potentially the edge PBX. (A PBX is a digital or analog telephone switchboard located on the subscriber premises and used to connect private and public telephone networks.)

VOATM Routing

ATM uses a Private Network-to-Network Interface (PNNI), a hierarchical link-state routing protocol that is scalable for global usage. In addition to determining reachability and routing within an ATM network, it is also capable of call setup.

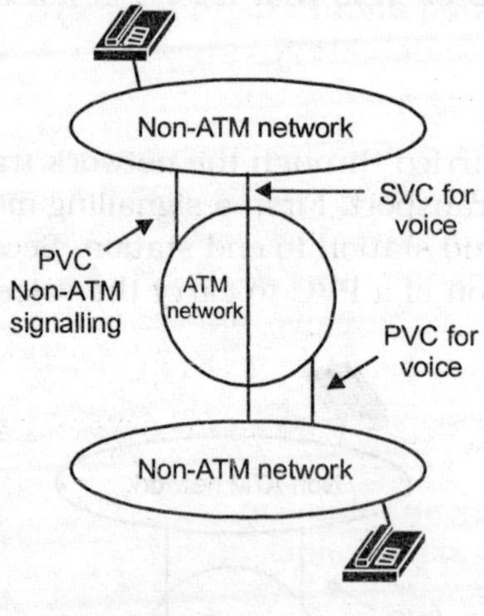

Figure 11.8 In the VoATM Signalling Translate Model, the ATM Network Interprets the Signalling from both non-ATM and ATM Network Devices

A Virtual Circuit (VC) call request causes a connection with certain QoS requirements to be requested through the ATM network. The route through the network is determined by the source ATM switch based on what it determines is the best path through the network, based on the PNNI protocol and the QoS request. Each switch along the path is checked to determine whether it has the appropriate resources for the connection.

When the connection is established, voice traffic flows between end stations as if a leased line existed between the two. This specification spells out routing in private networks. Within carrier networks, the switch-to-switch protocol is B-ICI. Current research and development of integrated non-ATM and ATM routing will yield new capabilities to build translate level voice and ATM networks.

11.5.2 Voice Over Frame Relay

Voice over Frame Relay enables a network to carry live voice traffic (for example, telephone calls and faxes) over a Frame Relay network. Frame Relay is a common and inexpensive transport that is provided by most of the large telcos.

VOFR Signalling

Historically, Frame Relay call setup has been proprietary by vendor. This has meant that products from different vendors would not interoperate. Frame Relay Forum FRF.11 establishes a standard for call setup, coding types, and packet formats for VoFR, and will provide the basis for interoperability between vendors in the future.

VOFR Addressing

Address mapping is handled through static tables-dialled digits mapped to specific PVCs. How voice is routed depends on which routing protocol is chosen to establish PVCs and the hardware used in the Frame Relay network. Routing can be based on bandwidth limits, hops, delay, or some combination, but most routing implementations are based on maximizing bandwidth utilization.

The two extremes for designing a VoFR network are

1. A full mesh of voice and data PVCs to minimize the number of network transit hops and maximize the ability to establish different QoS. A network designed in this fashion minimizes delay and improves voice quality, but represents the highest network cost.
2. Most Frame Relay providers charge based on the number of PVCs used. To reduce costs, both data and voice segments can be configured to use the same PVC, thereby reducing the number of PVCs required. In this design, the central site switch re-routes voice calls. This design has the potential of creating a transit hop when voice needs to go from one remote to another remote office. However, it avoids the compression and decompression that occurs when using a tandem PBX.

A number of mechanisms can minimize delay and delay variation on a Frame Relay network. The presence of long data frames on a low-speed Frame Relay link can cause unacceptable delays for time-sensitive voice frames. To reduce this problem, some vendors implement smaller frame sizes to help reduce delay and delay variation. FRF.12 proposes an industry standard approach to do this, so products from different vendors will be able to interoperate and consumers will know what type of voice quality to expect.

Methods for prioritizing voice frames over data frames also help reduce delay and delay variation. This, and the use of smaller frame sizes, are vendor-specific implementations. To ensure voice quality, the committed information rate (CIR) on each PVC should be set to ensure that voice frames are not discarded. Future Frame Relay networks will provide SVC signalling for call setup, and may also allow Frame Relay DTEs to request a QoS for a call. This will enhance VoFR quality in the future.

11.5.3 Voice Over IP

VoIP's appeal is based on its capability to facilitate voice and data convergence at an application layer. Increasingly, VoIP is being seen as the ideal last-mile solution for cable, DSL, and wireless networks because it allows service providers to bundle their offerings. VoIP also offers service providers the ability to provision standalone local loop bypass and long distance arbitrage services. To provide a VoIP solution, signaling, routing, and addressing must be addressed.

VOIP Signalling

VoIP signalling has three distinct areas: signalling from the PBX to the router, signalling between routers, and signalling from the router to the PBX. The corporate intranet appears as a trunk line to the PBX, which signals the corporate intranet to seize a trunk. Signalling from the PBX to the intranet may be any of the common signalling methods used to seize a trunk line, such as fax expansion module (FXS) or E&M signalling. In the future, digital signalling such as common channel signalling (CCS) or Q signaling (QSIG) will become available. The PBX then forwards the dialed digits to the router in the same manner in which the digits would be forwarded to a telco switch. Within the router the dial plan mapper maps the dialed digits to an IP address and signals a call establishment request to the remote peer that is indicated by the IP address. Meanwhile, the control channel is used to set up the Real-Time Control Protocol (RTCP) audio streams, and the Resource Reservation Protocol (RSVP) is used to request a guaranteed QoS.

When the remote router receives the call request, it signals a line seizure to the PBX. After the PBX acknowledges, the router forwards the dialled digits to the PBX and signals a call acknowledgement to the originating router. In connectionless network architectures such as IP, the responsibility for session establishment and signalling is with the end stations. To successfully emulate voice services across an IP network, enhancements to the signalling stacks are required.

For example, an H.323 agent is added to the router for standards-based support of the audio and signalling streams. The Q.931 protocol is used for call establishment and teardown between H.323 agents or end stations. RTCP is used to establish the audio channels themselves. A reliable session-oriented protocol, Transmission Control Protocol (TCP), is deployed between end stations to carry the signalling channels. Real-Time Transport Protocol (RTP), which is built on top of User Datagram Protocol (UDP), is used for transport of the real-time audio stream. RTP uses UDP as a transport mechanism because it has lower delay than TCP and because actual voice traffic, unlike data traffic or signalling, tolerates low levels of loss and cannot effectively exploit retransmission.

VOIP Addressing

An existing corporate intranet should have an IP addressing plan in place. To the IP numbering scheme, the voice interfaces appear as additional IP hosts, either as an extension of the existing scheme or with new IP addresses.

Translation of dial digits from the PBX to an IP host address is performed by the dial plan mapper. The destination telephone number, or some portion of the number, is mapped to the destination IP address. When the number is received from the PBX, the router compares the number to those mapped in the routing table. If a match is found, the call is routed to the IP host. After the connection is established, the corporate intranet connection is transparent to the subscriber.

VOIP Routing

One of the strengths of IP is the maturity and sophistication of its routing protocols. A modern routing protocol, such as Enhanced Interior Gateway Routing Protocol (EIGRP), is able to consider delay when calculating the best path. These are also fast converging routing protocols, which allow voice traffic to take advantage of the self-healing capabilities of IP networks. Advanced features, such as policy routing and access lists, make it possible to create highly sophisticated and secure routing schemes for voice traffic.

RSVP can be automatically invoked by VoIP gateways to ensure that voice traffic is able to use the best path through the network. This can include segments of arbitrary media, such as switched LANs or ATM networks. Some of the most interesting developments in IP routing are tag switching and other IP switching disciplines. Tag switching provides a way of extending IP routing, policy, and RSVP functionality over ATM and other high-speed transports. Another benefit of tag switching is its traffic engineering capabilities, which are needed for the efficient use of network resources. Traffic engineering can be used to shift traffic load based on different predicates, such as time of day.

VOIP and Delay

Routers and specifically IP networks offer some unique challenges in controlling delay and delay variation. Traditionally, IP traffic has been treated as "best effort," meaning that incoming IP traffic is allowed to be transmitted on a first-come, first-served basis. Packets have been variable in nature, allowing large file transfers to take advantage of the efficiency associated with larger packet sizes. These characteristics have contributed to large delays and large delay variations in packet delivery. RSVP allows network managers to reserve resources in the network by end station. The network manager can then allocate queues for different types of traffic, helping to reduce the delay and delay variation inherent in current IP networks.

The second part of supporting delay-sensitive voice traffic is to provide a means of prioritizing the traffic within the router network. RFC 1717 breaks down large packets into smaller packets at the link layer. This reduces the problems of queuing delay and delay variation by limiting the amount of time a voice packet must wait in order to gain access to the trunk.Weighted fair queuing, or priority queuing, allows the network to put different traffic types into specific QoS queues. This is designed to prioritize the transmittal of voice traffic over data traffic. This reduces the potential of queuing delay.

Applying Packet Voice

In today's networking, there are several attractive alternatives both to conventional public telephony and to leased lines. Among the most interesting are networking technologies based on a different kind of voice transmission, called packet voice. Packet voice appears to a network as data; thus it can be transported over networks normally reserved for data, where costs are often far less than in voice networks. Packet voice uses less transmission bandwidth than conventional voice, so more can be carried on a given connection. Whereas telephony requires as much as 64,000 bits per second (bps), packet voice often needs less than 10,000 bps. For many companies, there is sufficient reserve capacity on national and international data networks to transport considerable voice traffic, making voice essentially free.

Packet voice networks can be used in two broad contexts, differentiated by geography or by the types of users to be served. The economics and technology of the network may be unaffected by these factors, but there may be legal constraints in some areas for some combinations of these two contexts, and network users or operators should be aware of them.

Telecommunications is regulated within countries by national administrations, or arms of the governments, based on local regulations. In some countries, such as the United States, there may be multiple levels of regulatory authority. In all cases, treaties define the international connection rules, rates, and so forth. It is important for any business planning to use or build a packet voice network to ensure that it is operating in conformance with all laws and regulations in all the areas the network serves. This normally requires some direct research, but the current state of the regulations can be summarized as follows:

1. Within a national administration or telephony jurisdiction, it is almost always proper for a business to employ packet voice to support its own voice calling among its own sites. In such applications, it is normally expected that some of the calls transported on the packet voice network will have originated in the public phone network. Such outside calling over packet voice is uniformly tolerated in a regulatory sense, on the basis that the calls are from employees, customers, or suppliers and represent the company's business. When a packet voice connection is made between national administrations to support the activities of a single company—to connect two or more company locations in multiple countries—the application is uniformly tolerated in a regulatory sense.

In such a situation, an outside call placed from a public phone network in one country and terminated in a company site within another via packet voice may be a technical violation of national monopolies or treaties on long-distance service. Where such a call is between company employees or between employees and suppliers or customers, such a technical violation is unlikely to attract official notice. When a packet voice network is used to connect public calls within a company, the packet voice provider is technically providing a local or national telephone service and is subject to regulation as such.

When a packet voice network is used to connect public calls between countries, the packet voice provider is subject to the national regulations in the countries involved and also to any treaty provisions for international calling to which any of the countries served are signatories.

Thus, it is safe to say that companies could employ packet voice networking for any applications where traditional leased-line, PBX-to-PBX networking could be legally employed. In fact, a good model for deploying packet voice without additional concerns about regulatory matters is to duplicate an existing PBX trunk network or tie-line network using packet voice facilities.

If you regularly make long-distance phone calls, chances are you've already used **IP telephony** without even knowing it. IP telephony, known in the industry as **Voice-over IP (VoIP)**, is the transmission of telephone calls over a data network like one of the many networks that make up the Internet. While you probably have heard of VoIP, what you may not know is that many traditional telephone companies are already using it in the connections between their regional offices.

If you look at a typical phone conversation, much of this transmitted data is wasted. While you are talking, the other party is listening, which means that only half of the connection is in use at any given time.. Plus, a significant amount of the time in most conversations is **dead air** — for seconds at a time, neither party is talking. If we could remove these silent intervals, the file would be even smaller.

Data networks do not use circuit switching. Your Internet connection would be a lot slower if it maintained a constant connection to the Web page you were looking at. Instead of simply sending and retrieving data as you need it, the two computers involved in the connection would pass data back and forth the whole time, whether the data was useful or not. That's no way to set up an efficient data network. Instead, data networks use a method called **packet switching.**

Tiny Slices of Information

While circuit switching keeps the connection open and constant, packet switching opens the connection just long enough to send a small chunk of data, called a packet, from one system to another. What happens is this: The sending computer chops data into these small packets, with an address on each one telling the network where to send them. When the receiving computer gets the packets, it reassembles them into the original data.

Packet switching is very efficient. It minimizes the time that a connection is maintained between two systems, which reduces the load on the network. It also frees up the two computers communicating with each other so that they can accept information from other computers as well.

VoIP technology uses this packet-switching method to provide several advantages over circuit switching. For example, packet switching allows several telephone calls to occupy the amount of space occupied by only one in a circuit-switched network. Using PSTN, that 10-minute phone call consumed 10 full minutes of transmission time at a cost of 128 Kbps. With VoIP, that same call may have occupied only 3.5 minutes of transmission time at a cost of 64 Kbps, leaving another 64 Kbps free for that 3.5 minutes, plus an additional 128 Kbps for the remaining 6.5 minutes. Based on this simple estimate, another three or four calls could easily fit into the space used by a single call under the conventional system. And this example doesn't even factor in the use of data compression, which further reduces the size of each call.

Let's say that your company had equipment installed and a contract set up so that you can use VoIP. You have installed about a dozen telephones and a digital **private branch exchange** (PBX) in your office. A PBX is essentially a switch used to connect a number of phones (extensions) to each other and to one or more outside phone lines. In our example, the PBX is also a **gateway**

Gateways are used to connect devices on two different types of networks so that they can communicate with each other. Our PBX is a gateway because it converts the standard circuit-switched signal from each phone into digital data that can be sent over a packet-switched, IP-based network. **IP** stands for "Internet protocol," the language used by most data networks. Let's take another look at that typical telephone call, but this time using VoIP over a packet-switched network:

You pick up the receiver, which sends a signal to the PBX.

The PBX receives the signal and sends a dial tone. This lets you know that you have a connection to the PBX.

You dial the number of the party you wish to talk to. This number is then temporarily stored by the PBX.

Once you have entered the number, the PBX checks it to ensure that it is in a valid format.

The PBX determines whom to **map** the number to. In **mapping**, the number is attached to the IP address of another device called the **IP host.** The IP host is typically another digital PBX that is connected directly to the phone system of the number you dialled. In some cases, particularly if the party you are calling is using a computer-based VoIP client, the IP host is the system you wish to connect with.

A **session** is established between your company's PBX and the other party's IP host. This means that each system knows to expect packets of data from the other system. Each system must use the same protocol to communicate. The systems will implement two channels, one for each direction, as part of the session.

You talk for a period of time. During the conversation, your company's PBX and the other party's IP host transmit packets back and forth when there is data to be sent. The PBX at your end keeps the circuit open between itself and your phone extension while it forwards packets to and from the IP host at the other end.

You finish talking and hang up the receiver.

When you hang up, the circuit is closed between your phone and the PBX, freeing your line.

The PBX sends a signal to the IP host of the party you called that it is terminating the session. The IP host terminates the session at its end, too.

Once the session is terminated, the PBX removes the number-to-IP-host mapping from memory.

Probably one of the most compelling advantages of packet switching is that data networks already understand the technology. By migrating to this technology, telephone networks immediately gain the ability to communicate the way computers do. Of course, having the ability to communicate and understanding the methods of communication are two very different things. For telephones to communicate with each other and with other devices, such as computers, over a data network, they need to speak a common language called a **protocol.**

SIP and H.323

There are two major protocols being used for VoIP. Both protocols define ways for devices to connect to each other using VoIP. Also, they include specifications for audio **codecs.** A codec, which stands for **coder-decoder**, converts an audio signal into a compressed digital form for transmission and back into an uncompressed audio signal for replay.

The first protocol is **H.323**, a standard created by the **International Telecommunications Union** (ITU). **H.323** is a comprehensive and very complex protocol. It provides specifications for real-time, interactive videoconferencing, data sharing and audio applications such as IP telephony. Actually a suite of protocols, H.323 incorporates many individual protocols that have been developed for specific applications.

An alternative to H.323 emerged with the development of **Session Initiation Protocol (SIP)** under the auspices of the **Internet Engineering Task Force (IETF).** SIP is a much more streamlined protocol, developed specifically for IP telephony. Smaller and more efficient than H.323, SIP takes advantage of existing protocols to handle certain parts of the process. For example, **Media Gateway Control Protocol (MGCP)** is used by SIP to establish a gateway connecting to the PSTN system.

Calling Platforms

There are four ways that you might talk to someone using VoIP. If you've got a computer or a telephone, you can use at least one of these methods without buying any new equipment:

Computer-to-computer — You need software, a microphone, speakers, a sound card and an Internet connection, preferably a fast one like you would get through a cable or DSL modem. Computer-to-computer though has its issues since the telephone call is being placed by the computer must negotiate the computer's operating system, which in most cases it was not intended for.

Computer-to-telephone — This method allows you to call anyone (who has a phone) from your computer. Like computer-to-computer calling, it requires a software client.

Telephone-to-computer — A few companies are providing special numbers or calling cards that allow a standard telephone user to initiate a call to a computer user. The caveat is that the computer user must have the vendor's software installed and running on his or her computer.

Telephone-to-telephone — Through the use of Customer Premises Gateways, you can connect directly with any other standard telephone in the world. You enter the number you wish to call, and you are connected through an IP-based network.

11.6 DIAL-UP TECHNOLOGY

Dialup is simply the application of the Public Switched Telephone Network (PSTN) to carry data on behalf of the end user. It involves a customer premises equipment (CPE) device sending the telephone switch a phone number to direct a connection to. The AS3600, AS5200, AS5300, and AS5800 are all examples of routers that have the capability to run a PRI along with banks of digital modems. The AS2511, on the other hand, is an example of a router that communicates with external modems.

The carrier market has continued to grow, and there have been demands for higher modem densities. The answer to this need was a higher degree of interoperation with the telco equipment and the refinement of the digital modem: a modem capable of direct digital access to the PSTN. This has allowed the development of faster CPE modems that take advantage of the clarity of signal that the digital modems enjoy. The fact that the digital modems connecting into the PSTN through a PRI or a BRI can transmit data at more than 53 K using the V.90 communication standard attests to the success of the idea.

In 1979 the modulator-demodulator (modem) was introduced, and dialup networking was born. The early modems were slower and subject to proprietary communication schemes. Early uses of modems were for intermittent point-to-point WAN connections. Often, the call would come into a regular phone at a data center. An operator would hear modem tones and place the handset onto a special cradle that was the modem. In the late 1980s, the ITU-T began setting up V-series recommendations to standardize communications between both data communications equipment (DCE) and data terminal equipment (DTE). Early standards included these:

V.8—Standardized the method that modems use to initially determine the V-series modulation at which they will communicate. Note that this standard applies only to the communication session between the two DCE devices. This was later updated with V.8bis, which also specified some of the communication standards between the DTE devices going over the DCE's connection.

V.21, V.23, V.27ter, V.29—Defined 300, 600/1200, 2400/4800, and 9600 baud communications, respectively.

V.25, V.25bis, V.25ter—Served as a series of standards for automated dialling, answering, and control.

Modems increased greatly in sophistication in the late 1980s. This was due in part to the breakup of the Bell system in 1984. With the client premises equipment in the hands of free enterprise, competition spurred on the development of speedier connections. More recent standards include these:

V.32bis, V.34, V.90—Standardized 14400, 33600, and up to 56000 baud communication speeds.

V.110—Allowed an asynchronous DTE device to use an ISDN DCE (terminal adapter).

The first access servers were the AS2509 and the AS2511. The AS2509 could support 8 incoming connections using external modems, while the AS2511 could support 16. The AS5200 was introduced with 2 PRIs and could support 48 users using digital modems-this represented a major leap forward in technology. Modem densities have increased steadily, with the AS5300 supporting four and then eight PRIs. The AS5800 was later introduced to fill the needs of carrier class installations needing to handle dozens of incoming T1s and hundreds of user connections.

A couple of outdated technologies bear mentioning in a historical discussion of dialer technology. 56 Kflex is an older (pre-V.90) 56 K modem standard that was proposed by Rockwell. Cisco supports version 1.1 of the 56 Kflex standard on its internal modems, but it recommends migrating the CPE modems to V.90 as soon as possible. Another outdated technology is the AS5100. The AS5100 was a joint venture between Cisco and a modem manufacturer. The AS5100 was created as a way to increase modem density through the use of quad modem cards. It involved a group of AS2511s built as cards that were inserted into a backplane shared by quad modem cards, and a dual T1 card.

Today dialup is still used as an economical alternative (depending on the connection requirements) to dedicated connectivity. It has important uses as backup connectivity, in case the primary lines go down. Dialup also offers the flexibility to create dynamic connections as needed.

Dialup Connectivity Technology

This section provides information from various dialup options. Also included are advanced options for dialup connectivity and various dialup methods.

Plain Old Telephone Service

The regular phone lines used in voice calls are referred to as Plain old telephone service (POTS). They are ubiquitous, familiar, and easy to obtain; local calls are normally free of charge. This is the kind of service that the phone network was built on. Sounds carried over this service are sampled at a rate of 8000 times per second (using 8 bits per sample) in their conversion to digital signals so that sound can be carried on a 64 kbps channel at acceptable levels.

The encoding and decoding of voice is done by a piece of telco gear called a CODEC. The CODEC was needed to allow backward-compatibility with the old analog phones that were already in widespread use when the digital network was introduced. Thus, most phones found in the home are simple analog devices.

Dialup connectivity across POTS lines has historically been limited to about 33,600 bps via modem-often referred to as V.34 speeds. Recent improvements have increased the speed at which data can be sent from a digital source to a modem on a POTS line, but using POTS lines on both ends of the connection still results in V.34 connectivity in both directions.

Basic Rate Interface

Intended for home use, this application of ISDN uses the same copper as a POTS line, but it offers direct digital connectivity to the telephone network. A special piece of equipment known as a terminal adapter is required (although, depending on the country, it may be integrated into the router or DCE device). Always make sure to check—the plug used to connect to the wall socket looks the same whether it's the S/T or U demarcation point.

Normally, a Basic rate interface (BRI) interface has two B (bearer) channels to carry data, and one D (delta) channel to carry control and signalling information. Local telephone carriers may have different plans to suit local needs. Each B channel is a 64 K line. The individual 64 K channels of the telephone network are commonly referred to as digital service 0 (DS0). This is a common denominator regardless of the types of services offered, as will be shown later in this chapter.The BRI interface is a dedicated connection to the switch and will remain up even if no calls are placed.

T1/E1

The T1/E1 line is designed for use in businesses. T1 boasts 24 TDM channels run across a cable with 2 copper pairs. E1 offers 32 channels, although 1 is dedicated to frame synchronization. As is the case with the BRI, the T1/E1 connection goes directly into the telco switch. The connection is dedicated, so like a BRI, the T1/E1 remains connected and communicating to the switch all the time–even if there are no active calls. Each of the channels in the T1/E1 is just a B channel, which is to say that it's a 64-K DS0. The T1/E1 is also referred to as digital service 1 (DS1).

The North American T1 uses frames to define the timing between individual channels. For T1s, each frame has 24 9-bit channels (8 bits of data, 1 bit for framing). That adds up to 193 bits per frame. So, at 8000 of those per second, the T1 is carrying 1.544 Mbps between the switch and the customer premises equipment (CPE).

The E1 similarly uses frames for timing, but the E1 uses 32 8-bit channels for a 256-bit frame. Again at the 8000 Hz rate, the channel yields 2.048 Mbps of traffic between the switch and the CPE. Most of the world uses the E1.

Depending on the region, various line code and framing schemes will have to be used for the CPE and the switch to understand each other. For example, in North America, the encoding scheme most often seen is called binary 8 zero substitution (B8ZS), and the most common framing done is extended super frame (ESF). The telco through which the T1/E1 service is purchased must indicate which line code and framing should be used.

For dialup purposes, there are two types of T1/E1:

1. Primary Rate Interface (PRI) and
2. channel associated signalling (CAS).

PRI and CAS T1/E1s are normally seen in central locations that receive calls from remote sites or customers.

Primary Rate Interface

T1 Primary rate interface (PRI) service offers 23 B channels at 64 kbps at the cost of one D-channel (the 24th channel) for call signalling. Using NFAS to allow multiple PRIs to use a single D channel can minimize this disadvantage. E1 PRI service allows 30 channels, but it uses the 16th channel for ISDN signaling. The PRI service is an ISDN connection. It allows either voice-grade (modem) or true ISDN calls to be made and received through the T1/E1. This is the type of service most often seen in access servers because it fosters higher connection speeds.

Channel Associated Signalling

T1 Channel associated signalling (CAS) lines have 24 × 56K channels—part of each channel is borrowed for call signalling. This type of service is also called robbed-bit signalling. The E1 CAS still uses only the 16th channel for call signalling, but it uses the R2 international standard for analog call signals.

CAS is not an ISDN interface; it allows only analog calls to come into the access server. This is often done to allow an access server to work with a channel bank, and this scenario is seen more commonly in South America, Europe, and Asia.

MODEMS

From a terminology standpoint, a modem is considered data communication equipment (DCE), and the device using the modem is called data terminal equipment (DTE). As indicated earlier, modems must adhere to a number of communication standards to work with other modems: Bell103, Bell212A, V.21, V.22, V.22bis, V.23, V.32, V.32bis, V.FC, and V.34, to name a few.

Advances in access server technology have allowed the development of new standards to take advantage of better connectivity at the server end. These standards are X2, 56 Kflex, and V.90. X2 and 56 Kflex represent earlier proprietary standards that were made obsolete by V.90. The assumption made by all these standards is that the access server has digital connectivity to the telephone network.

Notice that the signal goes through only one analog conversion. Because the conversion is done on the client's side, traffic generated by the client modem is limited to V.34 speeds. The traffic coming from the access server is not subject to the noise problems that an analog conversion would introduce, so it can be sent at much higher speeds. Thus, the client can receive data at v.90 speeds but can send data at only V.34 speeds.

How does it really work?

Going from the DTE device, the data is sent through the UART, which handles buffering and flow control with the host. The data compressor passes the data to the packetizer, which puts a checksum on it and sends it on to the DSP. The packetizer also handles retransmits if the data doesn't get through to the other DCE. The data travels onward to the digital to analog processor, which pushes the data out the RJ11 jack to the phone line. Receiving data goes in the reverse process. In theory, V.90 modems could send data at 56 kbps, but because of limits placed on the phone lines by government agencies, 53 kbps is all that is currently possible.

PPP

PPP bears mentioning because it is so vital to the operation of dialup technologies. Until PPP came along in 1989, dialup protocols were specific to the protocol being used. To use multiple protocols, it was necessary to encapsulate any other protocols within packets of whatever protocol the dialup link was running. Many of the proprietary link methods (such as SLIP) didn't even have the capability to negotiate addressing. Fortunately, PPP does this and many more things with flexibility and extensibility. PPP connection establishment happens in three phases: Link Control Protocol (LCP), authentication, and Network Control Protocol (NCP).

LCP

LCP is the lowest layer of PPP. Because PPP does not follow a client/server model, both ends of the point-to-point connection must agree on the negotiated protocols. When negotiation begins, each of the peers wanting to establish a PPP connection must send a configure request (CONFREQ). Included in the CONFREQ are any options that are not the link default. These often include maximum receive unit, async control character map, authentication protocol, and the magic number. At this stage, the peers negotiate their authentication method and indicate whether they will support PPP multilink.

A Couple of Advanced Considerations

The Multilink Point-to-Point Protocol feature provides a load-balanced method for splitting and recombining packets to a single end system across a logical pipe (also called a bundle) formed by multiple links. Multilink PPP provides bandwidth on demand and reduces transmission latency across WAN connections. At the same time, it provides multivendor interoperability, packet fragmentation with proper sequencing, and load calculation on both inbound and outbound traffic. Multilink PPP works over the following interface types (single or multiple):

Asynchronous Serial Interfaces

1. BRIs
2. PRIs

Multichassis multilink PPP (MMP), on the other hand, provides the additional capability for links to terminate at multiple routers with different remote addresses. MMP can also handle both analog and digital traffic. This functionality is intended for situations in which there is a large pool of dial-in users, and a single access server cannot provide enough dial-in ports. MMP allows companies to provide a single dialup number to their users and to apply the same solution to analog and digital calls. This feature allows Internet service providers, for example, to allocate a single ISDN rotary number to several ISDN PRIs and not have to worry about whether a user's second link is on the same router. MMP does not require reconfiguration of telephone company switches.

AAA

Another technology that should be mentioned because of its importance is Authentication, Authorization, and Accounting (AAA). The protocols used in AAA can be either TACACS or RADIUS. These two protocols were developed in support of a centralized method to keep track of users and accesses made on a network. AAA is employed by setting up a server (or group of servers) to centrally administer the user database. Information such as the user's password, what address should be assigned to the user, and what protocols the user is allowed to run can be controlled and monitored from a single workstation. AAA also has powerful auditing capabilities that can be used to follow administratively important trends such as connection speeds and disconnect reasons. Any medium or large dialup installation should be using AAA, and it's not a bad idea for small shops, either.

What's a Dialer?

The term *dialer* has a few meanings, depending on the specifics of the configuration, but in general, it refers to the interface where the routing is actually happening. This is the interface that knows the address and phone number where the traffic is supposed to go. When looking at the routing table, the dialer interface should be the interface referenced for the next hop to reach the network on the other side. The dialer interface does not have to be the physical interface that is doing the dialing, but it can be made so by placing the configuration command **dialer in-band** in a physical interface. Thereafter, the interface becomes a dialer. For example, an async interface is not a dialer by default, but placing the configuration command **dialer in-band** in the async interface causes dialer behavior on that interface. For example, calls received by that async interface after applying the command will have an idle timeout applied to the connection from then on. An example of a physical interface that is also a dialer by default would be the BRI interface.

Beyond making physical interfaces into dialers, there are interfaces called dialer interfaces. These are logical interfaces that call upon real interfaces to place calls. The advantage of using a dialer interface is flexibility. A group of potential DDR links can share a handful of BRI interfaces. Dialer interface configuration comes in two flavors: dialer map-based (sometimes referred to as legacy DDR) and dialer profiles. Which method you use depends on the circumstances under which you need dial connectivity. Dialer map-based DDR was first introduced in IOS Version 9.0; dialer profiles were introduced in IOS Version 11.2.

Benefits and Drawbacks

The benefits of dialup are flexibility and **cost savings.** First, let's look at why flexibility is important. Intermittent connectivity is most often needed in mobile situations. A mobile workforce needs to be capable of connecting from wherever they are. Phone lines are normally available from wherever business is transacted, so a modem connection is the only reasonable choice for mobile users.

In long-distance situations, a user often dials into a local ISP and uses an IPSec-encrypted tunnel going back to a home gateway system that allows access to the rest of the corporate network. In this example, the phone call itself costs nothing, and an account with the local ISP could be significantly less expensive than the long-distance charges that would otherwise be incurred. As another example, a BRI attached at a central office located in an area that offers inexpensive rates on ISDN could have database servers configured to call out to other sites and exchange data periodically. Each site needs only one BRI line, which is significantly less expensive than dedicated links to each of the remote locations. Finally, in the case of a backup link, the savings are seen when the primary link goes down but business continues, albeit slower than normal.

Cost savings is a two-edged sword where dialup is concerned, however. The downside of a dialup line is that connection costs for a heavily used line are higher than the price of dedicated connectivity. Going over long distance raises the price even higher. There's also speed to consider. Dialup connectivity has a strong high-end bandwidth, particularly with the capability to tie channels together using PPP multilink, but dedicated connectivity through a serial port can outperform dialup connections.

Another consideration is **security.** Certainly, any PPP connection should be authenticated, but this presents anyone with the dialup number an opportunity to break into the system. A significant part of any dialup system's configuration concerns the capability to keep out unwanted guests. The good news is that it can be done, and AAA goes a long way toward dealing with this problem. However, it is a disadvantage to have potential intruders coming in through dialup lines.

11.7 GOPHER

In short, the Internet Gopher is a distributed document search and retrieval system. It combines the best features of browsing through collections of information and fully indexed databases. The protocol and software follow a client/server model and permit users on a heterogeneous mix of desktop systems to browse, search, and retrieve documents residing on multiple distributed server machines.

The reason for developing Gopher was the need for a campus-wide information system which enables anybody to be able to publish documents or information even with a small desktop computer. Gopher client software presents users with a hierarchy of items and directories much like a file system. In fact, the **Gopher interface** is designed to resemble a file system since a file system is a good model for locating documents and services. So if you are connected to a Gopher server you get a list of different items, similar to the display of a root directory from a PC. After selecting a menu item for example you get all the items included, similar to a subdirectory and so forth. If you select a file item for example the file is automatically transmitted and displayed at the client. It is not necessary for the file to reside on the same Gopher server where you got the information. A Gopher menu can include items from different Gopher servers and the user gets automatically connected to the server where the selected item points to and so on. The user does not know or care that the items up for selection may reside on many different machines anywhere on the Internet.

A simple example:

You would like to have a look at the menu of your canteen.

1. Start your Gopher client and connect to the main Gopher server.
2. Find an item which could include the menu and select it. For example: Facilities.
3. The sub-items of Facilities are displayed.
4. One of the items may be "Today's Menu" which is a file residing on the canteen's Gopher server.
5. If you select it your Gopher client automatically establishes a connection to the server pointed to in the item, retrieves and displays the file.

The path to the file could be very complex and Gopher servers around the world could be involved.

To implement the above mentioned hierarchy the Gopher client needs some information of the object type in order to display a file or a directory icon for example. The Gopher type is coded as a single digit at the beginning of each line. Following is a list of known Gopher types included :

- 0-Item is a file
- 1-Item is a directory
- 2-Item is a CSO (qi) phone-book server
- 3-Error
- 4-Item is a BinHexed Macintosh file
- 5-Item is a DOS binary archive of some sort
- 6-Item is a UNIX encoded file
- 7-Item is an Index-Search server

- 8-Item points to a text-based telnet session
- 9-Item is a binary file
- T-TN3270 connection
- s-Sound type. Data stream is a mulaw sound
- g-GIF type
- M-Item contains MIME data
- h-html type
- I-Image type
- i-"inline" text type.

Implementations

A Gopher client is implemented in OS/2 Warp V3.0 and Internet Connection V3.0 for Windows.

Veronica

As interesting as it can be to explore "Gopherspace", one day you might want to retrieve some information or a file from a Gopher server. The problem is how to get the right servers providing the information needed without calling up endless Gopher menus. Fortunately there is a way to make even Gophers easier to use.

This tool is called Veronica (Very Easy Rodent-Oriented Net-wide Index to Computerized Archives) and does for Gopherspace what *Archie* does for FTP sites. Veronica is a resource-discovery system providing access to information resources held on most (99% +) of the world's Gopher servers. In addition to native Gopher data, Veronica includes references to many resources provided by other types of information servers, such as WWW servers, usenet archives, and telnet-accessible information services.

Veronica queries are keyword-in-title searches. A simple query can be quite powerful because a large number of information servers are included in the index. Veronica is accessed through Gopher client software. A Veronica user submits a query (via a Gopher client) which may contain Boolean keyword expressions as well as special Veronica directives. The result of a Veronica search is a Gopher menu comprising information items whose titles contain the specified keywords. The results menu may be browsed like any other Gopher menu. In January 1995, 5057 Gopher servers were indexed. The index also includes items from approximately 5000 other servers, in cases where those servers are referenced on Gopher menus. These other servers include 3905 WWW servers and about 1000 TELNET-type services.

11.8 READY FAQS

1. *What are some ways of determine the IP address of my computer?*

Different operating systems use different ways of finding the IP address of the printer. Normally, you can view all information about your TCP/IP configuration by running some sort of configuration program. Here are some of the most common ways for the most common operating systems.

Windows NT:

Initiate a command prompt. Go to Start\Programs\Command Prompt. This will bring you to the old MS-DOS window. At the prompt, type "ipconfig". You will see your IP address and other TCP/IP configuration information.

Windows 9x:

Choose "Run" from the Windows Start menu. Type "winipcfg". You will see a GUI interface that you can use to view your TCP/IP configuration and IP address.

Windows 3.x:

There is no sure way of determining the IP address on a Windows 3.x host. If RPM 2.1.3 is currently installed and working, you can find the IP address by enabling "high detail" under "Network Logging" and restarting RPM. The log will now display the computer's current IP address.

UNIX:

From a command line, enter "ifconfig". This stands for interface configuration. This works on most UNIX systems.

2. How telephone works ?

Although we take it completely for granted, the telephone you have in your house is one of the most amazing devices ever created. If you want to talk to someone, all that you have to do is pick up the phone and dial a few digits. Instantly you are connected to that person and you can have a two-way conversation with him or her. The telephone network extends worldwide, so you can reach nearly anyone on the planet. When you compare that to the state of the world just 100 years ago, when it might have taken up to several weeks to get a one-way written message to someone, you realize just how amazing the telephone is!

The Telephone

Surprisingly, a telephone is one of the *simplest* devices you have in your house. It is so simple because the telephone connection to your house has not changed in nearly a century. If you have an antique phone from the 1920s, you could connect it to the wall jack in your house and it would work fine!

It only contains 3 parts and they are all simple:

1. A switch to connect and disconnect the phone from the network.
2. This switch is generally called the **hook switch.** It connects when you lift the handset. A speaker, which is generally a little 50 cent 8-ohm speaker of some sort
3. A microphone. In the past, telephone microphones have been as simple as carbon granules compressed between two thin metal plates. Sound waves from your voice compress and decompress the granules, changing the resistance of the granules and modulating the current flowing through the microphone.

That's it! You can dial this simple phone by rapidly tapping the hook switch—all telephone switches still recognize "pulse dialling" like this. If you pick the phone up and rapidly tap the switch hook 4 times, the phone company's switch will understand that you have dialled a 4, for example.

The only problem with the phone shown above is that when you talk you will hear your voice through the speaker. Most people find that annoying, so any real phone contains a device called a **duplex coil** or something functionally equivalent to block the sound of your own voice from reaching your ear. A modern telephone also includes a bell so it can ring and a touch-tone keypad and frequency generator. Still, it's pretty simple! In a modern phone there is an electronic microphone, amplifier and circuit to replace the carbon granules and loading coil. The mechanical bell is often replaced by a speaker and a circuit to generate a pleasant ringing tone. But a normal $6.95 telephone remains one of the simplest devices ever. Not only is a telephone a simple device, but the connection between you and the phone company is even simpler.

Your connection to the phone company consists of two copper wires. Usually they are red and green. The green wire is common, and the red wire supplies your phone with 6 to 12 volts DC at about 30 milliamps. If you think about a simple carbon granule microphone, all it is doing is modulating that current (letting more or less current through depending on how the sound waves compress and relax the granules), and the speaker at the other end "plays" that modulated signal. That's all there is to it!

Calling Someone on the Telephone Network

If you go back to the days of the manual switchboard, it is easy to understand how the larger phone system works. In the days of the manual switchboard, there was a pair of copper wires running from every house to a central office in the middle of town. The switchboard operator sat in front of a board with one jack for every pair of wires entering the office. Above each jack was a small light. A large battery supplied current through a resistor to each wire pair (in the same way you saw in the previous section). When someone picked up the handset on his or her telephone, the hook switch would complete the circuit and let current flow through wires between the house and the office. This would light the light bulb above that person's jack on the switchboard. The operator would connect his/her handset into that jack and ask who the person would like to talk to. The operator would then send a ring signal to the receiving party and wait for the party to pick up the phone. Once the receiving party picked up, the operator would connect the two people together in exactly the same way the simple intercom above was connected! It is that simple!

In a modern phone system the operator has been replaced by an electronic **switch.** When you pick up the phone, the switch senses the completion of your loop and it plays a **dial tone** sound so you know the switch and your phone is working. The dial tone sound is simply a combination of 350 hertz tone and a 440 hertz. You then dial the number using a touch-tone keypad. The different dialing sounds are made of pairs of tones, as shown here : If the number is busy, you hear a busy signal that is made up of a 480 hertz and a 620 hertz tone, with a cycle of 1/2 second on and 1/2 second off, like this:

Telephone Bandwidth

In order to allow more long-distance calls to be transmitted, the frequencies transmitted are limited to a **bandwidth** of about 3,000 hertz. All the frequencies in your voice below 400 hertz and above 3,400 hertz are eliminated. That's why someone's voice on a phone has a distinctive sound

The Telephone Network

The telephone network starts in your house. A pair of copper wires runs from a box at the road to a box (often called an "entrance bridge") at your house. From there the pair of wires is connected to each phone jack in your house (usually using red and green wires). If your house has two phone lines, then two separate pairs of copper wire run from the road to your house. The second pair is usually colored yellow and black inside your house.

Along the road runs a thick cable packed with 100 or more copper pairs. Depending on where you are located, this thick cable will run directly to the phone company's switch in your area, or it will run to a box about the size of a refrigerator that acts as a digital concentrator. The concentrator digitizes your voice at a sample rate of 8,000 samples per second and 8-bit resolution. It then combines your voice with hundreds of others and sends them all down a single wire (usually a coax cable or a fiber-optic cable) to the phone company office. Either way, your line connects into a **line card** at the switch so you can hear the dial tone when you pick up your phone.

If you are calling someone connected to the same office, then the switch simply creates a loop between your phone and the phone of the person you called. If it's a long-distance call, then your voice is digitized and combined with millions of other voices on the long-distance network. Your voice normally travels over a fiber-optic line to the office of the receiving party, but it may also be transmitted by satellite or by microwave towers.

In order to understand the computerized systems used today for routing, it is helpful to go back in time and look at how human beings once routed long distance calls. Think back to a time when a human being worked in a town's **central office.** The phone company would build the central office in the middle of town, and then run a pair of copper wires to every home. The operator would work in the central office. The operator would sit in front of a **switchboard,** and on this switchboard would be a collection of sockets—one socket for each of the phones in town. When you wanted to place a call:

You would pick up your phone.

- A light above your phone's socket would turn on.
- The operator would plug a jack into your socket and ask you whom you would like to talk to.
- The operator would then plug her jack into the receiving party's socket, send a ring signal down the line, and talk to the person who answered.
- The Operator would then plug a wire between your jack and the receiving party's jack to connect the two of you together.
- When the operator saw the lights go out above your jacks, they would remove the wire connecting the two sockets.

This was an incredibly simple system! To allow long distance calls in this simple system, the local phone company would add a line (or multiple lines) to connect to a **long distance office.** To make a long distance call to a person in this system, you would pick up your phone and tell the operator the long distance number of the person you are calling. Then:

- The operator would connect to one of the lines going to the long distance office.
- She would speak to the operator in the long distance office.
- The long distance operator would connect the local operator to another long distance office—the office for the area code of the person you are calling.
- The local would tell the long distance operator the number, and they would connect to another office.
- Eventually the local operator would be able to talk to the operator in the central office for the town that your calling party lives in.
- That operator would make a connection to you're calling party.
- Then the local operator would connect you to the long distance line, and you would be able to have your conversation.

As you can see, this system is still remarkably simple. Your call was patched together with direct, physical wires going from one office to the next. The long distance operator would keep track of the length of your call and create a billing record.

The first act of automation was to replace the local operator with a **mechanical switch.** When you placed a local call, the switch would connect you. To make a long distance call, you would dial "O" to speak to a human being, and the human being would connect the call through the long distance offices as before.

Computers allowed for the replacement of the long distance operators with computerized switches. The computers could create the connections and the billing records just like a human operator. Physical wires still connected you to the receiving party on each call, but the computer connected them together at each office. If, from Los Angeles, you dialled 1-212-555-1234 in New York, the 1 identified it as a long distance call, telling the local switch to connect to a long distance switch. The 212 told the long distance switch which long distance line to grab. Then the 555 told the long distance office in New York which local office to connect to. Then the local office would connect you to your party. The computers in each office would pass the number along to one another as digital data via data lines connected between the switches.

In today's world, there are two things that have changed:

- Physical wires no longer connect the offices together for each phone call. That system was incredibly expensive. Instead, a fiber optic line carries a digitized version of your voice. Your voice (along with thousands of others) becomes a stream of bytes flowing on a fiber optic line between offices. The difference in cost between "a pair of copper wires carrying a single conversation" and "a single fiber carrying thousands and thousands of conversations" is phenomenal.
- The phone company is no longer a monopoly. Instead, there are many different long distance and local carriers.

Today when you place a long distance call, the switch in the local office accesses a **database** that contains a record for each phone number connected to the switch. The database contains what's called a PIC code (Primary Interchange Carrier code), which indicates which long distance carrier you have chosen. [When you switch long distance carriers, this PIC code is what changes.] The switch looks up the PIC code for your number and then connects to a long distance switch for your long distance carrier. Your long distance carrier's switches route the call to the local carrier for your friend, and the local carrier completes the call to your friend.

SECTION A

DESCRIPTIVE QUESTIONS AND ANSWERS

Q. 1. *What is an Intranet ?*

Ans. An Intranet is the use of Internet technologies within an organization (or company) to achieve better results than the conventional means of data access and transfer. Intranet helps in cutting costs, easy and fast accessibility of day to day information.

Q. 2. *How is it different from "the" Internet ?*

Ans. Generally speaking an Intranet is different from an Internet in the following ways:

- Intranet is a network within the organization whereas Internet is a world wide network.
- Intranet has access to Internet but not vice-versa.

Q. 3. *How is an intranet solution better than a groupware solution ?*

Ans.
- cheaper
- versatile &
- flexible.

The bottom line difference between a WWW server and "collaborative" computing solutions such as Lotus Notes is design philosophy. Designed as a proprietary system in an area lacking widespread connectivity, Lotus Notes uses a proprietary database structure, which replicates data and does not provide quick access to remote databases.

Cheaper

The use of client browsers with one standard Window interface, offers the easy integration with other applications, such as electronic mail, faxes, calendaring, videoconferencing, and hot links within messages. As a single interface to a variety of information sources, the browser is cost-effective, highly efficient, and very easy to use.

Versatile

An Intranet server, eliminates the need to replicate database by providing users with easy access to source data. A single WWW server platform can support Internal and External applications for both internal information-sharing and external marketing on the Internet. Notes, on the other hand, is purely an internal application.

Flexible

The Intranet enables users to centralize their information resources in a single point-and-click environment-the browser-which is available on a variety of client platforms (PC, Mac, Unix,etc) Content can be easily accessed by browsers on any platform, in any location. With Notes, data distribution is in realtime, on an as-requested basis, over a public (or private) network.

Q. 4. *Is an Intranet faster than getting data over the Internet ?*

Ans. If the network is totally contained within a LAN, then you do get LAN speeds. *i.e.* the web server is connected via LAN to the client PC's. If you are connecting remote locations, and use the Internet as your backbone / transport, then your speed becomes dependent on the Internet itself, and the speeds by which you connect to it.

If performance is really the issue, you could also run your Intranet over private lines, such as frame relay. Then you can actually contract with the phone company for actual performance levels of speed. *i.e.* 56K, 256K, etc. Approximately Intranet operates at 10mbs-100mbs internal and 28.8k for remote access employees. After working for hours on the Intranet, the Internet is painfully slow at 28.8k or 14.4k from home. You WILL be surprised at the difference client machine speed makes on Intranet LAN-based access.It is not network bandwidth always, client speed very important!

Q. 5. *Can you setup an Intranet without a TCP/IP connection ? HOW ?*

Ans. If you are running Netscape Navigator to review how the pages look on my local machine try using a freeware dll file called mozilla.dll

You can perfectly be using the Netscape web browser links that reference local files. Instead of being a link like "http://www.foobar.com/index.shtmll" you get a link that looks like "file:\\c:\website\index.shtml". All links, references to graphics files, and everything else works fine. This would not necessarily apply to interactive features that use cgi scripts, java, etc. (although there might be a way to get these to work also).Consequently, it would seem that using this approach, you could set up a basic Intranet without webserver software, and without running tcp/ip stacks. Just put all the html files up on the Novell server, make sure that everybody's drives are mapped to a common standard , outfit all the clients with Netscape and Mozilla, and you've got a basic Intranet. If you want to do fancy java scripts, forms using cgi, etc., this might not work.

Q. 6. *Can you setup an Intranet without a Web server ?*

Ans. Yes. You can have your web browser point to the html files stored on a local drive. However you would probably need a server for more dynamic applications like forms, cgi, java etc.

Q. 7. *What is a firewall ? Where can i get more info on firewalls ?*

Ans. A firewall is any one of several ways of protecting one network from another untrusted network. The actual mechanism whereby this is accomplished varies widely, but in principle, the firewall can be thought of as a pair of mechanisms: one which exists to block traffic, and the other which exists to permit traffic. Some firewalls place a greater emphasis on blocking traffic, while others emphasize permitting traffic.

Q. 8. *What are the hardware and software components of an Intranet ?*

Ans. Intranet server hardware :

- intranet server software:
- tcp/ip stack
- browser/s
- firewall

advanced components :

- Hot Java
- Perl
- Shockwave

Q. 9. *Can I run an Intranet on a Novell Netware based network ?*

Ans. Yes. A simple setup can involve simple placing all your html files on a shared network drive and having your users point their browsers to this directory. ex. f:\intranet\home.htm If you need to support more advanced applications based in CGI, Java etc you will need to setup a web server. This can be TCP/IP based server. You can get Novells Web Server (link to www.novell.com) or any one of the servers available in the market.

Q. 10. *Is an Intranet simply a type of client-server system ?*

Ans. Loosely defined Yes. You can also interpret an Intranet solution as being a superset of client server systems. Some people refer to an Intranet solution as a "thin" client based client server system. Yet others say Intranets are client-server systems done right. Take your pick

Q.11. *What convention should we use for assigning IP addresses on an Intranet?*

Ans. The official document from Internic on conventions for assignment of IP addresses for Intranets.

Q.12. *What is an Extranet? How this is any different from intranet ?*

Ans. Loosely defined, an extranet is an intranet extended beyond the corporate boundaries. When selective access is provided to entities outside the organization and intranet becomes an extranet. For ex. if your company allows its suppliers, clients etc. to have access to your intranet, its an extranet. Access would of course be restricted by security means like :

- userids and passwords,
- encryption techniques etc.

Q. 13. *Security on intranets. Other than server authentication, what methods are there for restricting access to pages on an intranet?*

Ans. You can setup a CGI script to do authentication before the same CGI script serves the page to a user. Other than the CGI script and the server itself, a firewall can do authentication before allowing a user to get to the web server. The firewall method can't restrict which pages, just which servers.

Q. 14. *Intranet & Internet. Can an Intranet be designed entirely within the Internet* *with only password protected pages, or firewalls, separating the intranet from the internet? Or is a simple intranet network better?*

Ans. Yes, intranets and the internet can certainly coexist. In fact theoretically your entire intranet could be located at a remote site and your users can access the data using secure links. Cutting off your intranet from the outside world physically has its own advantages. The main advantage being a higher level of security. The down side is that if your organization has remote locations you will have to figure out some way of letting them in.

Q. 15. *What is VPI and VCI ?*

Ans. ATM is a connection orientated protocol and as such there is a connection identifier in every cell header which explicitly associates a cell with a given virtual channel on a physical link. The connection identifier consists of two sub-fields :

- the Virtual Channel Identifier (VCI) and
- the Virtual Path Identifier (VPI).

Together they are used in multiplexing, demultiplexing and switching a cell through the network. VCIs and VPIs are not addresses. They are explicitly assigned at each segment (link between ATM nodes) of a connection when a connection is established, and remain for the duration of the connection. Using the VCI/VPI the ATM layer can asynchronously interleave (multiplex) cells from multiple connections.

Q. 16. *How come an ATM cell is 53 bytes anyway?*

Ans. ATM cells are standardized at 53 bytes because it seemed like a good idea at the time! As it turns out, during the standardization process a conflict arose within the CCITT as to the payload size within an ATM cell. The US wanted 64 byte payloads because it was felt optimal for US networks. The Europeans and Japanese wanted 32 payloads because it was optimal for them. In the end 48 bytes was chosen as a compromise. So 48 bytes payload plus 5 bytes header is 53 bytes total.

The two positions were not chosen for similar applications however. US proposed 64 bytes taking into consideration bandwidth utilization for data networks and efficient memory transfer (length of payload should be a power of 2 or at least a multiple of 4). 64 bytes fit both requirements.

Europe proposed 32 bytes taking voice applications into consideration. At cell sizes >= 152, there is a talker echo problem. Cell sizes between 32-152 result in listener echo. Cell sizes <= 32 overcome both problems, under ideal conditions.

CCITT chose 48 bytes as a compromise. As far as the header goes, 10% of payload was perceived as an upper bound on the acceptable overhead, so 5 bytes was chosen.

Q. 17. *How does AAL5 work?*

Ans. Here is a very simplified view of AAL5 and AALs in general. AAL5 is a mechanism for segmentation and reassembly of packets. That is, it is a rulebook which sender and receiver agree upon for taking a long packet and dividing it up into cells. The sender's job is to segment the packet and build the set of cells to be sent. The receiver's job is to verify that the packet has been received intact without errors and to put it back together again.

Q. 18. *What is a DXI?*

Ans. The ATM DXI (Data Exchange Interface)is basically the functional equivalent of the SMDS DXI. Routers will handle frames and packets but not typically fragment them into cells; DSUs will fragment frames into cells as the information is mapped to the digital transmission facility.

The DXI, then, provides the standard interface between routers and DSUs without requiring a bunch of proprietary agreements. The SMDS DXI is simple 'cause the router does the frame (SMDS level 3) and the DSU does the cells (SMDS level 2). The ATM DXI is a little more complicated since it has to accommodate AAL3/4 and/or AAL5 (possibly concurrently).

Q. 19. *What is Goodput?*

Ans. When ATM is used to transport cells originating from higher-level protocols (HLP), an important consideration is the impact of ATM cell loss on that protocol or at least the segmentation processs. ATM cell loss can cause the effective throughput of some HLPs to be arbitrarily poor depending on ATM switch buffer size, HLP congestion control mechanisms, and packet size.

This occurs because during congestion for example, and ATM switch buffer can overflow which will cause cells to be dropped from multiple packets, running each such packet. The preceding and the remaining cells from such packets, which are ultimately discarded by the frame reassembly process in the receiver, are nevertheless transmitted on an already congested link, thus wasting valuable link bandwidth. The traffic represented by these "bad" cells may be termed as BADPUT. Correspondingly, the effective throughput, as determined by those cells which are successfully recombined at the receiver, can be termed as GOODPUT.

Q. 20. *Information about the classical IP over ATM approach.*

Ans. RFC1483 defines the encapsulation of IP datagrams directly in AAL5.Classical IP and ARP over ATM, defined in RFC1577, is targetted towards making IP run over ATM in the most efficient manner utilizing as many of the facilities of ATM as possible. It considers the application of ATM as a direct replacement for the "wires" and local LAN segments connection IP end-stations and routers operating in the "classical" LAN-based paradigm. A comprehensive document, RFC1577 defines the ATMARP protocol for logical IP subnets (LISs). Within an LIS, IP addresses map directly into ATM Forum UNI 3.0 addresses. For communicating out a LIS, an IP router must be used - following the classical IP routing mode.

Q. 21. *Are ATM cells delivered in order?*

Ans. Yes. The ATM standards specify that all ATM cells will be delivered in order. Any switch and adaptation equipment design must take this into consideration.

Q. 22. *What kind of technology is frame relay?*

Ans. Packet-switched technology.

Q. 23. *Name the two kinds of packet-switching techniques discussed in this chapter, and briefly describe each.*

Ans. In variable-length switching, variable-length packets are switched between various network segments to best use network resources until the final destination is reached. 2. Statistical multiplexing techniques essentially use network resources in a more efficient way.

Q. 24. *Describe the difference between SVCs and PVCs.*

Ans. A SVC, switched virtual circuit, is created for each data transfer and is terminated when the data transfer is complete. PVC, permanent virtual circuit, is a permanent network connection that does not terminate when the transfer of data is complete. Previously not widely supported by Frame Relay equipment, SVCs are now used in many of today's networks.

Q. 25. *What is the data-link connection identifier (DLCI)?*

Ans. The DLCI is a value assigned to each virtual circuit and DTE device connection point in the Frame Relay WAN. Two different connections can be assigned the same value within the same Frame Relay WAN-one on each side of the virtual connection.

Q. 26. *Describe how LMI frame relay differs from basic frame relay.*

Ans. LMI Frame Relay adds a set of enhancements, referred to as extensions, to basic Frame Relay. Key LMI extensions provide the following functionality: global addressing, virtual circuit status messages, and multicasting.

Q. 27. *Can an Intranet be designed entirely within the Internet with only password protected pages, or firewalls, separating the intranet from the internet? Or is a simple intranet network better?*

Ans. Yes, intranets and the internet can certainly coexist. In fact theoretically your entire intranet could be located at a remote site and your users can access the data using secure links. Cutting off your intranet from the outside world physically has its own advantages. The main advantage being a higher level of security. The down side is that if your organization has remote locations you will have to figure out some way of letting them in.

Q. 28. *What is client-server computing?*

Ans. Client/server is a computational architecture that involves client processes requesting service from server processes. Client/server computing is the logical extension of modular programming. Modular programming has as its fundamental assumption that separation of a large piece of software into its constituent parts ("modules") creates the possibility for easier development and better maintainability. Client/server computing takes this a step farther by recognizing that those modules need not all be executed within the same memory space. With this architecture, the calling module becomes the "client" (that which requests a service), and the called module becomes the "server" (that which provides the service). The logical extension of this is to have clients and servers running on the appropriate hardware and software platforms for their functions. For example, database management system servers running on platforms specially designed and configured to perform queries, or file servers running on platforms with special elements for managing files.It is this latter perspective that has created the widely-believed myth that client/server has something to do with PCs or Unix machines.

Q. 29. *What is a client process?*

Ans. The client is a process (program) that sends a message to a server process (program), requesting that the server perform a task (service). Client programs usually manage the user-interface portion of the application, validate data entered by the user, dispatch requests to server programs, and sometimes execute business logic. The client-based process is the front- end of the application that the user sees and interacts with. The client process contains solution-specific logic and provides the interface between the user and the rest of the application system. The client process also manages the local resources that the user interacts with such as the monitor, keyboard, workstation CPU and peripherals. One of the key elements of a client workstation is the graphical user interface (GUI). Normally a part of operating system *i.e.* the window manager detects user actions, manages the windows on the display and displays the data in the windows.

Q. 30. *What is a server process?*

Ans. A server process (program) fulfils the client request by performing the task requested. Server programs generally receive requests from client programs, execute database retrieval and updates, manage data integrity and dispatch responses to client requests. Sometimes server programs execute common or complex business logic. The server-based process "may" run on another machine on the network. This server could be the host operating system or network file server; the server is then provided both file system services and application services. Or in some cases, another desktop machine provides the application services. The server process acts as a software engine that manages shared resources such as databases, printers, communication links, or high powered-processors. The server process performs the back-end tasks that are common to similar applications.

Q. 31. *What is a two-tier architecture?*

Ans. A two-tier architecture is where a client talks directly to a server, with no intervening server. It is typically used in small environments (less than 50 users). A common error in client/server development is to prototype an application in a small, two-tier environment, and then scale up by simply adding more users to the server. This approach will usually result in an ineffective system, as the server becomes overwhelmed. To properly scale to hundreds or thousands of users, it is usually necessary to move to a three-tier architecture.

Q. 32. *What is a three-tier architecture?*

Ans. A three-tier architecture introduces a server (or an "agent") between the client and the server. The role of the agent is manyfold. It can provide translation services (as in adapting a legacy application on a mainframe to a client/server environment), metering services (as in acting as a transaction monitor to limit the number of simultaneous requests to a given server), or intelligent agent services (as in mapping a request to a number of different servers, collating the results, and returning a single response to the client.

Q. 33. *Shouldn't all 10Base-T networks just be upgraded to 100 Mbps? Why or why not?*

Ans. Not necessarily-if the current 10Base-T network is repeater-based, replacing the repeaters with 10/100 nonsaturating switches would result in an automatic *n* times increase in the average available bandwidth for each end station.

Q. 34. *Which 100Base version(s) are recommended? Why?*

Ans. 100Base-TX is recommended if the horizontal wiring is Category5 or better UTP. If the horizontal cabling is Category 3, 100BaseT4 can be used, but it may be difficult to acquire (some reports indicate that because 100Base-TX was available more than a year before T4, it captured as much as 95 percent of the market). 100Base-T2 is not available.

Q. 35. *Which 1000Base version(s) are recommended? Where would they be used?*

Ans. 1000Base-T, is recommended if the horizontal cabling is Category 5 or better UTP. 1000Base-SX can be used if the horizontal cabling is multimode optical fiber, as well as for some multimode backbones. 1000Base-LX can be used for either single-mode or multimode optical fiber. 1000Base-CX can be used for short-haul equipment-room jumpers up to 25 meters.

Q. 36. *What cable types should be used for new networks? For upgrading existing networks? Why?*

Ans. New or replacement UTP links may be Category 5E or better to allow for data rate growth to 1000 Mbps. Multimode fiber may be used as indicated in Table 7-5 for 1000Base-SX. (These fibers will also provide future support for shorter distances [between 100 and 300 meters, depending on the wavelength] at 10,000 Mbps.) To be truly future-proof and to ensure that you will be able to operate longer-distance backbones, choose single-mode fiber.

Q. 37. *How do you know when a network needs to be upgraded? Where do you start?*

Ans. There are several ways:

- Your users will tell you (but often only after they have crossed the frustration threshold).
- Your network management system should be capable of indicating the load characteristics for each DCE port.
- Your organization is considering adding new applications (such as multimedia) that will require more communication bandwidth.
- Your organization is growing, and there are not sufficient DCE ports in the right locations to accommodate the additional users.

After you have determined the need, you can consider the options. Remember that the network elements with the longest useful life (the link media, followed by the network servers and network switches) can also be the most expensive to replace. Choose with an eye to future growth, and consider reusing these elements wherever possible.

Q. 38. *What three frame types does a transparent bridge flood?*

Ans. Transparent bridges flood unknown unicast frames (where the bridge has no entry in its table for the destination MAC address), broadcast frames, and mulitcast frames.

Q. 39. *How does a bridge learn the relative location of a workstation?*

Ans. A bridge learns about the direction to send frames to reach a station by building a bridge table. The bridge builds the table by observing the source MAC address of each frame that it receives and associating that address with the received port.

Q. 40. *What two bridge PDUs does a transparent bridge generate, and what are they used for?*

Ans. Transparent bridges create either a configuration PDU or a topology-change PDU. Configuration PDUs help bridges learn about the network topology so that loops may be eliminated. Topology-change PDUs enable bridges to relearn the network topology whenever a significant change occurs when a segment may no longer have connectivity or when a new loop is created.

Q. 41. *What is the difference between forwarding and flooding?*

Ans. Bridges forward frames out a single interface whenever the bridge knows that the destination is on a different port than the source. On the other hand, bridges flood whenever the bridge does not know where the destination is located.

Q. 42. *After bridges determine the spanning-tree topology, they will take on various roles and configure ports into various modes. Specifically, the roles are root and designated bridges, and the modes are designated ports and root ports. If there are 10 bridges and 11 segments, how many of each are there in the broadcast domain?*

Ans. There is one and only one root bridge in a broadcast domain, and all other bridges are designated bridges. Therefore, there is one root bridge and nine designated bridges. There must be one designated port for each segment, so there are ten. Each bridge, except the root, must have one and only one root port. Therefore there are nine root ports.

Q. 43. *Describe a basic difference between transparent bridges and source-route bridges relative to the forwarding processes.*

Ans. In a transparent bridged environment, bridges determine whether a frame needs to be forwarded, and through what path based upon local bridge tables. In an SRB network, the source device prescribes the route to the destination and indicates the desired path in the RIF.

Q. 44. *Recall that the SRB standards do not specify how a source selects a path to the destination whenever multiple choices exist. The chapter listed four methods that a source could use to make the decision and said that the first received frame (path) was the most commonly used method. What assumptions might the source make about the network when using this method?*

Ans. The source may assume that the frame arrived first because of more bandwidth on the links, less congestion in the system, and less latency in the bridge equipment. Therefore, this may be a preferred route over the other choices.

Q. 45. *How do stations and bridges know if there is a source route defined in the frame?*

Ans. By the value of the RII bit. The RII is set if there is a RIF included in the frame.

Q. 46. *What problems might you anticipate in a large SRB network with many alternate paths?*

Ans. With this network topology, many explorer frames may propagate throughout the network. Because explorers are broadcast frames, they consume bandwidth throughout the entire broadcast domain and consume CPU cycles within end stations.

Q. 47. *Because only 4 bits are used to define bridge numbers, does this mean that there can be only 16 bridges (2^4=16)? Why or why not?*

Ans. No. This means only that there can be no more than 16 bridges in parallel between the same two adjacent rings.

Q. 48. *Can you have a large number of bridges attached to a central ring, all with the same bridge value?*

Ans. Yes, as long as none of the bridges directly interconnects the same two rings.

Q. 49. *A 12-bit value defines ring numbers. Can you have more than 4096 rings in the network (2^{12}=4096)? Why or why not?*

Ans. No, you cannot, because this value defines the total number of rings. Each ring number must be unique in the network.

Q. 50. *Describe the process of routing packets.*

Ans. Routing is the act of moving information across an internetwork from a source to a destination.

Q. 51. *What are some routing algorithm types?*

Ans. Static, dynamic, flat, hierarchical, host-intelligent, router-intelligent, intradomain, interdomain, link-state, and distance vector.

Q. 52. *Describe the difference between static and dynamic routing.*

Ans. Static routing is configured by the network administrator and is not capable of adjusting to changes in the network without network administrator intervention. Dynamic routing adjusts to changing network circumstances by analyzing incoming routing update messages without administrator intervention.

Q. 53. *Name the benefits of using IGRP instead of RIP.*

Ans. Despite its enduring success as an Interior Gateway Routing Protocol, RIP suffers from fundamental limitations that are not easily avoided. For example, it (and the subsequent RIPv2) is limited to a maximum of 16 hops per route. This tends to limit the size and complexity of a network that can be effectively routed with RIP. Other RIP limitations include its support for only equal-cost load balancing and its single, simple routing metric (hop count). IGRP was specifically designed to offer an alternative to RIP that was as easy to implement and administer as RIP, yet that did not suffer from these fundamental limitations.

Q. 54. *How can an administrator influence route selection?*

Ans. A network administrator can accept IGRP's default settings or can fine-tune network performance by manipulating any of IGRP's four routing metrics or their constant weights. These mathematical components of IGRP's composite routing metric offer remarkable latitude to network administrators by enabling them to emphasize or de-emphasize delay, link speed, historical reliability, or load levels in the selection of optimal routes.

Q. 55. *What is variance, and how does it affect multipath routing?*

Ans. Variance is another value that can be established and modified by a network administrator to fine-tune an IGRP network. In essence, variance enables a range of routing costs to be used to select multiple redundant paths of unequal cost to any given destination. Thus, variance is the mechanism by which IGRP supports unequal-cost load balancing.

Q. 56. *Identify and explain IGRP's stability features.*

Ans. IGRP uses holddowns, split horizons, and poison-reverse updates to improve operational stability. Holddowns prevent IGRP's interval updates from wrongly reinstating an invalid route. Split horizons help prevent routing loops by preventing a router from updating neighbors of any routing changes that it originally learned from those neighbors. Poison-reverse updates function similarly but are not limited to use between adjacent routers. Thus, they prevent large routing loops from occurring between nonadjacent routers.

Q. 57. *What timers are used by IGRP, and what is their function?*

Ans. IGRP features several functionally distinct timers, including an update timer, an invalid timer, a hold-time period, and a flush timer. The *update* timer specifies how frequently routing update messages should be sent. The *invalid* timer specifies how long a router should wait in the absence of routing-update messages about a specific route before declaring that route invalid. The *hold-time variable* specifies the holddown period. Finally, the *flush* timer indicates how much time should pass before a route should be flushed from the routing table.

Q. 58. *Name RIP's various stability features.*

Ans. RIP has numerous stability features, the most obvious of which is RIP's maximum hop count. By placing a finite limit on the number of hops that a route can take, routing loops are discouraged, if not completely eliminated. Other stability features include its various timing mechanisms that help ensure that the routing table contains only valid routes, as well as split horizon and holddown mechanisms that prevent incorrect routing information from being disseminated throughout the network.

Q. 59. *What is the purpose of the timeout timer?*

Ans. The timeout timer is used to help purge invalid routes from a RIP node. Routes that aren't refreshed for a given period of time are likely invalid because of some change in the network. Thus, RIP maintains a timeout timer for each known route. When a route's timeout timer expires, the route is marked invalid but is retained in the table until the route-flush timer expires.

Q. 60. *What two capabilities are supported by RIP 2 but not RIP?*

Ans. RIP 2 enables the use of a simple authentication mechanism to secure table updates. More importantly, RIP 2 supports subnet masks, a critical feature that is not available in RIP.

Q. 61. *What is the maximum network diameter of a RIP network?*

Ans. A RIP network's maximum diameter is 15 hops. RIP can count to 16, but that value is considered an error condition rather than a valid hop count.

Q. 62. *When using OSPF, can you have two areas attached to each other where only one AS has an interface in Area 0?*

Ans. Yes, you can. This describes the use of a virtual path. One area has an interface in Area 0 (legal), and the other AS is brought up and attached off an ABR in Area 1, so we'll call it Area 2. Area 2 has no interface in Area 0, so it must have a virtual path to Area 0 through Area 1. When this is in place, Area 2 looks like it is directly connected to Area 0. When Area 1 wants to send packets to Area 2, it must send them to Area 0, which in turn redirects them back through Area 1 using the virtual path to Area 2.

Q. 63. *Area 0 contains five routers (A, B, C, D, and E), and Area 1 contains three routers (R, S, and T). What routers does Router T know exists? Router S is the ABR.*

Ans. Router T knows about routers R and S only. Likewise, Router S only knows about R and T, as well as routers to the ABR in Area 0. The AS's separate the areas so that router updates contain only information needed for that AS.

Q. 64. *Name the four key technologies that are used by EIGRP.*

Ans. EIGRP employs four key technologies, including neighbor discover/recovery, Reliable Transport Protocol (RTP), Diffusing Update ALgorithm (DUAL) finite-state machine, and a modular architecture that enables support for new protocols to be easily added to an existing network.

Q. 65. *Explain why EIGRP is more efficient in operation than IGRP.*

Ans. Unlike most other distance vector routing protocols, EIGRP does not mandate a periodic update of routing tables between neighboring routers. Instead, it employs a neighbor discovery/recovery mechanism to ensure that neighbors remain aware of each other's accessibility. As long as a router receives periodic hello packets from its neighbors, it can assume that those neighbors remain functional. More importantly, it can assume that all of its routes that rely upon passage through those neighbors remain usable. Thus, EIGRP is much more efficient than conventional distance vector routing protocols because it imposes much less overhead on routers and transmission facilities during normal operation.

Q. 66. *How does RTP enable improved convergence times?*

Ans. RTP is responsible for providing guaranteed delivery of EIGRP packets between neighboring routers. However, not all of the EIGRP packets that neighbors exchange must be sent reliably. Some packets, such as hello packets, can be sent unreliably. More importantly, they can be multicast rather than having separate datagrams with essentially the same payload being discretely addressed and sent to individual routers. This helps an EIGRP network converge quickly, even when its links are of varying speeds.

Q. 67. *Why does EIGRP tag certain routes?*

Ans. EIGRP supports both internal and external routes. Routes that are internal to an AS are completely contained within that AS. External routes are those that are learned from neighbors that lie outside the AS. External routes are tagged with information that identifies their origin. This enables a network administrator to develop customized interdomain routing policies.

Q. 68. *Can IBGP be used in place of an IGP (RIP, IGRP, EIGRP, OSPF, or ISIS)?*

Ans. Yes and no. Remember that the next-hop information from EBGP is carried into IBGP. If IBGP does not have a route to reach the next hop, then the route will be discarded. Typically an IGP needs to be used to exchange routes to the next hop, but this can be achieved by using static routes on all the routers running IBGP. So, the answer is yes if you want to use and maintain static routes. Otherwise, the answer is no.

Q. 69. *Assume that a BGP router is learning the same route from two different EBGP peers. The AS_path information from peer 1 is {2345,86,51}, and the AS_path information from peer 2 is {2346,51}. What BGP attributes could be adjusted to force the router to prefer the route advertised by peer1?*

Ans. Weight and local preference. Both have a higher preference than AS path length.

Q. 70. *Can BGP be used only by Internet service providers?*

Ans. No. BGP can be used to scale large enterprise networks. A large network can be divided into segments, with each segment running an IGP. Routing information between segments could then be exchanged using BGP.

Q. 71. *If a directly connected interface is redistributed into BGP, what value will the origin attribute have for this route?*

Ans. Any redistributed route will have an origin of incomplete.

Q. 72. *What are the two routing protocols specified in the OSI suite?*

Ans. End System-to-Intermediate System (ES-IS) and Intermediate System-to-Intermediate System (IS-IS).

Q. 73. *Describe the OSI connectionless network protocol.*

Ans. OSI connectionless network service is implemented by using the Connectionless Network Protocol (CLNP) and Connectionless Network Service (CLNS). CLNP and CLNS are described in the ISO 8473 standard.

Q. 74. *Describe the OSI connection-oriented network protocol.*

Ans. OSI connection-oriented network service is implemented by using the Connection-Oriented Network Protocol (CONP) and Connection-Mode Network Service (CMNS).

Q. 75. *How are requests to services at the session layer made within OSI protocols?*

Ans. Requests are made at session-service access points (SSAPs), and SS-users are uniquely identified by using an SSAP address.

Q. 76. *Describe common-application service elements (CASEs).*

Ans. Common-application service elements (CASEs) are ASEs that provide services used by a wide variety of application processes. In many cases, multiple CASEs are used by a single application entity.

Q. 77. *Do I need to change my domain name server (DNS) information if I contract web hosting from another company?*

Ans. Often, web hosting companies and ISP's will request that you change the DNS Information for your domain name so that they can manage and make necessary zone file modifications for your domain name; *i.e.*, connecting your domain name to a website they may be hosting for you or setting your domain name's mail routing options.

Q. 78. *Do I need to own or register a DNS?*

Ans. You do not need to own or register your own DNS (domain name servers) in order to register a domain name or to sign up for email.

Q. 79. *How do I register a DNS on the Internet?*

Ans. In the same way that a domain name must be registered with a central registry to be recognized on the Internet, DNS (domain name servers) must also be registered with a central registry.Customers can register domain name servers through the online support interface, based on the following criteria: For .com, .net and .org domain names, you can register a DNS associated with your registered domain name through the online support interface. All other DNS registrations must be submitted to the official registrar for the domain name.

If your domain name meets the criteria for using the online interface to register your DNS, login to the interface using your username and password (typically established during the domain name registration process) and click the Modify DNS function in the interface. Enter the name of the DNS server you intend to register (example: dns1.myricha.com) and click submit.

In the event that the online support interface cannot translate the Name Server name into an IP Address, you will be prompted to enter the IP Address of the Name Server you are attempting to register. Enter this information and then click 'Yes' to submit the registration. A confirmation email will be sent to the administrative contact on file for the domain name. The DNS registration will not be completed until you check your email and follow the instructions to get to the final step in the confirmation process.

Once you have completed the confirmation process and the information you have provided is valid, the registration will be submitted to the registry. Please allow 24-72 hours for you DNS registration to be processed and updated by the registry.

Q. 80. *I have changed the authoritative DNS for my domain name to another company's DNS servers. Where can I go to make changes to IP addresses, domain aliases, MX records or SOA information?*

Ans. To make any changes to your IP Addresses, Domain Aliases, MX Records or SOA Information after you have changed the DNS servers listed as authoritative for your domain name from Vivek Limited's DNS to another company's DNS, you must contact the new DNS Administrators, since they are now responsible for creating and managing the zone file for your domain name.

Q. 81. *How long does it take for changes to DNS Information submitted through the online support interface to take effect?*

Ans. DNS changes must be confirmed via a link that is emailed to the contact email address on file for the domain name. The link accesses the final step in the confirmation process. Once this confirmation process is completed, it may take up to 72 hours for your DNS changes to be effective across the Internet.

Q. 82. *Why do I have different support functionality available for different domain names registered through Vivek Limited?*

Ans. If you have multiple domain names registered through Vivek Limited that have different functionality when you log into the online support interface, please check the following list for the capabilities available for the individual domain name:

You are able to edit DNS and contact information for a domain name, but have no access to IP addresses, domain aliases, MX records or SOA information: This basically means that the domain name uses Vivek Limited as its supporting registrar manager, but the domain name servers listed as authoritative for the domain name are administered through a different organization. Therefore, Vivek Limited cannot apply changes to the zone file information for the domain name. The DNS administrator of your domain name must make these changes for you.

You are able to edit IP addresses, domain aliases, MX records and SOA information for a domain name, but not contact information or DNS information: This means that the domain name lists Vivek Limited's domain name servers as authoritative for the domain name, but does not use Vivek Limited as its registrar manager. Therefore, Vivek Limited cannot offer the functionality to change your DNS information or contact information. You must make these changes with the registrar on file for your domain name.

Q. 83. *What are MIBs, and how are they accessed?*

Ans. A Management Information Base (MIB) is a collection of information that is organized hierarchically. MIBs are accessed using a network-management protocol such as SNMP. They are comprised of managed objects and are identified by object identifiers.

Q. 84. *SNMP uses a series of _____ and ______ to manage the network.*

Ans. Gets and Puts. SNMP uses a Get object and a Put object to manage devices on a network such as get counters.

Q. 85. *Name three of the seven fields of the SNMP v2 GETBULK.*

Ans. PDU Type, Request ID, Nonrepeaters, Max Repetitions, Variable Bindings (the variable bindings consists of variable object fields that make up the three remaining fields).

Q. 86. *What is the function of the RMON group matrix?*

Ans. This group stores statistics for conversations between sets of two addresses. As the device detects a new conversation, it creates a new entry in its table.

Q. 87. *What is RMON?*

Ans. Remote Monitoring (RMON) is a standard monitoring specification that enables various network monitors and console systems to exchange network-monitoring data.

Q. 88. *Multicast packets, CRC errors, runts, giants, fragments, and jabbers are elements of what RMON group?*

Ans. Statistics.

Q. 89. *Describe the process of routing packets.*

Ans. Routing is the act of moving information across an internetwork from a source to a destination.

Q. 90. *What are some routing algorithm types?*

Ans.

- Static,
- dynamic,
- flat,
- hierarchical,
- host-intelligent,
- router-intelligent,
- intradomain,
- interdomain,
- link-state, and
- distance vector.

Q. 91. *Describe the difference between static and dynamic routing.*

Ans. Static routing is configured by the network administrator and is not capable of adjusting to changes in the network without network administrator intervention. Dynamic routing adjusts to changing network circumstances by analyzing incoming routing update messages without administrator intervention.

Q. 92. *What are some of the metrics used by routing protocols?*

Ans. *Path length, reliability, delay, bandwidth, load, and communication cost.*

Q. 93. *Name the benefits of using IGRP instead of RIP.*

Ans. Despite its enduring success as an Interior Gateway Routing Protocol, RIP suffers from fundamental limitations that are not easily avoided. For example, it (and the subsequent RIPv2) is limited to a maximum of 16 hops per route. This tends to limit the size and complexity of a network that can be effectively routed with RIP. Other RIP limitations include its support for only equal-cost load balancing and its single, simple routing metric (hop count). IGRP was specifically designed to offer an alternative to RIP that was as easy to implement and administer as RIP, yet that did not suffer from these fundamental limitations.

Q. 94. *How can an administrator influence route selection?*

Ans. A network administrator can accept IGRP's default settings or can fine-tune network performance by manipulating any of IGRP's four routing metrics or their constant weights. These mathematical components of IGRP's composite routing metric offer remarkable latitude to network administrators by enabling them to emphasize or de-emphasize delay, link speed, historical reliability, or load levels in the selection of optimal routes.

Q. 95. *What is variance, and how does it affect multipath routing?*

Ans. Variance is another value that can be established and modified by a network administrator to fine-tune an IGRP network. In essence, variance enables a range of routing costs to be used to select multiple redundant paths of unequal cost to any given destination. Thus, variance is the mechanism by which IGRP supports unequal-cost load balancing.

Q. 96. *Identify and explain IGRP's stability features.*

Ans. IGRP uses holddowns, split horizons, and poison-reverse updates to improve operational stability. Holddowns prevent IGRP's interval updates from wrongly reinstating an invalid route. Split horizons help prevent routing loops by preventing a router from updating neighbors of any routing changes that it originally learned from those neighbors. Poison-reverse updates function similarly but are not limited to use between adjacent routers. Thus, they prevent large routing loops from occurring between nonadjacent routers.

Q. 97. *What timers are used by IGRP, and what is their function?*

Ans. IGRP features several functionally distinct timers, including an update timer, an invalid timer, a hold-time period, and a flush timer. The *update* timer specifies how frequently routing update messages should be sent. The *invalid* timer specifies how long a router should wait in the absence of routing-update messages about a specific route before declaring that route invalid. The *hold-time variable* specifies the holddown period. Finally, the *flush* timer indicates how much time should pass before a route should be flushed from the routing table.

Q. 98. *Name RIP's various stability features.*

Ans. RIP has numerous stability features, the most obvious of which is RIP's maximum hop count. By placing a finite limit on the number of hops that a route can take, routing loops are discouraged, if not completely eliminated. Other stability features include its various timing mechanisms that help ensure that the routing table contains only valid routes, as well as split horizon and holddown mechanisms that prevent incorrect routing information from being disseminated throughout the network.

Q. 99. *What is the purpose of the timeout timer?*

Ans. The timeout timer is used to help purge invalid routes from a RIP node. Routes that aren't refreshed for a given period of time are likely invalid because of some change in the network. Thus, RIP maintains a timeout timer for each known route. When a route's timeout timer expires, the route is marked invalid but is retained in the table until the route-flush timer expires.

Q. 100. *What two capabilities are supported by RIP 2 but not RIP?*

Ans. RIP 2 enables the use of a simple authentication mechanism to secure table updates. More importantly, RIP 2 supports subnet masks, a critical feature that is not available in RIP.

Q. 101. *What is the maximum network diameter of a RIP network?*

Ans. A RIP network's maximum diameter is 15 hops. RIP can count to 16, but that value is considered an error condition rather than a valid hop count.

Q. 102. *When using OSPF, can you have two areas attached to each other where only one AS has an interface in Area 0?*

Ans. Yes, you can. This describes the use of a virtual path. One area has an interface in Area 0 (legal), and the other AS is brought up and attached off an ABR in Area 1, so we'll call it Area 2. Area 2 has no interface in Area 0, so it must have a virtual path to Area 0 through Area 1. When this is in place, Area 2 looks like it is directly connected to Area 0. When Area 1 wants to send packets to Area 2, it must send them to Area 0, which in turn redirects them back through Area 1 using the virtual path to Area 2.

Q. 103. *Area 0 contains five routers (A, B, C, D, and E), and Area 1 contains three routers (R, S, and T). What routers does Router T know exists? Router S is the ABR.*

Ans. Router T knows about routers R and S only. Likewise, Router S only knows about R and T, as well as routers to the ABR in Area 0. The AS's separate the areas so that router updates contain only information needed for that AS.

Q. 104. *Name the four key technologies that are used by EIGRP.*

Ans. EIGRP employs four key technologies, including neighbor discover/recovery, Reliable Transport Protocol (RTP), Diffusing Update ALgorithm (DUAL) finite-state machine, and a modular architecture that enables support for new protocols to be easily added to an existing network.

Q. 105. *Explain why EIGRP is more efficient in operation than IGRP.*

Ans. Unlike most other distance vector routing protocols, EIGRP does not mandate a periodic update of routing tables between neighboring routers. Instead, it employs a neighbor discovery/recovery mechanism to ensure that neighbors remain aware of each other's accessibility. As long as a router receives periodic hello packets from its neighbors, it can assume that those neighbors remain functional. More importantly, it can assume that all of its routes that rely upon passage through those neighbors remain usable. Thus, EIGRP is much more efficient than conventional distance vector routing protocols because it imposes much less overhead on routers and transmission facilities during normal operation.

Q. 106. *How does RTP enable improved convergence times?*

Ans. RTP is responsible for providing guaranteed delivery of EIGRP packets between neighboring routers. However, not all of the EIGRP packets that neighbors exchange must be sent reliably. Some packets, such as hello packets, can be sent unreliably. More importantly, they can be multicast rather than having separate datagrams with essentially the same payload being discretely addressed and sent to individual routers. This helps an EIGRP network converge quickly, even when its links are of varying speeds.

Q. 107. *Why does EIGRP tag certain routes?*

Ans. EIGRP supports both internal and external routes. Routes that are internal to an AS are completely contained within that AS. External routes are those that are learned from neighbors that lie outside the AS. External routes are tagged with information that identifies their origin. This enables a network administrator to develop customized interdomain routing policies.

Q. 108. *Can IBGP be used in place of an IGP (RIP, IGRP, EIGRP, OSPF, or ISIS)?*

Ans. Yes and no. Remember that the next-hop information from EBGP is carried into IBGP. If IBGP does not have a route to reach the next hop, then the route will be discarded. Typically an IGP needs to be used to exchange routes to the next hop, but this can be achieved by using static routes on all the routers running IBGP. So, the answer is yes if you want to use and maintain static routes. Otherwise, the answer is no.

Q. 109. *Assume that a BGP router is learning the same route from two different EBGP peers. The AS_path information from peer 1 is {2345,86,51}, and the AS_path information from peer 2 is {2346,51}. What BGP attributes could be adjusted to force the router to prefer the route advertised by peer 1?*

Ans. Weight and local preference. Both have a higher preference than AS_path length.

Q. 110. *Can BGP be used only by Internet service providers?*

Ans. No. BGP can be used to scale large enterprise networks. A large network can be divided into segments, with each segment running an IGP. Routing information between segments could then be exchanged using BGP.

Q. 111. *If a directly connected interface is redistributed into BGP, what value will the origin attribute have for this route?*

Ans. Any redistributed route will have an origin of incomplete.

Q. 112. *What two types of messages are sent between systems in a ES-IS?*

Ans. Between ES and IS systems, IS hellos and ES hellos are sent at regular intervals to maintain the connections and to exchange subnetwork and network layer addresses.

Q. 113. *What link-state hierarchical routing protocol floods the network with link-state information when performing updates?*

Ans. Intermediate System-to-Intermediate System (IS-IS) is an OSI link-state hierarchical routing protocol that floods the network with link-state information to build a complete, consistent picture of network topology. To simplify router design and operation, IS-IS distinguishes between Level 1 and Level 2 ISs. Level 1 ISs communicate with other Level 1 ISs in the same area. Level 2 ISs route between Level 1 areas and form an intradomain routing backbone.

Q. 114. *How is the IS-IS metric figured on each link?*

Ans. IS-IS uses a single required default metric with a maximum path value of 1024. The metric is arbitrary and typically is assigned by a network administrator. Any single link can have a maximum value of 64, and path links are calculated by summing link values.

Q. 115. *Do I need to change my Domain Name Server (DNS) information if I contract web hosting from another company?*

Ans. Often, web hosting companies and ISP's will request that you change the DNS Information for your domain name so that they can manage and make necessary zone file modifications for your domain name; *i.e.*, connecting your domain name to a website they may be hosting for you or setting your domain name's mail routing options.

Q. 116. *Do I need to own or register a DNS?*

Ans. You do not need to own or register your own DNS (domain name servers) in order to register a domain name or to sign up for email.

Q. 117. *How do I register a DNS on the Internet?*

Ans. In the same way that a domain name must be registered with a central registry to be recognized on the Internet, DNS (domain name servers) must also be registered with a central registry.Customers can register domain name servers through the online support interface, based on the following criteria:

For .com, .net and .org domain names, you can register a DNS associated with your registered domain name through the online support interface. All other DNS registrations must be submitted to the official registrar for the domain name.

If your domain name meets the criteria for using the online interface to register your DNS, login to the interface using your username and password (typically established during the domain name registration process) and click the Modify DNS function in the interface. Enter the name of the DNS server you intend to register (example: dns1.myricha.com) and click submit.

In the event that the online support interface cannot translate the Name Server name into an IP Address, you will be prompted to enter the IP Address of the Name Server you are attempting to register. Enter this information and then click 'Yes' to submit the registration. A confirmation email will be sent to the administrative contact on file for the domain name. The DNS registration will not be completed until you check your email and follow the instructions to get to the final step in the confirmation process.

Once you have completed the confirmation process and the information you have provided is valid, the registration will be submitted to the registry. Please allow 24-72 hours for you DNS registration to be processed and updated by the registry. You must actually have a DNS in operation at a dedicated and unique IP Address (that is not yet registered as a DNS server) in order for the DNS server registration to be completed.

Q. 118. *I have changed the authoritative DNS for my domain name to another company's DNS servers. Where can I go to make changes to IP addresses, domain aliases, MX records or SOA information?*

Ans. To make any changes to your IP Addresses, Domain Aliases, MX Records or SOA Information after you have changed the DNS servers listed as authoritative for your domain name from Vivek Limited's DNS to another company's DNS, you must contact the new DNS Administrators, since they are now responsible for creating and managing the zone file for your domain name.

Q. 119. *How long does it take for changes to DNS Information submitted through the online support interface to take effect?*

Ans. DNS changes must be confirmed via a link that is emailed to the contact email address on file for the domain name. The link accesses the final step in the confirmation process. Once this confirmation process is completed, it may take up to 72 hours for your DNS changes to be effective across the Internet.

Q. 120. *Why do I have different support functionality available for different domain names registered through Vivek Limited?*

Ans. If you have multiple domain names registered through Vivek Limited that have different functionality when you log into the online support interface, please check the following list for the capabilities available for the individual domain name:

You are able to edit DNS and contact information for a domain name, but have no access to IP addresses, domain aliases, MX records or SOA information: This basically means that the domain name uses Vivek Limited as its supporting registrar manager, but the domain name servers listed as authoritative for the domain name are administered through a different organization. Therefore, Vivek Limited cannot apply changes to the zone file information for the domain name. The DNS administrator of your domain name must make these changes for you.

You are able to edit IP addresses, domain aliases, MX records and SOA information for a domain name, but not contact information or DNS information: This means that the domain name lists Vivek Limited's domain name servers as authoritative for the domain name, but does not use Vivek Limited as its registrar manager. Therefore, Vivek Limited cannot offer the functionality to change your DNS information or contact information. You must make these changes with the registrar on file for your domain name.

Q. 121. *What are MIBs, and how are they accessed?*

Ans. A Management Information Base (MIB) is a collection of information that is organized hierarchically. MIBs are accessed using a network-management protocol such as SNMP. They are comprised of managed objects and are identified by object identifiers.

Q. 122. *SNMP uses a series of _____ and _____ to manage the network.*

Ans. Gets and Puts. SNMP uses a Get object and a Put object to manage devices on a network such as get counters.

Q. 123. *Name three of the seven fields of the SNMP v2 GETBULK.*

Ans. PDU Type, Request ID, Nonrepeaters, Max Repetitions, Variable Bindings (the variable bindings consists of variable object fields that make up the three remaining fields).

Q. 124. *What is the function of the RMON group matrix?*

Ans. This group stores statistics for conversations between sets of two addresses. As the device detects a new conversation, it creates a new entry in its table.

Q. 125. *What is RMON?*

Ans. Remote Monitoring (RMON) is a standard monitoring specification that enables various network monitors and console systems to exchange network-monitoring data.

Q. 126. *Multicast packets, CRC errors, runts, giants, fragments, and jabbers are elements of what RMON group?*

Ans. Statistics.

Q. 127. *Which reference point for ISDN logical devices is relevant only in North America?*

Ans. U, the reference point between NT1 devices and line-termination equipment in the carrier network.

Q. 128. *What are the two speeds of ISDN PRI services?*

Ans. In North America and Japan, 23 B channels (1.472 Mbps) plus 1 D channel (64 kbps); in Europe and Australia, 31 B channels (1.984 Mbps) plus 1 D channel (64 kbps).

Q. 129. *Of the 48 bits in the ISDN physical layer frame formats, how many bits represent data?*

Ans. 36.

Q. 130. *Name the current versions of DSL technology.*

Ans. ADSL, SDSL, HDSL, HDSL-2, G.SHDL, IDSL, and VDSL.

Q. 131. *What are the two-line coding methods used for ADSL?*

Ans. DMT and CAP.

Q. 132. *Which versions of DSL offer symmetrical service?*

Ans. SDSL, HDSL, and HDSL-2.

Q. 133. *What symmetrical version of DSL offers multirate service over a single pair of wire?*

Ans. G.SHDSL

Q. 134. *How far of a reach can IDSL achieve from the CO?*

Ans. 26,000 feet.

Q .135. *What downstream and upstream rates are proposed for VDSL?*

Ans. The maximum downstream rate under consideration is between 51 and 55 Mbps over lines up to 1000 feet (300 m) in length. Downstream speeds as low as 13 Mbps over lengths beyond 4000 feet (1500 m) are also common. Upstream rates in early models will be asymmetric, just like ADSL, at speeds from 1.6 to 2.3 Mbps.

Q. 136. *What is a VPN?*

Ans. A VPN is a generic term that describes any combination of technologies that can be used to secure a connection through an otherwise unsecured or untrusted network.

Q. 137. *Explain the difference between L2TP's LAC and LSN.*

Ans. The LAC provides authentication and access concentration for remote users. After a remote user is authenticated, that user's communications session is then forwarded to the LSN, which provides access to that user's home network.

Q. 138. *What additional functionality does IPSec offer an L2TP implementation?*

Ans. L2TP's native security mechanisms build on the assumption that the nature of a point-to-point connection satisfies most of a remote user's security requirements. IPSec complements L2TP by offering a more robust set of technologies for authenticating remote users and for securing data in transit through foreign networks by encrypting data.

Q. 139. *What is a tunnel?*

Ans. A tunnel is a logical structure that encapsulates the frame and data of one protocol inside the Payload or Data field of another protocol. Thus, the encapsulated data frame may transit through networks that it would otherwise not be capable of traversing.

Q. 140. *What is the current standard?*

Ans. IPv4.

Q. 141. *What is the main reason for IPv6 being developed?*

Ans. The main issue surrounding IPv6 is addressing, or the lack of addressing. Many people believe that we are nearly out of the four billion addresses available in IPv4. IPv6 could be the solution to many problems, but IPv6 is still not fully developed and is not yet a standard.

Q. 142. *How many bits does the new expanded addressing provide?*

Ans. The expanded addressing moves us from 32-bit address to a 128-bit addressing method.

Q. 143. *What other benefits does expanded addressing provide?*

Ans. It provides newer unicast and broadcasting methods. Expanded addressing also injects hexadecimal into the IP address and moves from using "." to using ":" as delimiters.

Q. 144. *What are the new broadcast methods included in IPv6?*

Ans. Unicast, multicast, and anycast.

Q. 145. *What is unicast?*

Ans. Unicast is a communication between a single host and a single receiver.

Q. 146. *What is multicast?*

Ans. Multicast is communication between a single host and multiple receivers.

Q. 147. *What is anycast?*

Ans. Anycast is a communication between a single sender and a list of addresses.

Q. 148. *How many years did it take the telephone to reach 90 percent of the homes in the United States?*

Ans. The telephone was invented in 1875, and in 1970, 90 percent of American homes had a phone–it took 95 years.

Q. 149. *Which V series recommendations pertain to bits per second?*

Ans. V.21, V.23, V.27ter, V.29, V.32bis, V.34, and V.90.

Q. 150. *How many DS 0s are in a BRI, T1, and E1m respectively?*

Ans. Two in a BRI (although the D channel might be considered a third); 24 in a T1; and 32 in an E1.

Q. 151. *What is the flow of data going through a modem from the RJ 11 to the DTE?*

Ans. The data flows in the RJ 11 jack to the analog-to-digital converter. The DSP then gets the data and forwards it on to the packetizer, which sends the data to the data compressor. The decompressed data is then sent to the UART, which gets the data to the DTE device.

Q. 152. *What are the three phases of PPP negotiation? Why is the order significant?*

Ans. LCP, authentication, and NCP. LCP must complete first because it determines whether the link is viable and negotiates the link properties between the two peers. LCP also finds out whether authentication is needed. Authentication happens before network protocols are negotiated so that the network protocol negotiation will be capable of identifying the incoming user or host and assigning the appropriate network attributes.

Q 153. *How does interesting traffic relate to the idle timer?*

Ans. Interesting traffic determines whether the link will remain up or time out. Interesting traffic resets the idle timer to zero.

Q. 154. *Is a BRI interface a dialer? How would an async interface become a dialer?*

Ans. A BRI interface is a dialer. An async interface could become a dialer by having the **dialer in-band** configuration command entered into it.

Q. 155. *When is dialup connectivity appropriate to use? When isn't it appropriate?*

Ans. Dialup connectivity is adaptable but expensive. For intermittent connections or connections in which the endpoints move around, dialup is a convenient and sensible use. For permanent connectivity or links that stay up most of the time, it is not appropriate

Q. 156. *How do I share multiple hosts on my DSL line?*

Ans. To do so is largely dependent on how your DSL line is terminated to your CPE. If your provider gives you an Ethernet interface and multiple static IP addresses (many do), then you can simply use a 10BASE-T hub to connect a number of stations as you have IP addresses. After that, it gets more complex. If you have at least one valid IP address, you will need some type of gateway, proxy and/or network address translation (NAT) device. Matters are complicated further if your provider does not issue static IP addresses, which causes your gateway to require re-configuration each time the external IP address changes.

Q. 157. *Which reference point for ISDN logical devices is relevant only in North America?*

Ans. U, the reference point between NT1 devices and line-termination equipment in the carrier network.

Q. 158. *What are the two speeds of ISDN PRI services?*

Ans. In North America and Japan, 23 B channels (1.472 Mbps) plus 1 D channel (64 kbps); in Europe and Australia, 31 B channels (1.984 Mbps) plus 1 D channel (64 kbps).

Q. 159. *Of the 48 bits in the ISDN physical layer frame formats, how many bits represent data?*

Ans. 36.

Q. 160. *Name the current versions of DSL technology.*

Ans. ADSL, SDSL, HDSL, HDSL-2, G.SHDL, IDSL, and VDSL.

Q. 161. *What are the two-line coding methods used for ADSL?*

Ans. DMT and CAP.

Q. 162. *Which versions of DSL offer symmetrical service?*

Ans. SDSL, HDSL, and HDSL-2.

Q. 163. *What symmetrical version of DSL offers multirate service over a single pair of wire?*

Ans. G.SHDSL

Q. 164. *How far of a reach can IDSL achieve from the CO?*

Ans. 26,000 feet.

Q. 165. *What downstream and upstream rates are proposed for VDSL?*

Ans. The maximum downstream rate under consideration is between 51 and 55 Mbps over lines up to 1000 feet (300 m) in length. Downstream speeds as low as 13 Mbps over lengths beyond 4000 feet (1500 m) are also common. Upstream rates in early models will be asymmetric, just like ADSL, at speeds from 1.6 to 2.3 Mbps.

Q. 166. *What is a VPN?*

Ans. A VPN is a generic term that describes any combination of technologies that can be used to secure a connection through an otherwise unsecured or untrusted network.

Q. 167. *Explain the difference between L2TP's LAC and LSN.*

Ans. The LAC provides authentication and access concentration for remote users. After a remote user is authenticated, that user's communications session is then forwarded to the LSN, which provides access to that user's home network.

Q. 168. *What additional functionality does IPSec offer an L2TP implementation?*

Ans. L2TP's native security mechanisms build on the assumption that the nature of a point-to-point connection satisfies most of a remote user's security requirements. IPSec complements L2TP by offering a more robust set of technologies for authenticating remote users and for securing data in transit through foreign networks by encrypting data.

Q. 169. *What is a tunnel?*

Ans. A tunnel is a logical structure that encapsulates the frame and data of one protocol inside the Payload or Data field of another protocol. Thus, the encapsulated data frame may transit through networks that it would otherwise not be capable of traversing.

Q. 170. *What is the current standard?*

Ans. IPv4.

Q. 171. *What is the main reason for IPv6 being developed?*

Ans. The main issue surrounding IPv6 is addressing, or the lack of addressing. Many people believe that we are nearly out of the four billion addresses available in IPv4. IPv6 could be the solution to many problems, but IPv6 is still not fully developed and is not yet a standard.

Q. 172. *How many bits does the new expanded addressing provide?*

Ans. The expanded addressing moves us from 32-bit address to a 128-bit addressing method.

Q. 173. *What other benefits does expanded addressing provide?*

Ans. It provides newer unicast and broadcasting methods. Expanded addressing also injects hexadecimal into the IP address and moves from using "." to using ":" as delimiters.

Q. 174. *What are the new broadcast methods included in IPv6?*

Ans. Unicast, multicast, and anycast.

Q. 175. *What is unicast?*

Ans. Unicast is a communication between a single host and a single receiver.

Q. 176. *What is multicast?*

Ans. Multicast is communication between a single host and multiple receivers.

Q. 177. *What is anycast?*

Ans. Anycast is a communication between a single sender and a list of addresses.

Q. 178. *How many years did it take the telephone to reach 90 percent of the homes in the United States?*

Ans. The telephone was invented in 1875, and in 1970, 90 percent of American homes had a phone-it took 95 years.

Q. 179. *Which V series recommendations pertain to bits per second?*

Ans. V.21, V.23, V.27ter, V.29, V.32bis, V.34, and V.90.

Q. 180. *How many DS 0s are in a BRI, T1, and E1m respectively?*

Ans. Two in a BRI (although the D channel might be considered a third); 24 in a T1; and 32 in an E1.

Q. 181. *What is the flow of data going through a modem from the RJ 11 to the DTE?*

Ans. The data flows in the RJ 11 jack to the analog-to-digital converter. The DSP then gets the data and forwards it on to the packetizer, which sends the data to the data compressor. The decompressed data is then sent to the UART, which gets the data to the DTE device.

Q. 182. *What are the three phases of PPP negotiation? Why is the order significant?*

Ans. LCP, authentication, and NCP. LCP must complete first because it determines whether the link is viable and negotiates the link properties between the two peers. LCP also finds out whether authentication is needed. Authentication happens before network protocols are negotiated so that the network protocol negotiation will be capable of identifying the incoming user or host and assigning the appropriate network attributes.

Q. 183. *How does interesting traffic relate to the idle timer?*

Ans. Interesting traffic determines whether the link will remain up or time out. Interesting traffic resets the idle timer to zero.

Q. 184. *Is a BRI interface a dialer? How would an async interface become a dialer?*

Ans. A BRI interface is a dialer. An async interface could become a dialer by having the **dialer in-band** configuration command entered into it.

Q. 185. *When is dialup connectivity appropriate to use? When isn't it appropriate?*

Ans. Dialup connectivity is adaptable but expensive. For intermittent connections or connections in which the endpoints move around, dialup is a convenient and sensible use. For permanent connectivity or links that stay up most of the time, it is not appropriate

Q. 186. *How do I share multiple hosts on my DSL line?*

Ans. To do so is largely dependent on how your DSL line is terminated to your CPE. If your provider gives you an Ethernet interface and multiple static IP addresses (many do), then you can simply use a 10BASE-T hub to connect a number of stations as you have IP addresses. After that, it gets more complex. If you have at least one valid IP address, you will need some type of gateway, proxy and/or network address translation (NAT) device. Matters are complicated further if your provider does not issue static IP addresses, which causes your gateway to require re-configuration each time the external IP address changes.

Q. 187. *Can I have more than on xDSL line in my home?*

Ans. Yes, generally this is not a problem. The telephone company will provide as many lines, each on a separate copper pair into your house as you want. This may get expensive, but it has been done many times.

Q. 188. *How do I tune my xDSL line for maximum performance?*

Ans. There is little you can do to really tune your DSL line. You're generally relying on the cabling plant installed in your house all the way through to the provider's network. Since many types of xDSL service can run over what is jokingly referred to as CAT-0 cable, your speed is typically determined at provisioning time. If you are rewiring your home, it of course does make sense to perform a high quality wiring installation. In some cases, you can tune your operating systems to achieve higher performance through software tweaking. Although most systems are generally very fast in their default installations, some parameters such as TCP window size may greatly affect overall performance

Q. 189. *What is the effect of noise?*

Ans. Noise may be defined as the combination of unwanted interfering signal sources whether it comes from crosstalk, radio frequency interference, distortion, or random signals created by thermal energy. Noise impairs the detection of the smallest analog levels which may be resolved within the demodulator. The noise level along with the maximum clip level of an analog signal path set the available amplitude dynamic range. The maximum data rate of a modem is limited by the available frequency range (bandwidth) and signal-to-noise ratio (SNR) which is amplitude dynamic range. If more of either is available, more bits may be transferred per second. The information carrying limit was discussed theoretically by Claude Shannon and is known as Shannon's limit, or information theory.

Because modems run close to Shannon's limit today, no further advances will be made to traditional telephone line modems other than incremental improvement of V.90. The frequency range of the audio channel is very limited at about 4 kHz. V.34+ modems are limited to a maximum data rate of 33.6Kb/s by an SNR of about 36 dB caused mostly by network PCM quantization noise. While V.90 improves the SNR by utilizing the network PCM levels directly, it is still subject to Shannon's limit. xDSL modems take advantage of the spectrum above the telephone audio channel. While operating with somewhat less amplitude dynamic range they increase data rates by greatly increasing the frequency range of the communication signal (from about 10 kHz to over 1.0mHz). To do this they require the installation of special equipment at the central office and customer premise.

Q. 190. *How does the DSL line encapsulate my data?*

Ans. Most often, the CPE portion of the xDSL equipment provides an ATM PVC between it and the provider network. Between the CPE and the the end user equipment the data link layer is most often a 10BASE-T connection. PPP over ATM or Classical IP over ATM can also be used. If the CPE device is not an external device, such as a PCI card installed in a PC, the framing is usually ATM end-to-end. Regardless, the datalink encapsulation type means little to the end user, although a 10BASE-T interface is probably much more flexible for most users. If you're wondering why ATM is so prevalent in xDSL networking it is simply due to the fact that the organizations providing xDSL service, telco's, have a large investment in ATM based backbone equipment. By leveraging this investment, ATM all the way to the edge of their networks (your home) makes sense. Yes, there is some overhead in packaging your IP datagrams into individual 53 byte cells, but it is probably not as significant as you think. In the end, the link layer technology is not what users should be generally concerned unless one is significantly cheaper and/or faster than another.

Q. 191. *Why would applications require asynchronous communications?*

Ans. Performance is the most common reason.

Applications that perform a series of tasks that must be done sequentially cannot benefit from asynchronous communication. Applications that make only short duration remote operations have little need for asynchronous communication. Asynchronous communication can allow an application to perform addition tasks instead of waiting for tasks to complete. Applications that have a number of tasks that can be performed in any order can often benefit from distributed asynchronous communication. This becomes more important for applications that call lengthy remote operations. In order to benefit from asynchronous communication, an application must be able to perform some task after the request is issued but before the response is available. Tasks might include prompting for additional user input, displaying information, or making additional remote operation requests. Typical asynchronous communication candidates include applications that need to perform several lengthy database queries or complex calculations.

Q. 192. *Does corba support asynchronous communication?*

Ans. At the lowest level CORBA supports two modes of communication:

- A synchronous request/response which allows an application to make a request to some CORBA object and then wait for a response.
- A deferred synchronous request/response which allows an application to make a request to some CORBA object. An empty result will be returned immediately to the application. It can then perform other operations and later poll the ORB to see if the result has been made available.

At the lowest level, the CORBA deferred synchronous communication does allow a certain degree of asynchronous communication. Polling for responses represents only one form of asynchronous communication. Other more sophisticated asynchronous communication can only be achieved by developing an architecture on top of the lowest levels of CORBA.

Q. 193. *Are application threading and asynchronous communication related?*

Ans. No. They come from different families but hang out together a lot. Each has its own identity, but sometimes they can work together to make things go much more smoothly. Applications that wish to perform multiple concurrent tasks can use multiple threads instead of multiple asynchronous or deferred requests. Just as the distribution of operations across processes can allow for concurrent processing, performing tasks in different threads can allow for concurrent processing. Distribution supports concurrent processing across a network and threading supports concurrent processing within a particular machine. An application that needs to perform concurrent distributed requests can issue requests in different threads or issue asynchronous requests. The use of threading adds an additional set of complexities synchronization issues to the development process.

Q. 194. *What is the basic corba architecture?*

Ans. The CORBA architecture is designed to support the distribution of objects implemented in a variety of programming languages. This is achieved by defining an interface definition language that can be mapped to a number of existing languages. IDL is used to define the services offered by a particular distributed object. CORBA defines a wire protocol for making requests to an object and for the object to respond to the application making the request. The IIOP Protocol ensures interoperability between client applications and server based objects. CORBA then extends on this basic set of functionality by defining a set of low level services. These services are required by applications regardless of the exact nature of the applications. These services are defined in CORBA IDL. CORBA vendors preprocess the service IDL and then implement the service with varying degrees of robustness.

Q. 195. *How can corba enable client/server communication?*

Ans. A server is defined as an Interface in CORBA IDL. Data passing between the client and the server is defined as IDL structures, sequences, etc. The IDL is compiled with an IDL compiler and the generated code is included within the client and server processes. The server implements a particular interface. The implementation is the distributed object. Clients communicate with the object through an object reference. When an operation is performed on the object reference, network communication occurs, operation parameters are sent to the server and the actual distributed object executes the operation. It then returns any appropriate data to the client.

Q. 196. *Do any client/server limitations exist with corba?*

Ans. Some applications want to make distributed requests, but not wait for the response. Ideally, they want to be notified when the response is available. Threads can be used to allow applications to make more than one request or to continue performing other tasks while waiting for a response, but the thread making a request is blocked until the response is available. CORBA communication is basically a synchronous request/ response. This is true for all static invocations. Dynamic invocations do support a deferred request response. This means that an application can issue a request and poll for the response. CORBA communication can be used to notify applications when responses associated with earlier requests are available. This can lead to a more complex application architecture.

Q. 197. *What is the purpose of IDL?*

Ans. IDL stands for Interface Definition Language. Its purpose is to define the capabilities of a distributed service along with a common set of data types for interacting with those distributed services. IDL meets a number of objectives:

- Language Independence:
- Distributed service specification:
- Definition of complex data types:
- Hardware Independence:

Q. 198. *Do i program in idl no, it is an interface language? Applications are not programmed in idl.*

Ans. IDL is used to define two basic types of entities:

- Complex Data types shared between clients and servers: IDL supports 8 basic data types and allows complex data types to be composed of the basic types.
- Capabilities of Distributed Objects (CORBA Interfaces).

Q. 199. *Is idl a specification language, an implementation language, or both?*

Ans. A specification language. IDL makes a strong separation between the specification of an object and the implementation of that object. Programmers who use the interface of an object have no idea whatsoever how that object is implemented. For example, the object doesn't even need to be implemented using an OO programming language. This is called "Separation of Interface from Implementation," and is a very important concept in OO in general and in CORBA in particular.

Q 200. *Does my implementation need to use inheritance just because my idl intrerface uses inheritance?*

Ans. No. Even though a CORBA interface might utilize inheritance, the object implementation is not required to utilize inheritance. For example, given the following two IDL interfaces:

- interface Base { void f( ); };
- interface Derived : Base { void g( ); };

Suppose interface Base is implemented by class Base_impl and interface Derived is implemented by class Derived_impl. The key insight of this FAQ is that class Derived_impl does not need to inherit from class Base_impl. For example, Derived_impl could implement method f( ) directly, or it could contain a pointer to a Base_impl object and delegate f( ) to that object, or it could use some other technique.

Q. 201. *How does a corba object provide its services?*

Ans. A CORBA Object provides a set of services to its object references. In addition to the ORB and BOA, the CORBA Object requires two additional entities in order to respond to requests. First, something must listen for requests, next something must perform the operation, and third, something must issue the proper response based upon the results of the operation. These tasks are performed by the skeleton and the object implementation. Conceptually, the implementation object provides the actual operation "know-how" and the skeleton provides the networking "know-how". The skeleton and implementation, combine with the ORB and the BOA to support the full behavior of the particular CORBA Object.

Q. 202. *How are the skeleton and implementation object combined?*

Ans. **Derived:** In the derived approach, the implementation object "is" also a skeleton. This is usually obtained via inheritance. The ORB's IDL compiler would generate an appropriate skeleton class (based on the IDL interface and data types) and the developer would derive their own implementation class from it. The skeleton is able to listen to the network, de-marshall/re-marshall data types, etc. The implementation knows how and what to do within the body of the CORBA operations. A CORBA server will simply instantiate the implementation and tell the BOA that it "is ready". Since the implementation "is" also a skeleton, the CORBA Object will be able to respond to CORBA requests.

Delegated: In the delegated approach, The ORB's IDL compiler would generate an appropriate skeleton class (based on the IDL interface and data types) which would then delegate the actual operation execution to another class. The skeleton is still responsible for reading and writing to the network, de-marshall/re-marshall data types, etc. The implementation knows how and what to do within the body of the CORBA operations. While the implementation does not actually inherit from the skeleton, it still needs to implement the same set of minimal methods corresponding the to IDL operations. A CORBA server will need to instantiate the skeleton, instantiate the implementation, instruct the skeleton as to the where abouts of the implementation (often known as TIEing the skeleton and implementation together) and the tell the BOA that the skeleton "is ready"

Q. 203. *What is a distributed object?*

Ans. A distributed object is an object that can be accessed remotely. This means that a distributed object can be used like a regular object, but from anywhere on the network. An object is typically considered to encapsulate data and behavior. The location of the distributed object is not critical to the user of the object. A distributed object might provide its user with a set of related capabilities. The application that provides a set of capabilities is often referred to as a service. A Business Object might be a local object or a distributed object. The term business object refers to an object that performs a set of tasks associated with a particular business process.

Q. 204. *Are all distributed objects corba objects?*

Ans. No. A CORBA object is an object that obeys certain rules and which can be accessed via a particular protocol. A CORBA object is frequently also a distributed object, but it doesn't have to be. A distributed object is not necessarily a CORBA object. A distributed object might be a C++ object that can be accessed via a socket, RPC, or telephony. In order for a distributed object to be a CORBA object, it must be declared in IDL. The object can be implemented in a variety of programming languages.

Q. 205. *Why should i develop applications with distributed objects?*

Ans. For lots of reasons:

- Distributed objects might be used to share information across applications or users.
- Distributed objects might be used synchronize activity across several machines.
- Distributed objects might be used to increase performance associated with a particular task.
- Distributed objects might be used to connect applications running on PCs with information managed by UNIX processes or mainframes databases.
- Distributed objects might be used to allow people in different cities to contributed to a particular business process.
- Distributed objects can allow business processes to be modified or re-implemented without altering applications that use the distributed objects.
- Distributed objects are a way to distribute computing horsepower across a network of computers, which makes it easier to accommodate unpredictable growth. Centralized approaches frequently fail in such environments.

Q. 206. *How are distributed objects actually implemented?*

Ans. Typically a company will start by modeling their business processes. Next, the company will determine which business processes should be implemented as local objects and which should be implemented as distributed objects. Usually, the company will leverage a tool-kit that simplifies the distribution of those objects. There are many issues associated with simplifying distribution of objects. The tool-kit might also enhance the distribution with robust set of communication features. A company might select a particular CORBA implementation, and build their distributed objects on top of the third party package. The CORBA vendor simplifies distribution by implementing all low-level network development. An IDL compiler will process interface definition files into client and server side base classes. These base classes use low level network APIs (such as TCP/IP) to communicate. The vendor will most likely provide daemon processes that facilitate communication, the spawning of processes, the spawning of objects, and the storage of IDL used by a running system. A number of other utilities might also be provided. These could include debuggers, interface browsers or communication monitors.

SECTION B

OBJECTIVE QUESTIONS—SOLVED

Q. 1. *Which type of hub does a token ring topology use?*

Ans. A. Active B. Passive

C. Separate D. Token

E. Segmented

Q. 2. *You have a star topology network that has 32 users. Each of your three hubs can control 16 users. You have divided the users by department among the hubs. You have received six calls from the engineering department stating that they are unable to access the Windows NT Server. What is the most likely problem?*

Ans. A. The users do not know how to logon

B. The computers are unplugged

C. The Windows NT Server is down

D. The engineering hub is down

E. The router has been disconnected

Q. 3. *The sharing of information and services could best be described as a definition for:*

Ans. A. Shared processing B. Distributed processing

C. Collaborative computing D. Networking

Q. 4. *When networks in different cities are connected together, this is an example of:*

Ans. A. Wide Area Network B. Global LAN

C. Metropolitan Area Network D. Distributed Network

Q. 5. *Which of the following LAN devices is frequently a source of security concern because of its ability to process applications, share files, and perform network services in a peer-to-peer network?*

Ans. A. SQL Servers B. Routers

C. Switches D. Workstations

Q. 6. *You want to prevent users from downloading software on company workstations. What is this called?*

Ans. A. Desktop lookup B. Desktop lockup
C. Desktop lockdown D. Desktop lookdown

Q. 7. *Which of the following is a group of independent servers that are grouped together to appear like one server?*

Ans. A. Proxy Server B. SQL Server
C. Server Array D. Server Cluster

Q. 8. *Which of the following devices have similar security concerns because they provide file sharing, network connection, and application services? (Select all that apply.)*

Ans. A. Switches B. Routers
C. Workstations D. Servers

Q. 9. *You have added a new Web server to your network. Which of the following are sound practices when checking a Web server for security features? (Select all that apply.)*

Ans. A. Check with the vendor for the latest security patches for the Web software
B. Check the Web Server for any additional unused services
C. Check the Web Server for date of software distribution
D. Check the Internet for any reports of software vulnerabilities

Q. 10. *Your small company is growing and has decided to host a Web page and dedicate a server for email. What protocol is used to support email traffic?*

Ans. A. ARP B. DNS
C. SMTP D. IM

Q. 11. *Which of the following functions has an e-mail message relay agent?*

A. SMTP B. SNMP
C. S/MIME D. LDAP

Q. 12. *You desire to protect your e-mail server. What should you configure to protect your e-mail server? (Select all that apply.)*

Ans. A. SMTP relay settings B. SNMP relay settings
C. Antivirus software D. Access control permissions

Q. 13. *What is the primary purpose of an FTP server?*

Ans. A. Simplify storage of files
B. Allow for backup storage of files
C. Report security violations of files
D. Facilitate transfer of files

Q. 14. *Which of the following is frequently used to send and receive text-based files and messages, including router configurations and ACL information?*

Ans. A. File Transport Protocol (FTP)
B. Trivial File Transfer Protocol (TFTP)
C. Fast File Transfer Protocol (FFTP)
D. Trivial Transport Protocol (TTP)

Q. 15. *What is the primary function of a DNS server?*

Ans. A. Resolve 32-bit addresses in IPv4

B. Find other DNS servers

C. Resolve Fully Qualified Domain Names to IP addresses

D. Find MAC, 48-bit hardware addresses

Q. 16. *Which of the following is one of the most important tasks to perform when hardening a DNS server?*

Ans. A. Check the forward lookup zone for proper connections

B. Perform a DNS recursive query

C. Check the reverse lookup zone for proper connections

D. Restrict zone transfers to authorized computers

Q. 17. *Which of the following servers allows for a high volume of group network traffic and is a potential source for malicious code or DoS?*

Ans. A. FTP server B. NNTP server

C. DNS server D. File and Print server

Q. 18. *Which one of the following is an easy way to protect an NNTP server from malicious attacks?*

Ans. A. Implement a firewall protection plan on the NNTP server

B. Use a bastion host on the NNTP server

C. Implement virus scanning on the NNTP server

D. Turn off the NNTP server, because there is no way to protect a NNTP server from malicious attacks

Q. 19. *Because networks were created to share resources, file and print servers announce network shares by default. Which of the following provides the best hardening technique for file and print servers?*

Ans. A. Limit access to less than ten users at a time

B. Configure network shares to the default settings

C. Evaluate and set each folder share for the appropriate file and folder permissions

D. Audit all folders for successful access

Q. 20. *What is the primary network security concern with DHCP servers?*

Ans. A. Statically configured clients have the same address as DHCP clients

B. A cracker pretending to be the DHCP server, maliciously spoofs DHCP clients

C. The DNS server can be vulnerable to DHCP changes, causing clients to disconnect

D. The router is no longer available to DHCP clients

Q. 21. *Which of the following could pose a conflict of IP addressing for clients on your network, thereby removing them from your zone?*

Ans. A. A primary DHCP server B. A secondary DHCP server

C. A rogue DHCP server D. An Active Directory DHCP server

Q. 22. *Which of the following is actually considered a critical wireless device?*

Ans. A. AP B. WAP

C. WEP D. WLAN

Q. 23. *Which of the following are true statements about modems? (Select all that apply.)*

Ans. A. Modems use the telephone lines

B. Modem stands for modulator and demodulator

C. Modems are no longer used in secure networks

D. A modem's fastest transfer rate is 56 Kbps

Q. 24. *Modems can be configured to automatically answer any incoming call. Many user computers have modems installed from the manufacturer. What is the greatest security risk when dealing with modems in this situation?*

Ans. A. Remote access without network administrator knowledge

B. Local access without network administrator knowledge

C. Client access without network administrator knowledge

D. Server access without network administrator knowledge

Q. 25. *Which of the following are types of network cabling? (Select all that apply.)*

Ans. A. Twisted pair B. Token ring

C. Fiber optic D. Coaxial

Q. 26. *For which one of the following situations would a crossover cable be effective?*

Ans. A. Between a modem and a computer

B. Between a hub and a computer

C. Between two computers

D. Between a switch and a router

Q. 27. *What does CSMA represent?*

Ans. A. Carrier Sensing Minimal Access

B. Carrier Sensing Multiple Access

C. Carrier Sense Minimal Access

D. Carrier Sense Multiple Access

Q. 28. *Which of the following is a type of coax cabling transmission method? (Select all that apply.)*

Ans. A. Baseband B. Broadband

C. CSMA/CD D. CSMA/CA

Q. 29. *Which of the following is the greatest advantage of coax cabling?*

Ans. A. High security B. Physical dimensions

C. Long distances D. Easily tapped

Q. 30. *Which one of the following types of coax cabling has two outer conductors, or shields, and offers greater resistance and decreased attenuation?*

Ans. A. STP coax B. Dual-shielded coax

C. Multi-shielded coax D. Bi-coax

Q. 31. *Which of the following can transmit data at speeds of up to 16 Mbps?*

Ans. A. Category 1 UTP B. Category 2 UTP

C. Category 3 UTP D. Category 4 UTP

Q. 32. *Which of the following is not a property of twisted-pair cabling?*

Ans. A. Twisted-pair cabling is a relatively low-speed transmission

B. The wires can be shielded

C. The wires can be unshielded

D. Twisted-pair cable carries signals as light waves

Q. 33. *What is the media standard for most local network installations?*

Ans. A. Fiber B. CAT 3

C. CAT 5 D. Thinnet

Q. 34. *Which of the following is not a property of fiber optic cabling?*

Ans. A. Transmits at faster speeds than copper cabling

B. Easier to capture a signal from than copper cabling

C. Very resistant to interference

D. Carries signals as light waves

Q. 35. *What does fiber use to transmit data?*

Ans. A. Vibrations B. Sound

C. Electrical current D. Light

Q. 36. *Which of the following network cabling would you choose to install around a noisy room where machines were constantly running?*

Ans. A. Fiber B. STP

C. Coax D. UTP

Q. 37. *You've been told about radio frequency eavesdropping and want to protect your network from this threat. Which of the following media types would you choose in this situation?*

Ans. A. UTP B. STP

C. Coax D. Fiber

Q. 38. *Which of the following is most resistant to electrical and noise interference?*

Ans. A. STP B. UDP

C. Coax D. Fiber

Q. 39. *Which of the following is capable of conducting modulated light transmissions?*

Ans. A. Category 3 UTP B. Category 5 UTP
C. Fiber D. Coax

Q 40. *Which of the following is the most expensive to install and terminate?*

Ans. A. Fiber optic B. Coaxial cable
C. Category 4 UTP D. Category 5 UTP

Q. 41. *What are the terms for the two types of twisted-pair cables?*

Ans. A. Thinnet B. UTP
C. Thicknet D. STP

Q. 42. *What UTP category of cable is designed to carry voice transmission and is not designed to carry computer data?*

Ans. A. Category 5 B. Category 3
C. Category 1 D. Category 4

Q. 43. *Which coaxial cable is safest to put in tight areas, overheads and between walls?*

Ans. A. Plenum grade cable B. PVC grade cable
C. BNC grade cable D. UCC grade cable
E. Fire grade PVC cable

Q. 44. *What is the most popular type of twisted-pair cable for LANs?*

Ans. A. UTP B. Thick net
C. Thin net D. RJ-11
E. STP

Q. 45. *Select four statements about network cards.*

Ans. A. Sending adapter cards and receiving adapter cards must have the same transmission speeds
B. A buffer temporarily holds data in the network adapter card's transceiver
C. The network adapter card converts parallel data to serial data
D. Each network card has a unique address
E. Each network card has an internal transceiver built in (except for Thicknet)

Q. 46. *What is the least expensive network cabling type?*

Ans. A. Thinnet coaxial (10Base2) B. Twisted-pair (10BaseT)
C. Fiber optics D. Thicknet coaxial (10Base5)

Q. 47. *Which type of transmission technique uses single frequency digital signals?*

Ans. A. Baseband B. Broadband
C. Digiband D. Rubberband
E. UTBand

Q. 48. *You would choose Ethernet twisted-pair cabling for your network if which two of the following were true?*

Ans. A. You must be sure of data integrity up to 2000 feet on a single length of cable

B. You have a limited budget

C. You want simple computer-network connections

D. You want each computer to act as a repeater

Q. 49. *What is the term for signals from one line getting mixed with signals from another line causing corrupted network data?*

Ans. A. Attenuation B. Crosstalk

C. Plenumation D. Interference

Q. 50. *Name three advantages of using fiber-optic cable.*

Ans. A. It is less expensive than other types of cable

B. Data is more secure

C. It is easy to install

D. It is better for high speed, long distances, and high-volume data transmission

E. Best type of cable to be used in areas with high electrical interference

Q. 51. *RG-58 /U Coaxial cable consists of a core made up of solid ____ wire.*

Ans. A. Copper B. Lead

C. PVC D. Plenum

E. Glass

Q. 52. *Name a flexible coaxial cable that can emit poisonous gases if it burns and which should not be used in overheads.*

Ans. A. Plenum grade cable B. PVC grade cable

C. BNC grade cable D. STP grade cable

Q. 53. *Telephone wire is often used as a reference point and has a thickness of 22 AWG. Which wires are thicker than the 22 AWG telephone wires?*

Ans. A. 24 AWG B. 14 AWG

C. 8 AWG D. 1 AWG

E. 32 AWG

Q. 54. *Which category type of cable can support transmission up to 100 Mbps?*

Ans. A. Category 1 B. Category 3

C. Category 4 D. Category 5

Q. 55. *What is used to close each end of the Ethernet bus cable to absorb stray signals?*

Ans. A. BNC cable connector B. BNC T

C. BNC barrel D. BNC terminator

E. BNC BAT

Q. 56. *These are small connectors that connect two pins together to determine which circuits the network card will use.*

Ans. A. On-board ports B. External ports

C. Jumpers D. Barrels

Q. 57. *Usable bandwidth is best described as:*

Ans. A. The rate of speed at which a signal travels

B. The combination of the amplitude and frequency of a signal

C. The number of bits that can be transmitted in a unit of time

D. The amount of data transmitted minus the bytes required for error checking

Q. 58. *Shielded and unshielded are two common types of:*

Ans. A. Coaxial cable B. Twisted pair cable

C. Fiber optic cable D. Cable shielding techniques

Q. 59. *One method of reducing crosstalk between a pair of wires is to:*

Ans. A. Cut the wire B. Limit the strength of the signal

C. Limit the length of the cable D. Twist each pair of wires together

E. Ground one end of the cable

Q. 60. *Unshielded twisted pair wire standards include five categories. Their specifications include ___________.*

Ans. A. The transmission speed of data

B. The maximum length of the cable

C. The level of skill required to install the cable

D. The number of twisted pairs and number of twists per pair

E. Whether the cable is safe to use in ceilings

Q. 61. *A "punch-down block" is a device sometimes used with what type of cable?*

Ans. A. Shielded twisted pair B. Coax cable

C. Category 5 fiber optic cable D. Unshielded twisted pair

Q. 62. *A cable often associated with an IBM "type" specification is:*

Ans. A. Unshielded twisted pair B. Coaxial

C. Type 1 (shielded twisted pair) D. Fiber optic

Q. 63. *What is accomplished by using shielded twisted pair over unshielded twisted pair cable?*

Ans. A. Greatly reduces attenuation

B. Somewhat reduces interference and EMI

C. Allows longer cable segments before a repeater is needed

D. Requires using lower transmission speeds than Category 5

Q. 64. *The cable type most commonly used for "thin Ethernet" is:*

Ans. A. RG-59, 75 OHM B. RG-58, 50 OHM

C. Category 5 D. Category 3

E. RG-62, 93 OHM

Q. 65. *In order for a single coaxial cable segment to be properly installed, it should:*

Ans. A. Be grounded at one end, but terminated at both ends

B. Be grounded and terminated at both ends

C. Be terminated or grounded at one end only

D. Be terminated at both ends, but not grounded

Q. 66. *What are three characteristics of coaxial cable?*

Ans. A. Resists EMI better than UTP, but less than STP

B. Resists interference better than UTP or STP

C. Attenuates less rapidly than UTP, but faster than STP

D. Attenuates less rapidly than either UTP or STP

E. Supports longer cable lengths than STP

Q. 67. *What are two characteristics of fiber-optic cable?*

Ans. A. Able to support data rates similar to copper wire, but at much greater distances

B. Provide little security from eavesdropping

C. Unaffected by electrical interference

D. Well-suited to hazardous or high-voltage environments

E. Installation skills required are generally no greater than for copper wire

Q. 68. *A transmission type that is restricted to open environments and short distances would describe which of the following?*

Ans. A. High power, single-frequency B. Low power, multi-frequency

C. Low power, single-frequency D. Spread spectrum

E. Omni directional broadcast

Q. 69. *Microwave transmission may be _______________*

Ans. A. Used for non-line-of-sight installations

B. Terrestrial-based, line-of-sight

C. Relayed up to Earth satellites and back down to cover great distances

D. Omni-directional

E. Typically operated using unlicensed frequencies

Q. 70. *The location where the subscriber wiring responsibility ends and the phone company's responsibility begins is known as the:*

Ans. A. PSTN B. Demarc

C. Local loop D. Subscriber location

Q. 71. *A 16-bit ISA card can be inserted into which bus architecture?*

Ans. A. ISA only B. ISA and EISA

C. ISA, EISA, and Micro Channel D. ISA and PCI

E. ISA and PCMCIA

Q. 72. *How can network cards be configured?*

Ans. A. Software B. Plug-and-Play

C. Preconfigured D. Manually

E. By architecture

Q. 73. *What topology uses linear bus trunks that connect hubs while each hub connects to computers with the star topology?*

Ans. A. Star ring B. Star bus

C. Star wired ring D. Hub ring

Q. 74. *A logical topology where every signal is received by all devices:*

Ans. A. Star topology B. Synchronous topology

C. Multipoint topology D. Bus topology

E. Asynchronous topology

Q. 75. *Which topology requires a terminator at the cable ends?*

Ans. A. Ring topology B. Bus topology

C. Cellular topology D. Star topology

Q. 76. *Which of the following describes a ring topology?*

Ans. A. Signals are broadcast to all computers until the appropriate computer responds

B. All computers can transmit and receive simultaneously

C. Signals travel in one direction, passing through each computer

D. Failure of any one computer will not affect network performance

Q. 77. *Which of the following tasks are performed by an active hub?*

Ans. A. Repeat the incoming signal to the next computer

B. Regenerate the incoming signal before repeating it to the next computer

C. Generate an acknowledgement to the sending computer

D. Send a communication to the next computer to see if it is ready to receive the signal

E. Wait on the next router to become ready to receive the outgoing signal

Q. 78. *Which device can stop signal bounce?*

Ans. A. BNC Connectors B. Repeaters

C. Tokens D. Hubs

E. Terminators

Q. 79. *You have a Thinnet bus network and one of your workstation NICs has shorted a cable segment. How many computers are affected?*

Ans. A. Only the computer with the shorted NIC

B. Only the computers on the shorted segment

C. The entire network structure even across routers and bridges

D. The computer with the shorted NIC and the network server

Q. 80. *The three basic elements of networking are:*

Ans. A. Cabling, operating system, and storage devices

B. Clients, servers, and protocols

C. Applications, users, and transmission media

D. Data, applications, and peripherals

Q. 81. *In a peer-to-peer network, which of the following may act as both a client and server?*

Ans. A. A peer computer B. A dedicated server

C. A dedicated workstation D. A stand-alone computer

E. A repeater

Q. 82. *How can network cards be configured?*

Ans. A. Software B. Plug-and-Play

C. Preconfigured D. Manually

E. By architecture

Q. 83. *Identify two local area networks from the following configurations.*

Ans. A. One computer in California and one in Texas that use email and share documents.

B. Two computers and a printer connected by a network cable

C. 500 computers on different floors that are connected and share files

D. 200 computers all on the same floor that are configured as standalone computers

Q. 84. *When selecting a network board your decision should be based on which of the following?*

Ans. A. Phase B. Bandwidth or network speed

C. Topology D. PC Bus

E. Fault tolerance

Q. 85. *A client is going to add another twenty nodes to the network before the end* *of next month. These PCs will be running I/O intensive CAD/CAM applications. What PC bus architecture would you recommend?*

Ans. A. PCMCIA B. EISA

C. MCA D. VL-BUS

E. PCI

Q. 86. *The physical pathway a signal follows is best described as:*

Ans. A. The electromagnetic spectrum

B. The transmission medium

C. The use of headers to move data in the OSI model

D. A point-to-point connection

Q. 87. *A small business office with seven employees decides to implement a LAN because of increased business volume. Two more employees will be hired immediately and more will be added as the business expands. Everyone in the office has a computer, thus two more are to be added along with a new laser printer as part of the migration to a networking environment. What type of network would you recommend for this company?*

Ans. A. Peer-to-peer since the company will have under 10 users

B. Server-based since it will accommodate growth and provide for centralized security

C. No network since it would be less expensive to buy more laser printers than to install a LAN

D. A combination peer-to-peer and server-based network with departmental workgroups

Q. 88. *What are the three main categories of network documentation that should be maintained?*

Ans. A. The LAN system B. Resources used on the LAN

C. LAN user profiles D. History of the LAN

E. Server utilization statistics

Q. 89. *In wireless transmission, a component called a _____ offers an easy way to link buildings without using cable.*

Ans. A. transceiver B. access point

C. wireless bridge D. infrared point

E. foot bridge

Q. 90. When installing a manually configured adapter, what information must you know to avoid resource conflicts?

Ans. A. IRQ B. Number of bits

C. Base I/O port address D. Base Memory address

E. Operating System

Q. 91. *Which transmission technique uses amplifiers to regenerate analog signals at their original strength?*

Ans. A. Baseband B. Broadband
C. Rubberband D. Runningband
E. Bandwagon

Q. 92. *Which Ethernet topology specifications require the use of 50-ohm terminators at the end of each segment?*

Ans. A. 10Base-T B. 10Base2
C. 10Base5 D. 10Base-F
E. SCSI

Q. 93. *Name a device that acts as a central point of connection between different media segments:*

Ans. A. Hub B. Concentrator
C. Repeater D. Bridge
E. Router

Q. 94. *What is the name of a device that connects media segments without regenerating the signal?*

Ans. A. Active hub B. Intelligent hub
C. Passive hub D. Multiport repeater

Q. 95. *Your company has a large internal network that you would like to subnet into smaller parts. Which of the following devices can you use to separate your LAN and still protect critical resources? (Select all that apply.)*

Ans. A. An internal firewall
B. A router between subnets
C. A modem between computers
D. A switch between departments

Q. 96. *Which of the following are considered to be possible components of an ethernet LAN? (Select all that apply.)*

Ans. A. Access Point (AP) B. Coax
C. Fiber D. STP

Q. 97. *Which of the following devices is specially designed to forward packets to specific ports based on the packet's address?*

Ans. A. Specialty hub B. Switching hub
C. Port hub D. Filtering hub

Q. 98. *Your company receives Internet access through a network or gateway server. Which of the following devices is best suited to protect resources and subnet your LAN directly on the network server?*

Ans. A. DSL modem B. A multi-homed firewall

C. VLAN

D. A brouter that acts both as a bridge and a router

Q. 99. *What are some of the benefits of using a firewall for your LAN? (Select all that apply.)*

Ans. A. Increased access to Instant Messaging

B. Stricter access control to critical resources

C. Greater security to your LAN

D. Less expensive than NAT servers

Q. 100. *Which of the following are true about firewalls? (Select all that apply.)*

Ans. A. Filters network traffic

B. Can be either a hardware or software device

C. Follows a set of rules

D. Can be configured to drop packets

Q. 101. *Which of the following are true about firewall protection when using static packet filtering on the router? (Select all that apply.)*

Ans. A. Static packet filtering is less secure than stateful filtering

B. Static packet filtering is less secure than proxy filtering

C. Static packet filtering is more secure than dynamic packet filtering

D. Static packet filtering is more secure than stateful filtering

Q. 102. *A packet filtering firewall operates at which of the following OSI layers? (Select all that apply.)*

Ans. A. At the Application layer B. At the Transport layer

C. At the Network layer D. At the Gateway layer

Q. 103. *Firewalls are designed to perform all the following except:*

Ans. A. Limiting security exposures

B. Logging Internet activity

C. Enforcing the organization's security policy

D. Protecting against viruses

Q. 104. *Stateful firewalls may filter connection-oriented packets that are potential intrusions to the LAN. Which of the following types of packets can a stateful packet filter deny?*

Ans. A. UDP B. TCP

C. IP D. ICMP

Q. 105. *Which of the following systems run an application layer firewall using Proxy software?*

Ans. A. Proxy NAT B. Proxy client

C. Client 32 D. Proxy server

Q. 106. *Which of the following use routers with packet filtering rules to allow or deny access based on source address, destination address, or port number?*

Ans. A. Application layer firewall B. Packet filtering firewall

C. Router enhanced firewall D. enabled firewall

Q. 107. *Which of firewalls keeps track of the connection state?*

Ans. A. Application layer firewall

B. Packet filtering firewall

C. Router enhanced firewall

D. Stateful packet filtering firewall

Q. 108. *Network Interface card PROMs provide network security because ______.*

Ans. A. They have wireless networking

B. They allow remote-boot diskless startup

C. They block access to the server

D. They block access to the workstation

Q. 109. *Select four statements about network cards.*

Ans. A. Sending adapter cards and receiving adapter cards must have the same transmission speeds

B. A buffer temporarily holds data in the network adapter card's transceiver

C. The network adapter card converts parallel data to serial data

D. Each network card has a unique address

E. Each network card has an internal transceiver built in (except for Thicknet)

Q. 110. *The physical pathway a signal follows is best described as:*

Ans. A. The electromagnetic spectrum

B. The transmission medium

C. The use of headers to move data in the OSI model

D. A point-to-point connection

Q. 111. *A small business office with seven employees decides to implement a LAN because of increased business volume. Two more employees will be hired immediately and more will be added as the business expands. Everyone in the office has a computer, thus two more are to be added along with a new laser printer as part of the migration to a networking environment. What type of network would you recommend for this company?*

Ans. A. Peer-to-peer since the company will have under 10 users

B. Server-based since it will accommodate growth and provide for centralized security

C. No network since it would be less expensive to buy more laser printers than to install a LAN

D. A combination peer-to-peer and server-based network with departmental workgroups

Q. 112. *What are the three main categories of network documentation that should be maintained?*

Ans. A. The LAN system B. Resources used on the LAN

C. LAN user profiles D. History of the LAN

E. Server utilization statistics

Q. 113. *In wireless transmission, a component called a _____ offers an easy way to link buildings without using cable.*

Ans. A. transceiver B. access point

C. wireless bridge D. infrared point

E. foot bridge

Q. 114. *When installing a manually configured adapter, what information must you know to avoid resource conflicts?*

Ans. A. IRQ B. Number of bits

C. Base I/O port address D. Base Memory address

E. Operating System

Q. 115. *What interconnects LANs to create the image of a larger single LAN?*

Ans. A. Bridge B. Switch

C. Token ring D. Router

E. CPE

Q. 116. *Transparent bridging, encapsulated bridging, integrated routing and bridging, source-route bridging, source-route transparent bridging, and source-route transitional bridging are all examples of what?*

Ans. A. Nonrouted protocol support B. Routed protocol support

C. Bridging types D. Physical layer protocols

E. Network layer protocols

Q. 117. *On what kind of network is transparent bridging most commonly found?*

Ans. A. Ethernet B. IEEE 802.3

C. Token Ring D. FDDI

E. HDLC

Q. 118. *What is the functions of a transparent bridge?*

Ans. A. Connects two or more physical networks into one LAN.

B. Connects two hosts

C. Connect LANs with an independent transport connection

D. Was designed to be used with token rings

E. Incorporates more than one type of bridging

Q. 119. *What is the function of encapsulated bridging?*

Ans. A. To connect LANs with an independent transport connection, usually a serial or FDDI

B. To connect two or more physical networks into one LAN

C. To combined different types of bridging and routing

D. To determine a path for the packet

E. To connect two hosts

Q. 120. *Which of the following predetermines the destination of the entire route prior to sending data?*

Ans. A. Source-route bridging B. Transparent bridging

C. Encapsulated bridging D. Source-route transparent bridging

E. Source-route transitional bridging.

Q. 121. *Other than performing the functions of both SRB and transparent bridging, which are true statements about source-route transparent bridging?*

Ans. A. Does not translate between two bridging systems

B. Does not change frames from Ethernet to Token Ring networks

C. Traffic with routing information is handled by SRB

D. Traffic without routing information is handled by transparent bridging

E. Encapsulating a bridged frame inside another frame

Q. 122. *Which of the following can connect two hosts who use different types of bridging?*

Ans. A. Source-route translational bridging

B. Source-route transparent bridging

C. Source-route bridging

D. Integrated routing and bridging

E. Encapsulated bridging

Q. 123. *Source-route Bridging uses the Routing Information. Indicator, what is the Routing Information Indicators functions?*

Ans. A. To notice information in the frame

B. To decide whether the bit is set by the source to allow further investigation into the frame for control and routing information

C. To filter traffic

D. To police traffic

E. The solution will not work in this problem

Q. 124. *The RC field of the FIP is 3 bits and contains what?*

Ans. A. Specific route, all routes and all rings

B. Length of RIF

C. Direction

D. Largest frame

E. Bridge number and ring number

Q. 125. *The RD field of the RIF contains what?*

Ans. A. Specific route, all routes and all rings

B. Direct route

C. The largest frame

D. Ring number

E. Bridge number

Q. 126. *What is the function of the local ring command in the source bridge command?*

Ans. A. Identifies a network segment or ring in a bridged token ring network

B. Identifies the bridge connecting two rings

C. Identifies the number of target rings

Q. 127. *What is the function of the target ring command?*

Ans. A. Identifies the number of target rings.

B. Identifies the bridge connecting two rings.

C. Identifies a network segment or ring in a bridged token ring network.

D. Identifies the number of bridges crossed

Q. 128. *Which command enables automatic spanning for an interface?*

Ans. A. Source-bridge spanning B. Bridge group protocol ibm

C. Source-bridge bridge-group D. Source-bridge spanning tree

Q. 129. *What allows the interface to send certain routed frames to a destination?*

Ans. A. Proxy explorer B. Packet explorer

C. Routing information indicator D. Routing information field

Q. 130. *Select the true statements about the ring group command:*

Ans. A. It is a virtual ring with the transparent bridge group.

B. It is created by the source-bridge ring-group command.

C. It is the number assigned to the router.

D. It is a number between 1 and 4095.

E. It holds the vendor code.

Q. 131. *In the source-bridge transparent command, what does tb-group tell you?*

Ans. A. It is the transparent bridge group number.

B. This number connects with the source-route bridge.

C. It holds the vendor code.

D. It is a number between 1 and 4095.

E. It is the number assigned to the router.

Q. 132. *What does SRT do?*

Ans. A. Uses RII bit.

B. Notices the difference between frames using SRB and transparent bridging.

C. Chooses a destination path.

D. Use both SRB and transparent bridging.

Q. 133. *What function does source route translation bridging perform?*

Ans. A. Identifies SRT as a virtual bridge group.

B. SRT identifies TB as a pseudo ring.

C. Information from RIF is added or removed.

D. Notices the difference between frames using SRB and transparent bridging.

Q. 134. *What is the function of the source-bridge transparent command?*

Ans. A. Allows a bridge between TB configuration and SRB configuration.

B. Helps control traffic flow.

C. Enables SRB.

D. Enables TB.

Q. 135. *Which of the following is used to represent transparent bridging to the SRB?*

Ans. A. Ring group B. Pseudo ring

C. Bridge number D. tb-group

E. oui

Q. 136. *Which of the following is part of the source-bridge transparent command and informs you of the number assigned to the router?*

Ans. A. Bridge number B. Pseudo ring

C. Ring-group D. oui

E. tb-group

Q. 137. *Which of the following defines the SRB virtual ring?*

Ans. A. 10 B. 13

C. 1 D. 4

Q. 138. *Which entry tell you the number of frame bytes received for SRB?*

Ans. A. received icnt:bytes B. transmit cnt:bytes

C. max hp D. srb received

Q. 139. *Which entry tells you the number of all-routes explored?*

Ans. A. explorers B. all-rings

C. total D. TRO

Q. 140. *Which of the following are part of the show rif command?*

Ans. A. how B. idle
C. Routing Information Field D. spanning tree
E. seconds

Q. 141. *Which of the following apply to SRB?*

Ans. A. Uses explorer packets to find routing information about the network and sends it back to the host system.
B. Can verify with show source-bridge and show rif commands.
C. Can verify with show rif and show source commands.
D. Uses explorer packets to find other networks.

Q. 142. *Select the protocols that you CANNOT route:*

Ans. A. LAT B. MOP
C. NetBIOS D. TCP/IP
E. IPX/SPX

Q. 143. *You need to connect two physical, Ethernet networks into one LAN. You want the bridge to pass frames along one hop at a time based on tables, which associate end nodes with bridge ports. The bridge must not alter the data frame. Which type of bridging would you use?*

Ans. A. Transparent B. Encapsulated
C. Translational D. Source route
E. Integrated routing and bridging

Q. 144. *You have a network with FDDI media. You link it with another LAN across a serial link and use a transit bridge. What is another name for a transit bridge?*

Ans. A. Encapsulated B. Transparent
C. Translational D. Source route
E. Integrated routing and bridging

Q. 145. *How does source route bridging differ from transparent bridging?*

Ans. A. The source route bridge knows the whole route prior to sending the packet, the transparent bridge works on a hop by hop basis.
B. The transparent bridge knows the whole route prior to sending the packet, the source bridge works on a hop by hop basis.
C. Source routing is used with Token Ring, transparent bridging is associated with Ethernet.
D. Source routing is used with Ethernet, transparent bridging is associated with Token Ring.

Q. 146. *You have a network with two Token Ring segments. There are two routers connecting them—one uses source routing and the other uses transparent bridging. What kind of bridge can you employ to connect the two?*

Ans. A. Transparent B. Integrated Transparent
C. Translational D. Source-route Transparent Bridging
E. Integrated routing and bridging

Q. 147. *Which bridge would be appropriate to use to connect an Ethernet network using a transparent bridge and a token ring network using a source-route bridge?*

Ans. A. Source-Route Translation Bridge
B. Source-Route Transparent Bridge
C. Encapsulated Bridging
D. Gateway Bridge

Q. 148. *In the IP address 129.200.1.254, what is the network class and default subnet mask?*

Ans. A. Class A, 255.255.255.0 B. Class C, 255.255.255.0
C. Class A, 255.0.0.0 D. Class B, 255.255.0.0

Q. 149. *Assuming a default subnet mask, what is the network ID for a host with an IP address of 192.200.254.1?*

Ans. A. 192.200.254.0 B. 192.200.0.0
C. 192.0.0.0 D. 255.255.255.0
E. 255.255.255.255

Q. 150. *Scenario.*

Ans. The company network is routed and consists of 20 UNIX Machines, 30 Windows 2000 servers, 50 machines running Win2K Professional, and 1000 machines running Windows 98. All machines must communicate with one another. Routers connect the 14 subnets.

Required Objective To have a Win2K server act as a router between two subnets and have the route table updated automatically.

Optional Objectives

- To have the Microsoft machines initiate sessions with the servers using NetBIOS names.
- To have the UNIX machines and the Win2K machines be able to communicate using the FTP command. This includes the ability for a Microsoft or UNIX machine to initiate the FTP session.

Proposed Solution

- Enable the routing by placing multiple network adapters in the Win2K server and configure each with a different IP address. The IP address for card 1 will be 131.107.2.25 and the address for card 2 will be 131.107.3.26. These addresses are appropriate for the subnets to which the cards are cabled. The subnet mask is 255.255.255.0.
- Activate and configure RRAS.

- Enable and configure Routing Information Protocol version 2 (RIP2) for the Internet Protocol in RRAS.
- Manually configure appropriate IP addresses and masks on all the clients.
- Configure two of the Win2K servers to be WINS servers.
- Add the addresses of the WINS servers to the Microsoft client configurations.
- Add DNS to one of the Win2K servers.
- Create a zone that will include A records for all the UNIX machines.
- Enable WINS lookup for the zone.
- Add the address of the WINS server.
- Configure all the Microsoft and UNIX machines as DNS clients and provide the DNS server as their primary server.

The Proposed Solution

Ans. A. Achieves the required objective but doesn't achieve either of the optional objectives.

B. Achieves the required objective and one of the optional objectives.

C. Achieves the required objective and both of the optional objectives.

D. Doesn't achieve the required objective.

Q. 151. *Which of the following can be a Proxy Agent?*

Ans. A. MS Client 3.0 B. Windows for Workgroups 3.11

C. DOS 6.22 D. Unix

Q. 152. *Richa and Alankar Company has been assigned a Class C network address of 195.110.160.0. The network administrator, NetMan, has assigned a subnet mask of 255.255.255.224. How many subnets and valid IP addresses are possible with this configuration?*

Ans. A. 8 subnets, 32 addresses B. 6 subnets, 30 addresses

C. 4 subnets, 62 addresses D. 3 subnets, 5 addresses

Q. 153. *Richa is configuring a Class B network with address 132.117.0.0. She needs at least 60 subnets with room for 40 more within the next two years. She wants to select a subnet mask that will provide the maximum number of hosts on each subnet. Select the subnet mask she would use.*

Ans. A. 255.255.240.0 B. 255.255.248.0

C. 255.255.254.0 D. 255.255.224.0

Q. 154. *Goti is configuring a Class B network. He needs at least 1000 hosts on each subnet and wants to maximize the number of subnets. Select a subnet mask that will meet these requirements.*

Ans. A. 255.255.224.0 B. 255.255.252.0

C. 255.255.254.0 D. 255.255.248.0

Q. 155. *What are the three things to remember when doing a subnet mask?*

Ans. A. 2^n-2 B. Binary to hex conversion

C. Address class brakes D. Powers of 2 up to 10

E. Allows all ones in the subnet mask

Q. 156. *You want to use a WINS server to service 3 subnets with name registration. You want all Windows based computers on each subnet to register the computer name with the WINS Server. What should you do?*

Ans. A. Install a WINS proxy agent.

B. Install a DHCP relay agent on the routers between the subnets.

C. On the WINS server create a client reservation for each Windows based computer.

D. Configure each Windows based computer with the address of the WINS server.

Q. 157. *A dynamic router can only communicate with networks that it has a physically configured interface.*

Ans. A. True B. False

Q. 158. *You recently installed 4 new NT workstations on your subnet and you want to look at the routing table on the server to see if entries are there from the new clients. What command can you use from the server routing table?*

Ans. A. ARP -a B. ROUTE PRINT

C. TRACERT D. IPCONFIG /All

Q. 159. *You have a required objective of resolving host names and an optional objective of resolving NetBIOS names. Your solution is to configure a DHCP scope with WINS options and enable DHCP on all clients. You also configure the DHCP scope to provide the address for a DNS server.*

Ans. A. This solution meets both required and optional objectives

B. This solution meets no objectives

C. This solution meets only the optional objective

D. This solution meets only the required objective

Q. 160. *For all clients, you have a required objective of resolving host names and an optional objective of resolving NetBIOS names. You have both WIN95 and UNIX hosts. Your solution is to configure a DHCP scope with WINS options and enable DHCP on all clients. You also configure the DHCP scope to provide the address for a DNS server. You also install a WINS proxy agent and configure UNIX host to use DNS.*

Ans. A. This solution meets all objectives

B. This solution meets no objectives

C. This solution meets only the required objective

D. this solution meets only the optional objective

Q. 161. *If a client did not receive a new lease after the first default interval, it will* *contact any available server when what percentage of TTL has lapsed?*

Ans. A. 66% B. 70%
C. 87.5 D. 90%
E. 95%

Q. 162. *Because a client does not have the address of the DHCP server, it uses what source address?*

Ans. A. 255.255.255.255 B. 255.255.0.0
C. 0.0.0.255 D. 0.0.0.0
E. 127.0.0.1

Q. 163. *For clients that are non DHCP clients, it is important to ________ the scope addresses.*

Ans. A. Exclude B. Reserve
C. Insert D. Modify

Q. 164. *What is the most important entry in the "Add Reserved Clients" dialog box?*

Ans. A. IP Address B. Unique Identifier
C. Client Name D. Client Comments

Q. 165. *What is required during DHCP installation of NT servers?*

Ans. A. Static address B. DHCP address from DHCP server.
C. 255.255.255.255 D. 0.0.0.0

Q. 166. *A DHCP server requires at least how many scopes?*

Ans. A. Three B. Two
C. One D. Eight

Q. 167. *If the "Unique Identifier Field" is incorrectly typed, what will the DHCP server do?*

Ans. A. Assign the previous address
B. Assign the requested address temporarily
C. Assign any available address
D. Not assign any address

Q. 168. *If IP determines that the destination host is remote what will the ARP broadcast request?*

Ans. A. The IP address of the gateway.
B. The IP address of the Loopback .
C. The MAC address of the destination host.
D. The MAC address of the gateway.
E. The MAC address of the source host.

Q. 169. *In order for communication to occur a client must know both hardware and IP address information.*

Ans. A. True B. False

Q. 170. *To add a permanent entry in an ARP cache, which command can be used?*

Ans. A. arp -g B. arp -a
C. arp -s D. arp -d

Q. 171. *What is the default maximum length of time that a dynamic entry will remain in the ARP cache before it is updated?*

Ans. A. 5 minutes B. 10 minutes
C. 15 minutes D. 12 minutes

Q. 172. *Which three of the following are WINS Server requirements?*

Ans. A. NT Server B. NT Workstation
C. DHCP dynamic address D. Static address
E. Subnet Mask, Default Gateway

Q. 173. *Each host entry is limited to how many characters?*

Ans. A. 15 B. 16
C. 255 D. 256

Q. 174. *Our company has a routed internetwork that consists of 20 UNIX machines, 5 NT 4.0 Servers, 50 NT Workstations and 250 Windows 95 machines. We have standardized the Microsoft machine names to be 10 characters and the UNIX host names to be 20 characters. There is one NT Server on each of 5 subnets. We are running TCP/IP only and your goal is to eventually enable communications between all of these machines.*

Ans. **Required Objective**: To have the Microsoft client machines obtain their IP addresses, dynamically, from a central source instead of administrators adding them as static IP addresses.

Desired Objectives:

1. To have all the Microsoft machines use the utility, Microsoft Explorer, to map network drives, using machine and share names, and be able to map to all of the NT servers.
2. To have the Microsoft machines be able to FTP to the UNIX machines using Host names.

Solution: Install the DHCP server service on two of the Microsoft servers. Each server will be configured with a scope of addresses for each of the 5 subnets. We will make sure that the scopes do not have overlapping addresses. Configure each of the Microsoft client machines to obtain an IP address from a DHCP server. Configure the routers to forward BootP requests. Install the WINS server service on another of the NT servers to facilitate the resolution of IP addresses to the client names. On the DHCP server we will configure the server to provide to the client the WINS server's IP address and the node type of H-node. Configure these as Global options.

A. Achieves the Required Objective but does not achieve either of the optional objectives

B. Achieves the Required Objective and one of the optional objectives

C. Achieves the Required Objective and both of the optional objectives

D. Does Not Achieve the Required Objective

Q. 175. *Alankar wants to upload a file to the home office immediately, but the limited number of IP addresses available at his remote site have already been taken. DHCP is used at his site to assign IP addresses. Asim has just finished using his computer for the day, but the lease on his IP address is not up and will not be up for three more days. What can alankar do to make use of his address to send the file to the home office?*

Ans. A. Type "ipconfig /reset" at the command line on Asim's computer

B. Reset the lease duration on the DHCP server to 10 minutes

C. Type "ipconfig /release" at the command line on Asim's computer

D. Go into DHCP Client service on Asim's computer and reset his lease

Q. 176. *Your work group uses several laptops and regularly moves work locations. You want the WINS servers to automatically assign IP addresses as well as the IP addresses for the WINS server. What service must be running?*

Ans. A. DHCP B. DNS

C. SNMP D. WINS

Q. 177. *Consider the following network configuration: 4 Windows NT servers, 30 Windows 95 Computers, 120 NT workstations, and 10 computers running Windows for Workgroups 3.11. All network clients are using TCP/IP; but, only 45% of the network connections are used at any one time. There are 164 computers, but only 128 IP addresses are available. How can TCP/IP be configured to provide each user with an IP address?*

Ans. A. Use DHCP and set up client reservations that provide certain IP addresses to particular nodes at certain times.

B. Use DHCP to dynamically assign IP addresses, configure with short lease durations.

C. Use DNS to dynamically provide IP addresses to the users based on priority, utilizations, and needs.

D. Use WINS to assign the IP addresses, dynamically allocate IP address lease durations on an "as needed" basis.

Q. 178. *Our company has a routed internetwork that consists of 20 UNIX machines, 5 NT 4.0 Servers, 50 NT Workstations and 250 Windows 95 machines. We have standardized the Microsoft machine names to be 10 characters and the Unix host names to be 20 characters. There is one NT Server on each of 5 subnets. We are running TCP/IP only and your goal is to eventually enable communications between all of these machines. We are in the planning stages and settled on the following objectives:*

***Required Objective**: To have the Microsoft client machines obtain their IP addresses, dynamically, from a central source instead of administrators adding them as static IP addresses.*

Desired Objectives:

1. To have all the Microsoft machines use the utility Microsoft Explorer to map network drives using machine and share names. Be able to map to all of the NT servers.
2. Have the Microsoft Machines be able to FTP to the UNIX Machines using Host names.

Solution: We will install the DHCP server service on 2 of the Microsoft servers. Each server will be configured with a scope of addresses for each of the 5 subnets. We will insure that the scopes do not have overlapping addresses. We will configure each of the Microsoft client machines to obtain an IP address from a DHCP server. We will configure the routers to forward BootP requests, and install the WINS server service on another of the NT servers to facilitate the resolution of IP addresses to the names.

Ans. A. Achieves the Required Objective but does not achieve either of the optional objectives

B. Achieves the Required Objective and one of the optional objectives

C. Achieves the Required Objective and both of the optional objectives

D. Does Not Achieve the Required Objective

Q. 179. *Which is a function of NetBIOS?*

Ans. A. Provides a standard interface for applications and TCP/IP

B. Provides NetBIOS naming and session services

C. Provides a standard interface between NetBIOS applications and TCP/IP

Q. 180. *On a TCP/IP network, if I map a drive using the UNC path \\COMPUTER1\PUBLIC what address or addresses must be resolved to ensure communications?*

Ans. A. NetBios name to IP Address

B. NetBios name to Hardware address

C. IP address to Hardware address

D. WINS server name to Hardware address

E. Wins server name to DHCP server name

Q. 181. *Which is cached first?*

Ans. A. NetBIOS Name Cache B. ARP Cache

Q. 182. *Which two NetBIOS name resolution types have difficulty passing through routers?*

Ans. A. B-Node B. P-Node

C. M-Node D. H-Node

E. Enhanced B-Node

Q. 183. *NetBIOS names must be no more than how many bytes?*

Ans. A. 10 B. 12

C. 14 D. 15
E. 16

Q. 184. *What are three methods of NetBIOS name resolution?*

Ans. A. NetBIOS name cache B. LMHOSTS file
C. Nbtstat -n D. Local Broadcast

Q. 185. *Which port numbers are for forwarding B-Node broadcast?*

Ans. A. UDP Port 67 and 68 B. UDP Port 57 and 58
C. UDP Port 137 and 138 D. UDP Port 157 and 158

Q. 186. *At what percentage of the TTL lease does a WINS client attempt to refresh its registration?*

Ans. A. 30% B. 50%
C. 60% D. 80%

Q. 187. *Which of the following request new database entries?*

Ans. A. Pull Partner B. Push Partner

Q. 188. *All NetBIOS names are registered on a temporary basis in WINS so the same name can be used later by a different host if the original owner stops using it.*

Ans. A. True B. False

Q. 189. *WINS clients handle name registration differently by sending a name registration directly to the WINS server.*

Ans. A. True B. False

Q. 190. *Which is the default WINS client node type?*

Ans. A. B-Node B. H-Node
C. M-Node D. P-Node

Q. 191. *WINS server only replicates which of the following?*

Ans. A. New entries B. Entire database
C. Entire registry

Q. 192. *What helps non WINS clients solve browsing problems?*

Ans. A. WINS B. WINS Proxy agent
C. DHCP D. LMHOSTS files

Q. 193. *WINS was designed to eliminate the broadcast traffic associated with which type of broadcast?*

Ans. A. P-Node B. B-Node
C. H-Node D. M-Node

Q. 194. *If you want to create a Zone record to identify a mail server, what record do you create?*

Ans. A. CNAME record B. IN record
C. MX record D. NS record
E. PTR record

Q. 195. *What happens when a WINS server detects a duplicate address?*

Ans. A. Challenges the currently registered owner

B. Shuts down the PC making the request

C. If the current owner responds then a negative registration is sent to the WINS client attempting to register

Q. 196. *When is a default gateway necessary?*

Ans. A. When communicating outside your subnet if you have not configured the route in the local routing table

B. When connecting to the server

C. When connecting to PCs in your subnet

Q. 197. *Which is cached first?*

A. NetBIOS Name Cache B. ARP Cache

Q. 198. *You are in Subnet 1, you just connected to an FTP server in subnet 3 and downloaded files. Now you want to connect to a share name using NT explorer, but failed. What could be the problem?*

Ans. A. Your PC is not using DNS

B. Your PC is not using a default gateway

C. Your PC is not using WINS

D. The FTP Server is not using a default gateway

E. The FTP Server is not using WINS

Q. 199. *Remote Shell (RSH is used to run a ________ .*

Ans. A. Command on a server B. Process on another computer

C. Copies files between a NT computer another server

Q. 200. *What is the committee responsible for setting Internet standards and for managing the process of publishing RFCs?*

Ans. A. Internet Engineering Task Force (IETF)

B. Internet Research Task Force (IRTF)

C. Internet Review Board (IRB)

D. Internet Activities Board (IAB)

Q. 201. *A routing table defines the path to other __________.*

Ans. A. Servers B. Gateways

C. Networks

Q. 202. *The ARP cache is always checked for an IP address/hardware address mapping before broadcasting an ARP request.*

Ans. A. True B. False

Q. 203. *What is used to resolve host name to IP addresses?*

Ans. A. Hosts file B. DNS
C. WINS D. WINS Proxy
E. Networks file

Q. 204. *What utility should be used to verify each entry in the hosts file?*

Ans. A. TRACE B. NET USE
C. PING D. ARP
E. NBTSTAT

Q. 205. *You have three subnets connected to one BOOTP enabled router. What is the minimum number of DHCP servers required?*

Ans. A. One B. Two
C. Three

Q. 206. *You are using Internet explorer to connect to http:/charleston.af.mil and you received a "bad IP address" message. What are the two most likely causes?*

Ans. A. Your computer has an invalidated DNS configuration
B. There is no entry for charleston.af.mil on the DNS server
C. Your default gateway address is invalid
D. Your wins server address is invalid
E. Your wins server is down

Q. 207. *A Master Name Server can be installed in what two ways?*

Ans. A. Primary Server B. Secondary Server
C. Caching Only Server D. Wins Server
E. Tertiary Server

Q. 208. *If you would like to use more than one name to point to a single host you would create a(n):*

Ans. A. IN record B. MX record
C. ALIAS record D. CNAME record
E. NS record

Q. 209. *Which of the following is defined as the process of mapping a host name to IP address?*

Ans. A. NetBIOS name resolution B. ARP name resolution
C. Host Name resolution

Q. 210. *Immediately after an installation, the Microsoft DNS server is automatically a ______________.*

Ans. A. Caching Only Server B. Primary Server
C. Secondary Server D. Master Server
E. Principle Server

Q. 211. *The usual type of query for a Name Server to issue to a ROOT server is:*

Ans. A. RECURSIVE B. INCLUSIVE
C. REDUNDANT D. ITERATIVE
E. INVERSE

Q. 212. *Which of following devices discriminates between multicast and unicast packets?*

Ans. A. Multicast switch B. Bicast switch
C. Bicast router D. Multicast router

Q. 213. *Your primary concern is LAN security. You want to subnet your internal network with a device that provides security and stability. Which of the following devices do you choose to meet these needs?*

Ans. A. Static router B. Dynamic router
C. Static switch D. Dynamic switch

Q. 214. *Which of the following will help you to improve your LAN security? (Select all that apply.)*

Ans. A. Change user passwords frequently
B. Install a firewall program
C. Use a dynamic rather than static router
D. Use a proxy

Q. 215. *Which of the following is the most difficult to configure, but safest device to use on a LAN?*

Ans. A. Static router B. IP enabled router
C. Dynamic router D. RIP enabled router

Q. 216. *Which of the following statements are true about routers and bridges? (Select all that apply.)*

Ans. A. Bridges connect two networks at the Data Link Layer
B. Bridges are types of inexpensive routers
C. Routers are improved bridges
D. Routers connect two networks at the Network Layer

Q. 217. *Remember, routers work at the Network Layer of the International Standards Organization/Open Systems Interconnection (ISO/OSI) established sequence of OSI Layers. What is the correct and complete OSI sequence in order from user interface (Layer 7) to the delivery of binary bits (Layer 1)?*

Ans. A. Physical Layer, Network Layer, Data Link Layer, Transport Layer, Session Layer, Presentation Layer, Application Layer
B. Application Layer, Presentation Layer, Session Layer, Transport Layer, Network Layer, Data Link Layer, Physical Layer
C. Application Layer, Physical Layer, Session Layer, Transport Layer, Network Layer, Data Link Layer, Presentation Layer

D. Physical Layer, Data Link Layer, Network Layer, Session Layer, Transport Layer, Presentation Layer, Application Layer

Q. 218. *Most networks employ devices for routing services. Routers work at which of the following OSI layers?*

Ans. A. Transport B. Network

C. Presentation D. Session

Q. 219. *You manage a company network and the network budget. You want to minimize costs, but desire to prevent crackers from sniffing your local network (LAN). Which of the following devices would you recommend to meet your goals?*

Ans. A. Hub B. Switch

C. Router D. Firewall

Q. 220. *Which of the following statements apply to security concerns when using a switch in the LAN? (Select all that apply.)*

Ans. A. Switches use SSH to manage interfaces by default

B. Switches use Telnet or HTTP to manage interfaces

C. Switches are more secure than routers since they are internal to the LAN

D. Switches should be placed behind a dedicated firewall

Q. 221. *Which of following is a type of hub that forwards packets to an appropriate port based on the packet's address?*

Ans. A. Smart hub B. Switching hub

C. Routing hub D. Porting hub

Q. 222. *A company desires to use a private addressing scheme for their LAN users. What solution should they implement?*

Ans. A. NAT B. Honey pot

C. IDS D. Proxy server

Q. 223. *Which of the following is relatively more secure than proxy, because it assigns private IP addresses to the clients on your LAN, acting as a firewall?*

Ans. A. RADIUS

B. Internet Control Message Protocol (ICMP)

C. Network Address Translation (NAT)

D. ICMP Router Discovery Protocol (IRDP)

Q. 224. *What is the primary purpose for Network Address Translation (NAT)?*

Ans. A. Multiple users sharing one IP address for Instant Messenger (IM)

B. Hiding the IP addresses of the internal network from those outside of the network

C. Showing the IP addresses of the external network to clients on the internal network

D. Single users gaining access to multiple email accounts

Q. 225. *Which of the following are true statements about Network Address Translation (NAT)? (Select all that apply.)*

Ans. A. Provides for private addressing ranges for internal network

B. Hides the true IP addresses of internal computer systems

C. Ensures that private addresses can be globally routable

D. Translates private IP addresses into registered Internet IP addresses

Q. 226. *Which of the following is an example of a private IP address, which is not to be used on the Internet?*

Ans. A. 10.13.40.15 B. 131.10.42.5

C. 129.101.22.15 D. 193.10.143.105

Q. 227. *Which of the following is an example of a private IP address, which is not to be used on the Internet?*

Ans. A. 171.15.40.32 B. 172.46.32.2

C. 171.90.22.1 D. 172.16.12.5

Q. 228. *Which of the following is an example of a private IP address, which is not to be used on the Internet?*

Ans. A. 172.111.12.15 B. 192.168.141.15

C. 192.165.142.15 D. 19.176.134.15

Q. 229. *Which of the following applies to the networking concept of tunneling? (Select all that apply.)*

Ans. A. Private network data is encapsulated or encrypted

B. Public network data is encapsulated or encrypted

C. Private data is transmitted over a public network

D. Private network data is lost in a black hole

Q. 230. *There are several tunneling protocols. Which of the following are types of VPN remote computing tunneling protocols? (Select all that apply.)*

Ans. A. LP B. L2F

C. L2TP D. PPTP

Q. 231. *Which of the following hardening methods gives you the capability to deny access to one individual computer by IP address or computer name?*

Ans. A. NTFS permissions B. Authentication keys

C. PKI D. Access control lists

Q. 232. *Who is the technical advisory group responsible for setting Internet standards?*

Ans. A. Internet Architectural Authorities (IAA)

B. Internet Society (ISOC)

C. Internet Engineering Task Force (IETF))

D. Internet Architecture Board (IAB)

Q. 233. *If a resource requires a password for authentication, the visitor's browser prompts the user to enter a valid username and password. If the username and / or password are invalid the user will get which error?*

Ans. A. 403 B. 505
C. 911 D. 401

Q. 234. *What does the acronym IDS stand for?*

Ans. A. Intrusion Detection System B. Internet Detection Standard
C. Internet Detection System D. Intrusion Detection Standard

Q. 235. *Which of the following devices is used to monitor network traffic, including DoS attacks in real time?*

Ans. A. A host-based Intrusion Detection System
B. A network-based Intrusion Detection System
C. A router-based Intrusion Detection System
D. A server-based Intrusion Detection System

Q. 236. *Which of the following security devices acts more like a detective rather than a preventative measure?*

Ans. A. IDS B. DMZ
C. NAT D. Proxy

Q. 237. *Which of the following protocols is used to monitor network devices such as hubs, switches, and routers?*

Ans. A. SMTP B. SNMP
C. RIP D. OSPF

Q. 238. *You have been using a network monitor or protocol analyzer to monitor ethernet packets. One of the messages sent has an IP header protocol field value of "1". What does this value classify?*

Ans. A. UDP B. ICMP
C. IGMP D. TCP

Q. 239. *You have been using a network monitor or protocol analyzer to monitor ethernet packets. One of the messages sent has an IP header protocol field value of "6". What does this value classify?*

Ans. A. UDP B. ICMP
C. IGMP D. TCP

Q. 240. *Which one of the following is a small network device that is a security concern for network administrators because the device is easily misplaced?*

Ans. A. Workstation B. Server
C. Mobile device D. VPN

Q. 241. *Which of the following file systems allows for both file and folder level permissions?*

Ans. A. FAT B. FAT16
C. FAT32 D. NTFS

Q. 242. *You want to harden your Linux file system by modifying folder permissions. Which command allows you to change folder permissions on a Linux system?*

Ans. A. chmod B. ls
C. ls -l D. top

Q. 243. *When would you consider restoring a clean version of a file from a backup?*

Ans. A. When you are in a financial position to do so
B. When you have time to do so
C. When things are quiet at night
D. When a system file has become infected.

Q. 244. *For an anonymous user to upload, but not download files to the root directory of the FTP Server, what permission is needed?*

Ans. A. Execute B. Read Only
C. Change D. Write Only

Q. 245. *You wish to limit the number of users connecting to your FTP service at one time. How would you accomplish this?*

Ans. A. Control Panel, Internet Icon, FTP Tab, Limit Users To:______
B. Control Panel, Network Icon, Services Tab, FTP Service, Limit Users To: ______
C. ISM (MMC), Right Click FTP Service, Properties, Service Tab, Maximum Connections: ______
D. ISM (MMC), Right Click FTP Service, Properties, FTP Site, Limited To ______ Connections
E. There is no way to limit users on an FTP Service.

Q. 246. *What is the default port setting for incoming connections on an SMTP Site?*

Ans. A. 14 B. 21
C. 24 D. 25
E. 80

Q. 247. *You have a SMTP server in another domain, which does not use DNS, and want to set it up so that mail being directed through it contains the company's main domain name. What do you use?*

Ans. A. Register it with DNS
B. Specify a Fully Qualified Domain Name in delivery properties
C. Specify a Masquerade Domain in delivery properties
D. Specify a Smart Host Header in delivery properties

Q. 248. *Even in a large, mixed environment, TCP/IP is the protocol of choice for most networks. Which of the following protocols would you want to deny passage over your Firewall?*

Ans. A. TCP B. IP
C. IPX/SPX D. NetBEUI

Q. 249. *Which of the following is the best method to disable services?*

Ans. A. Verify the dependencies of all unused services before removing
B. Verify the dependencies of all active services before removing
C. Verify the dependencies of all unused services after removing
D. Verify the dependencies of all active services after removing

Q. 250. *There are several common TCP and UDP ports, some of which you may wish to disable. List the matching service provided by ports 20, 21, 23, 25, 42, 53, 67, 70, 80, 110, 119, 135, 139, 161, and 443. How many common ports do you recognize?*

Ans. A. At least 13 of the 15 ports B. At least 10 of the 15 ports
C. At least 5 of the 15 ports D. At least 2 of the 15 ports

Q. 251. *Your network administrator has found one of your unused server services enabled. What should you do?*

Ans. A. Disable the unused service for security reasons after verifying dependencies
B. Monitor the unused service for security reasons before verifying dependencies
C. Troubleshoot the unused service for security reasons and functionality
D. Maintain the enabled unused service for security reasons and functionality

Q. 252. ______ *is the primary transport protocol of the TCP/IP protocol suite.*

Q. 253. *The TCP/IP protocol that provides for source and destination addressing is* ______.

Q. 254. *The two most commonly used e-mail client protocols are* ______ *and* ______.

Q. 255. *The* ______ *TCP/IP utility is used to check the validity of a remote IP address.*

Q. 256. *TCP is a* ______ *communications protocol.*

Q. 257. *The Internet Protocol operates on the OSI model's* ______ *layer.*

Q. 258. *TCP and UDP are* ______ *layer protocols.*

Q. 259. ______ *is used to resolve an FQDN to its IP address.*

Q. 260. *The dynamic Windows-based service used to resolve NetBIOS names into their IP addresses is* ______.

Q. 261. *The* ______ *is typically the router interface that connects a network to the Internet.*

Q. 262. *Even in a large, mixed environment, TCP/IP is the protocol of choice for most networks. Which of the following protocols would you want to deny passage over your Firewall?*

Ans. A. TCP B. IP

C. IPX/SPX D. NetBEUI

Q. 263. *Which of the following is the best method to disable services?*

Ans. A. Verify the dependencies of all unused services before removing

B. Verify the dependencies of all active services before removing

C. Verify the dependencies of all unused services after removing

D. Verify the dependencies of all active services after removing

Q. 264. *There are several common TCP and UDP ports, some of which you may wish to disable. List the matching service provided by ports 20, 21, 23, 25, 42, 53, 67, 70, 80, 110, 119, 135, 139, 161, and 443. How many common ports do you recognize?*

Ans. A. At least 13 of the 15 ports B. At least 10 of the 15 ports

C. At least 5 of the 15 ports D. At least 2 of the 15 ports

Q. 265. *Your network administrator has found one of your unused server services enabled. What should you do?*

Ans. A. Disable the unused service for security reasons after verifying dependencies

B. Monitor the unused service for security reasons before verifying dependencies

C. Troubleshoot the unused service for security reasons and functionality

D. Maintain the enabled unused service for security reasons and functionality

Q. 266. *Who is the technical advisory group responsible for setting Internet standards?*

Ans. A. Internet Architectural Authorities (IAA)

B. Internet Society (ISOC)

C. Internet Engineering Task Force (IETF))

D. Internet Architecture Board (IAB)

Q. 267. *If a resource requires a password for authentication, the visitor's browser prompts the user to enter a valid username and password. If the username and / or password are invalid the user will get which error?*

Ans. A. 403 B. 505

C. 911 D. 401

Q. 268. *Which of the following protocols is used to monitor network devices such as hubs, switches, and routers?*

Ans. A. SMTP B. SNMP

C. RIP D. OSPF

Q. 269. *You have been using a network monitor or protocol analyzer to monitor ethernet packets. One of the messages sent has an IP header protocol field value of "1". What does this value classify?*

Ans. A. UDP B. ICMP
C. IGMP D. TCP

Q 270. *You have been using a network monitor or protocol analyzer to monitor ethernet packets. One of the messages sent has an IP header protocol field value of "6". What does this value classify?*

Ans. A. UDP B. ICMP
C. IGMP D. TCP

Q. 271. *Which one of the following is a small network device that is a security concern for network administrators because the device is easily misplaced?*

Ans. A. Workstation B. Server
C. Mobile device D. VPN

Q. 272. *Which of the following file systems allows for both file and folder level permissions?*

Ans. A. FAT B. FAT16
C. FAT32 D. NTFS

Q. 273. *You want to harden your Linux file system by modifying folder permissions. Which command allows you to change folder permissions on a Linux system?*

Ans. A. chmod B. ls
C. ls –l D. top

Q. 274. *When would you consider restoring a clean version of a file from a backup?*

Ans. A. When you are in a financial position to do so
B. When you have time to do so
C. When things are quiet at night
D. When a system file has become infected

Q. 275. *For an anonymous user to upload, but not download files to the root directory of the FTP Server, what permission is needed?*

Ans. A. Execute B. Read Only
C. Change D. Write Only

Q. 276. *You wish to limit the number of users connecting to your FTP service at one time. How would you accomplish this?*

Ans. A. Control Panel, Internet Icon, FTP Tab, Limit Users To:______
B. Control Panel, Network Icon, Services Tab, FTP Service, Limit Users To: ______
C. ISM (MMC), Right Click FTP Service, Properties, Service Tab, Maximum Connections: ______

D. ISM (MMC), Right Click FTP Service, Properties, FTP Site, Limited To ______ Connections

E. There is no way to limit users on an FTP Service.

Q. 277. *What is the default port setting for incoming connections on an SMTP Site?*

Ans. A. 14 B. 21

C. 24 D. 25

E. 80

Q. 278. *You have a SMTP server in another domain, which does not use DNS, and want to set it up so that mail being directed through it contains the company's main domain name. What do you use?*

Ans. A. Register it with DNS

B. Specify a Fully Qualified Domain Name in delivery properties

C. Specify a Masquerade Domain in delivery properties

D. Specify a Smart Host Header in delivery properties

Q. 279. *Which of the following terms defines RAS?*

Ans. A. Random Access Security B. Remote Access Security

C. Random Access Service D. Remote Access Service

Q. 280. *Usually, a RAS connection is a dial-up connection. What network connections also apply to RAS? (Select all that apply.)*

Ans. A. Client-Server B. ISDN

C. VPN D. DSL

Q. 281. *Your company has gone through several phone company changes to reduce costs. Last week, two new phone company employees indicated that they needed remote access to your company network and wanted to establish a permanent guest account on your RAS server for continued maintenance support. Which of the following actions are your best recommendations for this situation? (Select all that apply.)*

Ans. A. Agree with their requests so that maintenance costs are reduced

B. Recommend that user accounts be verified with strong authentication

C. Remove the guest account and create verifiable remote accounts

D. Create a phone company group account and place that inside the guest account

Q. 282. *Which of the following applies to PBX? (Select all that apply.)*

Ans. A. PBX stands for Private Branch Exchange

B. PBX allows for analog, digital, and data to transfer over a high-speed phone system

C. PBX stands for Public Broadcasting Exchange

D. PBX is used to carry analog messages and modem communication originating at the phone company

Q. 283. *You want to have a private communication between two sites that also allows for encryption and authorization. Which of the following is the best choice in this instance?*

Ans. A. Modem B. Firewall

C. VPN D. Bastion Host

Q. 284. *VPN tunnels have end points. Which of the following methods is used to offer Strong Authentication at each end point?*

Ans. A. DES B. Block cipher

C. Stream cipher D. Diffie-Hellman

Q. 285. *VPNs transfer encrypted data through tunneling technology. Which of the following performs fast data encryption and may be used with VPNs?*

Ans. A. Stream cipher B. RSA

C. DES D. IPSec

Q. 286. *You desire to secure a VPN connection. Which protocols should you use? (Select all that apply.)*

Ans. A. TLS B. IPSec

C. SSL D. L2TP

Q. 287. *What does ISDN work with besides MIB group with DDR?*

Ans. A. X.25 B. Frame Relay

C. OSPF D. IP

E. BGF

Q. 288. *ISDN is an end-to-end digital network, what are some benefits?*

Ans. A. Carries varied information such as video, audio and data.

B. It is faster than basic telephone services.

C. Transfers data faster than a modem.

D. It is wireless.

Q. 289. *What are the two access options for ISDN?*

Ans. A. BRI B. PRI

C. local telephone company D. a long distance provider

E. DDR

Q. 290. *Which of the following converts BRI signals into a form used by ISDN?*

Ans. A. TE1 B. NT2

C. NT1 D. TE2

E. TA

Q. 291. *What is part of the local exchange and terminates the local loop?*

Ans. A. LT B. ET

C. TE1 D. TE2

E. NT1

Q. 292. *What is part of the exchange, which communicates with other ISDN components?*

Ans. A. LT B. ET

C. NT1 D. NT2

E. TZ

Q. 293. *What references the points that connect into the NT2?*

Ans. A. R B. S

C. T D. U

E. none

Q. 294. *What command description would you use to configure the specific ISDN switch type?*

Ans. A. ISDN switch type and then type in the switch type

B. Just type in the switch type

C. ISDN switch type, the computer will then read the switch type

D. No command is needed, is automatic

E. switch type isdn and then type in the switch type

Q. 295. *What are the two numbers typically given when you first activate an ISDN line so that you can connect with a switch?*

Ans. A. spid numbers B. ldn

C. telephone number D. terminal number

E. BRI number

Q. 296. *Select the commands that can be used to verify MultiLink PPP operation:*

Ans. A. show dialer B. debug ppp multilink

C. show ip dialer D. list dialer

E. show multilink

Q. 297. *Choose all that apply in regards to ISDN service for DDR?*

Ans. A. Bandwidth on demand B. Multiple bearer channels

C. Screening incoming calls D. Dedicated, continuous connectivity

E. Multiprotocol supported

Q. 298. *What does ISDN work with besides MIB group with DDR?*

Ans. A. X.25 B. Frame Relay

C. OSPF D. IP

E. BGF

Q. 299. *ISDN works with X.25 and Frame Relay.*

ISDN is an end-to-end digital network, what are some benefits?

Ans. A. Carries varied information such as video, audio and data.

B. It is faster than basic telephone services.

C. Transfers data faster than a modem.

D. It is wireless.

Q. 300. *ISDN protocols that begin with "E" deal with.*

Ans. A. International Telephone Numbering Plan

B. International ISDN addressing

C. Concepts, structures and terminology

D. User Network Interface (UNI)

E. LAPD

Q. 301. *ISDN protocols that begin with "I" deal with.*

Ans. A. Concepts, structures and terminology

B. User Network Interfaces (UNI)

C. LAPD

D. ISDN network layer between switch and terminal

E. International ISDN addressing

Q. 302. *ISDN protocols that begin with "Q" deal with.*

Ans. A. International ISDN addressing

B. Concepts, structures and terminology

C. UNIs

D. LAPD

E. ISDN network layer between terminal and switch

Q. 303. *What are the two access options for ISDN?*

Ans. A. BRI B. PRI

C. local telephone company D. a long distance provider

E. DDR

Q. 304. *Which of the following converts BRI signals into a form used by ISDN?*

Ans. A. TE1 B. NT2

C. NT1 D. TE2

E. TA

Q. 305. *What is part of the local exchange and terminates the local loop?*

Ans. A. LT B. ET

C. TE1 D. TE2

E. NT1

Q. 306. *What is part of the exchange, which communicates with other ISDN components?*

Ans. A. LT B. ET

C. NT1 D. NT2

E. TZ

Q. 307. *What references the points that connect into the NT2?*

Ans. A. R B. S

C. T D. U

E. none

Q. 308. *What are the ISDN switch types used in the U.S. and Canada?*

Ans. A. AT&T 5ess and 4ess B. Northern Telecom DMS-100

C. VN2 D. NTT

E. Net3 and Net5

Q. 309. *What command description would you use to configure the specific ISDN switch type?*

Ans. A. isdn switch type and then type in the switch type

B. Just type in the switch type

C. isdn switch type, the computer will then read the switch type

D. No command is needed, is automatic

E. switch type isdn and then type in the switch type

SECTION C

ANSWERS OF SECTION B

1. **B.** Although ring is considered an active topology, the (MSAU) hubs are passive. The ring topology uses a passive hub topology because each NIC regenerates and repeats every signal that it receives. When a Token Ring Network is attached through hubs (MSAUs) they are passive because the signal is regenerated by the NICs in the computer.
2. **D.** When one hub goes down all computers connected to that hub will go down also. If a hub is linked to other hubs, those connections will be broken as well.
3. **D.** Networking arose from the need to share data.
4. **A.** As the geographical scope of a network grows by connecting users in different cities, the LAN grows into a WAN.
5. **D.** Workstations are a source of security concern in a LAN.
6. **C.** Desktop lockdown is the term used to prevent users from downloading software on company workstations.
7. **D.** A server cluster is a group of independent servers that are grouped together to appear like one server.
8. **C and D.** Workstations and servers have similar security concerns because they provide file sharing, network connection, and application services
9. **A, B and D.** The sound security practices include checking with the vendor for the latest security patches for Web software, checking for any additional unused services, and checking the Internet for any reports of software vulnerabilities.
10. **C.** Simple Mail Transfer Protocol (SMTP) is used to support email traffic.
11. **A.** Simple Mail Transfer Protocol (SMTP) works as a message relay agent.
12. **A, C and D.** To protect your email server you should configure your Simple Mail Transfer Protocol (SMTP) relay settings, antivirus software, and access control permissions.
13. **D.** The primary purpose of an FTP server is to facilitate file transfers.
14. **B.** Trivial File Transfer Protocol (TFTP) is frequently used to send and receive

text-based files and messages, including router configurations and ACL information.

15. **C.** The primary function of a DNS server is to resolve Fully Qualified Domain Names to IP addresses.

16. **D.** One of the most important tasks to perform when hardening a DNS server is to restrict zone transfers to authorized computer.

17. **B.** A Network News Transfer Protocol (NNTP) server, which runs on port 119, allows for a high volume of group network traffic and is a potential source for malicious code or Denial of Service (DoS) attacks.

18. **C.** One of the best ways to protect a NNTP server from malicious attack is to implement virus scanning on the NNTP server and use antivirus software.

19. **C.** Of the items listed, the best hardening technique for File and Print servers is to evaluate and set each folder share for the appropriate file and folder permissions.

20. **B.** Of the items listed, the primary network security concern with DHCP servers is that a cracker could pretend to be the DHCP server and maliciously spoof DHCP clients.

21. **C.** A rogue DHCP server could pose a conflict of IP addressing for clients on your network, thereby taking them away from your zone.

22. **A.** Access point is a critical wireless device.

23. **A, B.** The term modem stands for modulator and demodulator. Modems use telephone lines. DSL and cable modems are faster than 56 Kbps.

24. **A.** Remote access without network administrator knowledge is the greatest security risk when dealing with modems.

25. **A, C and D.** Twisted pair, fiber optic, and coaxial are types of network cabling. Token ring is a type of physical topology.

26. **C.** You use a crossover cable directly between two like components, like between two computers.

27. **D.** CSMA represents Carrier Sense Multiple Access.

28. **A and B.** Base band and broadband are the two common types of coax cabling transmission methods.

29. **C.** Of the choices listed for coax cabling, long distance is the best answer.

30. **B.** Dual-shielded coax has two outer conductors, or shields, and offers greater resistance and decreased attenuation.

31. **D.** Category 4 UTP is used in token ring networks and can transmit data at speeds of up to 16 Mbps.

32. **D.** Fiber optic cable carries signals as light waves.

33. **C.** CAT 5 twisted-pair cabling is the media standard for most local network installations.

34. **B.** Fiber optic cabling transmits at faster speeds than copper cabling, is very resistant to interference, and carries signals as light waves.

35. **D.** Fiber uses light to transmit data.

36. **A.** Fiber is the best choice in this situation.

37. **D.** Fiber protects against RF eavesdropping.

38. **D.** Fiber is most resistant to electrical and noise interference.

39. **C.** Fiber optic cable is a physical medium that is capable of conducting modulated light transmission.

40. **A.** Fiber optic cable is the most reliable cable type, but it is also the most expensive to install and terminate.

41. **B & D.** Unshielded Twisted Pair (UTP) and Shielded Twisted Pair (STP) cable are the two types of twisted-pair cables

42. **C.** UTP Category 1 cable is designed to only carry voice telephone signals. Prior to 1983 most of the installed telephone cable were Category 1. Today all new installations in the business world are requiring a minimum of Category 3 and a smart company will install Category 5 wiring for the higher data transfer bandwidth requirements.

43. **A.** Plenum cabling is made of special material that is fire resistant and is designed to give off less poisonous chemical fumes.

44. **A.** Unshielded Twisted Pair (UTP) cable is the easiest and most cost effective cabling structure for most LAN installations.

45. **A, C, D & E.** Each Network Interface Cards must have a unique network address. NICs will convert the parallel input from the computer bus into a serial output. NICs transmit at a certain speed and each receiving NIC must receive at the transmission speed of the sending NIC to be able to communicate.

46. **B.** UTP costs less per foot than any other network cable types. Fiber optic cable is the most expensive and hardest to work with.

47. **A.** Baseband signaling uses single frequency digital signaling. Baseband signals flow in the form of discrete pulses of electricity or light. Broadband transmissions travel analog (radio frequency) signals over separate inbound and outbound channels. Broadband networks provide simultaneous support for TV, data, voice, and other services on multiple transmission channels.

48. **B & C.** UTP Twisted pair is most efficient and cost efficient network topology today. In a token ring environment (not Ethernet), each NIC acts as a repeater. In an ARCnet environment, a single cable between a hub and a PC can be 2000 feet long.

49. **B.** Crosstalk occurs when data signals on one cable interfere with data signals on an adjacent cable

50. **B, D & E.** Fiber-optic is currently the most expensive cable and is not easy to install. Fiber optic cable is impervious to EM.

51. **A.** RG-58 A/U uses a stranded wire core, whereas RG-58 /U uses a solid copper wire core.

52. **B.** Polyvinyl Chloride cable is very flexible but gives off very poisonous gas if it burns. Plenum cable should be used in duct areas (plenum areas) because it is fire resistant and does not create toxic fumes when burning.

53. **B, C & D.** The AWG measures wire thickness in the manner of the larger the wire the smaller the number. As an example, telephone wire is normally 22 AWG whereas in your house, electrical wiring is normally 12 AWG to 14 AWG.

54. **D.** Category 5 certifies that UTP cable for data transmission can support up to 100 Mbps transfer rate. Category 1 is traditional (prior to 1983) telephone cable, capable of carrying voice but not data. Category 2 supports transmissions up to 4 Mbps. Category 3 supports transmissions up to 10 Mbps. Category 4 supports transmissions up to 16 Mbps.

55. **D.** Each end of a bus segment, whether it be coaxial cable or hub topology, must have a 50-**ohm** terminator. Without the BNC terminators, a bus network will not function properly.

56. **C.** Network Interface Cards can use jumpers to setup the interrupt and port that the card circuits will use.

57. **C.** In communications, bandwidth is the difference between the highest and lowest frequencies in a given range. Greater bandwidths mean faster data transfer rates.

58. **B.** Twisted pair cables are either shielded (STP) or unshielded (UTP). The actual number of pairs and the number twists per foot in a Twisted pair cable will vary.

59. **D.** The amount of shielding, the number of pairs, and the number of twists per pair all affect transmissions.

60. **A, B & D.** Category 1 is telephone (voice) cable (Category 1 UTP cannot carry data.) Category 2 transmits up to 4 Mbps Category 3 up to 10 Mbps Category 4 up to 16 Mbps Category 5 up to 100 Mbps. This answer (Whether the cable is safe to use in ceilings) is covered in the Fire Code Standards.

61. **D.** A punchdown block is a wiring terminal for cable that centralizes cabling location. It is sometimes used with unshielded twisted pair wiring.

62. **C.** IBM Type 1 standard label is STP consisting of two pair of 22 AWG wires surrounded by an outer braided shield used for computers and MAUs.

63. **B.** STP cable supports higher transmission rates over longer distances than UTP and somewhat reduces interference. The cable segments have a maximum length and should not be exceeded.

64. **B.** Thinnet commonly uses RG-58 A/U cable.

65. **A.** Coaxial cable segments must be grounded at one end but terminated at both ends.

66. **B, D & E.** Coaxial cable resists interference supports longer cable segments and attenuates less rapidly than either shielded twisted pair or unshielded twisted pair.

67. **C & D.** Fiber-optic cable is faster and more secure than copper wire cable but is more expensive and requires some expertise to install. Supporting 100 Mbps or more transmission rates, fiber-optic cable can use segment lengths of up to 6,562 feet. Because fiber-optic cable transmits light it is not susceptible to EMI and provides excellent protection against eavesdropping.

68. **C.**

69. **B & C.** Microwave systems are the most commonly used system for long distance transmission in the U.S. Using two directional antennas and two radio receivers at two line-of-sight points, communication can occur between satellite and ground sites, between two buildings, and across bodies of water or deserts.

70. **B.** Demarc is a term used to describe the location where the subscriber wiring responsibility ends and the telephone company's responsibility begins.

71. **B.** ISA cards may be either 8 or 16 bit and will fit in either a 16-or an EISA 32-bit slot.

72. **A, B & D.** A PCI Ethernet card is 32 bit and thus faster than a comparable 16-bit card. PCI specification is usually Plug and Play but some still tend to be PLUG and PRAY.

73. **B.** Star Ring and Star Bus use hubs to connect each segment of computers on the network.

74. **D.** Standard topologies are star, ring, and bus. Data is sent to all of the computers on the bus and accepted only by the computer whose address matches the address encoded in the original signal.

75. **B.** To stop a signal from bouncing, a terminator is placed at each end of the cable to absorb free signals.

76. **C.** A ring topology connects computers in a continuous loop with no terminated ends. Signals travel in a single direction until they reach the addressee. Since each computer acts as a repeater (a function of a token ring NIC), a failed computer will have a negative impact on network performance. Only one computer can transmit at a

77. **A & B.** Active hubs have the ability to regenerate and retransmit an incoming signal. Hubs do not generate acknowledgements or interrogations to computers on the network.time.

78. **E.** Within a bus topology, the terminator will absorb the cable signal to stop signal reflection. Repeaters amplify and resend signals. BNC barrel connectors connect two sections of Thinnet cable. A BNC Terminator closes each end of a bus cable to absorb any stray signals it receives. Tokens are signals passed around a ring topology.

79. **B.** A shorted NIC on a bus network will take down the entire network segment but not the entire network.

80. **A.** Organizations use networks primarily to share resources and enable online communication. Resources include data, applications, and peripherals. It is possible to have a wireless network

81. **A.** On a peer-to-peer network, each computer can act as both a client and the server computer. Peer-to-peer networks do not have dedicated servers.

82. **A, B & D.** A PCI Ethernet card is 32 bit and thus faster than a comparable 16-bit card. PCI specification is usually Plug and Play but some still tend to be PLUG and PRAY

83. **B & C.** To complete a network you must have a Topology (cable structure), a Network Interface Card, a Network Interface Card Driver, a Network Operating System and two or more Workstations or Servers

84. **B, C & D.** The selection of a network card must be made with the network topology and PC bus architecture in mind. There are four types of computer bus architectures: ISA, EISA, Micro Channel, and PCI. The network adapter card and the bus must match.

85. **E.** The PCI bus uses a 32-bit bus. PCI video cards are generally faster than VLB for graphics intensive operations and are Plug and Play. PCI is a 32-bit local-bus used in most Pentium computers and in the Apple Power Macintosh.

86. **B.** Local Area Networks are connected by some type of wire or cable, which acts as the transmission medium to carry data from one computer to another. The cabling is often referred to as the transmission medium.

87. **B.** Although a peer-to-peer LAN would work now, it appears that more employees will be hired and that a server-based LAN is the best choice to accommodate future growth.

88. **A, B & D.** The major categories of network documentation that should be maintained are the LAN system, resources used on the LAN, and the history of the LAN. Server Utilization is an important thing, a baseline should be done for a server so one can determine when it is being overworked. It is not as important as the main three. Records of user profiles (information, security access) is a good idea but should be in the backup files.

89. **C.** A wireless bridge can provide spread-spectrum radio technology using Ethernet and Token Ring bridging for up to 25 miles.

90. **A, C & D.** Configurable options that often must be set are the IRQ, the base I/O address, the base memory address, and transceiver settings.

91. **B.** Broadband systems use amplifiers to regenerate the analog signal along the topology structure. Analog signals which attenuate rapidly, are affected by electro-mechanical interference (EMI) and it needs to be regenerated often.

92. **B & C.** On a bus, only two terminators are used—one at each end. A network diagram that shows three terminators, for example, must be reworked so that it only has two—one at each end.

93. **A & B.** Hubs and concentrators act as a central point of connection between different media segments. In Ring Topology they are also called MAUs, SMAUs, or MSAUs.

94. **C.** A passive hub requires no electricity. Active hubs sometimes called multiport repeaters, regenerate and retransmit signals, requiring them to have electrical power to run.

95. **A, B and D.** Firewalls, routers, and switches will help you protect critical resources and separate your LAN.

96. **B, C and D.** Access Point (AP) is a component of a wireless LAN.

97. **B.** A switching hub is specially designed to forward packets to a specific port based on the packet's address.

98. **B.** A firewall is best suited to protect resources and subnet your LAN directly on the network or gateway server.

99. **B and C.** A firewall protects LAN resources from other networks.

100. **A, B, C and D.** All items listed are true about firewalls.

101. **A and B.** Static packet filtering is less secure than stateful filtering, proxy filtering, or dynamic packet filtering.

102. **B and C.** A packet filtering firewall operates at the Network or Transport layers.

103. **D.** Firewalls are designed to perform all the functions listed except protect against viruses.

104. **B.** Stateful firewalls may filter connection-oriented packets such as TCP.

105. **D.** Proxy server runs an Application layer firewall using proxy software.

106. **B.** A packet filtering firewall uses routers with packet filtering rules to allow or deny access based on source address, destination address, or port number.

107. **D.** A stateful packet filtering firewall keeps track of the connection state.

108. **B.** Remote-Boot PROMs allow computers with no hard drive or floppy drive to have access to the network through the use of their memory.

109. **A, C, D & E.** Each Network Interface Cards must have a unique network address. NICs will convert the parallel input from the computer bus into a serial output. NICs transmit at a certain speed and each receiving NIC must receive at the transmission speed of the sending NIC to be able to communicate.

110. **B.** Local Area Networks are connected by some type of wire or cable, which acts as the transmission medium to carry data from one computer to another. The cabling is often referred to as the transmission medium.

111. **B.** Although a peer-to-peer LAN would work now, it appears that more employees will be hired and that a server-based LAN is the best choice to accommodate future growth.

112. **A, B & D.** The major categories of network documentation that should be maintained are the LAN system, resources used on the LAN, and the history of the LAN. Server Utilization is an important thing, a baseline should be done for a server so one can determine when it is being overworked. It is not as important as the main three. Records of user profiles (information, security access) is a good idea but should be in the backup files.

113. **C.** A wireless bridge can provide spread-spectrum radio technology using Ethernet and Token Ring bridging for up to 25 miles.

114. A, C & D. Configurable options that often must be set are the IRQ, the base I/O address, the base memory address, and transceiver settings.

115. A. Bridges operate on the data link layer. They intersegment traffic creating a reduction in traffic.

116. A. Nonroutable traffic has no Layer 3, or network addressing and must be bridged. Along with the stated bridging types, Data Link Switching (DLSw) provides a way to transport SNA and NetBIOS traffic over a multiprotocol backbone. Remote source-route bridging (RSRB) can also be used to transport SNA traffic over IP networks.

117. A & B. Transparent bridging is named because end network nodes are not able to see the bridges, thus making them transparent. Transparent bridging is most commonly used on Ethernet and IEEE 802.3 networks.

118. A. Transparent bridging never changes the frame. Transparent bridges are transparent to end stations. They are used to connect two or more physical networks into one LAN.

119. A. Encapsulated bridging is the process of encapsulating a bridged frame inside another data link layer protocol, for example HDLC and de-encapsulating the packet on the opposite side of the link. Encapsulated bridging can also be called transit bridging when using FDDI. This causes the sending and receiving stations not to function on the FDDI medium.

120. A The source puts the whole source to destination route in the frame header of the inter-LAN frames. To find a destination the end stations send an explorer frame to find the location of the destination.

121. A, B, C & D.

122. A. Source-route translational bridging (SR/TLB) provides the functionality to connect two hosts that use different types of bridging.

123. A & B. The Routing Information Indicator is used in the 802.5 MAC header for identifying SRB traffic. The RII is the first byte in the source address in the 802.5 MAC frame and is bit 0.

124. A, B, C & D. The RC (Routing Control) field consists of Oxx, which is the specific route. 10x, which is all rings and all routes. 11x is the spanning route. It contains the RIF length of 5 bits. IT also figures the RIF direction. Finally, it has a code indicating the largest frame on it's way to its destination.

125. D. Both the ring number and bridge number are unique. The ring number is within the network and the bridge number connects two rings.

126. A. The local ring command is the number of interface rings. It is a decimal l number from 1-4095.

127. A. The target ring can also be a ring group.

128. B. The Cisco IOS global configuration command "bridge 'bridge-group' protocol ibm " is used to create a bridge group that runs the automatic spanning tree algorithm. The 'bridge-group' is a number in the range of 1–9.

129. A. This command helps to limit explorer traffic.

130. A, B & D. In the source-bridge transparent ring-group command the ring-group is a virtual group. This group is created by the source-bridge ring-group command. The source-bridge virtual ring is related to the transparent bridge group and is a number from 1 to 4095.

131. A & B. In the source-bridge transparent command the tb-group stands for the transparent bridge group number as well as the number related to the source-route bridge.

132. A & D. Source-Route Transparent bridging uses both transparent bridging and Source-Routing bridging. It does not, however, translate between the two protocols. It can forward both type end nodes and use spanning tree. It uses the RII to identify between SRB and transparent bridging. If RII bit is 1, then the bridge performs source routing because a RIF is in the frame. If the RII bit is 0, the bridge is transparent because there is no RIF in the frame.

133. A, B & C. SR/TLB translates between SRB and Transparent bridging. It can convert RIF, modify MTU size, and bit ordering only in Layer 2. Further, it helps add and remove RIF information and identify MAC address information.

134. A. Source-bridge transparent command enables communication between the SRB configuration and the TB configuration

135. B. The source-bridge transparent command uses a pseudo ring to represent the transparent bridge to the source-route bridge (the number is unique to the source-route bridged network).

136. A. The bridge number is the number assigned to the router.

137. A. 10 tells you that the ring group is number 10. The number 13 starts the transparent domain as a pseudo ring. The number 1 is the number to the bridge belonging to the transparent bridge domain. The number 4 is the transparent bridge that ties into the SRB domain.

138. A. max hp is length in hops for the maximum route descriptor.

receive cnt: bytes is the number of bytes and frames received.

transmit cnt: bytes is the number of bytes and frames transmitted.

Both received and transmitted are on the SRB interface.

139. B. Explorers details the explorer packets that a router has received and transmitted. All-rings is the number of all routes explored. Total tells you the total number of all all-routes explored and spanning explorers. The TR0 in the interface that receives the explorers.

140. A, B & C. The "show rif" command will tell you the way the rif was learned, the idle in minutes since the last response was received from the node, and the Routing Information Field, which lists the rif.

141. A & B

142. A, B & C. Some protocols (LAT, MOP, and NetBIOS) have no network-layer addressing so they can't be routed. IPX/SPX and TCP/IP are routable.

143. A. Transparent Bridging does not alter the data frame, it is never a source or destination for frames, and it makes the attached segments look like one cable. It is usually found on Ethernet networks.

144. A. Encapsulated Bridging is, also, called transit bridging. Networks on different media use an independent transport connection, normally FDDI or serial, to link the LANs. A data link layer protocol such as HDLC is used.

145. A & C. Source-Route Bridging (SRB) is used with Token Ring, developed by IBM. Transparent bridging bridges on a hop by hop basis. Source-Route Bridging knows the whole route prior to sending the packet. An explorer frame is used to discover the path.

146. D. Source-Route Transparent Bridging (SRT) is used in TokenRing to do both source-route and transparent bridging.

147. A. Source-Route Translational Bridging (SR/TLB) connects an Ethernet network using a transparent bridge and a Token Ring network using a source-route bridge. The bridge converts each frame to the other's format.

148. D. Class B, 255.255.0.0. The leftmost bits of the first octet are 10, which indicates that the network address is a Class B address. Although the predominant practice now is to use classless addresses, Windows 2000 chooses 255.255.0.0 as the default subnet when you enter this address into the "Internet Protocol (TCP/IP) Properties" dialog box.

149. A. 192.200.254.0. An address with a 192 value in the first octet is a Class C address because it ranges between 192 and 223 (*i.e.*, the leftmost bits in the first octet are 11). Because Class C networks have 24-bit subnets (*i.e.*, 255.255.255.0), the network portion is 192.200.254.0. The notation for classless subnetting is 192.200.254.0/24.

150. C. Achieves the required objective and both of the optional objectives. You've taken all the steps to enable dynamic routing, and the interface addresses are compatible with the assigned mask. You've properly configured a Windows 2000 server as a router whose route table will be updated automatically. By installing WINS and configuring the Microsoft clients to use WINS, you've met the first optional objective. You can communicate with the Win2K machines using the NetBIOS or machine names because WINS will resolve and return the IP addresses.

You've accomplished the second optional objective by installing a DNS server. The Microsoft machines can resolve the host name to the IP address of the UNIX machines because the records are part of the zone file. The Win2K machines can initiate an FTP session using the host name. The UNIX machines can resolve the Microsoft machine names because the DNS zone is configured to query the WINS server for the IP address of the Microsoft machines.

151. B. Because Workgroups 3.11 does not have a WINS Server. Wins Proxy agents must be NT.

152. B. The Class C subnet mask 255.255.255.224 provides 3 bits for subnet ID's and 5 bits for host **ID's.** This give a total of 6 subnets with 30 valid host addresses on each subnet.

153. C. To maximize the number of hosts, Gloria must minimize the bits used for subnets. The maximum number of subnets she needs is 100 (60 now and 40 for growth). It takes 7 bits to represent 100, so the smallest subnet mask she can use is 254 (11111110).

154. B. In a class B network there are 16 bits for host ID's. Taking 10 bits from that to represent 1000 host ID's leaves 6 bits for subnet ID's. The only subnet mask he can use is 252 (11111100). A smaller mask would provide fewer subnets; a larger mask would not provide enough host ID's per subnet. The subnet mask accommodates 62 subnets with 1022 class B hosts per subnet.

155. A, C & D.

156. D. To have a WINS enabled client you must configure it with the address of the WINS Server.

157. B. Dynamic routers automatically configure the routing tables.

158. B. ROUTE PRINT displays the contents of the local routing table on a Windows NT server.

159. A - DHCP centralizes and manages the allocation of TCP/IP configuration information by automatically assigning IP addresses to computers configured to use DHCP. Implementing DHCP eliminates some of the configuration problems associated with manually configuring TCP/IP.

160. A. Connectivity in Heterogeneous environments requires that all the processes necessary for DHCP, DNS servers, and WINS processes are completed.

161. C. This is automatic at 87.5% TTL.

162. D. The source address packet is 0.0.0.0 and the destination is 255.255.255.255.

163. A. A scope is a range of IP addresses that are available to be leased or assigned to clients.

164. B. The Unique Identifier field is what makes client reservations work. It must be configured with the MAC address of the NIC for the client.

165. A. While installing DHCP, a window appears to inform you that any adapters that were previously using DHCP will require static IP addressees.

166. C. A DHCP scope is the range of IP addresses a server can assign. At the very minimum, a DHCP server must have one scope.

167. D. The Unique Identifier field must be configured with the MAC address of the NIC for the client. Configuring this option incorrectly will cause the reservation to fail. See IPCONFIG/ALL.

168. D. If IP checks the destination IP address and determines that it is remote it will then check to see if a specific path is designated in the local routing table. If no particular entry is designated for the destination network then IP uses the default gateway. The source host first checks the Arp Cache for the default gateway's MAC or hardware address. If there is no entry then the ARP protocol broadcasts a request for the gateway's MAC address. The gateway issues an ARP reply containing its MAC address.

169. A. If a network is using TCP/IP as its protocol then it must use IP addresses. IP addresses are used by the INTERNET layer to identify the proper network and node that represents a destination host. On broadcast based networks such as Ethernet and Token Ring it is necessary to include the MAC or hardware address in another header of the destination packet. The destination host reads packets that are addressed to its hardware address and does not read packets addressed to other hardware addresses. Hardware addresses are resolved using the Address Resolution Protocol (ARP).

170. C. Type arp at the command prompt to see the proper syntax. ARP is used to display and modify the IP to MAC address translation tables, *i.e.*, the IP to NIC address tables. ARP-a displays current ARP entries. You may enter a static entry into the Arp cache by using the arp -s command.

171. B. The default is a 2 minute life for unused entries and a maximum 10 minute life for used entries. This may be changed by setting the "ARPCacheLife" parameter in the registry.

172. A, D & E. Before you install WINS, you must determine that your sever and clients meet the configuration protocol.

173. C. Each host entry is limited to 255 characters, and entries in the HOSTS file are not case sensitive.

174. B. To be a client of a DHCP server the client machine must be configured to obtain an address from a DHCP server. The DHCP server must be configured with a scope that will provide at least the IP address and subnet mask. The client must be configured to get an address from a DHCP server. To receive an address the Client sends a broadcast called a DHCP Discover packet that will not go through a router unless the router is configured to forward it. The scenario is a routed environment. They have configured forwarding of BootP packets at the routers.

This achieves the primary objective without having to include a DHCP server on each subnet. To be a WINS client the machine needs to be configured with the address of a WINS server.

If the WINS address is coming from a DHCP server, the DHCP must also configure the client to be an H-node. H-node means that the client will check the WINS server for name resolution before it tries using a subnet broadcast.

175. C. Since DHCP is in use, typing "ipconfig /release" at the command line on Asim's computer will release that IP address and allow DHCP to re-assign it to another user.

176. A. DHCP can be configured to automatically assign an IP address as well as the addresses of a WINS Server.

177. B. DHCP allows the dynamic assignment of IP addresses and can be configured with different lease durations. Client reservations can be made which designate a particular IP address for a particular host. They do not allow for setting IP addresses by time of day. With only 45% utilization of the network, DHCP with short lease durations should minimize the problems with keeping 164 users supplied with IP addresses, even with only 128 IP addresses available.

178. A. To be a client of a DHCP server the client machine must be configured to obtain an address from a DHCP server. The DHCP server must be configured with a scope that will provide at least the IP address and subnet mask. The client must be configured to get an address from a DHCP server. To receive an address the Client sends a broadcast called a DHCP Discover packet that will not go through a router unless the router is configured to forward it. The scenario is a routed environment. **They have configured** forwarding of BootP packets at the routers. This achieves the primary objective without having to include a DHCP server on each subnet. Neither of the optional objectives are achieved because they set up the WINS server but they did not configure the clients to use WINS.

179. C. A NetBIOS name is a unique 16-byte address used to identify a NetBIOS resource on the network. You can use the Nbtstat -n command to view your computer's NetBIOS name.

180. A & C. The NetBios name COMPUTER1, must be resolved to its IP address. This is done by WINS, HOSTS, LMHOSTS, DNS or broadcast. The IP address must be resolved to the Hardware address. This is done by an ARP broadcast.

181. A. If the DNS process is unsuccessful, the source host checks its local NetBIOS name cache.

182. A & C. If the name is not found in the name cache, the host sends a b-node broadcast to the local network, and if that fails to resolve the desired NetBIOS name, the host sends a directed request to the WINS (or NetBIOS) name server. An m-node machine will always broadcast before attempting point-to-point resolution.

183. E. A NetBIOS name is a unique 16-byte address used to identify a NetBIOS resource on the network.

184. A, B & D. Resolving a computer's NetBIOS name to an IP address is called NetBIOS name resolution. Note that typing nbtstat at a command prompt will display the nbtstat syntax, *e.g.*, nbtstat -c will display the remote name cache including the IP addresses.

185. C. For a router to forward broadcasts, forwarding of broadcast frames for UDP ports 137 and 138 must be enabled on the router.

186. B. Time To Live is the length of a lease. TTL function is announced within 50% of the total lease expiration for lease renewal.

187. A. Configure each server to be both a push and pull partner to replicate database entries between them.

188. A. The NetBIOS name is the name assigned to your computer.

189. A. WINS uses standard name registration, name renewal, and name release methods.

190. B. H-node is a combination of P-node and B-node. By default, an H-node functions as a P-node. If it is unable to resolve a name through the NetBIOS name server, it uses a broadcast to resolve the name.

191. A. When a WINS client initializes, it registers its NetBIOS name by sending a name registration request directly to the configured WINS server.

192. B & D. A WINS proxy agent extends the name resolution capabilities of the WINS server to non-WINS clients by listening for broadcast name resolution, and then forwarding them to a WINS server.

193. B. In large networks broadcasts increase the network load.

194. C. An MX record identifies a Mail Server. There is a field for preference if multiple mail servers exist.

195. A & C. If there is a duplicate name registered in the WINS database, the WINS server sends a challenge to the currently registered owner of the name. The challenge is sent as a name query request. The WINS server sends the challenge three times at 500-milisecond intervals.

196. A. To communicate with a host on another network, you must configure an IP address for the default gateway. TCP/IP sends packets that are destined for remote networks to the default gateway, but only if no other route is configured on the local host to the destination network. If you have not configured a default gateway, communications may be limited to the local network. A sample default gateway is 131.107.2.1.

197. A. If the DNS process is unsuccessful, the source host checks its local NetBIOS name cache.

198. C. Each time a WINS client starts, it registers its NetBIOS name IP address mapping with a configured WINS server. When a WINS client initiates a Windows NT command to communicate with another host, the name query request is sent directly to the WINS server instead of broadcasting it on the local network.

199. A. Enables connection of commands on a remote RSH server without logging on. This does not provide password protection.

200. D.

201. C.

202. A. The Arp Cache is always checked before broadcasting as a way to cut down on traffic. A thorough discussion of ARP is included in the Student Manual in Module 2: Architectural Overview of the TCP/IP

203. A, B & C. Unlike the LMHOSTS file, which is used for remote hosts only, the HOSTS file maps host names of both local and remote hosts to their IP addresses. A Domain Name System (DNS) server is a centralized online database that is used in UNIX environments to resolve fully qualified domain names (FQDNs) and other host names to IP addresses

204. C. The HOSTS file in a static file used to map host names to IP addresses. This file provides compatibility with the UNIX HOSTS file. The HOSTS file is used by PING and other TCP/IP utilities to resolve a host name to an IP address on both local and remote networks. The HOSTS file can be used to resolve NetBIOS NAMES (MicrosoftTCP/IP-32-specific).

205. A. DHCP is an extension of the BOOTP protocol which enables diskless clients to start up and automatically configure TCP/IP information to clients.

206. A & B. The DNS Server service obtains the default settings for the host name and domain name through the Microsoft TCP/IP properties dialog box.

207. A & B.

208. D. A CNAME record allows you to associate more than one name with an IP address. You can have many aliases for one IP address.

209. C. A Domain Name System (DNS) server is a centralized online database that is used in UNIX environments to resolve fully qualified domain names (FQDNs) and other host names to IP addresses.

210. A. After a default installation of the Microsoft DNS server, it is a caching-only server because it is not authoritative for any domains. It is configured with the addresses of the Root servers and can immediately begin resolving queries.

211. D.

212. D. A multicast router discriminates between multicast and unicast packets and informs switching devices what to do with the multicast packet.

213. A. The static router offers a stable table that you, as the network administrator, generate.

214. A, B and D. A dynamic router offers less security than a static router.

215. A. Of the items listed, a static router is the most difficult to configure, but safest device to use on a LAN.

216. A and D. Bridges connect two networks at the Data Link layer and routers connect two networks at the Network layer. Network spelled backward (kRowten) is similar to router with a silent k.

217. B. My useful mnemonic for this is "A Priest Says To Never Delay Praying."

218. B. Routers work at the Network layer. Network spelled backward (kRowten) is similar to Router with a silent k.

219. B. A switch will meet your goals for this situation.

220. B and D. Switches generally use Telnet or HTTP to manage interfaces and should be placed behind a dedicated firewall.

221. B. A switching hub forwards packets to an appropriate port based on the packet's address.

222. A. Network Address Translation (NAT) offers a private addressing scheme for LAN users, hiding their IP addresses from the Internet.

223. C. Network Address Translation (NAT) is relatively more secure than proxy, because it assigns private IP addresses to the client on your LAN, acting as a firewall.

224. B. Network Address Translation (NAT) has the primary purpose to shield the IP addresses of the internal network from those outside of the network.

225. A, B and D. NAT translates private IP addresses into registered Internet IP addresses, allows for private addressing ranges for internal networks, and is designed to hide the true IP addresses of internal computer systems.

226. A. The internal IP of 10.13.40.15 is an example of a private IP address reserved for internal networks, and not a valid address to use on the Internet. The Class A reserved addresses are 10.0.0.0-10.255.255.255.

227. D. The internal IP of 172.16.12.5 is an example of a private IP address reserved for internal networks, and not a valid address to use on the Internet. The Class B reserved addresses are 172.16.0.0-172.31.255.255.

228. B. The internal IP of 192.168.141.15 is an example of a private IP address reserved for internal networks, and not a valid address to use on the Internet. The Class C reserved addresses are 192.168.0.0-192.168.255.255.

229. A and C. With tunneling, private network data, which is encapsulated or encrypted, is transmitted over a public network.

230. B, C and D L2F, L2FP, and PPTP are used for VPN remote computing

231. D. Access control lists let you deny access to one individual computer by IP address or computer name.

232. D. The IAB is responsible for the broad view of the Internet, including standards and architecture.

233. D. An http error code will appear when an unsuccessful attempt is made to connect to a web **page.** 401—Unauthorized occurs on a protected web sitc when the server did not receive the correct password or encrypted identification.

234. A. IDS stands for Intrusion Detection System.

235. B. A network-based Intrusion Detection System monitors network traffic in real time.

236. A IDS is a security device that acts more like a detective rather than a preventative measure.

237. B. Simple Network Management Protocol (SNMP) is used to monitor network devices such as hubs, switches, and routers.

238. B. The IP header protocol field value of 1 = ICMP; 2 = IGMP; 6 = TCP; and 17 = UDP.

239. D. The IP header protocol field value of 6 = TCP; 1 = ICMP; 2 = IGMP; and 17 = UDP.

240. C. Mobile devices are smaller network devices, which are a security concern for network administrators because they are easily misplaced.

241. D. New Technology File System (NTFS) allows for both file and folder level permissions.

242. A. The command, chmod, allows you to change folder permissions on a Linux system.

243. D. When a system file has become infected, you should consider restoring a clean version of a file from a backup.

244. D. NTFS permissions must be used. Uploading to a directory requires only write access. To download from a directory, a user must have read permission. To run an application, execute permission is needed. To delete or modify information in a directory, Change permission is required.

245. D. You are limited to controlling the connections allowed by the FTP Service. One user could establish more than one connection; however by limiting the number of connections, you have set an upper limit to the number of users that can connect simultaneously.

246. D. Incoming and outgoing connection ports are both set to a default of 25.

247. C. A masquerade domain replaces any domain names used in the "From" lines of the header or the "Mail From" lines in the protocol with the domain name entered in the field.

248. D. NetBEUI should be denied passage over your firewall for security reasons.

249. A. When disabling services, verify the dependencies of all unused services before removing.

250. A. FTP = ports 20 (data) and 21 (session), Telnet = port 23, SMTP = port 25, Wins replication = port 42, DNS = 53, bootp = 67, IIS Gopher = 70, HTTP = 80, pop3 = 110, NNTP = 119, RPC = port 135, NetBIOS over IP = 139, SNMP =161, and SSL = 44

251. A. Verify that the unused service has no dependencies, then disable the service for security reasons.

252. TCP (Transmission Control Protocol)

253. IP (Internet Protocol)

254. POP3 (Post Office Protocol), IMAP (Interactive Mail Access Protocol).

255. PING (Packet Internet Groper)

256. Connection-oriented

257. Network

258. Transport

259. DNS (Domain Name System)

260. WINS (Windows Internet Name Service)

261. IP default gateway

262. d. NetBEUI should be denied passage over your firewall for security reasons.

263. A. When disabling services, verify the dependencies of all unused services before removing.

264. A. FTP = ports 20 (data) and 21 (session), Telnet = port 23, SMTP = port 25, Wins replication = port 42, DNS = 53, bootp = 67, IIS Gopher = 70, HTTP = 80, pop3 = 110, NNTP = 119, RPC = port 135, NetBIOS over IP = 139, SNMP =161, and SSL = 44.

265. A. Verify that the unused service has no dependencies, then disable the service for security reasons.

266. D. The IAB is responsible for the broad view of the Internet, including standards and architecture.

267. D. An http error code will appear when an unsuccessful attempt is made to connect to a web page. 401—Unauthorized occurs on a protected web site when the server did not receive the correct password or encrypted identification.

268. B. Simple Network Management Protocol (SNMP) is used to monitor network devices such as hubs, switches, and routers.

269. B. The IP header protocol field value of 1 = ICMP; 2 = IGMP; 6 = TCP; and 17 = UDP.

270. D. The IP header protocol field value of 6 = TCP; 1 = ICMP; 2 = IGMP; and 17 = UDP.

271. C. Mobile devices are smaller network devices, which are a security concern for network administrators because they are easily misplaced.

272. D. New Technology File System (NTFS) allows for both file and folder level permissions.

273. A. The command, chmod, allows you to change folder permissions on a Linux system.

274. D. When a system file has become infected, you should consider restoring a clean version of a file from a backup.

275. D. NTFS permissions must be used. Uploading to a directory requires only write access. To download from a directory, a user must have read permission. To run an application, execute permission is needed. To delete or modify information in a directory, Change permission is required

276. D. You are limited to controlling the connections allowed by the FTP Service. One user could establish more than one connection; however by limiting the number of connections, you have set an upper limit to the number of users that can connect simultaneously.

277. D. Incoming and outgoing connection ports are both set to a default of 25.

278. C. A masquerade domain replaces any domain names used in the "From" lines of the header or the "Mail From" lines in the protocol with the domain name entered in the field.

279. D. RAS stands for Remote Access Service.

280. B, C and D. A Remote Access Service (RAS) connection can be a dial-up connection or network connection using ISDN, DSL, VPN, or cable modem

281. B and C. Recommend that user accounts be verified with strong authentication, remove the guest account, and create verifiable remote accounts.

282. A and B. PBX stands for Private Branch Exchange, which allows for analog, digital, and data to transfer over a high-speed phone system.

283. C. A Virtual Private Network (VPN) provides for a private communication between two sites that also permits encryption and authorization.

284. D. Diffie-Hellman provides Strong Authentication used to verify the VPN tunnel end points.

285. C. DES performs fast data encryption and may be used with VPNs.

286. B and D. IPSec and L2TP are protocols that work together to create a secure VPN connection.

287. A & B. ISDN works with X.25 and Frame Relay.

288. A, B & C. The obvious benefits of ISDN (Integrated Services Digital Network) are the ability to transfer data, video and voice. ISDN can be used in place of basic telephone service in homes were ISDN service is available.

289. A & B. BRI has two 64 kbps bearer channels plus one 46 kbps data channel. BRI connects to an NT1. PRI is available in North America and Japan. It has 23 bearer channels and one 64 kbps D channel. In Europe PRI has a 30 B channel and one D channel.

290. C. TE1 is used to designate a router as a device having native ISDN interface. NT2 is for ISDN lines at the customer site which are switched using a customer switch. TE2 is used to designate a router as a device needing a TA for BRI signals. TA is used to convert EIA/TIA-232, V.35 signals into BRI signals.

291. A. BRI has two 64 kbps bearer channels plus one 46 kbps data channel. BRI connects to an NT1. PRI is available in North America and Japan. It has 23 bearer channels and one 64 kbps D channel. In Europe PRI has a 30 B channel and one D channel.

292. B. The LT (Local Termination) is the portion of the local exchange that terminates the local loop. The ET (Exchange Termination) is the portion of the exchange that communicates with other ISDN components.

293. B. S provides references to the points that connect into the NT2. R is the point that references between a non-ISDN compatible device and terminal adapter. T is the same as S, it references outbound connections form the NT2. U references the connection between NT1 and ISDN owned by the phone company.

294. A.

295. A & B. The spid number identifies the subscribed service. This number is assigned by the ISDN service provider. The ldn is optional and is a local dial number.

296. A & B. The "show dialer" command displays information about exiting multilinks. The "debug ppp multilink" is used to display event information about multilinks.

297. A, B, C & E.

298. A & B.

299. A, B & C. The obvious benefits of ISDN (Integrated Services Digital Network) are the ability to transfer data, video and voice. ISDN can be used in place of basic telephone service in homes were ISDN service is available.

300. A & B. E.163 is used for International Telephone Numbering Plan and E.164 is used for International ISDN addressing.

301. A & B. I.100 series is used for concepts, structures and terminology. I.400 Series is used for UNIs.

302. D & E.

303. A & B. BRI has two 64 kbps bearer channels plus one 46 kbps data channel. BRI connects to an NT1. PRI is available in North America and Japan. It has 23 bearer channels and one 64 kbps D channel. In Europe PRI has a 30 B channel and one D channel.

304. C. TE1 is used to designate a router as a device having native ISDN interface. NT2 is for ISDN lines at the customer site which are switched using a customer switch. TE2 is used to designate a router as a device needing a TA for BRI signals. TA is used to convert EIA/TIA-232, V.35 signals into BRI signals.

305. A. BRI has two 64 kbps bearer channels plus one 46 kbps data channel. BRI connects to an NT1. PRI is available in North America and Japan. It has 23 bearer channels and one 64 kbps D channel. In Europe PRI has a 30 B channel and one D channel.

306. B. The LT (Local Termination) is the portion of the local exchange that terminates the local loop. The ET (Exchange Termination) is the portion of the exchange that communicates with other ISDN components.

307. B. S provides references to the points that connect into the NT2. R is the point that references between a non-ISDN compatible device and terminal adapter. T is the same as S, it references outbound connections form the NT2. U references the connection between NT1 and ISDN owned by the phone company.

308. A & B. France uses VN2 and VN3. Japan uses NTT. United Kingdom uses Net3 and Net5.

309. A. The Cisco IOS global configuration command "isdn switch-type switch-type" is used to configure a switch at a CO. (Central Office-telephone switching location) The switch-type that you enter is a service provider switch type.

SECTION D

OBJECTIVE QUESTIONS—UNSOLVED

Q. 1. *Asynchronous protocols are widely used in ______.*

A. repeaters B. routers

C. modems D. bridges

Q. 2. *______ frame the data unit in asynchronous transmission.*

A. Error control bits B. Start and stop bits

C. Flags D. ACK characters

Q. 3. *______ layer protocols contain rules for line discipline, flow control, and error handling.*

A. Data link B. Network

C. Physical D. Transport

Q. 4. *The gaps between characters in asynchronous transmission are ______ in length.*

A. variable B. fixed-size

C. exactly one character D. one bit

Q. 5. *Since asynchronous protocols are ______, they are being replaced by synchronous protocols.*

A. expensive to implement B. inherently slow

C. require complex hardware D. require complex software

Q. 6. *XMODEM, BLAST, and Kermit are all ______ protocols.*

A. character-oriented B. bit-oriented

C. synchronous protocols D. asynchronous protocols

Q. 7. *In an XMODEM exchange, the sender can receive ______ frame.*

A. an ACK B. a NAK

C. a CAN D. any of the above

Q. 8. *The most widely used asynchronous protocol is ______.*

A. XMODEM B. YMODEM

C. BLAST D. Kermit

Q. 9. In XMODEM and Kermit, the sender waits for ______ before transmission begins.

A. an ACK B. a NAK

C. a CAN D. any of the above

Q. 10. *Kermit is a ______.*

A. terminal emulation program B. file transfer protocol

C. LAN D. A and B

Q. 11. *Kermit uses the ______ character to notify the receiver that a control character is next.*

A. DEL B. DLE

C. # D. Ctrl

Q. 12. *Control information in a system using ______ protocol are characters from an existing character encoding system.*

A. an asynchronous B. a character-oriented

C. a bit-oriented D. B and C

Q. 13. *Control information in a system using ______ protocol can be just one or a multiple number of bits.*

A. an asynchronous B. a character-oriented

C. a bit-oriented D. B and C

Q. 14. *BSC operates in the ______ mode.*

A. simplex B. half-duplex

C. full-duplex D. duplex

Q. 15. *BSC uses ______ for flow control.*

A. stop-and-wait ARQ B. go-back-n ARQ

C. selective-reject ARQ D. any of the above

Q. 16. *In BSC, an ______ means that a frame was accepted.*

A. ACK B. ACK0

C. ACK1 D. B and C

Q. 17. *Control characters for a character-oriented protocol can be represented by ______.*

A. one character B. two characters

C. three characters D. any of the above

Q. 18. *A BSC frame starts with a ______ character.*

A. SOH B. SYN

C. BCC D. STX

Q. 19. *In BSC, the character following the ______ character is data.*

A. SOH B. SYN

C. BCC D. STX

Q. 20. *In BSC, the header follows the ______ character.*

A. SOH B. SYN
C. BCC D. STX

Q. 21. *In BSC, the BCC character can follow the ______ character.*

A. ITB B. ETX
C. ETB D. any of the above

Q. 22. *How many ETX characters are in one message?*

A. 1 B. 2
C. 3 D. depends on how the message is split

Q. 23. *How many ETB characters in one message?*

A. 1 B. 2
C. 3 D. depends on how the message is split

Q. 24. *What is the purpose of a BSC control frame?*

A. establishes connections B. flow and error control
C. terminates connections D. all of the above

Q. 25. *When message data is mistaken for control data, this is called a lack of ______.*

A. synchronization B. data transparency
C. flow control D. line discipline

Q. 26. *How does the BSC protocol handle message data that looks like control data?*

A. byte stuffing B. bit stuffing
C. frame mapping D. byte mapping

Q. 27. *In BSC, a region of message data can be made transparent by inserting a ______ character before the STX character and before the ETX, ITB, or ETB character.*

A. SYN B. SOH
C. DLE D. BCC

Q. 28. *______ is the basis for all bit-oriented protocols in use today.*

A. SDLC B. HDLC
C. PPP D. LAP

Q. 29. *AN HDLC ______ station sends commands.*

A. primary B. secondary
C. combined D. A and C

Q. 30. *AN HDLC ______ station sends responses.*

A. primary B. secondary
C. combined D. B and C

Q. 31. *AN HDLC ______ station sends both commands and responses.*

A. primary B. secondary

C. combined D. none of the above

Q 32. *In a ______ configuration, an HDLC primary station and several secondary stations are connected.*

A. an unbalanced B. a symmetrical

C. a balanced D. an asymmetrical

Q. 33. *In an HDLC ______ configuration, the connected stations each consist of two logical stations (primary and secondary).*

A. unbalanced B. symmetrical

C. balanced D. asymmetrical

Q. 34. *In an HDLC ______ configuration, both stations are of the combined type.*

A. unbalanced B. symmetrical

C. balanced D. asymmetrical

Q. 35. *In an HDLC ______ configuration, a physical station can send both commands and responses.*

A. unbalanced B. symmetrical

C. balanced D. B and C

Q. 36. *In HDLC, the ______ describes which station has control of the link.*

A. station type B. configuration

C. mode of communication D. any of the above

Q. 37. *In the HDLC ______, the secondary device must have permission from the primary before it can transmit.*

A. NRM (Normal Response Mode)

B. ARM (Asynchronous Response Mode)

C. ABM (Asynchronous Balanced Mode)

D. any of the above

Q. 38. *There are ______ types of HDLC frames.*

A. 1 B. 2

C. 3 D. 4

Q. 39. *An HDLC ______ is used to transport user data and control information.*

A. I-frame B. S-frame

C. U-frame D. A-frame

Q. 40. *An HDLC ______ can transport system management information.*

A. I-frame B. S-frame

C. U-frame D. A-frame

Q. 41. *The HDLC flag field is ______.*

A. 01000010 B. 01010101

C. 10000001 D. 01111110

Q. 42. *HDLC inserts a redundant 0 bit after the ______ consecutive 1 bit in the message data.*

A. fifth B. sixth

C. seventh D. eighth

Q. 43. *If the HDLC flag field pattern is found in the message data field, it needs to be altered through ______.*

A. bit stuffing B. byte stuffing

C. bit synchronization D. byte synchronization

Q. 44. If the HDLC receiver counts more than six but less than fifteen consecutive 1s, this signifies ______.

A. data B. a flag

C. an abort D. an idle channel

Q. 45. *If the HDLC receiver counts fifteen or more consecutive 1s, this signifies ______.*

A. data B. a flag

C. an abort D. an idle channel

Q. 46. *If the HDLC receiver counts exactly six consecutive 1s, this signifies ______.*

A. data B. a flag

C. an abort D. an idle channel

Q. 47. *If the HDLC receiver counts exactly five consecutive 1s, this signifies ______.*

A. data B. a flag

C. an abort D. an idle channel

Q. 48. *When primary station A sends an HDLC frame to secondary station B, the address field contains the ______*

A. physical address of station A B. physical address of station B

C. logical address of station A D. logical address of station B

Q. 49. *When secondary station B sends an HDLC frame to primary station A, the address field contains the ______*

A. physical address of station A B. physical address of station B

C. logical address of station A D. logical address of station B

Q. 50. *In a five-byte HDLC address field, ______ in a 0 bit and ______ in a 1 bit.*

A. 2 bytes end; 3 bytes end B. 3 bytes end; 2 bytes end

C. 4 bytes end; 1 byte ends D. 1 byte ends; 4 bytes end

Q. 51. *If the least significant bit of a byte in an HDLC address field is 1, this means there are ______ more address bytes.*

A. 0 B. 1

C. 2 D. 3

Q. 52. *If the first two bits of an HDLC control field both 1s, this signifies ______.*

A. an I-frame B. an S-frame

C. a U-frame D. an E-frame

Q. 53. *All HDLC control fields contain ______.*

A. N(S) bits B. N(R) bits

C. a P/F bit D. code bits

Q. 54. *The HDLC ______ indicate the number of the frame being sent.*

A. N(S) bits B. N(R) bits

C. P/F bit D. code bits

Q. 55. *The HDLC ______ for acknowledgement.*

A. N(S) field is B. N(R) field is

C. P/F bit is D. code bits are

Q. 56. *______ contains both N(S) and N(R) bits.*

A. An I-frame B. An S-frame

C. A U-frame D. none of the above

Q. 57. *______ contains neither N(S) nor N(R) bits.*

A. An I-frame B. An S-frame

C. A U-frame D. none of the above

Q. 58. *______ is sent when acknowledgement is needed but there is no user data to transmit.*

A. An I-frame B. An S-frame

C. A U-frame D. none of the above

Q. 59. *The HDLC control field in ______ is increased to two bytes in the extended mode.*

A. an I-frame B. an S-frame

C. a U-frame D. a and b

Q. 60. *The HDLC P/F bit means poll when the frame is sent by a ______ station to a ______ station.*

A. secondary; primary B. primary; secondary

C. secondary; combined D. secondary; secondary

Q. 61. *The HDLC P/F bit means final when the frame is sent by a ______ station to a ______ station.*

A. secondary; primary B. primary; secondary

C. secondary; combined D. secondary; secondary

Q. 62. *An HDLC frame uses ______ for error detection.*

A. checksum B. VRC
C. LRC D. CRC

Q. 63. *In an HDLC S-frame the N(R) field can contain ______.*
A. the number of the next frame expected
B. the number of a damaged frame
C. the number of address bytes
D. a and b

Q. 64. *Negative acknowledgement requires an HDLC S-frame with the code field set to ______.*
A. 01 B. 10
C. 11 D. A or C

Q. 65. *Polling or selecting requires an HDLC S-frame with the code field set to ______.*
A. 00 B. 01
C. 10 D. A or C

Q. 66. *The HDLC U-frame has a ______ bit code field.*
A. 2 B. 3
C. 4 D. 5

Q. 67. *The U in U-frame stands for ______.*
A. unsupervised B. unilateral
C. unnumbered D. unicast

Q. 68. *Mode setting is handled by the ______ -frame.*
A. I B. S
C. U D. any of the above

Q. 69. *Disconnection and initialization are handled by the ______ frame.*
A. I B. S
C. U D. any of the above

Q. 70. *A secondary station has three data frames to send in response to a poll. The P/F bit for the first frame is ______, for the second frame it's ______, and for the third (last) frame it's ______.*
A. 1; 1; 1 B. 0; 0; 0
C. 1; 0; 0 D. 0; 0; 1

Q. 71. *The data link control portion of most LAN protocols in use today is based on ______.*
A. ANSI B. FDDI
C. SDLC D. HDLC

Q. 72. *Project 802 was started by the Computer Society of the ______.*

A. ANSI B. IEEE
C. AEA D. EIA

Q. 73. *In Project 802, the data link layer consists of the ______ sublayer and the ______ sublayer.*

A. LAN; MAC B. LLC; MAC
C. CSMA; LLC D. LLC; PDU

Q. 74. *In a LAN defined by Project 802, the ______ sublayer of the data link layer is non-architecture specific.*

A. CSMA B. MAC
C. LLC D. A and B

Q. 75. *Project 802 specifies functions in the ______ of the OSI model.*

A. bottom layer B. bottom 2 layers
C. bottom 3 layers D. bottom 4 layers

Q. 76. *IEEE 802.1 is concerned with ______ issues in LANs and MANs.*

A. error handling B. networking
C. internetworking D. flow control

Q. 77. *The ______ sublayer, as specified in Project 802, is LAN specific and deals with contention issues.*

A. CSMA B. MAC
C. LLC D. A and C

Q. 78. *Ethernet, Token Ring, and Token Bus are all different types of ______.*

A. LANs B. MANs
C. WANs D. VANs

Q. 79. *The ______ is the data unit at the LLC level.*

A. HDLC B. PDU
C. SSAP D. MAC

Q. 80. *DSAP and SSAP are both ______ fields.*

A. control B. user data
C. error control D. address

Q. 81. *The first bit of the ______ field in the PDU indicates the type of PDU (command or response).*

A. DSAP B. SSAP
C. HDLC D. LLC

Q. 82. *The first bit of the ______ field in the PDU indicates the destination type (individual or group).*

A. DSAP B. SSAP
C. HDLC D. LLC

Q. 83. *The PDU ______ field is identical to the HDLC ______ field.*

A. control; information B. control; control

C. control; PAD D. control; FCS

Q. 84. *A PDU frame can be ______.*

A. an I-frame B. an S-frame

C. a U-frame D. any of the above

Q. 85. *The flag, CRC, and station address fields are added to the PDU at the ______ layer.*

A. physical B. LLC

C. MAC D. network

Q. 86. *Which of the following is an IEEE Project 802 standard?*

A. Ethernet B. Token Ring

C. Token Bus D. All of the above

Q. 87. *______ signal is digital.*

A. A baseband B. A broadband

C. An Ethernet D. None of the above

Q. 88. *______ signal is analog.*

A. A baseband B. A broadband

C. An Ethernet D. None of the above

Q. 89. *A 100Base-T Ethernet LAN has a data rate of ______ Mbps.*

A. 1 B. 10

C. 100 D. 1000

Q. 90. *A 10Base2 Ethernet LAN has a data rate of ______ Mbps.*

A. 1 B. 2

C. 10 D. 100

Q. 91. *A 10Base5 Ethernet LAN has a maximum cable length of ______ meters (assume no repeaters, bridges, or other such devices).*

A. 5 B. 10

C. 100 D. 500

Q. 92. *The Ethernet access method ______.*

A. involves a token B. involves time registers

C. involves input and output queues

D. is CSMA/CD

Q. 93. *The T in 10Base-T and 100Base-T indicates the ______.*

A. data rate B. cable type

C. signal type D. access type

Q. 94. *A collision cannot occur on a ______ LAN.*

A. Ethernet
B. Token Ring
C. FDDI
D. B or C

Q. 95. *On an Ethernet LAN, when a collision is detected, the sending station ______.*

A. continues to send the transmission
B. quits sending the transmission
C. notifies the destination of an error
D. a and c

Q. 96. *A station on ______ network is identified by a unique 6-byte physical address.*

A. an Ethernet
B. a Token Ring
C. an FDDI
D. all of the above

Q. 97. *An Ethernet LAN uses ______ signals.*

A. Manchester encoded
B. differential Manchester encoded
C. differential PSK
D. PSK

Q. 98. *The error detection information for the IEEE 802.3 frame is found in the ______ field.*

A. SFD
B. PDU
C. CRC
D. preamble

Q. 99. *The ______ and ______ fields of the IEEE 802.3 frame have the same functions as the flag field in HDLC.*

A. PDU; CRC
B. PDU; SFD
C. preamble; CRC
D. preamble; SFD

Q. 100. *Which field in the IEEE 802.3 frame consists entirely of alternating 1s and 0s?*

A. preamble
B. SFD
C. PDU
D. CRC

Q. 101. *Thick coaxial cable is the medium for the ______ standard.*

A. 10Base5
B. 10Base-T
C. 10Base2
D. 1Base5

Q. 102. *The ______ function is to check for voltages and collisions on the line.*

A. cable terminator
B. transceiver
C. AUI
D. NIC

Q. 103. *In a 10Base5 Ethernet LAN, a station is connected to the coaxial cable through ______ and ______.*

A. a MAU; an AUI
B. a NIC; a MAU
C. an AUI; a NIC
D. a MAU; a terminator

Q 104. *A vampire tap is a connector found in a ______.*

A. thin Ethernet LAN B. thick Ethernet LAN
C. twisted-pair Ethernet LAN D. StarLan

Q. 105. *A BNC-T connector is used in a ______.*

A. thin Ethernet LAN B. thick Ethernet LAN
C. twisted-pair Ethernet LAN D. StarLan

Q. 106. *The 10Base5 maximum segment size is ______ that of the 10Base2 maximum segment size. (Assume no networking devices.)*

A. the same as B. less than
C. greater than twice D. none of the above

Q. 107. *The 10Base5 data rate is ______ that of the 10Base2 data rate.*

A. the same as B. less than
C. greater than twice D. none of the above

Q. 108. *The "T" in 10Base-T stands for ______.*

A. twisted-pair cable
B. the 10Mbps data rate
C. the telephone-like jack used for connection
D. the thousand-foot hub-to-station length

Q. 109. *Daisy chaining is often used by ______ networks to increase the number of stations per hub.*

A. 10Base5 B. 10Base2
C. 10Base-T D. 1Base5

Q. 110. *Which implementation of IEEE 802.3 has the lowest data rate?*

A. 10Base5 B. 10Base2
C. 10Base-T D. StarLan

Q. 111. ______ *Ethernet features a device that can route a frame directly to the destination station.*

A. Switched B. Fast
C. Gigabit D. All of the above

Q. 112. *The collision domain of Ethernet is limited to ______ meters.*

A. 2.5 B. 25
C. 250 D. 2500

Q. 113. *100Base-TX, 100Base-T4, and 100Base-FX are types of ______ Ethernet.*

A. Switched B. Fast
C. Gigabit D. 100Base-X

Q. 114. ______ *Ethernet can utilize the wiring (voice-grade UTP) existing in most buildings.*

A. 100 Base-TX B. 100 Base-FX
C. 100 Base-T4 D. A and B

Q. 115. *In Gigabit Ethernet the 1000Base-SX and 1000Base-LX implementations specify ______ as the medium.*

A. STP B. UTP
C. optical fiber D. A or B

Q. 116. Token Bus is physically configured like ______.

A. Ethernet B. Token Ring
C. FDDI D. all of the above

Q. 117. Token Bus operates under a collision-free environment similar to ______.

A. Ethernet B. Token Ring
C. CSMA/CD D. all of the above

Q. 118. *On a Token Ring LAN, a station can reserve the token by entering its priority code in the access control field of the ______ frame.*

A. data/command B. token
C. abort D. A or B

Q. 119. *The ______ field in a Token Ring frame is equivalent to the HDLC flag field.*

A. SD B. AC
C. FC D. FS

Q. 120. *A Token Ring frame can be identified as a token frame by a bit in the ______ field.*

A. SD B. AC
C. FC D. ED

Q. 121. *In Token Ring, the ______ sets the bits in the frame status field to indicate that the frame has been copied.*

A. sender B. receiver
C. monitor D. A and B

Q. 122. *In Token Ring, the ______ sets the bits in the frame status field to indicate that the frame has already been around the ring.*

A. sender B. receiver
C. monitor D. A and B

Q. 123. *The Token Ring AC field contains ______ information.*

A. priority B. frame type
C. reservation D. all of the above

Q. 124. *The Token Ring ______ field is present only on the data/command frame.*

A. SD B. AC
C. ED D. FS

Q. 125. *The Token Ring ______ frame consists of just the start and end delimiters.*

A. data/command B. token
C. abort D. command

Q. 126. *The Token Ring abort frame is sent by ______.*

A. the sending station B. the receiving station
C. a monitor D. A and C

Q. 127. *In a Token Ring LAN, a frame is ______ at each station.*

A. examined B. regenerated
C. encapsulated D. A and B

Q. 128. *The purpose of connecting each Token Ring station to an automatic switch is to ______.*

A. multiplex frames B. bypass an inactive station
C. prevent errors D. increase the data rate

Q. 129. *A multistation access unit is most often used in ______ LAN.*

A. an Ethernet B. a Token Ring
C. an FDDI D. A and B

Q. 130. *An FDDI LAN can use ______ as a medium.*

A. any metallic cable B. copper cable
C. fiber optic cable D. B or C

Q. 131. *Token Ring and FDDI both use ______ as an access method.*

A. CSMA B. CSMA/CD
C. token passing D. HDLC

Q. 132. An FDDI synchronous data frame means that ______.

A. the information is real-time
B. the information is not real-time
C. the information comes from the SDLC protocol
D. the information is time-division multiplexed

Q. 133. *Each station on an FDDI ring has a ______ register while there is just one ______ register for the entire FDDI ring.*

A. SA; TTRT B. TTRT; SA
C. AMT; SA D. SA; TRT

Q. 134. *The ______ register holds a value equal to twice the ______.*

A. AMT; TTRT B. TTRT; AMT
C. AMT; SA D. TTRT; SA

Q. 135. *If a token traverses the FDDI ring in a time greater than the ______, the ring gets reinitialized.*

A. SA B. TTRT
C. TRT D. AMT

Q. 136. *The ______ is the average time required for a token to circulate the ring exactly once.*

A. SA B. TTRT
C. AMT D. TAM

Q. 137. *The sum of the ______ should be a value close to the TTRT.*

A. SAs B. TTRTs
C. AMTs D. TAMs

Q. 138. *The ______ is a measure of an actual cycle time while the ______ is an average cycle value set at ring initialization.*

A. TRT; THT B. THT; TRT
C. THT; TTRT D. TRT; TTRT

Q. 139. *The THT is a function of the ______ and ______.*

A. AMT; TTRT B. TTRT; TRT
C. SA; TTRT D. AMT; SA

Q. 140. *The ______ is always 0 when the token arrives at an FDDI station.*

A. TTRT B. TRT
C. THT D. SA

Q. 141. *An FDDI station sends asynchronous data as long as the ______ value is positive.*

A. TTRT B. TRT
C. THT D. SA

Q. 142. *When the token leaves an FDDI station, the TRT value is ______.*

A. 0 B. some positive value
C. some negative value D. greater than TTRT but less than SA

Q. 143. *FDDI specifies ______ encoding prior to NRZ-I encoding.*

A. 4B/5T B. 3B/4B
C. 5B/4B D. 4B/5B

Q. 144. *Which of the following is not a protocol in the FDDI standard?*

A. PMD B. PHY
C. MAC D. HDLC

Q. 145. *Which type of FDDI node has two MICs?*

A. DAS B. SAS
C. DAC D. A and C

Q. 146. *Which type of FDDI node has one MIC?*

A. DAS B. SAS

C. DAC D. A and C

Q. 147. *How many MICs are need for a DAC connecting 3 workstations to an FDDI ring?*

A. 2 B. 3

C. 4 D. 5

Q. 148. *In FDDI, when all synchronous data have been sent and the THT value is still positive, ______.*

A. no asynchronous data can be sent

B. asynchronous data can be sent

C. all asynchronous data have been sent

D. any of the above

Q. 149. *One MAU can support ______ stations.*

A. 5 B. 8

C. 32 D. any number of

Q. 150. *An MAU is a device used in ______.*

A. Ethernet B. Token Ring

C. FDDI D. all of the above

Q. 151. *An SAS is a device used in ______.*

A. Ethernet B. Token Ring

C. FDDI D. all of the above

Q. 152. *A multiplexer ______ several transmission streams while a demultiplexer ______ them.*

A. combines; separates B. compresses; decompresses

C. encrypts; decrypts D. separates; combines

Q. 153. *One ______ can be made of many ______.*

A. channel; paths B. path; channels

C. path; links D. channel; links

Q. 154. *Which of the following is a digital multiplexing method?*

A. FDM B. asynchronous TDM

C. synchronous TDM D. B and C

Q. 155. *Which is not a basic multiplexing method?*

A. FDM B. TDM

C. WDM D. MDM

Q. 156. ______ *is an analog multiplexing technique usually involving signals that are not in the visible light frequencies.*

A. FDM B. TDM
C. WDM D. MDM

Q. 157. *______ is a digital multiplexing technique usually involving signals that are not in the visible light frequencies.*

A. FDM B. TDM
C. WDM D. MDM

Q. 158. *______ is an analog multiplexing technique usually involving signals in the visible light frequencies.*

A. FDM B. TDM
C. WDM D. MDM

Q. 159. *In FDM, the bandwidth of the link must be ______ the sum of the bandwidths of the signals to be combined.*

A. equal to B. less than
C. greater than D. an order of magnitude greater than

Q. 160. *In FDM, if five signals are to be multiplexed, at least ______ carriers, each of a different frequency, must be modulated.*

A. 1 B. 5
C. 6 D. 10

Q. 161. *FDM uses ______ to prevent modulated signals from overlapping.*

A. physical hardware devices B. carrier frequencies
C. guard bands D. demultiplexers

Q. 162. *In FDM, the ______ signals can all have the same frequency range.*

A. modulating B. carrier
C. modulated D. B or C

Q. 163. The FDM demultiplexer uses a series of ______ to decompose the multiplexed signal into its constituent signals,

A. guard bands B. filters
C. repeaters D. amplifiers

Q. 164. *WDM is very similar in concept to ______.*

A. asynchronous TDM B. synchronous TDM
C. FDM D. AM or FM

Q. 165. *If the sum of the data rates of the sending devices is X, TDM can be applied when the data rate capacity of the transmission medium is ______.*

A. less than X B. greater than X
C. one half X D. two times X

Q. 166. *In ______ the multiplexer allocates exactly the same time slot to each device at all times.*

A. synchronous TDM B. asynchronous TDM
C. FDM D. WDM

Q. 167. *In ______, if a device has no data to send, its time slot remains empty.*

A. synchronous TDM B. asynchronous TDM
C. FDM D. WDM

Q. 168. In synchronous TDM, a ______ is a complete cycle of time slots, including one or more slots dedicated to each sending device.

A. filter B. carrier
C. signal D. frame

Q. 169. *What is the efficiency of a system using synchronous TDM if 2 of the 5 devices have nothing to send?*

A. 20% B. 50%
C. 60% D. 100%

Q. 170. *In synchronous TDM, if device X has data to send, the data go to ______ in the frame.*

A. the next available slot B. a preassigned slot
C. the first slot D. none of the above

Q. 171. *In asynchronous TDM, if device X has data to send, the data go to ______ in the frame.*

A. the next available slot B. a preassigned slot
C. the first slot D. none of the above

Q. 172. *In synchronous TDM, if device X has no data to send, what happens to its allotted slot?*

A. The next device in line takes it.
B. An error message is sent.
C. The bit pattern 01010101 is sent.
D. The slot remains empty.

Q. 173. *In synchronous TDM, each frame is filled with data from the devices in a fixed order. We call this ______.*

A. interleaving B. synchronization
C. switching D. line discipline

Q. 174. ______ *allow the demultiplexer to synchronize with the incoming stream.*

A. Slots B. Framing bits
C. Demultiplexing bits D. Trailers

Q. 175. *In synchronous TDM, if ten devices are each sending data at the rate of 2000 bps, what is the data rate for the line carrying the multiplexed signals?*

A. 2000 bps B. 20,000 bps
C. greater than 20,000 bps D. less than 20,000 bps

Q. 176. *What is the major weakness of asynchronous TDM?*

A. There aren't enough slots in each frame.

B. There are too many slots per frame.

C. Each slot requires an address.

D. All of the above

Q. 177. *What is the major weakness of synchronous TDM?*

A. Some slots may remain empty.

B. There aren't enough slots.

C. The slots are too small.

D. All of the above.

Q. 178. *Which type of multiplexing takes data from one high-speed line and breaks it into portions that can be sent across several lower-speed lines simultaneously?*

A. Asynchronous TDM B. Synchronous TDM

C. FDM D. Inverse multiplexing

Q. 179. *The most common dial-up service used by a person making a home telephone call is ______.*

A. analog switched service B. analog leased service

C. switched/56 service D. digital data service

Q. 180. *The bandwidth on a local loop is between ______.*

A. 0 Hz to 400 Hz B. 0 Hz to 4000 Hz

C. 1000 Hz to 4000 Hz D. 4000 Hz to 8000 Hz

Q. 181. *A line can have less attenuation and less distortion if it is ______.*

A. switched B. conditioned

C. unconditioned D. dedicated

Q. 182. *In the analog hierarchy, twelve voice channels are multiplexed to create a ______.*

A. group B. super group

C. master group D. jumbo group

Q. 183. *In the analog hierarchy, a ______ consists of 60 independent voice channels.*

A. group B. super group

C. master group D. jumbo group

Q. 184. *In the analog hierarchy, a ______ consists of 600 independent voice channels.*

A. group B. super group

C. master group D. jumbo group

Q. 185. *In the analog hierarchy, a ______ consists of 3600 independent voice channels.*

A. group B. super group

C. master group D. jumbo group

Q. 186. *Which digital service requires a DSU?*

A. switched/56 service B. DDS

C. DS D. A and B

Q. 187. *Which of the following about switched/56 service is true?*

A. Subscribers need modems.

B. Data is analog.

C. A DSU changes the analog data to digital.

D. Sender and receiver must both subscribe to the service.

Q. 188. ______ *is a digital leased line with a maximum data rate of 64 Kbps.*

A. DS B. DDS

C. Switched/56 service D. Analog switched service

Q. 189. *In the DS service hierarchy,* ______ *resembles DDS.*

A. DS-0 B. DS-1

C. DS-2 D. DS-3

Q. 190. *A DS-0 service is a single digital channel of* ______.

A. 4000 Kbps B. 2000 Kbps

C. 1000 Kbps D. 64 Kbps

Q. 191. *A DS-4 service can be composed of 4032* ______ *channels.*

A. DS-0 B. DS-1

C. DS-2 D. DS-3

Q. 192. *A DS-4 service is implemented by a* ______.

A. DS line B. T-4 line

C. DS-4 line D. none of the above

Q. 193. *T lines can be used for* ______.

A. digital data transmission

B. digital voice transmission

C. regular telephone transmission

D. any of the above

Q. 194. *For a telephone voice transmission to use a T-line, the signal must be* ______ *before being multiplexed.*

A. synchronized B. modulated

C. sampled D. filtered

Q. 195. *A T-1 line can handle* ______ *multiplexed voice channels.*

A. 6 B. 12

C. 18 D. 24

Q. 196. *A T-1 frame has ______ slot(s) of ______ bit(s) each plus ______ bit(s) for synchronization.*

A. 24; 8; 1 B. 8; 24; 1
C. 24; 1; 8 D. 8; 1; 24

Q. 197. A T-1 line carries ______ frames per second.

A. 193 B. 24
C. 8000 D. 1.544

Q. 198. *A ______ allows a T line to be shared.*

A. DSU B. CSU
C. DSU/CSU D. splitter

Q. 199. *A T line that is shared by several customers is called a______.*

A. fractional T line B. DSL
C. shared T line D. switched/56 line

Q. 200. *Europeans use a version of T lines called ______.*

A. A lines B. B lines
C. D lines D. E lines

Q. 201. *The link between a telephone user and the telephone network is called ______.*

A. the MTSO B. the local loop
C. DSL D. the common carrier

Q. 202. *The bit rate for users of ADSL is higher in the ______ direction than in the ______ direction.*

A. downstream; upstream B. upstream; downstream
C. sending; receiving D. none of the above

Q. 203. *ADSL divides the bandwidth of a ______ cable into three bands.*

A. coaxial B. fiber-optic
C. twisted-pair D. any of the above

Q. 204. In ADSL, a(n) ______ KHz band is used for downstream communication.

A. 4 B. 25
C. 175 D. 800

Q. 205. *In ADSL, a(n) ______ KHz band is used for POTS.*

A. 4 B. 25
C. 175 D. 800

Q. 206. *In ADSL, a(n) ______ KHz band is used for upstream communication.*

A. 4 B. 25
C. 175 D. 800

Q. 207. *ADSL uses a modulation technique called ______.*

A. differential modulation technique

B. carrierless amplitude/phase

C. discrete multitone technique

D. downstream modulation technique

Q. 208. *What kind of modulation is used by ADSL?*

A. PSK B. FSK

C. QAM and FDM D. PCM

Q. 209. *What kind of multiplexing is used by ADSL?*

A. FDM B. Asynchronous TDM

C. Synchronous TDM D. WDM

Q. 210. Which ADSL-based technology allows different data rates depending on the type of communication?

A. RADSL B. HDSL

C. SDSL D. VDSL

Q. 211. In RADSL, cost is assessed according to ______.

A. the amount of use time B. the time of use

C. the data rate required D. all of the above

Q. 212. *What ADSL-based technique uses 2B1Q encoding?*

A. RADSL B. HDSL

C. SDSL D. VDSL

Q. 213. *What kind of encoding does a T-1 line use?*

A. PSK B. FSK

C. ASK D. AMI

Q. 214. *What data rate can HDSL attain?*

A. 56 Kbps B. 100 Kbps

C. 2 Mbps D. 8 Mbps

Q. 215. Which DSL technology uses echo cancellation to create a full-duplex transmission?

A. RADSL B. HDSL

C. SDSL D. VDSL

Q. 216. *To which DSL technology is SDSL most similar?*

A. RADSL B. HDSL

C. SDSL D. VDSL

Q. 217. *To which DSL technology is VDSL most similar?*

A. RADSL B. HDSL

C. SDSL D. ADSL

Q. 218. *What type of medium does VDSL use?*

A. Coaxial cable B. Twisted-pair cable

C. Fiber-optic cable D. Any of the above

Q. 219. *What type of medium does FTTC use?*

A. Fiber-optic cable B. Coaxial cable

C. Twisted-pair cable D. A plus c

Q. 220. *What kind of network uses FTTC?*

A. Telephone network B. Cable TV network

C. Radio network D. A and B

Q. 221. *Reliable communication means that ______.*

A. errors must be detected B. errors must be corrected

C. noise must be eliminated D. A and B

Q. 222. *If the ASCII "m" character is received as an "n" character, this is known as a ______.*

A. single-bit error B. burst error

C. character error D. byte error

Q. 223. *If the ASCII "7" character is received as the "5" character, this is known as a ______.*

A. single-bit error B. burst error

C. character error D. byte error

Q. 224. *If data were sent at 54 Kbps, what duration of noise would cause a single-bit error?*

A. 54 microseconds B. 5.4 microseconds

C. 18.5 microseconds D. 18.5 milliseconds

Q. 225. *A 2-microsecond duration of noise caused a single-bit error. What is the minimum data rate?*

A. 500 kbps B. 50 kbps

C. 50 Mbps D. 500 Mbps

Q. 226. *A single-bit error is more likely in a ______ transmission while a burst error is more likely in a ______ transmission.*

A. serial; parallel B. parallel; serial

C. serial; multiplexed D. duplex; parallel

Q. 227. *Data are being sent at 30 Mbps. An external electrical surge of 0.01 seconds affects the transmission. What is the maximum number of bits that can be affected?*

A. 3000 B. 30,000

C. 300,000 D. 3,000,000

Q. 228. *Which of the following is an error detection method?*

A. Multiplexing B. Redundancy
C. Reciprocity D. Conditioning

Q. 229. *Another name for VRC is ______.*

A. LRC B. CRC
C. checksum D. parity check

Q. 230. *Which type of redundancy check do the upper layers primarily use?*

A. VRC B. CRC
C. LRC D. Checksum

Q. 231. *VRC, LRC, and CRC are normally implemented in the ______ layer(s) for use in the ______ layer.*

A. upper; data link B. network; data link
C. physical; data link D. data link; physical

Q. 232. *Checksum is an error detection method used primarily by the ______.*

A. physical layer B. data link layer
C. lower layers D. upper layers

Q. 233. *The most common and least expensive error detection mechanism is ______.*

A. VRC B. CRC
C. LRC D. checksum

Q. 234. *In the VRC method of error detection, redundancy consists of ______.*

A. one data unit B. one bit
C. one byte D. any of the above

Q. 235. *For even parity, after adding the redundant bit, the number of ______.*

A. 0s should be even B. 0s should be odd
C. 1s should be even D. 1s should be odd

Q. 236. *For even parity, after adding the redundant bit, the number of 0s ______.*

A. should be even
B. should be odd
C. should be less than the number of 1s
D. we cannot say

Q. 237. *Which method can detect all single-bit errors?*

A. CRC B. VRC
C. LRC D. All of the above

Q. 238. VRC can detect ______.

A. all single-bit errors
B. burst errors if the number of errors is odd

C. burst errors if the number of errors is even

D. a and b

Q. 239. If a block of bits contains eight data units with sixteen bits per data unit, how many bits is the LRC?

A. 8 B. 16

C. 17 D. 32

Q. 240. *If we use LRC for error detection on a block of bits containing eight data units with sixteen bits per data unit, how many total data units are sent?*

A. 8 B. 9

C. 16 D. 32

Q. 241. *Which data link layer redundancy technique is most powerful?*

A. VRC B. LRC

C. CRC D. checksum

Q. 242. *For CRC, the redundant bits are ______.*

A. appended to the original data unit

B. subtracted from the original data unit

C. interleaved with the original data unit

D. sent in a separate data unit

Q. 243. *For CRC, a remainder of 0s at the receiver indicates the data ______.*

A. are missing B. are good

C. are bad D. need to be retransmitted

Q. 244. *The CRC divisor is ______.*

A. the same number of bits as the CRC

B. one more bit than the CRC

C. one less bit than the CRC

D. unrelated in size to the CRC

Q. 245. In the CRC generator, the dividend for the CRC technique consists of ______.

A. the data only B. the data plus n 0 bits

C. the data plus the CRC D. the data plus the divisor

Q. 246. In the CRC checker, the dividend for the CRC technique consists of ______.

A. the data only B. the data plus n 0 bits

C. the data plus the CRC D. the data plus the divisor

Q. 247. *For CRC, a non-zero remainder at the checker indicates the data are ______.*

A. missing B. good

C. bad D. duplicated

Q. 248. *The CRC ______ is at the receiver site while the CRC ______ is at the sender site.*

A. generator; checker
B. generator; divisor
C. checker; generator
D. checker; redundant

Q. 249. *The CRC remainder consists of ______.*

A. the quotient
B. the divisor
C. the bits left over from division
D. the bits added to the divisor

Q. 250. *What do the CRC generator and checker share in common?*

A. the quotient
B. the divisor
C. the remainder
D. the dividend

Q. 251. *For CRC, which of the following determines the length of the burst error that can be detected?*

A. The number of non-zero coefficients
B. The degree of the polynomial
C. The number of negative coefficients
D. All of the above

Q. 252. ______ *is an acceptable CRC polynomial.*

A. $x^3 + x^2 + x + 1$
B. $x^3 + x^2 + x$
C. $x^3 + x^2$
D. x^3

Q. 253. *What is the largest burst error that a polynomial of degree 32 can detect?*

A. 4 bits
B. 8 bits
C. 16 bits
D. 32 bits

Q. 254. *Why is $x^3 + x^2 + x$ unacceptable as a CRC polynomial?*

A. It is divisible by x.
B. It is not divisible by (x+1).
C. It is not divisible by x.
D. A and B

Q. 255. *What does the CRC divisor look like if the polynomial is $x^{10} + x^9 + x + 1$?*

A. 11000000011
B. 11110000000
C. 11000000010
D. 10100010100

Q. 256. *What is the polynomial given the CRC divisor of 11011?*

A. $x^4 + 2x^2 + x + 1$
B. $x^4 + x^3 + 2x + 1$
C. $x^4 + x^3 + x + 1$
D. $x^5 + x^4 + x^2 + x$

Q. 257. *For a CRC-32, the divisor is ______ bits in length.*

A. 31
B. 32
C. 33
D. none of the above

Q. 258. *For a CRC-32, the remainder is ______ bits in length.*

A. 31
B. 32
C. 33
D. none of the above

Q. 259. *CRC can detect ______.*

A. all burst errors

B. all burst errors of length less than or equal to the degree of the polynomial

C. any type of error

D. all of the above

Q. 260. *In the checksum error detection method, segments are added together using ______ arithmetic.*

A. sign-and-magnitude B. one's complement

C. two's complement D. any of the above

Q. 261. *In checksum generation the checksum is ______.*

A. all 0s

B. all 1s

C. the sum of the one's complement addition

D. the complement of the one's complement addition

Q. 262. *In checksum calculation at the receiver, the data unit is accepted if the final result is ______.*

A. all 0s B. all 1s

C. all 0s or all 1s D. the numeric value 1

Q. 263. ______ *is an error correction method.*

A. LRC B. CRC

C. The checksum D. Hamming encoding

Q. 264. *The sum of a one's complement addition of a data unit is 00001111. The checksum is therefore ______.*

A. 00001111 B. 11110000

C. 10101010 D. 00010000

Q. 265. *In the formula 2r >= m + r + 1, what is r?*

A. The number of bits in error

B. The number of bits in the data unit

C. The number of redundant bits

D. The error location

Q. 266. *In the formula 2r >= m + r + 1, what is m?*

A. The number of bits in error

B. The number of bits in the data unit

C. The number of redundant bits

D. The error location

Q. 267. *For a 16-bit data unit, what is the minimum r that satisfies 2r >= m + r + 1?*

A. 3 B. 4

C. 5 D. 6

Q. 268. *For a 32-bit data unit, what is the minimum r that satisfies 2r >= m + r + 1?*

A. 3 B. 4

C. 5 D. 6

Q. 269. *If r is 1 in the formula 2r >= m + r + 1, what is the minimum size of the data unit?*

A. 0, no data unit possible B. 1

C. 2 D. 3

Q. 270. *If r is 5 in the formula 2r >= m + r + 1, what is the maximum size of the data unit?*

A. 5 B. 16

C. 26 D. 32

Q. 271. *For a transmittable unit of 11 bits (data plus redundant bits), there are ______ states for error detection.*

A. 4 B. 7

C. 11 D. 12

Q. 272. *For a transmittable unit of 5 bits (data plus redundant bits), there are ______ states for error detection.*

A. 2 B. 3

C. 4 D. 6

Q. 273. *The ______ code is a method to determine the position of the bit in error.*

A. Humming B. Hanning

C. Hamming D. Dijkstra

Q. 274. *A redundancy bit in the Hamming code is calculated using ______.*

A. VRC B. LRC

C. CRC D. checksum

Q. 275. *The frequency range of visible light is ______ than the frequency range used in radio communication.*

A. lower B. higher

C. the same as D. depends on the medium

Q. 276. *Which of the following is usually not classified as a guided medium?*

A. Twisted-pair cable B. Fiber-optic cable

C. Coaxial cable D. Troposphere

Q. 277. ______ *consists of 2 conductors twisted round each other.*

A. Twisted-pair cable B. Fiber-optic cable

C. Coaxial cable D. Microwave cable

Q. 278. ______ *has an inner conductor and an outer conductor separated by insulation.*

A. Twisted-pair cable B. Fiber-optic cable
C. Coaxial cable D. All of the above

Q. 279. *Category 5 UTP cables ______ Category 1 cables.*

A. transmit data at lower rates than
B. transmit data at higher rates than
C. are unsuitable for voice transmission compared to
D. have less twists per foot than

Q. 280. *UTP is popular in LAN technology due to its ______.*

A. flexibility B. low cost
C. ease of installation D. all of the above

Q. 281. *The most frequently used UTP connector is ______.*

A. category 5 connector B. EIA 232
C. RJ45 D. JR45

Q. 282. One of the benefits of encasing a twisted-pair cable in a metal foil covering is the ______.

A. reduction of crosstalk B. increase of crosstalk
C. increase in flexibility D. decrease in costs

Q. 283. ______ *cable carries signals of higher frequency ranges than* ______ *cable.*

A. Twisted-pair; coaxial B. Twisted-pair; fiber-optic
C. Coaxial; twisted-pair D. None of the above

Q. 284. *The outer metallic sheath in coaxial cable functions as ______.*

A. a connector B. a second conductor
C. a shield against noise D. B and C

Q. 285. *The most popular connector used with ______ cable is the BNC.*

A. twisted-pair B. shielded twisted-pair
C. coaxial D. fiber-optic

Q. 286. *A ______ is a device that prevents the signal at the end of a bus backbone from echoing back on to the line.*

A. repeater B. horn antenna
C. T-connector D. terminator

Q. 287. *The core of an optical fiber is ______.*

A. glass B. plastic
C. metal D. A or B

Q. 288. *Light travels at ______ in a vacuum.*

A. 300,000 km/s B. 300,000 miles/s
C. 300,000 m/s D. 186,000 m/s

Q. 289. *Light travels at ______ in the atmosphere.*

A. less than 186,000 miles/s B. greater than 186,000 miles/s

C. 186,000 miles/s D. 186,000 m/s

Q. 290. *As a beam of light goes from the air into a body of water, its speed ______.*

A. increases B. decreases

C. remains the same D. doubles

Q. 291. The angle of ______ is measured with respect to the vertical axis.

A. incidence B. reflection

C. refraction D. all of the above

Q. 292. When the angle of ______ is 90 degrees the angle of ______ is equal to the critical angle.

A. incidence; refraction B. refraction; incidence

C. refraction; reflection D. reflection; refraction

Q. 293. *There is no reflection until the angle of incidence is greater than the ______ angle.*

A. critical B. refractive

C. horizontal D. vertical

Q. 294. *When a light beam is reflected back into the medium, the angle of ______ equals the angle of ______.*

A. incidence; reflection B. incidence; refraction

C. reflection; refraction D. refraction; recursion

Q. 295. *In which propagation mode does the light source move through the core in different paths?*

A. Multimode step-index B. Multimode graded-index

C. Single mode D. A and B

Q. 296. *In which propagation mode is the core a uniform single density?*

A. Multimode step-index B. Multimode graded-index

C. Single mode D. A and C

Q. 297. *In which propagation mode is the core of varying density?*

A. Multimode step-index B. Multimode graded-index

C. Single mode D. A and B

Q. 298. *A beam of light is least distorted in a ______ fiber.*

A. Multimode step-index B. Multimode graded-index

C. Single mode step-index D. A and B

Q. 299. *The ______ surrounds the ______ in a fiber-optic cable.*

A. fiber; cladding B. core; fiber

C. core; cladding D. cladding; core

Q. 300. *An ______ provides a light source that can be focused to a very narrow range allowing control over the angle of incidence.*

A. ILD B. LED

C. IED D. EFF

Q. 301. *As a light source for fiber-optic cable, ______ though inexpensive, can only be used for short-distance use.*

A. ILD B. LED

C. IED D. EFF

Q. 302. *______ cable is not susceptible to most noise that is electrical in nature.*

A. Twisted-pair B. Shielded twisted-pair

C. Coaxial D. Fiber-optic

Q. 303. *For refraction to occur, the ______ must be of a lower density than the ______.*

A. cladding; core B. core; cladding

C. cladding; jacket D. core; Teflon coating

Q. 304. *The transmission of a signal through fiber-optic cable is most affected by ______.*

A. electric motors B. heat

C. lightning D. external light

Q. 305. *Which factor makes twisted-pair cable superior to fiber-optic cable?*

A. Signal attenuation B. Noise resistance

C. Bandwidth range D. Cost

Q. 306. *Which factor makes fiber-optic cable superior to twisted-pair cable?*

A. Cost B. Maintenance

C. Robustness D. Bandwidth range

Q. 307. *The section of the electromagnetic spectrum defined as radio communication is divided into ______ bands.*

A. 5 B. 6

C. 7 D. 8

Q. 308. *The two highest radio communication bands use frequencies propagated mainly through ______.*

A. space B. the ionosphere

C. the troposphere D. the atmosphere

Q. 309. *Radio communication ranges from a frequency of ______ to a frequency of ______.*

A. 3 KHz; 300 MHz B. 3 KHz; 300 GHz

C. 3 MHz; 300 GHz D. 3 GHz; 300 THz

Q. 310. *When radio waves travel from the lowest portion of the atmosphere, hugging the earth, this is called _______ propagation.*

A. surface B. tropospheric

C. ionospheric D. line-of-sight

Q. 311. *Long-range radio navigation uses frequencies in the _______ ranges.*

A. VLF and LF B. LF and MF

C. MF and HF D. HF and UHF

Q 312. *AM radio uses frequencies in the _______ range.*

A. LF B. MF

C. HF D. EHF

Q. 313. *CB radio uses frequencies in the _______ range.*

A. LF B. MF

C. HF D. EHF

Q. 314. *FM radio uses frequencies in the _______ range.*

A. LF B. MF

C. HF D. VHF

Q. 315. *Mobile telephones use frequencies in the _______ range.*

A. UHF B. MF

C. HF D. EHF

Q. 316. *In the transmission of terrestrial microwaves, _______ can regenerate the signal at each antenna.*

A. repeaters B. bridges

C. routers D. any of the above

Q. 317. *In a ______ a wide range of incoming waves is directed to a common point called the focus.*

A. repeater B. satellite

C. parabolic dish antenna D. any of the above

Q. 318. *Terrestrial microwave communication can use _______ for transmission.*

A. repeaters B. parabolic dish antennas

C. horn antennas D. all of the above

Q. 319. *What is the advantage of using a satellite in microwave communication?*

A. The limitations imposed on distance by the earth's curvature is reduced.

B. Remote areas can be serviced.

C. Leasing time or frequencies is relatively inexpensive.

D. All of the above

Q. 320. *Frequencies for satellite communication are in the ______ range.*

A. millihertz B. megahertz
C. gigahertz D. terahertz

Q. 321. *A geosynchronous orbit is 22,000 miles from earth at the ______.*

A. north pole B. tropic of capricorn
C. equatorial plane D. A and B

Q. 322. *The minimum number of geosynchronous satellites needed to cover the earth is ______.*

A. 1 B. 2
C. 3 D. 4

Q. 323. *In cellular telephony, a ______ is a service area containing an antenna and controlled by the cell office.*

A. cell B. MTSO
C. local loop D. band

Q. 324. *One ______ controls many ______.*

A. cell; MTSOs B. antenna; MTSOs
C. cell; antennas D. MTSO; cells

Q. 325. *The MTSO is responsible for ______.*

A. coordinating communication between the cell offices and the telephone central office
B. connecting cells
C. recording call information and billing
D. all of the above

Q. 326. *Cell size is a function of ______.*

A. weather conditions B. population
C. latitude D. MTSO type

Q. 327. *Each cell can access ______ channels.*

A. 40 B. 400
C. 416 D. 432

Q. 328. *An MTSO searches for the location of a mobile phone by sending query signals to each cell in a process called ______.*

A. transmitting B. paging
C. receiving D. handoff

Q. 329. *The MTSO can change the channel carrying a call through a process called ______.*

A. transmitting B. paging
C. receiving D. handoff

Q. 330. *Handoff is necessary when ______.*

A. a mobile phone initiates a call to a land phone
B. a land phone initiates a call to a mobile phone
C. a mobile phone calls a mobile phone
D. the mobile phone moves from one cell to another

Q. 331. ______ *is a cellular data standard providing low-speed digital service.*

A. FM　　B. ASCS
C. CDPD　　D. OSI

Q. 332. *A received signal is often not exactly the same as the original signal due to ______.*

A. attenuation　　B. distortion
C. noise　　D. all of the above

Q. 333. *When a signal loses energy in overcoming the resistance of a medium, this is called ______.*

A. attenuation　　B. distortion
C. noise　　D. all of the above

Q. 334. *The purpose of ______ is to compensate for an attenuated signals loss.*

A. an antenna　　B. an amplifier
C. a transmitter　　D. an LED

Q. 335. *The ______ measures the relative strengths of two signals or a signal at two different points.*

A. decibel　　B. power
C. Shannon capacity　　D. signal-to-noise ratio

Q. 336. *A loss of 3 dB is equivalent to ______.*

A. losing 3 times the power　　B. losing half the power
C. gaining 3 times the power　　D. gaining half the power

Q. 337. *What formula calculates the dB of a signal at points 1 and 2 (P1and P2)?*

A. dB = P2/P1　　B. dB = log10(P2/P1)
C. dB = 10log10 (P2/P1)　　D. dB = 10 (P2/P1)

Q. 338. *When a signal changes its form or shape, this type of transmission impairment is called ______.*

A. attenuation　　B. distortion
C. noise　　D. all of the above

Q. 339. *The performance of transmission media is often measured by ______.*

A. throughput　　B. propagation speed
C. propagation time　　D. all of the above

Q. 340. *Throughput is usually measured in ______.*

A. bps B. decibels

C. wavelengths D. power

Q. 341. *Propagation speed is usually measured in ______.*

A. decibels B. wavelengths

C. power D. m/s

Q. 342. *The propagation time is ______.*

A. distance / propagation speed

B. propagation speed / distance

C. distance / decibel

D. distance / wavelength

Q. 343. *The ______ of a sine wave is dependent on its frequency and its medium.*

A. amplitude B. phase

C. wavelength D. any of the above

Q. 344. *The wavelength is the distance a simple signal can travel ______.*

A. in one second B. in one ms

C. in one period D. none of the above

Q. 345. *In the formula ? = c/f, c is the ______.*

A. wavelength B. frequency

C. speed of light in a vacuum D. propagation speed

Q. 346. *One micron is ______ meters.*

A. 0.01 B. 0.001

C. 0.000001 D. 0.000000001

Q. 347. *The Shannon capacity formula gives us the ______ for a channel.*

A. theoretical highest bandwidth

B. theoretical highest data rate

C. maximum decibels available

D. signal-to-noise ratio

Q. 348. *What is the theoretical highest data rate for a common telephone line?*

A. 3.486 Kbps B. 34.86 Kbps

C. 348.6 Kbps D. 3486 Kbps

GLOSSARY

A

AAA—Authentication, Authorization and Accounting.

Access server—An access server acts as a concentration point for dial-in and dial-out connections.

AAR—Automatic Alternate Routing

ACF—Advanced Communications Function

ACK—Acknowledge Character

ADCCP—Advanced Data Communications Control Procedures

ALC—Access Line Charge

ANI—Automatic Number Identification

ANSI—American National Standards Institute

ARC—Attached Resource Computer

ARS—Automatic Route Selection

ARU—Automatic Response Unit

ASA—American Standards Association

ASCII—American (National) Standard Code for Information Interexchange

ADSL—Asynchronous digital subscriber line

API—Application programming interface

ARP—Address resolution protocol.

ABBREVIATED DIALING—The ability of a telephone user to reach frequently called numbers by using less than seven digits. Synonym: Speed Dialing.

ACCESS-(1)—Point at which entry is gained into a circuit or a network. May be switched or dedicated. (2) Ability to obtain data from a storage device or peripheral. (3) Type of connection between CPE and network.

ACCESS CONTROL-(1)—Action taken to permit ordinary use of the components of a communications system. (2) The tasks performed by hardware, software and administrative controls to monitor system operation, ensure data integrity, perform user identification, record system access and changes and grant users access.

ACCESS LINE—A circuit between a subscriber and a switching center. Any line giving access to a larger system or network. Also, the private lines feeding a common control switching arrangement or enhanced private switched communications service switch from a PBX.

ACCESS METHOD-(1)—A technique for moving data, voice or video between main storage and input/output devices. (2) In local area networks, the technique and/or program code used to determine use of the communications medium by granting access selectively to individual stations.

ACKNOWLEDGE CHARACTER (ACK)— A transmission control character transmitted as an affirmative response to a connecting station or to a sender.

ADDRESS-(1)—In a communications network, the identifying designation of an entity that is physically and/or logically distinct. (2) The destination of a message. (3) In software, a location that can be specifically referred to in a program. It can refer to a storage location, a terminal, a peripheral device, a cursor location or any other unit or component in a computer network.

ALLOCATE—To assign a resource for use in performing a specific task.

ALTERNATE ROUTE—A secondary communications path used to reach a destination if the primary path is unavailable.

AMERICAN STANDARD CODE FOR INFORMATION INTERCHANGE (ACSII)—A code with seven information signals plus one parity check signal, designed for interworking between computers (*i.e.*, the transmittal of text). The most popular coding method used by computers for converting letters, numbers, punctuation and control codes with digital form.

AMPLIFIER-(1)—Device which receives an input signal in wave form and outputs a magnified signal. (2) Electronic device used to increase signal power or amplitude.

ANALOG—A transmission method employing a continuous (rather than pulsed or digital) electrical signal that varies in amplitude or frequency in response to changes of sound, light, position, etc., imposed on a transducer in the sending device; opposite of digital.

ANALOG SIGNAL—A signal in the form of a continuous varying physical quantity such as voltage -which reflects variations in some quantity; or loudness in the human voice as opposed to digital.

ANSWERBACK—A signal sent by a data receiver to a data transmitter indicating it is ready to receive data, or is acknowledging the receipt of data. [The answerback is typically part of the "handshaking" between devices.]

APPEND—To change or alter a file or program.

APPLICATION LAYER—The top layer of the OSI seven-layer logical structure for data services; the end-user layer.

APPLICATIONS SOFTWARE—The instructions that direct the hardware to perform specific functions. Common software applications include payroll, inventory control and electronic spreadsheets.

ARCHITECTURE—The interaction between hardware and software in a computing system to achieve the most economic, efficient, secure, rapid or low-maintenance system.

ASSIGN—To give a new value to a variable during the running of a program.

ASYNCHRONOUS TRANSMISSION-(1)—A mode of data communications transmission in which time intervals between transmitted characters may be of unequal length. (2) Transmission independently controlled by start and stop elements at the beginning and end of each character. Synonym: start-stop transmission.

ATM—Asynchronous transfer mode.

ATTENUATION—Reduction in power level due to line resistance, leakages or induction which results in the received signal being lower in volume than the original transmitted signal. [In optical fiber systems there are other causes of attenuation, such as absorption, scattering and losses into radiation modes. It is usually expressed in decibel (dB).]

AUDIBLE RINGING TONE—The information tone sent back to the calling party to indicate the called line is being rung.

AUDIO RESPONSE UNIT (ARU)—Output device which provides a spoken response to digital inquiries from a telephone or other device. The response is usually assembled by a computer from a prerecorded vocabulary of words.

AVAILABILITY-(1)—The degree to which a system or resource is operable and not in a state of congestion or failure at any given point in time. (2) The percentage of total trunks in a group which can be accessed by a particular switch.

B

BBER—Background Bit Error Rate

BCC—Block Check Character

BCD—Binary Coded Decimal

BER—Bit Error Rate

BEX—Broadband Exchange

BISYNC—Binary Synchronous Transmission

BLERT—Block Error Rate Test

bps—Bits Per Second

BSC—Binary Synchronous Transmission

BACKGROUND BIT ERROR RATIO (BBER)—(1) The ratio of the number of bits in error to the total number of bits received, exclusive of error bursts, over a special measurement period. (2) The error performance of the system under normal operation and does not include error bursts caused by line switching, maintenance, activity, etc. [An end-to-end BBER is not specified for digital private line because of the varying error distribution of access connection.]

BACKGROUND ERRORS—Errors that occur during the normal operation of the system. They generally occur one at a time or a few at a time.

BAND-(1)—The range of frequencies between two defined limits. (2) In reference to WATS, one of the six specific geographic service areas as defined by Sprint.

BANDWIDTH-(1)—The difference between the top and bottom limiting frequencies of a continuous frequency band. (2) Indicates the information-carrying capacity of a channel. Analog transmission usually expressed in kHz or MHz; digital transmission, bps, Mbps. Fiber-optic bandwidth is usually given as its capacity to transmit information in a specific time period for a specific length. (*e.g.* 10 Mbps/KM.) (3) Expressed in different measurements depending on transmission type.

BAUD-(1)—A unit of signalling speed. (2) A unit of data transmission speed measured in bits per second. [The speed in baud is the number of discreet conditions or signal elements per second. If each event represents only one bit condition, then baud is the same as bits per second.]

BAUD RATE—A measure of signalling speed in data communications that specifies the maximum number of signal elements transmitted each second. [Over dial-up telephone lines, 300 and 1200 baud are most common. For most purposes, at slow speeds, a baud rate is the same as the speed in bits per second. Baud rate is the same as bit rate if all bits have the same length.]

BINARY—A number system based upon twos rather than tens and that uses only two characters, zero (0) and one (1).

BINARY DIGIT—Unit of information in two-level digital notation which may be 0 or 1. A member selected from a binary set.

BINARY SYNCHRONOUS TRANSMISSION (BSC OR BISYNC)—(1) Data transmission in which synchronization of characters is controlled by timing signals generated at the sending and receiving stations. (2) A half-duplex, character-oriented data communications protocol. Contrast with asynchronous transmission.

BIPOLAR—Literally, having two poles. An input signal is bipolar when one electrical voltage polarity represents a logically true input and its opposite polarity represents a logically false input. Contrast with unipolar.

BIT-(1)—The smallest unit of coded information. (2) A pulse whose presence or absence indicates data. Abbreviation for binary digit.

BIT DURATION—(1) Equivalent to the time that it takes one encoded bit to pass a point on the transmission medium. (2) In serial communications, a relative unit of time measurement used for comparison of delay times where the data rate of a transmission channel can vary (for example propagation delay, access latency).

BIT RATE OR BANDWIDTH—The rate at which bits (binary digits) are transmitted over a communications path. Normally expressed in bits per second (bps). [The bit rate is not to be confused with the data signalling rate which measures the rate of signal elements being transmitted.]

BIT TRANSFER RATE—The number of bits transferred per unit time, usually expressed in bits per second (bps).

BIT-ORIENTED—Describes a communications protocol or transmission procedure where control information is encoded in fields of one or more bits; oriented toward full-duplex link operation.

BIT MAP—A matrix of dots, all of the same density, that form an image.

BITS PER SECOND (BPS)—The rate at which data transmission (binary digits) is measured. See bit rate.

BRIDGE, BRIDGING—Equipment and techniques used to match circuits to each other ensuring minimum transmission impairment. [Bridging is normally required on multipoint data channels were several local loops or channels are interconnected.]

BGP—Boarder gateway protocol.

BRI—Basic rate interface.

BROADBAND—(1) A transmission facility having a bandwidth of greater than 20 kHz and, therefore, capable of higher-speed data transmission. (2) Analog transmission technique used with data and video transmissions that provides multiple channels for users through frequency division multiplexing.

BROADCAST—Transmission to a number of receiving locations simultaneously. [Normally associated with a multidrop line, where a number of terminals share the line] buckets-(1) In Sprint billing software, an electronic file or folder in which records are kept until invoice processing occurs. (See Suspense File.) (2) In data, a storage unit.

BUFFER—(1) A high-speed area of storage that is temporarily reserved for use in performing the input/output operation into which data is read or from which data is written. (2) Used to accumulate data into blocks of sufficient size to be handled efficiently by a processor or terminal. Synonym: I/O area.

BULLETIN BOARD—An electronic message center accessible through computer-aided communication lines.

BURST—A sequence of signals in data communications counted as one unit in accordance with some specific criterion or measure.

BURST ERRORS—Bits or signals lost due to such problems as line switching or multiplex switching. [Typically involves a few thousand errors or lost bits at a time.]

BUS—(1) A heavy conductor, or group of conductors, to which several units of the same type of equipment may be connected. (2) A path or channel for transmitting electrical signals and data, usually between a computer and peripheral equipment.

BUSY—Call condition in which transmission facilities are already in use. Synonym: off-hook condition.

byte - (1) The representation of a character. (2) A group of eight bits makes a byte. Typically a 16-bit "word" is itself divided into two bytes for handling. (3) Unit of measurement used to rate storage capacity of disks; usually the smallest addressable unit of information in a data store or memory. One thousand bytes is a kilobyte; one million bytes is a megabyte.

C

CCITT—Consultative Committee on International Telegraph and Telephone

CODEC—Coder-Decoder

CPS—Characters Per Second

CPU—Central Processing Unit

CRC—Cyclic Redundancy Check

CSMA—Carrier Sense Multiple Access

CSMA/CD—Carrier Sense Multiple Access with Collision Detection

CACHE MEMORY—A high-speed, buffer-type memory filled at medium speed from the main memory. [Programs and instructions found in the cache memory can be operated at higher speeds without the necessity of loading another segment.]

carrier-(1) A company authorized by appropriate regulatory agencies to provide communications services. (2) A continuous frequency capable of being modulated or impressed with a second information carrying signal.

CARRIER MODULATION—A signal at some fixed amplitude and frequency which is combined with an information bearing signal in the modulation process to produce and output a signal suitable for transmission.

CAP—Cable service access protocol.

CORBA—Common object request broker architecture.

CMOT—Communication Management information Protocol over TCP/IP.

CARRIER SYSTEM—A method for providing several communications channels over a single path. Accomplished by modulating the data, voice or video transmissions onto a higher frequency carrier wave, then recovering it at the receiving end through a process of demodulation (See Frequency Division Multiplexing.)

CATEGORIES OF SERVICE—Basic and enhanced, as defined by the Federal Communications Commission (FCC). [Basic service refers to transmission capacity for the movement of information; for example residential telephone service. Enhanced service combines basic service with computer processing; for example Electronic Yellow Pages.]

CHANNEL—(1) The smallest subdivision of a transmission system by means of which a single type of communication service is provided, for example, a voice channel or a data channel. (2) A communications path via a carrier or microwave radio. (3) In data communications, a path for electrical transmission between two or more points. (4) Within a computer, the electronic paths along which data flows between the input-output units of a computer and the customer premises equipment (CPU). Synonym: circuit, facility, line, link or path.

CHANNEL CAPACITY—The maximum bit rate that can be handled by a channel.

CHANNEL, FOUR-WIRE—A two-way circuit, each with backup, where the signals simultaneously follow separate and distinct paths in opposite directions in the transmission medium.

CHARACTER—(1) Any alphabetical letter, digit or special symbol. (2) In data transmission, the representation of a letter number or symbol by a specific code made up of binary digits.

CHARACTER-ORIENTED—A communications protocol or transmission procedure that carries control information encoded in fields of one or more bytes.

CIRCUIT—A path for the transmission of electromagnetic signals; includes all conditioning and signalling equipment. Synonym: facility.

CIRCUIT SWITCHING—(1) A method of communications, where an electrical connection between calling and called stations is established on demand for exclusive use of the circuit until the connection is released. (2) A switching system that completes a dedicated transmission path from sender to receiver at the time of transmission. See also: packet switching, store and forward, message switching.

COAXIAL CABLE—Cable consisting of an outer conductor surrounding an inner conductor, separated from each other by insulating material. It can carry a much higher bandwidth than a wire pair.

CODEC—Equipment containing a coder plus a decoder. Used to convert analog signals to digital form for transmission over a digital medium and back again to the original analog form.

COMMUNICATION—Transmission of intelligence between two points (origin and reception) without alteration of sequence or structure of the information content. See also data communication.

COMMUNICATIONS TERMINAL—Any device which generates or receives electrical or tone signals that can be transmitted over a communications channel.

COMPUTER—A device capable of solving problems or manipulating data by accepting data, performing prescribed operations on the data and supplying the results of these operations. Various types of computers are: analog computer, digital computer, calculator.

CONCATENATION—(1) To unite in a series; to link together; to chain. (2) The linking of transmission channels (phone lines, coaxial cable, optical fiber) end-to-end.

CONFIGURATION—The interconnection and programming of independent machines or equipment to operate as a system.

CROSSTALK—Transmission noise caused by energy "leaking" from one channel to another on the same facility. [In analog voice communications, crosstalk makes conversation on one circuit accidentally audible on another.]

CYCLIC REDUNDANCY CHECK—Error detection technique. [Using a polynomial, a series of two eight-bit block check characters are generated that represent the entire block of data. The block check characters are incorporated into the transmission frame, then checked at the receiving end.

D

dB—Decibel

DCA—Distributed Communications Architecture

DES—Data Encryption Standard

DHCP—Dynamic Host Configuration Protocol

DS—Digital Signal

DS0—Digital Signal level zero

DS1—Digital Signal level one

DS3—Digital Signal level three

DTE—Digital Transmission Equipment

DE—Discard eligibility.

DHCP—Dynamic host configuration protocol.

DLCI—Data link connection identifier.

DMT—Discrete multitone devices.

DCN—Distributed computer N/W.

DATA—(1) Units of information. (2) Any representation, such as characters or analog quantities, to which meaning is or may be assigned.

DATA COMMUNICATIONS— (1) Transfer of information between a source and a destination via one or more data links, according to appropriate protocols. (2) Transmission and reception of data, often including operations such as coding, decoding and validation.

DATA CONVERSION—Process of changing information from one form of representation to another.

DATA ENCRYPTION STANDARD (DES)— A cryptographic algorithm designed by the National Bureau of Standards to encipher and decipher data using a 64-bit key.

DATALINK CONTROL—Second layer in the International Standards Organization reference model for Open Systems Interconnection (OSI). Synonym: protocol.

DATA TERMINAL EQUIPMENT (DTE)—(1) Provides for the communications control function (protocol). (2) Any piece of equipment at which a communications path begins or ends.

DEADLOCK—Unresolved contention for the use of a resource.

DECIBEL (DB)— (1) A unit of measure represented as a ratio of two voltages, currents or powers. (2) Measurement of transmission loss or gain.

DELAY DISTORTION—Noise or echo resulting from the non-uniform speeds of various signal components of transmissions through a transmission medium(s).

DEMODULATION—Conversion of a signal from either digital or analog to its original form. Antonym: modulation.

DENIAL—all condition that occurs when no circuits are available and a busy tone is returned to the calling party. [This situation is distinctly different from delay in that denial is not time-related and can only be measured in terms of the percentage of calls denied.] See blocking.

DHCP—Stands for "Dynamic Host Configuration Protocol". This protocol is based on BOOTP and BOOTP clients can still connect to a DHCP server. DHCP allows for dynamic allocation of network addresses and configurations to newly attached hosts, as well as recovery and reallocation of network addresses through a leasing mechanism. Rather than an administrator visiting each computer on a network and entering configuration data (IP address, default router, network mask, DNS server, NTP [Network Time Protocol] server, etc.), all computers are configured the same-to use DHCP. When the computers boot, they receive all of this configuration information from the DHCP server. If configuration information needs to change it can be edited in one place, the database, and each affected computer will receive the update.

DIAL-UP LINE—(1) A communications circuit that is established by a switched circuit connection. (2) Any circuit available over the public switched network.

DIGITAL SIGNAL (DS)— (1) A nominally discontinuous electrical signal that changes from one state to another in discreet steps. (2) A signal that is time-wise discontinuous (*i.e.*, discreet) and can assume a limited set of values. Antonym: analog.

DIGITAL TECHNOLOGY— Method of storing, processing and transmitting information through the use of electronic or optical pulses that represent binary digits or bits (0 and 1).

DIGITAL TRANSMISSION SYSTEM—A transmission system in which information is transmitted in a series of pulses, and in which the signal can be regenerated. See also pulse modulation and time division multiplexing.

DISCRETE—Pertains to separate and distinct parts of data such as holes in a card or graphic characters.

DISTORTION—(1) Any change from the original wave form or signal. (2) Normally, non-predictable changes which interfere with interpretation of the result.

distributed systems-Arrangements wherein an organization's computer complex has many separate computing facilities interfaced and working in a cooperative manner.

DNS—Stands for "Domain Name System". This service maps an internet domain name to an IP address and visa versa. ITCom already runs a production DNS service. By integrating this service into this project a synergy can be achieved. Most DHCP/DNS systems require manual configuration of the associated data. This project plans to automate much of this process. A new computer is plugged into the network. The user authenticates and DHCP and DNS servers are automatically configured with the appropriate data.

DUPLEX— (1) Two units in one. (2) Simultaneous two-way independent transmission. Synonym: full duplex.

E

E & M SIGNALLING—Method of receiving and transmitting signals. (Originally stood for ear and mouth).

EXTERNAL BINARY CODED DECIMAL INTERCHANGE CODE (EBCDIC)—A transmission system used by several IBM and IBM-compatible data terminals which consists of eight data bits, each of which represents a particular number, letter or character.

ECHO—A distortion that occurs when a signal is reflected or otherwise returned (on the same wire on which the speaker is speaking) with sufficient magnitude and delay as to be perceived by the speaker. [Typically, a problem on satellite circuits.]

ELECTRONIC MAIL—(1) The electronic transmission of letters, messages and memos from one computer to another. (2) A computer-aided method of communication where an individual sends an on-line message to another individual via dial-up or dedicated access.

ENABLE—(1) To prepare a circuit for operation. (2) To allow an item to function.

ENCODING—(1) Inscribing or imprinting Magnetic Ink Character Recognition (MICR) characters on checks, deposits and other documents to be processed by a MICR reader. (2) The introduction of data on a medium such as a magnetic strip on plastic cards.

ENCRYPTION—Conversion of data into code form for security purposes during transmission and decoding at the receiving end.

EIGRP—Enhanced interior gateway routing protocol

ERP—Exterior routing protocol

EGP—Exterior gateway protocol

ERLANG—(1) A unit of traffic intensity. (2) One erlang is the intensity at which one traffic path would be continually occupied.

ERROR—(1) A difference between a computer value and the theoretically correct value. (2) A malfunction that is not reproducible. (3) In data communications, any unwanted change in the original contents of a transmission.

ERROR BURST—Results of an event that causes a lengthy stream of consecutively transmitted bits to be defective. [Retransmission is the normal correction procedure in the event of an error burst.]

ERROR RATE—Ratio of the number of signal elements (or data) incorrectly received to the total number transmitted. (2) The probability of an error occurring during the transmission of a message.

ETHERNET—A packet-switched data local area network (LAN) design by Xerox Corp. which employs CSMA-CD as access control mechanism.

EXCHANGE (EX)— (1) A room or building equipped so that telephone lines terminating there may be interconnected as required. The equipment may include manual or automatic switching equipment. (2) A telephone switching center; an aggregate of traffic-carrying devices, switching stages, controlling and signalling means at a network node that enables subscriber lines and/or other telecommunication circuits to be interconnected as required by individual callers. (3) The territory served by an exchange, within which local service rates apply; also known as the exchange area or local service area.

F

FDM—Frequency Division Multiplexing

FACILITY—A transmission path between two or more locations without terminating or signaling equipment. [Addition of terminating equipment would produce either a channel, a central office line or a trunk. Various types of signalling would also be used depending on the application.]

FAULT TOLERANCE—The level of ability within a program or system to operate properly even if errors occur.

FEEDBACK—(1) Return of part of the output of a machine, process or system to the computer as input for another phase; typically used for surveillance, self-correcting maintenance or control purposes. (2) Means of comparing or providing actual performance which can be compared with planned performance.

FIBER OPTICS— (1) A means of providing a high-speed transmission, using light to send images through a flexible bundle of glass fibers. (2) The use of light as the primary medium in an actual application.

FIBER-OPTIC TRANSMISSION SYSTEM (FOTS)— A means of sending data by coded light pulses through small diameter glass fibers. [Information is transferred by modulating the transmitted light. These modulated signals are detected by light-sensitive semiconductor devices (photodiodes).]

FIBER-OPTIC CABLE—A bundle of thin filaments of glass or other transparent materials used as the medium for transmitting coded light pulses that represent data, images or sound.

FDDI—Fiber distributed data interface.

FM—Frequency modulation.

FMM—Fault management mechanism.

FILE—(1) An organized, named collection of records treated as a unit. (2) The storage media on which these records are kept.

FILE SERVER—A station or microprocessing computer dedicated to providing file and mass data storage services to the other stations on the local network. [Often found in Local Area Network (LAN) applications.]

FIRMWARE—Computer programs that are embodied in a physical device that can form part of a machine.

FLOW CONTROL—The procedure for controlling the rate of transfer of packets between two designated points in a data network; used to prevent data loss during transmission.

FORWARD ERROR CORRECTION—Technique for regenerating lost data transmissions or errored messages; retransmission of any information by the transmitter. [Typically, this is accomplished by adding bits to each transmitted character or code clock using a predetermined algorithm. It doesn't need a feedback channel, and therefore may be used with a one-way transmission system.]

FREQUENCY DIVISION MULTIPLEXING (FDM)— Method of transmitting two or more signals by dividing the available transmission frequency into narrower bands and using each as a separate channel.

FREQUENCY MODULATION (FM)—Transmission method in which the frequency of the carrier wave is changed to correspond to changes in the signal wave.

full duplex - See duplex.

G

G.711— CCITT recommendation detailing a 74 kbps, 7-kHz bandwidth audio coding algorithm.

G.722—CCITT recommendation detailing a 32 kbps, 3.4-kHz bandwidth audio coding algorithm.

GIGABYTE—One billion or one thousand million 10^9 bytes.

H

Hz—Hertz

H.221—CCITT recommendation regarding frame structure for audiovisual teleservices.

H.230—CCITT recommendation regarding frame-synchronous control and indication signals for audiovisual systems.

H.242—CCITT recommendation regarding a system for establishing communication between audiovisual terminals using digital channels up to 2 Mbps.

HALF DUPLEX—Alternating the direction of transmission of signals between two terminals or computers but not transmitting in both directions simultaneously. Contrast with duplex.

HANDOFF—Process by which a cellular radio telephone call is transferred from one cell site to another.

HANDSET—That portion of the telephone containing the transmitter and receiver which is designed to be hand-held when the telephone is in use.

HANDSHAKE—A preliminary exchange of predetermined signals performed by modems and/or terminals and computers to verify that a communications link has been established and data transmission can proceed.

HARDWIRE—To directly attach or dedicate a cable or line between units of equipment.

HERTZ (HZ)—International standard unit of frequency. [Replaces, and is identical to, the older unit cycles-per-second.]

I

IC—Interexchange Carrier

IDN—Integrated Digital Network

ISDN—Integrated Services Digital Network

ISO—International Organization for Standardization

ISP—Internet Service Provider

ITU—International Telecommunications Union

IXC—Interexchange Carrier

IN-BAND SIGNALLING— (1) A type of transmission using an alternate current (AC) signal (usually 2,600 Hz) within the normal voice band. (2) An audible signal transmitted end-to-end on a long voice circuit without intermediate signaling equipment; requires that signalling equipment be arranged for "tone on when idle" operation.

INPUT/OUTPUT (I/O CHANNEL)—(1) A general term for equipment used to communicate with a computer. (2) The process of transmitting information from an external source to the computer, or from the computer to an external source. (3) Buffer area for the temporary storage of data.

INTEGRATED SERVICES DIGITAL NETWORK (ISDN)—A switched network providing end-to-end digital connectivity for the simultaneous transmission of voice, data, video, imaging and fax over several multiplexed communications channels. Employs high-speed, out-of-band signalling protocols that conform to international standards. [Since signalling and communications are separate, the configuration reduces network blockage and provides faster connectivity for users.]

INTERACTIVE—(1) A conversational mode between a user and computer system. (2) Action in more than one direction, either simultaneously or sequentially.

ICMP—Internet control message protocol.

IDSL—Integrated digital subscriber line.

IDRP—Interdomain routing protocol.

IGRP—Interior gateway routing protocol.

IP—Internet protocol.

IDL—Interface definition language.

ISDN—Integrated service digital network.

IRP—Interior routing protocol.

IPv6—Internet protocol version 6.

IDRP—Interdomain routing protocol.

INTERCEPT—To stop a telephone call placed to an improper number and redirect that call to an operator or a recording.

INTERCONNECT—(1) Arrangement that permits the connection of customers telecommunications equipment to a common carrier network. (2) Industry name for manufacturers, excluding AT&T and Bell companies, who provide telephone premises equipment.

INTERFACE—(1) A hardware and software link between two devices. (2) The junction or point of interconnection between two systems of equipment having different characteristics. For example, a computer card that allows users to transmit data using a variety of telecommunications modes.

INTERFERENCE—(1) Unwanted noise, crosstalk or signal deviations on communications channels that result from natural or man-made occurrences. (2) Anything not properly a part of the signal or call being transmitted.

International Organization for Standardization (ISO) — An organization that promotes the development of standards to facilitate the international exchange of goods and services as well as develops mutual cooperation in areas of intellectual, scientific, technological and economic activity.

INTERNET SERVICE PROVIDER (ISP)—An entity that provides attachment to the Internet.

INTERRUPT—Stop a process in such a way that it can be resumed.

ISDN—The Integrated Services Digital Network (ISDN) Dial-In Service operates like standard telephone service but is completely digital, allowing you to connect to the U-M campus network (UMnet) and the Internet from off campus at much higher speeds than with a regular analog modem.

IT Communications Engineer - ITD Staff who work with the department through the Network Analyst to design the services required by the customer. May be involved directly with the department on particularly complex installations.

J

jack—A connecting device having springs which make electrical contact with mating contacts of a plug.

K

k—Kilo (1000 in decimal notation)

kb—Kilobit

kbps—Kilobit Per Second

kHz—Kilohertz

KEY SYSTEM—A telecommunications system with multi-button telephone sets on which more than one outside line terminates, allowing several people to answer or use more than one line. [All hardware is typically located on subscriber premises.]

L

LASER—A device which transmits an extremely narrow and coherent beam of electromagnetic energy in the visible light spectrum. [Acronym for Light Amplification by Stimulation of Emission of Radiation.]

latency—Time interval between when a network station seeks access to a transmission channel and access is granted or received.

LAYER—(1) Related processes, activities or information that constitute one level in a hierarchy or network platform. (2) Related communications-processing functions that comprise one level in a hierarchy of functions within the OSI reference model.

LEASED LINE— Any communication channel leased for exclusive use from a common carrier. Synonym: private line.

LEAST COST ROUTING (LCR)—Method for automatic selection of the least costly facility for transmission of a call. Synonyms: Most Economical Route Selection (MERS); Route Optimization; Automatic Route Selection; Flexible Route Selection.

LEVEL—(1) A group of related functions, activities or occurrences. (2) Expressed as the relative signal strength at a fixed point in a communications circuit .

LINE—Any communications path between two or more points, including satellite or microwave channels. See channel.

LINE CONDITIONING—Adjustment and control of the properties of a leased line to bring its characteristics within specified tariff limits; generally improves the frequency response and delay considerations of the line. [Line conditioning services provided by telephone carriers are designated as Type C or D (example C1, C2 or C4).]

L2TP—Layer 2 tunnelling protocol.

LLC—Logical link control.

LMI—Local management interface.

LINK—A communications path between two nodes in a network.

LINK LAYER—(1) The logical entity in the OSI model relative to transmission of data between adjacent network nodes. (2) The second processing level in the OSI model, between the physical and the network layers.

LOCAL LOOP—(1) The communications lines/services between the telephone subscriber and the LEC switching center. (2) The local connection between the end user and Class 5 central office or end office.

LOOP—(1) A closed circuit. (2) The single connection from a switching center to an individual telecommunications instrument.

LOOP BACK—A method of performing transmission tests on a circuit which does not require the assistance of personnel at the distant end.

LADT—Local Area Data Transport

LAN—Local Area Network

LLC—Logical Line Control

M

Mega—one million.

M/W—Microwave

Mbps—Megabits Per Second (or Million of Bits Per Second)

MDF—Main Distribution Frame

MHz—Megahertz

MODEM—Modulator/Demodulator

MU—Message Unit

MUX—Multiplexer

MAIN DISTRIBUTION FRAME (MDF)—A steel bar framework that is the major cross connect point for COs and TOCs. Used to interconnect loop cable pairs and line equipment terminals on a switching system. Synonym : Main Frame.

MAINFRAME—A central processing unit.

MEDIUM—(1) Material on which computer data is recorded, for example, magnetic tape, floppy diskette, winchester disk. (2) Any material substance that can be used for the propagation of signals from one point to another. (3) The communications forum chosen on marketing promotions and/or customer information.

MEGA—(1) A Greek word meaning one million. (2) A prefix in the international system of measurements; for example: megabytes, that is one million bytes (10^6).

MEGABYTE—Literally 1,000,000 bytes; usually 1024 x 1024 bytes.

MEGAHERTZ (MHz)—1,000,000 (10^6) cycles per second.

MESSAGE—Complete transmission of data or text. Sometimes used interchangeably with block.

MESSAGE UNIT (MU)—Standard against which charges for messages based on time and distance are measured.

MICROWAVE—Any electromagnetic wave in the radio frequency spectrum above 890 megahertz.

MIB—Management information base.

MIME—Multi purpose mail extension

MGCP—Media gateway control protocol.

MMP—Multi chassis multilink PPP.

MPE—Manchester phase encoding.

MSK—Minimum shift keying.

MILLISECOND—One-thousandth of a second.

MODE—(1) The most common or frequent value in a frequency distribution. (2) A particular form or variety of software.

MODEM—[Contraction of Modulator-Demodulator.] A device which modulates and demodulates signals on a carrier frequency and allows the interface of digital terminals with analog carrier systems. [A modem is also known as a dataset.]

MODULATION—Alterations in the characteristics of carrier waves, usually impressed on the amplitude and/or the frequency, for the purpose of transferring information.

MODULE—(1) A unit of something. (2) A unit of code performing a distinct function.

MULTIPLEX—(1) To interleave or simultaneously transmit two or more messages on a single channel. (2) A communications arrangement where multiple devices share a common transmission channel, though only one may transmit at a time.

MULTIPLEXER—Hardware device that allows handling of multiple variable speed signals over a single, higher speed channel.

MULTIPLEXING—Process or equipment that combines data from two or more individual circuits onto a higher speed circuit for transmission. [Two methods are used: (1) Frequency division where all channels are transmitted at the same time. (2) Time division where several messages timeshare a channel.]

MULTIPOINT—(1) Line or channel connecting more than two different service points. (2) Circuit having points served by three or more switches.

MULTITASKING—System that can run two or more programs at the same time. [Apple's Multifinder, A T & T's UNIX and IBM's OS/2 are multitasking operating systems. By contrast, MS-DOS is a single-tasking operating system.]

MUX—[Abbreviation for multiplexing] The process or equipment for combining a number of paths into a single path or bit stream for transmission.

N

NANOSECOND (NS, NSEC)—One-thousandth-millionth (or billionth) of a second. (10^{-9} second.) network-(1) System of mutually-communicating devices (for example: computers, terminals, peripheral devices, process controllers) connected in common and for a purpose by one or more transmission facilities. (2) A collection of switches connected to one another by transmission facilities.

NETWORK ADMINISTRATOR—Departmental Staff member responsible for administering and maintaining a network.

NETWORK ARCHITECTURE—The philosophy and organizational concept for enabling communications between equipment at multiple locations; detailed specifications outlining the processors, terminals and transmission media, protocols and software to be used to accomplish accurate communications.

NETWORK LAYER—The logical network entity that services the transport layer in the OSI model. It is responsible for ensuring that data passed to it from the transport layer is routed and delivered through the network.

NETWORK TOPOLOGY—(1) Describes the physical and logical relationship of nodes in a network. (2) The schematic arrangement of the links and nodes of a network, typically either a star, ring, tree or bus topology, or some hybrid combination thereof.

NFS—Network file system.

NIC—Network interface card.

NRZ—Non-return to zero.

NVT—Network virtual terminal.

NETWORK TRUNKS—Circuits connecting switching centers.

NETWORK VIRTUAL TERMINAL—A communications concept wherein a variety of DTEs, with different data rates, protocols, codes, and formats, are accommodated in the same network. This is done as a result of network processing, where each device's data is converted into a network standard format, then converted into the format of the receiving device at the destination end.

NIBBLE—Popular name for four bits, or half a byte. Also spelled nybble.

NODE—(1) In network topology, a terminal of any branch of a network or a terminal common to two or more branches of a network. (2) In a switched network, the switching points, including patch and control facilities. (3) In a data network, the location of a data station which interconnects data transmission lines. (4) A point in a standing wave at which the amplitude is at a minimum. Synonyms: junction point, nodal point, vertex, null.

NOISE—(1) Unplanned energy introduced onto a communications path, resulting in transmission errors. Undesirable signals bearing no desired information. (2) The unpredictable difference between the observed data and the true process.

O

OBJECT PROGRAM—(1) Fully compiled or assembled software that is ready to be loaded into the computer. (2) The output from processing a source program through an assembler or compiler. Synonym: object code.

OPTICAL FIBER—Any filament or fiber made of dielectric materials that is used to transmit light and/or to guide signals. [Optical fiber typically consists of a core, that carries the signal and cladding, a substance with a slightly higher refractive index than the core, which surrounds the core and serves to reflect the light signal back into it.]

OFC—Optical fiber communication.

OSI—open system interconnection.

OUT-OF-BAND—(1) Any entity outside an assigned range, scope or magnitude. (2) Any frequency outside the spectrum used for voice.

OUT-OF-BAND SIGNALLING—Use of a separate data link which is not in the voice circuit to transmit call set-up and ANI information from carrier to carrier, or from carrier to customer.

OVERFLOW—(1) Switching equipment which operates when the traffic load exceeds the capacity of the regular equipment. (2) Traffic which is handled on overflow equipment. (3) Traffic which exceeds switching capacity and is lost. (4) The carry digit in a digital computer. (5) Intermediate message storage which serves as an extension of in-transit storage to preclude system saturation; an example, magnetic tape.

P

PABX—Private Automatic Branch Exchange

PAD—Packet Assembler/Disassembler

PAM—Pulse Amplitude Modulation

PAX—Private Automatic Exchange

PBX—Private Branch Exchange

PCM—Pulse Code Modulation

PSN—Public Switched Network

PACKET ASSEMBLER/DISASSEMBLER (PAD)—(1) A non-adjustable resistance network used to insert transmission loss into a circuit. (2) To fill a block with dummy data, usually zeros or blanks. PAD character — A fill character inserted when insufficient data characters are present to satisfy a field length requirement.

PARITY—A constant state or equal value.

PARITY BIT—A check character or bit appended to an array of binary digits to make the sum of the digits, including the check bit, always odd or always even.

PARITY CHECKING—One of the oldest error checking techniques. Character bit patterns are forced into parity (total number of bits odd or even) by adding a 1 or 0 bit as appropriate, as they are transmitted. The parity (odd or even) is then verified upon receipt by the receiving device.

PATCH—(1) To make an improvised modification. (2) To change a software routine in a rough or expedient way. (3) A temporary electrical connection.

PBX TRUNK—Connects a customer's PBX to another PBX, central office (CO), remote CO or Sprint switch. (See Private Branch exchange).

PHYSICAL LAYER—Within the OSI model, lowest level of network processing below the link layer that is concerned with the electrical, mechanical and handshaking procedures over the interface that connects a device to a transmission medium (example, RS-232-C).

POLLING—Process by which a computer checks the readiness of other units to transmit or receive signals and information.

PORT—(1) Entrance or access point to a computer, multiplexer network or device where signals may be supplied, extracted or observed. (2) The place where a peripheral device is connected to a computer.

PAM—Pulse amplitude modulation.

PRI—Primary rate interface.

PPTP—Point to point tunnelling protocol.

PPP—Point to point protocol.

PRIVATE AUTOMATIC BRANCH EXCHANGE (PABX)—Small, local, automatic telephone office serving extensions in a business complex and providing access to the public network.

PRIVATE AUTOMATIC EXCHANGE (PAX)—Small, local, automatic telephone office, normally serving extensions in a business complex, typically without external lines to the public network.

PRIVATE BRANCH EXCHANGE (PBX)—Small, local, telephone office-either manually or automatically operated-serving extensions in a business complex and providing access to the public domain.

PROTOCOL—A set of formalized conventions governing the format and relative timing of message exchange in a communications network.

PROTOCOL CONVERSION—Process of translating communications formats and timing, which would otherwise be incompatible, into messages understood by the network. Performed by a dedicated device, a software package loaded onto an existing system or by a value-added (intelligent) network.

PULSE—A signal that can be wholly described by a constant amplitude and the duration time. (2) Signal form typically used internally in computers, terminals and other business machines as well as in communications facilities.

PULSE CODE MODULATION (PCM)—Method of sampling information signals at regular intervals and transmitting the samples as a series of pulses in coded form which represent the amplitude of the information signal at that time.

PULSE MODULATION—Method of varying the amplitude, frequency or phase of information-bearing signals into a series of pulses. [Typical methods involve modifying the amplitude (PAM), width or duration (PDM) or position (PPM). The most common pulse modulation technique in telephone work is pulse code modulation (PCM).]

PULSE-LINK REPEATER—A device used to magnify signals in a telephone circuit and re-transmit corresponding pulses to another signalling circuit.

Q

QUEUE—(1) To arrange or form in a line. (2) A waiting line. (3) A series of elements, one waiting behind the other. (4) A temporary delay in providing service caused by the inability of the particular system to handle the number of messages or calls attempted (example, a call queued for the least expensive route).

QAM—Quadrature amplitude modulation.

QoS—Quality of service.

QSK—Quadrature shift keying.

R

RADIO COMMON CARRIER (RCC)—A communications carrier that provides radio paging and mobile telephone services to the public.

RANDOM ACCESS MEMORY (RAM)—Portion of a computer storage which can be accessed non-sequentially and is considered the working memory.

READ ONLY MEMORY (ROM)—Portion of computer memory which is programmed electrically by the manufacturer, is unchangeable and is unaffected by a power loss.

REPEATER—(1) A device which serves as an interface between circuits, receiving signals from one circuit and transmitting them to the other. (2) A one- or two-way device which amplifies an input signal for retransmission. (3) A device that amplifies, reshapes, retimes or performs a combination of these functions on an input pulse for re-transmission.

REVERSE CHANNEL—A simultaneous data path in the reverse direction over a half-duplex facility; used for positive/negative acknowledgements of previously received data blocks.

RARP—Reverse address resolution protocol.

RIP—Routing information protocol.

RMI—Remote method invocation.

RPC—Remote procedure call.

RZ—Return to zero.

S

SNA—Systems Network Architecture

SNMP—Simple Network Management Protocol

SPC—Single Point Connection

SS7—Signalling System #7

STP—Signalling Transfer Point

SX—Simplex Signalling

SECONDARY CHANNEL—Low-speed channel established on a four-wire circuit over which diagnostic or control information is passed. [User data is passed on the primary, high-speed channels of the circuit.]

SDSL—Synchronous digital subscriber line.

SMTP—Simple mail transfer protocol.

SNMP—Simple network management protocol.

SMDS—Switched multi megabit services.

SESSION—(1) Connection between two stations that allows them to communicate. (2) Meeting or period devoted to a particular activity.

SESSION LAYER—Layer 5 of the Open Systems Interconnection (OSI) model, responsible for binding and unbinding logical links between end users and maintaining an orderly dialogue between them.

SIDEBAND—Set of frequencies which are produced on either side of the carrier signal as a result of the modulation process. [Upper sidebands (USB) are higher in frequency than the carrier; lower sidebands (LSB) are below the frequency of the carrier. Various modulation techniques make use of one or both of the sidebands.]

SIGNAL—An intentional introduction of energy onto a communications path, resulting in the transmission of information. Contrast with noise.

Signal-to-noise ratio-Relative power of the signal information to the noise in a specified bandwidth, usually expressed in decibels (dB). [As the ratio decreases on a line, it becomes more difficult to distinguish between information and non-information (noise).]

SIGNALLING—(1) Use of signals for communication. (2) Method of conveying signals over a circuit. (3) The exchange of electrical information other than by speech. (4) Means of establishing and controlling connections in a communications network.

SIGNING AUTHORITY—Departmental Staff responsible for authorizing an expenditure.

SIMPLE NETWORK MANAGEMENT PROTOCOL(SNMP)—A protocol used to manage devices on a network.

SIMPLEX—One-way data transmission, with no capability for changing direction.

STATISTICAL MULTIPLEXING - A time-division interleaving technique in which time slots are dynamically allocated on the basis of need or to equipment with data to be transmitted.

STOP BIT—In asynchronous transmission, the bit that indicates the end of a block of data.

STORE-AND-FORWARD—(1) Technique in which a message is received from the originator and held in storage until a circuit to the addressee becomes available. (2) Transmittal of complete network messages or packets into storage before sending them forward to the next center. (3) Capture of transaction data on magnetic media for subsequent batch input to a computer.

SUBNET—A computer network composed of all devices whose IP addresses have the same prefix. Dividing a network into subnets is useful for both security and performance reasons.

SWITCH—An electronic device which opens or closes circuits, changes operating parameters or selects paths either on a space or time division basis.

SWITCHED 56/64 KBPS DATA TRANSMISSION—Provides users with the end-to-end capability to transport high-speed data (up to 64 kbps) over the public network.

SWITCHED LINE—One of a series of lines that can be interconnected to all other lines through a switching center; a line on the public telephone network. Contrast with leased line.

SWITCHED MESSAGE NETWORK—Any network service providing interconnection of message devices such as teletypewriters.

SWITCHED NETWORK—A multipoint network with circuit switching capabilities.

SWITCHING CENTER—Location where an incoming call/message is automatically or manually directed to one or more outgoing circuits.

SYNC CHARACTER—Character or defined bit pattern used by a receiving terminal to adjust its clock and achieve synchronization with the master clocking device.

SYNCHRONIZATION—Process of adjusting a receiving terminal or switch clock to match the transmitting system's master clock.

SYNCHRONOUS—Having a constant time interval between successive bits, characters or events. [Synchronous transmission uses no redundant information (such as the start and stop bits in asynchronous transmission) to identify the beginning and end of characters; thus it is faster and more efficient than asynchronous transmission.]

SYNTAX—Rules governing structure in a programming language.

SYNTAX ERROR—System response to a mistake in its instructions, such as a transposition of characters or an omission of a character or word.

SYSTEM DESIGN—Specifications of the working relations between all the parts of a system in terms of their characteristic actions.

SYSTEM RELIABILITY—Probability that a system will perform its specified task properly under stated conditions of environment.

T

t1—(1) A 1.544 circuit with the equivalent of 24 analogs. (2) The basic 24-channel 1.544 Mbps pulse code modulation system used in the United States.

T-CARRIER—General designation of any digital transmission system.

TABLE DRIVEN—A logical computer process in which a user-entered variable is matched against an array of predefined values. Frequently used logical process in network routing, access security and modem operation.

TELEPHONE—Device which converts acoustical energy (sound) into electrical energy for transmission to a distant point.

TERMINAL EQUIPMENT—Devices, apparatuses and associated interfaces used to forward information to a local customer or distant point.

TERMINATION—(1) Item such as a port that is connected to the end point of a circuit or equipment. (2) The points on a switching network to which a trunk or line may be attached.

TIME OUT—Set waiting period before a terminal system performs some action. [Typical uses include a poll release (when a terminal is disconnected if the time-out period elapses before keying resumes) or an access time-out.]

TIME-SHARING—The sharing of available processing time on a single computer system among multiple simultaneous users.

TOKEN BUS—Local network access mechanism and topology in which all stations actively attached to the bus listen for a broadcast token or supervisory frame. Stations wishing to transmit must receive the token before doing so; however, the next physical station to transmit is not necessarily the next physical station on the bus. Bus access is controlled by preassigned priority algorithms.

TOKEN PASSING—Local area network access technique in which participating stations circulate a special bit patter (the token) that grants network access to each station in sequence; often used in networks with a ring topology.

TOKEN RING—Local network access and topology in which a supervisory frame or token is passed from station to station in sequential order. Stations wishing to gain access to the network must wait for the token to arrive before transmitting data. In a token ring, the next logical station receiving the token is also the next physical station on the ring.

TOPOLOGY—Logical or physical arrangement of stations on a network in relation to one another. See bus, ring, star and tree.

TRACE—Technique used in trouble shooting and/or debugging computer programs and equipment.

T1—Same as DS1

TAP—T1 Access Partitioning

TRANSMISSION—The electrical transfer of a signal, message or other form of data from one location to another without unacceptable loss of information content due to attenuation, distortion or noise.

TRANSMISSION LEVEL—Level of signal power, normally 1,000 Hz, which should be measured at a particular reference point.

TRANSMISSION SPEED—Number of pulses or bits transmitted in a given period of time, usually expressed as bits per second (bps) or words per minute (wpm).

TRANSPORT LAYER—In the OSI model, the network processing entity responsible for the end-to-end control of transmitted data and the optimized use of network resources; works in conjunction with the underlying network, data, link and physical layers.

TCP—Transmission control protocol.

TFTP—Trivial file transfer protocol.

U

U-M IT COMMUNICATIONS ADVISORY COMMITTEE—A committee with cross campus representation that makes recommendations to IT Communications Services on product direction.

UDLC--Universal Data Link Control

UDP—User datagram protocol.

V

VOIP—Voice over IP.

VOATM—Voice over ATM.

VOFR—Voice over frame relay.

VDSL—Very high data rate DSL.

VPN—Virtual private network.

VALUE ADDED NETWORK (VAN)—A public data communications network that provides basic transmission facilities (generally leased by the VAN vendor from a common carrier) plus additional, enhanced services such as computerized switching, temporary data storage, error detection and correction, electronic mail service and packet switching.

W

WAIT STATE—Condition of a central processing unit when all operations are suspended.

WIDEBAND—Facilities or circuits where bandwidths are greater than that required for one voice channel.

WAN—Wide Area Network

X

X—A series of CCITT recommendations for data transmission over public data networks.

X.21— A CCITT recommendation which specifies a general purpose interface between data circuit-terminating equipment for synchronous operation on public data networks.

X.25—A CCITT recommendation which specifies an interface between data terminal equipment for terminals operating in the packet mode on public data network.

INDEX

T

U

V

W

X

FIREWALL MEDIA

(An imprint of Laxmi Publications Pvt. Ltd.)

Computer Books *for School, BCA, MCA, IGNOU, DOEACC and Engineering Students and Professionals*

ISBN	TITLE	AUTHOR	PRICE	PAGES
	.NET			
8170087155	**Building Business Intelligence Applications with .Net**	Robert Ericsson	Rs. 295.00	404
8170083567	**Learning VB.Net Through Applications**	Clayton Crooks	Rs. 295.00	450
8131800865	**Magic of C# with .Net Frame Work**	Shibi Panikkar, Kumar Sanjeev	Rs. 495.00	950
8170082471	**Magic of ASP.Net with C#**	Shibi Panikkar, Kumar Sanjeev	Rs. 395.00	828
8170089662	**ASP.Net Interview Questions and Answers**	J. Rajaram	Rs. 95.00	175
	A TO Z SERIES			
8170083214	**Access 2002 from A to Z**	Julia Kelly, Stephen L. Nelson	Rs. 75.00	185
8170083222	**Excel 2002 from A to Z**	Stephen L. Nelson	Rs. 75.00	193
8170083230	**Front Page 2002 from A to Z**	Heather Williamson	Rs. 85.00	219
8170083249	**Outlook 2002 from A to Z**	Stephen L. Nelson	Rs. 75.00	202
8170083257	**Page Maker 7 from A to Z**	Marc Campbell	Rs. 75.00	202
8170083265	**PowerPoint 2002 from A to Z**	Stephen L. Nelson	Rs. 75.00	202
8170083273	**Windows XP from A to Z**	Pat Coleman	Rs. 95.00	249
8170083281	**Word 2002 from A to Z**	Stephen L. Nelson	Rs. 75.00	199
817008329X	**XML from A to Z**	Heather Williamson	Rs. 75.00	200
8170083303	**Dreamweaver 4 from A to Z**	Heather Williamson	Rs. 85.00	215
	BEGINNERS & GENERAL INTEREST			
817008248X	**Shortcuts to Success in Computing**	Dheeraj Mehrotra	Rs. 55.00	110
8170083311	**Pictorial Computer Dictionary**	Dheeraj Mehrotra	Rs. 45.00	156
8170083486	**Pocket Net Browser**	Dheeraj Mehrotra	Rs. 95.00	302
8170084261	**1000 IT Quizzes**	Dheeraj Mehrotra	Rs. 75.00	120
8131800679	**Information Technology Bible**	Remesh Bangia	Rs. 295.00	567
8131800377	**Fundamentals of Information Technology Including MS Office**	Dinesh Maidasani, Jai Narayan Yadav	Rs. 175.00	356
813180089X	**Fundamentals of Information Technology Including MS Office (Hindi Medium)**	Dinesh Maidasani, Jai Narayan Yadav	Rs. 175.00	425
8170089719	**Foundations of Computer Science**	Ashok Arora	Rs. 250.00	386

Please write for a free color Firewall Media Catalog for details on the above books.

ISBN	TITLE	AUTHOR	PRICE	PAGES
	CALL CENTERS			
8170082196	**Call Centers Made Easy**	Stephen Medcroft	Rs. 195.00	310
	CISCO			
8170087481	**Enabling IP Routing with Cisco Routers**	R. Das, K. Chakrabarty	Rs. 295.00	486
817008749X	**Designing Networks with Cisco**	H. Pasricha, D. Jagu	Rs. 195.00	316
8170087503	**Cisco IP Routing Protocols: Troubleshooting Techniques**	V. Anand, K. Chakrabarty	Rs. 295.00	409
	DATABASES			
8170089530	**DBMS—Complete Practical Approach**	Sharad Maheshwari, Ruchin Jain	Rs. 350.00	656
8170082404	**Learn to Program Visual Basic-Examples**	John Smiley	Rs. 295.00	482
8170082412	**Learn to Program Visual Basic-Databases**	John Smiley	Rs. 325.00	653
8170082420	**Learn to Program Visual Basic-Objects**	John Smiley	Rs. 325.00	670
817008475X	**IT Resources-Access 2002 VBA Programming Access**	Michele Amelot	Rs. 195.00	424
8170084512	**The Power of Oracle 9i**	Rajiv Parida, Vinod Sharma	Rs. 475.00	1035
8170088518	**Principles and Implementation of Data Warehousing**	Rajiv A. Parida	Rs. 295.00	487
817008864X	**DBA Study Guide OCP Prep Guide**	Nazar Abdul	Rs. 295.00	474
8170088658	**Oracle 11i—The Complete Reference**	Rashmi Anandi	Rs. 495.00	975
8131800067	**Toxonomy of Database Management System**	Aditya Kumar Gupta	Rs. 75.00	146
8131800385	**Introduction to SQL and PL/SQL**	Sharad Maheshwari, Ruchin Jain	Rs. 200.00	389
	DOEACC 'O' LEVEL			
8170088089	**DOEACC 'O' Level Model Test Papers**	Ramesh Bangia	Rs. 175.00	296
8170089115	**DOEACC 'O' & 'A' Level Programming & Problem Solving Through 'C' Language (Model Test Paper with Solutions)**	Mukesh Sharma	Rs. 95.00	213
8170089069	**DOEACC 'O' & 'A' Level Business Systems (Model Test Paper with Solutions)**	Mukesh Sharma	Rs. 100.00	252
8170085640	**Programming and Problem Solving Through "C" Language**	Harsha Priya, R. Ranjeet	Rs. 95.00	306

ISBN	TITLE	AUTHOR	PRICE	PAGES
8170084474	**IT Tools and Applications**	Ramesh Bangia	Rs. 145.00	370
8170085594	**Business Systems**	Ramesh Bangia	Rs. 175.00	452
8170089514	**Internet & Web Design**	Ramesh Bangia	Rs. 150.00	300

ELECTRONIC COMMERCE

8170085497	**Electronic Commerce**	Pete Loshin, John Vacca	Rs. 295.00	472
817008119X	**E-Commerce**	Mamta Bhusry	Rs. 95.00	215
8170083524	**Marketing in the Cyber Age**	Kurt Rohner	Rs. 295.00	223

HARDWARE/EMBEDDED SYSTEMS

8170087473	**Essential Electronics for PC Technicians**	John W. Farber	Rs. 295.00	546
8170086264	**Grid Computing: A Practical Guide to Technology and Applications**	Ahmar Abbas	Rs. 295.00	408
8170088186	**CD Cracking Uncovered Protection Against Unsanctioned CD Copy**	Kris Kaspersky	Rs. 295.00	422
8170083435	**Practical Linux Programming: Device Drivers, Embedded Systems and the Internet**	Ashfaq A. Khan	Rs. 295.00	420
8170083575	**TCP/IP Application Layer Protocols for Embedded Systems**	M. Tim Jones	Rs. 295.00	460
8131800520	**PC Repair and Maintenance : A Practical Guide**	Joel Rosenthal, Kevin irwin	Rs. 195.00	362
8131800768	**The A+ Certification and PC Repair Handbook**	Christopher A Crayton, Joel Z. Rosenthal	Rs. 495.00	888

INTERNET & WEB TECHNOLOGY

8170083206	**The Internet Handbook for Writers, Students and Teachers**	Mary McGuire, Linda Stilborne	Rs. 195.00	276
8170084776	**Way in-Internet Getting Started**	Elizabeth Bramire	Rs. 95.00	165
8170088976	**Web Technology**	Ramesh Bangia	Rs. 250.00	560
8170087163	**Web Design with Macromedia Studio MX 2004**	Eric Hunley	Rs. 295.00	558
8170083400	**Professional Web Design (Techniques and Templates)**	Clint Eccher	Rs. 295.00	425
8170088046	**HTML, XHTML, CSS and XML**	Teodoru Gugoiu	Rs. 195.00	355
8170083583	**FrontPage 2000 for Visual Learners**	Chris Charuhas	Rs. 95.00	200
8170083591	**HTML & Java Script for Visual Learners**	Chris Charuhas	Rs. 95.00	200

ISBN	TITLE	AUTHOR	PRICE	PAGES
8170083605	**The Visual Learners Guide to Managing Web Projects**	Chris Charuhas	Rs. 95.00	130
8170083613	**Dreamweaver 4 for Visual Learners**	Chris Charuhas	Rs. 95.00	200
8170084768	**IT Resource-Implementing XML: Managing and Formatting Data**	Johhny Brochard	Rs. 125.00	279
8170089476	**Design Your Web World**	Sunil Jalota	Rs. 75.00	146

KEEPING AHEAD SERIES

ISBN	TITLE	AUTHOR	PRICE	PAGES
8170084652	**Keeping Ahead-Exchange 2000 Server**	Philippe Levesque	Rs. 145.00	285
8170084660	**Keeping Ahead-Windows 2000 Professional**	Jose Dardoigne	Rs. 175.00	388
8170084679	**Keeping Ahead-Windows 2000 Server**	Philippe Mathon	Rs. 175.00	360
8170084687	**Keeping Ahead-Linux Administration Kernel Version 2.0 to 2.2**	Bruno Guèrin	Rs. 125.00	240
8170084695	**Keeping Ahead-Using Linux Kernel Version 2.0 to 2.2**	Bruno Guèrin	Rs. 125.00	258
8170084709	**Keeping Ahead-Java 2**	Benjamin Aumaille	Rs. 145.00	284
8170084717	**Keeping Ahead-SQL Server 7**	Joelle Mosset	Rs. 145.00	329
8170084725	**Keeping Ahead-JavaScript and VBScript**	Benjamin Aumaille	Rs. 145.00	313
8170084733	**Keeping Ahead-C++ Programming Language**	Bruno Dubois	Rs. 125.00	234
8170084741	**Keeping Ahead-TCP/IP in the NT Environment**	Bruno Ferec	Rs. 125.00	230

MCSE

ISBN	TITLE	AUTHOR	PRICE	PAGES
817008489X	**MCSE-Administering SQL Server 7.0**	Jerome Gabillaud	Rs. 295.00	580
8170084903	**MCSE-Networking Essentials**	Jose Dordoigne	Rs. 245.00	453
8170084911	**MCSE-Windows 2000 Professional**	Jose Dordoigne	Rs. 325.00	665
817008492X	**MCSE-Windows 2000 Server**	Phillippe Mathon	Rs. 345.00	712

MULTIMEDIA AND ANIMATION

ISBN	TITLE	AUTHOR	PRICE	PAGES
8170088208	**3DS Max 6 Animation with Character Studio 4 and Plug-Ins**	Boris Kulagin, Dmitry Morozov	Rs. 175.00	216

Please write for a free color Firewall Media Catalog for details on the above books.

ISBN	TITLE	AUTHOR	PRICE	PAGES
8170088216	**Adobe Audition: Soundtracks for Digital Video**	Roman Petelin, Yury Petelin	Rs. 195.00	278
8170086205	**Building A Digital Human**	Ken Brilliant	Rs. 295.00	380
8170086213	**Making Digital Videos**	Ben Long	Rs. 295.00	284
8170087171	**Illustrating with Macromedia Flash ™ MX2004**	Robert Firbaugh	Rs. 245.00	366
8170082439	**Multimedia Basics-Technology (Vol. I)**	Andreas Holzinger	Rs. 195.00	312
8170082447	**Multimedia Basics-Learning (Vol. II)**	Andreas Holzinger	Rs. 195.00	326
8170082455	**Multimedia Basics-Design (Vol. III)**	Andreas Holzinger	Rs. 195.00	280
8170083532	**Maya Feature Creature Creations**	Todd Palamar	Rs. 295.00	376
8170083540	**Sound Forge Power**	Scott R. Garrigus	Rs. 195.00	344
8131800288	**Multimedia and Web Technology**	Ramesh Bangia	Rs. 395.00	878
813180044X	**Photoshop CS**	Shruti Lal	Rs. 195.00	434

NETWORKING

ISBN	TITLE	AUTHOR	PRICE	PAGES
817008721X	**Networking Essentials**	Jose Dordoigne	Rs. 195.00	453
8170089328	**TCP/IP Distributed System**	Vivek Acharya	Rs. 250.00	474
8170087023	**Computer Networks**	Ajit Kumar Singh	Rs. 95.00	181
8131800148	**The Real—world Network Troubleshooting Manual**	Alan Sugano	Rs. 295.00	396
817008203X	**Telecom & Networking Glossary**	Robert Mastin	Rs. 300.00	250
8170082048	**Data Networking Made Easy**	Karen Patten	Rs. 360.00	350
8170082056	**Digital Convergence**	Andy Covell	Rs. 300.00	234

OFFICE AUTOMATION

ISBN	TITLE	AUTHOR	PRICE	PAGES
8170089891	**Desk Top Publishing**	Dinesh Maidasani	Rs. 150.00	311
8170087805	**Learning Computer Fundamentals, MS Office and Internet & Web Technology**	Dinesh Maidasani	Rs. 95.00	301
8170087686	**MS-Word 2000 Thumb-Rules and Details**	Snigdha Banerjee	Rs. 175.00	390
8170089239	**Computer Accounting with Tally 7.2**	Firewall Media	Rs. 195.00	330

ON YOUR SIDE SERIES

ISBN	TITLE	AUTHOR	PRICE	PAGES
8170084830	**On your Side-Powerpoint 2002**	Andrew Blackburn	Rs. 145.00	282
8170084849	**On your Side-Excel 2002**	Adrienne Tommy	Rs. 125.00	275

Please write for a free color Firewall Media Catalog for details on the above books.

ISBN	TITLE	AUTHOR	PRICE	PAGES
8170084857	On your Side-Word 2002	Adrienne Tommy	Rs. 125.00	289
8170084865	On your Side-Access 2002	Adrienne Tommy	Rs. 125.00	303
8170084873	On your Side-Frontpage 2002	Andrew Blackburn	Rs. 95.00	245
8170084881	On your Side-Windows XP	Adrienne Tommy	Rs. 125.00	310

OPERATING SYSTEMS

ISBN	TITLE	AUTHOR	PRICE	PAGES
8170087236	Linux—A Practical Approach	B. Mohamed Ibrahim	Rs. 95.00	187
8170088623	Red Hat Linux Study Guide	Vijay Shekhar	Rs. 350.00	635
8170088631	Red Hat Linux-The Complete Bible	Vijay Shekhar	Rs. 545.00	1176
8170089581	Unix and Shell Programming	Archana Verma	Rs. 80.00	137
8170089131	Operating System Concepts	P.S. Gill	Rs. 95.00	181
8170083427	The MS-Windows XP Professional Handbook	Louis Columbus	Rs. 295.00	330
8170084784	Way in-Windows XP Home Edition	Andrew Blackburn	Rs. 95.00	183
8170086221	Cyber Rookies—Operating System Fundamentals	D. Irtegov	Rs. 295.00	498

PROGRAMMING

ISBN	TITLE	AUTHOR	PRICE	PAGES
8170087791	The Art of Programming Through Flowcharts & Algorithms	Anil Bikas Chaudhuri	Rs. 95.00	160
8170086248	Preventative Programming Techniques: Avoid and Correct Common Mistakes	Brian Hawkins	Rs. 295.00	322
8170083443	Learning Computer Programming : It's not about Languages	Mary Farrell	Rs. 295.00	375
8170086256	Object-Oriented Programming: From Problem Solving to Java	José M. Garrido	Rs. 295.00	360
817008931X	Object-Oriented Programming-Concept and Implementation	A. Rajesh	Rs. 95.00	182
8170089107	Java: J2SE-5 A Practical Approach	B. Mohammad Ibrahim	Rs. 175.00	332
8170089409	Advance Java	Gajendra Gupta	Rs. 175.00	305
8170088038	Assembly Language Programming for Intel Processors Family	Vasile Lungu	Rs. 295.00	577
8170088178	The Assembly Programming Master Book	Vlad Pirogov	Rs. 395.00	726
813180075X	Java Messaging	Eric Bruno	Rs. 295.00	480

ISBN	TITLE	AUTHOR	PRICE	PAGES
	PROGRAMMING - C#, C, C++			
8170083702	**The Power of C#**	Rajiv Parida	Rs. 295.00	576
8170085632	**Mastering Graphics Programming in 'C'**	Sudhir Dawra	Rs. 145.00	286
8170088879	**Programming in C and Numerical Analysis**	J.B. Dixit	Rs. 350.00	355
8170087074	**Mastering C Programs**	J.B. Dixit	Rs. 195.00	434
8170081262	**Programming in C**	J.B. Dixit	Rs. 295.00	506
8170087619	**Unix and C Programming**	Ashok Arora, Shefali Bansal	Rs. 295.00	606
817008878X	**C Interview Questions and Answers**	J. Rajaram	Rs. 75.00	139
8170089034	**Pragmatic C**	R.K. Jangda	Rs. 150.00	258
8170086140	**Data Structure for 'C' Programming**	Ajay Kumar	Rs. 145.00	290
8170081270	**Programming in C++**	J.B. Dixit	Rs. 260.00	602
8170088194	**Hackish C++ Pranks & Tricks**	Michael Flenov	Rs. 245.00	326
8170082889	**Basics of C++ Programming**	Nishant Kundalia	Rs. 95.00	168
8170083648	**Mastering C++ Programs**	J.B. Dixit	Rs. 295.00	598
817008623X	**Cyber Rookies—C++ Programming Fundamentals**	Chuck Easttom	Rs. 295.00	417
8131800202	**Data Structure using C++**	N. Jayalakshmi	Rs. 65.00	126
8170089123	**C++ Made Easy**	T.D. Malhotra	Rs. 250.00	449
8131800393	**C++ & Introduction to C#**	T.D. Malhotra, Rajeev A. Parida, A. Rajesh	Rs. 200.00	440
8131800350	**OOPS with C++**	M. Jaya Prasad	Rs. 150.00	317
	SECURITY			
8170083419	**Computer Forensics : Computer Crime Scene Investigation**	John Vacca	Rs. 445.00	731
8131800156	**Computer Evidence (Collection and Preservation)**	Christopher L.T. Brown	Rs. 295.00	394
8170083494	**Firewall Architecture for the Enterprise**	Norbert Pohlmann, Tim Crothers	Rs. 295.00	480
8170086272	**Net Spies**	Andrew Gauntlett	Rs. 195.00	210
3826607546	**Firewall Systems**	Norbert Pohlmann	Rs. 1630.00	544
8131800504	**Homeland Security Techniques and Technologies**	Jesus Mena	Rs. 295.00	346

Please write for a free color Firewall Media Catalog for details on the above books.

ISBN	TITLE	AUTHOR	PRICE	PAGES
	ENGINEERING AND TECHNOLOGY			
817008718X	**Human Aspects of Software Engineering**	James E. Tomayko, Orit Hazzan	Rs. 195.00	338
8131800032	**Management Information Systems**	Avdhesh Gupta, Anurag Malik	Rs. 195.00	400
8170087953	**Human Computer Interaction**	Rajendra Ranjan Kumar	Rs. 95.00	210
8170088097	**Structured System Analysis and Design**	Preeti Gupta	Rs. 125.00	192
817008802X	**Autocad 2005 for Engineers**	Ionel Simion	Rs. 175.00	271
8170088054	**Digital Signal Processing Fundamentals**	Ashfaq A. Khan	Rs. 295.00	391
8131800164	**Digital Communication System Using System VUE**	Dennis Silage	Rs. 295.00	365
8170089719	**Foundations of Computer Science**	Ashok Arora	Rs. 250.00	386
817008363X	**Practical Project Management**	Ivan Bayross	Rs. 195.00	342
8131800806	**Digital Signal Processing using MATLAB and Wavelets**	Michael Weeks	Rs. 350.00	452
8131800792	**Classical Electrodynamics**	Hans C. Dhanian	Rs. 395.00	620
8131800512	**The Software Vulnerability Guide**	Herbert H. Thompson, Scott G. Chase	Rs. 195.00	368
8131800776	**Robot Modelling and Kinematics**	Rachid Manseur	Rs. 295.00	380
8131800369	**System Software**	M. Joseph	Rs. 95.00	185
	STRAIGHT TO THE POINT SERIES			
8170084601	**STTP : Word 2002**	Corinne Hervo	Rs. 45.00	154
817008461X	**STTP : Excel 2002**	Corinne Hervo	Rs. 45.00	153
8170084628	**STTP : Dreamweaver 4**	Corinne Hervo	Rs. 45.00	135
8170084636	**STTP : Flash 5**	Corinne Hervo	Rs. 45.00	183
8170084644	**STTP : Photoshop 6**	Corinne Hervo	Rs. 45.00	152
817008881X	**STTP : MS Office 2000**	Dinesh Maidasani	Rs. 125.00	290
8170086100	**STTP : MS Office 2003**	Dinesh Maidasani	Rs. 145.00	288
8170087651	**STTP : MS Word 2003**	Firewall Media	Rs. 60.00	150
8170088011	**STTP : Photoshop CS**	Firewall Media	Rs. 60.00	150
8170088143	**STTP : MS Excel 2003**	Firewall Media	Rs. 60.00	150
8170088151	**STTP : CorelDraw 12**	Firewall Media	Rs. 60.00	150
8131800105	**STTP : 3ds MAX 7**	Dinesh Maidasani	Rs. 95.00	182
8131800083	**STTP : Auto CAD 2006**	Dinesh Maidasani	Rs. 95.00	190
8131800245	**STTP : CorelDraw X3**	Dinesh Maidasani	Rs. 75.00	188

ISBN	TITLE	AUTHOR	PRICE	PAGES
8131800253	**STTP : Dreamweaver 8**	Dinesh Maidasani	Rs. 75.00	148
8131800237	**STTP : Photoshop CS2**	Dinesh Maidasani	Rs. 75.00	172
8170088380	**STTP : Tally 7.2**	Firewall Media	Rs. 175.00	322
8131800091	**STTP : Flash 8**	Dinesh Maidasani	Rs. 95.00	180
8131800407	**STTP : My SQL 5.0**	Dinesh Maidasani	Rs. 85.00	166
8131800458	**STTP : Microsoft Power Point 2003**	Dinesh Maidasani	Rs. 75.00	142

STUDIO FACTORY

ISBN	TITLE	AUTHOR	PRICE	PAGES
8170084792	**Studio Factory—Photoshop 6**	Christophe Aubry	Rs. 175.00	364
8170084806	**Studio Factory—Flash 5**	Sami Ben Yahiya	Rs. 145.00	314
8170084814	**Studio Factory—Dreamweaver Ultradev 4**	Phillippe Chatellier	Rs. 95.00	240
8170084822	**Studio Factory—Dreamweaver 4**	Christophe Aubry	Rs. 175.00	373
8170087643	**Studio Factory—Dreamweaver MX**	Christophe Aubry	Rs. 195.00	407
8170087627	**Studio Factory—Flash MX**	Arnaud Blanche	Rs. 145.00	337
817008766X	**Studio Factory—Photoshop 7**	Cyril Guerin	Rs. 195.00	420

LAXMI PUBLICATIONS (P) LTD

113, Golden House, Daryaganj, New Delhi-110002

Phone : **011 - 43 53 25 00**

Fax : **011 - 43 53 25 28**

EMAIL : info@laxmipublications.com

Website : www.laxmipublications.com

BRANCHES

- 129/1, IIIrd Main Road, IX Cross, Chamrajpet, **Bangalore** (*Phone* : 080-26 61 15 61)
- 26, Damodaran Street, T. Nagar, **Chennai** (*Phone* : 044-24 34 47 26)
- 43/1394D, St. Benedict's Road, Ernakulam North, **Cochin** (*Phone* : 0484-239 70 04)
- Pan Bazar, Rani Bari, **Guwahati** (*Phones* : 0361-254 36 69, 251 38 81)
- 4-2-453, Ist Floor, Ramkote, **Hyderabad** (*Phone* : 040-24 75 02 47)
- Adda Tanda Chowk, N.D. 365, **Jalandhar City** (*Phone* : 0181-222 12 72)
- 106/A, Ist Floor, S.N. Banerjee Road, **Kolkata** (*Phones* : 033-22 27 37 73, 22 27 52 47)
- 18, Madan Mohan Malviya Marg, **Lucknow** (*Phone* : 0522-220 95 78)
- 142-C, Victor House, Ground Floor, N.M. Joshi Marg, Lower Parel (W), **Mumbai** (*Phones* : 022-24 91 54 15, 24 92 78 69)
- Radha Govind Street, Tharpagna, **Ranchi** (*Phone* : 0651-230 77 64)